The Analogical Mind

The Analogical Mind

Perspectives from Cognitive Science

edited by Dedre Gentner, Keith J. Holyoak, and
Boicho N. Kokinov

A Bradford Book
The MIT Press
Cambridge, Massachusetts
London, England

This book was set in Sabon by Best-set Typesetter Ltd., Hong Kong and was printed and bound in the United States of America.

Library of Congress Cataloging-in-Publication Data

The analogical mind : perspectives from cognitive science / edited by Dedre Gentner, Keith J. Holyoak, and Boicho N. Kokinov.
    p. cm.
    Includes bibliographical references and index.
    ISBN 0-262-07206-8 (hardcover : alk. paper)—ISBN 0-262-57139-0 (pbk. : alk. paper)
    1. Symbolism (Psychology)—Congresses. 2. Analogy—Congresses.
3. Similarity (Psychology)—Congresses. 4. Cognition—Congresses.
I. Gentner, Dedre. II. Holyoak, Keith James, 1950– III. Kokinov, Boicho N.
BF458 .A53   2001
169—dc21   00-057889

Contents

Preface

The volume editors and the majority of the authors of chapters in this book spent several days together in the summer of 1998 at a workshop entitled "Advances in Analogy Research: Integration of Theory and Data from the Cognitive, Computational, and Neural Sciences," which was held at the New Bulgarian University in Sofia, Bulgaria. The researchers in attendance included those studying analogy from a wide variety of perspectives: cognitive, developmental, and comparative psychology; artificial intelligence; cognitive linguistics; brain studies and neuro-psychology; and philosophy. They spanned a wide geographical range, bringing together eastern and western Europeans with North Americans and Pacific Rim dwellers. This pooling of research insights from all over the world was extremely rewarding. The researchers spent four days (July 17–20) in intensive discussions, starting in the early morning and finishing late at night. About 60 papers were presented at the workshop, which were published in the conference proceedings (Holyoak, Gentner, and Kokinov 1998).

The Sofia workshop served as a launching pad for this more focused volume. A limited number of the workshop participants were invited to write extended chapters for the current volume, and a few other major researchers who had not been able to attend also joined in the book project. Many ideas that emerged during the discussions held at the workshop were incorporated into the chapters of this volume. We would therefore like to thank, first of all, the participants who made this endeavor possible.

Art and science have always needed the support of generous patrons. We wish to thank our sponsors for their contribution to the success of the Sofia workshop on analogy as well as of this book project. These sponsors include the Cognitive Science Society, the United States Air Force European Office of Aerospace Research and Development, and the Fulbright Commission-Sofia. We also wish to thank the Soros Open Society Fund in Sofia and the Open Society Institute in Budapest for supporting the International Summer School in Cognitive Science, which ran in parallel with the analogy workshop at the New Bulgarian University. The overlapping summer school provided many young students with the opportunity to immerse themselves in the analogy workshop, and also allowed some of the authors represented in this volume to teach at the summer school.

We would also like to thank the hosts and local sponsors of the workshop—the Central and East European Center for Cognitive Science and the Department of Cognitive Science and Psychology at the New Bulgarian University, Sofia. Their staff and students made the stay in Sofia pleasant and enjoyable for all the visitors and provided a creative and stimulating environment. We are especially grateful to Guergana Erdeklian and Iliana Haralanova, as well as the members of the AMBR research group, for organizing the workshop.

Each of the editors of this volume owes particular debts of gratitude. Dedre Gentner's work on this volume was completed during a sabbatical fellowship at the Center for Advanced Study in the Behavioral Sciences, with support provided by the William T. Grant Foundation, award 95167795. Her research related to the volume was supported by ONR grant N00014-92-J-1098 and NSF grant SBR-9511757. Keith Holyoak would like to acknowledge the support provided by the James McKeen Cattell Foundation, which made it possible for him to complete his work on this project during a sabbatical year. His research related to this volume was supported by Grant SBR-9729023 from the National Science Foundation. Boicho Kokinov worked on this volume while visiting the Institute of Psychology at the Italian National Research Council (CNR) in Rome. His stay was supported by a joint project of CNR and the Bulgarian Academy of Sciences on "Context and Emergent Cognition." His research related to this volume has been supported both by the Institute of Mathematics and Informatics at the Bulgarian Academy of Sciences and by the Central and East European Center for Cognitive Science at the New Bulgarian University.

We are particularly grateful for the early and generous support of The MIT Press, which made this volume possible. Our editorial work was greatly aided by the efforts of Amy Brand and the rest of the staff at the press. Finally, we thank Kathleen Braun of Northwestern University's Psychology Department for organizing and assembling the chapters.

Reference

Holyoak, K., Gentner, D., and Kokinov, B., eds. (1998). Advances in analogy research: Integration of theory and data from the cognitive, computational, and neural sciences. Sofia: New Bulgarian University Press.

Contributors

Miriam Bassok
Department of Psychology
University of Washington

Consuelo Boronat
Center for Cognitive Neuroscience
Neurology Department
Temple University School of Medicine

Brian F. Bowdle
Department of Psychology
Indiana University

Fintan Costello
Department of Computer
Applications
Dublin City University

Kevin Dunbar
Department of Psychology
McGill University

Gilles Fauconnier
Department of Cognitive Science
University of California, San Diego

Kenneth D. Forbus
Computer Science Department
Northwestern University

Dedre Gentner
Department of Psychology
Northwestern University

Usha Goswami
Institute of Child Health
University College London

Brett Gray
School of Psychology
University of Queensland

Graeme S. Halford
School of Psychology
University of Queensland

Douglas R. Hofstadter
Center for Research on Concepts and
Cognition
Indiana University

Keith J. Holyoak
Department of Psychology
University of California, Los Angeles

John E. Hummel
Department of Psychology
University of California, Los Angeles

Mark T. Keane
Department of Computer Science
University College Dublin

Boicho N. Kokinov
Central and East European Center for
Cognitive Science
Department of Cognitive Science and
Psychology
New Bulgarian University

Arthur B. Markman
Department of Psychology
University of Texas at Austin

C. Page Moreau
Department of Marketing
Cox School of Business
Southern Methodist University

David L. Oden
Department of Psychology
La Salle University

Alexander A. Petrov
Department of Psychology
Carnegie Mellon University

Steven Phillips
Information Science Division
Electrotechnical Laboratory

David Premack
Somis, California

Cameron Shelley
Philosophy Department
University of Michigan

Paul Thagard
Philosophy Department
University of Waterloo

Roger K. R. Thompson
Whitely Psychology Laboratories
Franklin and Marshall College

William H. Wilson
Computer Science and Engineering
University of New South Wales

Phillip Wolff
Department of Psychology
University of Maryland, College Park

1
Introduction: The Place of Analogy in Cognition

Keith J. Holyoak, Dedre Gentner, and Boicho N. Kokinov

Thinking about Relational Patterns

The celebration of the turn of a century is called a "centennial," and few people get to celebrate more than one of them. Even rarer is the celebration of the turn of a millennium. What should we call it? Why, a "millennial," of course. No need for prior experience, or even a dictionary—a simple verbal analogy provides an appropriate term to mark the dawn of the third thousand-year period of the Julian calendar. Not so simple, however, are the mental operations that underlie this pervasive form of human thinking. This volume is a kind of millennial marker in analogy research, a set of papers that collectively lay out the "state of the art" in our current scientific understanding of the mental processes involved in the use of analogy in cognition.

A millennial, though it may simply be a side effect of arbitrary calendar conventions, somehow seems to call attention to the way in which the present state of humanity connects to the broad sweep of our evolutionary and cultural history. If we consider what it means to be human, certain cognitive capabilities loom large—capabilities that subserve language, art, music, invention, and science. Precisely when these capabilities arose in the course of human evolution is unclear, but it seems likely they were well developed at least fifty thousand years ago, based on archeological findings of standardized stone tools and jewelry in East Africa. About forty thousand years ago, the Cro-Magnon people in southwestern Europe created magnificent cave paintings as well as statues and musical instruments, suggesting mental capabilities comparable to our own. We have been human for quite some time already.

What cognitive capabilities underlie our fundamental human achievements? Although a complete answer remains elusive, one basic component is a special kind of symbolic ability—the ability to pick out patterns, to identify recurrences of these patterns despite variation in the elements that compose them, to form concepts that abstract and reify these patterns, and to express these concepts in language. Analogy, in its most general sense, is this ability to think about relational patterns. As Douglas **Hofstadter** (chap. 15, this volume) argues, analogy lies at the core of human cognition.

Although we believe that analogy is indeed a central component of human cognition, it is not quite the exclusive province of our species. Indeed, we can illustrate the basic idea of a relational pattern using an example that is within the capacity of another primate species, the chimpanzee. Consider the pairs of geometric forms displayed in figure 1.1. It is readily apparent (at least to a typical adult human) that pair A is the "same" as the standard in a way in which pair B is not (because the two triangles in pair A have the same shape, just as do the two circles in the standard). But where is this "sameness" that connects the standard and pair A? It does not reside in the physical forms, which overlap not at all. Rather, it resides in the identity of the *relation* between the two triangles and the *relation* between the two squares—"sameness of shape," a shared relational pattern. In order to solve this problem one has to *explicitly* represent the relations between the objects and to match them. This type of explicit relational match has been shown to be within the capacity of a handful of chimpanzees that have received training with physical symbols for the concept "same." The first such symbol-trained chimpanzee to exhibit relational matching was Sarah (Premack 1978), whose analogy abilities are discussed by David **Oden**, Roger **Thompson**, and David **Premack** (chap. 14).

Critically, explicit relational matching is extremely difficult for chimpanzees that lack special training in symbol use, and apparently impossible for monkeys (Thompson and Oden 1998). In contrast to any other type of animal, analogy use develops spontaneously in very young members of the human species (see **Goswami**, chap. 13). The ability to

Standard

Pair A   Pair B

Figure 1.1
A test of relational matching. Pair A exhibits the same relation as does the standard ("same shape"), whereas pair B does not.

perceive and explicitly represent relational patterns thus appears to be intimately connected to the development of general representational abilities in humans (Gentner and Rattermann 1991).

The more complex the analogies, the more complex the representations they require. To draw an analogy, whole systems of connected relations are matched from one domain to another (Gentner 1983). To model this process, computational models must be able to build and maintain complex representational structures. Although this requirement is easily satisfied in models that make use of explicit symbols for individual concepts (see **Forbus**, chap. 2, and **Kokinov and Petrov**, chap. 3), it is much more difficult to satisfy it using models that represent symbols as patterns of activation over a neural substrate (**Holyoak and Hummel**, chap. 4, and **Wilson, Halford, Gray, and Phillips**, chap. 5; Plate 1998; Kanerva 1998). Solving this representational problem is one of the major goals for current modeling efforts.

A more specific aspect of this representational requirement for relational processing is to distinguish relational roles (e.g., "lover" and "beloved" in the relation "love") from the particular fillers of the role (e.g., "John" and "Mary"), while at the same time capturing the fact that those particular fillers are bound to the role. Providing a solution to this "binding problem" poses particular challenges for models that attempt to show how analogical processing might be realized in a neural architecture. Presumably, this difficult problem was solved in some manner during the evolution of the primate nervous system. Although we know little as yet about the neural substrate for processing relational patterns, progress has been made in understanding the cognitive operations involved.

Yet another representational problem arises from the need for flexible, dynamically changing, and context-sensitive representations. Often the representations of both target and source domains seem to change during the analogy-making process to fit each other as well as to fit the current context (see **Fauconnier**, chap. 7; Hofstadter and the Fluid Analogies Research Group 1995; **Hofstadter**, chap. 15; Kokinov 1998; and **Kokinov and Petrov**, chap. 3). This sort of dynamic reorganization of human representations is difficult for both symbolic and connectionist models.

From Gilgamesh to the Microbiology Lab

Although analogy has likely been a human cognitive ability for tens of thousands of years, its direct expression in the historical record awaited the development of written language. Uses of analogies—explicit mention of relational likenesses between distinct situations—are found in the world's earliest preserved literature. In the Babylonian epic *Gilgamesh*, written about four thousand years ago, the hero grieves over the corpse of his friend Enkidu (translated by Ferry 1993):

> . . . Gilgamesh covered
Enkidu's face with a veil like the veil of a bride.
He hovered like an eagle over the body,
or as a lioness does over her brood.

In the same era, an ancient Egyptian poet (translated by Merwin 1968) wrote

> Death is before me today
> like the sky when it clears
> like a man's wish to see home after numberless years of captivity.

In ancient India, more than 2,500 years ago, concrete analogies were used to express abstract philosophical ideas. For example, in the Upanishads (translated by Mitchell 1989) it is written that

As a man in sexual union with his beloved
is unaware of anything outside or inside,
so a man in union with Self knows nothing, wants nothing,
has found his heart's fulfillment and is free of sorrow.

Analogies have figured in poetry across all times and cultures (see Washburn, Major, and Fadiman 1998, for these and many other examples). One basic function of analogy—perhaps its most ancient—is especially apparent in poetry. This is the transfer of emotions, a topic discussed by Paul **Thagard** and Cameron **Shelley** (chap. 10). The Babylonian text makes us feel that Gilgamesh's grief is as profound as the love of a bridegroom for his bride, his watchfulness and protectiveness as intense as those of an eagle or a lioness. Although the Egyptian writer says nothing directly about his emotions at the prospect of death, the analogies in that poem suggest a (perhaps surprising) sense of expectant joy at a long-awaited release, like that of a captive granted freedom. And the Indian poet uses his analogy with the experience of sexual union to convey not only an intellectual sense of what it means to be connected with the Self, but even more forcefully the emotional intensity of the experience. Emotional experiences are notoriously difficult or impossible to convey by literal language; but by connecting the relational pattern of a novel experience with that of a familiar, emotion-laden one, analogy provides a way of recreating a complex pattern of feelings.

The historical records of many cultures provide ample illustrations of the role of analogy in literature, religion and philosophy (see Holyoak and Thagard 1995). As Greek and Roman civilizations gave birth to Western science, analogy was enlisted as a tool for advancing this new kind of systematic and empirically verifiable analysis. At least two thousand years ago, the earliest recorded use of analogy to develop an enduring scientific theory produced the hypothesis that sound is propagated in the form of waves. During the reign of the emperor Augustus, a Roman architect and engineer named Vitruvius described the nature of sound by analogy to water waves (1960:138–139):

Voice is a flowing breath of air, perceptible to the hearing by contact. It moves in an endless number of circular rounds, like the innumerably increasing circular waves which appear when a stone is thrown into smooth water, and which keep on spreading indefinitely from the centre unless interrupted by narrow limits, or by some obstruction which prevents such waves from reaching their end in due formation.

The wave theory of sound became the seed of a new and insightful abstraction: the general conception of waves as a mode of transmission of patterns across space. This abstraction continued to be developed over the course of centuries. At first simply a qualitative explanation of sound transmission, the wave theory was eventually given a mathematical formulation. In the seventeenth century a wave theory of light was developed, by analogy with the wave theory of sound. The progression from highly specific, single-case analogies to more abstract concepts or schemas is one of the most powerful roles that analogy plays in cognition. This progression has been observed not only for scientific, mathematical, and problem-oriented concepts (see **Bassok**, chap. 12), but also for metaphorical concepts in everyday language (see **Gentner, Bowdle, Wolff, and Boronat**, chap. 6).

Although the development of large-scale theories based on analogy is a relatively rare event in science, smaller-scale uses are commonplace. Kevin **Dunbar** (chap. 9) describes some of his research on the use of analogies as they occur "on-line" in the activities of microbiology laboratories. In many situations, such as being faced with a series of unexpected findings, scientists will propose hypotheses based on analogical transfer from known examples (e.g., the possible function of a mysterious gene in one organism may be inferred from a similar and better-understood gene in a different organism).

The role of analogy in thinking manifests itself in many different cognitive tasks. The chapters in this volume give a sense of the scope of the human activities that involve analogy. These include the use of metaphor (**Gentner, Bowdle, Wolff, and Boronat**, chap. 6), conceptual blends (**Fauconnier**, chap. 7), translation (**Hofstadter**, chap. 15), scientific reasoning, political debate (**Dunbar**, chap. 9), creative design (Ward 1998), humor, empathy (**Thagard and Shelley**, chap. 10), computer-aided tutoring (**Forbus**, chap. 2), decision-making and choice (**Markman and Moreau**, chap. 11), mathematical problem-solving (**Bassok**, chap. 12), high-level perception (**Hofstadter**, chap. 15), memory recall (**Kokinov and Petrov**, chap. 3), and infant imitation (**Goswami**, chap. 13). Analogy is certainly not the sole basis for cognition (see **Keane and Costello**, chap. 8); but taken as a whole, these diverse manifestations of analogy support the claim that it forms a critical part of the core of cognition.

Analogy in Cognitive Science

The topic of analogy has a special place in the field of cognitive science. Modern cognitive science arose as a discipline in the final half-century of the millennium just ended—scarcely a tick on the clock of human life on earth. Although several converging factors led to the development of cognitive science, perhaps the most critical was an analogy—that between human information processing and the processing performed by the digital computer. This basic analogical insight, that cognition can be systematically analyzed as a form of computation, guided early work on such cognitive processes as memory, attention, perception, and problem-solving.

Although an analogy provided a major part of the foundation of cognitive science at its inception, the study of analogy itself as a cognitive process did not receive much attention until somewhat later. Modern views of analogy can be traced to such pioneering influences as the philosopher Mary Hesse (1966), whose treatise on analogy in science argued that analogies are powerful forces in discovery and conceptual change. For some time, however, most research on analogy, both in artificial intelligence (Evans 1968) and in psychology (Piaget, Montangero, and Billeter 1977; Sternberg 1977) focused on four-term analogy problems of the sort used in intelligence tests (e.g., *cat is to kitten as dog is to what?*), rather than on the richer analogies used in science and everyday life.

About 1980, several research projects in artificial intelligence and psychology began to take a broader view of analogy. Researchers in artificial intelligence started to grapple with the use of complex analogies in reasoning and learning (Winston 1980; Schank 1982; Carbonell 1983, 1986; Hofstadter 1984). This exploration led to a more general focus on the role of experience in reasoning and the relationships among reasoning, learning, and memory, giving rise to an approach termed "case-based" reasoning (e.g., Kolodner 1993). In contrast to rule-based approaches to reasoning (the approach that was dominant in artificial intelligence at the time), case-based reasoning emphasized the usefulness of retrieving and adapting cases or analogs stored in long-term memory when deriving solutions to novel problems.

In psychology, Gentner (1982, 1983; Gentner and Gentner 1983) began working on mental models and analogy in science. She was struck by the idea that in analogy, the key similarities lie in the *relations* that hold within the domains (e.g., the flow of electrons in an electrical circuit is analogically similar to the flow of people in a crowded subway tunnel), rather than in features of individual objects (e.g., electrons do not resemble people). Moreover, analogical similarities often depend on *higher-order* relations—relations *between* relations. For example, adding a resistor in series to a circuit *causes* (a higher-order relation) a decrease in flow of electricity, just as adding a narrow gate in the subway tunnel would decrease the rate at which people pass through. In her structure-mapping theory, Gentner set forth the view that analogy entails finding a structural alignment, or mapping, between domains. This alignment between two representational structures is characterized by structural parallelism (consistent, one-to-one correspondences between mapped elements) and systematicity—an implicit preference for deep, interconnected systems of relations governed by higher-order relations, such as causal, mathematical, or functional relations. Gentner and her colleagues carried out empirical studies to provide evidence for relational alignment (Gentner and Clement 1988; Markman and Gentner 1993), including alignments based on higher-order relations (Clement and Gentner 1991). The structure-mapping theory was eventually instantiated in computer simulations of analogical mapping and inference (the SME program; Falkenhainer, Forbus, and Gentner 1989) and analogical retrieval (the MAC/FAC program; Forbus, Gentner, and Law 1995; see **Forbus**, chap. 2, and **Gentner et al.**, chap. 6). It has been extended to ordinary similarity (Gentner and Markman 1997) and applied in diverse areas such as decision-making (Markman and Medin 1995; **Markman and Moreau,** chap. 11) and cognitive development (Gentner and Medina 1997).

Over this period, Holyoak and his collaborators (Holyoak 1985; Gick and Holyoak 1980) also investigated the role of analogy in complex cognitive tasks. Their initial focus was on the role of analogy in problem solving, which led to a strong concern for the role of pragmatics in analogy—how current goals and context guide the interpretation of an analogy. Gick and Holyoak (1983) provided evidence that analogy can provide the seed for forming new relational categories, by abstracting the relational correspondences between examples into a schema for a class of problems. Analogy was viewed as a central part of human induction (Holland et al. 1986). Holyoak and Thagard developed a multiconstraint approach to analogy in which similarity, structural parallelism, and pragmatic factors interact to produce an interpretation. They developed simulation models of analogical mapping and inference (ACME; Holyoak and Thagard 1989) and retrieval (ARCS; Thagard et al. 1990) based on algorithms for simultaneously satisfying multiple constraints. Thagard (1989, 2000) extended the constraint-satisfaction approach to other cognitive tasks, such as evaluating explanations and making decisions, and showed how analogy could interact with other constraints in these broader contexts (see **Thagard and Shelley**, chap. 10). Hummel and Holyoak (1997) developed a new computer simulation, LISA, that was based on the multiconstraint theory of analogy but introduced representational and processing assumptions more consistent with the operation of human memory as instantiated in a neural architecture (**Holyoak and Hummel**, chap. 5).

Since the late 1980s, the efforts of many cognitive scientists have contributed to an emerging consensus on many issues concerning analogy (e.g., Gentner 1989; Halford 1993; Hummel and Holyoak 1997; Keane, Ledgeway, and Duff 1994; Kokinov 1988, 1994; Ross 1989). The process of analogical thinking can be usefully decomposed into several basic constituent processes. In a typical reasoning scenario, one or more relevant analogs stored in long-term memory must be *accessed*. A familiar analog must be *mapped* to the target analog to identify systematic correspondences between the two, thereby aligning the corresponding parts of each analog. The resulting mapping allows analogical *inferences* to be made about the target analog, thus creating new knowledge to fill gaps in understanding. These inferences need to be evaluated and possibly *adapted* to fit the unique requirements of the target. Finally, in the aftermath of analogical reasoning, *learning* can result in the generation of new categories and schemas, the addition of new instances to memory, and new understandings of old instances and schemas that allow them to be accessed better in the future. All current computational models of analogy deal with some subset of these basic component processes, and progress has been made in integrating them (e.g., **Forbus**, chap. 2; Kokinov 1994; **Kokinov and Petrov**, chap. 3). In various ways and with differing emphases, all current models make use of some combination of structural information about the form of the analogs, an assessment of the similarity between the episode elements, and pragmatic information about the goals that triggered the reasoning episode.

One of the more general contributions of analogy research to cognitive science is that it has served as an example of the way in which multiple disciplines can jointly contribute to our understanding of cognition. The chapters in this volume illustrate many of these diverse but interrelated approaches to analogy, which include psychological experiments, naturalistic observation, linguistic analyses, and computer simulation. In addition to research on analogy use by adult humans, important findings have emerged from studies of the development of analogy abilities in children and the capabilities of other primates, notably chimpanzees.

Overview of the Book

The first section of this volume presents four chapters that describe theories of analogical thinking that are instantiated in running computer models. The first two chapters take a similar approach, both arguing for integration of analogy models with models of other cognitive processes, and both using localist symbolic representations of concepts. Kenneth **Forbus** provides a review of computational models developed within the framework of the structure-mapping theory, which include models of analogical retrieval (MAC/FAC), mapping and inference (SME), and learning (Phineas). His chapter describes the ways in which these models can operate together, and in combination with models of other forms of commonsense reasoning, to simulate reasoning in knowledge-rich domains such as commonsense qualitative physics. The chapter emphasizes the integration constraint on analogy models—the need to show how models of component processes can be integrated to perform complex reasoning tasks based on large quantities of information.

Boicho **Kokinov** and Alexander **Petrov** take an integrative approach that tries to bring analogy and memory together. Their chapter addresses phenomena emphasized by constructivist approaches to memory, such as memory distortions and memory illusions, and show how these phenomena interact with analogy-making. They provide evidence for omissions, blending of episodes, intrusions from generic knowledge, and effects of context, priming, and order in analogical reminding, and they explain these phenomena in terms of interactions among memory, mapping, and perception. The chapter presents the latest development of their AMBR model, which simulates these phenomena by the parallel work and interplay of many subprocesses. This model uses dynamic emergent representations and computations performed by a society of hybrid micro-agents. AMBR is built on a general cognitive architecture, which makes it possible to integrate analogy with other cognitive processes and to provides a basis for unified explanations of phenomena such as context-sensitivity that cut across virtually all cognitive processes.

Whereas the models in the SME family, and also AMBR, are based on localist representations of meaning, the next two chapters explore the potential use of distributed representations of relational knowledge within neural-network architectures. Within localist-symbolic models the operations needed to bind fillers to roles and to build hierarchical knowledge structures are straightforward; in contrast, these requirements of analogical thinking pose major hurdles when treated within neural networks. William **Wilson**, Graeme **Halford**, Brett **Gray**, and Steven **Phillips** describe the STAR-2 model, which provides mechanisms for computing analogies using representations based on the mathematics of tensor products. This model is directly related to a general theory of the relationship between the complexity of relational representations and human capacity limits. STAR-2 provides mechanisms for mapping complex knowledge structures using a combination of chunking and unchunking, serial processing of propositions, and constraint satisfaction. Simulations show that the model successfully scales up to handle complex mapping problems.

Keith **Holyoak** and John **Hummel** describe LISA, an integrated model of analogical access, mapping, inference, and learning that is based on the use of neural synchrony to code role bindings in working memory. Their chapter argues for the psychological and neural plausibility of this approach, which provides an account of how complex analogies can be processed within a system with inherent constraints on the capacity of working memory—constraints that also apply to biological symbol systems, such as that underlying human reasoning. Simulations show that the model scales up to handle realistic mapping problems based on large-scale knowledge representations. In addition to describing computational tests of the model, the chapter reviews various psychological experiments that test LISA's predictions about the role of working memory in constraining human analogical mapping, as well as research showing that the human prefrontal cortex may be a critical part of the neural substrate for relational reasoning.

In the second section of the volume, seven chapters address the roles that analogy plays in a wide range of complex cognitive tasks. The first three of these focus on processes closely linked to language. Dedre **Gentner**, Brian **Bowdle**, Phillip **Wolff**, and Consuelo **Boronat** show that analogical processing can account for much of the phenomenology of metaphor. One general issue that is explored is whether and when metaphor processing is based on on-line analogical mapping versus the more direct application of pre-stored conceptual categories. Their chapter presents a unified framework for the processing of analogy, similarity, and metaphor. It also reviews evidence for the "career of metaphor" hypothesis, which proposes that novel metaphors are processed as structural alignments based on specific analogical comparisons, whereas conventional metaphors are based on abstract meanings that are the product of repeated mappings.

The chapter by Gilles **Fauconnier** discusses conceptual blending, a cognitive operation that appears closely related to both metaphor and counterfactual reasoning. As his chapter documents with a variety of examples, people have a remarkable facility to integrate aspects of two situations to construct a novel mental representation that goes beyond either one (such as an imaginary "race" between two boats sailing a similar course, but a century apart in time). The chapter illustrates how analogy may serve as one component of more complex cognitive processes that also draw upon other mental operations. Fauconnier also argues for the dynamic construction of these blended representations.

Mark **Keane** and Fintan **Costello** address a different type of generative process that operates in language—various forms of conceptual combinations based on compound phrases, such as "soccer mom." Their chapter contrasts alternative theories of how conceptual combinations are interpreted, focusing on a theory based on multiple constraints (diagnosticity, plausibility, and informativeness). Their constraint theory (contrary to some previous claims) posits that conceptual combination does not depend on structural alignment, suggesting possible limits on the role of analogy in linguistic interpretation. At the same time, the chapter suggests how analogy may be related to a broader class of constraint-based mechanisms for performing complex cognitive tasks.

The chapter by Kevin **Dunbar** draws a contrast between the relative difficulty of triggering spontaneous use of analogies between remote domains in the psychology laboratory with the relatively frequent spontaneous use of analogies in a variety of naturalistic settings. The evidence discussed includes detailed observations of the use of analogies by scientists in microbiology laboratories, as well as analyses of analogies used in political debate. Whereas the scientific analogies that were observed tended to be drawn between relatively similar domains (e.g., between one type of virus and another), the political analogies often connected more remote topics (e.g., between governments and families). The political analogies also tended to have a strong emotional component. Interestingly, experimental work described in Dunbar's chapter suggests that the task of producing meaningful analogs encourages deeper relational encodings than does simply comprehending an individual analog. This chapter provides a good example of how naturalistic observations can be combined with controlled experiments to raise issues that might be overlooked if the phenomenon is studied only in the laboratory.

The chapter by Paul **Thagard** and Cameron **Shelley** explores the role played by analogy in situations that tap into emotions. These include the use of analogies as persuasive arguments, the use of metaphors in poetry, and the experience of empathy between one person and another. Their chapter argues that the transfer of emotions by analogy is best understood as part of a broader system for establishing coherence among beliefs, attitudes, and feelings. The chapter illustrates this overarching framework using the HOTCO model of how emotional coherence can be integrated with cognitive coherence using computational principles based on constraint satisfaction.

Arthur **Markman** and Page **Moreau** discuss the role of analogy in decision-making, focusing on the selection of a preferred option from among a set of alternatives. The chapter describes how cross-domain analogies can function to frame decisions and thereby guide the choice of actions. Analogy also plays a role in choosing between options within one choice problem. In particular, experimental studies have shown that alignable differences—differences in values on corresponding dimensions or predicates—have a greater impact on choices than do nonalignable differences. Such evidence indicates that structure-mapping plays a role in making decisions among options.

The chapter by Miriam **Bassok** reviews research on the role of analogical mapping in solving mathematical word problems. In general, the application of mathematical knowledge to a concrete problem requires that the specific entities of the problems be mapped onto mathematical elements so as to align the relations in the concrete situation with the mathematical relations of the equation. Importantly, semantic and pragmatic knowledge about the specific entities and the relationships among them is likely to influence the preferred mappings. For example, symmetrical semantic relationships such as that between co-hyponyms of a common category (e.g., tulips and daffodils) seem to invite the symmetrical arithmetic operation of addition, whereas asymmetrical relationships such as containment (e.g., tulips and vases) invite the asymmetrical operation of division. More generally, the mapping of problem statements into equations is guided by schemas that suggest plausible relationships between the problem elements. This chapter exemplifies some of the important implications of analogy research for education.

The third section of the book includes two chapters that respectively address the development of analogical thinking in children and the possibility that nonhuman primates are capable of some form of analogy use. Usha **Goswami** reviews research on young children's analogical capacities, focusing on the earliest signs of sensitivity to relational similarity. Although children's performance varies with familiarity of the relations and other task factors, it is clear that basic analogical capabilities are present in preschool children. Early forms of imitation, such as facial imitation of gestures, may be precursors of more general analogical abilities. Analogy appears to be a powerful tool for reasoning and learning that arises early in the course of normal child development.

As we mentioned earlier, the chimpanzee Sarah was the first nonhuman primate observed to solve relational matching tasks, including four-term analogy problems. David **Oden**, Roger **Thompson**, and David **Premack** describe an extensive series of reanalyses of data from tests of Sarah's analogy ability, with the goal of assessing the possibility that her successes might be attributable to simpler nonanalogical strategies. The tasks Sarah performed were demanding, including tests of not only her ability to comprehend analogy problems, but also her ability to construct analogies by arranging items in a systematic manner on a board. These reanalyses confirm not only that Sarah can solve analogy problems, but also that she does so preferentially even in situations in which a simpler associative strategy would suffice. Our human analogical abilities appear to be shared to some extent with the best-educated members of cognitively sophisticated animals such as nonhuman primates.

Finally, the book concludes with an essay by Douglas **Hofstadter**, in which he argues for a broad view of analogy as the very core of cognition. His chapter draws links between analogy, high-level perception, and the formation of abstract categories. He emphasizes the fluidity of analogies and concepts—the way in which they vary as they mold themselves to fit specific situations—and suggests that this fluidity permits remindings that connect new experiences with memories of remote events that are relationally similar. Analogy, in the broad view taken in his chapter, encompasses tasks ranging from everyday application of simple concepts to the complex cross-linguistic mappings required to translate structured poetry from one language to another.

Taken as a whole, the chapters collected in this volume provide a broad and detailed portrait of the state of analogy research at the millennial divide. Much has been learned about this core cognitive process, particularly in the past two decades. The progress in understanding analogy has been manifested in several ways. First, the study of analogy has engendered and sustained collaborations between researchers in psychology and artificial intelligence, with significant influences from philosophy, linguistics, and history of science; the methods of cognitive neuroscience are also beginning to be applied. Second, the empirical and computational work has led to a substantial degree of convergence between researchers in the field, indicating the stability of many of the fundamental theoretical assumptions. Finally, theories of analogy have been extended to account for phenomena in areas that are near relatives, such as metaphor and mundane similarity, as well as to more distant cousins, such as categorization and decision making. Systematic efforts are under way to integrate our understanding of analogical mechanisms with models of other cognitive processes and thus to view human cognition in a unified way.

The field of analogy research has indeed made progress. Nonetheless, the most important message of this volume is the large number of open questions that remain to be solved. A full understanding of analogy remains a challenge for the researchers of the new millennium.

Acknowledgments

Preparation of this chapter was supported by NSF Grant SBR-9729023 to John Hummel and Keith Holyoak, by NSF Grant SBR-95-11757 and ONR Grant N00014-92-J-1098 to Dedre Gentner, and by a joint CNR-BAS grant to Boicho Kokinov.

References

Carbonell, J. G. (1983). Learning by analogy: Formulating and generalizing plans from past experience. In R. S. Michalski, J. G. Carbonell, and T. M. Mitchell, Eds., *Machine learning: An artificial intelligence approach*, 137–161. Palo Alto, CA: Tioga.

Carbonell, J. G. (1986). Derivational analogy: A theory of reconstructive problem solving and expertise acquisition. In R. S. Michalski, J. G. Carbonell, and T. M. Mitchell, Eds., *Machine learning: An artificial intelligence approach*, vol. 2, pp. 371–392. Los Altos, CA: Morgan Kaufman.

Clement, C. A., and Gentner, D. (1991). Systematicity as a selection constraint in analogical mapping. *Cognitive Science* 15:89–132.

Evans, T. G. (1968). A program for the solution of geometric-analogy intelligence test questions. In M. L. Minsky, Ed., *Semantic information processing*, pp. 271–353. Cambridge, MA: MIT Press.

Falkenhainer, B., Forbus, K. D., and Gentner, D. (1989). The structure-mapping engine: Algorithm and examples. *Artificial Intelligence* 41:1–63.

Ferry, D. (1993). *Gilgamesh: A new rendering in English*. New York: Farrar, Straus and Giroux.

Forbus, K. D., Gentner, D., and Law, K. (1995). MAC/FAC: A model of similarity-based retrieval. *Cognitive Science* 19:141–205.

Gentner, D. (1982). Are scientific analogies metaphors? In D. S. Miall, Ed., *Metaphor: Problems and perspectives*, pp. 106–132. Brighton: Harvester Press.

Gentner, D. (1983). Structure-mapping: A theoretical framework for analogy. *Cognitive Science* 7:155–170.

Gentner, D. (1989). The mechanisms of analogical learning. In S. Vosniadou and A. Ortony, Eds., *Similarity and analogical reasoning*, pp. 199–241. Cambridge: Cambridge University Press.

Gentner, D., and Clement, C. (1988). Evidence for relational selectivity in the interpretation of metaphor. In G. H. Bower, Eds., *The psychology of learning and motivation*, vol. 22, pp. 307–358. New York: Academic Press.

Gentner, D., and Gentner, D. R. (1983). Flowing waters or teeming crowds: Mental models of electricity. In D. Gentner and A. L. Stevens, Eds., *Mental models*, pp. 99–129. Hillsdale, NJ: Erlbaum.

Gentner, D., and Markman, A. B. (1997). Structure mapping in analogy and similarity. *American Psychologist* 52:45–56.

Gentner, D., and Medina, J. (1997). Comparison and the development of cognition and language. *Cognitive Studies: Bulletin of the Japanese Cognitive Science Society* 4:112–149.

Gentner, D., and Rattermann, M. J. (1991). Language and the career of similarity. In S. A. Gelman and J. P. Brynes, Eds., *Perspectives on thought and language: Interrelations in development*, pp. 225–277. London: Cambridge University Press.

Gick, M. L., and Holyoak, K. J. (1980). Analogical problem solving. *Cognitive Psychology* 12:306–355.

Gick, M. L., and Holyoak, K. J. (1983). Schema induction and analogical transfer. *Cognitive Psychology* 15:1–38.

Halford, G. S. (1993). *Children's understanding: The development of mental models*. Hillsdale, NJ: Erlbaum.

Hesse, M. (1966). *Models and analogies in science*. Notre Dame, IN: Notre Dame University Press.

Hofstadter, D. (1984). The CopyCat Project: An experiment in nondeterminism and creative analogies. AI Memo No. 775. Cambridge, MA: MIT.

Hofstadter, D., and the Fluid Analogies Research Group. (1995). *Fluid concepts and creative analogies*. New York: Basic Books.

Holland, J. H., Holyoak, K. J., Nisbett, R. E., and Thagard, P. (1986). *Induction: Processes of inference, learning, and discovery*. Cambridge, MA: MIT Press.

Holyoak, K. J. (1985). The pragmatics of analogical transfer. In G. H. Bower, Ed., *The psychology of learning and motivation*, vol. 19, pp. 59–87. New York: Academic Press.

Holyoak, K. J., and Thagard, P. (1989). Analogical mapping by constraint satisfaction. *Cognitive Science* 13:295–355.

Hummel, J. E., and Holyoak, K. J. (1997). Distributed representations of structure: A theory of analogical access and mapping. *Psychological Review* 104:427–466.

Kanerva, P. (1998). Dual role of analogy in the design of a cognitive computer. In K. J. Holyoak, D. Gentner, and B. N. Kokinov, Eds., *Advances in analogy research: Integration of theory and data from the cognitive, computational, and neural sciences*, pp. 164–170. Sofia: New Bulgarian University Press.

Keane, M. T., Ledgeway, T., and Duff, S. (1994). Constraints on analogical mapping: A comparison of three models. *Cognitive Science* 18:387–438.

Kokinov, B. N. (1988). Associative memory-based reasoning: How to represent and retrieve cases. In T. O'Shea and V. Sgurev, Eds., *Artificial intelligence III: Methodology, systems, applications*, pp. 51–58. Amsterdam: Elsevier.

Kokinov, B. N. (1994). A hybrid model of analogical reasoning. In K. J. Holyoak and J. A. Barnden, Eds., *Advances in connectionist and neural computation theory*, vol. 2, *Analogical connections*, pp. 247–318. Norwood, NJ: Ablex.

Kokinov, B. N. (1998). Analogy is like cognition: Dynamic, emergent, and context-Sensitive. In K. J. Holyoak, D. Gentner, and B. N. Kokinov, Eds., *Advances in analogy research: Integration of theory and data from the cognitive, computational, and neural sciences*, pp. 96–105. Sofia: New Bulgarian University Press.

Kolodner, J. (1993). *Case-based reasoning*. San Mateo, CA: Morgan Kaufmann.

Markman, A. B., and Gentner, D. (1993). Structural alignment during similarity comparisons. *Cognitive Psychology* 25:431–467.

Markman, A. B., and Medin, D. L. (1995). Similarity and alignment in choice. *Organizational Behavior and Human Decision Processes* 63:117–130.

Merwin, W. S. (1968). *Selected translations 1948–1968*. New York: Atheneum.

Mitchell, S. (1989). *The enlightened heart: An anthology of sacred poetry*. New York: HarperCollins.

Piaget, J., Montangero, J., and Billeter, J. (1977). La formation des correlats. In J. Piaget, Ed., *Recherches sur L'abstraction reflechissante*, pp. 115–129. Paris: Presses Universitaires de France.

Plate, T. (1998). Structured operations with distributed vector representations. In K. J. Holyoak, D. Gentner, and B. N. Kokinov, Eds., *Advances in analogy research: Integration of theory and data from the cognitive, computational, and neural sciences*, pp. 154–163. Sofia: New Bulgarian University Press.

Premack, D. (1978). On the abstractness of human concepts: Why it would be difficult to talk to a pigeon. In S. Hulse, H. Fowler, and W. K. Honig, Eds., *Cognitive processes in animal behavior*, pp. 423–451. Hillsdale, NJ: Erlbaum.

Ross, B. (1989). Distinguishing types of superficial similarities: Different effects on the access and use of earlier problems. *Journal of Experimental Psychology: Learning, Memory, and Cognition* 15:456–468.

Schank, R. C. (1982). *Dynamic memory*. New York: Cambridge University Press.

Sternberg, R. J. (1977). *Intelligence, information processing, and analogical reasoning: The componential analysis of human abilities*. Hillsdale, NJ: Erlbaum.

Thagard, P. (1989). Explanatory coherence. *Behavioral and Brain Sciences* 12:435–467.

Thagard, P. (2000). *Coherence in thought and action*. Cambridge, MA: MIT Press.

Thagard, P., Holyoak, K. J., Nelson, G., and Gochfeld, D. (1990). Analog retrieval by constraint satisfaction. *Artificial Intelligence* 46:259–310.

Thompson, R., and Oden, D. (1998). Why monkeys and pigeons, unlike certain apes, cannot reason analogically. In K. J. Holyoak, D. Gentner, and B. N. Kokinov, Eds., *Advances in analogy research: Integration of theory and data from the cognitive, computational, and neural sciences*, pp. 38–48. Sofia: New Bulgarian University Press.

Vitruvius (1960). *The ten books on architecture*. Translated by M. H. Morgan. New York: Dover.

Ward, T. (1998). Mental leaps versus mental hops. In K. J. Holyoak, D. Gentner, and B. N. Kokinov, Eds., *Advances in analogy research: Integration of theory and data from the cognitive, computational, and neural sciences*, pp. 221–230. Sofia: New Bulgarian University Press.

Washburn, K., Major, J. S., and Fadiman, C., Eds. (1998). *World poetry: An anthology of verse from antiquity to our time*. New York: Quality Paperback Book Club.

Winston, P. H. (1980). Learning and reasoning by analogy. *Communications of the ACM* 23:689–703.

I

Computational and Theoretical Approaches

2

Exploring Analogy in the Large

Kenneth D. Forbus

2.1 Introduction

There has been solid progress in the scientific understanding of the phenomena of analogy and similarity, as the work discussed in this volume attests. One of the drivers of this progress has been research on cognitive simulations that model a variety of phenomena in analogy, similarity, and retrieval (Gentner and Holyoak 1997). My goal here is to highlight what I believe is a promising new direction for cognitive simulation of analogy and similarity. To date, most models have focused on exploring the fundamental phenomena involved in matching, inference, and retrieval. Although there is still much to be discovered about these processes, I believe that it is now critical to focus more on exploring analogy "in the large": simulating the roles comparison plays in larger-scale cognitive processes. Along with many of the researchers represented in this volume, I believe that analogy is one of the core processes of cognition. This makes it crucial to ensure that the processes that we propose can play their intended role in cognition. This new focus on what might be called *large-scale analogical processing* can provide new understanding of the fundamental processes as well as yield new insights into the cognitive processes that rely on them.

This chapter begins with a brief review of SME and MAC/FAC, our simulations of matching and retrieval. Next I lay out several arguments for exploring analogy in the large, including why it is now very feasible and what we can learn by such explorations. A new constraint on cognitive simulations, the *integration constraint*, is proposed: a cognitive simulation of some aspect of analogical processing should be usable as a component in larger-scale cognitive simulations. I believe that the implications of this new constraint for cognitive simulation of analogy are far reaching. After that, two explorations of larger-scale phenomena are described. First, I describe a theoretical framework in which we model commonsense reasoning as an interplay of analogical and first-principles reasoning. Second, I describe how SME and MAC/FAC have been used in a case-based coach that is accessible to engineering thermodynamics students worldwide via electronic mail. These examples show that exploring analogy in the large can provide new insights and new challenges to our simulations. Finally, the broader implications of this approach are discussed.

2.2   SME and MAC/FAC: A Brief Review

Structure-mapping theory (Gentner 1983, 1989) provides an account of comparison processes that is consistent with a growing body of psychological evidence (Gentner and Markman 1997). These computations have been simulated with SME (Falkenhainer, Forbus, and Gentner 1989; Forbus, Ferguson, and Gentner 1994), which in turn has been used as a module in other simulations and in performance systems. SME takes as inputs two structured propositional representations, the *base* (about which more is presumably known) and the *target*. These descriptions are internal symbolic representations, with predicate/argument structure. They can include *attributes*, which are unary predicates indicating features, *relations* that express connections between entities, and *higher-order relations* that express connections between relations.

Given a base and target, SME computes a *mapping* (or a handful of them). Each mapping contains a set of *correspondences* that align particular items in the base with items in the target, and *candidate inferences*, which are statements about the base that are hypothesized to hold in the target by virtue of these correspondences. SME operates in polynomial time (Forbus and Oblinger 1990), and can also incrementally extend its mappings as more information is added to the base and/or target (Forbus, Ferguson, and Gentner 1994).

MAC/FAC (Forbus, Gentner, and Law 1995) models similarity-based retrieval. The MAC stage first uses a simple, nonstructural matcher to filter out a few promising candidates from a (potentially immense) memory of structured descriptions. The FAC stage then evaluates these candidates more carefully, using SME to provide a structural match, and thus the correspondences and candidate inferences that indicate how the reminded information may be relevant to the current situation. Scalability comes from the simplicity of MAC: the MAC stage lends itself to implementation in parallel (including connectionist) hardware. MAC/FAC has been used successfully to model various aspects of similarity-based retrieval (Forbus, Gentner, and Law 1995).

The purpose of computational models is to generate insights, and these in turn should lead to new psychological work. This has indeed happened with SME and MAC/FAC. Some of the psychological research that has used ideas from SME and MAC/FAC produced the following results:

• Systematicity and structural consistency influences interpretation of analogies (Clement and Gentner 1991).

• Structural consistency influences inference in analogical reasoning (Clement and Gentner 1991; Keane 1996; Spellman and Holyoak 1992, 1996; Markman 1997) and in category-based induction (Lassaline 1996; Wu and Gentner 1998).

• Systematicity influences inference in analogical reasoning and category-based induction (Clement and Gentner 1991; Wu and Gentner 1998).

• Ordinary similarity comparisons use processes of structural alignment and mapping, that is, similarity is like analogy (Gentner 1989; Gentner and Markman 1995, 1997; Markman and Gentner 1993; Medin, Goldstone, and Gentner 1993).

• Similarity-based retrieval is surface-driven, but similarity-based reasoning is structurally driven (Gentner, Rattermann, and Forbus 1993; see also Holyoak and Koh 1987; Ross 1989).

A number of SME's psychological predictions have been confirmed by experiments with human subjects, including

• Online processing of similarity and analogy is influenced both by object richness and by relational depth (Gentner and Rattermann 1991; Markman and Gentner 1993; Rattermann and Gentner 1998).

• Early in development, object matches win over relational matches (*relational shift*) because of inadequate relational knowledge (Gentner and Toupin 1986; Gentner 1988; Gentner and Rattermann 1991; see Goswami (1992); chap. 13, this volume; and Halford (1987, 1993) for related positions).
• Learning higher-order domain relations enables children to perform relational mappings (Gentner and Rattermann 1991; Kotovsky and Gentner 1996; Rattermann and Gentner 1998; Goswami and Brown 1989).

There are several psychological phenomena that we have not tried to capture so far within SME. One of these is working memory limitations, which are being explored in LISA (Hummel and Holyoak 1997). Another, which we are just beginning to investigate, is predictions about processing time within a mapping, which have been addressed by IAM (Keane 1990, 1997) and SIAM (Goldstone 1994; Goldstone and Medin 1994).

2.3   Arguments for Large-Scale Analogical Simulations

I am suggesting that we devote relatively more of our effort to large-scale analogical simulation over studying analogy and similarity in isolation. This may sound strange from the perspective of other areas of cognitive science, where isolating processes is both highly valued and notoriously difficult to achieve. In cognitive psychology, for instance, studying any process must be done in the context of multiple concurrent processes, most of whose character is still conjectural. Rarely can single processes be isolated with absolute certainty. Of all the methods in cognitive science, cognitive simulation has the most direct access to isolated processes because one can, with appropriate assumptions, create simulations of very specific slices of hypothesized systems and particular processes. This is a signature strength of the method and can provide clarity of a sort that is quite difficult for other methods to achieve. Why work against a method's strength?

This ability to zero in on a specific process is indeed a major strength of simulation studies. However, it can also be a major weakness: the assumptions one makes about the surrounding systems become critical. Too many simulations have only been tested in single tasks or toy domains, with no particular cross-checks as to their assumptions about the properties of representations and other processes posited. To avoid myopia, we must look up, to larger units of analysis encompassing a broader range of phenomena.

2.3.1 The Integration Constraint

The ubiquity of structural alignment in cognition, as suggested by recent results in cognitive science, lends support to the need for larger-scale simulation studies. It appears that the same component processes are used in a range of cognitive processes spanning from visual perception to problem solving to learning to conceptual change. Models of these component processes must be capable of the same ubiquity. This suggests what I call the *integration constraint*: a cognitive simulation of an analogical process, such as matching or retrieval, should be able to serve as a component in simulations of larger-scale cognitive processes.

The integration constraint represents a new, and very difficult, challenge. As discussed in section 2.7, no model can yet be said to fully satisfy it, although some are coming closer than others. This very difficulty is exactly what makes it worthwhile: ultimately, our models need to be capable of human-level performance.

2.3.2 Other Components Are Coming Together

The scale of phenomena that can be simulated is increasing. This is due to the confluence of several effects.

· Better understanding of how to build AI systems. The various components that are needed to build larger-scale simulations, such as reasoning systems, natural language processing, and vision, are becoming more available. There is also an explosion in technologies for connecting heterogeneous software components, which ultimately should simplify experimentation.

· Tremendous increases in available computing power and memory. It seems likely that Moore's law, which predicts a doubling of capacity every eighteen months, will last until at least 2010.

• Increased interest in creating larger-scale systems that can tackle real problems. For example, computers are now widespread enough that there is significant interest in making them radically easier to use, by making software that better understands its users and what they are doing. This provides new settings for research.

The scale of what can be accomplished has changed. For example, the SOAR cognitive architecture has been used to create "software pilots" that operate in shared virtual worlds with humans. In one recent large-scale exercise (Jones et al. 1999), all U.S. military tactical and logistics flights were carried out by SOAR pilots. These pilots communicated with their human comrades through speech, using simulated radio channels.

In what sense are these SOAR pilots cognitive simulations? No one compared their millisecond-to-millisecond performance against human pilots doing a similar task, as might be the goal in using a simulation of a single pilot to evaluate an interface. Here, the goal was a larger unit of analysis, the tactical behavior occurring second to second. These pilots had to operate in the simulated world in a manner that enabled them to be treated as human by their collaborators, in a wide variety of circumstances. That kind of robust capability, to be able to perform successfully over a range of complex situations in a humanlike way, is a powerful measure of success for a large-scale simulation.

An argument often raised against larger-scale simulations is that the number of underconstrained assumptions required becomes unmanageable. It is true that, given the state of knowledge about cognitive processes in general, the number of underconstrained assumptions about any process or representation (including its very existence, as the debates on the existence of prototypes in category research illustrate!) remains high, and that adding more processes increases the number of assumptions involved. However, the need to work in concert with other processes invokes new constraints: if, for example, one process, P1, exploits the results of another process, P2, then P2's output must be compatible with P1's input. Thus studies of analogical encoding, for example, require studying the likely kinds of representations created by the human visual system (Ferguson 1994; Ferguson, Aminoff, and Gentner 1996). Small-scale simulations still require assumptions about their inputs, but such assumptions are all too often made without any justification. Being used as a component in a larger simulation shines new light on those assumptions.

Every cognitive simulation has both aspects that are intended to be models of human processing and aspects that are not. Large-scale cognitive simulations do not necessarily need to make more assumptions than small-scale simulations, if they limit the range of their claims. Even if, say, a natural language module is not something that the simulation authors would bet on as a psychological model, it still can be used beneficially in a larger simulation if it decreases the reliance on hand-coded representations.

Ultimately, we will build larger-scale simulations because, without them, we cannot explore via simulation the same range of human cognition that other areas of cognitive science can explore. Unless we increase the size of our unit of analysis, we cannot use simulation to explore problem solving, learning, and conceptual change. This increase will not be without costs: for example, it requires substantially more work to build large systems than it does to build small systems. Moreover, looking at the macro puts the micro out of focus—reaction times are unlikely to be a useful measure at this larger scale, and more emphasis will have to be placed on content-oriented measures, such as errors, patterns of misconceptions, and models learned. But what we gain from this shift is the ability to model human behavior at a grander scale, reducing the gap between what people do and what our simulations of them can do.

2.3.3   Large-Scale Analogical Processing as a Source of Constraints

I have argued that looking at larger-scale analogical processing can provide useful insights and constraints on the component processes involved. A concrete example is provided by Phineas, a system created by Brian Falkenhainer in the late 1980s. The experience in creating Phineas led to substantial changes in SME. Let us look more closely at this example, to see how large-scale analogical processing works.

Phineas (Falkenhainer 1987, 1990) learned physical domain theories by analogy with previously understood examples. In addition to SME, its design exploited several other modules that have themselves been used in other projects.

• QPE (Forbus 1990) is a qualitative simulator using Qualitative Process theory (Forbus 1984). Given a theory describing the qualitative laws of a domain and a specific situation, QPE produced predictions of the kinds of behaviors that could occur in that situation. This description, called an *envisionment*, describes behavior symbolically, in terms of states and transitions between them.

• DATMI (Decoste 1990) is a measurement interpretation system. It takes as input an envisionment, as produced by QPE, and a specific behavior, described in terms of measurements. It figures out how the specific behavior can be explained in terms of the states of the envisionment.

The architecture of Phineas is shown in figure 2.1.

The best way to illustrate how Phineas worked is by example. Phineas started with the description of the behavior of a physical system, described in qualitative terms. In one test, Phineas was given the description of the temperature changes that occur when a hot brick is immersed in cold water. Phineas first attempted to understand the described behavior in terms of its current physical theories, by using QPE to apply these theories to the new situation and qualitatively simulate the kinds of behaviors that can occur, and using DATMI to construct explanations of the observations in terms of the simulated possibilities. In this case, Phineas did not have a model of heat or heat flow, so it could not find any physical processes to explain the observed changes. In such circumstances Phineas turned to analogy to seek an explanation.

To derive an explanation, Phineas attempted to find an analogous behavior in its database of previously explained examples. These examples were indexed in an abstraction hierarchy by their observed behaviors. Based on global properties of the new instance's behavior, Phineas would select a potentially analogous example from this hierarchy. When evaluating a potential analog, Phineas used SME to compare the behaviors, generating a set of correspondences between different physical aspects of the situations. These correspondences were then used with SME to analogically infer an explanation for the new situation, based on the explanation for the previously understood situation. Returning to our immersed brick example, the most promising candidate explanation is a situation where liquid flow causes two pressures to equilibrate. To adapt this explanation for the original behavior Phineas created a new

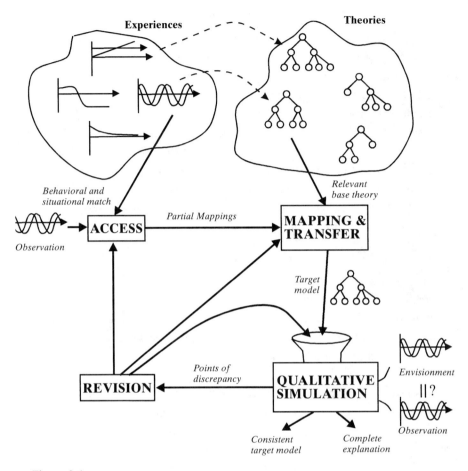

Figure 2.1
The architecture of Phineas, a system that used structure-mapping to learn qualitative mental models of physical domains.

process, PROCESS-1 (which we will call heat flow for simplicity), which is analogous to the liquid flow process, using the correspondences between aspects of the two behaviors. In this new physical process, the relationships that held for pressure in the liquid flow situation are hypothesized to hold for the corresponding temperature parameters in the new situation.

Generating the initial physical-process hypothesis via analogical inference is only the first step. Next, Phineas has to ensure that the hypothesis is specified in enough detail to actually reason with it. For instance, in this case it is not obvious what the analog to liquid is, nor what constitutes a flow path, in the new heat flow situation. It resolved these questions by a combination of reasoning with background knowledge about the physical world (e.g., that fluid paths are a form of connection, and that immersion in a liquid implies that the immersed object is in contact with the liquid) and by additional analogies. Falkenhainer calls this the *map/analyze cycle*. Candidate inferences were examined to see if they can be justified in terms of background knowledge, which may in turn lead to further matching to see if the newly applied background knowledge can be used to extend the analogy further. Eventually, Phineas would extend its candidate theory into a form that can be tested, and proceeded to do so by using the combination of QPE and DATMI to see if the newly extended theory can explain the original observation.

We believe that Phineas provides a model for the use of analogy in learning, and indeed for the role of analogy in abduction tasks more generally. The least psychologically plausible part of Phineas's operation was its retrieval component, in which a domain-specific indexing vocabulary was used to filter candidate experiences (although it might be a reasonable model of expert retrieval). On the other hand, Phineas's map/analyze cycle and its method of using analogy in explanation and learning were, we believe, plausible in their broad features as a psychological model.

In addition to providing insights about the use of analogy in learning and abduction, our experience with Phineas led to several changes in SME itself.

· The need to match nonidentical relational predicates in physical models led to a new way to relax the identicality constraint.[1] *Minimal ascension*

(Falkenhainer 1988) allows nonidentical relational predicate matches when they support a larger relational overlap and have a close common superordinate.

• The map/analyze cycle involves incrementally extending a match, when new items are added to the base or target. In Phineas this ability was provided by mechanisms external to SME; since then, SME (v3) itself has been made incremental (Forbus, Ferguson, and Gentner 1994).

• When constructing a new theory by analogy, the correspondences between entities suggested by the mapping between similar behaviors must be used to carry over the explanatory theory from the base to the target, to provide the starting point for the theory of the new domain. This experience was one of the factors that led to the introduction of pragmatic constraints (Forbus and Oblinger 1990; Forbus, Ferguson, and Gentner 1994), a simple mechanism for task information to influence the mapping process by requiring or excluding correspondences.

• Although the Phineas examples all ran fine with the original SME exhaustive merge algorithm, plans to move to larger examples led to replacing the exhaustive merge algorithm with a linear-time greedy algorithm (Forbus and Oblinger 1990) that produces at most a handful of mappings.

Each of these innovations has been used in subsequent systems for larger-scale tasks. For instance, the ability to express constraints on correspondences is useful in reasoning from historical precedents. When reasoning about what a specific country might do in a crisis, one wants to find a precedent that is similar to the current situation, but in which the country in question maps to itself. More distant precedents might be considered but are less preferred in this task than precedents involving the same country.

2.4   Example: Mental Models

An active area of research in cognitive science is studying *mental models* (Gentner and Stevens 1983), the models people use in reasoning about the physical world. Understanding mental models is a central issue for cognitive science because they appear important in reasoning about complex physical systems, in making and articulating predictions about the world, and in discovering causal explanations for what happens around us. Mental-models research also offers practical benefits. In an increasingly technological society, understanding the nature of mental models for complex physical systems could help people learn better mental models, which in turn could reduce accidents and improve productivity (Norman 1988).

A key intuition often associated with mental models is that they are *runnable*, that is, there is a sense of deriving answers via mental simulation rather than logical reasoning. An appealing explanation for runnability is that mental-model reasoning is like watching a movie of a physical system with your mind's eye. It does seem likely that spatial mental models rely in part on visual computations (e.g., Schwartz 1999). However, we know of no evidence suggesting that the data needed for full quantitative simulation are available in commonsense reasoning tasks, nor do we know of any evidence that people have a mental simulation facility capable of using such information. Consider predicting the pattern of liquid that will appear on a rug if a half-full cup of coffee is knocked off a table. Our visual apparatus is powerful enough to describe the shape of the patterns that result. However, we are not capable of predicting what specific shapes will result in advance. Solving this problem to a high degree of accuracy involves computational fluid dynamics; it seems quite unlikely that we are capable of performing such a prodigious feat mentally.

If we aren't watching a high-fidelity simulation, then what are we doing? One possibility is that we are doing some kind of simulation, but a *qualitative* simulation (de Kleer and Brown 1984; Forbus 1984; Bredeweg and Schut 1991; White and Frederiksen 1990). Qualitative physics research has developed a variety of techniques for reasoning from first principles about physical situations, even with very little information. The results of qualitative simulation involve high-level, conceptual descriptions of physical values and their changes, typically involving sign information (e.g., that a parameter is increasing, decreasing, or constant) and ordinal relationships between parameters (i.e., relative rates of flows, temperatures relative to phase transition boundaries). The systems of qualitative mathematics developed in this research succinctly capture the kinds of conceptual relationships people often use when describing interactions between continuous parameters (e.g., "heat rising causes temperature to rise").

Although the representations of qualitative physics are appealing as models of the contents of human mental representations of commonsense physics, the qualitative simulation algorithms developed to date are problematic as models of human reasoning. Current qualitative simulation algorithms operate via first-principles reasoning over general-purpose axiomatic knowledge. They often produce a huge number of possible behaviors (hundreds or even thousands) even for relatively simple situations (Kuipers 1994). The reason for this is that qualitative simulation, because of the decreased resolution of information about a state, tends to be ambiguous. In a quantitative simulation there is a unique next state. But in qualitative simulations there can be several next states, corresponding to different transitions that are logically consistent with the resolution of the qualitative state information. Each of these potential next states has several next states in turn, and so the number of simulation states in general grows exponentially. To be sure, there are some industrial applications where exploring every possible behavior—what is called *envisioning* (de Kleer 1979)—is necessary. Unfortunately, this exponential behavior makes such algorithms seem psychologically implausible, given how easily people reason about everyday physical situations.

A second problem with first-principles qualitative simulation algorithms as models of human commonsense reasoning is that their predictions tend to include a large number of spurious behaviors (Kuipers 1994), behaviors that logically follow from the low-resolution qualitative descriptions that they use as input but are not in fact physically possible. In engineering applications, such behaviors are generally pruned by using more detailed knowledge (e.g., specific equations or numerical values). But that is not a viable option for modeling the common sense of the person on the street, who is capable of making reasonable predictions even without such detailed information.

We (Forbus and Gentner 1997) suggest that the solution to this puzzle lies in our use of within-domain analogies (e.g., literal similarity) in commonsense reasoning. We claim that a psychological account of qualitative reasoning should rely heavily on analogical reasoning in addition to reasoning from first principles. Qualitative predictions of behavior can be generated via analogical inference from prior observed behaviors described qualitatively. Prediction based on experience reduce the problems of purely first-principles qualitative reasoning, because they are limited to what one has seen. The set of observed behaviors, barring misinterpretations, does not include physically or logically impossible occurrences. Predicted behaviors that are physically impossible might still be generated, because an experience might be applied to a situation containing differences that make it irrelevant, but there would still be many fewer of them than would be generated by a first-principles algorithm. Moreover, predictions from experience have the advantage of being more likely, inasmuch as they have actually occurred, rather than simply being logically possible, which greatly reduces the number of predicted behaviors.

The fact that people store and remember behaviors of physical systems is uncontroversial. But how far literal similarity can go in explaining physical reasoning is still an open question. A major issue is generativity: How flexibly can past experiences be used to make new predictions, and especially predictions about novel systems and/or configurations?

We believe there are three factors that make memory-based reasoning more generative than some might otherwise expect. First, qualitative representations reduce differences. Assuming that people store and use qualitative representations of situations and behavior, then two situations that vary only in quantitative details will look identical with respect to the qualitative aspect of their behavior. Second, analogical reasoning can generate predictions for novel situations. For commonsense reasoning, within-domain analogies (i.e., predicting what will happen when pouring coffee into a cup based on previous experiences pouring coffee into a different cup) should provide a reliable guide to action. Third, multiple analogies can be used to piece together models for complex systems (Spiro et al. 1989).

2.4.1   The Hybrid Similarity Model of Commonsense Reasoning

There is psychological evidence that the same comparison processes used for cross-domain analogical thinking are also used for within-domain comparisons, in tasks ranging from visual perception to conceptual change (Gentner and Markman 1997). It would be surprising if such processes were not used in commonsense physical reasoning. However, memory-based reasoning along is insufficient to explain our ability to use general-purpose, domain-independent physical knowledge—something that we undeniably do, even if there is disagreement over how much of it people do routinely and under what circumstances. Consequently, we suspect that commonsense reasoning arises from the interplay of analogical and first-principles reasoning.

The model we are creating differs from our previous model (Forbus and Gentner 1986), in that we now suspect that the kinds of knowledge and processes that we previously divided into stages are actually tightly interwoven. Specifically, we now believe that comparison processes play a central role throughout the span of expertise. Our assumptions include the following:

· The representational constructs of qualitative physics are psychologically plausible as part of the constituents of human mental models.
· People encode varying amounts of detailed information about the values of continuous properties, in addition to qualitative properties.
· People sometimes use domain-independent principles of qualitative reasoning and situation-independent general knowledge of particular domains.
· Much of people's knowledge is highly context-specific, that is, many principles of qualitative reasoning people use are domain-specific, and much of their knowledge about a domain is tied to situations or classes of situations within that domain.

This view is very different than the standard view in qualitative physics, where domain knowledge is completely generic. The best way to see the implications of this view is to consider a simple example: pouring too much coffee into a cup, leading to it overflowing. Consider this sequence of states of knowledge about that kind of situation:

1. A remembered behavior concerning a specific cup at a specific time, for example, more coffee pouring into your favorite cup leading to it flowing over the top and spilling on your desk. The behavior's description probably includes many concrete details, such as visual descriptions of the objects and their behaviors.
2. A remembered behavior concerning a specific cup at a specific time, including a causal attribution relating different factors or events, for

example, the overflow was caused by continuing to pour coffee once the cup was full. This attribution might come about by someone's explaining the situation to you, or by analogy with an explanation given for another situation, or by the application of a more general principle. Additional qualitative relations might be included, such as blaming the overflow event on pouring a liquid, with the rate of overflow depending on the rate of pouring.

3. A generalization that coffee cups can overflow if you keep filling them up with liquid. This generalization might be formed by successive comparisons of very concrete situations, conservatively stripping away details that are not common across otherwise similar situations. Visual properties may be gone, but many aspects of the descriptions are still very concrete—coffee cups instead of containers, for instance, or even coffee instead of any liquid. More qualitative relationships may be included.

4. A generic domain theory of containers, liquids, and flow that supports limit analysis (Forbus 1984), for example, the coffee cup is a container, the coffee in it is a contained liquid, therefore one limit point in the quantity space for the level of the contained liquid is the height of the cup's top, and a qualitative transition in behavior will occur when the level (which is rising due to its being the destination of a liquid flow, which is the only thing happening that is affecting the amount of coffee in the cup) reaches the height of the top of the cup.

All of these states of knowledge can be used to make predictions. The first state of knowledge represents pure memory. Making a prediction with this kind of knowledge involves using the candidate inferences from a literal similarity match. The last state of knowledge represents the sort of explanation that would be generated by first-principles qualitative simulators. This state of knowledge supports reasoning purely from first principles, but this knowledge can also be used to explain new situations by analogical abduction, based on previous explanations.

The knowledge states in this sequence are samples from a continuum of knowledge about the physical world. The states in between represent what we suspect might be very common in human mental models: intermediate levels of generalization and explanation, where partial explanations have been constructed in a conservative fashion (e.g., generalizing across liquids but still restricted to coffee cups). They are examples of what we could call *situated rules*, pieces of knowledge that are partially abstracted but still partially contextualized.

From an applications perspective, situated rules are the bane of good knowledge-engineering practice. When engineering a domain theory, one strives for generality and broad coverage. In that context, the use of partially abstracted, partially contextualized knowledge represents a failure of analysis.[2] But the situations faced by knowledge engineers and by human learners are very different. Human learning is often initially conservative (Forbus and Gentner 1987; Gentner and Medina 1998; Medin and Ross 1989). Situated rules provide an intermediate form of knowledge between concrete or slightly schematized descriptions of behaviors and the mechanism-based ontologies of standard qualitative physics.

We conjecture that situated rules are used to express principles of qualitative physics as well as knowledge about particular domains. That is, it seems likely that there is a range of knowledge about physical reasoning, varying from concrete, situated rules applicable to a small class of situations to the kinds of overarching, general principles encoded in performance-oriented qualitative reasoning systems. English speakers commonly use the phrase "what goes up must come down," and other language communities have similar expressions. How many of those speakers know that, assuming classical continuity, this statement implies the existence of an instant of time between going up and going down where the vertical velocity is zero? There is a large terrain between knowing nothing and having a broad-coverage general theory, and that terrain is not empty.

We have not yet created a cognitive simulation of our hybrid analogical/first-principles account of qualitative reasoning, but most of the components required have already been created. Let us see how these pieces might fit together to make predictions:

Let the input be a (partial) description of a physical situation. An augmented version of *generate and test* could be used to make predictions as follows:

1. Retrieve similar behaviors (using MAC/FAC). The candidate inferences from mapping these remembered behaviors onto the observed behavior provide additional expectations about the current situation, and hypotheses about the states to follow, based on what happened in

the remembered behavior. The state transitions hypothesized in the candidate inferences form the initial set of predictions.

2. If qualitative simulation rules or procedures are available for generating new behaviors (either by association with this type of task or because they are retrieved by MAC/FAC along with the behaviors used in the previous step), use them to expand the set of predictions.

3. If qualitative simulation rules or procedures are available for evaluating the consistency of possible transitions (from the same sources as the previous step), use them to filter the set of predictions.

4. If there are multiple predictions remaining, estimate their relative likelihood. Return the best, or several, if others are close to the best.

The first step provides quick recognition of familiar behaviors. If the overlap with the current situation is high and the behavior predicted unique, processing may stop at this point, depending on task demands. The second step augments this recognition by domain-specific or first-principles consequences. The third step provides an opportunity for applying exceptions and caveats ("if it were overflowing, you would see coffee coming down the outside of the cup" and "strong acid dissolves coffee cups"). In the fourth step, we suspect that a variety of methods are used to estimate relative likelihood, ranging from domain-specific knowledge ("filling a wax paper cup with hot coffee usually causes it to leak") to estimates of relative frequency based on accessibility in memory ("I've never seen a ceramic coffee cup shatter when it was filled").

Although much work lies ahead in exploring this hybrid qualitative simulation approach, it already illustrates how analogical processing ideas can be used to tackle larger-scale phenomena. The decomposition of analogical processing into units, and the existence of concrete models for those units, provides a vocabulary for analyzing more complex psychological phenomena.

2.5 Example: Case-Based Coaching

A second benefit of exploring analogy in the large is that it can lead to interesting new kinds of applications. These applications are both useful in their own right, and help establish the capabilities of the simulation software in real-world tasks. Such systems, as a whole, are typically not cognitive simulations: performance, rather than fidelity, is their goal. However, such systems can still provide interesting insights for cognitive modeling in two ways. First, they can provide insights about the information processing requirements of a class of tasks, which in turn provides bounds on the required capabilities for people to carry out those tasks. Second, systems that produce explanations as part of their tasks must produce explanations that are considered plausible by their human users. This provides an information-level constraint on the knowledge that is used in a task.

One important application of analogy is *case-based coaching*. Good instructors typically use analogies and examples in helping learners master material. When a learner needs help in solving a problem, a coach might suggest that a specific principle or technique from an example might be relevant, and show the learner how it might be applied in their situation. We have used SME and MAC/FAC to create such a case-based coach, to help students who are learning engineering thermodynamics.

Engineering thermodynamics involves transformations of heat and work. It is the science underlying engines, power plants, refrigerators, and cryogenic systems. Typically taught to college sophomores, it is one of the toughest courses in the engineering curriculum. We have developed software intended to help students learn engineering thermodynamics by providing an *articulate virtual laboratory* (Forbus and Whalley 1994) where students can safely tackle design projects in a scaffolded environment that provides explanations. The program, called CyclePad (Forbus 1997; Forbus et al. 1998), presents its users with a schematic interface on which they design their cycles by "wiring up" components (e.g., turbines, pumps) and making assumptions about numerical values (e.g., pressures, temperatures, flow rates) and properties of the components and the working fluid involved (e.g., choosing water versus some other substance, modeling a turbine as adiabatic). CyclePad uses AI techniques to derive the consequences of a student's assumptions, detect physically impossible combinations of assumptions, and provide explanations for its derivations on demand.

CyclePad is used by a large number of students at a variety of geographically distributed sites. We use a *distributed coach*, where part of the coaching software is embedded in CyclePad itself and part of the coaching services are provided via electronic mail. The "onboard" facilities are lightweight and well tuned, providing rapid feedback for students. The email facility, called the *CyclePad Guru*, enables us to experiment with different coaching techniques without requiring our users to download new software. This is especially important for case-based coaching, since cases often include a variety of media that can be centralized on a server rather than distributed en masse to each student.

The email-based coach works like this. An email dialog in CyclePad offers students several kinds of queries. For our purposes, the only relevant query is a request for design help, which invokes the case-based coach. Design help concerns how to improve the student's design, for example, how one might increase the efficiency of a cycle or lower its operating costs. The student's query is sent via email to an agent colony, RoboTA (Forbus and Kuehne 1998), at Northwestern. The coach's response is sent back via email. Assuming the student's question made sense, this email contains up to two suggestions about how the student might change the design to improve it. (If the student has not finished analyzing his or her design yet or it is contradictory, this is pointed out instead.) These suggestions are based on MAC/FAC retrieving plausible entries from a library of design transformations, and using SME's candidate inference mechanism to generate specific advice about how to apply the transformation used in the case to the student's design. Let us see how this works.

The structural and teleological aspects of the student's design is used as a probe to MAC/FAC.[3] (We found that numerical aspects of the student's design were irrelevant, and hence we filter them out.) The cases in the MAC/FAC memory pool include a description of a design, a problem with that design, and a transformation that modifies the original design in a way that solves this problem. Each reminding includes the SME match created by the FAC stage for that reminding, which is the analogical match between that case and the student's design. A reminding might give rise to several suggestions since SME can generate more than one mapping for a comparison. Each mapping potentially contains a suggestion. For example, a plan to improve turbine efficiency by increasing turbine inlet temperature is applicable in three different ways to a design that has three turbines. Recall that a candidate inference of a mapping is a statement in the base (here, the case) that is suggested by the correspondences of the mapping as possibly holding in the target (here, the student's design). Candidate inferences are the source of advice. Box 2.1 shows the candidate inferences when the coach is reminded of reheat given a Rankine cycle.

Suggestions are filtered in two ways to ensure that they are relevant. First, the candidate inferences must include the case's transformation— otherwise, there is no advice to give. Second, the candidate inferences must include a statement of the form

(implies <*structural/functional properties of cycle*>
   (applicable <*plan of case* >))

Each case is guaranteed to include a statement of this form due to the way cases are created, outlined below. The antecedents are exactly those properties that must be true for the case's transformation to make sense. For example, neither of the suggestions in box 2.1 would make sense for a cycle that did not have heater. All of the antecedents for the implication must have correspondences in the suggestion's mapping, without skolems,[4] in order for the case to be applicable to the student's design.

The suggestions generated by MAC/FAC are prioritized according to the complexity of the transformation they suggest, with simpler transformations being preferred, and on the structural quality of the candidate inference (Forbus et al. 1998). At most two suggestions are selected to be used for generating advice, to avoid overloading the students. If MAC/FAC did not produce at least two suggestions, the case that it was reminded of is removed from the pool and MAC/FAC is run again, using the student's design as a probe as before. This iterative process continues at most N times (currently $N = 2$), until the requisite number of suggestions are generated.

Advice is generated from each suggestion by a module that translates CyclePad's internal representations into understandable English. Box 2.2 shows the advice generated from the candidate inferences in box 2.1. The advice generator treats structural transformations differently from

Box 2.1
The suggestions generated by the CyclePad Guru, using MAC/FAC to retrieve cases that contain suggested design improvements. Cases are generated automatically by domain experts, using the learning environment and a case compiler

```
Suggestions for <Desc WM of Rankine Cycle>:
Suggestion <Use INCREASE-RANKINE-BOILER-T>:
    1 step
    support = .085 extrapolation = 0.66
    normalized = 0.45 overlap = .408
    combined = .944
<Mapping 153 Candidate Inferences>
(BOILER htr1)
(CONDENSER clr1)
(IMPLIES (AND (TURBINE tur1 s2 s3)
              (HEATER htr1 s1 s2))
    (APPLICABLE (:SKOLEM :dsn-tr)))
(TRANSFORMATION-OF (:SKOLEM :dsn-tr)
        (STEPS (ASSIGN (T s2) (:SKOLEM :+))))
Suggestion <Use REHEAT-RANKINE-CYCLE>:
    16 steps
    support = 0.03 extrapolation = .846
    normalized = .404 overlap = .134
    combined = .567
<Mapping 172 Candidate Inferences>
(BOILER htr1)
(CONDENSER clr1)
(IMPLIES (AND (TURBINE tur1 s2 s3)
              (COOLER clr1 s3 s4))
    (APPLICABLE (:SKOLEM :dsn-tr)))
(TRANSFORMATION-OF (:SKOLEM :dsn-tr)
        (STEPS (DISCONNECT (OUT tur1) (IN clr1) s3)
               (INSERT-DEVICE (:SKOLEM heater)
                        (:SKOLEM htr2))
               (CONNECT (OUT tur1) (IN (:SKOLEM htr2))
                        (:SKOLEM s5))
               (INSERT-DEVICE (:SKOLEM turbine)
                        (:SKOLEM tur2))
               (CONNECT (OUT (:SKOLEM htr2))
                        (IN (:SKOLEM tur2))
                        (:SKOLEM s6))
               (CONNECT (OUT (:SKOLEM tur2)) (IN clr1)
                        (:SKOLEM s7))
               (INVOKE-ASN (SATURATED (:SKOLEM s5)))
               (ASSIGN (DRYNESS (:SKOLEM s5))
                        (:SKOLEM 1.0))
               (INVOKE-ASN (REHEATER (:SKOLEM htr2)))
               (INVOKE-ASN (ISOBARIC (:SKOLEM htr2)))
               (INVOKE-ASN (MATERIAL-OF (:SKOLEM htr2)
                        (:SKOLEM molybdenum)))
               (INVOKE-ASN (FUEL-OF (:SKOLEM htr2)
                        (:SKOLEM natural-gas)))
               (INVOKE-ASN (ISENTROPIC (:SKOLEM tur2)))
               (INVOKE-ASN (MATERIAL-OF (:SKOLEM tur2)
                        (:SKOLEM molybdenum)))
               (INVOKE-ASN (SATURATED (:SKOLEM s7)))
               (ASSIGN (DRYNESS (:SKOLEM s7)) (:SKOLEM 1))))
```

Box 2.2
Advice for a student generated from the suggestions of box 2.1. The step-by-step instructions on carrying out the transformation are generated from the candidate inferences generated during retrieval

---

I have 2 suggestions.
= =

Suggestion #1
Your problem reminds me of a method: increasing boiler temperature in a Rankine cycle.
Increasing the boiler temperature increases the efficiency of the cycle.
You can find out more about this at
http://www.qrg.ils.nwu.edu/thermo/design-library/turank.htm.
Here is how you might apply this to your design:
1. Increase T (S2).
= =

Suggestion #2
Your problem reminds me of a method: reheat in a Rankine cycle. Reheat adds another heater and another
turbine. The second heater, a reheater, heats up the working fluid at the turbine
outlet, and the second turbine extracts yet more work from that. This increases efficiency because more heat
is being added when the steam is still at a reasonably high temperature.
You can find out more about this at
http://www.qrg.ils.nwu.edu/thermo/design-library/reheat.htm.

Here is how you might do this with your design:

1. Disconnect the outlet of TUR1 from the inlet of CLR1.
2. Create a new heater, which we'll call HTR2.
3. Connect the outlet of TUR1 to the inlet of HTR2. Let's refer to the properties of the working fluid there
as S5.
4. Create a new turbine, which we'll call TUR2.
5. Connect the outlet of HTR2 to the inlet of TUR2. Let's refer to the properties of the working fluid there
as S6.
6. Connect the outlet of TUR2 to the inlet of CLR1. Let's refer to the properties of the working fluid there
as S7.

You might find the following assumptions relevant or useful:

1. Assume that the working fluid at S5 is saturated.
2. Assume quality (S5) = 1.0000 [0–1]
3. Assume that HTR2 is a reheater.
4. Assume that HTR2 works isobarically.
5. Assume that HTR2 is made of molybdenum.
6. Assume that HTR2 burns natural-gas.
7. Assume that TUR2 works isentropically.
8. Assume that TUR2 is made of molybdenum.
9. Assume that the working fluid at S7 is saturated.
10. Assume quality (S7) = 1.0000 [0–1]
= =

---

other suggestions. This is because structural transformations must be followed in order to implement the suggestion, whereas the other assumptions may or may not be relevant to the student's particular situation. We believe that forcing the student to think carefully about which assumptions make sense is good exercise for them. In box 2.2, for example, it is suggested that the new components be made of molybdenum, which a student should recognize as unusual and expensive. If the suggestion is about modifying parameter values rather than structural changes, qualitative descriptions of relative changes in value are used in the advice. The advice also includes a URL describing the case in detail, using hypertext supplied by the case's author, encouraging the student to learn more by following up in the Web-based design library.

New cases in the coach's design library are automatically generated by a *case compiler*. To add a case, instructors provide two snapshots of a CyclePad design, one before and one after their transformation. They also specify the goals of the transformation, in terms of changes in parameter values (i.e., what parameters must have increased or decreased), some strings to be used in templates, and a URL pointing to a detailed rationale for that case. While we insist that the Web page for the case include an explanation of the case, this explanation is in natural language: case authors only need to be thermodynamics experts, not AI experts. The case compiler uses CyclePad to analyze the before and after design snapshots. It uses a record of user actions stored internally with each dumped design to construct the description of the transformation that leads from one to the other, and augments the case description with this plan, the problems it is intended to solve, and the applicability condition described earlier. (It also checks to ensure that the transformation actually achieves the claimed goals, since even experts can make mistakes.) Adding the new case to the MAC/FAC memory is simple, because no indexing is required: the structured representations needed to support reasoning also suffice for retrieval, since the content vectors needed by the MAC stage are automatically computed from them.

Our case library currently consists of fourteen cases, averaging seventy-four expressions involving twenty-three entities each. Retrieval and advice generation is very quick: less than five seconds on the average, with no more than six seconds at most, on a 200 MHz Pentium Pro. This performance comes from two factors. First, the MAC stage provides significant filtering, with only two or three cases proposed for processing by SME each time. Second, SME now uses a polynomial-time greedy algorithm in its merge step, making its overall complexity quadratic in the size of descriptions compared (Forbus, Ferguson, and Gentner 1994). The coach has been continuously available to CyclePad users since February 1998.

Our use of SME and MAC/FAC provides two significant advantages over the state of the art in case-based coaching. Most case-based coaching systems use very weak machine-understandable representations—often lists of features—complemented by student-friendly media, such as video. This requires hand-encoding and indexing of every new case, a labor-intensive process that is a major cost in creating and maintaining such systems. Furthermore, the lack of rich formal representations (e.g., proofs or causal arguments) makes it impossible for a software coach to show a student just how the principle illustrated by the case might apply to their situation. Our use of MAC/FAC means that domain experts can use CyclePad and a case compiler to extend the design library without any knowledge of how CyclePad's representations operate nor any knowledge of how the retrieval software operates. Our use of SME enables us to ensure that the advice can actually be applied to the student's problem, and generate step-by-step instructions showing them how to do so. Thus MAC/FAC functions as a black-box retriever and SME functions as an explanation and inference generator.

Although the CyclePad Guru is an application of analogical processing, it is interesting to see how its use of these models connects to psychological considerations. First, by using a psychologically motivated model of retrieval, we avoid the by-hand indexing that plagues most CBR systems, as noted earlier. Second, it may at first glance seem paradoxical that MAC/FAC produces good remindings, given the evidence on the difficulty of analogical retrievals. However, its behavior actually fits the psychological data quite well: the cases are in the same domain as the student's problems, so it is retrieving literal similarities, rather than cross-domain analogies. Moreover, its encoding processes for cases correspond more to experts than novices, which again is a factor that facilitates retrieval.

2.6 Scaling Up: How Structure-Mapping Fares

These examples suggest that structure-mapping can go the distance: the ability to handle large, complex representations that are automatically generated to help with real problems is encouraging. Although our work on hybrid qualitative simulation is still in progress, the clarity that can be achieved by casting larger-scale process models in terms of pre-existing component process models suggests that this perspective is a valuable theoretical tool. The case-based coach suggests that structure-mapping can be effectively applied to complex, real-world problems.

Two other application efforts in progress are worthy of mention, because they give some indication of the scale that is involved in some of the tasks that people find straightforward. Under the DARPA High Performance Knowledge Base program,[5] we have been using SME and MAC/FAC to tackle two kinds of human reasoning: reasoning from historical precedents about international crises, and critiquing battlefield courses of action by analogy. These are tasks that experts do daily and that novices can understand the results of easily (even if they have trouble solving the problem by themselves).

These complex real-world tasks provide interesting data points concerning the size of descriptions that need to be handled for scaling up to handle the breadth of human analogical reasoning. In crisis management, we worked with the two competing teams, one led by SAIC and the other by Teknowledge/Cycorp. Each team had its own large knowledge base, and did all of the encoding of historical case information and associated background knowledge about countries. Cases tended to be hundreds of propositions in size, with some being well over two thousand propositions in size. In the battlefield critiques, the knowledge base was built by a collaborative team, with the contents of cases being created by drafting tools and natural-language parsing tools that produced representations, which were on the order of a thousand propositions each. Although these descriptions were rich enough to (mostly) handle the problems thrown at them, we suspect that people would be able to reason with far more knowledge than these systems would, given the same inputs. In crisis management, where a formal evaluation was performed, our average score was 2.3 out of 3, which was quite respectable given the difficulty of the problem.[6]

Tackling problems of this magnitude led us to develop some extensions to SME. The most interesting of these are *automatic case extraction* and *dynamic case expansion*. With automatic case extraction, the propositions that constitute a case are drawn from a larger knowledge base according to properties of the task, rather than being prepackaged as a combined experience. While our particular implementation of this operation is not intended to be psychologically plausible (i.e., pattern-matching and backward-chaining reasoning), how dynamically determined are the descriptions used in analogical reasoning, and by what means, is an interesting issue worth exploring. With dynamic case expansion, incremental additions are made to the contents of a case based on the progress of the match so far. This is useful in exploring complex analogies. For example, the SAIC Year-Two scenario description consisted of 2,341 propositions and the SAIC Operation Desert Shield description consisted of 2,159 propositions. Directly matching both of these descriptions leads to creating hundreds of thousands of match hypotheses. But by starting with a "small" initial subset (778 versus 663 propositions), the match could be grown to include the relevant subset of the information (ultimately 1,513 by 1,605 propositions) in a tractable manner.

The Phineas experience, our first large-scale analogical processing simulation, led to substantial changes in SME. The HPKB experience, aside from performance tuning, has led to fewer internal changes in SME, but significantly expanded the ways it can interact with large knowledge bases. We find this relative stability encouraging: It suggests that SME can evolve to go the distance.

2.7 The Integration Constraint Revisited

Now that we have seen some examples of large-scale analogical processing, let us return to the integration constraint and consider what lessons we might learn, in order to improve simulation models of analogical processing.

Processes need to operate in a range of domains. Modeling human performance in a domain naturally requires assumptions about how that domain is represented. Domain-specific representation assumptions are often core components of a theory, as in the assumptions about qualitative representations made earlier. But models of similarity processes, to capture their ability to operate across multiple domains, need to avoid domain-specific assumptions. For example, CopyCat (Hofstadter and Mitchell 1994) and TableTop (French 1995) each provide suggestive models of similarity for a specific domain and task. Unfortunately, their use of hand-coded domain-specific correspondences and matching algorithms means that for each new domain a new system must be created (Forbus et al. 1997). This makes it hard to see how these principles might generalize to other arenas.

Systems must be able to scale up. Real-world analogical processing tasks often involve descriptions that are much larger than the traditional test cases for analogy simulations. Scaling up to larger descriptions and larger memories is a serious challenge. ARCS (Thagard et al. 1990), for example, worked with small examples, but fell apart on larger memories[7] (Forbus, Gentner, and Law 1995). IAM's (Keane 1990, 1997) purely serial mapping strategy can be led astray by syntactic garden paths and miss larger potential matches, a problem that will likely be more severe as the size of descriptions grows.

Candidate inferences must be structurally sound. To produce coherent advice, for example, in suggesting to a student how to improve their design, the candidate inferences of an analogy need to follow the 1:1 constraint and parallel connectivity constraint. ACME's ability to produce many-to-one mappings, though intuitively appealing in some ways, leads to candidate inferences that are psychologically implausible (Markman 1997).

Processes must have realistic resource requirements. For example, SME originally produced an exhaustive enumeration of mappings. Although convenient for studying the possible outcomes of an analogy, the idea of judging among dozens of mappings is psychologically highly implausible, and the factorial worst-case computational complexity even more so (Falkenhainer, Forbus, and Gentner 1989). This caused us to replace the exhaustive merge algorithm with a greedy algorithm that produces only a few intepretations (Forbus and Oblinger 1990). A good example in this regard is LISA (Hummel and Holyoak 1997), an evolving model which places a priority on operating under strong working-memory constraints—a design choice that makes scaling up more of a challenge.

Tailorability in processing should be avoided. Hand-tuning an algorithm for specific examples reduces its explanatory power and compromises its ability to be integrated into larger-scale models. For example, central to LISA is its use of serial activation—the pattern of which is currently set by hand.

Constraints can emerge from the interaction of processes. Gentner and Clement (1988) argued that the best way to capture the influence of goals and task-specific constraints on analogy is in terms of their role in setting up the inputs and evaluating the outputs of a fixed-analogy engine. The use of automatic case extraction in crisis management and the evaluation of candidate inferences in the case-based coach provide supporting evidence for this argument.[8] By contrast, ACME's mingling of semantic similarity, pragmatic relevance, and structural consistency within the mapping engine itself led to the problematic many-to-one mapping described earlier. On the other hand, we have found that very limited forms of "advice" to the mapping engine, based on task constraints (e.g., requiring or excluding correspondences [Forbus and Oblinger 1990]) can be valuable in real problems.

These lessons are sobering. Clearly we are a long way from achieving models that fully satisfy the integration constraint. However, it is equally clear that the field is making significant progress, and there is every reason to believe that this progress will continue.

2.8   Discussion

My suggestion in this chapter has been that the basic mechanisms of comparison and retrieval are understood well enough that more of the field's energy should be focused on what might be called *large-scale analogical processing*, that is, exploring the roles analogical processing plays in other cognitive processes. This has always been a central concern of cognitive psychologists, of course. My argument is that now it should become a central concern for cognitive simulation as well. Creating larger-scale simulations of cognitive phenomena is an exciting new frontier, opened up by the combination of progress in cognitive science and the Moore's Law expansion of available computational power. Exploring this frontier leaves behind the stultifying world of microworlds that provide no general insights and wind-up toy models that cannot scale up to realistic phenomena. This challenge makes sense only now because research on cognitive simulation of analogy has climbed up past the foothills of the phenomena and, from the ridge we are standing on, can now see new peaks, representing new phenomena to explore.

There is of course a second frontier opening up: progress in neuroscience has lead to the intriguing possibility of modeling analogical processing on the microscale, so to speak. This complementary direction has its own promises and perils that others can speak of more knowledgeably than can I. Happily, the solid consensus that has been achieved at the information and algorithm levels of understanding (in the sense of Marr [1982]) provides a canvas to which explorers in both directions can contribute results.

New frontiers are always difficult, and inertia is a powerful force. However, for progress to continue, I believe that scaling up is crucial. The most serious danger in foregoing investigations of analogy in the large is intellectual myopia. All too often, researchers are tempted to keep tuning the microstructure of a simulation and arguing over fine details, ignoring the fact that their simulation cannot possibly scale to handle kinds of cognitive processing that human beings clearly do. Exploring the microstructure of the processes of mapping and retrieval are still important enterprises, to be sure, but they cannot continue to dominate analogy research. Arguably, they will not even be the major source of constraints on models in the foreseeable future: given what we have learned so far about how analogy and similarity work, I believe that we will learn more by exploring their roles in other processes than by exclusively focusing on them in isolation. Simulating the use of mapping in discourse (cf. Boronat and Gentner, in preparation), the roles of analogy in argumentation (cf. Spellman and Holyoak 1992), and the use of analogy in conceptual change and scientific discovery (cf Gentner et al. 1997) are all examples of simulation challenges that will help us discover much more about the nature of analogy and similarity. There is a mo n-tain range of phenomena to be explored, and it will not be explored by playing "King of the Foothill."

See you in the mountains.

Acknowledgments

This work has been carried out in collaboration with Dedre Gentner. The case-based coaching work described here has been done in collaboration with John Everett, Mike Brokowski, Leo Ureel, Sven Kuehne, and Julie Baher. This research is supported by the Cognitive Science and Artificial Intelligence Programs of the Office of Naval Research. Research on CyclePad was supported by the Applications of Advanced Technology program of the National Science Foundation. Valuable discussions with Dedre Gentner, Ron Ferguson, Sven Kuehne, Art Markman, Keith Holyoak, and John Hummel helped shape this chapter.

Notes

1. The *tiered identicality constraint* of structure-mapping states that the default criterion for matching relational statements is that the predicates involved be identical. Nonidentical functions are allowed to match because they provide cross-dimensional mappings. We are currently exploring predicate decomposition as another method to achieve partial matches among relations.

2. See, for example, the *No function in structure* principle of de Kleer and Brown (1984), which is clearly violated by situated rules.

3. Teleology refers to how a design achieves its intended function. CyclePad automatically derives teleological information from the structure of a student's design, ascribing a role to each component in the cycle (i.e., "this mixer is acting as a jet ejector") using a Bayesian recognition architecture (Everett 1995, 1999.)

4. Skolem constants are introduced in candidate inferences when the projected base fact contains an entity that is not part of the mapping (Falkenhainer, Forbus, and Gentner 1986, 1989). Each such entity gives rise to a skolem, indicating that some entity in the target domain must be identified (or postulated) to play its role before the candidate inference can be used.

5. http://projects.teknowledge.com/HPKB/.

6. The specifications for the challenge problems can be found at http://www.iet.com/Projects/HPKB/.

7. This was due in part to the normalization algorithm used in the winner-take-all network valuing absolute size over relative fit (Holyoak, personal communication). As Forbus, Gentner, and Law (1994) report, the ARCS algorithm could also be improved by replacing ARCS's semantic similarity constraint with structure-mapping's tiered identicality constraint.

8. The crisis management system also involved the evaluation of candidate inferences, and task constraints are built into the case compiler used with the case-based coach, but these were not mentioned here for the sake of brevity.

References

Boronat, C., and Gentner, D. (in preparation). Novel metaphors are processed as generative domain mappings.

Bredeweg, B., and Schut, C. (1991). Cognitive plausibility of a conceptual framework for modeling problem solving expertise. *Proceedings of the thirteenth annual conference of the Cognitive Science Society*, pp. 473–479. Hillsdale, NJ: Erlbaum.

Clement, C. A., and Gentner, D. (1991). Systematicity as a selection constraint in analogical mapping. *Cognitive Science* 15:89–132.

de Kleer, J. (1979). The origin and resolution of ambiguities in causal arguments. *Proceedings of the sixth international joint conference on Artificial Intelligence*, pp. 197–203. San Mateo: Morgan Kaufmann.

de Kleer, J., and Brown, J. S. (1984). A qualitative physics based on confluences. *Artificial Intelligence* 24:7–83.

Decoste, D. (1991). Dynamic across-time measurement interpretation. *Artificial Intelligence* 51(1–3):273–341.

Everett, J. O. (1995). A theory of mapping from structure to function applied to engineering domains. Paper presented at the fourteenth international joint conference on Artificial Intelligence, Montreal.

Everett, J. O. (1999). Topological inference of teleology: Deriving function from structure via evidential reasoning. *Artificial Intelligence*, 113(1–2):149–202.

Falkenhainer B. (1987). An examination of the third stage in the analogy process: Verification-based analogical learning. In *Proceedings of IJCAI-87*. Los Altos: Morgan-Kaufmann.

Falkenhainer, B. (1990). A unified approach to explanation and theory formation. In Shrager and Langley, Eds., *Computational Models of Scientific Discovery and Theory Formation*. San Mateo, CA: Morgan Kaufmann Publishers.

Falkenhainer, B., Forbus, K., and Gentner, D. (1986). The structure-mapping engine. *Proceedings of AAAI-86*, pp. 272–277. Philadelphia, PA. AAAI Press.

Falkenhainer, B., Forbus, K., and Gentner, D. (1989). The Structure-mapping engine: Algorithm and examples. *Artificial Intelligence* 41:1–63.

Ferguson, R. W. (1994). MAGI: Analogy-based encoding using symmetry and regularity. In A. Ram and K. Eiselt, Eds., *Proceedings of the sixteenth annual conference of the Cognitive Science Society*, pp. 283–288. Mahwah, NJ: Erlbaum.

Ferguson, R. W., Aminoff, A., and Gentner, D. (1996). Modeling qualitative differences in symmetry judgments. *Proceedings of the eighteenth annual conference of the Cognitive Science Society*, pp. 334–339. Hillsdale, NJ: Erlbaum.

Forbus, K. D. (1984). Qualitative process theory. *Artificial Intelligence* 24(1):85–168.

Forbus, K. D. (1990). The qualitative process engine. In D. S. Weld and J. de Kleer, Eds., *Readings in qualitative reasoning about physical systems*, pp. 220–233. San Mateo, CA: Morgan Kaufmann.

Forbus, K. (1997). Using qualitative physics to create articulate educational software. *IEEE Expert* **12**(3):32–41.

Forbus, K., Everett, J. O., Ureel, L., Brokowski, M., Baher, J., and Kuehne, S. (1998). Distributed coaching for an intelligent learning environment. *Proceedings of the twelfth international workshop on qualitative reasoning*, pp. 57–64. Melo Park, CA: AAAI Press.

Forbus, K., Ferguson, R., and Gentner, D. (1994). Incremental structure-mapping. *Proceedings of the sixteenth annual conference of the Cognitive Science Society*, pp. 313–318.

Forbus, K., and Gentner, D. (1986). Learning physical domains: Towards a theoretical framework. In R. Michalski, J. Carbonell, and T. Mitchell, Eds., *Machine learning: An artificial intelligence approach*, vol. 2, pp. 311–348. San Mateo, CA: Morgan-Kauffmann.

Forbus, K., and Gentner, D. (1997). Qualitative mental models: Simulations or memories? *Proceedings of the eleventh international workshop on qualitative reasoning*, pp. 99–104. Cortona, Italy.

Forbus, K., Gentner, D., and Law, K. (1995). MAC/FAC: A model of similarity-based retrieval. *Cognitive Science* **19**(2):141–205.

Forbus, K., Gentner, D., Markman, A., and Ferguson, R. (1997). Analogy just looks like high-level perception: Why a domain-general approach to analogical mapping is right. *Journal of Experimental and Theoretical Artificial Intelligence* **4**:185–211.

Forbus, K., and Kuehne, S. (1998). RoboTA: An agent colony architecture for supporting education. *Proceedings of second International Conference on Autonomous Agents*, pp. 455–456. ACM Press.

Forbus, K., and Oblinger, D. (1990). Making SME greedy and pragmatic. *Proceedings of the twelfth annual conference of the Cognitive Science Society*. Hillsdale, NJ: Erlbaum.

Forbus, K., and Whalley, P. (1994). Using qualitative physics to build articulate software for thermodynamics education. *Proceedings of AAAI-94*, pp. 1175–1182. Menlo Park: AAAI Press.

French, R. M. (1995). *The subtlety of similarity*. Cambridge, MA: MIT Press.

Gentner, D. (1983). Structure-mapping: A theoretical framework for analogy. *Cognitive Science* **7**:155–170.

Gentner, D. (1988). Metaphor as structure mapping: The relational shift. *Child Development* **59**:47–59.

Gentner, D. (1989). The mechanisms of analogical learning. In S. Vosniadou and A. Ortony, Eds., *Similarity and analogical reasoning*, pp. 199–241. London: Cambridge University Press.

Gentner, D., Brem, S., Ferguson, R. W., Wolff, P., Markman, A. B., and Forbus, K. D. (1997). Analogy and creativity in the works of Johannes Kepler. In T. B. Ward, S. M. Smith, and J. Vaid, Eds., *Creative thought: An investigation of conceptual structures and processes*, pp. 403–459. Washington, DC: American Psychological Association.

Gentner, D., and Clement, C. (1988). Evidence for relational selectivity in the interpretation of analogy and metaphor. In G. H. Bower, Ed., *The psychology of learning and motivation, advances in research and theory*, vol. 22, pp. 307–358. New York: Academic Press.

Gentner, D., and Forbus, K. D. (1991). MAC/FAC: A model of similarity-based access and mapping. *Proceedings of the thirteenth annual conference of the Cognitive Science Society*, pp. 504–509. Chicago, IL.

Gentner, D., and Holyoak, K. J. (1997). Reasoning and learning by analogy: Introduction. *American Psychologist* 52:32–34.

Gentner, D., and Markman, A. B. (1995). Similarity is like analogy: Structural alignment in comparison. In C. Cacciari, Ed., *Similarity in language, thought and perception*, pp. 111–147. Brussels: BREPOLS.

Gentner, D., and Markman, A. B. (1997). Structure mapping in analogy and similarity. *American Psychologist* 52:45–56.

Gentner, D., and Medina, J. (1998). Similarity and the development of rules. *Cognition* 65:263–297.

Gentner, D., and Rattermann, M. J. (1991). Language and the career of similarity. In S. A. Gelman and J. P. Brynes, Eds., *Perspectives on thought and language: Interrelations in development*, pp. 225–227. London: Cambridge University Press.

Gentner, D., and Rattermann, M. J. (forthcoming). Deep thinking in children: The case for knowledge change in analogical development. *Behavioral and Brain Sciences*.

Gentner, D., Rattermann, M. J., and Forbus, K. D. (1993). The roles of similarity in transfer: Separating retrieval from inferential soundness. *Cognitive Psychology* 25:524–575.

Gentner, D., and Stevens, A., Eds. (1983). *Mental Models*. Hillsdale, NJ: LEA Associates.

Gentner, D., and Toupin, C. (1986). Systematicity and surface similarity in the development of analogy. *Cognitive Science* 10:277–300.

Goldstone, R. L. (1994). Influences of categorization on perceptual discrimination. *Journal of Experimental Psychology: General* 123(2):178–200.

Goldstone, R. L., and Medin, D. L. (1994). Time course of comparison. *Journal of Experimental Psychology: Learning, Memory and Cognition* 20(1):29–50.

Goswami, U. (1992). *Analogical reasoning in children*. Hillsdale, NJ: Erlbaum.

Goswami, U., and Brown, A. L. (1989). Melting chocolate and melting snowmen: Analogical reasoning and causal relations. *Cognition* 35:69–95.

Halford, G. S. (1987). A structure-mapping approach to cognitive development. The neo-Piagetian theories of cognitive development: Toward an interpretation. *International Journal of Psychology* 22(5–6):609–642.

Halford, G. S. (1993). *Children's understanding: The development of mental models.* Hillsdale, NJ: Erlbaum.

Hofstadter, D. R., and Mitchell, M. (1994). The CopyCat project: A model of mental fluidity and analogy-making. In K. J. Holyoak and J. A. Barnden, Eds., *Advances in connectionist and neural computation theory,* vol. 2, *Analogical connections,* pp. 31–112. Norwood, NJ: Ablex.

Holyoak, K. J., and Koh, K. (1987). Surface and structural similarity in analogical transfer. *Memory and Cognition* 15:332–340.

Holyoak, K. J., and Thagard, P. (1989). Analogical mapping by constraint satisfaction. *Cognitive Science* 13(3):295–355.

Hummel, J. E., and Holyoak, K. J. (forthcoming). LISA: A computational model of analogical inference and schema induction. *Psychological Review.*

Jones, R. M., Laird, J. E., Nielsen, P. E., Coulter, K. J., Kenny, P., and Koss, F. V. (1999). Automated intelligent pilots for combat flight simulation. *AI Magazine* 20(1): 27–41.

Keane, M. T. (1990). Incremental analogising: Theory & model. In K. J. Gilhooly, M. T. G. Keane, R. H. Logie, and G. Erdos, Eds., *Lines of thinking,* vol. 1. Chichester: Wiley.

Keane, M. T. (1997). What makes an analogy difficult? The effects of order and causal structure on analogical mapping. *Journal of Experimental Psychology: Learning, Memory and Cognition* 23(4):946–967.

Keane, M. T. (1996). On adaptation in analogy: Tests of pragmatic importance and adaptability in analogical problem solving. *The Quarterly Journal of Experimental Psychology* 49/A(4):1062–1085.

Kotovsky, L., and Gentner, D. (1996). Comparison and categorization in the development of relational similarity. *Child Development* 67:2797–2822.

Kuipers, B. (1994). *Qualitative reasoning: Modeling and simulation with incomplete knowledge.* Cambridge, MA.: MIT Press.

Lassaline, M. E. (1996). Structural alignment in induction and similarity. *Journal of Experimental Psychology: Learning, Memory, and Cognition* 22(3):754–770.

Markman, A. B. (1997). Constraints on analogical inference. *Cognitive Science* 21(4):373–418.

Markman, A. B., and Gentner, D. (1993). Structural alignment during similarity comparisons. *Cognitive Psychology* 25:431–467.

Marr, D. (1982). *Vision: A computational investigation into the human representation and processing of visual information.* San Francisco, CA: W. H. Freeman.

Medin, D. L., Goldstone, R. L., and Gentner, D. (1993). Respects for similarity. *Psychological Review* 100(2):254–278.

Medin, D. L., and Ross, B. H. (1989). The specific character of abstract thought: Categorization, problem-solving, and induction. In R. J. Sternberg, Ed., *Advances in the psychology of human intelligence*, vol. 5, pp. 189–223. Hillsdale, NJ: Erlbaum.

Norman, D. A. (1988). *The psychology of everyday things*. New York: Basic Books.

Rattermann, M. J., and Gentner, D. (1998). The effect of language on similarity: The use of relational labels improves young children's performance in a mapping task. In K. Holyoak, D. Gentner, and B. Kokinov, Eds., *Advances in analogy research: Integration of theory and data from the cognitive, computational, and neural sciences*, pp. 274–282. Sofia: New Bulgarian University Press.

Ross, B. H. (1989). Distinguishing types of superficial similarities: Different effects on the access and use of earlier problems. *Journal of Experimental Psychology: Learning, Memory and Cognition* 15(3):456–468.

Schwartz, D. L. (1999). Physical imagery: Kinematic versus dynamic models. *Cognitive Psychology* 38:433–464.

Spellman B. A., and Holyoak, K. J. (1992). If Saddam is Hitler then who is George Bush? Analogical mapping between systems of social roles. *Journal of Personality and Social Psychology* 62(6):913–933.

Spellman, B. A., and Holyoak, K. J. (1996). Pragmatics in analogical mapping. *Cognitive Psychology* 31:307–346.

Spiro, R. J., Feltovich, P. J., Coulson, R. J., and Anderson, D. K. (1989). Multiple analogies for complex concepts: Antidotes for analogy-induced misconception in advanced knowledge acquisition. In S. Vosniadou and A. Ortony, Eds., *Similarity and analogical reasoning*, pp. 498–531. Cambridge: Cambridge University Press.

Thagard, P., Holyoak, K. J., Nelson, G., and Gochfeld, D. (1990). Analog retrieval by constraint satisfaction. *Artificial Intelligence* 46:259–310.

White, B., and Frederiksen, J. (1990). Causal model progressions as a foundation for intelligent learning environments. *Artificial Intelligence* 42:99–157.

Wu, M., and Gentner, D. (1998). Structure in category-based induction. *Proceedings of the twentieth annual conference of the Cognitive Science Society*, pp. 1154–1158. Hillsdale, NJ: Erlbaum.

3

Integrating Memory and Reasoning in Analogy-Making: The AMBR Model

Boicho N. Kokinov and Alexander A. Petrov

3.1 Reuniting Memory and Reasoning Research: An Appeal for a Second Marriage after Their Divorce

Three blind men were exploring an elephant. The first of them, who happened to reach the leg, described the elephant as something like a tree trunk—high and of cylindrical shape. The second one grasped the ear and described the elephant as something like a blanket—flexible, thin, and covering a large surface. The third grasped the trunk and formed an image of a long and flexible pipe-shaped object like a hose. For a long time they argued about the right conception of the elephant.

We cognitive scientists are often in the role of those blind researchers trying to understand human cognition. Because it is a huge and complex object of study, each of us approaches it from a certain perspective and studies only a tiny bit of it. Although we do not misrepresent the whole of cognition with the particular object of study, say memory or analogy, we tend to think of mechanisms that could explain the tiny fraction we have focused on. To continue the elephant story, when "trunk specialists" observe the fluid that comes out when the trunk is cut, they tend to hypothesize that it is an olfactory secretion. "Leg specialists" also observe a fluid coming out when the leg is cut but have a very different hypothesis about it—it must be some filling of the leg. The fact that this fluid is one and the same in all cases (blood) and has the same function can be discovered only when these scientists come together and consider the elephant as a whole. They need to explore the interactions between various parts (e.g., that an infection in the leg might cause complications

Figure 3.1
Cognitive scientists study human cognition in small fractions and often do not recognize its underlying unity.

in the trunk) and to postulate general principles and systems (like the cardiovascular system).

There is nothing wrong with separating cognition into pieces and studying them. The practice of "carving nature at its joints" dates at least as far back as the dialogues of Plato. "Scientists try to study systems that are sufficiently closed to be predictable and sufficiently small to be understandable" (Hunt 1999:8). Big and complex systems are hardly manageable. Studies of isolated parts have led to very important achievements in understanding the mechanisms of human cognition and analogy-making in particular.

However, studies of components should be done with awareness of the fact that the separation of human cognition into various processes is just a convenient tool and not a reality. They should be complemented with explorations of the interactions among various cognitive processes, that is, instead of being carved, the "joints of nature" have to be studied.

Early philosophers like Aristotle considered thinking and memory in an integrated way. The doctrine of associationism explained human thinking by means of the content and organization of human memory. Later, as science developed and psychology became an experimental science, researchers tended to analyze simple and separate faculties of the human mind in order to be able to study them experimentally. Nowadays we have a huge pile of facts about both memory and reasoning (and analogical reasoning in particular). The problem is that these two research communities do not speak to each other often. As a result, facts established in one of the fields are often neglected and ignored in the other.

We feel the time has come to try to put the pieces back together. This chapter makes an attempt to reintegrate research on analogy-making with research on memory. Keith Holyoak and John Hummel (chap. 5, this volume) present another attempt in a similar direction—they integrate analogy with memory and learning. Kenneth Forbus (chap. 2, this volume) also appeals for integrating analogy models with models of large-scale cognitive processes. He presents an integrated model of commonsense thinking based on analogical reasoning and reasoning from first principles. Douglas Hofstadter (chap. 15, this volume) argues that analogy-making might be the core of many cognitive processes from perception to categorization to translation of poetry. Gilles Fauconnier (chap. 7, this volume) integrates analogy with conceptual blending. Paul Thagard and Cameron Shelley (chap. 10, this volume) integrate analogy with emotions. Arthur Markman and Pase Morean (chap. 11, this volume) integrate analogy-making with decision-making. These are all small but important steps in the direction of reintegrating our knowledge about human cognition. It seems that cognitive science has matured enough to pursue these steps.

Modeling has too many degrees of freedom. A phenomenon can often be modeled in several different ways and it is difficult to evaluate the model based on this single phenomenon alone. That is why it is important to restrict the space of possible models by bringing to bear as many constraints as possible. Several types of constraints can be exploited:

• Behavioral constraints—these come from psychological experiments and describe the behavior that should be generated by the model under different circumstances (the richer the set of circumstances the better).
• Biological constraints—these come from the neurosciences and describe the restrictions on the model arising from the known organization of the brain and body.
• Evolutionary and developmental constraints—these come from developmental psychology and animal research and restrict the complexity and type of mechanisms as well as their evolution and development.
• Architectural constraints—these come from theoretical considerations and require coherence among the mechanisms underlying human cognition so that they can function together and interact.

In addition, we can differentiate between specific and general constraints. Typically, when modeling a specific phenomenon we tend to concentrate on the constraints known to apply to that specific phenomenon. Thus when studying analogy we tend to collect data *with respect to analogy*. The utility of these data is clear, and we try to draw from as many sources as we can: psychological, neurological, evolutionary, and developmental. Very often, however, we ignore data that are not directly related to analogy but are nevertheless very useful because of their relation to other cognitive processes that in turn relate to analogy. If we consider analogy as an integrated phenomenon in the complex structure of human mind, we need to pay attention to these general constraints as well.

This is, of course, an overambitious task that is clearly beyond the scope of this chapter. However, it is an important motivation of the current work. This chapter describes only a few steps on the way toward integrating analogy back again into human cognition. Special emphasis is put on some general behavioral and architectural constraints and particularly on the integration of analogy-making and memory.

Section 3.2 presents a highly selective and biased review of the literature on memory. It concludes with a summary of the behavioral and architectural constraints on analogy models as seen by the authors. Section 3.3 reviews the AMBR research program. Finally, section 3.4 describes AMBR2—the current version of the AMBR model—which tries to bring memory and analogy back together.

3.2   Reconstructing the Dinosaur: The Dynamic and Constructive Nature of Human Memory

Is memory a storehouse or an action? There is no consensus on a single and unified theory of memory or even on a single general metaphor for memory (Roediger 1980; Koriat and Goldsmith 1996). The classical metaphor of memory describes it as a physical space where items are stored and later on searched for and retrieved. This metaphor has been very powerful and even dominant in the history of psychology. It uses some well-known source domains such as libraries, storehouses, and computers and thus helps us to transfer many inferences about memory. That is why the storehouse metaphor is so widespread. Even our terminology is influenced by it, so that we speak about storage and retrieval from memory.

On the other hand, starting with Sir Frederick Bartlett (1932), the spatial metaphor has been under continuous fire and a new dynamic and constructive view on human memory has emerged. One particularly notable new metaphor is due to Ulric Neisser (1967). He likens human memory to the constructive work of a paleontologist who uses a small set of bone fragments as well as general knowledge about dinosaurs and other similar animals in order to reconstruct and piece together the skeleton: "out of a few bone chips, we remember the dinosaur" (p. 285).[1]

According to the spatial metaphor, memory traces are "stable objects" or "information structures" placed in a store. The "retrieval" process then attempts to locate and select the appropriate ones given a probe. Once a particular memory trace has been retrieved, all the information stored in it is accessible. In other words, memory consists of static structures and active processes. The former simply lie there, possibly indexed and organized in some useful way, while the latter operate on them when necessary. The constructive view (Bartlett 1932; Neisser 1981; Barclay 1986; Brewer 1988; Metcalfe 1990; Schacter 1995; McClelland 1995; Whittlesea 1997) takes a different perspective. It does not separate structures from processes and considers memory as a constructive process. Memory traces are conceptualized as temporary states constructed on the spot rather than as "fortune cookies" cracked open to reveal the message contained in them.

There are no true and false metaphors, and each metaphor could be useful in certain contexts. The question is which metaphor would be more useful in the context of analogy-making and problem solving. The two schools of thought have been conducting experiments in different ways. The proponents of the first metaphor have experimented mostly with simple artificial material—lists of words, lists of numbers, sets of pictures, and so on. The dependent measure of main interest has been the success/failure ratio (or d' in more recent studies). In contrast, the protagonists of the second school have been studying memory in more natural settings.[2] They have been interested in autobiographical memory, in memory for complex events or stories (like a party or a witnessed burglary or car accident). Under these circumstances, what is really interesting is not whether people remember the event or not, but rather what details they do remember and what types of errors they make. Focusing on the errors people make in recalling from memory became an important source of insights. Thus the main message sent across by the storehouse metaphor is that one may have trouble finding the book in the library or perhaps that the book might have been spoiled. However, one cannot find a book that does not exist in the library, one cannot find a modified (rewritten) book, and so forth. In contrast, the second metaphor easily communicates the message that because the paleontologist *reconstructs* the skeleton (even though constrained by the given fossils) the result might be quite different from the reality. It might even be the case that the reconstructed skeleton has not existed or even that it cannot exist. The reconstruction might also be a skeleton of a centaur—a nonexistent mixture of two or more kinds of animals. The paleontologist might make a second reconstruction that could be different from the first one because something new was learned in between, or some fossils have disappeared, or new ones were found.

The empirical question is whether such phenomena happen with human memory, and the answer is yes. During the long history of the second school much evidence has been gathered for false and illusory memories, memory distortions, and so on (see Schacter 1995b for a recent review). These constructive-memory effects are especially likely when the episode that is to be recalled is complex and agrees with commonsense knowledge. These are the exact characteristics of the sources for many analogies—past problem-solving episodes, familiar events, and real-world situations rather than lists of words. Therefore, we argue that the constructivist view of memory is highly relevant to analogy research and can bring important behavioral constraints for the modeling endeavor. The next section reviews some of the evidence supporting this position.

3.2.1   Human Memory: Sharp, Complete, and Fixed or Blurry, Partial, and Flexible?

Brown and Kulik (1977) suggested the existence of a special type of memory for important events in our life, which they called *flashbulb memory*. They claimed that "it is very like a photograph that indiscriminately preserves the scene in which each of us found himself when the flashbulb was fired" (p. 74). They presented the results of a study which demonstrated that most Americans had a very vivid memory about the assassination of John F. Kennedy, including details about the place they were, the informant, the ongoing event, and so on. So, they supported Livington's idea for a special neurobiological mechanism called *Now print!* that is triggered when we evaluate an event as very important for us. The flashbulb memory theory has inspired a whole line of research and many controversial results have been obtained (Neisser and Harsch 1992; Conway 1995). What is clear nowadays is that there are differences in the degree of vividness and the details that we retain about different events. It is also clear that even "flashbulb memories" are partial and probably also distorted. For the sake of accuracy, we must point out that Brown and Kulik wrote in the same article that "a flashbulb memory is only somewhat indiscriminate and is very far from complete" (p. 75).

Now, if even flashbulb memories are not complete, what about our ordinary memories? Bartlett (1932) showed that people ignore many important details of a story. Nickerson and Adams (1979) tested the memory Americans have for a commonly used object such as a penny. It turned out that on average each element was omitted by 61 percent of the participants. Some elements, such as the text *Liberty*, were omitted by 90 percent of the participants. Others, such as *United States of America*, *E Pluribus Unum*, and even *one cent*, were omitted by about

50 percent of them. And, of course, each of us has had personal experiences when we could recall an episode but not some important aspects of it, such as the name of the person, the color of his or her eyes, or the place where we met.

Our inability to recall the details might mean that we have simply not attended and encoded them; in this case memory would not be responsible for the omissions. However, on a particular occasion in a specific context one might be able to recall these specific details. This means that the details are encoded, but one cannot *always* reproduce them. There is a huge number of studies of the effect context plays on our ability to recall or recognize objects and events (see Davies and Thomson 1988 for a review). These studies show that although some details can be recalled on one occasion, they may not be recalled on another. Thus Salaman (1982) and Spence (1988), in their reports on involuntary reminding, also claim that people are reminded about the same episode on different occasions at different level of detail, omitting various aspects of the event. Godden and Baddeley (1975) had divers study the material either on the shore or twenty feet under the sea. The divers were then asked to recall the material in either the same or a different environment. Participants clearly showed superior memory when they were asked to recall in the same context in which they studied. Similar environmental context effects on recall have been found in numerous experiments (for an overview see Smith 1988). Human memory turned out to be mood-dependent as well (for a review see Guenther 1988). Thus when in an elated mood participants tend to produce more "happy" memories, while when in a depressed mood they tend to produce more unhappy memories. Just having some cookies in the waiting room may influence them to produce more "positively colored life experiences" (Isen et al. 1978).

Many experiments have also demonstrated robust context effects on recognition. For example, Craik and Kirsner (1974) and Kolers and Ostry (1974) have shown that the same voice (vs. different) and same typography (vs. different) facilitate performance in a memory recognition test for words. Davies (1988) provides an exhaustive review of the experimental studies of memory for faces and places. The review shows that recognizing a face in an familiar context is much easier than recognizing it in an unusual one. Thus, for example, Thomson, Robertson, and Vogt (1982) manipulated systematically the setting in which a given person was observed, the activity this person was performing, and the clothing of the person. They found that all three factors had significant effects on a later face-recognition test.

Implicit memory has also been shown to be context-specific. Thus priming effects are decreasing with every single difference between study and test conditions (Tulving and Schacter 1990; Roediger and Srinivas 1993).

To summarize, people make many omissions and describe objects and events only partially, but they do so in a context-sensitive manner: different omissions on different occasions. There is an apparent hyper-specificity of human memory, which leads us to think that all aspects of an episode are encoded and all of them facilitate our memory for that episode, but on any occasion only a very small part of them can be reproduced. The conclusion we draw is that memory representations are very flexible and context-dependent. This challenges the classic view of memory as consisting of stable representations of past episodes and objects. Spence (1988) also concluded that memories for episodes have "no clear boundaries"— neither in the details they describe, nor in the timing of the episode (when it starts and when it ends). He suggested that the "enabling context" which triggered the involuntary memory for the episode sets an "acceptance level," which is then used to filter out some aspects of the episode.

Barsalou has demonstrated that concepts also change their structure in different contexts. He suggested a context-sensitive representation of concepts—they are constructed on the spot rather than retrieved from memory (Barsalou 1982; Barsalou and Medin 1986; Barsalou 1987; Barsalou 1993). He studied the variability of the graded structure of concepts and demonstrated that it is highly context-sensitive. It varies substantially with changes in linguistic context and with changes in point of view. High variability occurs both within and between individuals (Barsalou 1987). Moreover, people can dynamically change their judgments of typicality when the context changes. In a related study, Barsalou (1993) demonstrated context effects on the characterization of concepts. He came to the conclusion that "invariant representations of categories do not exist in human cognitive systems. Instead, invariant representations of categories are analytic fictions created by those who study them" (Barsalou 1987:114). Furthermore, he claimed that "people have the ability to construct a wide range of concepts in working memory for the same category. Depending on the context, people incorporate different information from long-term memory into the current concept that they construct for a category" (p. 118).

The conclusion is that explaining the context-sensitive character of human memory for both episodes and concepts probably requires much more dynamic and flexible representations, which can be constructed on the spot rather than retrieved prepacked from some static memory store.

3.2.2   Are There False Memories and Memory Illusions?

The extensive literature on this topic shows clearly that there is much evidence for false memories, that is, "memories" for aspects of events that did not occur. Moreover, in many cases people strongly believe in these false memories. False memories arise by two major means: either by blending two or more episodes, or by intrusions from some generic knowledge or schema. We will briefly review both aspects.

3.2.2.1   Blending of Episodes   The study of this phenomenon probably starts with the wave of research surrounding the interference theory of forgetting. Although the theory itself has long been forgotten, the experimental facts that were established remain important. Basically, these studies showed the interference between the traces of two learning events. The participants studied two different lists of items. Later on, at the test session, they mixed up items from the two lists. Just to mention one particular example out of many: Crowder (1976) has demonstrated an interference effect between pair-associations learned on two different occasions. A similar effect was observed by Deese (1959), who demonstrated false memories for nonstudied but strongly associated items.

Loftus and her colleagues (Loftus 1977, 1979; Loftus and Palmer 1974; Loftus, Miller, and Burns 1978; Loftus, Feldman, and Dashiel 1995) developed a new paradigm for studying memory for complex real-world events such as crimes and accidents. These studies typically involve two sessions. On the first session the participants watch a slide show or a movie about some event, and on the second session they answer questions or listen to narratives describing the same event. The second session provides some misinformation about the event. It has been demonstrated that even though the context of learning and the sources were very different in the two sessions, there was blending between the two episodes in participants' memory. In a recent review, Loftus, Feldman, and Dashiel (1995) report: "In some studies, the deficits in memory performance following exposure to misinformation have been dramatic, with performance difference exceeding 30%. With a little help from misinformation, subjects have recalled seeing stop signs when they were actually yield signs, hammers when they were actually screwdrivers, and curly-haired culprits when they actually had straight hair" (p. 48). Moreover, the same authors have shown that in many cases people do believe they have really seen the mistaken element.

Neisser and Harsch (1992) have also demonstrated that people can have vivid memories and believe strongly in them though in fact they are false. They interviewed people immediately after the *Challenger* accident and asked them to write down a report of how they learned about the accident, what they were doing, where they were, and so on. One year later the experimenters asked the same subjects whether they still remember the accident and how they learned about it. People claimed they had very vivid ("flashbulb") memories about every single detail. However, the stories they told on the second interview were often very different from the ones they had written on the previous one. Many participants were shocked when confronted with their original versions. Moreover, even in the face of this indisputable evidence (and what could be more convincing than an archive report written in one's own handwriting) some people still maintained that their second versions reflected better their memory of the accident. The exaggerated form of this memory distortion is called *confabulation* (Schacter 1995b; Moscovitch 1995). Neuropsychological patients with this symptom report their own biography in a very creative way. The misinformation effects of Loftus, the distorted *Challenger* reports told to Neisser and Harsch, and the confabulation of patients were attributed by Schacter (1995b) to the same possible cause: people's failure to distinguish between various sources of information about an event; that is to say from episode blending or *source confusion*.

Because the pieces that are used in the memory-reconstruction process come from real (although different) episodes, the (false) memories constructed in this way can be very vivid and people can strongly believe they are real.

Blending of objects (as opposed to episodes) seems possible as well. Several experiments are particularly informative in this respect. McClelland and Mozer (1986) have shown that people can mix two items (words in this case) and produce an nonexistent item which is composed of phonetic elements from the original items (e.g., producing *land* out of *lane* and *sand*). Reinitz, Lammers, and Cochran (1992) presented people with human faces and asked them to learn them. Later on, on the test session, the participants were shown some novel faces that had not been presented before but were constructed out of elements of faces presented previously. This manipulation produced an illusion of memory for the novel faces (i.e., many participants "recognized" them as seen during the learning session). Finally, Nystrom and McClelland (1992) produced a blending of sentences which they called *synthesis errors*. About 10 percent of all errors were false recognitions of sentences in which one word came from one old sentence and another from a second one. The participants were asked to rate the confidence of their judgments, and 40 percent of the synthesis errors received the highest possible ranking. One particularly important observation that McClelland (1995) makes based on a simulation of these data is that "intrusions from the other sentence rush in when the most active trace provides no information" (p. 78).

3.2.2.2 Intrusions from Generic Knowledge

Another type of false memories comes from intrusions from generic knowledge. Thus Bartlett (1932) showed that episodes are remembered in terms of generic schemata and their representations are systematically shifted or changed in order to fit these schemata. He demonstrated, for example, the intrusions of expectations and rationalizations which were part of participant's schematic knowledge, but were not part of the real event (in this case a folktale). Research on autobiographical memory has also provided evidence that people use generic knowledge to fill in missing elements as well as to change existing elements in order to fit them into a schema

(Barclay 1986). It has also been shown that people systematically reconstruct their past in order to fit into their current self-image schema (Neisser 1998; Neisser and Jopling 1997).

Sulin and Dooling (1974) had their subjects read a brief paragraph about a wild and unruly girl. Then in one of the conditions they mentioned that the name of the girl was Helen Keller, whereas in the other condition they called her Carol Harris. Later on, they tested the rote memory of the participants for the sentences of the story. The test demonstrated robust false recognition of a completely novel sentence—"She was deaf, dumb, and blind"—in the first condition but not in the second. This intrusion obviously came from the generic knowledge the participants had about Helen Keller.

Loftus and Palmer (1974) demonstrated that subjects may claim they have seen broken glass in a car accident, whereas there was no broken glass in the slide show they had observed. Moreover, the percentage of subjects making this wrong reconstruction depended on the wording of the question (*smashed into* versus *hit*). In other words, the reconstructed episode contained intrusions from generic knowledge about car crashes. Similar results have been obtained in numerous other experiments summarized by Loftus, Feldman, and Dashiel (1995) as follows: "Subjects have also recalled non-existing items such as broken glass, tape recorders, and even something as large and conspicuous as a barn in a scene that contained no buildings at all" (p. 48).

Williams and Hollan (1981) used the think-aloud technique to study how people recollect the names of their classmates. They found that the participants in the experiment typically first looked for a specific context (e.g., a swimming pool or a specific trip), then searched this context to find the corresponding classmate(s) who were part of that context, and finally verified the information. Williams and Hollan described memory retrieval as a reconstructive and recursive process of problem solving. Partial information about a target item is used to construct a partial description of the item and this description is then used to recover new fragments. A new description is constructed and the process continues recursively. Obviously the result will depend on the starting point and in particular on the specific context in which the memory reconstruction takes place. Kolodner (1984) also found that people tend to construct details that they do not remember. The reconstruction is based on general schemata for similar events. Thus, for example, a person would say, "I must have gone to a hotel," and then possibly remember the specific hotel they were accommodated in.

Tulving (1983) also endorses the constructivist idea that memory traces result from a synthesis between stored information and current retrieval information. Schacter (1995b) provides additional data from brain studies and argues that the fact that many cortical areas are jointly involved in the recollection process suggests that information from various sources is being collected in order to reconstruct the episode.

Summarizing the results from this section, we may conclude that there are no clear-cut boundaries between episodes, or between episodes and generic knowledge. Episodes may become blended and elements of generic knowledge may be instantiated and implanted into an episode as if they had been part of the event. Which particular elements from other episodes or from generic knowledge will intrude depends on the context of recall.

3.2.3   Dynamics of Recollection and Order Effects

Recollecting an episode is not an instantaneous process. It takes time, which according to Anderson and Conway (1997) may run up to fifteen seconds in a laboratory experiment. Sometimes reminding is sponta-neous, but recalling an episode may also be an effortful process. Even spontaneous memories come into our minds in portions.

As remembering is a slow and gradual process, we may be interested in the order in which various aspects of the event are being recalled. It turns out that this order may differ on different occasions (Salaman 1982; Spence 1988). The order in which the elements of the episode are recalled must have an effect on the mapping in analogy-making. We call these effects *memory order effects* (to contrast them with the order effects due to the timing of perceiving—see the end of section 3.2.4.3).

Ross and Sofka (1986), in an unpublished work, describe a protocol analysis they performed on remindings of old episodes. They presented subjects with problems and asked them which old problems they were reminded of. They found that reminding was slow and gradual rather than an instantaneous process, and that it runs in parallel and interacts with mapping. In particular, Ross and Sofka found that the subjects relied on the established mapping to recall details about the old episode. In other words, this study suggests that the mapping process (and, more broadly, reasoning) influences and guides the memory process.

Here is how Ross (1989) summarized these results: "other work (Ross and Sofka 1986) suggests the possibility that the retrieval may be greatly affected by the use. In particular, we found that subjects, whose task was to recall the details of an earlier example that the current test problem reminded them of, used the test problem not only as an initial reminder but throughout the recall. For instance, the test problem was used to probe for similar objects and relations and to prompt recall of particular numbers from the earlier example. The retrieval of the earlier example appeared to be interleaved with its use because subjects were setting up correspondences between the earlier example and the test problem during the retrieval" (p. 465).

This study was, however, performed in the context of a pure memory task. Subjects were not asked to solve the problems; they were rather asked to recall the problems they were reminded of. The next section looks at the complex interactions between memory, reasoning and perception in the context of problem solving.

3.2.4   Interplay between Memory, Reasoning, and Perception in Analogy-Making: Interaction Effects

Unfortunately, most of the research on memory has concentrated on deliberate and voluntary remembering. This applies both to the classical storehouse tradition and the constructive ecological tradition. The pure memory tasks, such as free recall, cued recall, and recognition tests, all have the drawback that they study memory in isolation. What we really need for understanding the complex interactions between memory and reasoning is the study of spontaneous remembering, that is, remindings that happen spontaneously in the context of a problem-solving activity. In particular, we are interested in spontaneous remindings of analogous situations and problems.

On the other side, the sparse research on memory within an analogy-making framework has ignored the constructive view on memory and has concentrated on how people select the most appropriate episode from the vast set of episodes in long-term memory. We will not review these studies in any detail because Hummel and Holyoak (1997) have done this already; we will only mention some basic findings. It has been established that the existence of similar story lines or similar objects (objects with similar properties) is a crucial factor for analogical remind-ing (Holyoak and Koh 1987; Ross 1989; Gentner, Rattermann, and Forbus 1993). That is why remote analogies are very rare and difficult to achieve (Gick and Holyoak 1980). However, Dunbar (chap. 9, this volume) demonstrates that people, both in natural settings and in the experimental laboratory, are able to produce remote analogies based on shared relations in both domains. Actually, the role of similarity between the relations in both domains has never been seriously studied. What has been studied and established is that structural correspondence (similar objects playing similar roles in similar relations) does not have much effect on reminding. It can possibly facilitate reminding under certain circumstances, but only when there is general similarity between the domains or story lines (Ross 1989; Wharton, Holyoak, and Lange 1996). Dunbar (chap. 9, this volume) and Ross and Bradshaw (1994) present evidence for encoding effects on remindings, that is, that reminding is facilitated when the subjects perform similar operations on the material at study and test, and when they focus on the same aspects (relations or properties) in both cases. Spencer and Weisberg (1986) have found context effects indicating that even the same or similar environmental context can facilitate reminding. Unfortunately, there is not much research on the dynamics of the process of reminding (or reconstruct-ing), on the completeness and accuracy of the resulting descriptions of the old episodes, and on how these reconstructions depend on the target problem.

The following subsections review briefly some results obtained by the AMBR research group illustrating the possible effects reasoning can have on reminding, memory on reasoning, and perception on memory and reasoning.

3.2.4.1 Omissions, Blendings, and Intrusions in Spontaneous Remind-ings in Analogy-Making: Effects of Reasoning on Memory   A recent experiment looked at human memory in the context of analogical

problem solving. It was designed as a replication of Holyoak and Koh's (1987) experiment 1. A think-aloud method was used, however, and the accuracy of the base story was measured as it was being recalled. The participants were college students taking an introductory cognitive science course. As part of the class on thinking, they discussed the radiation problem and its solution. Three to seven days later they were invited by different experimenters to participate in a problem-solving session in an experimental lab. They had to solve a version of the light-bulb problem. Almost all subjects (except one who turned out not to have attended the class discussing the tumor problem) constructed the convergence solution and explicitly (in most cases) or implicitly made analogies with the radiation problem. We were interested in how complete and accurate their spontaneous descriptions of the tumor problem story were.

It turned out that remembering the radiation problem was not an all-or-nothing event. Different statements from the story were recollected and used with varying frequency. Thus the application of several X-rays on the tumor was explicitly mentioned by 75 percent of the sixteen students participating in the experiment; the statement that high-intensity rays will destroy the healthy tissue was mentioned by 66 percent of the subjects; and the statement that low-intensity rays will not destroy the tumor was mentioned by only 25 percent. Finally, no one mentioned that the patient would die if the tumor was not destroyed. All this demonstrates partial recall of the base. Our hypothesis is that the elements that tend to be reproduced are the ones that correspond to pragmatically important elements in the target. This hypothesis remains to be tested and corresponding experiments are under development.

On the other hand, there were some insertions, that is, "recollections" of statements that were never made explicit in the source domain description. Thus one subject said that the doctor was an oncologist, which was never explicated in the radiation problem description (nor should it be necessarily true). Another subject claimed that the tumor had to be burned off by the rays, which was also never formulated in that way in the problem description.

Finally, there were borrowings from other possible bases in memory. Thus one subject said that the tumor had to be "operated by laser beams" while in the base story an operation was actually forbidden. Such blendings were very frequent between the base and the target. Thus seven out of the eleven subjects who spontaneously retold the base (radiation) story mistakenly stated that the doctor used laser beams (instead of X-rays) to destroy the tumor. This blending evidently results from the correspondence established between the two elements and their high similarity.

In summary, the experiment has shown that remindings about the base story are not all-or-nothing events and that subjects make omissions, insertions, and blendings with other episodes influenced by the correspondences established with the target problem.

3.2.4.2 Priming: Effects of Memory on Reasoning Memory in its turn, having its own life independent of reasoning, can influence the reasoning process. One example of this is the influence that our immediate or very recent past has on reasoning. Thus people are always in a particular memory state when they start solving a problem. This state is determined by what they have been doing and thinking about immediately before they switched to the new task. This state will typically be unrelated to the current problem but can nevertheless have an influence on how it is solved. This memory state is characterized by the person's currently active concepts, generic facts, rules, particular past episodes, goals, plans, and so on. In an attempt to partially control this memory state, Kokinov (1990, 1994a) carried subjects through a series of problem-solving tasks. The problems were chosen from a variety of domains (algebra, geometry, physics, commonsense, etc.), so that there were no apparent relations among them. The problems were presented to the subjects one by one and in different orders in the different experimental groups. Each presentation consisted of a series of ten problems, two of which were covertly related and hence anticipated to interact. The expected interaction was that the early problem would prime the other, that is, induce a memory state that would facilitate solving the later problem.

The experiment demonstrated that when the target problem was preceded by different priming problems subjects may solve it in different ways. The solution of the priming problem was known to the subjects in advance (it was a commonsense problem such as how to prepare tea in a mug). Therefore, the only effect that this priming presentation had on the subjects was to make certain concepts, facts, rules, or episodes more accessible. This turned out to be crucial for the following problem-solving process, as the performance of the subjects in the task rose from 12 percent to 44 percent. In some cases we demonstrated that people can be influenced to find different solutions of the same problem depending on the specific priming provided. The experiment also studied the dynamics of the process by manipulating the length of the time interval between the priming and target problem (by making people solve distractor problems in between). The results showed that the priming effect decreased exponentially with the course of time and disappeared within about twenty-five minutes in this particular study. Thus immediately after priming the rate of successful performance was 44 percent, about five minutes later it declined to 29 percent, and after twenty-five minutes it was back at the control level of 12 percent. Schunn and Dunbar (1996) have also demonstrated priming effects on problem solving. Their results indicate that subjects were not aware of the priming effect.

Kokinov (1989) demonstrated that memory about general facts such as "which is the lightest chemical element?" is also sensitive to recent experience. The experiment demonstrated priming effects on recall of such general facts. Many experiments have demonstrated priming effects on particular concepts. For instance, studies in social psychology have demonstrated that a particular priming can affect the use of various prototypes in characterizing a person or person's behavior (see Bargh 1994 for a review).

3.2.4.3   Context Effects: Effects of Perception on Reasoning   Based on a prediction derived from an earlier simulation of analogy-making (Kokinov 1994a), the AMBR research group started to look for context effects, that is, how the perception of incidental elements of the environment during the problem-solving process can alter it. Thus Kokinov and Yoveva (1996) conducted an experiment on problem solving in which seemingly irrelevant elements of the problem solver's environment were manipulated. The manipulated material consisted of drawings accompanying other problems which happened to be printed on the same sheet of paper. There was no relation between the problems, and the subjects did not have to solve the second problem on the sheet. However, these seemingly irrelevant pictures proved to play a role in the problem-solving process, as we obtained different results with the different drawings. We used Clement's (1988) spring problem as target:

Two springs are made of the same steel wire and have the same number of coils. They differ only in the diameters of the coils. Which spring would stretch further down if we hang the same weights on both of them?

The problem description was accompanied by the picture in figure 3.2.

In different experimental conditions the drawings used to accompany a second unrelated problem on the same sheet of paper were different: a comb, a bent comb, and a beam (figure 3.3).

The results obtained in these experimental conditions differed significantly. In the control condition (no second picture on the same sheet of paper) about half of the subjects decided that the first spring will stretch more, the other half "voted" for the second one, and only a few said

Figure 3.2
Illustration accompanying the target problem.

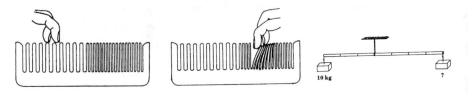

Figure 3.3
Illustrations accompanying the irrelevant problems in the various experimental conditions. (Reproduced from Kokinov and Yoveva 1996, copyright, Cognitive Science Society, Incorporated, used by permission.)

they will stretch equally. In the *comb* condition considerably more subjects suggested that the first spring will stretch more. In the *bent-comb* condition considerably more subjects preferred the second spring. Finally, in the *beam* condition more subjects than usual decided that both springs will stretch equally. Our interpretation is that the illustrations activate certain memory elements that, once activated, start to play a role in the problem-solving process. For example, the image of the bent comb probably activates concepts such as "bending" and facts such as "thicker teeth are more difficult to bend." This knowledge is then transferred (incorrectly in this case) by mapping teeth to springs, bending to stretching, and concluding that "thicker springs are more difficult to stretch."

Similar results, although not that dramatic, were obtained in the think-aloud experiment described in section 3.2.4.1. Subjects who had to solve the lightbulb problem were divided into two groups. In the control group there were no other problems on the sheet of paper, whereas in the context group the following problem was presented on the same sheet (figure 3.4).

The voting results from the parliamentary elections in a faraway country have been depicted in the following pie chart. Would it be possible for the largest and the smallest parties to form a coalition which will have more than 2/3 of the seats?

The results were the following: in the context group *all* seven subjects who produced the convergence solution to the lightbulb problem used *three* laser beams (7:0), while in the control group no one said three: two subjects said they would use *two or three* beams and the rest said they would use either *two* or *several* beams (2:5). The difference is significant at the 0.01 level.

Figure 3.4
Illustration accompanying the context problem.

Finally, Kokinov, Hadjiilieva, and Yoveva (1997) have demonstrated that subjects were not aware of the manipulations and the possible context effect of the second illustration. The context condition was contrasted with an explicit-hint condition in which subjects were invited to use the same picture during the problem-solving process. The results from the hint condition were significantly different. Moreover, in some cases when a hint was given to use the picture, subjects were less successful in solving the target problem compared to the control condition, while when they seemingly ignored the picture they were still influenced by it and showed better performance compared to the control. The results from all the experiments described in this subsection demonstrate that sometimes perceiving small changes of a seemingly arbitrary element of the environment can radically change the outcomes of the problem-solving process (blocking it, or guiding it in a specific direction).

Another effect that perception can have on reasoning has been demonstrated by Keane, Ledgeway, and Duff (1994). They have shown that the specific order of perceiving the elements of the target can also influence the problem-solving process. We call these *perceptual order effects* to contrast with the *memory order effects* described in section 3.2.3. We hypothesize that the mapping process in its turn influences perception. For example, the currently established mapping may guide the attention and thus influence the selection of details to be perceived and their order. We do not have experimental support for this hypothesis yet. We call this potential influence *mapping effect on perception*.

The conclusion from this short review is that perception, memory, and reasoning strongly interact during the problem-solving process and must be studied and modeled together. The next subsection attempts to summarize all these results and to describe the constraints they entail for models of analogy-making.

3.2.5   General and Specific Behavioral and Architectural Constraints on Models that Integrate Analogy and Memory

Let us briefly summarize the findings related to reminding of an analogical episode in a problem-solving context. The specific findings about remindings in analogy-making are reviewed by Hummel and Holyoak

(1997). They are almost skipped in the present review inasmuch as they are well known; however, these findings are presented in table 3.1. The foregoing review focused on more general characteristics of human memory that should be taken into account when modeling analogical remindings. These data, although well known as well, are often ignored in analogy models. They are also summarized in table 3.1.

When modeling a cognitive process or subprocess we often focus on those data and characteristics that are highly specific for this process and we forget about features that cut across all cognitive processes. Because the focus of this chapter is on human analogy-making, we have to take into account both its specific and universal features. Moreover, we should not only be able to account for those universal features, but we should also model them in a unified way. Stated differently, our treatment of the universal features in models of analogy-making should allow equivalent treatment of the same features in models of other cognitive processes as well. This is analogous to the unified understanding of the role of blood in all parts of the elephant body presented in the introduction.

One such very important aspect of all human cognitive processes is their context-sensitivity, that is, their dynamic adaptation to the specific context. This property should be explained for memory, for reasoning, and for perception, in a unified way. Doing so requires that we build our models on a general cognitive architecture, and that this architecture provides basic mechanisms that ensure context-sensitivity of all cognitive processes.

Representations of episodes and generic knowledge should be appropriate not only for analogy-making, but for all possible cognitive processes that might need them. This does not mean that there should be unique and universal representations of episodes or concepts—on the contrary, people may well have several complementary representations of the same concept or the same episode. However, all representations should be accessible to all cognitive processes. Of course, some might be more suitable for one task than others. Box 3.1 summarizes the architectural constraints on analogy models.

Reviewing the existing models of analogy-making, and especially those of them that involve reminding of an old episode—ARCS (Thagard, Holyoak, Nelson, and Gochfeld 1990), MAC/FAC (Forbus, Gentner, and

Table 3.1
Behavioral constraints on modeling the interactions between analogy, memory, and perception

Type of finding	Finding	Reference to a section in the text
Findings specific for analogy-making	• *Similarity effect*: semantic similarity between story lines, objects, properties, and possibly relations in both domains is crucial for analogical reminding	3.2.4
	• *Structural effect*: structural correspondence (similar objects playing similar roles) plays a very restricted role in analogical reminding and operates only when there is general similarity between the domains	3.2.4
	• *Encoding effect*: similarity between encoding and test conditions (type of task and focus on similar aspects) plays a role in reminding	3.2.4
	• *Schema effect*: the presence of generalizations of several analogous experiences from the past assists analogical reminding	3.2.4
	• *Familiarity effect*: familiar analogs have advantage during reminding	3.2.4
	Memory order effect: the order of recalling the elements of the old episode influences the mapping	3.2.3
	• *Perceptual order effect*: the order of perceiving the elements of the target influences the mapping	3.2.4.3
	• *Mapping effect on memory*: the mapping process influences the recall of details of the old episode(s) and their order	3.2.3
	• *Mapping effect on perception*: the mapping process influences the encoding of details of the target and their order (no experimental support for this potential effect)	3.2.4.3

Findings about human memory in general	
• *Omissions:* details of the episodes are recalled selectively depending on the context	3.2.1 and 3.2.4.1
• *Blending:* episodes are blended; intrusions from other episodes take place, especially when important elements are not available in the dominant episode	3.2.2.1 and 3.2.4.1
• *Schematization:* intrusions from generic knowledge take place	3.2.2.2 and 3.2.4.1
• *Context-sensitive representation of episodes and objects* (effects on reminding, recognition, priming)	3.2.1
• *Context-sensitive representation of concepts*	3.2.1
• *Gradual recall and order of recall:* episode elements may be recalled in different order	3.2.3
• *Priming effects on episodes*	3.2.4.2
• *Priming effects on generic knowledge,* including facts and concepts	3.2.4.2
• *Environmental context effects:* perception of accidental elements from the environment may play a role in reminding and mapping	3.2.4.3

Box 3.1
Architectural constraints on analogy models

- Analogy models should be built on a general cognitive architecture.
- Analogy models should be integrable with models of other cognitive processes.
- Models of different processes and subprocesses should use unified representations.
- A unified set of basic architectural mechanisms should support more complex mechanisms in models of different processes.
- The cognitive architecture should ensure context-sensitivity of all cognitive processes.

Law 1995), AMBR1 (Kokinov 1994a), and LISA (Hummel and Holyoak 1997)—we will notice that they fail to incorporate most of the behavioral and architectural constraints described here.[3] Invariably these models use the storehouse metaphor of memory. Their long-term memory "stores" a collection of frozen representations of past episodes (prepared by the author of the model). One or more of these episodes are "retrieved" during the problem solving process and serve as a base for analogy. The very idea of having encapsulated centralized and frozen representations of base episodes is at least questionable, but it underlies most analogy-making models (figure 3.5).

Both ARCS and MAC/FAC have centralized representations of past episodes, and the aim of the retrieval mechanism is to select the best one. The intactness and accuracy of the episode representation is taken for granted. Copycat (Hofstadter 1984, 1995; Mitchell 1993) and Tabletop (Hofstadter 1995; French 1995) lack episodic memory, but they do have more dynamic representation of concepts. The Metacat system (Marshall and Hofstadter 1998; Marshall 1999) stores problem-solving episodes in memory, but it also seems to do it in a very centralized way—by storing a package of variables. LISA is based on distributed representations, but only in working memory. The long-term memory consists of centralized localist representations of the episodes. Moreover, when retrieved in working memory all propositions of a given episode are switched from "dormant" to "active" state at one and the same moment.

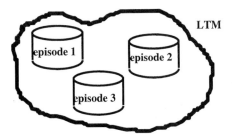

Figure 3.5
Centralized and frozen representations of episodes in long-term memory.

This implies that the system keeps for each episode a complete list of the propositions that participate in it. This amounts to a centralized and frozen representation. Thus even in this model, which relies on distributed representations, the episodes are static constructions—no omissions, no blending, no insertions are envisaged. However, we do believe that this model has the potential to be developed further to reflect these requirements, based on its ability for partial activation of memory elements. AMBR1 too is based on the storehouse metaphor and depends on stable and complete representations of episodes. Thus the current chapter presents the new version of the model—AMBR2—which has been developed further to meet these requirements.

3.3   Analogy-Making in a DUAListic Society: The AMBR View of Analogy

Associative Memory-Based Reasoning (AMBR) has been proposed as a model of human reasoning in problem solving, unifying analogy, deduction, and induction (Kokinov 1988). Since its inception in 1988 the model has gradually been developed. The first fully implemented version that got up and running was reported by Kokinov (1994a). We will refer to it as AMBR1. Various simulation experiments on analogy-making and priming effects on problem solving were performed with it. The work on the model and the aspiration for generality and lack of ad hoc decisions led to the formulation of a core of general principles, representation scheme, and basic mechanisms that formed the general cognitive architecture DUAL (Kokinov 1989, 1994b, 1994c, 1994d, 1997). Later on, an AMBR research group was established at the New Bulgarian University. The group developed a new portable implementation of both DUAL and AMBR. More importantly, it introduced many conceptual improvements and new mechanisms resulting into a new version of the model called here AMBR2 (Kokinov 1998; Kokinov, Nikolov, and Petrov 1996; Petrov 1998; Petrov and Kokinov 1998, 1999). In parallel with the modeling efforts, various psychological experiments tested some predictions of the model (Kokinov 1990, 1992; Kokinov and Yoveva 1996; Kokinov, Hadjiilieva, and Yoveva 1997; Kokinov 1998).

3.3.1 Basic Principles of the AMBR Research Program

The AMBR research program has always followed a number of methodological principles which have provided strategic guidance in our efforts to understand human cognition (table 3.2). These principles set some very high requirements on the model design. Successive versions of DUAL and AMBR satisfied them to different degrees, often at very rudimentary levels. Many of the requirements are far from being completely satisfied yet. However, it is important to keep them in mind and to push the research closer and closer to their satisfaction. Or to put it differently, these principles make us aware of important limitations of our current models and specify the direction to look for better ones.

The first principle reflects our belief stated in the introduction that the time has come to reintegrate human cognition. This principle requires that analogy should be studied together with other forms of thinking, perception, memory, learning, and language. It is also very important to explore the interactions among these cognitive processes.

The second principle is a recursive application of the first one at the finer grain size of the various subprocesses of analogy-making. According to our current understanding, these processes include representation-building of the target, analogical reminding, dynamic re-representation of the target and source, mapping, transfer, evaluation, and learning. The second principle dictates that all of them should be studied together and their interactions should be explored.

The third principle is an implication of the first two. It claims that in order to integrate analogy-making mechanisms and integrate human cognition as a whole, we should not build small isolated models of separate "stages." We should rather combine the piecemeal models developed so far into bigger unified models based on a single cognitive architecture. This general architecture should ensure the compatibility of the models and their ability to interact. Moreover, it should bring harmony to the whole system of cognition, that is, it should ensure that the various models follow the same principles, use the same representations, and depend on a common set of basic mechanisms.

Apart from the methodological principles, the research program has followed certain principles which cannot be claimed to be the universal truth. These are decisions that the AMBR group has made in order to reflect some general behavioral constraints or particular philosophical views. We are fully aware that alternative principles can probably serve the same role, and that our selection reflects our personal views and choices. That is why we call them design principles.

The first design principle is based on our understanding that the dramatic context-sensitivity of human cognition as a whole and of human thinking in particular cannot be easily captured by models based on centralized control. Subtle changes in the environment or the memory state can result in abrupt changes in behavior. It is difficult to imagine a centralized system that accounts for that and does not fall prey to the frame problem. The central processor would have to go through all elements of the environment and assess their potential relevance to the problem at hand. Context-sensitivity seems to arise much more naturally within a distributed system where many small processors look for local changes in their respective elements of the environment and/or the memory state. The overall behavior of such system emerges from the local activities of the individual processors. We call a computation *emergent* when no explicit a priori specification of either what is computed or how it is computed exists in the system (Kokinov, Nikolov, and Petrov 1996). Thus the first design principle calls for emergent context-sensitive computation.

The second design principle reflects the evidence presented in section 3.2 that human memory does not consist of frozen stable representations of events and concepts. Much more dynamic, flexible, and context-sensitive representations are required. Thus the second principle

Table 3.2
Methodological and design principles of AMBR and DUAL

Methodological principles	• Integrating analogy-making with memory, perception, learning, reasoning, i.e., reintegrating human cognition • Integrating various subprocesses of analogy-making such as representation building, analogical reminding, mapping, transfer, evaluation, learning, i.e., reintegrating analogy • Grounding the model of analogy-making in general cognitive architecture
Design principles	• Dynamic context-sensitive emergent computation • Dynamic context-sensitive emergent representations • Integrating symbolic and connectionist processing by microlevel hybridization

proclaims the use of emergent context-sensitive representations. This means that the particular representation of the episode or concept used on particular occasion should emerge from the collective work of many smaller units and should reflect the context-relevant features and structures of the corresponding object of interest. Again it seems improbable that the representations of the many concepts and episodes needed on each particular occasion could be crafted by a centralized mechanism.

Finally, the third design principle reflects our belief in the need for complementary ways of describing human cognition. Such a complex object could hardly be explained by a simple and coherent set of principles or axioms. That is why we strongly believe that human cognition should be modeled by using two or more complementary approaches each reflecting certain aspects of the reality. So, we have adopted both symbolic and connectionist approaches (thus displeasing both camps). We have, however, integrated them at the microlevel, that is, at the level of small processing units, rather than at the level of cognitive processes. Having both symbolic and connectionist aspects at the microlevel in the underlying architecture makes both of them available for use by all cognitive processes.

3.3.2 The DUAListic Society: A General Cognitive Architecture
Let us imagine that someone has the idea to establish an art museum in the capital of Utopia. The curator discusses it with friends, and some of

them decide to join the project. These enthusiasts in turn solicit their friends or colleagues. Gradually a number of people get involved in the enterprise, each in a different way: some provide money, others expertise in a specific type of art, and so on. The level of participation also differs—some spend years on the project, others participate only incidentally; some donate a lot of money, others only give a small amount. The outcome of the whole project depends on so many people and circumstances that no one can foresee the result in advance.

Now, suppose the project was successful and the government of the neighboring country Antiutopia invites the same curator to build a similar art museum. Will the result be the same? Never! First of all, not all people who contributed to the first project will be interested in the second one for all sorts of reasons. But even if we imagine that exactly the same people carry out the second project, they will certainly build a different museum. The degree of their involvement will differ. Their experience with the first project will influence the choices they make on the second. Their resources and the timing of their contributions will differ as well. For example, if a philanthropist makes the same donation as before but does it a little earlier, the architect may start with a different budget and hence design a different building.

The DUAL cognitive architecture adopts a multiagent approach to meet the design requirements listed in table 3.2. Both computations and representations in the architecture are distributed over a big number of *microagents*. Each piece of knowledge is represented by a *coalition* of agents and each computation is carried out by a whole team of locally communicating agents. Moreover, these coalitions of agents are not fixed in advance. Instead, they are formed dynamically via communication among the agents, in a way that depends on the context. Thus in different contexts different groups of agents work on the same task (or slightly different groups but with different level of participation and with different timing), and may eventually produce different outcomes at the global level (figure 3.6). This is how context effects on all cognitive processes are explained in DUAL (Kokinov 1994b, 1994c).

The DUAL agents are relatively simple and serve both representational and computational roles. A microagent might, for example, represent a simple proposition, or stand for a concept or a particular object.

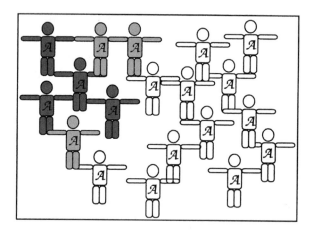

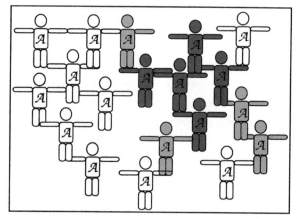

Figure 3.6
Different sets of agents are active and take part in the computation in different contexts. The filling pattern corresponds to the level of participation of the agent. (Reproduced from Kokinov 1994c, copyright, Cognitive Science Society, Incorporated, used by permission.)

However, no agent possesses all the knowledge that the system has for that concept or object—it is distributed over several agents instead. The same agents carry out the information processing in the architecture. There is no central processor that operates on the agents; they do all the work themselves.

The participation of each agent in the whole process is graded. For example, the agent might loudly announce its knowledge so that all interested parties can use it. On another occasion the same agent might whisper so that only the closest and most attentive neighbors can hear it. The same principle of graded participation applies to the information-processing activities of the agents as well. An agent might be highly involved and work very fast on some tasks or be quite indifferent and work slowly on others. Even the same task may elicit different involvement in different contexts. The degree of participation of an agent depends on its motivational power. The motivational power reflects the relevance of the knowledge the agent has to the current task and context.

The microagents are hybrid. They consist of symbolic and connectionist aspects. The connectionist aspect calculates an activation level for each agent. This is how the "motivational power" suggested earlier is operationalized in DUAL. The activation level estimates the relevance of the agent to the current task and context. It is updated continuously according to connectionist rules.

Each agent has a symbolic aspect as well. It has a symbolic processor that can do simple symbol manipulations such as comparing two lists or sending a marker to another agent. Each agent interacts only with a few neighbors, and any computation that spans over large populations of agents is carried out through massive exchange of messages. Communication is carried out through *links* between the agents: permanent or temporary. The same links are used both for connectionist and symbolic exchange—that is, for spreading activation and messages.

The activation level computed by the connectionist part is used to determine the speed of the symbolic processor. Active agents work quickly, moderately active agents work slowly, and the processors of inactive agents cannot run at all. This dualistic way of operation of the agents is very important. There are two separate but interdependent aspects of the computation—the connectionist aspect calculates context relevance while the symbolic aspect carries out the reasoning process. The two types of computation are done in parallel and influence each other. The context evolves continuously and provokes changes of the activation levels, which in turn alters the speed and availability of the symbolic processors, thus guiding the reasoning process. Reciprocally, the reasoning process sets new goals, shifts the attention to different aspects of the environment, and opens new lines for communication between agents. All this influences the activation levels calculated by the connectionist aspect.

Concepts, episodes, and objects are represented in a distributed way over a set of agents forming a coalition. The agents in a coalition are linked together so that when some members are active the remaining members tend to become active too. The weight of the link measures the strength of this coupling of the activation levels. Coalitions might be tight or weak depending on the weights of the respective links.

Finally, agents live in a big community that corresponds to the long-term memory of the system. Most agents are permanent but there are also temporary agents. There is a working-memory threshold. All agents, permanent or temporary, whose activation levels are above the threshold belong to the working memory. This active segment of the community is responsible for the outcome of all current computations. Most links within the community of agents are stable. They are established by the past experience of the system—something like old friendships or long-term business partnerships. The agents, however, can also establish new temporary connections. The possibility of establishing new temporary agents and links adds very important dynamism to the architecture. The topology of the network changes temporarily to adapt to the task. Table 3.3 outlines the meaning of some key DUAL terms.

DUAL has adapted the Society of Mind idea of Marvin Minsky (1986) as a basis for the cognitive architecture. The need for distributed and emergent computation and representation leads naturally to the idea that human cognition can be considered to be the product of the collective behavior of many simple microagents. Compared to Minsky's proposal, however, DUAL is more dynamic and less predetermined, inasmuch as new agents can be created on the fly and new links can be established between the agents. The emergent computation property of the DUAL system would also probably be at odds with some of Minsky's views.

It is closer to another recent implementation of the Society of Mind idea, namely, the Copycat, Tabletop, and Metacat systems designed by Douglas Hofstadter and the Fluid Analogies Research Group (Hofstadter 1995, Mitchell 1993, French 1995, Marshall 1999). These systems are also highly emergent and are based on the interaction between *codelets* that are very similar to DUAL agents. There are a number of signifi-

Table 3.3
DUAL basic terms

DUAL term	Meaning
Agent (or Microagent)	• The basic computational unit in DUAL
Hybridization	• Each agent has both symbolic and connectionist aspects
Communication	• Via preestablished long-term links or via temporary links created on the spot. Both activation and symbolic structures are exchanged over the links
Coalitions	• Distributed representation of concepts, episodes, and objects
Large communities	• Long-term memory
Motivational power	• Activation level as computed by the connectionist part of the agent; reflects the estimated relevance of the agent to the current context
Graded and variable participation	• Variable individual speed of symbolic processing of each agent determined by its motivational power

cant differences between DUAL and these systems, however. While the working memory in DUAL is not a separate storage, Copycat and Tabletop maintain a separate storage area called *Workspace* where copies of the codelets run and construct representations. Another important difference is that DUAL is a deterministic system, and the variability of its behavior derives from the ceaseless stream of influences from the environment and from the system's own recent internal states. In other words, the variations in context are responsible for the changes in behavior. In contrast, Hofstadter's systems are internally stochastic in nature, and he believes that this is important for explaining creativity and human cognition in general.

Compared to a connectionist system, DUAL agents are more complicated and are not exact copies of each other, thus forming a heterogeneous system. Another difference is the dynamic reorganization of the network of agents described above. On the other hand, DUAL as it currently stands does not have learning abilities and its agents are predesigned by the programmer rather than evolving with experience. We would like to add learning capabilities to the future versions of the architecture.

3.3.3   The AMBR1 Model

The first version of the AMBR model (Kokinov 1994a) integrated memory, mapping, and transfer and simulated analogy-making in a commonsense domain—boiling water and preparing tea and coffee in the kitchen and in the forest. The most interesting example of analogy-making that this model addressed involved the following target problem:

Suppose you are in the forest and you want to heat some water, but you have only a knife, an ax, and a matchbox. You do not have a container of any kind. You can cut a vessel of wood, but it would burn in the fire. How can you heat the water in this wooden vessel?

This is not an easy problem for human beings. Only about 12–14 percent of the participants in several psychological experiments have been able to solve it (Kokinov 1990, 1994a). Solving this problem required that the participants recall a common situation involving heating tea in a plastic cup. All Bulgarian students participating in the experiments knew how to solve the latter problem using an immersion heater—an electric appliance that is put directly into the water and heats it without melting the plastic cup. This method of boiling water for tea is very popular in Bulgarian dormitories. Nonetheless, only 12 percent of the participants were reminded of this situation and were able to successfully make the analogy—to heat the knife and put it in the water. The reason is that the typical way of boiling water is by using a teapot on a hot plate. Most participants tried to use this source and failed to solve the problem, as the wooden vessel would burn in the fire. The priming studies described earlier used this same target problem, but as an experimental manipulation the subjects were primed with the plastic cup problem in advance. The immediate priming raised the percentage of successful solutions to 44 percent. Four to five minutes after he priming the success rate dropped to 29 percent. Finally, after twenty-four minutes the priming disappeared and the results were at the base level of 12–14 percent. The simulation experiments with the AMBR1 model have replicated the qualitative trends of these data. Basically, without priming the model was not able to solve the problem. When primed with the immersion heater situation it found the solution and the degree of this facilitation depended on the residual activation of the immersion heater situation.

The simulation experiments with AMBR1 have also made the prediction that if during the problem-solving process the subjects perceive a stone, they may use it instead of the knife for heating the water. This prediction was tested in a subsequent experiment (Kokinov and Yoveva 1996). In this experiment an illustration of the situation in the forest has been added to the textual description and there were some stones to be seen by the river. The prediction was confirmed—the subjects who saw the illustration produced significantly more solutions involving stones than the subjects in the control condition (without illustration).

Thus AMBR1 has been successfully used in studying some interactions between memory (priming), perception (context effects), and reasoning (problem solving).

Remindings in AMBR1 are based on the connectionist mechanism of spreading activation. The sources of this activation are the perceived elements and the goals of the system. Mapping is a complex emergent process based on the local marker-passing and structure-comparison processes. Mapping is implemented by a form of constraint satisfaction network similar to ACME (Holyoak and Thagard 1989). There are, however, a number of important differences that reflect our striving for psychological validity.

· The model has more realistic working-memory requirements because not all possible hypotheses are constructed, only those that seem plausible and relevant to the current context. Thus a hypothesis is constructed only when (and if) at least one agent finds a justification for it. The justification might be on the grounds of either semantic similarity or structural consistency.
· Mapping and memory processes run in parallel and thus can interact.
· The hypotheses are constructed dynamically. As different agents run at different speeds, some agents (the more relevant ones) establish their hypotheses earlier than others. This head start helps the early hypotheses gain activation.

· The constraint satisfaction network is constructed as part of the overall network of agents in the system. The activation can thus pass back and forth between the hypotheses and the representations of concepts and episodes. This allows for an interaction between memory and mapping tailored to the particular context.

· The semantic similarity is computed dynamically and is context dependent. The computations are done by a marker-passing process and the markers are guided, restricted, speeded up, or slowed down depending on the activation level of the agents which are processing the markers, that is, depending on the particular context.

· The structure-correspondence process is not limited by the n-ary restriction that was characteristic for all other models at that time (see Hummel and Holyoak 1997; chap. 5, this volume). Once the semantic similarity between two relations has been detected, AMBR1 can map them even if they do not have the same number of arguments. This is because the marker passing mechanism disambiguates the correspondence between arguments of the two propositions. The disambiguation is based on the semantics of the arguments which is represented in the network of agents. LISA (Hummel and Holyoak 1997) has recently solved the n-ary restriction in a similar way—the distributed representations of predicates capture the argument semantics.

The 1994 version of the AMBR model implemented only some of the AMBR principles as listed in table 3.2. AMBR1 is based on dynamic context-sensitive computation, but it has rigid and frozen representation of episodes. This is because there is an agent for each episode which points to all agents representing its various aspects. Thus the knowledge of the episode is distributed over a coalition of agents but this coalition is centralized—it has a leader which enumerates all the members of the group. This simplifies the mapping and transfer processes a lot because the system (and more specifically this agent) can use the list of mapped and unmapped propositions to guide the mapping. As we have argued in section 3.2, however, such a representation of episodes is psychologically implausible. This was one of the major reasons to develop a second version of the model.

3.3.4 The AMBR2 Model

The AMBR2 model described in more detail in the next section is a step further on the road delineated by the AMBR principles. Like its predecessor, it relies on emergent context-sensitive computations and implements them in an even more decentralized way. The big improvement, however, is that the episode representations are also emergent and context sensitive in AMBR2.

Concepts and objects are represented in the same way as in AMBR1—knowledge is distributed over a coalition of agents, but the coalition still has a leader which contains a list of the members (or more often of some of the members). The reason for having leaders of coalitions is that concepts and objects typically have names and thus these names are associated with the leaders. However, typically only part of the coalition becomes activated enough to become part of working memory, and thus we will use a partial context-dependent description of the concept or object as suggested by Barsalou (1993).

Episodes are, however, more complex and unique experiences and in most cases one cannot expect a name for an episode (other than using a general category name). Thus there is no need to have a leader of the coalition. For that reason in AMBR2 episodes are represented not only in a distributed but also a decentralized way. This means that no agent in the system knows all the agents of that coalition. Thus the coalitions become even more fuzzy and dynamic and even more susceptible to context influences.

Mapping and transfer are difficult to achieve in the absence of full lists of propositions on both sides. It is difficult to know what is mapped and what is not, when enough correspondences have been found, what remains to be transferred, and so on. "Difficult" does not mean "impossible," however. Solutions to some of these problems have been found; for others they are still to be sought. The current version implements memory and mapping but not transfer. The simulations are in the same commonsense domain as AMBR1 but the knowledge base has been more than doubled. Both episodic and semantic knowledge has been added. These simulations explore the interplay between memory and mapping in various ways and demonstrate how most of the requirements listed in section 3.2 are fulfilled in AMBR2.

3.4   Integration of Memory and Reasoning in AMBR2

This section describes how the general architectural principles discussed earlier can be specified to produce a self-contained functional system— in this case a model of analogy making. First the memory and reasoning mechanisms are described as emerging from the collective behavior of a set of agents. Then the interaction between memory and reasoning is explained. And finally, the section concludes with a brief description of several simulation experiments performed with the model.

3.4.1   Collective Memory in AMBR2

Memory in AMBR is a collective phenomenon, just as in human society history is based on the memory of all members of the society. Each individual remembers a small piece of an entire event, a certain aspect of it from a certain point of view. Some individuals compare the versions held by others and draw conclusions about the relationships and correspondences. Thus the history of the event is gradually reconstructed and different individuals would offer different reconstructions. The global history emerges from all these local stories and is a collective product. Whenever a question about a certain event arises, the answer is constructed by the individuals who happened to be around with the partial knowledge they have. Thus there is never an ultimate truth about the event—each time the story is a bit different, but the stories also share a great deal. An interesting aspect of the AMBR view is that there are no historians—no special individuals write and keep the history. History is "written" and kept by the people who make it. Various individuals act in the social world. They communicate with each other and remember these communicative acts. Thus history is a by-product of acting.

3.4.1.1   Distributed and Decentralized Representations in AMBR   The representation scheme used in DUAL and AMBR is framelike, where the slot fillers are only pointers or lists of pointers to other agents (Kokinov 1989). As a consequence the actual fillers are represented by separate agents. Thus even a simple proposition like "the water is in the teapot" will be represented by a small coalition of four agents (figure 3.7). From

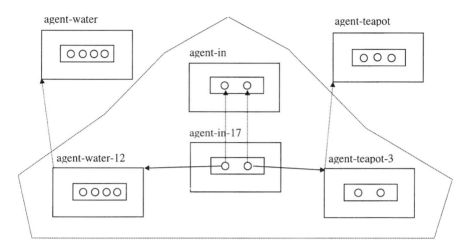

Figure 3.7
Representation of the proposition "the water is in the teapot" by a coalition of four agents.

a strictly connectionist point of view of this is a localist representation because it is symbolic. From a different perspective, however, it is also distributed because it is the whole coalition which represents the proposition and many different propositions will overlap their representations with this one, for example, "the teapot is green," "the water is hot," and so on. If it happens that only *agent-in*, *agent-in-17*, and *agent-water-12* are activated, the meaning will change, since this partial coalition will represent "the water is in something." This representation, although distributed, is highly centralized because there is a leader of the coalition (*agent-in-17*) that knows *all* coalition members.

A particular object such as a stone would also be represented by a centralized coalition, with the leader standing for the object itself and each member standing for some of its properties or relations to other objects or classes of objects. In this case, however, the leader will not know directly all the members of the coalition; it might know only a few of them. Thus the leader would definitely not have a list of all agents representing the properties of the object, far less all its participations in various episodes. Concepts are represented in the same way— distributed and centralized, with the leaders having only a partial list of the coalition members. Thus pieces of generic knowledge might be floating around in the space of coalitions and be associated with many coalitions but possibly not listed in any of them. For example, the fact that teapots are typically made of metal is a piece of generic knowledge that participates in several coalitions, such as the coalition representing the concept *teapot*, the coalition representing *metal*, and the coalition representing materials or *made-of* relations.

Another peculiar aspect of the representation scheme is the relationship between concepts and their instances. The leader of the coalition representing an object will probably always have a pointer to the concept (corresponding to the class of objects), but the leader of the coalition corresponding to the concept will only occasionally have a pointer to the object representation. The reason is that we consider it psychologically improbable to have complete list of all instances of a given category. Moreover, such a huge number of links from the concept to its instances would render these links useless, because the fan-out effect prevents any activation whatsoever to reach the instances. That is why a more flexible decision was taken, namely that such "top-down" links are established to a very restricted number of instances—the most familiar ones and the most recently used ones. As time passes by, different sets of instances will be pointed to because of the different recent usages or because new instances became familiar. This organization of the knowledge has an impact on the reminding process, because seeing a stone in the target situation will not automatically activate all stones and therefore all situations involving stones (an assumption that is true for models like MAC/FAC, ARCS, and LISA).

Finally, the episodes are represented in a distributed and decentralized way. They are represented by rather big coalitions that do not have leaders, that is, none of the members of the coalition has a list (even partial) of its members. There is a special member of the coalition which "stands for" the particular time and place location (it may be considered as a simple unique tag rather than a vector in some abstract space) and all members of the coalition point to it. This is the only way in which one can recognize that all these agents represent aspects of the same event. However, there are no pointers coming out of this special agent, that is, it does not list any of the coalition members.

Goals are represented as propositions that have the special tag of being a goal of the system. Thus whenever they get activated they are recognized as goals and put on the goal list. New goals can be established by the reasoning mechanisms or old goals can be reactivated.

3.4.1.2 Spreading Activation The connectionist mechanism of spreading activation is the basic memory mechanism. Because the activation level of an agent determines its participation in both the representation and computation process, this mechanism has a pervasive influence on all other processes. It calculates a dynamic estimate of the relevance of each individual agent to the current context as defined by the goals, perception, and memory state. Based on this estimated relevance, it determines the motivational power and therefore the level of participation of each agent (i.e., its speed of processing and visibility to other agents). Because the outcomes depend on the participation level of all agents and its timing, we can describe AMBR functioning as context-guided emergent processing.

The connectionist processor of each agent computes the activation level and output activation from its inputs. There is spontaneous decay that forces each agent to lose activation according to an exponential law in the absence of external support. The particular activation function used is described by the following equation:

$$\left| \begin{array}{l} \dfrac{da}{dt} = -d \cdot a(t) + E \cdot net(t) \cdot [M - a(t)] \\ a(t_0) = a_0 \end{array} \right.$$

where *a(t)* is the activation level as a function of time, *net(t)* is the net input to the agent, M is the maximum activation level, d is the decay rate, and E is a parameter determining the excitation rate. In addition, there is a threshold (not explicated in the equation above) that clips small activation values back to zero. The sources of activation are the input and goal nodes. The input node is linked to all agents corresponding to elements of the environment that are currently perceived, and the goal node is linked to all the agents-leaders of coalitions that represent a currently active goal. Because the decay rate is low, there are significant amounts of residual activation. Thus the "previous" memory state influences the current one, giving rise to priming effects.

There are only excitatory links in the long-term memory. Inhibitory links are also built dynamically during processing, for example, in the constraint satisfaction network described in the next subsection. In this latter case spreading activation is used for relaxation of the constraint satisfaction network.

3.4.2   Collective Reasoning in AMBR2

This subsection describes the mechanisms for mapping that result from the collective behavior of many agents in the system. Mapping is performed by gradually building and relaxing a constraint satisfaction network (CSN) similarly to ACME (Holyoak and Thagard 1989, 1995). In sharp contrast to ACME, however, the network is built incrementally and in a distributed way by the independent operation of many agents that base their decisions only on local information. The CSN's function is to integrate the local opinions of the various agents and find a globally consistent mapping at the level of the coalition of hypothesis. It consists of temporary *hypothesis agents* and temporary excitatory and inhibitory links between them. In contrast to ACME, however, this net is tightly interconnected with the main network of permanent agents. Hypotheses receive activation from permanent agents and pass activation back to them. This feature ensures that the CSN works in harmony with the rest of the system and integrates this mechanism with others. Suppose, for example, that a particular concept is highly relevant in the current context. This is reflected by a high degree of activation of the corresponding agents in its coalition. This results in building more and stronger hypotheses based on that concept. And vice versa, if a particular hypothesis gains a lot of support and becomes very active, it activates the concepts and episodes that are linked to it and thus fosters the establishment of more and stronger hypotheses of a similar type (related to the same concept or episode).

Let us now describe briefly the main participants in the construction of the CSN. Although, it can be said that practically all active agents at a particular instance of time participate in the construction of the network, we can separate two main mechanisms for constructing new hypothesis agents: the *marker-passing mechanism* and the *structure-correspondence mechanism*. In addition, other mechanisms are responsible for synchronizing the network construction and avoiding duplication of hypotheses, inasmuch as they are built by decentralized local mechanisms. Next, mechanisms responsible for the promotion and selection of the winning hypotheses will be described. And finally, mechanisms for integrating generic knowledge in the mapping process will be presented.

3.4.2.1 Computing Semantic Similarity Dynamically by a Marker-Passing Mechanism
Each permanent agent in the system is capable of marker passing. When it receives some markers it passes them over to its neighboring superclass agents with a speed proportional to its activation level. Whenever an agent that is the leader of a coalition representing an instance (object, property, or relation) enters the working memory, it emits a marker. This marker propagates upward through the superclasses hierarchy (there might be more than one superclass of a given class). It signals in this way indirectly to other agents the presence of an instance of that particular type. An intersection of two markers originating from two different instances (one from the target and another from permanent memory) means that these instances belong to the same class at a certain level of abstraction and thus are considered similar. This provides a justification for establishing a hypothesis that these two instances might correspond. The agent that detects the intersection constructs a new temporary agent representing such hypothesis. In this way semantic similarity between relations, properties, or objects in both domains plays a role in the CSN construction. Moreover, because the speed of processing of markers depends on the relevance of the corresponding agents to the current context (estimated by their activation level), the similarity computed in this dynamic fashion is context-sensitive.

3.4.2.2 Ensuring Structural Consistency by a Local Structure-Correspondence Process
The structure-correspondence mechanism is based on the ability of hypothesis agents to construct other hypothesis agents that will correspond to hypotheses consistent with the one they are standing for. There are both top-down and bottom-up hypothesis construction. Top-down construction is initiated when a hypothesis is

established that two propositions correspond to each other. This should result in constructing hypotheses about the correspondence of their parts (e.g., arguments) as well as constructing excitatory links between them. Bottom-up construction is initiated when a hypothesis is established about the correspondence between instances of two concepts. This should result in establishing correspondences between the concepts themselves. If such a more general hypothesis is established, this will facilitate the construction of more hypotheses at the instance level of the same type or will make them stronger. For example, in the preceding case, when the two propositions are put into correspondence, this will result in the construction of a hypothesis about the corresponding relations of which they are instances. This will facilitate the later construction of other hypotheses about correspondences between propositions involving that same relations. All this work is performed locally by the hypothesis agents once they have been established. This mechanism ensures the emergence of global structural consistency in the winning hypotheses from the CSN as prescribed by the systematicity principle (Gentner 1983).

3.4.2.3   Consolidating the CSN: Secretaries and Life Cycle of Hypothesis Agents

The fact that the hypotheses are established locally by individual agents complicates things, because it is perfectly possible that two independent agents find different justifications to establish one and the same correspondence (e.g., semantic similarity vs. structural consistency). This would result in establishing two different hypothesis agents standing for the same correspondence but competing with each other. To avoid this AMBR possesses certain mechanisms for merging such duplicate hypotheses. Instead of two agents with one justification each, the system ends up with a single hypothesis with two (and then three, etc.) justifications.

AMBR2 achieves all this by means of local interactions only. The so-called *secretaries* are instrumental in this respect. Each permanent agent keeps track of the hypothesis agents relating to it. To simplify the presentation we can assume that there is a secretary associated with each agent. (In the actual implementation each agent does all the bookkeeping itself.) All hypotheses are created as *embryo hypotheses*. Each embryo issues "registration requests" to the respective secretaries. The latter check their records and determine, locally, whether the hypothesis represents a unique correspondence or duplicates an existing one. In the former case the embryo is allowed to become a *mature hypothesis*. In the latter case the embryo resigns in favor of the established hypothesis that represents the same correspondence. The secretaries make sure they handle all links dealing with justifications, with non-identical but conflicting hypotheses, and so on. The net effect of their coordinated efforts is that the constraint satisfaction network is built gradually by decentralized addition of nodes (i.e., hypothesis agents) and links.

3.4.2.4   Dynamic Promotion and Selection of Winning Hypotheses
The phases of building the CSN and its relaxation are not separated in AMBR. The secretary of each object, relation, or concept maintains a current winner hypothesis at each point in time. This allows the transfer and evaluation processes to start in parallel with the mapping; they need not wait until it finishes. This opens the possibility for backward influences of the transfer and evaluation processes on the mapping. For example, it may turn out that the currently winning hypothesis is not interesting or not valid in the target domain and thus can be abandoned at a relatively early stage of the mapping. The process of selecting the best hypotheses is continuously running and is performed locally by the secretaries of the agents. Because they have registered all hypotheses that involve the current agent, they may decide which of these hypotheses is the most promising one. Of course, one would like to avoid a very early decision that cancels all the efforts by other agents to construct alternative hypotheses. On one hand, one would like early-established hypotheses to have some priority, because their early construction reflects the fact that the agents who constructed them have been highly active and therefore highly relevant to the context. On the other hand, hypotheses that arrive later might form a better and more consistent coalition that might provide a better global match. That is why the hypotheses are rated continuously by the secretaries, but promoted only gradually depending on many factors including the strength of their competitors and the duration of the time period in which they have led the competition. Thus if a hypothesis maintains its leading status long enough and

is sufficiently ahead of its competitors (in terms of activation), it is promoted into a *winner hypothesis* and the evaluation and transfer mechanisms may use it as a starting point.

3.4.3   Interaction between Memory and Reasoning in AMBR2

This section describes several simulation experiments performed with AMBR2 that illustrate the interactions between memory and reasoning, and in some cases also perception, in the process of analogy-making. The experiments are of two types: case studies and aggregate statistics. The case studies track certain runs in detail, zooming into the specific mechanisms of the model. Aggregate statistics are collected over hundreds of runs of the system and disclose its overall tendency to produce certain solutions more readily than others. In the latter case we exploit the fact (described in section 3.4.1.1) that there could be only a restricted number of links from general concepts to their instances. Thus, one hundred variations of the knowledge base have been generated by randomly sampling which instances are connected and which are not. In addition, some associative links have also been established at random. Only about 4 percent of the approximately three thousand links in the overall long-term memory are changed from run to run, but as the results that follow will show, these changes are enough to produce a wide variety of solutions to identical target problems.

3.4.3.1   Perceptual Order Effects   Suppose a student reads the description of some problem from a textbook. The text is read sequentially and the internal representation of this text would tend to be constructed sequentially too. In the AMBR2 model this process can be crudely approximated by attaching the temporary agents representing the target sequentially to the activation sources of the system (i.e., the goal node and input node). In a more elaborated model these elements will be constructed by the perceptual mechanisms. When some target elements are perceived and/or declared as goals earlier than others, they start receiving activation earlier. This enables them in turn to activate their coalition partners in the network. These agents enter the working memory more vigorously than the agents related to the target elements that have not been perceived yet. Moreover, earlier elements establish hypotheses earlier, which in turn reinforces their advantage. The net result is that the order of presentation of the target problem will affect all subsequent work on the problem. Specifically, source analogs involving elements which are semantically similar to a given target element are used more frequently when this target element is presented earlier to the system.

A simulation experiment was designed to highlight this order effect. The experiment consisted of three conditions involving the same target problem:

There is a teapot and some water in it. There is an egg in the water. The teapot is made of metal. The color of the egg is white. The temperature of the water is high. What will the outcome of this state of affairs be?

The long-term memory contained many episodes, three of which were most related to this particular target. Two episodes dealt with heating liquids and one with coloring Easter eggs. The target problem was run three times on the set of one hundred knowledge base variants, yielding a total of three hundred runs. In the control condition all target elements were presented simultaneously to the system at the beginning of the run. In the *hot water* condition, the agents representing that the water was hot were presented first, followed after a certain delay by the agents representing the teapot and its material. The *color-of* relation was presented last. In the *colored egg* experimental condition, the agents were presented in reverse order. The dependent variable was the frequency of activating and mapping the various source episodes.

The results were straightforward. In the control condition 48 percent of the runs were dominated by one of the two water-heating source analogs and 35 percent by the red-egg analog. When the target elements involving high temperatures were presented early (the *hot water* condition), these percentages changed to 74 percent and 5 percent, respectively. On the other hand, when the presentation began by the proposition that the color of the egg was white (the *colored egg* condition), the frequencies were 18 percent vs. 67 percent. Given that all runs involved exactly the same target problem and the same set of one hundred knowledge base variants, the experiment demonstrated clearly that AMBR2 was sensitive to the order in which target elements are presented to the system.

Thus the interaction of the subprocesses of perception, episode recall, and mapping in AMBR predicts *perceptual order effects* in analogy-making. A psychological experiment testing this prediction is currently being carried out by the AMBR research group.

3.4.3.2 Influence of Mapping on Episode Recall As stated throughout this chapter the various subprocesses of analogy-making in AMBR run in parallel and can interact. The interaction takes different forms, including influences that supposedly later "stages" exert on supposedly earlier ones. This subsection reviews a case study that focuses on the influence of mapping on episode recall. The full details of this simulation experiment are reported elsewhere (Petrov and Kokinov 1998).

Such "backward" influences seem strange at first glance. How can a system map a source episode to the target if the source has not even been retrieved? The key here is that episodes are represented by decentralized coalitions in AMBR2 and thus can be brought to the working memory element by element. As soon as some members of a coalition become active, the mapping mechanisms can start constructing hypotheses relating these elements to various elements of the target. If these hypotheses do well in the constraint satisfaction network, their activation levels rise and part of this high activation propagates back to the LTM members that have generated them. In other words, if some (partially recalled) propositions from some source episode turn out to be structurally consistent with some target propositions, the source elements receive additional support from the constraint satisfaction network. This allows them to bring more of their coalition members above the working memory threshold. The latter then construct new hypotheses thus opening new opportunities to receive activation from the highly active target elements, and so forth.

A simulation experiment was designed to highlight and test this sequence of mutual facilitation. It consisted of two experimental conditions, both of which solved the same target problem over exactly the same knowledge base. In the *parallel condition* the AMBR model operated in its normal manner—the mechanisms for mapping and memory worked in parallel. In the *serial condition* the mechanisms were artificially forced to work serially—first to activate episodes from memory, pick up the most active one, and only then map it to the target. The model produced different results in these two conditions. When all mechanisms worked in parallel, they succeeded in identifying a structurally isomorphic analog, activating it fully from LTM, and mapping it to the target problem. The serial condition resulted in activation of a superficially similar but structurally inappropriate base. (The relations that were crucial for successful transfer of the solution were cross-mapped.) This simulation not only explains the mapping effect of recall, but also sheds light on the mechanisms of the structural effect (table 3.1). Other models (MAC/FAC, ARCS) have to incorporate patches which perform partial mapping in order to explain the structural effect. AMBR2 explains it just by the fact that both recall and mapping run in parallel and thus mapping can influence recall.

3.4.3.3 Blending of Episodes   More than 1,300 runs of the AMBR2 system have been performed on different target problems and with different concepts and episodes in LTM. A typical pattern in these simulations is that early during a run the spreading activation mechanism brings to the working memory an assortment of agents belonging to different episodes. These elements are recalled from LTM based solely on their semantic similarity to some target element. As more and more hypothesis agents are being constructed, however, the constraint satisfaction network begins to influence the pattern of activation over the entire community of agents. The dynamics of the CSN usually drives it into a state of minimum energy that corresponds to a consistent mapping between the target and one specific source episode.

Occasionally, however, the system produces blends in which two or more sources are partially mapped to the target. The exact conditions for the emergence of such blends are yet to be explored, but the simulations so far have revealed that they are certainly possible, albeit rare. Blends tend to happen when none of the episodes in the long term memory matches the target well enough or when the appropriate episode is superseded by another one (e.g., as a result of a priming or context effect). Under these circumstances one of the sources maps to some fraction of the target and another source maps to the rest. This is possible in AMBR because the mapping is done element by element and the pressure to stay within the dominant source episode is soft (i.e., implemented via the constraint satisfaction mechanisms) rather than enforced in an all-or-none fashion.

3.4.3.4 Incorporating Generic Knowledge into Episode Representations: The Instantiation Mechanism The instantiation mechanism extends the episode representations with elements derived from generic knowledge. This is a kind of re-representation of the episode performed during recall and under the pressure of mapping (Kokinov and Petrov 2000). The instantiation mechanism thus exemplifies the interaction between memory and reasoning in one of its most sophisticated forms. Memory, deduction, and analogy meet together at this point. The episode representation is partially recalled from memory and partially inferred from generic knowledge, whereas the whole reconstructive process aims at aligning the episode with the current target.

The main ideas behind the instantiation mechanism are the following. The spreading activation typically brings agents belonging to various coalitions into working memory. Some of the agents belong to coalitions representing various episodes; other agents belong to coalitions representing generic knowledge. Each agent undertakes various actions whose ultimate goal is to establish a correspondence between the agent in question and some agent from the target problem. These actions include emission of markers, creation of hypotheses, and "acts of cooperation" within the coalition (e.g., sending activation to poor members). Not all aspirations of the agents can be satisfied, however, because the target agents act selectively (and thereby press for one-to-one mapping). This generates competition for the "valences" of the target problem. The epicenter of this competition is in the constraint-satisfaction network, but it reverberates throughout the working memory because the success of the hypotheses in the CSN depends on the support they receive from the other agents, and vice versa.

Two scenarios are possible at this point. The first happens when there is an episode that can use up all valences of the target, and in addition all members of the coalition representing this episode have been activated and held in working memory. Under these circumstances the hypotheses relating this episode to the target will form a complete and coherent set of pairwise correspondences and are likely to win the competition. Sometimes, however, the dominant episode cannot saturate all valences of the target. This leaves some target elements with no counterparts in the (active portion of the) dominant episode. These free valences then invite elements from other coalitions to intrude. If the intruders come from other episodes, we get blending. If the intruders represent pieces of generic knowledge, they become starting points for the instantiation mechanism.

Suppose, for example, that the target problem involves a bowl and it is explicitly represented that this bowl is made of wood. Suppose further that the episode that currently dominates the mapping involves a teapot but no information about the material of this teapot is available in the working memory. This might be either because this information has never been attended and encoded, or because it is represented by a loose part of the coalition and fails to reach the threshold. Finally, suppose the generic knowledge that teapots are typically made of metal has been activated (due to the salient *made-of* relation in the target). Under these circumstances the working memory contains agents (organized in small coalitions) representing the two propositions that, on one hand, teapots are generally made of metal and, on the other hand, the target bowl is made of wood. A hypothesis representing the tentative correspondence between these two propositions is established in the CSN. In the absence of any strong competitor from the dominating base episode, this hypothesis gains activation and hence comes on the top of the list maintained by the secretary of the *made-of* proposition in the target. The rating performed by this secretary detects that the top hypothesis involves a generic statement and triggers the instantiation mechanism by sending a message to the respective hypothesis-agent.

The instantiation process is carried out via a complicated sequence of messages exchanged between the agents. The net result of this process is that a *specific proposition* is generated to replace the *general proposition* currently mapped to the (specific) proposition in the target. In the example above, the new proposition states that the specific teapot in the base episode (rather than teapots in general) is made of metal. New temporary agents are constructed to represent this new proposition. In other words, the representation of the base episode is extended to include a statement inferred from generic knowledge. The new elements added to the episode representation can be both relations and objects. The instantiation mechanism tries to use existing agents from the old coalition whenever possible and generates new agents only upon necessity. In our example, the existing teapot will be used because it already corresponds to the bowl in the target. (This is the same bowl that is made of wood and that introduced *made-of* relations to begin with.)

Once the agents representing the new proposition are added to the working memory, they carry out the same activities that all permanent agents do upon entering WM. In other words, the mapping mechanism operates uniformly across all elements—it does not matter whether they are activated from LTM (gradually over time) or are constructed by instantiation (gradually over time). However, there is a built-in bias in favor of hypotheses about specific propositions over hypotheses about general ones. In addition, the new specific instances receive strong support from their coalition members because the episode overall has strong positions in the competition. Thus when the instantiation mechanism adds specific propositions to WM, the respective specific hypotheses tend to replace the hypotheses about general propositions even though the latter have appeared earlier in the constraint-satisfaction network.

In summary, the instantiation mechanism augments the description of an episode with objects and propositions that are specific instances of some generic concepts and propositions. On one hand, the specific propositions constructed in this way can be considered as deductions from generic knowledge. On the other hand, however, they are constructed only when needed to fill some free valences in the target, that is, guided by the analogy. That is why the instantiation process is a nice example of the interplay between deduction, analogy, and memory.

It is easy to see how the instantiation mechanism can run in the complementary direction too (although this feature is not implemented in the existing version of AMBR). The same basic sequence of events, with slight modifications, can be used to augment the description of the target so that it aligns better with the past episode that currently dominates the mapping. This constitutes a form of analogical transfer that is also backed up by generic knowledge and is yet another nice example of the interplay between deduction, analogy, and memory.

3.5 Conclusions

This chapter tries to draw a bridge between analogy and memory research. Based on the findings established in both areas we have presented the behavioral and architectural constraints that, in our view, realistic models of analogy-making should reflect. These constraints are summarized in table 3.1 and box 3.1. The AMBR research program was presented as a step-by-step attempt to build a model satisfying these constraints. Finally, the current version of the model—AMBR2—was described, along with a discussion of how it faces some of the challenges to cognitive models of analogy-making. The explanations provided by AMBR2 to these challenging phenomena are briefly summarized in table 3.4.

Finally, we are fully aware that all models are false, AMBR included. Some models are useful, however, and we hope AMBR might shed some light on the mysteries of analogy-making and on the role that dynamic context-sensitive emergent computations and representations may play in some of them. We also hope that the approach presented in this chapter will bring us one step further along the route toward seeing the elephant as a whole again.

Acknowledgments

This chapter reports the results of a project that started in 1988. It has been continuously supported by the Institute of Mathematics and Informatics at the Bulgarian Academy of Sciences (BAS) since its inception. During the last eight years it has also been supported by the Department of Cognitive Science and Psychology and the Central and East European Center for Cognitive Science at the New Bulgarian University (NBU). The project has also been supported by grants from the Bulgarian National Science Fund. This chapter was written during the stay of the first author at the Institute of Psychology at the Italian National Research Council (CNR) in Rome, which was supported by a grant provided jointly by CNR and BAS. The second author worked on the paper while occupying a postdoctoral position at the Department of Psychology at Carnegie Mellon University, which was made possible by grant AFOSR F49620-99-10086 awarded to John R. Anderson.

Table 3.4
Explanations provided by AMBR2 to the phenomena listed in table 3.1 as challenges to analogy models

Findings	Explanation provided by AMBR
Similarity effect: semantic similarity between story lines, objects, properties, and possibly relations in both domains is crucial for analogical reminding	• Reminding is based on the spreading activation mechanism which is sensitive to similarity. There is no difference between properties and relations in that respect. The only requirement is that the element is encoded in the episode representation.
Structural effect: structural correspondence (similar objects playing similar roles) plays a very restricted role in analogical reminding and operates only when there is general similarity between the domains	• This effects is explained by the parallel work of mapping and memory and the backward influence of mapping on reminding as described in section 3.4.3.2.
Encoding effect: similarity between encoding and test conditions (type of task and focus on similar aspects) plays a role in reminding	• There are two reasons for this effect. First, as explained above, relations (or properties) have to be encoded; otherwise the spreading activation mechanism cannot activate them. Second, since agents represent both declarative and procedural knowledge, the operations performed by the agents, if the same in the two conditions, can facilitate processing.
Schema effect: the presence of generalizations of several analogous experiences from the past assists analogical reminding	• In this case activation needs to spread only in one direction—from instances "up" to class descriptions—and thus it avoids the insecure way "down." The way down is insecure because of a fan effect and because each AMBR concept has explicit links to only a few instances rather than all of them (section 3.4.1.1).
Familiarity effect: familiar analogs have advantage during reminding	• The more familiar an episode, the stronger the coalition, and the stronger the links to it (both "top-down" links from concepts and "lateral" links from other episodes).

Effect	Explanation
Perceptual order effect: the order of perceiving the elements of the target influences the mapping	• Target elements that are encoded earlier can establish hypotheses earlier (section 3.4.3.1). Early hypotheses have a head start in the constraint satisfaction network.
Memory order effect: the order of recalling the elements of the old episode influences the mapping	• The earlier an element passes the working-memory threshold, the earlier it gets a chance to establish hypotheses and participate in the mapping. Early hypotheses have a head start in the constraint satisfaction network.
Mapping effect on memory: the mapping process influences the recall of details of the old episode(s) and their order	• This effect is explained by the parallel work and interaction between memory and mapping. The backward influence of mapping has been simulated as described in section 3.4.3.2.
Mapping effect on perception: the mapping process influences the encoding of details of the target and their order	• The current version of AMBR does not account for this effect yet because of its rudimentary perceptual capabilities. In a future version the perceptual subprocess will run in parallel with mapping (and with everything else) and will be influenced by it.
Omissions: details of the episodes are recalled selectively depending on the context	• Most episodes are represented by relatively loose coalitions. In such coalitions the activation of a few members does not necessarily bring the remaining members above the threshold.
Blending: episodes are blended; intrusions from other episodes take place, especially when important elements are not available in the dominant episode	• This is explained by coactivation of elements of several coalitions when none of them is really dominating (section 3.4.3.3). This is especially true when the more active coalition lacks important elements and thus leaves free valences to the competing episode.
Schematization: intrusions from generic knowledge take place	• The instantiation mechanism adds new elements to episodes by specializing generic facts and propositions (section 3.4.4). The instantiation mechanism is triggered and guided by the mapping.

Table 3.4
(continued)

Findings	Explanation provided by AMBR
Context-sensitive representation of episodes and objects (effects on reminding, recognition, priming)	• This is a direct consequence of the fact that context is represented by the whole state of activation over the memory elements and that the relevance of each element is estimated by its activation. Therefore the representations are always biased and influenced by the context.
Context-sensitive representation of concepts	• The same is true for the representation of concepts.
Gradual recall and order of recall: episode elements may be recalled in different order	• Episodes are represented in a distributed and decentralized way. They are recalled gradually as various elements pass the working memory threshold at different times.
Priming effects on episodes	• The priming effects are explained by residual activation from previously solved problems. The residual activation decays with time (section 3.4.1.2).
Priming effects on generic knowledge, including facts and concepts	• The same as above.
Environmental context effects: perception of accidental elements from the environment may play a role in reminding and mapping	• Perception activates certain memory elements which then take part in the computation. Thus even accidental elements, once activated by perception, participate in the process of reasoning and can influence it in various ways.

We would like to thank first of all the AMBR research group at NBU for the long-lasting and fruitful collaborations and lively discussions. This group has involved the following people at various stages: Vassil Nikolov, Marina Yoveva, Kalina Hadjiilieva, Silvia Ivanova, Milena Leneva, Ivailo Milenkov, Radu Luchianov, Maurice Greenberg, Sonya Tancheva, Slavea Hristova, Iliana Haralanova, and Alexandrina Bahneva. We are also grateful to our colleagues and mentors Peter Barnev, Encho Gerganov, and Elena Andonova, who supported the research over the years and from whom we have learned a lot. We would also like to thank Keith Holyoak, Dedre Gentner, Ken Forbus, Larry Barsalou, Brian Ross, Douglas Hofstadter, Pentti Kanerva, John Hummel, Robert French, John Anderson, Dario Salvucci, Cristiano Castelfranchi, and Maria Miceli for many insightful discussions and their comments on earlier drafts of this text which helped greatly to improve it. Finally, we would like to thank all participants of the Sofia Workshop on Analogy who provided cooperative and useful discussions of our work.

Notes

1. This is actually a nice example of conceptual blending (Fauconnier, chap. 7, this volume).
2. Dunbar (chap. 9, this volume) presents a nice example of naturalistic studies in analogy-making.
3. At the same time, there are many pure-memory models that do try to capture some of the general behavioral findings listed in table 3.1; for example, Sparse Distributed Memory (Kanerva 1988), MINERVA (Hintzman 1988), CHARMA (Metcalfe 1990), and Trace Synthesis Model (McClelland 1995). These models will not be discussed here because they do not address problem-solving issues.

References

Anderson, S., and Conway, M. (1997). Representations of autobiographical memories. In M. Conway, Ed., *Cognitive models of memory*, pp. 217–246. Hove, UK: Psychology Press.

Barclay, C. (1986). Schematization of autobiographical memory. In D. Rubin, Ed., *Autobiographical memory*, pp. 82–99. Cambridge: Cambridge University Press.

Bargh, J. (1994). The four horsemen of automaticity: Awareness, intention, efficiency and control in social cognition. In R. Wyer and T. Srull, Eds., *Handbook of social cognition*, vol. 1, *Basic processes*, pp. 1–40. Hillsdale, NJ: Lawrence Erlbaum Associates.

Barsalou, L. (1982). Context-independent and context-dependent information in concepts. *Memory and Cognition* 10:82–93.

Barsalou, L. (1987). The instability of graded structure: Implications for the nature of concepts. In U. Neisser, Ed., *Concept and conceptual development: Ecological and intellectual actors in categorization*, pp. 101–140. Cambridge: Cambridge University Press.

Barsalou, L. (1993). Flexibility, structure, and linguistic vagary in concepts: Manifestations of a compositional system of perceptual symbols. In A. Collins, S. Gathercole, M. Conway, and P. Morris, Eds., *Theories of memory*, pp. 29–101. Hillsdale, NJ: Lawrence Erlbaum Associates.

Barsalou, L., and Medin, D. (1986). Concepts: Fixed definitions or context-dependent representations? *Cahiers de Psychologie Cognitive* 6:187–202.

Bartlett, F. (1932). *Remembering*. Cambridge: Cambridge University Press.

Brewer, W. (1988). Memory for randomly sampled autobiographical events. In U. Neisser and E. Winograd, Eds., *Remembering reconsidered: Ecological and traditional approaches to the study of memory*, pp. 21–90. Cambridge: Cambridge University Press.

Brown, R., and Kulik, J. (1977). Flashbulb memories. *Cognition* 5:73–99.

Clement, J. (1988). Observed methods for generating analogies in scientific problem solving. *Cognitive Science* 12:563–586.

Conway, M. (1995). *Flashbulb memories*. Hillsdale, NJ: Lawrence Erlbaum Associates.

Conway, M. (1996). Failures of autobiographical remembering. In D. Herrmann, M. Johnson, C. McEvoy, C. Hertzog, and P. Hertel, Eds., *Basic and applied memory, research*, vol. 1, *Theory in context*, pp. 295–315. Hillsdale, NJ: Lawrence Erlbaum Associates.

Craik, F., and Kirsner, K. (1974). The effect of speaker's voice on word recognition. *Journal of Experimental Psychology* 26:274–284.

Crowder, R. (1976). *Principles of learning and memory*. Hillsdale, NJ: Lawrence Erlbaum Associates.

Davies, G. (1988). Faces and places: Laboratory research on context and face recognition. In G. Davies and D. Thomson, Eds., *Memory in context: Context in memory*, pp. 35–53. Chichester: John Wiley and Sons.

Davies, G., and Thomson, D. (1988). *Memory in context: Context in memory*. Chichester: John Wiley and Sons.

Deese, J. (1959). On the prediction of occurrence of particular verbal intrusions in immediate recall. *Journal of Experimental Psychology* 58:17–22.

Forbus, K., Gentner, D., and Law, K. (1995). MAC/FAC: A model of similarity-based retrieval. *Cognitive Science* 19:141–205.

French, R. (1995). *The subtlety of sameness: A theory and computer model of analogy-making.* Cambridge, MA: MIT Press.

Gentner, D. (1983). Structure-mapping: A theoretical framework for analogy. *Cognitive Science* 7:155–170.

Gentner, D. (1989). The mechanisms of analogical learning. In S. Vosniadou and A. Ortony, Eds., *Similarity and analogical reasoning*, pp. 199–241. New York: Cambridge University Press.

Gentner, D., Rattermann, M., and Forbus, K. (1993). The roles of similarity in transfer: Separating retrievability from inferential soundness. *Cognitive Psychology* 25:524–575.

Gick, M., and Holyoak, K. (1980). Analogical problem solving. *Cognitive Psychology* 12:306–355.

Godden, D. R., and Baddeley, A.D. (1975). Context-dependent memory in two natural environments: On land and under water. *British Journal of Psychology* 66:325–331.

Guenther, K. (1988). Mood and memory. In G. Davies and D. Thomson, Eds., *Memory in context: Context in memory*, pp. 57–80. Chichester: John Wiley and Sons.

Hintzman, D. (1988). Judgements of frequency and recognition memory in a multiple-trace model. *Psychological Review* 95:528–551.

Hofstadter, D. (1984). The Copycat Project: An experiment in nondeterminism and creative analogies. AI Memo No. 775. Cambridge, MA: MIT.

Hofstadter, D., and the Fluid Analogies Research Group (1995). *Fluid concepts and creative analogies: Computer models of the fundamental mechanisms of thought.* New York: Basic Books.

Holyoak, K., and Koh, K. (1987). Surface and structural similarity in analogical transfer. *Memory and Cognition* 15(4):332–340.

Holyoak, K., and Thagard, P. (1989). Analogical mapping by constraint satisfaction. *Cognitive Science* 13:295–355.

Holyoak, K., and Thagard, P. (1995). *Mental leaps: Analogy in creative thought.* Cambridge, MA: MIT Press.

Hummel, J., and Holyoak, K. (1997). Distributed representation of structure: A theory of analogical access and mapping. *Psychological Review* 104:427–466.

Hunt, E. (1999). What is a theory of thought? In R. Sternberg, Ed., *The nature of cognition*, pp. 3–49. Cambridge, MA: MIT Press.

Isen, A., Shalker, T., Clark, M., and Karp, L. (1978). Affect, accessibility of material in memory, and behavior: A cognitive loop? *Journal of Personality and Social Psychology* 36:1–12.

Kanerva, P. (1988). *Sparse distributed memory.* Cambridge, MA: MIT Press.

Keane, M., Ledgeway, K., and Duff, S. (1994). Constraints on analogical mapping: A comparison of three models. *Cognitive Science* **18**:387–438.

Kokinov, B. (1988). Associative memory-based reasoning: How to represent and retrieve cases. In T. O'Shea and V. Sgurev, Eds., *Artificial intelligence III: Methodology, systems, applications*, pp. 51–58. Amsterdam: Elsevier.

Kokinov, B. (1989). About modeling some aspects of human memory. In F. Klix, N. Streitz, Y. Waern, and H. Wandke, Eds., *Man-computer interaction research MACINTER-II*, pp. 349–359. Amsterdam: Elsevier Science.

Kokinov, B. (1990). Associative memory-based reasoning: Some experimental results. *Proceedings of the twelfth annual conference of the Cognitive Science Society*, pp. 741–749. Hillsdale, NJ: Lawrence Erlbaum Associates.

Kokinov, B. (1992). Inference evaluation in deductive, deductive, and analogical reasoning. *Proceedings of the fourteenth annual conference of the Cognitive Science Society*, pp. 903–908. Hillsdale, NJ: Lawrence Erlbaum Associates.

Kokinov, B. (1994a). A hybrid model of reasoning by analogy. In K. Holyoak and J. Barnden, Eds., *Advances in connectionist and neural computation theory*, vol. 2, *Analogical connections*, pp. 247–318. Norwood, NJ: Ablex.

Kokinov, B. (1994b). The DUAL cognitive architecture: A hybrid multi-agent approach. *Proceedings of the eleventh European Conference of Artificial Intelligence*, pp. 203–207. London: John Wiley and Sons.

Kokinov, B. (1994c). The context-sensitive cognitive architecture DUAL. *Proceedings of the sixteenth annual conference of the Cognitive Science Society*, pp. 502–507. Hillsdale, NJ: Lawrence Erlbaum Associates.

Kokinov, B. (1994d). Flexibility versus efficiency: The DUAL answer. In P. Jorrand and V. Sgurev, Eds., *Artificial intelligence: Methodology, systems, applications*, pp. 321–330. Singapore: World Scientific Publishers.

Kokinov, B. (1997). Micro-level hybridization in the cognitive architecture DUAL. In R. Sun and F. Alexander, Eds., *Connectionist-symbolic integration: From unified to hybrid approaches*, pp. 197–208. Hillsdale, NJ: Lawrence Erlbaum Associates.

Kokinov, B. (1998). Analogy is like cognition: Dynamic, emergent, and context-sensitive. In K. Holyoak, D. Gentner, and B. Kokinov, Eds., *Advances in analogy research: Integration of theory and data from the cognitive, computational, and neural sciences*, pp. 96–105. Sofia: New Bulgarian University Press.

Kokinov, B., Hadjiilieva, K., and Yoveva, M. (1997). Explicit vs. implicit hint: Which one is more useful? In B. Kokinov, Ed., *Perspectives on cognitive science*, vol. 3, pp. 176–183. Sofia: New Bulgarian University Press.

Kokinov, B., Nikolov, V., and Petrov, A. (1996). Dynamics of emergent computation in DUAL. In A. Ramsay, Ed., *Artificial intelligence: Methodology, systems, applications*, pp. 303–311. Amsterdam: IOS Press. [Available on-line: http://www.andrew.cmu.edu/~apetrov/publications/dyn_em_comp/abstract.html]

Kokinov, B., and Petrov, A. (2000). Dynamic extension of episode representation in analogy making in AMBR. *Proceedings of the twenty-second annual conference of the Cognitive Science Society*, pp. 274–279. Hillsdale, NJ: Lawrence Erlbaum Associates. [Avaliable on-line: http://www.andrew.cmu.edu/~apetrov/publications/rerepres/abstract.html]

Kokinov, B., and Yoveva, M. (1996). Context effects on problem solving. *Proceedings of the eighteenth annual conference of the Cognitive Science Society*, pp. 586–590. Hillsdale, NJ: Lawrence Erlbaum Associates.

Kolodner, J. (1984). *Retrieval and organizational strategies in conceptual memory*. Hillsdale, NJ: Lawrence Erlbaum Associates.

Kolers, P., and Ostry, D. (1974). Time course of loss of information regarding pattern analyzing operations. *Journal of Verbal Learning and Verbal Behavior* **13**:599–612.

Koriat, A., and Goldsmith, M. (1996). Memory metaphors and the real-life/laboratory controversy: Correspondence versus storehouse conceptions of memory. *Behavioral and Brain Sciences* **19**:167–228.

Loftus, E. (1977). Shifting human color memory. *Memory and Cognition* **5**:696–699.

Loftus, E. (1979). *Eyewitness testimony*. Cambridge, MA: Harvard University Press.

Loftus, E., Feldman, J., and Dashiell, R. (1995). The reality of illusory memories. In D. Schacter, Ed., *Memory distortions: How minds, brains, and societies reconstruct the past*, pp. 47–68. Cambridge, MA: Harvard University Press.

Loftus, E., Miller, D., and Burns, H. (1978). Semantic integration of verbal information into a visual memory. *Journal of Experimental Psychology: Human Learning and Memory* **4**:19–31.

Loftus, E., and Palmer, J. (1974). Reconstruction of automibile destruction: An example of interaction between language and memory. *Journal of Verbal Learning and Verbal Behavior* **13**:585–589.

Marshall, J. (1999). *Metacat: A self-watching cognitive architecture for analogy-making and high-level perception*. Ph.D. dissertation, Indiana University at Bloomington.

Marshall, J., and Hofstadter, D. (1998). Making sense of analogies in Metacat. In K. Holyoak, D. Gentner, and B. Kokinov, Eds., *Advances in analogy research: Integration of theory and data from the cognitive, computational, and neural sciences*, pp. 118–123. Sofia: New Bulgarian University Press.

McClelland, J. (1995). Constructive memory and memory distortions: A parallel distributed processing approach. In D. Schacter, Ed., *Memory distortions: How minds, brains, and societies reconstruct the past*, pp. 69–90. Cambridge, MA: Harvard University Press.

McClelland, J., and Mozer, M. (1986). Perceptual interactions in two-word displays: Familiarity and similarity effects. *Journal of Experimental Psychology: Human Perception and Performance* 12(1):18–35.

Metcalfe, J. (1990). Composite holographic associative recall model (CHARM) and blended memories in eyewitness testimony. *Journal of Experimental Psychology: General* 119:145–160.

Minsky, M. (1986). *The society of mind.* New York: Simon & Schuster.

Mitchell, M. (1993). *Analogy-making as perception: A computer model.* Cambridge, MA: MIT Press.

Moscovitch, M. (1995). Confabulation. In D. Schacter, Ed., *Memory distortions: How minds, brains, and societies reconstruct the past*, pp. 226–251. Cambridge, MA: Harvard University Press.

Neisser, U. (1967). *Cognitive psychology.* New York: Appleton Century Crofts.

Neisser, U. (1981). John Dean's memory: A case study. *Cognition* 9:1–22.

Neisser, U. (1998). Stories, selves, and schemata: A review of ecological findings. In M. Conway, S. Gathercole, and C. Cornoldi, Eds., *Theories of memory*, vol. 2, pp. 171–186. Hove: Psychology Press.

Neisser, U., and Harsch, N. (1992). Phantom flashbulbs: False recollections of hearing the news about *Challenger.* In E. Winograd and U. Neisser, Eds., *Affect and accuracy in recall: Studies of "flashbulb memories"*, pp. 9–31. Cambridge: Cambridge University Press.

Neisser, U., and Jopling, D., Eds. (1997). *The conceptual self in context: Culture, experience, self-understanding.* New York: Cambridge University Press.

Nickerson, R., and Adams, M. (1979). Long-term memory for a common object. *Cognitive Psychology* 11:287–307.

Nystrom, L., and McClelland, J. (1992). Trace synthesis in cued recall. *Journal of Memory and Language* 31:591–614.

Petrov, A. (1998). *A dynamic emergent computational model of analogy-making based on decentralized representations.* Ph.D. dissertation, New Bulgarian University.

Petrov, A., and Kokinov, B. (1998). Mapping and access in analogy-making: Independent or interactive? A simulation experiment with AMBR. In K. Holyoak, D. Gentner, and B. Kokinov, Eds., *Advances in analogy research: Integration of theory and data from the cognitive, computational, and neural sciences*, pp. 124–134. Sofia: New Bulgarian University Press. [Available on-line: http://www.andrew.cmu.edu/~apetrov/publications/ice_cube/abstract.html]

Petrov, A., and Kokinov, B. (1999). Processing symbols at variable speed in DUAL: Connectionist activation as power supply. In *Proceedings of the sixteenth international joint conference on Artificial Intelligence*, vol. 2, pp. 846–851. [Available on-line: http://www.andrew.cmu.edu/~apetrov/publications/energy/abstract.html]

Reinitz, M., Lammers, W., and Cochran, B. (1992). Memory-conjunction errors: miscombination of stored stimulus features can produce illusions of memory. *Memory and Cognition* 20:1–11.

Roediger, H. (1980). Memory metaphors in cognitive psychology. *Memory and Cognition* 8:231–246.

Roediger, H., and Srinivas, K. (1993). Specificity of operations in perceptual priming. In P. Graf and M. Masson, Eds., *Implicit memory: New directions in cognition, development, and neuropsychology*, pp. 17–48. Hillsdale, NJ: Lawrence Erlbaum Associates.

Ross, B. (1989). Distinguishing types of superficial similarities: Different effects on the access and use of earlier problems. *Journal of Experimental Psychology: Learning, Memory, and Cognition* 15:456–468.

Ross, B., and Bradshaw, G. (1994). Encoding effects of remindings. *Memory and Cognition* 22:591–605.

Ross, B., and Sofka, M. (1986). Remindings: Noticing, remembering, and using specific knowledge of earlier problems. Unpublished manuscript.

Salaman, E. (1982). A collection of moments: A study of involuntary memories. In U. Neisser, Ed., *Memory observed*, pp. 49–63. San Francisco: W. H. Freeman.

Schacter, D., Ed. (1995a). *Memory distortions: How minds, brains, and societies reconstruct the past.* Cambridge, MA: Harvard University Press.

Schacter, D. (1995b). Memory distortion: History and current state. In D. Schacter, Ed., *Memory distortions: How minds, brains, and societies reconstruct the past*, pp. 1–43. Cambridge, MA: Harvard University Press.

Schunn, C., and Dunbar, K. (1996). Priming, analogy, and awareness in complex reasoning. *Memory and Cognition* 24:271–284.

Smith, S. (1988). Environmental context-dependent memory. In G. Davies and D. Thomson, Eds., *Memory in context: Context in memory*, pp. 13–34. Chichester: John Wiley and Sons.

Spence, D. (1988). Passive remembering. In U. Neisser and E. Winograd, Eds., *Remembering reconsidered: Ecological and traditional approaches to the study of memory*, pp. 311–325. Cambridge: Cambridge University Press.

Spencer, R., and Weisberg, R. (1986). Context-dependent effects on analogical transfer. *Memory and Cognition* 14:442–449.

Sulin, R., and Dooling, D. (1974). Intrusion of a thematic idea in retention of prose. *Journal of Experimental Psychology* 103:255–262.

Thagard, P., Holyoak, K., Nelson, G., and Gochfeld, D. (1990). Analog retrieval by constraint satisfaction. *Artificial Intelligence* 46:259–310.

Thomson, D., Robertson, S., and Vogt, R. (1982). Person recognition: The effect of context. *Human Learning* 1:137–154.

Tulving, E. (1983). *Elements of episodic memory.* New York: Oxford University Press.

Tulving, E., and Schacter, D. (1990). Priming and human memory systems. *Science* **247**:301–306.

Wharton, C., Holyoak, K., and Lange, T. (1996). Remote analogical reminding. *Memory and Cognition* **24**(5):629–643.

Whittlesea, B. (1997). Production, evaluation, and preservation of experiences: Constructive processing in remembering and performance tasks. *The Psychology of Learning and Motivation* **37**:211–264.

Williams, D., and Hollan, J. (1981). The process of retrieval from very long-term memory. *Cognitive Science* **5**:87–119.

4

The STAR-2 Model for Mapping Hierarchically Structured Analogs

William H. Wilson, Graeme S. Halford, Brett Gray, and Steven Phillips

Although the importance of analogy in human cognition has long been recognized (e.g., Piaget 1950; Spearman 1923), and understanding of human analogical reasoning accelerated in the 1980s (Gentner 1983, 1989; Gick and Holyoak 1983), the explanatory potential of analogy has not been fully recognized. Computational modeling has advanced rapidly, as is clear from the chapters in this volume, and this has been accompanied by increasingly wide applications. A role has been been proposed for analogy in a variety of cognitive phenomena including scientific understanding (chap. 9, this volume; Gentner and Gentner 1983), political reasoning (Holyoak and Thagard 1995) and children's mathematics (English and Halford 1995). Analogy is recognized as a natural mechanism for human reasoning, since it is possible from an early age (Goswami 1992; Halford 1993) and can even be performed by some nonhuman primates such as chimpanzees (Oden, Thompson, and Premack 1998; Premack 1983). However, despite recognition of the power and widespread availability of analogy, it is not yet as widely used in modeling human cognition as we might have expected.

Part of the reason why the explanatory potential of analogy in human cognition has been underutilized might be that it has sometimes been difficult to demonstrate its effects on human problem solving in the laboratory. Analogy is a structure-preserving map from a base or source to a target (Gentner 1983), but unless participants are given extensive training on the base analog, they tend to focus on superficial attributes rather than recognizing relations that form the deeper basis for the analogy (Gick and Holyoak 1983). This is by contrast with real-life analogies where structural correspondences between situations tend to be more readily recognized. The chapter by Kevin Dunbar in this volume is very timely in indicating possible reasons for the paradox that effective analogical reasoning occurs so readily in naturalistic settings yet is so difficult to demonstrate in laboratories. Analogies in real life tend to be idiosyncratic and ephemeral, often lasting only as long as necessary to solve a problem, and then being forgotten. Most importantly, people are more likely to focus on structural aspects when they generate analogies for themselves. These factors makes analogical reasoning difficult to manipulate experimentally. If research such as that by Dunbar and his collaborators leads to more effective techniques for promoting analogical reasoning in laboratory studies, it might increase experimentation on the explanatory power of analogy.

We have argued elsewhere (e.g., Halford 1993) that there is potential for analogy theory, in combination with capacity theory, to explain phenomena in cognitive development. We will briefly review some examples to indicate the kind of hypotheses that can be generated.

Analogy as a Mechanism in Children's Reasoning

Developmental research on analogy has tended to focus on age of attainment (e.g. Goswami 1992; chap. 13, this volume) rather than on the role of analogy as a model of children's reasoning. However we will illustrate its explanatory potential in two domains, transitive inference and class inclusion. It is well established that transitive inference can be performed by ordering premise elements into an array (Riley and Trabasso 1974; Sternberg 1980a, 1980b), and Halford (1993) has pointed out that this can be interpreted as mapping premises into an ordering schema, as shown in figure 4.1a. Given premises such as "Tom is taller than James, Mike is taller than Tom," we can construct the order Mike, Tom, James. At first sight this might not seem to be a case of analogy, but on reflection we see that it amounts to assigning the three names to slots in an ordering schema. We all learn ordering schemas such as top-bottom or left-right at an early age, and they can function effectively as templates for ordering. The template is really the base for an analogy, and the ordered set of names is the target. This illustrates that analogy may play

A

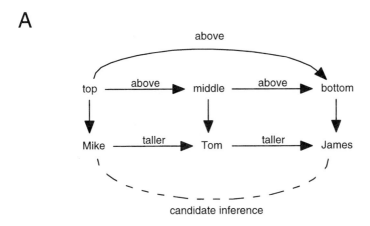

B

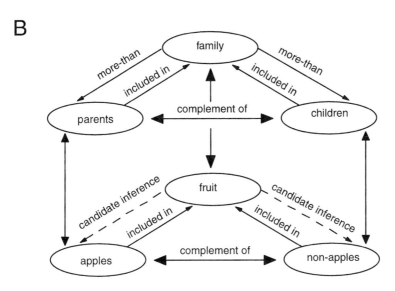

Figure 4.1
A. Transitive inference schema mapped to ordering schema. B. Class inclusion
problem mapped to family schema.

a subtle role in a lot of situations where it has not been recognized. Consequently, analogy theory, as it has been developed over the last two decades, has a lot of unrecognized potential for generating hypotheses about such tasks.

We have been interested in generating hypotheses based on the processing demands of analogical mapping. The load occurs in this case because in order to map Mike, Tom, and James into top, middle, and bottom respectively, both premises must be considered. The premise "Tom is taller than James," taken alone, only tells us that Tom should go in top or middle position, and that James should go in middle or bottom position. Similarly for the premise "Mike is taller than Tom." To assign Mike, Tom, and James uniquely to ordinal positions, both premises must be considered jointly. It is the integration of the premises, each of which represents a binary relation, into a ternary relation, that imposes the processing load for both children (Halford, Maybery, and Bain 1986) and adults (Maybery, Bain, and Halford 1986). This provides a possible explanation for the difficulty which young children experience with transitive inference (Andrews and Halford 1998).

Another task that young children have found difficult for reasons that have not been easy to explain is class inclusion (Halford 1993) as shown in figure 4.1b. A class inclusion problem for children might entail presenting a small set of apples and oranges and asking, "are there more fruit or more apples?" Unlike transitive inference, the basis of solution is not known, and analogy theory can help fill this gap. In principle, the problem can be solved by mapping into a familiar schema that is isomorphic to the inclusion hierarchy. A suitable schema would be the family, because it includes parents and children. Fruit can be mapped into family, apples into (say) parents, and nonapples into children. Family is more numerous than parents, and this becomes a candidate inference for the target. By reverse mapping, it can be concluded that fruit are more numerous than apples.

The difficulties children have with these tasks can be explained by the complexity of information that must be processed to perform the correct mapping (Halford 1993). Notice that, in order to determine the correct mapping, it needs to be recognized that fruit and family are superordinates, whereas apples-nonapples, and parents-children, are subordinates.

The difficulty of recognizing this is that the status of a category as super-ordinate or subordinate is not inherent in the category, but is defined by its relation to other categories. For example, neither fruit nor family is inherently a superordinate. If the hierarchy had been fruit, meat, and food, fruit would have been a subordinate and food a superordinate. Fruit is a superordinate because it includes a subordinate and its com-plement, that is apples and nonapples. Similarly, family is a superordi-nate because it includes parents and children. To determine the correct mapping, relations between the three classes must be taken into account. This means mapping a ternary relation, between fruit, apples, nonapples to another ternary relation, between family, parents, children, as shown in figure 4.1a. Mapping ternary relations imposes a high processing load (Halford, Wilson, and Phillips 1998a) for both adults and children, which explains one source of difficulty.

Analogy in Mathematics Education
Another little-recognized application for analogy occurs in mathematics education, where concrete aids representing mathematical concepts have been analyzed as analogs. Differences in effectiveness can be explained by the complexity of the information that is required to determine the mapping from the analog to the concept represented (Halford 1993; English and Halford 1995).

Analogy Theory in Reasoning
There is also scope for analogy theory to have a greater explanatory role in logical inference. Some models are based on formal inference rules (Braine 1978; Rips 1989) but most theorists have chosen to model reasoning on the basis of alternative psychological mechanisms such as memory retrieval (Kahneman and Tversky 1973) mental models (Johnson-Laird 1983; Johnson-Laird and Byrne 1991) or pragmatic rea-soning schemas (Cheng and Holyoak 1985). There are also models based on more specialized mechanisms such as cheater detection (Cosmides 1989; Cosmides and Tooby 1992).

The major issues here can be exemplified in the Wason Selection Task (Wason 1968) shown in figure 4.2. In this task participants are given four cards containing p, $\sim p$, q, $\sim q$ (where $\sim p$ means not-p) and

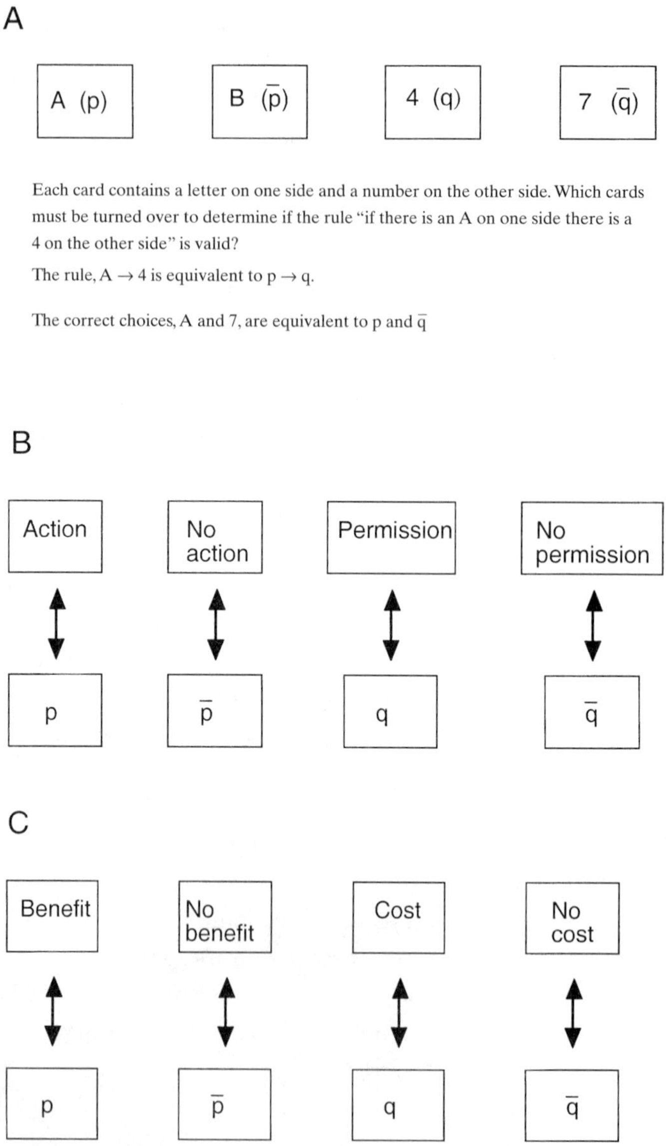

A

| A (p) | B ($\bar{p}$) | 4 (q) | 7 ($\bar{q}$) |

Each card contains a letter on one side and a number on the other side. Which cards must be turned over to determine if the rule "if there is an A on one side there is a 4 on the other side" is valid?

The rule, A $\rightarrow$ 4 is equivalent to p $\rightarrow$ q.

The correct choices, A and 7, are equivalent to p and $\bar{q}$

B

| Action | No action | Permission | No permission |

$\updownarrow$ $\updownarrow$ $\updownarrow$ $\updownarrow$

| p | $\bar{p}$ | q | $\bar{q}$ |

C

| Benefit | No benefit | Cost | No cost |

$\updownarrow$ $\updownarrow$ $\updownarrow$ $\updownarrow$

| p | $\bar{p}$ | q | $\bar{q}$ |

Figure 4.2
A. Wason Selection Task. B. Wason Selection Task mapped to permission schema.
C. Wason Selection Task mapped to social contract schema.

asked which cards must be turned over to test the rule $p \rightarrow q$ (p implies q). The correct choices, p and $\sim q$, are rarely chosen in abstract versions of the task (see reviews by Evans 1982, 1989). The literature on techniques for improving performance on this task includes evidence for an effect of analogy (e.g., Cox and Griggs 1982), but the scope for improvement has probably increased because of greater understanding of analogical reasoning processes. An example of this is that the improvement induced by pragmatic reasoning schemas, such as permission (Cheng and Holyoak 1985), appears to be interpretable as analogical reasoning.

The general form of the permission schema is that in order to perform action p, it is necessary to have permission q. The disconfirming case is p and $\sim q$, where the action is performed without permission. Pragmatic reasoning schemas are sometimes interpreted as being specialized for deontic reasoning (Oaksford and Chater 1994; Rips 1994; Almor and Sloman 1996), but it appears to have been overlooked that they may be utilized by analogical mapping. We will use the definition of pragmatic reasoning schemas as structures of general validity that are induced from ordinary life experience. This includes not only deontic rules such as permission and obligation, but other rules such as prediction and cause, and also extends to social contract schemas such as cheater-detection. As figure 2b shows, the elements and relations presented in the WST task can be mapped into a permission or prediction schema. This can be done by application of the principles that are incorporated in contemporary computational models of analogy (Falkenhainer, Forbus, and Gentner 1989; Gray et al. 1997; Hummel and Holyoak 1997; Mitchell and Hofstadter 1990), and no special mechanism is required. Most of the major findings attributed to different formats might be more parsimoniously interpreted in terms of analogical mapping.

In this theory, a possible reason why induction of a permission schema improves performance is that, as table 4.1 shows, permission is isomorphic to the conditional. Extending this argument, a possible reason for the tendency to respond in terms of the biconditional $p \leftrightarrow q$, is that in the standard version of the task participants may interpret the rule as a prediction. As table 4.1 shows, prediction is isomorphic to the biconditional (Halford 1993). It implies that the importance of permission is not

Table 4.1
The structure of the permission schema

Permission schema		Action → Permission	Permission (Symbolic)	Schema $A \to P$	Conditional $A\ P\ A \to P$	Biconditional (Prediction) $A \leftrightarrow P$
Action	permission	allowed	A P	+	1 1 1	1
Action	no permission	not allowed	A P̄	−	1 0 0	0
No action	permission	allowed	Ā P	+	0 1 1	0
No action	no permission	allowed	Ā P̄	+	0 0 1	1

that it is deontic, but that it is isomorphic to the conditional. As the canonical interpretation of the task is based on the truth-functional definition of the conditional, this mapping produces more responses that are deemed to be correct. By contrast, a lot of the errors produced by the standard version of the task are attributable to the rule being interpreted as a biconditional. This is what would be expected if the task were mapped into the prediction schema, because prediction is isomorphic to the biconditional.

Although we would not suggest that this argument accounts for all the effects associated with either the Wason Selection Task (WST) or pragmatic reasoning schemas, it does serve to illustrate that analogy can serve as the basic mechanism even in tasks such as WST that might normally be considered to entail logical reasoning. Analogical mapping explanations of WST performance are not confined to schemas such as permission and prediction, but will apply in principle to any schema with a structure sufficiently close to the WST problem to permit a mapping to be made. It therefore has potential to subsume other explanations, including those based on social contract theory.

Cosmides and Tooby (1992) have argued that performance in the WST does not reflect general purpose reasoning mechanisms, but is based on a cheater detection schema that has evolved because of its adaptive value in a social environment. Thus the rule $p \rightarrow q$ can be represented as:

"If you take the benefit, then you pay the cost" (benefit $\rightarrow$ cost).

The correct choice, p and $\sim q$, corresponds to cases where the benefit is taken without paying the cost. One specific prediction made by social contract theory is that the choices should be the same if the rule is switched:

"If you pay the cost, then you take the benefit" (cost $\rightarrow$ benefit).

Social contract theory predicts that favored choices with the switched rule will continue to be those where the benefit is taken without paying the cost. However because the rule is now "cost $\rightarrow$ benefit," the logically correct choices, corresponding to p and $\sim q$, are those where cost is paid and the benefit is not accepted. The data favor the social contract theory prediction, that is, cases where the benefit is taken without paying the cost, are chosen.

It is possible however that the cheater detection schema could be used by analogical mapping as shown in figure 4.2c. The rule benefit → cost is isomorphic to the conditional. It is really another interpretation of the permission rule. Therefore, although Cosmides and Tooby may well be correct in their claim that cheater detection is a powerful schema for reasoning about the WST, the phenomena they observe are quite consistent with the principle that performance on the task reflects a general purpose, analogical reasoning process.

The tendency to make the same choices with the original and switched rules might simply reflect a tendency by participants to transform the rule to a more familiar form. Thus the rule "If you pay the cost, then you take the benefit" might be transformed to "If you take the benefit, then you pay the cost." They might switch rules based on the principle of the complementarity of rights (Holyoak and Cheng 1995). There is plenty of evidence throughout cognition and cognitive development that the problem participants solve may be very different from the one that the experimenter intends (e.g., Cohen 1981). The undoubtedly powerful tendency to apply the cheater-detection schema, irrespective of the surface form of the problem, might simply reflect a universal tendency to map the problem into a familiar schema. Viewed this way, cheater-detection is another reasoning schema that is isomorphic to the conditional, and the reasoning mechanism might be another case of analogy.

Analogy and Relations in Higher Cognition
We have been exploring the potential of relational knowledge to provide a basis for the theory of higher cognitive processes. We have argued that the implicit-explicit distinction may be captured by the contrast between associations and relations (Phillips, Halford, and Wilson 1995) and that the theory of relational knowledge captures the properties of higher cognition and accounts for processing capacity limitations (Halford, Wilson, and Phillips 1998a, 1998b). This theory has been implemented as a neural net model (Halford, Wilson, and Phillips 1998a). Analogy plays a central role in this theory, so it is essential to demonstrate that analogy can be implemented in the architecture of the neural net model. That is the primary purpose of the STAR model of analogy, to be presented next.

The STAR Model of Analogy

The Structured Tensor Analogical Reasoning (STAR) model of analogical reasoning (Halford et al. 1994) is a neural net model, and the representations used are designed to be consistent with human processing capacity limitations.

An analogy is a structure-preserving map from a base or source to a target (Gentner 1983). The structure of base and target are coded in the form of one or more propositions. An analogical mapping between base and target consists of a mapping of the propositions in the base to the propositions in the target. Each proposition consists of a binding between a relation-symbol (e.g., bigger-than or CAUSE) and a number of arguments (e.g. bigger-than[dog, cat] or CAUSE[pressure-difference, water-flow]). A proposition is like a relational instance in that a proposition with n arguments and an n-ary relation both comprise a subset of the cartesian product of n sets. However a proposition, unlike a relational instance, need not be true. True and false propositions correspond to different subsets of the cartesian product (Halford, Wilson, and Phillips 1998a, section 2.2.2).

The STAR-1 Model

The problem for any neural net model of analogy is how to represent the propositions that comprise the base and target of the analogy. This is essentially the same problem as how to represent relational instances. There are two major classes of approaches to this problem. One is based on a synchronous oscillation model (Hummel and Holyoak 1997; Shastri and Ajjanagadde 1993) while the other is based on product operations such as circular convolution (Plate 1998) or tensor products (Smolensky 1990). Our approach is based on a tensor product representation of relational knowledge. The first version, which we now designate STAR-1, (Halford et al. 1994), is briefly described later. A further development, STAR-2, is described in detail in this chapter.

Our approach to representing propositions and relational instances is to represent the relation symbol and each argument by a vector. The binding is represented by computing the tensor product of the vectors. Thus the n-ary relation R on $A_1 \times A_2 \times \ldots \times A_n$ is represented in a tensor product space $V_R \otimes V_1 \otimes V_2 \otimes \ldots \otimes V_n$. The vectors used to represent concepts in each space V_i are orthnormal (i.e., orthogonal to each other and of length 1). To illustrate, binary relational instances mother-of(mare, foal) and loves(woman, baby) are represented by $v_{mother-of} \otimes v_{mare} \otimes v_{foal}$ and $v_{loves} \otimes v_{woman} \otimes v_{baby}$. The representing vectors $v_{mother-of}$ and v_{loves} are orthogonal, and so are the pairs v_{mare} and v_{woman}, and v_{foal} and v_{baby}. The representation handles all of the properties of relational knowledge as well as providing a natural explanation for limits to human information processing capacity (Halford, Wilson, and Phillips 1998a).

Information can be retrieved from this representation using a generalized dot-product operation. For example the query "what is mare the mother of?" can be answered by defining the probe mother-of(mare, -) and computing the dot product of the tensor product representing the probe with the tensor product representing the proposition, thus;

$$v_{mother-of} \otimes v_{mare} \cdot v_{mother-of} \otimes v_{mare} \otimes v_{foal} = v_{foal}.$$

Any one or more components of the proposition can be retrieved in this way, as we will illustrate.

Other propositions can be superimposed on the same representation. Thus mother-of(mare,foal) and mother-of(cat,kitten) can be superimposed by adding the corresponding tensor products:

$$v_{mother-of} \otimes v_{mare} \otimes v_{foal} + v_{mother-of} \otimes v_{cat} \otimes v_{kitten}.$$

Simple proportional analogies of the form A is to B as C is to what (A:B::C:?) were simulated by superimposing an appropriate set of propositions on the same neural net representation as shown in figure 4.3. We define a tensor product representation, T, of a set of propositions as:

$$T = v_{mother-of} \otimes v_{mare} \otimes v_{foal} + v_{mother-of} \otimes v_{cat} \otimes v_{kitten} + \ldots$$
$$+ v_{larger-than} \otimes v_{mare} \otimes v_{rabbit} + v_{larger-than} \otimes v_{cat} \otimes v_{kitten}.$$

It is important that not all the stored propositions contribute to the required mapping. A proportional analogy such as cat:kitten::mare:? can be solved by using the retrieval operation defined above. First we use "cat" and "kitten" as input, and the output is all the relation-symbols of the propositions that have "cat" in the first argument position and "kitten" in the second argument position. Thus the analogy

A.   **B.**

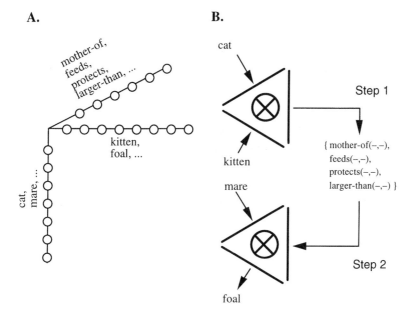

Figure 4.3
Neural net representation of binary relations used in STAR-1 solution of proportional analogy *cat:kitten::mare:foal*.

cat:kitten::mare:foal can be performed by the following operations, as illustrated in figure 4.3B.

$$v_{cat} \otimes v_{kitten} \cdot T = B_p = v_{mother\text{-}of} + v_{feeds} + v_{protects} + \cdots + v_{larger\text{-}than}$$

This output is called a "relation-symbol bundle" and comprises the sum of the relation-symbols that are bound to cat and kitten. The relation-symbol bundle is then used as input in the second step:

$$B_p \otimes v_{mare} \cdot T = w_1 \cdot v_{foal} + w_2 \cdot v_{rabbit}.$$

With w_1 and w_2 being the weighting of each vector in the output bundle, $w_1 > w_2$ due to foal's satisfying more propositions in T than rabbit satisfies.

The ambiguity in the output is realistic, because cat:kitten::mare:rabbit is a valid, though not very satisying, analogy. Just as a cat is larger than a kitten, a mare is larger than a rabbit. However the solution "foal" is more satisfying because the arguments mare-foal are bound to more relation-symbols than the pair mare-rabbit. Thus we have mother-of(mare,foal), feeds(mare,foal), protects(mare,foal), larger-than(mare, foal), whereas the only proposition with the argument pair mare-rabbit is larger-than(mare,rabbit). The fact that $w_1 > w_2$ reflects the larger number of relation-symbols bound to mare and foal.

STAR-1 was also able to perform other forms of analogy, including those in which the relation-symbol was missing, and those where a base had to be retrieved. It also incorporated realistic processing capacity constraints, and was in fact the first model to do so. A metric for quantifying the complexity of structures that can be processed in parallel was required, and it was also necessary to explain how problems that exceed this capacity are processed. We proposed that a metric in which complexity of relations is quantified by the number of arguments is the best for this purpose (Halford et al. 1994; Halford, Wilson, and Phillips 1998a).

Capacity and Complexity

It is important that a model of human analogical reasoning should conform to human processing capacity limitations. This in turn raises the question of how to quantify processing capacity. The STAR model is designed to conform to the theory that capacity limitations can be defined by the complexity of relations that can be processed in parallel (Halford 1993; Halford et al. 1994; Halford, Wilson, and Phillips 1998a). In this section we will outline the relational complexity approach to defining processing capacity limitations.

The number of arguments of a relation corresponds to the dimensionality of the space on which the relation is defined. An N-ary relation can be thought of as a set of points in N-dimensional space. Each argument provides a source of variation, or dimension, and thereby makes a contribution to the complexity of the relation. A unary relation (one argument) is the least complex, and corresponds to a set of points in uni-dimensional space. A binary relation (e.g., BIGGER-THAN) has two arguments, and is defined as a set of points in two-dimensional space. A ternary relation has three arguments (e.g., love-triangle is a ternary relation, and has arguments comprising three people, two of whom love a third) is defined on three-dimensional space, and so on.

Relations of higher dimensionality (more arguments) impose higher processing loads. The working memory literature, plus some specific experimentation, has led to the conclusion that adult humans can process a maximum of four dimensions in parallel, equivalent to one quaternary relation (Halford, Wilson, and Phillips 1998a).

The tensor product representation provides a natural explanation for observations that processing load increases as a function of the arity of relations, and also explains why processing capacity would be limited to relations with only a few arguments. As figure 4.3A illustrates, the number of binding units equals the product of number of units in all vectors, and increases exponentially with the number of arguments. Representation of an n-ary relation requires $n + 1$ vectors, one for the relation symbol and one for each argument. If the relation symbol and each argument are represented by a vector with m elements, then the number of binding units for an n-ary relation is m^{n+1}.

Structures more complex than quaternary relations must be processed by either conceptual chunking or segmentation. *Conceptual chunking* is recoding a concept into fewer dimensions. Conceptual chunks save processing capacity, but the cost is that some relations become temporarily inaccessible. *Segmentation* is decomposing tasks into steps small enough not to exceed processing capacity, as in serial processing strategies.

Even a relatively simple analogy, such as that between heat-flow and water-flow shown in figure 4.4 has a structure that is too complex to be processed entirely in parallel by humans. Consequently it is segmented into propositions that do not exceed processing capacity, and which are processed serially. The most efficient way to do this is to construct a hierarchical representation, as illustrated for heat-flow and water-flow in figure 4.4. However STAR-1 was not able to process hierarchically structured knowledge representations. This therefore was the primary motivation for STAR-2.

The STAR-2 Model

STAR-2 processes complex structures that are represented hierarchically, as illustrated in figure 4.4. Each argument is either an element, representing a basic object (e.g., water) or a chunked proposition (e.g., waterflow is a chunked representation of the proposition flow[vesselA, vesselB,

Water-flow

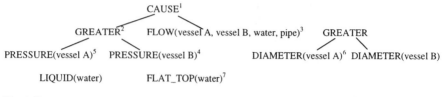

Heat-flow

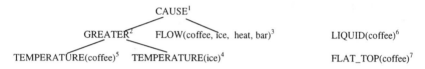

Mappings

Focus No.	Water-flow	Heat-flow	Final Overall Mapping Score
1	Cause Term	Cause Term	
1	CAUSE	CAUSE	1
1	Greater Pressure Term	Greater Temperature Term	
1	Flow Term	Flow Term	
2	GREATER	GREATER	1
2	Pressure Vessel A Term	Temperature Coffee Term	
2	Pressure Vessel B Term	Temperature Ice Term	
3	FLOW	FLOW	1
3	vessel A	coffee	0.9743
3	vessel B	ice	1
3	water	heat	0.8535
3	pipe	bar	1
4	PRESSURE	TEMPERATURE	1
6	Diameter Vessel A Term	Liquid Term	
6	DIAMETER	LIQUID	1
7	Flat Top Term	Flat Top Term	
7	FLAT_TOP	FLAT_TOP	1
7	water	coffee	0.5117

Figure 4.4
Analogical mapping between the relational structures representing water-flow and heat-flow. The hierarchical structures represent the domains used as input. The superscript numbers within the relational instances represent the order of focus of the model. We use the word "Term" to refer to a chunked relational instance. In this domain the model initially focused on the causal terms and then moved on to the "greater" terms and so on (represented by numbers 1 and 2). The mappings section presents the mappings in the order that they were formed, along with the focus in which they were formed and the final overall mapping score of the mappings. Mappings that are formed in multiple focuses are only reported the first time they are formed.

water, pipe]). The height of a proposition in a hierarchy gives an indication of how much chunked structure it contains. First-order propositions have elements as arguments, while higher-order propositions have chunked propositions as arguments. First-order propositions are of height 2, and the height of a higher-order proposition is the height of the highest unchunked argument plus one.

The STAR-2 model forms mappings between domains containing multiple propositions while conforming to the working memory limitation of only mapping a single pair of quaternary propositions at a time. In order to do this, the model sequentially selects corresponding pairs of propositions from the base and target. The relation symbols and arguments in each selected pair of propositions are mapped in parallel before a new base and target pair of propositions are selected. The sequential selection of pairs of propositions can be seen as a form of segmentation, sequentially focusing on propositions of acceptable dimensionality in order to form a mapping between higher dimensional concepts (e.g., the heat-flow and water-flow domains). Both the parallel mapping of relation-symbols and arguments as well as the sequential selection of proposition pairs are performed by constraint satisfaction networks, indicating a degree of computational similarity between the sequential focus selection and the parallel mapping processes.

The model consists of three main structures: the focus selection network, the argument-mapping network, and the information storage structures, which include a map-storing network. To illustrate the process of the model and the interaction of these structures we will consider the heat-flow/water-flow analogy (figure 4.4). The basic steps involved in the model are as follows:

1. Initially, the information storage structures are established to represent the domains being mapped. These structures store information such as similarity of items in the domains, salience of propositions, item types (e.g., relation symbol, number, animal) and chunked-proposition/unchunked-proposition associations. This information is specified as input to the model.

2. The focus selection network is established and used to select a single base/target pair of propositions that will form the first pair of

propositions to be mapped (i.e., the first focus). This selection is influenced by a number of heuristics detailed later. In the heat-flow/water-flow example the causal propositions of each domain were selected, largely due to their height and the "Cause" relation symbol that was common to the propositions in the base and target.

3. The argument mapping network is established and forms mappings between the relation symbols and arguments of the currently selected propositions. In the heat-flow/water-flow example the mappings formed were Cause ↔ Cause, and the propositions Greater Pressure ↔ Greater Temperature and Flow ↔ Flow. These mappings are then stored in the map-storing network, which maintains a store of all the mappings currently formed.

4. Connectivity in the focus selection network is modified to incorporate the mappings formed in step 3 and to ensure that previously selected propositions are not reselected. The network then selects another pair of propositions to be mapped. In the example, the Greater Pressure proposition and the Greater Temperature proposition are selected due to their height and the mapping formed between them in step 3. These propositions then form the next focus.

5. The argument-mapping network is then reestablished to map the relation-symbols and arguments of the current propositions. The mappings Greater ↔ Greater, Pressure(Vessel A) ↔ Temperature(Coffee) and Pressure(Vessel B) ↔ Temperature(Ice) were formed and stored in the map-storing network.

6. The model then repeatedly:

   a. Updates the connectivity to the focus selection network.

   b. Selects a new pair of propositions.

   c. Maps the components of the selected propositions in the argument-mapping network.

   d. Stores the new mappings in the map-storing network, until a termination criterion is met. The order of selection of propositions in the example is indicated by the superscript numbers in figure 4.4 and the order of mappings formed is also indicated in the figure.

On termination of the algorithm, all mappings for the analogy are retrievable from the map-storing network. We will now consider each of the components of the model in more detail.

Argument-Mapping Network
This is a constraint satisfaction network[1] and consists of up to five rows
and five columns of mapping nodes. Each row corresponds to either
the relation-symbol or an argument position of the currently selected
base proposition, while each column corresponds to either the relation-
symbol or an argument position of the currently selected target proposition. Each mapping node, therefore, represents a potential mapping
between a relation-symbol/argument in the base proposition and a
relation-symbol/argument in the target proposition.

An example of the network is shown in figure 4.5, mapping the top
proposition of water-flow to heat-flow. That is, it is mapping the causal
relation between pressure difference and water-flow to the causal relation
between temperature difference and heat flow. Each of the nodes has an
associated activation value that is updated by the excitatory and inhibitory
input from each of the other nodes. Inhibitory connections between all
nodes in the same row or column tend to make mappings unique; that is,
each base element is mapped to at most one target element and vice versa.
Excitatory connections exist between all nodes not in the same row or
column to allow a stable growth of activation. When the activations
stabilize, winning nodes are selected due to their greater activation, and
indicate the mapping adopted. The shaded nodes in figure 4.5 show the
winning nodes, that represent mapping of the relation-symbol and arguments of the base to the relation-symbol and arguments of the target.

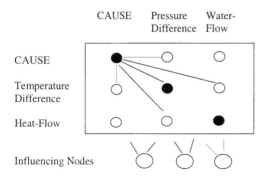

Figure 4.5
Argument-mapping network. The dotted lines represent inhibitory connections
while the full lines represent excitatory connections.

Mapping heuristics bias the mappings selected in the network towards conforming to various informational constraints. They are implemented by influencing nodes that provide constant excitatory or inhibitory input to the mapping nodes, biasing them toward or away from becoming winning nodes. These influencing nodes include:

· *Corresponding argument positions* This node provides a bias toward mapping relation-symbol to relation-symbol, and to mapping arguments in corresponding positions in base and target. For example, if the proposition $R(a,b)$ was being matched to the proposition $R'(c,d)$ then there would be a bias toward the mappings $R \leftrightarrow R'$, $a \leftrightarrow c$, $b \leftrightarrow d$.

· *Similarity* There is a bias to map identical or similar entities. Semantic *similarity* of items is specified as input to the model, and identical items are identified through a common label.

· *Type* Items are initially specified with a *type* such as relation symbol, object, number or animal and there is a bias to map items of identical or previously mapped types. As mappings of the elements of the domains are formed and stored in the map-storing network (detailed later), the corresponding types of elements also form type mappings, which are also stored to the map-storing network. These mappings then influence later instances of the argument-mapping network.

· *Salience* Items are initially specified with a *salience*, and there is a bias toward mapping pairs of items with a higher salience and a bias away from mappings between items with a difference in salience.

· *Consistency* There is a bias toward mappings that are consistent with previous mappings and a bias against mapping unlike components, such as elements to propositions, or relation-symbols to arguments. The strength of potential mappings is derived from the map storing network in the form of a mapping score (detailed later) as each argument mapping network is instantiated. This allows connectivity to be established that biases toward strong mappings, but is not a hard constraint so one-to-many and many-to-many mappings can still be formed if implied by the domains.

Focus Selection Network
The focus selection network (see figure 4.6) is a two-layer constraint satisfaction network designed to select the pair of propositions that will

Columns Correspond to Target Terms

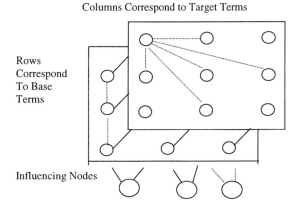

Rows
Correspond
To Base
Terms

Influencing Nodes

Figure 4.6
Focus selection network. The dotted lines represent inhibitory connections while the full lines represent excitatory connections.

form the next focus, to be passed on to the argument-mapping network. Each layer has a structure similar to the argument-mapping network. Within a layer each row represents a proposition from the base, and each column a proposition from the target. Thus each node represents a base/target pair of chunked propositions. For example, in the water-flow/heat-flow analogy in figure 4.4, one node represents the pair of causal propositions from base and target. The constraint satisfaction process eventually results in a winning node that indicates the next pair of propositions to be mapped.

Layer 1 (the lower layer) is influenced by many of the same sources of activation as the mapping network, with additional heuristics, biasing toward selecting propositions with similar height in the hierarchy, similar numbers of arguments and with corresponding relation-symbols and arguments.

Excitatory connections are placed between focus selection nodes in which the propositions represented by one node are arguments to the propositions represented by the other node. For example, referring to figure 4.4, in the heat-flow/water-flow domain an excitatory connection exists between the node representing the pair of CAUSE propositions (superscript 1) and the node representing the pair of FLOW propositions (supercript 3). This connectivity provides a bias toward matching similarly shaped tree structures. To illustrate, if the node representing the pair of CAUSE propositions developed a significant activation, the excitatory connection to the node representing the pair of FLOW propositions would increase the activation of this node and also the node representing the pair of GREATER propositions (superscript 2). Over the entire analogy this will mean that nodes in the corresponding positions in the heat-flow and water-flow trees will support each other. The connectivity results in layer 1's settling to a state in which a group of nodes develops a strong activation, representing a set of consistent base/target proposition pairs potentially to be mapped.

The first layer is influenced by a number of heuristics through influencing nodes, including heuristics based on the height and height difference of propositions, salience, similarity, types associated with propositions and common or previously mapped propositions, arguments, and relation-symbols. The connectivity from the influencing nodes can be modified between runs of the network to accommodate newly formed mappings. For example, in the heat-flow/water-flow analogy, if the argument mapping network had been loaded with the pair of CAUSE propositions, resulting in mappings being formed between the pair of GREATER and the pair of FLOW propositions, excitatory connectivity from the appropriate influencing node to the nodes representing the GREATER and FLOW proposition pairs will be established and increase the likelihood of these proposition pairs winning in the next selection.

Layer 2 is designed to select a single winning pair of chunked propositions from the set of winning terms in layer 1. Within layer 2, inhibitory connections are formed from each mapping node to every other mapping node. This connectivity forms competition between all the layer 2 mapping nodes and therefore results in a final, stable state of only one node winning. This single winning node represents the pair of chunked propositions that becomes the next focus.

The connectivity between layer 1 and layer 2 is displayed in figure 4.6. It is unidirectional so layer 2 cannot affect layer 1. An excitatory connection is formed from each node in layer 1 to the corresponding node in layer 2. This connectivity results in strong units (winning nodes) of layer 1 providing strong input to the corresponding unit in layer 2, and losing nodes of layer 1 providing no significant input to layer 2. Additional connectivity is formed between unit i in layer 1 and unit j in layer 2 if the chunked propositions represented by unit i are arguments to the propositions represented by unit j or vice versa. This corresponds to the excitatory connections between mapping nodes in layer 1, and provides a bias for layer 1's winning nodes that are part of a layer 1 "winning tree." If a pair of chunked propositions has already been a successful focus, then the weight of the connections between the units in layer one and the unit in layer 2 representing these chunked propositions, as well as all other units in the same row or column, is set to 0. This stops the input to these units, and ensures that a previous focus, or foci inconsistent with it, will not be selected in future focus selections.

In addition to the above, connectivity is formed from some of the influencing nodes in layer 1 to the focus selection nodes in layer 2. While the influencing nodes in layer 1 biased which combination of nodes (tree) would win, in layer 2 the bias is to which of the nodes in the winning combination becomes the focus. The heuristics for influencing connectivity to layer 2 are based on the height of propositions and common or previously mapped relation symbols.

Information-Storage Structures

Information-storage structures are used to store information about the entities (propositions, elements and relation-symbols) in the base and target. A number of tensor networks store information about similarity between pairs of entities, salience of entities, entity-type associations and chunked proposition—unchunked proposition associations. In addition to these networks, a rank 2 tensor "mapping tensor" (or "map-storing network") is used to store mappings between entities as they are formed by the argument mapping network.

Mapping scores are designed to reflect the uniqueness of mappings from base to target, and also the salience of the mapped entities. Uniqueness is a soft constraint, and nonunique mappings can occur if an element in the target is mapped to different base elements, or vice versa, on different foci. When a base item a is mapped to a target item b, a weighted form of the tensor product $a \otimes b$ is superimposed on the mapping tensor. If a mapping formed by the argument-mapping network is the same as one stored from a previous focus, the new mapping is still superimposed on the mapping tensor to increase the strength of the mapping. Corresponding type mappings are stored as each atomic element and relation-symbol mapping is stored.

To reflect salience, the tensor product $a \otimes b$ is weighted by multiplying the resulting binding units by either:

1. The average salience of the two propositions that formed the focus from which the mapping was made.
2. The single specified salience if only one of the two propositions has a specified salience.
3. The average of all specified saliences of propositions if neither of the two propositions has a specified salience.

This weighting results in mappings formed in salient foci being considered more important than mappings formed in less salient foci.

The first step in computing the mapping score is to retrieve the vector bundle comprising all target (base) elements mapped to base (target) item a, from the mapping tensor. The "base-to-target mapping score" for the a-b mapping is calculated as follows:

base-to-target mapping score = b · vector_bundle/|vector_bundle|

where vector_bundle is the vector retrieved from the calculation a · mapping tensor

This mapping score will be in the range 0 to 1 and indicates the degree of uniqueness of the mapping. A value of 0 means that b has never been mapped to a, and 1 means that b is the only item mapped to a. A value between 0 and 1 (exclusive) indicates the number of items, including b, that have been mapped to a. The higher the value the greater the strength of the a-b mapping relative to other mappings into which a has entered.

The target to base mapping score can be calculated in an analogous manner, but it is not necessarily equal to the base to target mapping score (e.g., if item a in the base was mapped to several items in the target, including b, but item b was only mapped to item a in the base). To provide an overall indication of the strength of the a-b mapping, an overall mapping score is calculated as follows:

overall mapping score = (base to target mapping score + target to base mapping score) / 2.

This overall mapping score is used to determine biases in the argument-mapping network and the focus selection network.

Termination Criteria

In the current implementation a test for termination occurs when either the focus selection network selects a previous focus, or a focus that is inconsistent with a previous focus, or the argument-mapping network converges to a state in which a set of mappings cannot be interpreted from the result. The percentage of chunked propositions in the smaller domain that have formed a focus is calculated and labeled as the percentage focused. If this percentage focused is greater than 90 percent, then the algorithm terminates and has successfully found an analogy. Successful termination also occurs when all chunked propositions in the smaller domain have formed a focus. None of the tested domains required a failure termination.

Analogies Solved

In addition to heat flow/water flow, a number of other analogies have been solved by the model. These include:

The *Rutherford analogy* between the structure of the solar system and the structure of the hydrogen atom has more propositions than heat-flow/water-flow and has a more complex structure, but is successfully handled by the STAR-2. The same representation adopted for SME (Falkenhainer, Forbus, and Gentner 1989) was used, as shown in figure 4.7. This included a structured representation of the solar system involving the gravitational attraction of the sun and planets, the mass difference of the sun and planets and the revolution of the planets around the sun. The corresponding structure of the atom was partly represented, omitting some of the higher order relations. Irrelevant details were added to both the solar system and the atom in the form of the temperature difference of the sun and planets and the mass difference of the electron and the nucleus.

STAR-2 successfully mapped all the corresponding structures of the two domains, initially focusing on the highest available corresponding causal relationships, and then moving down the corresponding structures. Once the corresponding structures were mapped, STAR then went

Solar System

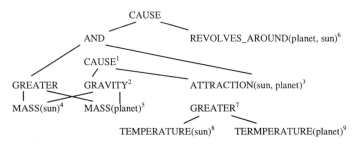

Atom

Mappings

Focus	Solar System	Atom	Final Overall Mapping Score
1	Attraction Cause Term	Attraction Cause Term	
1	CAUSE	CAUSE	1
1	Gravity Term	Opposite Sign Term	
1	Attraction term	Attraction term	
2	GRAVITY	OPPOSITE_SIGN	1
2	Sun Mass Term	Neutron Charge Term	
2	Planet Mass Term	Electron Charge Term	
3	ATTRACTION	ATTRACTION	1
3	sun	neutron	1
3	planet	electron	1
4	MASS	CHARGE	1
6	Revolves Term	Revolves Term	
6	REVOLVES_AROUND	REVOLVES_AROUND	1
7	Greater Temerature Term	Greater Mass Term	
7	GREATER	GREATER	1
7	Sun Temperature Term	Neutron Mass Term	
7	Planet Temperature Term	Electron Mass Term	
8	TEMPERATURE	MASS	1

Figure 4.7
Domain and mappings for the Rutherford analogy.

on to map the irrelevant sun/planet temperature difference to the irrelevant electron/nucleus mass difference.

The *jealous animals* problem is an analogy between isomorphic children's stories where animals play the roles in the story (Gentner and Toupin 1986) (see figure 4.8). A number of versions were tested in which the corresponding animals' similarity was varied as well as the presence of higher order propositions (see Holyoak and Thagard 1989 for details of these analogies). The model correctly solved most versions of the analogy, but also made incorrect mappings on versions that are difficult for humans (e.g., where animal similarity worked against the structurally correct mappings). Six versions, designed to vary systematicity (defined by existence of higher-order relations) and transparency (defined as the same animal filling corresponding roles in base and target stories) in the same manner as Gentner and Toupin, were tested. Animal similarity was specified as an element similarity in the input. The solutions produced by STAR-2 to this analogy corresponded closely to those found by Gentner and Toupin (1986). For the systematic versions, all representations resulted in correctly mapped corresponding chunked propositions and relation-symbols. For the unsystematic versions, the case where animal similarity worked against the structurally correct solution resulted in incorrect mappings of animals, relation-symbols, and propositions. The other cases were mapped correctly.

Addition/Union was solved by ACME to demonstrate the ability to find isomorphisms without semantic or pragmatic information (Holyoak and Thagard 1989). It is an analogy between the properties of associativity, commutativity, and the existence of an identity element on numeric addition and set union. The properties of addition and union are in fact isomorphic and involve higher-order propositions, but have no common relation-symbols or arguments between the two domains (see figure 4.9). STAR-2 solves this analogy despite the lack of common items.

In the representation solved by ACME all propositions were considered to be single level (height = 1), with additional elements introduced to represent intermediate results of additions (unions). For example, commutativity of addition ($a + b = b + a$) would be represented as *Sum* (a, b, c), *Sum* (b, a, d), *Number_equal* (c, d). In this form STAR-2 was unable to solve the analogy, as there were no heuristics to distinguish

Jealous Animals (dog, seal, penguin)

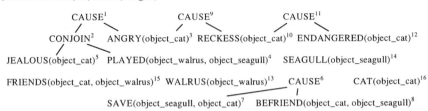

CAUSE[1]   CAUSE[9]   CAUSE[11]

CONJOIN[2]   ANGRY(object_dog)[3]   RECKESS(object_dog)[10]   ENDANGERED(object_dog)[12]

JEALOUS(object_dog)[5]   PLAYED(object_seal, object_penguin)[4]   PENGUIN(object_penguin)[14]

FRIENDS(object_dog, object_seal)[15]   SEAL(object_seal)[13]   CAUSE[6]   DOG(object_dog)[16]

SAVE(object_penguin, object_dog)[7]   BEFRIEND(object_dog, object_penguin)[8]

Jealous Animals (cat, walrus, seagull)

CAUSE[1]   CAUSE[9]   CAUSE[11]

CONJOIN[2]   ANGRY(object_cat)[3]   RECKESS(object_cat)[10]   ENDANGERED(object_cat)[12]

JEALOUS(object_cat)[5]   PLAYED(object_walrus, object_seagull)[4]   SEAGULL(object_seagull)[14]

FRIENDS(object_cat, object_walrus)[15]   WALRUS(object_walrus)[13]   CAUSE[6]   CAT(object_cat)[16]

SAVE(object_seagull, object_cat)[7]   BEFRIEND(object_cat, object_seagull)[8]

Mappings

Focus No.	(dog, seal, penguin)	(cat, walrus, seagull)	Overall mapping score
1	Conjoin Cause Angry Term	Conjoin Cause Angry Term	
1	CAUSE	CAUSE	1
1	Conjoin Term	Conjoin Term	
1	Angry Term	Angry Term	
2	CONJOIN	CONJOIN	1
2	Jelous Term	Jelous Term	
2	Played Term	Played Term	
3	ANGRY	ANGRY	1
3	object_dog	object_cat	
4	PLAYED	PLAYED	1
4	object_seal	object_walrus	
4	object_penguin	object_seagull	1
5	JEALOUS	JEALOUS	1
6	Save Cause Befriend Term	Save Cause Befriend Term	
6	Save Term	Save Term	
6	Befriend Term	Befriend Term	
7	SAVE	SAVE	1
8	BEFRIEND	BEFRIEND	1
9	Angry Cause Reckless Term	Angry Cause Reckless Term	
9	Reckless Term	Reckless Term	
10	RECKLESS	RECKLESS	1
11	Reckless Cause Endangered Term	Reckless Cause Endangered Term	
11	Endangered Term	Endangered Term	
12	ENDANGERED	ENDANGERED	1
13	Seal Term	Walrus Term	
13	SEAL	WALRUS	1
14	Penguin Term	Seagull Term	
14	PENGUIN	SEAGULL	1
15	Friends Term	Friends Term	
15	FRIENDS	FRIENDS	1
16	Dog Term	Cat Term	
16	DOG	CAT	1

Figure 4.8

Domain and mappings for a version of the jealous animals domain. Note the similar animals in corresponding roles. Other versions had no similar animals or similar animals in crossed roles. Another group of versions was similar but had no higher-order relations.

ADDITION

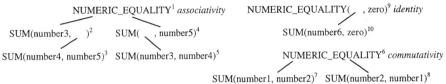

UNION

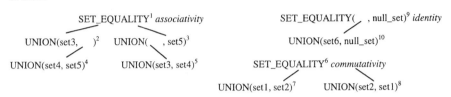

Mappings

Focus	Addition	Set	Final overall mapping score
1	Associativity Term	Associativity Term	
1	NUMERIC_EQUALITY	SET_EQUALITY	1
1	Sum Number 3_45 Term	Union Set 3_45 Term	
1	Sum Number 34_5 Term	Union Set 34_5 Term	
2	SUM	UNION	1
2	number3	set3	1
2	Sum Number 4_5 Term	Union Set 4_5 Term	
3	Sum Number 3_4 Term	Union Set 3_4 Term	
3	number5	set5	1
4	number4	set4	1
6	Commutativity Term	Commutativity Term	
6	Sum Number 1_2 Term	Union Set 1_2 Term	
6	Sum Number 2_1 Term	Union Set 2_1 Term	
7	number1	set1	1
7	number2	set2	1
9	Identity Term	Identity Term	
9	Sum Number 6_0 Term	Union Set 6_null Term	
9	zero	null_set	1
10	number6	set6	1

Figure 4.9
Domain and mappings for the Addition/Union analogy. Number$_i$ and set$_i$ refer to numeric and set variables, while the labels in italics are added to help identify chunked terms.

between the many first-level propositions, a lot of which adopted the same relation-symbol (sum or union). STAR was, however, able to solve the same problem with the domains re-represented to incorporate chunking and higher-order relations. In the modified representation commutativity of addition would be represented as follows:

Sum (a, b) chunk as sum_ab, and considered to be a number.

Sum (b, a) chunk as sum_ba and consider to be a number.

Number_equal (sum_ab, sum_ba) chunk as commutativity.

The representation containing higher-order relations corresponds to our introspections when performing this analogy, and appears to be more cognitively realistic. In a complex physics equation, components would be chunked and higher-order relations adopted that use the chunked components. For example, velocity is distance divided by time, but velocity is normally chunked as a single variable (e.g., d/t is chunked into v). Then v is used to represent acceleration $= (v_2 - v_1)/(t_2 - t_1)$. Here, acceleration could be considered a higher-order concept than velocity, rather than both single-level concepts with intermediate values used to hold the results (as ACME's representation would imply).

Adopting these hierarchical representations, STAR was able to successfully map the entire analogy representing commutativity, associativity, and identity. It would first focus on a pair of higher-order propositions (associativity of union and addition) and then focus on the arguments of the selected higher-order propositions, moving down the hierarchical structure. It would then repeat this for commutativity and identity existence.

The *boy-dog analogy* (Holyoak and Thagard 1989) is an analogy in which the base and target have isomorphic structure, but there are no higher order propositions and no common relation symbols or arguments (see figure 4.10). The basic version is difficult for humans to solve, and it is not clear how participants succeed on it. One possibility would be backtracking, that is partially undoing an incorrect solution. Backtracking was not used in STAR-2 because there does not yet appear to be definitive evidence that humans partially undo a failed attempt at analogy. Alternatively, participants might start the analogy again, avoiding previously incorrect solutions. Neither approach is implemented in

Boy

FIRST[1]
|
SMART(bill)[3]   SMART(steve)[2]   TALL(bill)[4]   TALL(tom)[5]   TIMID(tom)[6]

Dog

FIRST[1]
|
HUNGRY(rover)[3]   HUNGRY(fido)[2]   FRIENDLY(rover)[4]   FRIENDLY(blackie)[5]   FRISKY(blackie)[6]

Mappings

Focus	Boy	Dog	Final overall mapping score
1	First Term	First Term	
1	FIRST	FIRST	1
1	Smart Steve Term	Hungry Fido Term	
2	SMART	HUNGRY	1
2	steve	fido	1
3	Smart Bill Term	Hungry Rover Term	
3	bill	rover	1
4	Tall Bill Term	Friendly Rover Term	
4	TALL	FRIENDLY	1
5	Tall Tom Term	Friendly Blackie Term	
5	tom	blackie	1
6	Timid Tom Term	Frisky Blackie Term	
6	TOM	FRISKY	1

Figure 4.10
Domain and mappings for the Boy/Dog (smart Bill) analogy. The diagram represents a version where a corresponding pair of relational instances were presented first (indicated by the First Term). The basic version does not contain the First Term, and the model failed to find a correct mapping. Other versions also did not include the First Term, but had 1 (or 5) corresponding relation-symbols specified with a similarity value. These versions were also solved correctly.

STAR-2 as it stands, with the result that it fails the basic version of the boy-dog analogy. However, humans are more successful with a modified order of presentation or additional information about similarities of relation symbols (See Keane, Ledgeway, and Duff 1994 for details on the versions of this analogy). Order of presentation was handled in STAR-2 by an additional higher-order proposition indicating which proposition was presented first (see figure 4.10). Two additional versions with different sets of similarity ratings were also used. In accordance with human results, STAR-2 failed the basic analogy but was able to form all of the modified analogies.

Conclusion

The STAR-2 model of analogical mapping maps complex analogies through a combination of serial and parallel processing. Base/target pairs of propositions are selected sequentially while mappings between the components of the propositions are formed in parallel. This corresponds to a form of segmentation over capacity-limited relational domains and thus conforms to observed psychological capacity limitations in the complexity of relations that can be processed in parallel. The model has been tested on five analogies and displays a correspondence with psychological results.

Note

1. Constraint satisfaction networks have been used in a number of PDP analogy models since first introduced by ACME. A detailed explanation of constraint satisfaction operational mechanics as well as details of ACME can be found in Holyoak and Thagard (1989).

References

Almor, A., and Sloman, S. A. (1996). Is deontic reasoning special? *Psychological Review* **103**(2):374–380.

Andrews, G., and Halford, G. S. (1998). Children's ability to make transitive inferences: The importance of premise integration and structural complexity. *Cognitive Development* **13**:479–513.

Braine, M. D. S. (1978). On the relation between the natural logic of reasoning and standard logic. *Psychological Review* **85**:1–21.

Cheng, P. W., and Holyoak, K. J. (1985). Pragmatic reasoning schemas. *Cognitive Psychology* **17**:391–416.

Cohen, L. J. (1981). Can human irrationality be experimentally demonstrated? *Behavioral and Brain Sciences* **4**:317–370.

Cosmides, L. (1989). The logic of social exchange: Has natural selection shaped how humans reason? Studies with the Wason selection task. *Cognition* **31**:187–276.

Cosmides, L., and Tooby, J. (1992). Cognitive adaptations for social exchange. In J. H. Barkow, L. Cosmides, and J. Tooby, Eds., *The adapted mind: Evolutionary psychology and the generation of culture*, pp. 163–228. New York: Oxford University Press.

Cox, J. R., and Griggs, R. A. (1982). The effects of experience on performance in Wason's selection task. *Memory and Cognition* 10(5):496–502.

English, L. D., and Halford, G. S. (1995). *Mathematics education: Models and processes*. Hillsdale, NJ: Erlbaum.

Evans, J. S. B. T. (1982). *The psychology of deductive reasoning*. London: Routledge and Kegan Paul.

Evans, J. S. B. T. (1989). *Bias in human reasoning: Causes and consequences*. Hillsdale, NJ: Lawrence Erlbaum Associates.

Falkenhainer, B., Forbus, K. D., and Gentner, D. (1989). The structure-mapping engine: Algorithm and examples. *Artificial Intelligence* 41:1–63.

Gentner, D. (1983). Structure-mapping: A theoretical framework for analogy. *Cognitive Science* 7:155–170.

Gentner, D. (1989). *The mechanisms of analogical reasoning*. Cambridge: Cambridge University Press.

Gentner, D., and Gentner, D. R. (1983). Flowing waters or teeming crowds: Mental models of electricity. In D. Gentner and A. L. Stevens, Eds., *Mental models*, pp. 99–129. Hillsdale, NJ: Lawrence Erlbaum Associates.

Gentner, D., and Toupin, C. (1986). Systematicity and surface similarity in the development of analogy. *Cognitive Science* 10:277–300.

Gick, M. L., and Holyoak, K. J. (1983). Schema induction and analogical transfer. *Cognitive Psychology* 15:1–38.

Goswami, U. (1992). *Analogical reasoning in children*. Hillsdale, NJ: Lawrence Erlbaum Associates.

Gray, B., Halford, G. S., Wilson, W. H., and Phillips, S. (2000). A neural net model for mapping hierarchically structured analogs. In R. Heath, B. Nayes, A. Heathcote, & C. Hooker, Eds., *Proceedings of the fourth conference of the Australasian Cognitive Science Society, University of Newcastle*, NSW, Australia.

Halford, G. S. (1992). Analogical reasoning and conceptual complexity in cognitive development. *Human Development* 35:193–217.

Halford, G. S. (1993). *Children's understanding: the development of mental models*. Hillsdale, N. J.: Erlbaum.

Halford, G. S., Maybery, M. T., and Bain, J. D. (1986). Capacity limitations in children's reasoning: A dual task approach. *Child Development* 57:616–627.

Halford, G. S., Wilson, W. H., Guo, J., Gayler, R. W., Wiles, J., and Stewart, J. E. M. (1994). Connectionist implications for processing capacity limitations in analogies. In K. J. Holyoak and J. Barnden, Eds., *Advances in connnectionist and neural computation theory*, vol. 2, *Analogical connections*, pp. 363–415. Norwood, NJ: Ablex.

Halford, G. S., Wilson, W. H., and Phillips, S. (1998a). Processing capacity defined by relational complexity: Implications for comparative, developmental, and cognitive psychology. *Behaviorial and Brain Sciences* 21:803–864.

Halford, G. S., Wilson, W. H., and Phillips, S. (1998b). Relational processing in higher cognition: Implications for analogy, capacity and cognitive development. In K. Holyoak, D. Gentner, and B. Kokinov, Eds., *Advances in analogy research: Integration of theory and data from the cognitive, computational, and neural sciences*, pp. 57–73. Sofia: New Bulgarian University Press.

Holyoak, K. J., and Cheng, P. W. (1995). Pragmatic reasoning with a point of view. *Thinking and Reasoning* 7(4):289–313.

Holyoak, K. J., and Thagard, P. (1989). Analogical mapping by constraint satisfaction. *Cognitive Science* 13(3):295–355.

Holyoak, K. J., and Thagard, P. (1995). *Mental leaps: Analogy in creative thought*. Cambridge, MA: MIT Press.

Hummel, J. E., and Holyoak, K. J. (1997). Distributed representations of structure: A theory of analogical access and mapping. *Psychological Review* 104:427–466.

Johnson-Laird, P. N. (1983). *Mental models*. Cambridge: Cambridge University Press.

Johnson-Laird, P. N., and Byrne, R. M. J. (1991). *Deduction*. Hillsdale, NJ: Lawrence Erlbaum Associates.

Kahneman, D., and Tversky, A. (1973). On the psychology of prediction. *Psychological Review* 80(4):237–251.

Keane, M. T., Ledgeway, T., and Duff, S. (1994). Constraints on analogical mapping: A comparison of three models. *Cognitive Science* 18:387–438.

Maybery, M. T., Bain, J. D., and Halford, G. S. (1986). Information processing demands of transitive inference. *Journal of Experimental Psychology: Learning, Memory and Cognition* 12(4):600–613.

Mitchell, M., and Hofstadter, D. R. (1990). The emergence of understanding in a computer model of concepts and analogy-making. *Physica D* 42(1–3):322–334.

Oaksford, M., and Chater, N. (1994). A rational analysis of the selection task as optimal data selection. *Psychological Review* 101:608–631.

Oden, D. L., Thompson, R. K. R., and Premack, D. (1998). Analogical problem-solving by chimpanzees. In K. Holyoak, D. Gentner, and B. Kokinov, Eds., *Advances in analogy research: Integration of theory and data from the cognitive, computational, and neural sciences*, pp. 38–48. Sofia: New Bulgarian University Press.

Piaget, J. (1950). *The psychology of intelligence*. London: Routledge and Kegan Paul.

Plate, T. A. (1998). Structured operations with distributed vector representations. In K. Holyoak, D. Gentner, and B. Kokinov, Eds., *Advances in analogy research: Integration of theory and data from the cognitive, computational, and neural sciences*, pp. 154–163. Sofia: New Bulgarian University Press.

Phillips, S., Halford, G. S., and Wilson, W. H. (1995). The processing of associations versus the processing of relations and symbols: A systematic comparison.

Paper presented at the seventeenth annual conference of the Cognitive Science Society, Pittsburgh, PA.

Premack, D. (1983). The codes of man and beasts. *Behavioral and Brain Sciences* **6**:125–167.

Riley, C. A., and Trabasso, T. (1974). Comparatives, logical structures and encoding in a transitive inference task. *Journal of Experimental Child Psychology* **17**:187–203.

Rips, L. J. (1989). The psychology of knights and knaves. *Cognition* **31**:85–116.

Rips, L. (1994). *The psychology of proof: Deductive reasoning in human thinking.* Cambridge, MA: MIT Press.

Shastri, L., and Ajjanagadde, V. (1993). From simple associations to systematic reasoning: A connectionist representation of rules, variables, and dynamic bindings using temporal synchrony. *Behavioral and Brain Sciences* **16**(3):417–494.

Smolensky, P. (1990). Tensor product variable binding and the representation of symbolic structures in connectionist systems. *Artificial Intelligence* **46**(1–2):159–216.

Spearman, C. E. (1923). *The nature of intelligence and the principles of cognition.* London: Macmillan.

Sternberg, R. J. (1980a). Representation and process in linear syllogistic reasoning. *Journal of Experimental Psychology: General* **109**:119–159.

Sternberg, R. J. (1980b). The development of linear syllogistic reasoning. *Journal of Experimental Child Psychology* **29**:340–356.

Wason, P. C. (1968). Reasoning about a rule. *Quarterly Journal of Experimental Psychology* **20**:273–281.

5

Toward an Understanding of Analogy within a Biological Symbol System

Keith J. Holyoak and John E. Hummel

Knowledge Representation in Models of Analogy

The past two decades have seen extraordinary growth in the investigation of analogical thinking. This work has included extensive experimental study as well as naturalistic observation of analogy use (e.g., Dunbar, chap. 9, this volume), theoretical analyses of the component processes involved in analogical transfer, and detailed simulations that instantiate theories of analogy in running computer programs (e.g., Forbus, chap. 2, and Kokinov and Petrov, chap. 3, this volume). Although many issues remain controversial, a remarkable degree of consensus has been reached about the basic nature of analogical thinking. A number of component processes have been distinguished (retrieval of a source analog from long-term memory, mapping of source to target in working memory, generation and evaluation of inferences, and induction of relational schemas). All these component processes depend in part on representations with a predicate-argument (or role-filler) structure, especially relations (predicates with multiple arguments) and higher-order relations (predicates that take propositions as arguments). The centrality of relational representations to analogy was first clearly articulated in Gentner's (1983) structure-mapping theory of mapping, and has been acknowledged in all major models of analogy. In addition to the role of structure, it is generally accepted that analogy use is guided by semantic similarity of concepts and by the goals of the analogist. The combined influence of structural, semantic, and pragmatic constraints was emphasized by the multiconstraint model of Holyoak and Thagard (1989, 1995).

Particularly given the interdisciplinary nature of work on analogy, the field can be viewed as one of the exemplary products of modern cognitive science. Analogy provides an important example of what appears to be a highly general cognitive mechanism that takes specific inputs from essentially any domain that can be represented in explicit propositional form, and operates on them to produce inferences specific to the target domain. At its best, analogy supports transfer across domains between analogs that have little surface resemblance but nonetheless share relational structure, and generates both specific inferences and more general abstractions from as few as two examples. These properties make analogy a central example of the power of explicit symbolic thought, which distinguishes the cognition of humans and perhaps other primates from that of other species. They also provide a major challenge for computational models, particularly types of neural-network models that depend on huge numbers of training examples and that exhibit severely restricted transfer to novel inputs (Holyoak and Hummel 2000; Marcus 1998).

Because analogical thinking depends on representations that can explicitly express relations, all major computational models of analogy have been based on knowledge representations that express the internal structure of propositions, binding values to the arguments of predicates (or equivalently, fillers to relational roles). Such representations constitute symbol systems (Newell 1980, 1990). Most models have used traditional symbolic representations based on variants of predicate calculus, in which localist symbols are bound to roles by virtue of their positions in ordered lists. (This is true not only of models of analogical reasoning, but of symbolic models of cognitive processes, generally; cf. Holyoak and Hummel 2000.) For example, the proposition "John loves Mary" might be represented by the code *loves (John, Mary)*. Models based on such representations include SME (Falkenhainer, Forbus, and Gentner 1989; Forbus, chap. 2, this volume), ACME (Holyoak and Thagard 1989), ABMR (Kokinov 1994; chap. 3, this volume), and IAM (Keane, Ledgeway, and Duff 1994). These systems are broadly similar in that they take symbolic, propositional representations as inputs, use localist representations of individual concepts, and perform complex symbolic operations to generate plausible sets of candidate mappings.

Despite the considerable success such models have achieved in simulating aspects of human thinking, several reservations have been expressed about their psychological plausibility and potential for extension (Hummel and Holyoak 1997). First, the algorithms used in these models have typically ignored the capacity limits of human working memory, which their processing requirements appear to exceed. Although the working-memory requirements for mapping can be reduced by using incremental algorithms to serialize processing (Keane, Ledgeway, and Duff 1994; Forbus, Ferguson, and Gentner 1994), these algorithms provide no principled basis for estimating the maximum working-memory capacity available for mapping; that decision is left to the intuitions of the modeler. Second, none of these models have achieved a full integration of the major steps in analogical thinking (access, mapping, inference, and learning; but see Forbus, chap. 2, and Kokinov and Petrov, chap. 3, this volume, for discussions of major integrative modeling efforts). The major models perform mapping and inference, and some have been combined with models of access (ACME with ARCS; Thagard et al. 1990; and SME with MAC/FAC; Forbus, Gentner, and Law 1995). However, none of these models have fully integrated a domain-independent learning component capable of inducing new abstractions from analogical mappings (including mappings between nonidentical predicates).

For several years, we and our colleagues (Holyoak and Hummel 2000; Hummel and Holyoak 1992, 1993, 1996, 1997, forthcoming; Hummel, Burns, and Holyoak 1994; Hummel et al. 1994) have been working to develop a new architecture for analogical thinking and other forms of relational reasoning. Our aim is to develop a model with greater psychological and ultimately biological fidelity than previous efforts. Although we are far from achieving this goal, we believe cognitive science can benefit from a new focus on *biological* symbol systems—knowledge representations that capture the symbolic nature of human (and other primate) cognition, and might potentially be realized in the brain. Our models are high-level abstractions of possible neural representations and processes, being based on densely connected networks of local computing elements. Our aim is to relate models of analogy to cortical functions, particularly the role of the prefrontal cortex in relational reasoning (see Benson 1993; Grafman, Holyoak, and Boller 1995; Shallice and Burgess 1991 for reviews of prefrontal functions). These models also consititute relatively concrete proposals about the possible interface between perception and cognition (e.g., Hummel and Holyoak, forthcoming).

We will provide an overview of our current model of analogical thinking and show how it provides a unified account of the major stages of analogical processing. We will also sketch our initial effort at integrating abstract reasoning about relations with a perception-like module that can be used to make transitive inferences based on linear orderings. Finally, we will describe some recent behavioral and neuropsychological studies that connect relational reasoning with human working memory and the functions of prefrontal cortex.

Symbolic Connectionism: The LISA Model

At the heart of our effort is a neural-network model of analogy called LISA (Learning and Inference with Schemas and Analogies), and the principles of symbolic processing on which it is based. LISA represents an approach to building symbolic representations in a neurally inspired computing architecture—an approach that we term *symbolic connectionism* (Hummel and Holyoak 1997; Holyoak and Hummel 2000).

Dynamic Binding in a Symbolic-Connectionist Model

We have argued that one basic requirement for relational reasoning is the ability to represent roles (relations) independently of their fillers (arguments), which makes it possible to appreciate what different symbolic expressions have in common, and therefore to generalize flexibly from one to the other. What gives a symbolic representation its power is precisely this capacity to bind roles to their fillers dynamically (i.e., to create the bindings as needed), and to represent the resulting bindings independently of the roles and fillers themselves (i.e., without changing the representation of the roles or fillers; Fodor and Pylyshyn 1988; Holyoak and Hummel 2000).

The symbolic-connectionist framework that we have been developing seeks to realize these properties of symbol systems using the tools available in neurally plausible computing architectures. Specifically, symbolic-connectionist models (Holyoak and Hummel 2000; Hummel and Holyoak 1997) and their precursors (Hummel and Biederman 1992; von der Malsburg 1981) use synchrony of firing to bind representations of roles to representations of their fillers. The basic idea is that if two elements are bound together, then the neurons (or units in an artificial neural network) representing those elements fire in synchrony with one another; elements that are not bound together fire *out* of synchrony. For example, to represent "Jim loves Mary," the units for Jim would fire in synchrony with the units for lover, while Mary fires in synchrony with beloved. To represent "Mary loves Jim," the very same units would be placed into the opposite synchrony relations, so that Mary fires in synchrony with lover while Jim fires in synchrony with beloved. Binding by synchrony satisfies the computational requirements for dynamic binding in a symbol system in that it permits the system to express binding information both explicitly and independently of the representation of the bound elements (synchronizing "Jim" with "lover" on one occasion and "Mary" with it on another need not affect the representation of "lover" at all). As a basis for a biological theory of symbolic processing, binding by synchrony has the additional advantage of neural plausibility; there is growing evidence that real nervous systems use synchrony of firing as a basis for binding (see e.g., Singer 1999 for a recent review). As discussed later, symbolic connectionism—as an *algorithmic* theory of symbol systems—also provides a natural account of the fact that humans have a limited working-memory capacity.

Analog Representation, Retrieval and Mapping

We will now sketch the LISA model and its approach to analog retrieval and mapping. These operations are described in detail (along with simulation results) by Hummel and Holyoak (1997). The core of LISA's architecture is a system for actively (i.e., dynamically) binding roles to their fillers in working memory (WM) and encoding those bindings in long-term memory (LTM). Case roles and objects are represented in WM as distributed patterns of activation on a collection of *semantic units* (small circles in figure 5.1); case roles and objects fire in synchrony when they are bound together and out of synchrony when they are not.

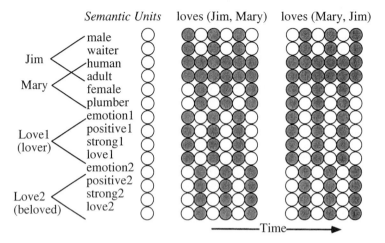

Figure 5.1
Representation of propositions in LISA's working memory (WM). Objects and relational roles are represented as patterns of activation distributed over a collection of semantic units. Objects are bound to relational roles in LISA's WM by synchrony of firing. Active semantic units are depicted in dark gray and inactive units in while.

Every proposition is encoded in LTM by a hierarchy of *structure units* (see figures 5.1 and 5.2). At the bottom of the hierarchy are *predicate* and *object* units. Each predicate unit locally codes one case role of one predicate. For example, *love1* represents the first (agent) role of the predicate "love" and has bidirectional excitatory connections to all the semantic units representing that role (e.g., *emotion1, strong1, positive1,* etc.); *love2* represents the patient role and is connected to the corresponding semantic units (e.g., *emotion2, strong2, positive2,* etc.). Semantically related predicates share units in corresponding roles (e.g., *love1* and *like1* share many units), making the semantic similarity of different predicates explicit. Object units are just like predicate units except that they are connected to semantic units describing things rather than roles. For example, the object unit *Mary* might be connected to units for *human, adult, female,* and so on, whereas *rose* might be connected to *plant, flower,* and *fragrant.*

Subproposition units (*SPs*) bind roles to fillers (objects or other propositions) in LTM. For example, "love (Jim, Mary)" would be represented

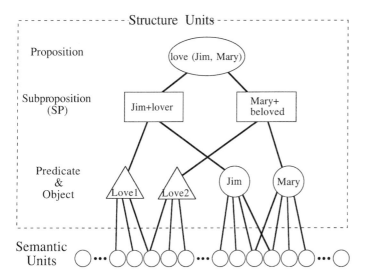

Figure 5.2
Representation of a proposition in LISA's long-term memory (LTM). Predicate units (triangles) and object units (circles) have bidirectional excitatory connections to semantic units describing the corresponding relational role (or object), and bind those semantics together in LTM. Role-filler bindings are encoded into LTM by subproposition (SP) units (rectangles), which have excitatory connections with the corresponding role and filler. Collections of role-filler bindings are bound into complete propositions by means of proposition (P) units, which have excitatory connections with the corresponding SPs.

by two SPs, one binding Jim to the agent of loving, and the other binding Mary to the patient role (figure 5.1). The *Jim + agent* SP has bidirectional excitatory connections with *Jim* and *love1*, and the *Mary + patient* SP has connections with *Mary* and *love2*. *Proposition (P)* units reside at the top of the hierarchy and have bidirectional excitatory connections with the corresponding SP units. P units serve a dual role in hierarchical structures (such as "Sam knows that Jim loves Mary"), and behave differently according to whether they are currently serving as the "parent" of their own proposition or the "child" (i.e., argument) of another (Hummel and Holyoak 1997). It is important to emphasize that structure units do not encode semantic content in any direct way. Rather, they serve only to store that content in LTM, and to generate (and respond to) the corresponding synchrony patterns on the semantic units.

The final component of LISA's architecture is a set of *mapping connections* between structure units of the same type in different analogs.[1] Every P unit in one analog shares a mapping connection with every P unit in every other analog; likewise, SPs share connections across analogs, as do objects and predicates. For the purposes of mapping and retrieval, analogs are divided into two mutually exclusive sets: a *driver* and one or more *recipients*. Retrieval and mapping are controlled by the driver. (There is no necessary linkage between the driver/recipient distinction and the more familiar source/target distinction.)

LISA performs mapping as a form of guided pattern matching. As P units in the driver become active, they generate (via their SP, predicate and object units) synchronized patterns of activation on the semantic units (one pattern for each role-argument binding). The semantic units are shared by all analogs, so the patterns generated by a proposition in one analog will tend to activate one or more similar propositions in other analogs in LTM (analogical access) or in WM (analogical mapping). Mapping differs from retrieval solely by the addition of the modifiable mapping connections. During mapping, the weights on the mapping connections grow larger when the units they link are active simultaneously, permitting LISA to learn the correspondences generated during retrieval. These connection weights serve to constrain subsequent memory access and mapping. By the end of a simulation run, corresponding structure units will have large positive weights on their mapping connections, and noncorresponding units will have strongly negative weights.

This algorithm accounts for a large number of findings in human analog retrieval and mapping, including the role of working memory in mapping, the effects of analog similarity and size on analog retrieval, and some complex asymmetries between retrieval and mapping (see Hummel and Holyoak 1997). Of particular interest is LISA's account of the role of working memory—and the implications of its limitations—in analogical mapping. Binding by synchrony is inherently capacity-limited, in the sense that it is possibly to have only a finite number of separate role-filler bindings simultaneously active and mutually out of synchrony with one another. Let us refer to the set of currently active but mutually desynchronized bindings as the *phase set* (the set of bindings that are firing out of phase with one another). The phase set is the set of bindings LISA can process "all at once," so the maximum size of the phase set corresponds to the capacity of LISA's working memory. A reasonable estimate for this capacity in humans is about four to six bindings (i.e., two or three propositions; see Hummel and Holyoak 1997). That is, under plausible estimates of the capacity of human working memory, LISA can "think about" at most two or three propositions at once. As a result, analog retrieval and mapping are largely serial operations in LISA, in which propositions are mapped in packages consisting of at most three (and more often one).

The serial nature of LISA's mapping algorithm matters because mappings discovered early on can, by virtue of the mapping connections thereby acquired, strongly influence the mappings discovered later. Mapping performance therefore depends heavily on the order in which LISA maps the propositions, and on which propositions it considers together in the same phase set.[2] (Putting two or more propositions into the same phase set effectively allows LISA to consider them in parallel, so that the mappings established for one do not influence those established for others.) This property leads to some counterintuitive predictions about human performance, a number of which we are actively testing. For example, as elaborated later in this chapter, LISA predicts that any manipulation that leads human reasoners to group propositions in working memory in a way that aids mapping—including simply drawing a box around a pair of statements, and instructing subjects to "think about these statements together"—will improve performance on difficult mapping tasks. Preliminary tests (Kubose, Holyoak, and Hummel 1999) show that this prediction is correct. Importantly, this prediction derives directly from the intrinsic limitations on LISA's working memory.

Inference and Schema Induction

Augmented with unsupervised learning and intersection discovery, LISA's approach to mapping supports inference and schema induction as a natural extension (Holyoak and Hummel 2000; Hummel and Holyoak 1996). Consider an analogy between two pairs of lovers: Jim loves Mary,

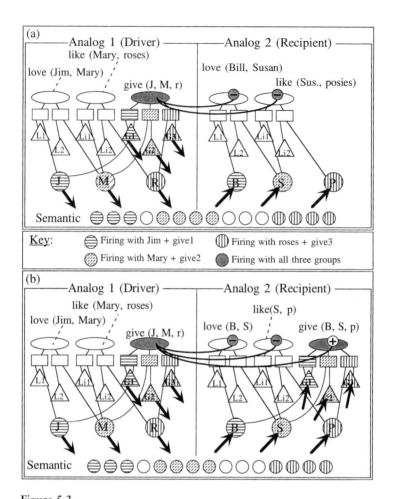

Figure 5.3
Illustration of analogical inference in LISA. (a) When *give (Jim, Mary, roses)* fires in the driver, it inhibits (via mapping connections; arcs terminating in dark circles) all the existing propositions in the recipient. (b) This situation serves as a cue to build new structure units (here, Give1, Give2, Give3, the P unit for *give (Bill, Sally, posies)*, and the corresponding SPs). LISA connects these newly created structure units to one another and to active existing structure units (here, the object units *Bill, Sally,* and *posies*). Structure units are connected together when they fire in synchrony.

Mary likes roses, and Jim gives Mary roses; Bill loves Susan, and Susan likes posies. Based on the analogy between these situations, a reasonable inference to draw is that Bill will give Susan posies. LISA draws this inference based on the known mappings (Jim to Bill, Mary to Susan, etc.) and some simple routines for unsupervised learning. When the proposition "Jim gives Mary roses" is called into working memory (in the driver), nothing in the Bill/Susan story matches it. This failure-to-match serves as a cue to LISA to infer a new proposition in the (recipient) Bill/Susan analog. Based on the correspondences (established during mapping) between John and Bill, Mary and Susan, and roses and posies, LISA infers that Bill will give Susan posies (see Holyoak and Hummel 2000; Hummel and Holyoak 1996 for details).[3]

Schema induction in LISA is performed by a similar set of operations. Consider the previous "love and flowers" analogy, and let there be a third "analog" as yet devoid of any structure units (i.e., it contains no units specifying predicate roles, objects, role-object bindings, or propositions). Like any other analog, this analog receives input from the semantic units. During mapping, units in the recipient analog (Bill and Susan in the previous example) feed activation back to the semantic units to which they are attached. As a result, semantic units connected to structure units in both the driver and the recipient tend to receive about twice as much input—and therefore become about twice as active—as semantic units connected to one analog but not the other. That is, semantics that are common to both the driver and the recipient are tagged as such by taking high activation values. The unsupervised learning algorithm, which operates during both analogy-based inference and schema induction, is sensitive to the activations of the semantic units. The result is that, when units are created in the schema analog (by the same mapping-based algorithm that drives the creation of units during inference), those units connect much more strongly to the highly active (shared) semantic units than to the less active (unshared) units. The same learning algorithm that is responsible for analogy-based inference causes the schema to perform a kind of intersection discovery, encoding what is common to the two analogs from which it is induced, and ignoring the rest. Figure 5.4 illustrates this process for one proposition in the "love and flowers" analogy.

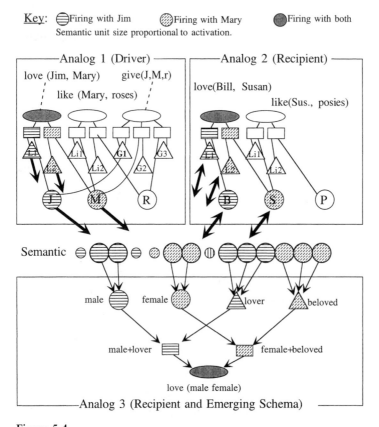

Figure 5.4
Illustration of schema induction in LISA. When *love (Jim, Mary)* fires in the driver (Analog 1), it activates *love (Sill, Susan)* in the recipient (Analog 2). The recipient feeds activation back to the semantic units, so that semantic units common to the driver and the recipient (depicted as large circles) tend to get about twice as active as those that belong to one but not the other (depicted as small circles). Units in the emerging schema (Analog 3) selectively learn connections to highly active semantic units, thereby encoding what is common to Analogs 1 and 2 (here, the abstract proposition *love (male, female)*).

The Perception–Cognition Interface

The type of symbolic-connectionist architecture embodied in LISA may provide a basis for modeling the relationship between perceptual and cognitive representations. This possibility is supported by the close theoretical links between LISA and models of perception, such as Hummel and Biederman's (1992; Hummel and Stankiewicz 1996) JIM model of object recognition. LISA's most basic operations, which perform analog access by guided pattern classification, rest on representations and processes that permit the classification of distributed representations of structure. The upper layers of the JIM model perform exactly the same function (except that in JIM the representations are structural descriptions of object shape). As such, it is no accident that LISA resembles (and operates like) the upper layers of JIM. The architectures and operations necessary for structural description (of visually perceived shapes) and LISA-style analogical mapping are closely related.

Another parallel between LISA and JIM arises from their shared approach to the representation of structure. LISA can solve analogies that violate what we have termed the *n*-ary restriction (Hummel and Holyoak 1997), mapping (for example) a proposition with two arguments onto a subset of a different proposition with three. The missing case role poses no special difficulty for LISA because the meaning of each individual role is specified by a set of active semantic units. Similarly, JIM can map a two-part structural description of an image onto a three-part structural description stored in memory (a capacity that permits JIM to recognize objects based on a subset of their parts, as when one part is invisible because it is occluded by another surface). LISA's freedom from the *n*-ary restriction and JIM's capacity to recognize objects from a subset of their parts both result from the fact that the basic elements (case roles or object parts) are not tied to specific positions in a list or vector. Most models of analogy represent case roles as elements in an ordered list (but see Kokinov 1994 for an important exception, the AMBR model, which like LISA is free of the *n*-ary restriction). Similarly, most models of object recognition (e.g., Poggio and Edelman 1990; Ullman and Basri 1991) represent object features as elements in a vector of coordinates. Coding elements as a list (or vector) yields models that are highly sensitive to the number of elements (case roles or features) in the to-be-compared structures. For example, the match between a four-element feature vector and a five-element vector in memory is mathematically undefined. LISA's departure from this representational convention (like JIM's) frees it from this kind of sensitivity to list (or vector) position.

LISA's freedom from the n-ary restriction, and its natural connections to perceptual processing, have been exploited in an extended version of the model that solves transitive inference problems (Hummel and Holyoak, forthcoming). Transitive inferences require the integration of at least two binary relations (e.g., Bill is taller than Charles, Abe is taller than Bill) to derive deductive consequences (e.g., Abe is taller than Charles). Many researchers have proposed that people reason about transitive relations by exploiting the properties of spatial arrays (e.g., Huttenlocher 1968). The general hypothesis is that, given statements such as "A is greater than B" and "B is greater than C," we map A, B, and C onto locations in a spatial array (e.g., with A near the top, B in the middle and C at the bottom). Given this mapping, the machinery that computes spatial relations from visual images can easily compute that A is above (greater than) C, that A is at the top (greatest), and that C is at the bottom (least). Indeed, for a model that computes spatial relations from visual images, the "inference" that A is above C is not an inference at all, but rather a simple observation. In addition to empirical evidence suggesting the use of a mental array to make transitive inferences in three-term series problems (e.g., DeSoto, London, and Handel 1965; Huttenlocher 1968), the mental array hypothesis is also supported by the inverse distance effect commonly found when people make comparative judgments about terms in series of four to sixteen items (e.g., Potts 1972, 1974; Woocher, Glass, and Holyoak 1978). That is, the further apart two items are in an ordered series, the faster people can decide which is greater or lesser. The distance effect is readily accounted for by perceptual discriminability of items in an array, but has no ready explanation in terms of logical inference rules. The mental array hypothesis is also appealing for its simplicity and economy: given that we come equipped with routines for processing transitive relations in the domain of visual perception, it seems natural to assume that these same routines might be recruited in aid of reasoning about transitive relations in nonvisual domains.

In spite of the appeal of the mental array hypothesis, a detailed account of exactly how these operations might work has remained elusive. Developing a process model of transitive inference is further complicated by evidence indicating that transitive reasoning depends on limited-capacity working memory (Maybery, Bain, and Halford 1986). For example, the abilities of preschool children to make transitive inferences appear to be subject to capacity limitations (Halford 1984), and transitive inference can be greatly impaired by damage to the prefrontal cortex, the apparent neural substrate for the form of working memory required for integrating relations (Waltz et al. 1999). An additional complication is that transitive inference depends on linguistic representations, which are not specifically spatial (Clark 1969; Sternberg 1980). How might nonvisual representations and processes communicate with the machinery of visuospatial processing for transitive reasoning, and how might the resulting algorithms give rise to the behavioral properties of human transitive reasoning?

To perform transitive inferences, LISA is equipped with a Mental Array Module (MAM; see figure 5.5), a specialized module for manipulating visuospatial relations. Like any other analog in LISA, MAM contains a collection of object and predicate units, which have connections to the semantic units that are shared by all analogs. In MAM, predicate units represent the roles of the *greater-than* relation (which we will designate "greater-subject," *gS*, and "greater-referent," *gR*) and the *less-than* relation (less-subject, *lS*, and less-referent, *lR*). Object units represent locations (values) in a spatial array. In contrast to an "ordinary" analog, MAM also contains an array of *location-and-relation*, L × R, units (Hummel and Biederman 1992), each of which represents a conjunction of one relational role at one location in the array. For example, the L × R unit *6-gS* represents any object whose location (value) is 6 and is greater than the location (value) of some other object. Each L × R unit has excitatory connections to the corresponding relation and location units (horizontal and vertical gray lines in figure 5.5), and mediates the communication between them. These units make it possible to compute categorical relations (such as *greater-than* (A, B)) given specific values (such as A = 6 and B = 4) as input, and vice versa.

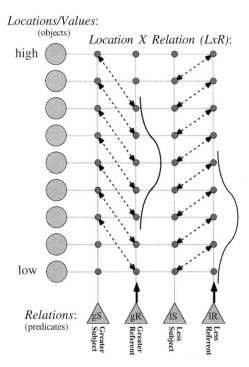

Figure 5.5
Architecture of the Mental Array Module (MAM). See text for details.

Reasoning about transitive relations by mapping objects to locations in a spatial array requires finding a mapping from categorical relations to specific values. Not only does such a mapping require violating the *n*-ary restriction, but it is inherently underconstrained: given only the knowledge that A is greater than B, there is no unique assignment of A and B to values in the array. In order to bootstrap the mapping from categorical relations to specific values, MAM contains two additional sets of connections, which amount to heuristic "guesses" about the likely value of an object based on the relational role(s) to which it is bound. First, the referent relations, *gR* and *lR*, activate their corresponding L × R units in a Gaussian pattern (Gaussian curves in figure 5.5). For example, *gR*, the referent role of the *greater-than* relation, strongly excites the L × R unit corresponding to *greater-referent at location 5 (5-*

gR), and more weakly excites those surrounding location 5 (the strength of excitation falls off according to a Gaussian function). This pattern of excitation corresponds to the assumption: given no knowledge about an object except that it is the referent of a *greater-than* relation, assume that that object has a medium value. (Location 5 is the center of the array.) Similarly, *lR*, the referent role of the *less-than* relation, excites L × R units in a Gaussian pattern centered over location 3 (below the center). These connections correspond to the assumption: given no knowledge except that an object is the referent of a less-than relation, assume that the object has slightly less than a medium value. Whereas *greater-than* is an unmarked relation, *less-than* is the marked form of the relation (Clark 1969). In LISA, markedness manifests itself in the assumption that an object has a smaller-than-average value. For example, told that Abe is taller than Bill (the unmarked form), LISA assumes that Bill (the referent) is of average height; but told that Bill is shorter than Abe, it assumes that Abe (the referent) is shorter than average.

The second set of additional connections in MAM (dashed diagonal arrows in figure 5.5) capture the logical dependencies among the referent and subject roles of the *greater-than* and *less-than* relations. L × R units representing the referent role of *greater-than* excite all L × R units representing the subject role of the *greater-than* relation at values two *above* themselves. For example, L × R unit 5-*gR* (greater-referent at location 5) excites unit 7-*gS* (greater-subject at location 7), and vice-versa (i.e., the connections are reciprocal): whatever the value, V_r, of the object bound to the referent role of the *greater-than* relation, the value, V_s, of the object bound to the subject role must be greater than that (i.e., $V_s > V_r$). Conversely, L × R units representing the referent role of the *less-than* relation excite L × R units for the subject role of that relation one unit *below* themselves, and vice versa: whatever the value, V_r, of the object bound to the referent role of a *less-than* relation, the value, V_s, of the object bound to the subject role must be less than that (i.e., $V_s < V_r$). Markedness manifests itself in these connections as the distance between connected L × R units representing the unmarked relation relative to the distance between L × R units representing the marked relation. The former is twice the latter, corresponding to the assumption that the arguments of an unmarked relation are likely to be less similar than the arguments of a marked relation: Told that Bill is shorter than Abe (the marked form), LISA will assign Bill and Abe to more similar heights than when told that Abe is taller than Bill.

The MAM representation, coupled with suitable processing assumptions (see Hummel and Holyoak, forthcoming), successfully simulates the pattern of response times observed in speeded transitive-inference tasks in which the markedness of the comparatives (in both premises and question) and the order of the premises were systematically varied (Sternberg 1980). Note that, although LISA reasons about transitive relations by mapping objects to locations in a spatial array (mapping categorical relations to analog values), it does not generate any sort of literal "image" of objects in specific locations. Rather, it is sufficient to bind symbolic representations of the objects (object units in the architecture of LISA) to symbolic representations of their values or magnitudes (object units in MAM). Indeed, for the purposes of computing the relations among objects, this symbolic representation of magnitude is superior to any literal image-based representation of objects in specific locations (see Hummel and Biederman 1992). Like the representation the JIM uses to compute spatial relations, the symbolic representation of magnitude in MAM specifies all and *only* that which is relevant to the relation of interest—namely, the values or magnitudes that need to be compared. A literal image, by contrast, would specify (implicitly or explicitly) all manner of irrelevant visual information. More generally, the visual representations that make contact with higher cognition may depend on symbolic structural descriptions that make explicit what it is necessary to know and discard the rest. (See Hummel 2000 for similar arguments about the nature of object recognition, and Pylyshyn 1973 for similar arguments about the nature of visual imagery.) The LISA model augmented with MAM suggests the beginnings of an account of how cognitive and perceptual processing interact within a biological symbol system.

Working Memory and Relational Reasoning

Recall that symbolic-connectionist models have inherent capacity limits due to the fact that it is only possible to have a finite number of groups of units simultaneously active (i.e., in working memory) and mutually *out* of synchrony with one another. (Although we have discussed the limits of dynamic binding in terms of the limits on binding by synchrony, the principle is the same regardless of what kind of tag is used for binding; see Hummel and Stankiewicz 1996.) That is, there is a limit on how much LISA can "think about" at any one time. In contrast to models that discover mappings by massively parallel constraint satisfaction (such as ACME; Holyoak and Thagard 1989), mapping in LISA requires systematic serial processing combined with limited parallel constraint satisfaction. This limit on LISA's capacity for parallel processing imposes an upper bound on the complexity of reasoning tasks that LISA can reliably solve, which in turn leads to predictions about human performance in such tasks. Specifically, we predict that people will be unable to reliably solve problems that require processing more than four to six role-bindings in parallel. In addition, they may perform suboptimally on problems within their capacity limit if they are not led to make full use of their available resources, or if their effective capacity is reduced by a secondary task. We will now describe a set of simulations that reveal how LISA can "scale up" to handle large mapping problems despite its working-memory limits. We will then review a number of experimental studies that bear upon the relationship between working memory and relational reasoning.

Scaling Up: How LISA Can Map Large Analogs Despite Limited Capacity

One of the apparent paradoxes of human analogical thinking is that people have great difficulty mapping some small, spartan analogs, yet easily map other analogs that are much larger and might seem more complex. For example, Hummel and Holyoak (1997) showed that LISA, like college students, is unable to reliably map the "boys and dogs" analogs (Holyoak and Thagard 1989)—two isomorphic analogs, each consisting of just three objects and three attributes (one-place predicates) expressed in five propositions. This analogy problem is hard because the semantics of the two analogs provide no clues to the mapping, and the structural constraints exceed LISA's (and presumably people's) working-memory capacity.

In contrast, even very large analogs can be mapped reliably if rich semantic constraints guide the corespondences between the two situations (e.g., Spellman and Holyoak 1996). Many naturalistic examples of analogies used in argumentation have this property (see Dunbar, chap. 9, this volume). For example, in 1991 President George Bush used an analogy between the Persian Gulf crisis and World War II to argue for American intervention after Saddam Hussein of Iraq invaded and occupied Kuwait. This analogy, which centered on a mapping between Saddam Hussein and Adolf Hitler, was highly effective in eliciting support for Bush's policy. Identifying the major corespondences is clearly within the capabilities of college students, as was tested and confirmed by Spellman and Holyoak (1992). This is true even though the two analogs are quite large and far from isomorphic (e.g., Bush and the United States of 1991 might map onto either Franklin Roosevelt and the United States of World War II, or to Winston Churchill and Great Britain).

Spellman and Holyoak (1992, experiment 2) had groups of college students read short descriptions of World War II that were intended to bias the preferred mapping by placing greater emphasis on either the roles of Roosevelt or Churchill, and either the United States or Great Britain. The ACME model (Holyoak and Thagard 1989), which uses parallel constraint satisfaction without any working-memory limits, was able to provide a qualitative simulation of the dominant mapping patterns produced by human subjects in each of the four conditions. The simulation was based on large representations (76 propositions for the Gulf crisis scenario, and 112–124 propositions for each of the four World War II histories), including numerous propositions based on higher-order predicates such as "cause," which take propositions as arguments. As far as we know, this remains the largest analogical mapping problem shown to be solvable by people that has ever been simulated by a computer model.

To assess LISA's ability to scale up to such large examples, we applied LISA to the same set of four analogy problems (mappings from each of the four World War II analogs to the Gulf analog). Although the analogs are large and the mapping is complicated by various many-to-one possible correpondences, finding the correspondences is aided by rich semantic connections that can guide the mapping (e.g., similar relations such as "attacking" that map to one another). To test LISA, we converted the ACME representations used by Spellman and Holyoak (1992) to representations suitable for LISA, maintaining informational equivalence as much as possible. Simple semantic-feature representations were created for each predicate and object, with feature overlap of predicates reflecting the similarity of predicates as had been specified for ACME. Propositions based on one-place predicates for ACME were coverted to object features for LISA.

One run was performed for each of the four versions of the mapping problem. In each case the World War II analog served as the driver. (The subjects tested by Spellman and Holyoak 1992 were informed about the mapping task before reading the description of World War II, a procedure that presumably encouraged them to map from World War II to the Gulf scenario in an incremental fashion as they read the history.) Propositions were fired one at a time, in an order determined by the order of mention of the corresponding facts in the English versions read by subjects (roughly, a paragraph describing the actions of Hitler and Germany that started World War II, followed by a paragraph focusing on the actions of either Churchill or Roosevelt, followed by a paragraph focusing on the actions of either Britain or the United States). The first proposition fired was selected to establish a mapping between Saddam Hussein and Hitler, which was specified for human subjects and marked as "presumed" in the ACME simulation. As the propositions included at most three arguments, the effective phase set used by LISA was three, well within human working-memory limits. LISA went through each proposition in the driver analog one time only.

Table 5.1 presents a summary of LISA's preferred mappings for the people and countries that were mapped by subjects in Spellman and Holyoak's (1992) study, based on the weights acquired on the connections from the Gulf scenario to the World War II scenario (the direction in which subjects were queried). For comparison, table 5.1 also indicates the ordinal rank of each mapping in the human data by a superscript (e.g., a superscipt of 1 indicates the most frequent human response). In general, LISA's preferred mappings correspond to those most frequently given by people: Saddam Hussein mapped strongly to Hitler and Iraq to Germany; and President Bush mapped to either Churchill or Roosevelt,

Table 5.1
LISA's mappings from World War II to the Persian Gulf War for each of the
biased histories used by Spellman and Holyoak (1992, experiment 2)

Biased History				
If Saddam is Hitler then who is . . .	Churchill Britain	Churchill U.S.	FDR Britain	FDR U.S.
Iraq?	[1]Germany (1.00)	[1]Germany (1.00)	[1]Germany (1.00)	[1]Germany (1.00)
Bush?	[1]Churchill 1 (0.68)	[1]Churchill 1 (0.81)	[1]FDR (0.77)	[1]FDR (0.62)
United States?	[1]Britain (0.96) [2]United States (0.78)	[2]United States (0.77) [1]Britain (0.59)	[1]United States (0.91) [2]Britain (0.90)	[1]United States (0.95) [2]Britain (0.78)
Kuwait?	[1]Poland (0.78)	[1]Poland (0.84)	[2]Poland (0.81) [1]Austria (0.49)	[1]Poland (0.86) [2]Austria (0.46)
Saudi Arabia?	[1]France (0.69)	[1]France (0.51)	[2]France (0.49)	[3]Austria (0.53) [2]France (0.46)

Note: Numbers in parentheses are weights on the strongest mapping connections (maximum = 1). All mappings with strengths above .20 are reported. Super-
scripts indicate the ordinal frequencies of mappings generated by human subjects.

depending on which World War II leader was emphasized in the biased
history. People's preferred mapping for the United States of the Gulf
situation tended to be controlled by their mapping for President Bush
(rather than by the country emphasized in the history). LISA's strongest
mapping followed the same pattern for three of the four conditions. Like
people, LISA mapped Kuwait (the "victim" nation in the Gulf war) onto
either Poland or Poland and Austria (comparable victims of German
aggression in World War II).

The main deviation between LISA's performance and that of people is that LISA produced strong mappings of the United States to both the United States and to Britain, whereas people generally gave just one of these mappings. (As a side effect, LISA missed the possible mapping of Saudi Arabia to Britain, given by a small plurality of subjects in the two conditions in which they mapped the United States to the United States rather than to Britain.) A closer examination of LISA's performance suggests a possible reason for this discrepancy. LISA fires the driver propositions sequentially, and after processing the propositions focusing on the leader in World War II it acquired a strong mapping not only of Bush to that leader (Churchill or Roosevelt), but also of the United States to the corresponding country (Britain or the United States). When the run was stopped at that point, LISA gave the same single mapping of the United States as most subjects did. However, if the run continued through the propositions of the final paragraph (as in all the runs summarized in table 5.1), then whichever country was emphasized in the ending of the history also became a strong mapping. It is possible that subjects in Spellman and Holyoak's (1992) study tended to commit themselves to mappings as soon as possible, and therefore paid little attention to the final paragraph of the history they were reading (since they did not need even to read it to answer the mapping questions).

In general, then, these simulation results establish that LISA can find sensible mappings for large, ambiguous, and semantically rich analogies of the sort that people are able to map. LISA does so within psychologically realistic limits on its working memory, in this case focusing on just one driver proposition at a time (rather than all one hundred or more, as the ACME or SME model would do). Moreover, the sequential nature of LISA's operation leads to new and testable predictions (e.g., that when mappings are ambiguous, people's tendency to give multiple mappings may be increased if they are encouraged to process the analogs as fully as possible before giving mapping responses).

Grouping Effects and Mapping Asymmetries

Although there is clear evidence that analogical inferences can be asymmetrical (e.g., Bowdle and Gentner 1997), most models of analogy predict that the actual mapping process is inherently symmetrical. In

LISA, however, mapping is a directional, capacity-limited, and sequential process. The directional aspect of mapping follows from the driver/recipient distinction. If a driver analog contains more propositions than WM can hold, then propositions must be fired individually or in small groups. In this case, it matters which propositions are fired first, and which are fired together. This property of LISA's operation leads to predictions about the influence of grouping propositions on mapping performance. For example, if the text of the driver analog is thematically connected (e.g., by causal relations) in a way that encourages a beneficial ordering and grouping of propositions, then mapping may be more accurate than if the text consists of causally unrelated propositions. Keane (1997) reported findings consistent with this prediction. He demonstrated that performance mapping two structurally isomorphic analogs improves if one analog contains causal content, even if the other does not.

LISA accounts for Keane's finding in terms of the impact of causal content on the way propositions are grouped and ordered for firing in the driver analog. LISA therefore predicts that this facilitory effect of causal content should be asymmetrical: if the driver contains causal content but the recipient does not, then that content may facilitate mapping by virtue of how it influences the grouping and ordering of propositions for firing. By contrast, if the recipient contains causal content but the driver does not, then that content should provide no benefit relative to a condition in which neither the driver nor the recipient has casual content. Of course, the best performance is expected when both the driver and recipient contain causal content, in which case the causal content can aid mapping not only by encouraging optimal grouping and ordering, but also by mapping directly (i.e., the causal statements in one analog will map onto the causal statements in the other by virtue of their shared casual roles; see Kubose, Holyoak, and Hummel 1999).

Our group has extended Keane's procedure to test this predicted asymmetrical effect of causal content on analogical mapping. Kubose, Holyoak, and Hummel manipulated the driver/recipient status by having subjects first answer questions about one or the other analog, and then asking directed mapping questions (i.e., for each object and relation in the driver, subjects were asked to provide the corresponding element from the recipient). As LISA predicts, mapping performance was best (i.e., most accurate) when both analogs had causal content, next best when the driver (rather than the recipient) had causal content, and equally poor when the recipient (rather than the driver) had causal content as when neither had causal content.

Other experiments conducted by Kubose, Holyoak, and Hummel (1999) also supported LISA's interpretation of causal effects on mapping as being mediated (at least in part) by selective grouping of propositions. For example, LISA predicts that *anything* that promotes appropriate grouping of propositions in the driver should facilitate mapping, whether it is thematic causal content or simply a box drawn around the appropriate statements, accompanied by an instruction to "think about these statements together." To test this prediction, Kubose, Holyoak, and Hummel presented subjects with two noncausal analogs and asked them to identify the correspondences between elements. In one condition, two propositions in the driver were optimally grouped for subjects simply by drawing a box around the critical sentences and asking subjects to consider them together (the "good box" condition). In other conditions, control subjects either had no box (and no instructions to group propositions; the "no box" condition), or else they were instructed to group propositions that LISA predicted would not facilitate mapping (the "bad box" condition). As predicted, mapping performance in the good-box condition exceeded that in both the no-box and bad-box conditions.

Other recent experiments in our laboratory (Waltz et al. 2000) have tested a different type of prediction LISA makes about the role of working memory in mapping. In accord with the theory of relational complexity developed by Halford and his colleagues (Halford and Wilson 1980; Halford, Wilson, and Phillips 1998; see Wilson et al., chap. 4, this volume), LISA predicts that the complexity of mappings is constrained by the availability of WM resources to maintain multiple role bindings concurrently. It follows that restricting WM by adding dual-task requirements (e.g., a phonological working-memory load), which are known to compete for WM capacity (e.g., Dunbar and Sussman 1995; Hitch and Baddeley 1976; Gilhooly et al. 1993) will impair the ability to make relationally complex mappings.

In order to test this prediction, we asked subjects to map a set of stimuli with ambiguous mappings. These stimuli, created by Markman and Gentner (1993), are pairs of pictures (e.g., a man bringing groceries to a woman; a woman feeding nuts to a squirrel) in which one element of the first picture (e.g., the woman) can map to either of two elements in the second (the woman, on the basis of perceptual similarity, or the squirrel, based on the shared role of recipient-of-food). For such cross-mapped objects (which require relational, rather than feature-based mappings), we found that adding a dual-task requirement, such as maintaining a concurrent digit load or generating random digits, caused a shift from relational to more direct perceptual similarity as the basis of mappings. LISA predicts this shift because finding the relational match is more dependent on WM resources, which are reduced by a concurrent memory load. In addition, Tohill and Holyoak (2000) have shown similar reductions in relational matches when subjects' anxiety level is increased *prior* to the mapping task (by a difficult backward-counting task). The detrimental impact of anxiety on relational mapping is consistent with theories of anxiety that emphasize its restrictive impact on WM resources (Eysenck and Calvo 1992).

All these recent studies point to a general conclusion: analogical mapping is highly sensitive to the specific information that is processed together in working memory. Relational mappings can be encouraged by manipulations that lead reasoners to consider multiple structurally informative propositions together, and is hindered by manipulations that reduce the effective capacity of working memory.

Neuropsychological and Neuroimaging Studies of Relational Reasoning

We have also begun to investigate the neural locus of the operations that support relational reasoning (Waltz et al. 1999). Investigations by our group have revealed selective deficits in relational processing in tasks similar to analogy, such as simple variants of Raven's Progressive Matrices problems (see Carpenter, Just, and Shell 1990), for patients with focal degeneration of the prefrontal cortex. The patients tested were diagnosed with frontotemporal dementia (FTD), a dementing syndrome resulting in the degeneration of anterior regions of cortex (Brun et al. 1994). In the early stages of FTD, degeneration tends to be localized to either prefrontal or anterior temporal cortical areas, with eventual involvement throughout all cortical regions in advanced stages. This makes possible the division of patients with mild FTD into two sub-groups. In the frontal variant of FTD, damage is initially localized in pre-frontal cortex. Patients with the temporal variant of FTD often exhibit semantic dementia, characterized by impairments in semantic knowledge (Graham and Hodges 1997).

Waltz et al. (1999) found that, relative to patients with damage to anterior temporal cortex, patients with degeneration of prefrontal cortex show dramatic impairment in the ability to make inferences requiring the integration of multiple relational representations. For example, performance on a set of matrix problems showed striking differences between patients with damage to prefrontal cortex and those with damage to anterior temporal cortex and normal controls in the ability to integrate multiple relational premises. The two patient groups did not differ either from each other or from normals in the average proportion of correct responses given to problems not requiring relational integra-tion (i.e., problems with variation on at most one dimension). However, on problems that required integration (those with variations on two dimensions), patients with prefrontal cortical damage were catastrophi-cally impaired compared to patients with anterior temporal lobe damage as well as normal controls.

To complement such neuropsychological studies, we (Kroger et al. 1998; Kroger 1998) have also begun to perform neuroimaging studies to investigate the neural basis of relational processing in normal college students. Previous functional imaging studies of reasoning have shown involvement of the same areas of cortex as are activated in working-memory tasks, especially the dorsolateral area of prefrontal cortex (e.g., Prabhakaran et al. 1997), but have not systematically manipulated rela-tional complexity. We constructed materials matched closely in terms of visuospatial attributes, but varying in relational complexity (Halford and Wilson 1980; Halford, Wilson, and Philips 1998). An initial experiment used variants of Raven's Progressive Matrices problems that vary the number of relations that that must be considered to find the solution.

These problems are more complex versions of the matrix problems used with FTD patients by Waltz et al. (1999), suitable for use with normal college students. The problems varied relational complexity over five levels, defined in terms of the number of monotonic variations (0–4) across rows and columns of the matrices (e.g., a circle increasing in size across rows). Solution times increased as relational complexity increased, confirming that this task taps into increasingly complex cognitive processes. Functional magnetic resonance imaging revealed increasing activation in both dorsolateral prefrontal cortex and parietal cortex across levels of complexity. These findings are consistent with the hypothesis that the dorsolateral prefrontal cortex is involved in manipulating relations among display elements, while the elements themselves are represented in more modality-specific posterior cortical areas (parietal cortex in the case of visuospatial matrix problems).

In addition to testing matrix problems with FTD patients, Waltz et al. (1999) obtained converging evidence for a selective role of prefrontal cortex in relational integration using a transitive-inference task. Transitive inference requires integration of two binary relations (e.g., Bill is taller than Charles; Abe is taller than Bill) based on a shared role filler (Bill). Waltz et al. found that patients suffering from degeneration of frontal cortex performed at chance on transitive-inference problems such as the preceding example, in which the premises are scrambled so that solving them requires integration of multiple relations. However, if problems are stated so that the people are introduced in order of height (e.g., Abe is taller than Bill; Bill is taller than Charles), then it is possible to find the solution using a chaining strategy that does not require relational integration. Patients with prefrontal degeneration were able to solve problems stated in this canonical ordering as well as age-matched normals. In contrast to frontal patients, patients with degeneration in anterior temporal cortex performed all transitive-inference tasks (including those that could not be solved by chaining) as well as age-matched controls—with near-perfect accuracy.

Findings such as these strongly suggest that prefrontal cortex must be centrally involved in the kind of working memory that is responsible for relational integration. LISA provides an account of why working memory (and in particular, the working memory associated with prefrontal cortex) is essential for relational reasoning in tasks such as transitive inference. In particular, the LISA/MAM model that we described earlier provides a straightforward account of these findings in terms of the role of the mapping connections in the model's ability to integrate relations (Hummel et al. 1998). The mapping connections play a central role in LISA's ability to integrate *greater-than* (A, B) with *greater-than* (B, C) for the purposes of mapping A, B, and C to unique locations in the spatial array: It is the connection from B to a particular location (established when *greater-than* (A, B) fires) that makes it possible to keep B at that location and place C at a lower location when *greater-than* (B, C) fires. Without this critical connection, C in the context of *greater-than* (B, C) would map to exactly the same location as B in the context of *greater-than* (A, B). The resulting representation would be useless for deciding which object is greatest and which least. And indeed, run with its mapping connections disabled, LISA, like frontal patients, performs randomly on the transitive inference task.

In this context, it is tempting to speculate that the "mapping connections" of LISA may be realized neurally as neurons in prefrontal cortex with dynamically reassignable response properties—that is, neurons that can represent X on one occasion (e.g., the mapping of B to location 5) and Y on another (see note 1; also Hummel and Holyoak 1997).

Conclusion

Symbolic connectionism, as instantiated in models such as LISA, offers a possible account of the general form of a biological symbol system that underlies human (and other primate) relational reasoning. LISA provides a solution to the problem (forcefully posed by Fodor and Pylyshyn 1988) of representing knowledge over a distributed set of units while preserving systematic relational structure. Like previous models based on traditional symbolic representations, LISA is able to retrieve and map analogs based in large part on structural constraints. But in addition, LISA is able to capitalize on its distributed representations of meaning to integrate analog retrieval and mapping with a flexible mechanism for analogical inference and schema induction.

A key aspect of LISA, given its use of dynamic binding, is that analogical processing (and relational reasoning in general) is heavily constrained by working-memory resources. In order to make relationally complex mappings, the reasoner must be able to consider multiple role bindings together. The neuropsychological and neuroimaging results support the hypothesis that relational processing may form the core of an executive component of prefrontal working memory (Robin and Holyoak 1995). In other words, relational integration—and specifically, dynamic variable binding—may be the "work" done by working memory. We can now begin to see not only what mappings can be computed by human reasoners, but also how they may be computed, and what regions of the brain are necessary for computing them. The task of reconciling computational models of high-level reasoning with the operating principles of neural systems has only begun, but will surely be a major project for cognitive neuroscience in the new millennium.

Acknowledgments

Preparation of this chapter was supported by NSF Grant SBR-9729023. Jessica Choplin provided valuable assistance with the simulations of the Gulf War analogies. We thank Ken Forbus and Mark Keane for helpful comments on a previous draft.

Notes

1. In a more biologically realistic implementation, mapping connections might take the form of units rather than connections. Mapping connections need not preexist in long-term memory; rather, they might be "wired up" as needed in working memory by neurons with modifiable receptive fields.

2. In LISA simulations reported to date, the firing order and groupings of propositions in the phase set was set by the programmer; however, an automated algorithm is currently under development. We postulate that the flow of control in the driver is dependent on factors that influence text coherence (e.g., causal links and argument overlap). In the large-scale simulations reported in the present chapter, firing order was simply matched to order of mention in the corresponding texts read by human subjects.

3. Specifically, the mapping algorithm assigns negative mapping weights to all pairs of units it knows do not map. For example, because Jim maps to Bill, it cannot also map to poppies; the *Jim* unit therefore has a negative mapping connection to the *poppies* unit. Whenever the active units in the driver inhibit (via mapping connections) all the units in the recipient, LISA interprets this situation as an indication that nothing in the recipient matches.

References

Benson, D. F. (1993). Prefrontal abilities. *Behavioral Neurology* 6:75–81.

Bowdle, B. F., and Gentner, D. (1997). Informativity and asymmetry in comparisons. *Cognitive Psychology* 34:244–286.

Brun, A., Englund, B., Gustafson, L., Passant, L., Mann, D. M. A., Neary, D., and Snowden, J. S. (1994). Clinical and neuropathological criteria for frontotemporal dementia. *Journal of Neurology, Neurosurgery and Psychiatry* 57:416–418.

Carpenter, P. A., Just, M. A., and Shell, P. (1990). What one intelligence test measures: A theoretical account of the processing in the Raven Progressive Matrices Test. *Psychological Review* 97:404–431.

Clark, H. H. (1969). Linguistic processes in deductive reasoning. *Psychological Review* 76:387–404.

DeSoto, C., London, M., and Handel, S. (1965). Social reasoning and spatial paralogic. *Journal of Personality and Social Psychology* 2:513–521.

Dunbar, K., and Sussman, D. (1995). Toward a cognitive account of frontal lobe function: Simulating frontal lobe deficits in normal subjects. In J. Grafman, K. J. Holyoak, and F. Boller, Eds., *Structure and functions of the human prefrontal cortex. Annals of the New York Academy of Sciences*, vol. 769, pp. 289–304. New York: New York Academy of Sciences.

Eysenck, W. E., and Calvo, M. G. (1992). Anxiety and performance: The processing efficiency theory. *Cognition and Emotion* 6:409–434.

Falkenhainer, B., Forbus, K. D., and Gentner, D. (1989). The structure-mapping engine: Algorithm and examples. *Artificial Intelligence* 41:1–63.

Fodor, J. A., and Pylyshyn, Z. W. (1988). Connectionism and cognitive architecture: A critical analysis. In S. Pinker and J. Mehler, Eds., *Connections and symbols*, pp. 3–71. Cambridge, MA: MIT Press.

Forbus, K. D., Ferguson, R. W., and Gentner, D. (1994). Incremental structure mapping. In A. Ram and K. Eiselt, Eds., *Proceedings of the sixteenth annual conference of the Cognitive Science Society*, pp. 313–318. Hillsdale, NJ: Erlbaum.

Forbus, K. D., Gentner, D., and Law, K. (1995). MAC/FAC: A model of similarity-based retrieval. *Cognitive Science* 19:141–205.

Gentner, D. (1983). Structure-mapping: A theoretical framework for analogy. *Cognitive Science* 7:155–170.

Gilhooly, K. J., Logie, R. H., Wetherick, N. E., and Wynn, V. (1993). Working memory and strategies in syllogistic-reasoning tasks. *Memory and Cognition* 21:115–124.

Grafman, J., Holyoak, K. J., and Boller, F., Eds. (1995). *Structure and functions of the human prefrontal cortex*. New York: New York Academy Sciences.

Graham, K. S., and Hodges, J. R. (1997). Differentiating the roles of the hippocampal complex and the neocortex in long-term memory storage: Evidence from the study of semantic dementia and Alzheimer's disease. *Neuropsychology* 11:77–89.

Halford, G. S. (1984). Can young children integrate premises in transitivity and serial order tasks? *Cognitive Psychology* 16:65–93.

Halford, G. S., and Wilson, W. H. (1980). A category theory approach to cognitive development. *Cognitive Psychology* 12:356–411.

Halford, G. S., Wilson, W. H., and Phillips, S. (1998). Processing capacity defined by relational complexity: Implications for comparative, developmental, and cognitive psychology. *Behavioral and Brain Sciences* 21:803–864.

Hitch, G. J., and Baddeley, A. D. (1976). Verbal reasoning and working memory. *Quarterly Journal of Experimental Psychology* 28:603–621.

Holyoak, K. J., and Hummel, J. E. (2000). The proper treatment of symbols in a connectionist architecture. In E. Dietrich and A. Markman, Eds., *Cognitive dynamics: Conceptual change in humans and machines*, pp. 229–263. Mahwah, NJ: Erlbaum.

Holyoak, K. J., Novick, L. R., and Melz, E. R. (1994). Component processes in analogical transfer: Mapping, pattern completion, and adaptation. In K. J. Holyoak and J. A. Barnden, Eds., *Advances in connectionist and neural computation theory*, vol. 2, *Analogical connections*, pp. 130–180. Norwood, NJ: Ablex.

Holyoak, K. J., and Thagard, P. (1989). Analogical mapping by constraint satisfaction. *Cognitive Science* 13:295–355.

Holyoak, K. J., and Thagard, P. (1995). *Mental leaps: Analogy in creative thought*. Cambridge, MA: MIT Press.

Hummel, J. E. (2000). Where view-based theories break down: The role of structure in shape perception and object recognition. In E. Dietrich and A. Markman, Eds., *Cognitive dynamics: Conceptual change in humans and machines*, pp. 157–185. Mahwah, NJ: Erlbaum.

Hummel, J. E., and Biederman, I. (1992). Dynamic binding in a neural network for shape recognition. *Psychological Review* 99:480–517.

Hummel, J. E., Burns, B., and Holyoak, K. J. (1994). Analogical mapping by dynamic binding: Preliminary investigations. In K. J. Holyoak and J. A. Barnden, Eds., *Advances in connectionist and neural computation theory*, vol. 2, *Analogical connections*, pp. 416–445. Norwood, NJ: Ablex.

Hummel, J. E., and Holyoak, K. J. (1992). Indirect analogical mapping. In *Proceedings of the fourteenth annual conference of the Cognitive Science Society*, pp. 516–521. Hillsdale, NJ: Erlbaum.

Hummel, J. E., and Holyoak, K. J. (1993). Distributing structure over time. *Behavioral and Brain Sciences* 16:464.

Hummel, J. E., and Holyoak, K. J. (1996). LISA: A computational model of analogical inference and schema induction. In *Proceedings of the eighteenth annual conference of the Cognitive Science Society*, pp. 352–357. Hillsdale, NJ: Erlbaum.

Hummel, J. E., and Holyoak, K. J. (1997). Distributed representations of structure: A theory of analogical access and mapping. *Psychological Review* **104**:427–466.

Hummel, J. E., and Holyoak, K. J. (forthcoming). A process model of human transitive inference. In M. L. Gattis, Ed., *Spatial schemas in abstract thought.* Cambridge, MA: MIT Press.

Hummel, J. E., Melz, E. R., Thompson, J., and Holyoak, K. J. (1994). Mapping hierarchical structures with synchrony for binding: Preliminary investigations. In A. Ram and K. Eiselt, Eds., *Proceedings of the sixteenth annual conference of the Cognitive Science Society*, pp. 433–438. Hillsdale, NJ: Erlbaum.

Hummel, J. E., and Stankiewicz, B. J. (1996). An architecture for rapid, hierarchical structural description. In T. Inui and J. McClelland, Eds., *Attention and performance XVI: Information integration in perception and communication*, pp. 93–121. Cambridge, MA: MIT Press.

Hummel, J. E., Waltz, J. A., Knowlton, B. J., and Holyoak, K. J. (1998). A symbolic connectionist model of the impact of prefrontal damage on transitive reasoning. *Journal of Cognitive Neuroscience Supplement* **10**:58.

Huttenlocher, J. (1968). Constructing spatial images: A strategy in reasoning. *Psychological Review* **75**:550–560.

Keane, M. T. (1997). What makes an analogy difficult? IAM predicts the effects of order and causal relations on analogical mapping. *Journal of Experimental Psychology: Learning, Memory, and Cognition* **23**:1–22.

Keane, M. T., Ledgeway, T., and Duff, S. (1994). Constraints on analogical mapping: A comparison of three models. *Cognitive Science* **18**:387–438.

Kokinov, B. N. (1994). A hybrid model of reasoning by analogy. In K. J. Holyoak and J. A. Barnden, Eds., *Advances in connectionist and neural computation theory*, vol. 2, *Analogical connections*, pp. 247–318. Norwood, NJ: Ablex.

Kroger, J. K. (1998). *Human processing of relationally complex representations: Cognitive and neural components.* Ph.D. dissertation, University of California, Los Angeles.

Kroger, J. K., Holyoak, K. J., Bookheimer, S. Y., and Cohen, M. S. (1998). Processing relationally complex representations in Raven's Progressive Matrices: An fMRI study. *Society for Neuroscience Abstracts 24.*

Kubose, T. T., Holyoak, K. J., and Hummel, J. E. (1999). Strategic use of working memory in analogical mapping. Manuscript.

Marcus, G. F. (1998). Rethinking eliminative connectionism. *Cognitive Psychology* **37**:243–282.

Markman, A. B., and Gentner, D. (1993). Structural alignment during similarity comparisons. *Cognitive Psychology* **23**:431–467.

Maybery, M. T., Bain, J. D., and Halford, G. S. (1986). Information-processing demands of transitive inference. *Journal of Experimental Psychology: Learning, Memory, and Cognition* 12:600–613.

Newell, A. (1980). Physical symbol systems. *Cognitive Science* 4:135–183.

Newell, A. (1990). *Unified theories of cognition.* Cambridge, MA: Harvard University Press.

Poggio, T., and Edelman, S. (1990). A neural network that learns to recognize three-dimensional objects. *Nature* 343:263–266.

Potts, G. R. (1972). Information processing strategies used in the encoding of linear orderings. *Journal of Verbal Learning and Verbal Behavior* 11:727–740.

Potts, G. R. (1974). Storing and retrieving information about ordered relationships. *Journal of Experimental Psychology* 103:431–439.

Prabhakaran, V., Smith, J. A. L., Desmond, J. E., Glover, G., and Gabrieli, J. D. E. (1997). Neural substrates of fluid reasoning: An fMRI study of neocortical activation during performance of the Raven's Progressive Matrices Test. *Cognitive Psychology* 33:43–63.

Pylyshyn, Z. (1973). What the mind's eye tells the mind's brain: A critique of mental imagery. *Psychological Bulletin* 80:1–24.

Robin, N., and Holyoak, K. J. (1995). Relational complexity and the functions of prefrontal cortex. In M. S. Gazzaniga, Ed., *The cognitive neurosciences*, pp. 987–997. Cambridge, MA: MIT Press.

Shallice, T., and Burgess, P. (1991). Higher-order cognitive impairments and frontal lobe lesions in man. In H. S. Levin, H. M. Eisenberg, and A. L. Benton, Eds., *Frontal lobe function and dysfunction*, pp. 125–138. New York: Oxford University Press.

Shastri, L., and Ajjanagadde, V. (1993). From simple associations to systematic reasoning: A connectionist representation of rules, variables and dynamic bindings using temporal synchrony. *Behavioral and Brain Sciences* 16:417–494.

Singer, W. (1999). Response synchronization: A universal coding strategy for the definition of relations. In M. S. Gazzaniga, Ed., *The new cognitive neurosciences*, pp. 325–338. Cambridge, MA: MIT Press.

Spellman, B. A., and Holyoak, K. J. (1992). If Saddam is Hitler then who is George Bush? Analogical mapping between systems of social roles. *Journal of Personality and Social Psychology* 62:913–933.

Spellman, B. A., and Holyoak, K. J. (1996). Pragmatics in analogical mapping. *Cognitive Psychology* 31:307–346.

Sternberg, R. J. (1980). Representation and process in linear syllogistic reasoning. *Journal of Experimental Psychology: General* 109:119–159.

Thagard, P., Holyoak, K. J., Nelson, G., and Gochfeld, D. (1990). Analog retrieval by constraint satisfaction. *Artificial Intelligence* 46:259–310.

Tohill, J. M., and Holyoak, K. J. (2000). The impact of anxiety on analogical reasoning. *Thinking and Reasoning* 6:27–40.

Ullman, S., and Basri, R. (1991). Recognition by linear combinations of models. *IEEE Transactions on Pattern Analysis and Machine Intelligence* 13:992–1006.

von der Malsburg, C. (1981). The correlation theory of brain function. Internal Report 81–2. Department of Neurobiology, Max-Planck-Institute for Biophysical Chemistry.

Waltz, J. A., Knowlton, B. J., Holyoak, K. J., Boone, K. B., Mishkin, F. S., de Menezes Santos, M., Thomas, C. R., and Miller, B. L. (1999). A system for relational reasoning in human prefrontal cortex. *Psychological Science* 10:119–125.

Waltz, J. A., Lau, A. Grewal, S. K., and Holyoak, K. J. (2000). The role of working memory in analogical mapping. *Memory and Cognition.*

Woocher, F. D., Glass, A. L., and Holyoak, K. J. (1978). Positional discriminability in linear orderings. *Memory and Cognition* 6:165–173.

II

Arenas of Analogical Thought

6

Metaphor Is Like Analogy

Dedre Gentner, Brian F. Bowdle, Phillip Wolff, and Consuelo Boronat

Metaphor is pervasive in language and thought: in scientific discovery (Gentner 1982; Gentner and Jeziorski 1993; Gruber 1995; Nersessian 1992), in literature (Gibbs 1994; Lakoff and Turner 1989; Miller 1993; Steen 1989) and in everyday language (Glucksberg and Keysar 1990; Hobbs 1979; Lakoff and Johnson 1980). Yet despite a considerable amount of research, surprisingly little is known about how metaphors are psychologically processed.

In this chapter we present an approach that unifies metaphor with processes of analogy and similarity. We first lay out the analogy approach to metaphor and delineate some limitations. In the first section we ask whether large-scale conceptual metaphors such as *Love is a journey* or *The mind is a computer* can be modeled as extended structural mappings between domains. Our research suggests that the answer is *yes* for novel metaphors, but not for conventional metaphors. In the second section we describe research that shows that the real-time processing of nominal metaphors can be captured by detailed models from analogy. In the third section we lay out a theory—the *career of metaphor*—of how metaphoric representation changes as a metaphor evolves from novel to conventional. In the fourth section we discuss implications of these ideas.

One reason metaphor[1] is challenging is its range of types, as in the following list:

1. A man is not necessarily intelligent because he has plenty of ideas, any more than he is a good general because he has plenty of soldiers (Chamfort).
2. My job is a jail.

3. His eyes were burning coals.

4. Tires are like shoes.

5. On a star of faith pure as the drifting bread, /As the food and flames of the snow (Dylan Thomas).

Metaphors (1) and (2) could be considered analogies—comparisons that share primarily relational information. But metaphors can also be based on common object attributes, as in (3), or both, as in (4). Most of the metaphors studied in the psychological literature are analogies—that is, they convey chiefly relational commonalities: for example, *Encyclopedias are gold mines, My job is a jail*. According to structure-mapping theory, such relational metaphors convey that a system of relations holding among the base objects also holds among the target objects, regardless of whether or not the objects themselves are intrinsically similar. The centrality of relations during metaphor comprehension has been confirmed by a number of studies. For example, people's interpretations of metaphors tend to include more relations than simple attributes, even for statements that suggest both types of commonalities (e.g., Gentner and Clement 1988; Shen 1992; Tourangeau and Rips 1991). Further, Gentner and Clement (1988) found that subjects' judgments of the aptness of metaphors was positively correlated with the judged relationality of their interpretations of these metaphors, but was either negatively correlated or unrelated to the attributionality of their interpretations.

According to structure-mapping theory (Gentner 1983, 1988; Gentner and Markman 1997), analogical mapping is a process of establishing a *structural alignment* between two represented situations and then projecting inferences. Structure-mapping theory assumes the existence of structured representations made up of objects and their properties, relations between objects, and higher-order relations between relations. An alignment consists of an explicit set of correspondences between the representational elements of the two situations. The alignment is determined according to *structural consistency* constraints: (1) one-to-one correspondence between the mapped elements in the base and target, and (2) parallel connectivity, in which the arguments of corresponding predicates also correspond. In addition, the selection of an alignment is guided by the *systematicity principle*: a system of relations connected by higher-order constraining relations such as causal relations is preferred over one with an equal number of independent matches. Systematicity also guides analogical inference: people do not import random facts from base to target, but instead project inferences that complete the common system of relations (Bowdle and Gentner 1997; Clement and Gentner 1991).

Although analogy provides the strongest evidence for structure-mapping, alignment and mapping processes also apply in ordinary similarity (Gentner and Markman 1997; Markman and Gentner 1993; Medin, Goldstone, and Gentner 1993). For several years, we have run our main analogy simulation, SME (the Structure-mapping Engine), as an overall similarity engine. It forms matches at all levels, from object attributes to higher-order relations, and then sets about combining these into the best overall alignment. Because of the systematicity bias, relational alignments tend to win out, as in the case of examples (1) and (2). However, SME can also derive attributional solutions, as in (3), as well as interpretations that preserve both relational and attributional information, as in (4). (Indeed, SME's "favorite" class of comparisons, all else being equal, is literal similarity, in which there is a high degree of overlap in both object and relational information.)

Examples (1)–(4) all show structural consistency—one-to-one correspondences and parallel connectivity. Example (5) is more challenging. It belongs to a class of literary metaphors that lack clear one-to-one mappings and are characterized by many cross-weaving connections, with no clear way of deciding exactly which correspondences should hold (Gentner 1982; Gentner, Falkenhainer, and Skorstad 1988). These kinds of metaphors seem to require processes such as metonymy and phonological matching in addition to alignment and mapping (see Fauconnier 1990, this volume; Fauconnier and Turner 1998 for further examples and analyses of complex metaphors.)

Structure-mapping makes a number of predictions that should follow if metaphors are processed like analogies. In the next two sections we consider the evidence. The first section asks whether extended metaphoric systems—which intuitively bear a strong resemblance to analogical systems—are in fact processed as analogical mappings between domains. The second section asks whether individual metaphors are processed by alignment and mapping.

Conceptual Metaphors as Extended Analogical Mappings

The presence of extended metaphoric systems is a striking feature of our language. People use analogies and metaphors from familiar concrete domains to discuss less familiar or abstract domains: e.g., flowing water for electricity (Gentner and Gentner 1983) or a long journey for marriage (Quinn 1987). Extended metaphors can evoke a whole system of knowledge, as when the computer metaphor, with its notions of encoding, storage, and retrieval, is applied to cognition.

Lakoff and his colleagues have documented many large-scale metaphoric systems in everyday language, such as the *argument as container* metaphor exemplified above, or the *love as a journey* metaphor: "The road was rough and steep but we carried on. . . . If we pull together we can surmount these hard times. We're having a rocky time and I'm not sure we're going to make it" (Lakoff and Johnson 1980; Lakoff and Turner 1989; Turner 1987). Many other domain-level metaphors have been described: marriage as a contract (Quinn 1987); the use of spatial terms to describe abstract dimensions such as economic prosperity or affective state (Nagy 1974); and the use of progeneration terms to express ideas like causality or preeminence, as in *mother of battles* (Turner 1987).

This research investigates the processing of extended metaphors during comprehension. In particular, we ask whether such metaphors are processed as mappings from one domain to the other during on-line comprehension—that is, whether participants establish and use a system-mapping between an initial domain (the base domain) and a second domain (the target domain) to process an extended metaphor. The presence of systems of metaphors between domains suggests that such metaphors are processed as systematic analogies (Gentner and Gentner 1983; Kittay 1987). But there are other possibilities. It could be that the metaphoric sentences in an extended metaphoric discourse are each processed separately and locally, with no connection across the sets of metaphoric phrases; or even that these seemingly metaphoric phrases are so conventionalized that their figurative meanings are directly available in the lexicon as alternate word senses. For example, the sentence *Ida gave Joe a great idea* could be processed as an on-line metaphor in which *give*, which normally means to *cause a change in possession*, is mapped onto something like to *cause a change in cognitive state* (Gentner 1975; Gentner and France 1988). But it is also possible that the meaning to *cause a change in cognitive state* has become conventionalized as a possible meaning sense of *give*, in which case there need be no metaphorical mapping, merely a lexical look-up. Such cases may have originated as novel comparisons and become entrenched (the *cognitive archaeology* possibility). Thus, possibilities range from on-line generative mappings (the strongest claim) through the localist possibility that metaphors are simply processed and then discarded, to the weakest claim, that apparent metaphors might simply be processed as instances of multiple word senses (as polysemous word entries).

Localist Theories

There is little empirical evidence on the on-line processing of extended metaphors. With few exceptions, most theories of the processing of metaphor have emphasized local interactions between pairs of terms and ignored large-scale domain interactions. Many such theories are variants of the comparison view (Black 1962), in which finding the meaning of a metaphor involves finding the set of features that the base and target share (e.g., Malgady and Johnson 1980; Marschark, Katz, and Paivio 1983; Ortony 1979). For example, Ortony's (1979) influential salience imbalance theory of metaphor asserted that metaphoricity arises from an imbalance in the salience of the common features such that high-salient features in the base are matched with low-salient features of the target. In contrast, Glucksberg and Keysar's (1990) class-inclusion theory of metaphor, in explicit rejection of comparison theories, argues that metaphors are statements of category membership. A metaphor such as *my job is a jail* is understood by assigning the target of the metaphor (*my job*) to the category of which *jail* is the prototypical example: e.g., *confining institutions*. Glucksberg, McGlone, and Manfredi (1997) elaborated the category approach in their *attributive categorization* model. In this model, potential categories are generated and projected from the base while sets of modifiable dimensions are simultaneously identified in the target. For example, in the above metaphor, the base, *jail*, projects its *confining institutions* category while the target, *job*, yields its modifiable dimensions: working conditions, degree of flexibility, and so on. The interpretation of the metaphor is thus an interaction between the category prototypically associated with the base and the dimensions that characterize the target. In this model, the base and target enter into processing in role-specific ways throughout the comprehension process.

The category approach can account for the finding that metaphors are asymmetrical: for example, the fact that *Some surgeons are butchers* and *Some butchers are surgeons* mean very different things, as noted by Ortony (1979) (see also Camac and Glucksberg 1984; Ortony et al. 1985). (However, other approaches can also account for asymmetry, as we will see.) The category-based approach is "localist:" it assumes that a metaphor conveys a categorical relation between a particular pair of terms. Thus this approach addresses single metaphors and not extended systems of metaphors.

Domain-Mapping Theories

One of the first theories aimed at large-scale domain-mappings was the domain-interaction hypothesis, proposed by Rumelhart and Abrahamson (1973) for analogies and by Tourangeau and Sternberg (1981, 1982) for metaphors (see also Tourangeau and Rips 1991). These theories used a multidimensional space model of mental representation and postulated that in metaphor, the dimensional structure of the base domain is mapped onto the dimensional structure of the target. Thus the metaphor *Brezhnev is a hawk* specifies an implicit mapping from the domain of birds to the domain of politicians, and states (with the appropriate dimensional substitutions) that Brezhnev's relative position among politicians—high in aggressiveness and political power—is the same as the hawk's among birds—high in ferocity and in strength. Tourangeau and Sternberg (1982) proposed that a good metaphor is one that, first, involves two very different domains and thus has high between-domain distance; and, second, shows low within-space distance between the base and target items in their very distant respective spaces: for example, *Brezhnev* and *hawk* occupy the same relative position in their domain spaces. Tourangeau and Sternberg found support for the theory's prediction that within-space closeness is positively correlated with aptness, as well as a trend in favor of the second prediction—that between-domain distance should be positively correlated with aptness.

Kelly and Keil (1987) found evidence that metaphors can promote alignment across domains. Their participants rated concepts from two topic areas—say, periodicals and food—on semantic differential scales. Participants in the experimental condition then paraphrased and rated the aptness of four metaphors linking the two domains: for example, *The Wall Street Journal is the spinach of newspapers and magazines*. Then they again performed the same rating task. The experimental participants showed a shift in their ratings relative to a control group: pairs that made good metaphors became more similar in their semantic differential ratings and pairs that made poor metaphors became less similar. These findings are consistent with the claim that metaphors can induce large-scale domain-mappings.

The mental space representation of conceptual structures used in much of this earlier research has limited representational capabilities. It can represent dimensional structure, such as the ordering of members of a domain on attributes such as size or ferocity, but it cannot capture many other relations that are important in metaphor, such as causal structure, progeneration, and higher-order perceptual schemas (see Markman 1999). Nevertheless, these findings offer general support for the domain-mapping hypothesis.

A related approach from linguistics is Kittay and Lehrer's (1981) semantic field theory, which asserts that people understand metaphors through mapping the lexical fields that characterize the two domains. Metaphorically linking two domains alters one's view of one or both domains and this restructuring of domain(s) makes inferences about the target domain possible (Kittay 1987; Kittay and Lehrer 1981). For example, Kittay and Lehrer (1981) analyzed Wordsworth's poem comparing the history of Venice to the life history of a woman, in which the rise and decline of the city are likened to the youth and age of a noble-woman, Venice's inception in liberty (as a republic) is likened to a high-born birth, and so on.

Albritton, McKoon, and Gerrig (1995) found evidence suggesting that extended metaphors can result in schemalike long-term memory representations. Recognition of sentences from metaphorical passages was faster when both the target sentence and the preceding (priming) sentence shared a connection to the metaphor-based schema than when they did not. This research suggests that online mappings are created, but it does not test this directly, for participants made their recognition judgments *after* the reading metaphoric passages. Our research, presented below, takes up the issue of how extended metaphoric systems are processed on line. It uses reading time measures to determine whether participants are sensitive to the consistency of metaphoric mappings between domains during comprehension.

Lakoff and his colleagues argue for domain-level metaphors in a stronger sense than the foregoing researchers. They suggest that people possess large-scale conceptual metaphors such as "life as a journey" or "justice as balancing" (Lakoff and Johnson 1980; Lakoff and Turner 1989; Turner 1987, 1991). They have documented a large number of conceptual mappings that they propose are used to interpret metaphors and to inform their target domains. For example, Lakoff and Johnson (1980:90, 91) list examples of the *An argument is a journey* metaphor:

- We have *set out* to prove that bats are birds.
- *So far*, we've seen that no current theories will work.
- We will *proceed* in a *step-by-step* fashion.
- This observation *leads* to an elegant solution.
- He *strayed* from the main argument.
- Do you *follow* my argument?
- We have *covered a lot of ground* in our argument.

According to Lakoff (1990), metaphors are comprehended by invoking global mappings. Thus, this theory accounts for extended metaphor by postulating that people invoke a domain-level, prestored conceptual mapping when they encounter a local instance of the metaphor. To account for novel metaphors, Lakoff and Turner (1989) state that conceptual metaphors can be extended to new occurrences of existing domain-mappings (see also Gibbs 1990, 1994). Finally, a strong tenet of Lakoff's view is that metaphors do not draw on existing similarities, but rather *create* similarities by providing structure for the target domain.

Lakoff's claims about the psychology of metaphor have been controversial. For example, Murphy (1996, 1997) has noted difficulties in interpreting one of Lakoff's major theoretical claims, the *invariance hypothesis*: "Metaphorical mappings preserve the cognitive topology (that is, the image-schema) of the source domain, in a way consistent with the inherent structure of the target domain" (Lakoff 1993:215). One problem for the invariance hypothesis is the existence of multiple metaphors for the same target: e.g., *love is a journey*, *love is a disease*, *love is a fire*. Gibbs (1996) has defended the conceptual metaphor position on this last point, arguing that many abstract domains can be construed in several different ways, and therefore can accept metaphors from multiple base domains. However, a more serious challenge to the invariance principle is that the *same* base domain can provide different structures for different targets. For example, compare three metaphors that all use the base domain of *fire*: *knowledge is a fire* (one may pass the flame to others); *love is a fire* (its heat may consume the lover); *envy is a fire* (it burns upward toward its object, covering it with smoke). It is hard to argue that an invariant image-schema from *fire* is informing all these metaphors. It seems much more likely that our representations of *fire* include multiple schemas, and that which one is invoked depends on the alignment with the target domain. A related question is whether metaphors are understood by invoking preexisting conceptual metaphors, as Lakoff's theory suggests, or whether novel interpretations also occur. Finally, Murphy challenges Lakoff's claim that metaphors *create* meaning in the target, as opposed to reflecting parallels.

Despite these theoretical concerns, it is clear that Lakoff has identified an important phenomenon. Our research aims to capture the phenomena of large-scale mappings in a psychologically grounded account. We seek to explain how conceptual metaphors are processed and how they are learned. Are metaphors understood in terms of long-standing conceptual metaphors, or can mappings be constructed online, as most analogy theories assume? Structure-mapping theory suggests that metaphors are processed as structural alignments, based on some initial relational commonalties. Then further inferences are projected from the more concrete or familiar base to target. Thus, alignment highlights parallel structure (consistent with Murphy's position), and inference-projection creates new knowledge in the target. This last fits with Lakoff's emphasis on new knowledge, but with the proviso that inference projection is guided by an initial alignment. This means that abstract domains are not structured de novo by concrete domains, but rather begin with some structure of their own and accept further structure from a commensurable concrete domain. Alignment serves to provide the needed constraint on possible conceptual metaphors.

Structure-mapping provides a natural mechanism for explaining how extended domain mappings are processed (Gentner 1982, 1983, 1988; Gentner and Clement 1988; Gentner and Markman 1997). Two key features that support extended mappings are the *systematicity bias* in interpretation and inference and the *incremental mapping* mechanism (Falkenhainer, Forbus, and Gentner 1989; Forbus, Gentner, and Law 1995; Gentner 1983; Gentner and Markman 1997). The systematicity bias—the preference for alignments that form deeply interconnected structures—fits with evidence that people naturally interpret analogy and metaphor by mapping connected systems of belief, rather than independent features. For example, Clement and Gentner (1991) asked people which of two common facts was most important to an analogy and, in another experiment, which new fact could be predicted from an analogy. For both tasks, participants were strongly influenced by systematicity: they were more likely to infer a new fact, and more prone to call a given fact important, if it was connected to a common causal structure. Systematicity is related to people's preference for relational interpretations of metaphors. Gentner and Clement (1988) found that adults interpreted metaphors such as *Plant stems are drinking straws* by invoking common relational systems (e.g., *They both convey liquids to nourish living things*) rather than object commonalties (e.g., *Both are long and thin*). Furthermore, adults (but not children) considered metaphors more apt when they found interpretations based on relational structure (Gentner 1988; Gentner, Rattermann, and Forbus 1993).

The second line of computational support for extended mappings is *incremental mapping*. An analogical mapping can be extended by adding further assertions from the base domain to the mapping (Burstein 1983; Novick and Holyoak 1991). For example, Keane and Brayshaw's (1988) IAM model simulates Keane's finding that subjects' initial mappings can influence their subsequent correspondences. We have adapted this technique to create an incremental version of SME, called ISME. After creating a mapping between the initial base and target representations, ISME can extend the analogy by fetching further information from the base and seeking correspondences in the target that are consistent with the ongoing mapping. It thus enlarges the analogical mapping (Forbus, Ferguson, and Gentner 1994).

Assuming that a plausible process model can be provided for conceptual metaphors, there still remains the question of their psychological status. Are they cognitive mappings, or merely ways of talking? It is impossible to read the examples assembled by Lakoff and Johnson (1980), Turner (1987, 1991) Sweetser (1990), and others without feeling that at least some of them reflect psychologically real domain mappings. However, despite the intuitive appeal of the conceptual metaphor hypothesis, it would be rash to assume such a conclusion without more direct evidence. The perils of relying on intuition in interpreting metaphorical language are made clear in Keysar and Bly's (1995) study of the illusory transparency of idioms. They gave people archaic English idioms (for which the meanings are no longer current) in different contexts. People who heard *The goose hangs high* in the context of a sad story thought that it expressed sadness (a dead goose); those who heard it in a happy story thought it expressed happiness (a plentiful larder). More tellingly, both groups were confident that they would have arrived at the same interpretations without the story; they felt that their interpretation could be derived simply from the idiom. Keysar and Bly went on to suggest that the perceived transparency of an idiomatic expression increases with repeated use of an expression, and is not dependent on a genuine conceptual connection.

Researchers who study metaphor face the same difficulty as Keysar and Bly's subjects, of separating what they know to be the standard meaning of a conceptual metaphor from what the metaphor by itself suggests. These findings show that a feeling of transparency is not *by itself* evidence of a conceptual psychologically real mapping. A sense of transparency does not tell us whether the meaning is derivable from a systematic pattern or is simply learned by frequent lexical exposure. What is needed are techniques that go beyond speakers' intuitions.

In order to establish the conceptual role of domain mappings, we must first lay out the set of alternatives. There are at least four broad possibilities. The strongest possibility, as discussed above, is that metaphors *create* meaning (Lakoff 1990). In analogical processing terms, this would imply a purely *projective mapping*: the target domain is organized and structured in terms of conceptual systems borrowed from the more readily observable base domain. People actively use the metaphorical base domain to think about the target. The second possibility is *structural parallelism* in the domain representations, as suggested by Murphy (1996). Due to inherent similarities in the referent domains, parallel systems of semantic relations could evolve independently in two domains. Metaphors linking the two domains would then reflect structural alignment between the two parallel domain representations (Gentner and Markman 1997; Medin, Goldstone, and Gentnter 1993). In this case the two domains would share conceptual systems, but neither is derived from the other.

The third possibility is *cognitive archaeology*: systematic metaphors represent conceptual systems initially mapped from a particular base domain to a target domain, but which now exist as abstract systems that can apply to both domains. Such metaphoric relics would testify to the prior importance of a given analogical mapping in shaping the construal of the target domain in cultural history, they would not entail online mappings from the concrete domain during reasoning. However, they need not be purely local. To the extent that such systems preserve interconnections between their parts, they may still be processed as global systems in the target domain rather than in terms of individual assertions. The fourth and weakest possibility is *local lexical relations* (a kind of highly local cognitive archaeology). In this case, there are no large-scale systematic mappings; metaphors consist simply of individual polysemies and/or homophonies. For example, a term like *icy* could have concrete word senses, such as "made of frozen water; hard, cold," and also abstract word senses, such as "emotionally aloof, rigid, unyielding." A related possibility is that the two senses are stored as separate homophonic lexical entries. Either way the phenomenon would be purely lexical. It would entail neither large-scale structuring nor online mapping processes.

To settle these questions requires investigating the online processing of metaphors belonging to extended systems. Unfortunately, as noted above, most metaphor research has concentrated on individual metaphors—usually nominal metaphors of the form "An X is a Y." Much of this research has centered on testing the dual-stage hypothesis, proposed by Clark and Lucy (1975) and Kintsch (1974), which asserts that people first attempt to process linguistic material literally, and only if it cannot be understood literally do they try to process it nonliterally (Miller 1979; Searle 1976). Tests of this view typically compare processing of literal and figurative sentences (see Hoffman and Kemper 1987 for a review) and does not address the current question of whether and how people respond to systematic domain mappings.

Testing the Domain-Mapping Hypothesis
Gentner and Boronat set out to investigate whether extended metaphors are processed on-line as domain mappings (Boronat 1990; Gentner and Boronat 1992, in preparation; Gentner 1992). One potential obstacle to this kind of investigation is the fact that metaphorical language is often almost invisible. People use conventionalized metaphors such as *the weight of evidence* or *his spirits sank* without apparently noticing their metaphorical basis. Asking subjects for explicit judgments could interfere with natural processing. To get around this problem, we developed an indirect technique that does not require explicit choices. Our method is based on the phenomenon that mixed metaphors can be jarring and even humorous, as illustrated by these examples from the *New Yorker*:

This college is standing on a launching pad ready to flex its muscles

or

Reynaud was under the thumb of a mistress who was in the pocket of the pro-Axis party in France.

If such shifts of metaphor slow down processing, this suggests a disruption in the mapping process. Such a disruption would be consistent with the claim that people comprehend metaphors by setting up structurally consistent, systematic domain mappings. When two mappings are inconsistent, the resulting incongruity is then noticed. We used this mixed-metaphor technique to test the importance of consistency and systematicity in the comprehension of extended metaphors. All the experiments followed the same logic, which can be illustrated with the following examples:

(1)   Was Anna still boiling mad when you saw her?
      No, she was doing a slow simmer.

(2)   Was Anna still a raging beast when you saw her?
      No, she was doing a slow simmer.

The initial sentences in (1) and (2) communicate roughly the same meaning. Both passages have the same final sentence. However, the last sentence in passage (2) involves a rather startling switch from the mapping set up in the first sentence (ANGER IS A BEAST) to the mapping in the final sentence (ANGER IS HEAT). In contrast, passage (1) uses the ANGER IS HEAT mapping throughout. Example (1), which maintains the same base to target mapping throughout, is *a consistently extended* metaphor. Example (2), which switches from one base domain to another, is *inconsistently extended:* the final sentence disrupts the metaphor set up by the first sentence. If participants take longer to read the last sentence in passage (2) than in passage (1), this will be support for the domain-mapping hypothesis, that people construct base-to-target mappings when they read extended metaphors, and that they naturally extend these mappings in a structurally consistent manner across connected base systems within the base and target.

We first describe two studies that used novel metaphors from existing conceptual mappings, as exemplified in box 6.1 (for more detail, see Boronat 1990; Gentner and Boronat 1992, in preparation; Gentner and Wolff 2000). The major contrast was between passages that used the same base throughout (*consistent*), and those in which the base was switched at a key point (*inconsistent*). The metaphor switch always occurred in the last sentence, for which reading times were collected. The consistent and inconsistent passages had the same story line and the same last sentence, but differed in the global metaphor used. For example, a short story about a debate was written using two different global metaphors[2] (see table 6.1). The consistent passage used the global metaphor A DEBATE IS A RACE: for example, ... *he had to steer his course carefully in the competition*. The inconsistent passage used the

Box 6.1
Sample metaphoric passages utilizing novel metaphors (Gentner and Boronat 1992, in preparation)

Note: Metaphoric terms are in italics. They were presented in normal typeface to subjects. Passages were presented a sentence at a time.

Consistent: *A Debate is a Race*

Dan saw the big debate as a *race*: he was determined to win it. He knew that he had to *steer his course* carefully in the competition. His strategy was to go *cruising through* the initial points and then make his move. After months of debating practice, Dan knew how to present his conclusions. If he could only *keep up the pace*, he had a good chance of winning. Before long, he felt the audience was receptive to his arguments. Then, he *revved up* as he made his last key points. His skill left his opponent *far behind him* at the *finish line*.

Inconsistent: *A Debate is a War*

Dan saw the big debate as a *war*: he was determined to be victorious. He knew that he had to use every *weapon* at his command in the competition. He mapped out his strategy to insure he established a *dominant position*. After months of debating practice, Dan knew how to present his conclusions. If he could only *marshall his forces*, he had a good chance of winning. Before long, he felt the audience was receptive to his arguments. Then, he *intensified the bombardment* as he made his last key points. His skill left his opponent *far behind him* at the *finish line*.

Literal control:

Dan's topic in the big debate was "how to win a *race*": he had to be convincing. His first argument was on the proper way to *steer a course* in a competition. He argued strongly for *cruising through* initial laps and then making a move. After months of debating practice, Dan knew how to present his conclusions. If he could prove the need to *keep up the pace*, he had a good chance to win. Before long, he felt the audience was receptive to his arguments. His concluding remarks focused on *revving up* near the end of a race. His skill left his opponent *far behind him* at the *finish line*.

global metaphor, A DEBATE IS A WAR: for example, . . . *he had to use every _weapon_ at his command in the competition*. For both passages, the last sentence used the RACE metaphor: for example, *His skill left his opponent _far behind him_ at the _finish line_*. For the consistent passage, this represents a continuation of the global metaphor. However, for the inconsistent passage, the critical final sentence presents a switch between global metaphors: from A DEBATE IS A WAR to A DEBATE IS A RACE. The domain-mapping hypothesis predicts that the last sentence will be read more quickly following a consistent global metaphor than following an inconsistent global metaphor, because the former continues an established base to target mapping, whereas the latter disrupts it.

A literal control condition was also included to check for the possibility that such a mapping consistency effect, if observed, could be attributed to mere associative priming between the words in a passage and the words in the final sentence. The literal control passages contained all of the metaphoric terms of their matched consistent-metaphor passages, but these terms were used literally. Thus these subjects encountered the *terms* from the metaphoric base domain in the passage, but encountered the metaphor itself for the first time in the final test sentence. If these subjects read the final sentence as quickly as subjects in the consistent condition, it would suggest that any facilitation for the consistent condition over the inconsistent condition could be due merely to lexical priming.

The predictions are as follows. Localist metaphor theories, such as the class-inclusion theory of Glucksberg and Keysar (1990; Glucksberg, McGlone, and Manfredi 1997), would predict no difference between the two metaphoric conditions, since the key (metaphoric) sentence is the same. A modality-oriented view emphasizing differences between metaphoric and literal modes would also predict no difference between the two metaphor conditions, but would predict an advantage for both kinds of metaphor passages over the literal control passages. This is because the metaphoric last sentences should be faster to process after metaphoric than after literal material. Finally, the domain-mapping account predicts that test metaphors will be read faster in the consistent condition than in the inconsistent or literal control conditions.

Box 6.2
Sample metaphoric passage utilizing conventional metaphors

Consistent: *A Debate is a Journey*

Dan wanted to *guide* the audience *through* his debate speech. He did not *stray* from his *line* of argument. He showed that the opposition's arguments went off in the wrong *direction*. He won the debate because he *oriented* the judges to his interpretation.

Inconsistent: *A Debate is a War*

Dan wanted to *devastate* the audience with his debate arguments. He did not *desert* his *line* of argument. He *attacked* the opposition's arguments from the start. He won the debate because he *oriented* the judges to his interpretation.

Literal Control Passage:

Dan's *directions guided* him *through* the building to the debate room. He did not *stray* from the *lines* drawn on the map. He was well prepared to discuss problems with the opposition's arguments. He won the debate because he *oriented* the judges to his interpretation.

The results showed a mapping consistency effect: subjects read the last sentence significantly faster when it extended the existing mapping than when it drew on a new metaphoric mapping or followed a literal control passage. This finding supports the claim that processing extended metaphors involves alignment and mapping, and that people readily incrementally extend such mappings. These findings lend support to the claim that large-scale domain metaphors are psychologically real.

The evidence so far supports the domain-mapping hypothesis for novel metaphors.[3] But what about conventional metaphors? In two studies, Gentner and Boronat used passages that contained conventional metaphors, as exemplified in box 6.2. In many cases these metaphors came from the same global metaphors as the novel metaphors—e.g., DEBATE AS A RACE—but here the individual metaphors were conventional. We reasoned that conventionalization might result in lexical storage—in metaphorical meanings coming to be stored with the base term. In this case, for highly conventional metaphors the metaphorical interpretation would simply be an alternate word sense. There should be no particular cost for switching global metaphors, since comprehension would simply involve finding the appropriate word sense. On this account, we would predict no advantage in time to read the last sentence for consistent metaphors over inconsistent metaphors.

The results were quite different from the first set of findings. Consistent with our speculations, when highly conventional metaphors were used, there was no apparent cost of shifting between global metaphors: subjects were not significantly slowed by a shift in the global metaphor. This supports the "alternate word sense" account for conventional metaphors. This finding is convergent with research suggesting that conventionalization results in a shift in metaphor processing from on-line active interpretation to retrieval of stored meanings (Bowdle and Gentner 1995, 1999). We return to this point later.

Summary

According to the domain-mapping hypothesis, people construct base-to-target mappings when they read extended metaphors, and extend these mappings in a structurally consistent manner across connected systems within the base and target. This predicts that metaphoric sentences will be read faster when they extend an ongoing mapping than when they require a new mapping, even when the conveyed meaning in the target is equivalent—the mapping consistency effect. In contrast, a localist account of metaphor—in which the passage metaphors are understood as local categorizations and then dropped—would predict no difference in reading time for the last lines of consistently and inconsistently mapped passages, since the same metaphors are being read and the meaning in the target is the same for both conditions.

We found evidence for a mapping consistency effect, but only for novel metaphors. Highly conventional metaphors were processed in a localist manner. We speculate that conventional metaphors behave like borderline idioms, with lexically stored figurative interpretations. This prediction is consistent with other evidence that highly familiar idiomatic and metaphorical meanings are stored and processed at a lexical level (Blank 1988; Blasko and Connine 1993; Cacciari and Tabossi 1988; Gentner and Wolff 1997; Gibbs 1980, 1985, 1994; Gibbs and O'Brien 1990; Swinney and Cutler 1979).

The present results for novel metaphors are consistent with domain-mapping theories such as that of Rumelhart and Abrahamson (1973) and Tourangeau and Sternberg (1982) and with research suggesting that metaphors can be processed as large-scale conceptual systems (Allbritton, McKoon, and Gerrig 1995; Gibbs 1990, 1994; Nayak and Gibbs 1990; but see Glucksberg, Brown, and McGlone 1993). They argue against the kind of localist frame that is implicit in much current research. Theories that focus on single metaphors, such as Glucksberg and Keysar's (1990) class-inclusion theory of metaphor, cannot explain the links between extended metaphors, because they have no mechanisms for linking several discrete base-to-target mappings. Thus they cannot explain the pattern found for novel metaphors. However, as just noted, we believe a localist account may fit well with some kinds of conventional metaphors.

What Analogy Can Tell Us about the Processing of Individual Metaphors

Structure-mapping makes a number of predictions about the processing of individual metaphors that should follow if metaphors are processed like analogies. SME serves as a process model to motivate these predictions. The Structure-mapping Engine (SME) (Falkenhainer, Forbus, and Gentner 1989; Forbus, Ferguson, and Gentner 1994; Forbus, Gentner, and Law 1995) uses a local-to-global[4] alignment process to arrive at a structural alignment of two representations. Figure 6.1 shows SME's three stages of mapping. In the first stage, SME begins blind and local by matching all identical predicates in the two representations. Semantic similarity between predicates is captured through a decomposition into partial identities.[5] This initial mapping is typically inconsistent, containing many-to-one matches. In the second phase these local matches are coalesced into structurally consistent connected clusters (called *kernels*). The kernels are essentially partial mappings—connected sets of

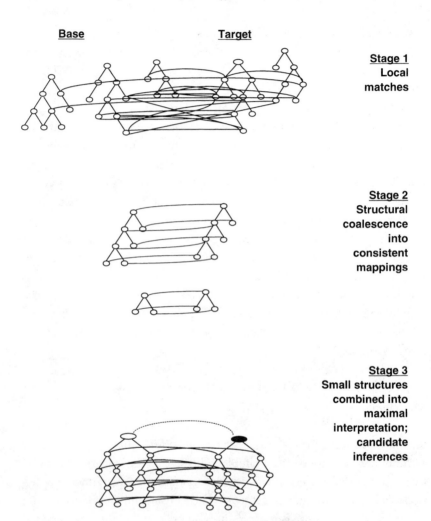

Figure 6.1
Overview of the algorithm used by the Structure-mapping Engine.

structurally consistent corresponding base-target pairs. They are given structural evaluations that depend not only on the sheer number of predicates but also on the depth of the system (Forbus and Gentner 1989).

Finally, in the third stage the kernels are merged into one or a few structurally consistent global interpretations (mappings displaying *one-to-one correspondences* and *parallel connectivity*). The challenge in finding the global interpretation is to find large, deep interpretations without having to exhaustively produce all possible interpretations, which would be psychologically implausible. SME uses a *greedy merge* algorithm (Forbus and Oblinger 1990) that operates in linear time.[6] It begins with the maximal kernel and then adds the largest kernel that is structurally consistent with the first one, continuing until no more kernels can be added without compromising consistency. It then carries out this process beginning with the second largest kernel to produce a second interpretation.

SME then produces a structural evaluation of the interpretation(s), using a kind of cascadelike algorithm in which evidence is passed down from predicates to their arguments. This method is used—both here and for the individual kernel evaluations mentioned earlier—because it favors deep systems over shallow systems, even given equal numbers of matches (Forbus and Gentner 1989). Up to this point, the processing has been a role-neutral process of alignment. Now, however, a directional inference process takes place. Predicates connected to the common structure in the base, but not initially present in the target, are projected as *candidate inferences* in the target. Thus, structural completion can lead to spontaneous unplanned inferences.

SME has several psychologically appealing features. First, it begins blindly, without needing to know the point of the comparison. Its alignment process begins by making large numbers of local matches, many of them mutually inconsistent. The global interpretations emerge by coalescing these matches in a manner that honors structural consistency and systematicity. Second, SME can derive two or three simultaneous interpretations of an analogy, capturing the finding that people can notice more than one interpretation of a metaphor. In particular, SME can derive literal and metaphorical interpretations simultaneously (We will return to this point.). Third, inference occurs as a natural outcome of comparison, without special intention. This capacity to produce unanticipated inferences fits with the psychological intuition that inferences often arise unbidden in analogy, and may even surprise the reasoner.

This framework gives rise to several processing predictions. In particular,

• Metaphor comprehension begins with a symmetric (nondirectional) alignment process.
• If an alignment is found, then further inferences are directionally projected from base to target.
• Thus, directionality in metaphor comprehension arises *after* the initial stage of processing.

Directionality in Metaphor

According to the process model embodied in SME, metaphor comprehension begins with a symmetric alignment process: the representations of base and target are placed in correspondence and the largest and deepest consistent alignment(s) is found. At first glance, this claim of initially symmetric metaphor processing may seem far-fetched. After all, directional inference is one of the signature phenomena of metaphor: for example, in the metaphor *A rumor is a virus*, ideas such as contagion and sanitary habits are projected from the base concept, *virus*, to the target concept, *rumor*. Another symptom of metaphors' directionality is their nonreversability. For example, if the above metaphor is reversed, the result—*A virus is a rumor*—seems pointless. In other cases, reversing the terms radically changes the meaning. For example, *The acrobat is a hippopotamus* suggests a clumsy acrobat, while the reverse metaphor, *The hippopotamus is an acrobat*, suggests a graceful hippopotamus (Gentner and France 1988).

Ortony (1979) was the first to point out the importance of directionality for theories of metaphor. He proposed that metaphoricity arises through *salience imbalance*, when high-salient features of the base match with low-salient features of the target. Although empirical tests have not supported salience imbalance as the *cause* of metaphoricity (Gentner and Clement 1988; Tourangeau and Rips 1991), Ortony's insight that directionality is more important in metaphor than in literal similarity still stands. There is abundant evidence that reversing metaphors affects their perceived aptness and interpretability (Gentner and Clement 1988; Glucksberg and Keysar 1990; Glucksberg, McGlone, and Manfredi 1997; Miller 1993; Ortony 1979; Ortony et al. 1985). For these reasons, most models of metaphor and analogy have assumed that processing is asymmetric throughout.

But in fact, there are at least three basic possibilities, as shown in figure 6.2. The strongest is that there is an initial *temporal asymmetry*. Processing begins with the base; after information is accessed or abstracted from the base, it is projected from the base to the target. A second possibility is that there is an *initial processing asymmetry*. Processing begins simultaneously with both terms, but is differentiated from the start in role-specific ways (Glucksberg, McGlone, and Manfredi 1997). The third possibility, predicted by structure-mapping and operationalized in SME, is *initial symmetry followed by processing asymmetry*. The initial stage is a role-neutral alignment stage; it is followed by a directional process of inference projection.

The first possibility, that processing temporally begins with the base, is explicitly or implicitly held by schema-projection models of analogy, such as Greiner's (1988) NLAG model or Keane and Brayshaw's (1988) IAM model. This processing order is also inherent in Glucksberg and Keysar's (1990) class-inclusion model of metaphor, in which metaphors are understood by finding or creating the category of which the base is the prototypical member and then applying this category to the target.

Gentner and Wolff (1997; Wolff and Gentner 1992) found evidence against temporal asymmetry using a priming method. We reasoned that if metaphor processing begins by accessing or deriving an abstraction from the base, and then projecting it to the target, then metaphor processing should be facilitated if the base term is presented just before the metaphor. In contrast, if the initial step is one of alignment, then there will be no special advantage for seeing the base over the target; either term will give a little advance information, and neither is sufficient to get very far.

To decide this issue, we measured subjects' time to interpret metaphors that were primed by either the base term or the target term. Initial projection models with temporal asymmetry predict faster comprehension given base priming than given target priming. The initial alignment

Three Processing Algorithms for
Analogy, Similarity, and Metaphor

1. Initial Projection:
Temporal Asymmetry

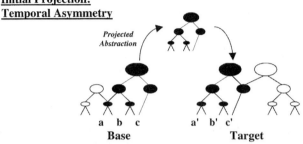

2. Initial Abstraction:
Processing Asymmetry

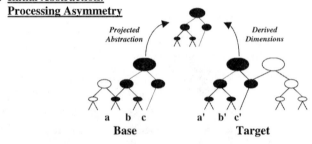

3. Initial Alignment

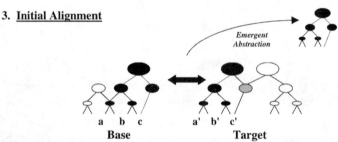

Figure 6.2
Three classes of process models. Model 1 shows initial projection of an abstraction from base to target. Model 2 shows initial projection of an abstraction from the base, along with dimensions from the target. Model 3 shows initial alignment, with subsequent extraction of the common abstraction.

model predicts no difference between base and target priming. Further, the initial alignment model predicts an advantage for high-similarity metaphors over low-similarity metaphors, because high (metaphoric or relational) similarity should facilitate initial alignment. The results were consistent with alignment-first processing. High-similarity metaphors were interpreted faster than low-similarity metaphors, and no base advantage was found across a series of experiments.[7]

Partly in response to these findings, Glucksberg, McGlone, and Manfredi (1997) proposed a more elaborated model (Model 2) in which there is a *processing* asymmetry, but not a temporal asymmetry, between the terms of a metaphor. In their *attributive category model*, processing begins simultaneously with both terms, but is differentiated from the outset in role-specific ways. The base term provides an abstract category that can be used to characterize the target, and the target provides dimensions along which it can be characterized. The base abstraction meets the dimensions derived from the target to form the interpretation. This proposal preserves Glucksberg and Keysar's position that metaphors are inherently class-inclusion statements, and that processing is directional from the start, but allows for Gentner and Wolff's finding of no general base advantage in priming.

For example, in *My surgeon is a butcher*, a category such as *one who cuts flesh crudely* is derived from the base term, *butcher*, while a set of dimensions, such as *skill level* and *income level*, is derived from the target term, *surgeon*. The base category is combined with the target dimensions to produce the metaphor interpretation. As evidence for role-specific processing, Glucksberg and his colleagues showed that metaphors were faster to be comprehended when primed by *unambiguous* bases—that is, bases that uniquely exemplify a particular category—than by *ambiguous* bases, and by *high-constraint* targets—that is, targets that strongly constrain the attributive dimensions along which they can be characterized—than by *low-constraint* targets. However, this study did not demonstrate that these effects were role-specific. That is, there was no test of the equally important *negative* prediction—that low ambiguity in the target and high constraint in the base would *fail* to facilitate comprehension. Lacking such a demonstration, it remains possible that degree of ambiguity and degree of constraint are both simply aspects of the *informa-*

tivity of terms with respect to the metaphoric interpretation; and that high-informative terms (not surprisingly) facilitate comprehension of metaphor to a greater degree than low-informative terms.

At this point, it seemed that the two groups had reached a kind of priming stalemate. Recall that in structure-mapping, the initial stage of metaphor processing is a symmetric alignment process; directional inference projection does not occur until after the representations are aligned (Bowdle and Gentner 1997; Falkenhainer, Forbus, and Gentner 1989; Forbus, Gentner, and Law 1995; Gentner and Markman 1997; Gentner and Wolff 1997; Wolff and Gentner 1992, 2000, in preparation). For example, given the metaphor *My surgeon is a butcher*, an initial (symmetric) alignment process would yield the common system *one who cuts flesh*. Then role-specific inference processes would project further ideas connected to this schema from the base to the target: for example, the idea of *cutting crudely and without regard for the health of the flesh*. Thus the question was how to test between processing that begins role-neutral and ends role-specific (as in structure-mapping) and processing that begins with two simultaneous role-specific processes (as in the attributive category model), that is, between Models 2 and 3 in figure 6.2.

What was needed was a better way to probe initial stages of processing. Wolff and Gentner (2000) found such a technique by adapting a metaphor interference technique originally pioneered by Glucksberg, Gildea, and Bookin (1982) and extended by Keysar (1989). In Glucksberg et al.'s task, participants were simply asked to judge statements as literally true or false. There were three basic kinds of statements: true class-inclusion statements (e.g., *Some birds are robins*), false class-inclusion statements (e.g., *Some birds are apples*), and metaphorical statements (e.g., *Some jobs are jails*). Subjects were told to respond "true" only for the first class, the literally true statements. Response times were recorded. As expected, participants could speedily classify correct class-inclusion statements as true and false statements as false. The key finding was that participants found it hard to reject metaphors: they were slower to respond "false" to metaphors than to ordinary false statements. The fact that metaphoric meaning interfered with literal true-false judgments was an important finding in the history of metaphor, for it implies that processing of metaphorical meanings begins *before* a true-false literal judgement has occurred.

For present purposes, the beauty of Glucksberg et al.'s interference effect is that it appears to tap into the initial processing stages. Metaphoric interference effects appear at about 1,200 milliseconds, well below the two to four seconds typically required for full comprehension of metaphor. Thus the metaphor interference technique offers a way to probe very early metaphoric processing.

Our technique was simply to repeat the task used by Glucksberg, Gildea, and Bookin (1982) and Keysar (1989), with one key alteration: We included reversed metaphors—e.g., *Some handcuffs are contracts*—as well as forward metaphors—e.g., *Some contracts are handcuffs*. (See Wolff and Gentner, 2000, for details.) According to Glucksberg, McGlone, and Manfredi's (1997) attributive category account, initial processing is role-specific. If the terms are in reversed order, the sentence should simply seem anomalous, because the category provided by the base will not fit with the dimensions provided by the target. (All the metaphors were pre-tested to ensure that they were strongly directional, so that only the forward direction made sense.) Thus, metaphoric interference is expected only when the terms are in the forward order; a reversed ordering of the terms should lead to no more interference than an ordinary false statement. In contrast, if the initial process is structural alignment, then the early stages should be role-neutral; only later should subjects detect the bizarreness of the reversed metaphors. Hence, structure-mapping predicts that metaphoric interference (1) should be independent of the order of the terms; and (2) should increase with the similarity between base and target (because, as noted above, high similarity facilitates alignment).

The results were fairly dramatic. In the first study, we replicated Glucksberg et al.'s interference effect: Metaphors took longer to reject than ordinary false statements, indicating early processing of metaphoric meaning. The key finding, however, was that reversed metaphors showed just as much interference as forward metaphors. (Time to say *false* was 1,118 msec for forward and 1,111 msec for reversed metaphors; these times did not significantly differ from each other, but both were longer than the 1,064 msec found for ordinary false statements.) That interference effects were independent of the order of the base and target terms is strong evidence for initial role-neutral processing, even for highly directional metaphors.

In the second study, we again probed initial processing, this time using metaphors that seemed particularly apt for revealing role-specific processing—namely, high-conventional metaphors, whose base terms have stock metaphorical senses associated with them. We reasoned that such metaphors should be particularly likely to show directional role effects. As before, initial projection theories predict strong effects of direction, and no early effects of similarity. Initial alignment theories such as structure-mapping predict strong early effects of similarity and not of direction.

The results were again striking. We again found symmetric interference effects. Even highly conventional metaphors showed no direction dependence in interference effects.[8] Further, interference effects occurred only for high-similarity metaphors. This result is exactly what would be expected if the initial processing of a metaphor were structural alignment. These results are evidence for initial alignment theories and against initial projection theories.

In the third study, we verified that the metaphors were directional when processed to completion. According to the structure-mapping model, the initial alignment process is followed by directional projection of inferences. Thus metaphoric directionality should emerge if people are allowed to complete the comprehension process. To test this prediction, we gave subjects the same metaphors as in the prior studies and asked them to judge whether or not the metaphor was comprehensible. If later processing is directional, as predicted by structure-mapping theory, then forward metaphors should be rated as more comprehensible than reversed metaphors.

This result is exactly what was found. Participants judged forward metaphors ($M = .75$) to be comprehensible about twice as often as reversed metaphors ($M = .37$). Further, forward metaphors were comprehended in less time than reversed metaphors ($M = 1,644$ ms for forward, $M = 1,778$ ms for reversed). The third prediction of the structure-mapping model, that high-similarity metaphors should be easier to comprehend than low-similarity metaphors was also borne out. High-similarity metaphors were more likely to be judged comprehensible than low-similarity metaphors.

In sum, the results support a process model in which an early symmetrical alignment process is followed by later directional processing. Early processing of metaphors, as tapped by the interference effect, is symmetrical. However, when full processing is allowed, a pronounced asymmetry appears between forward and reversed metaphors. Overall, the pattern fits the structure-mapping claim of initially symmetric processing followed by later directional projection of inferences.

Implications for Models of Analogy

Models of analogical processing, like models of metaphor, differ in whether they begin with a directed projection process, followed by matching and verification, or with a symmetric matching process, followed by directed projection. The former class includes explanation-based-learning models of analogy (Kedar-Cabelli 1988), abstraction-based models such as Greiner's (1988) NLAG, Keane and Brayshaw's (1988) IAM, and possibly Hummel and Holyoak's (1997) LISA model, which operates in driver-recipient mode rather than by alignment,[9] as well as incremental projection models such as that of Keane, Ledgeway, and Duff (1994). The latter class includes alignment-first models: SME (Falkenhainer, Forbus, and Gentner 1989) and ACME (Holyoak and Thagard 1989). The findings reviewed here are strong evidence for initially symmetric, role-neutral processing and, more generally, for alignment-based models of analogy and metaphor.

The Career of Metaphor

The alert reader may have noticed that conventional metaphors have differed from novel metaphors in several ways in the studies described so far. In the first section, novel metaphors, but not conventional metaphors, showed mapping consistency effects in processing extended metaphors (Gentner and Boronat 1992). In the second section, the one exception to our general finding of equivalence between base and target priming was that highly conventional, low-similarity metaphors showed a base priming advantage (Gentner and Wolff 1997) (See note 7). In this section we lay out a theory of how conventional metaphoric meanings arise and how the representation and processing change as a metaphor progresses from novel to conventional.

We propose an account of metaphor and polysemy that we call the *career of metaphor* hypothesis: Novel metaphors are processed as structural alignments between the concrete or literal representations of the base and target, but as repeated comparisons are made, the metaphorical meaning is gradually abstracted and comes to be associated with the base term (Bowdle and Gentner 1995, 1999, in preparation; Gentner and Wolff 1997, 2000; Wolff and Gentner 1992, 2000, in preparation). We know from research on analogical problem solving that the alignment of two relationally similar situations can lead to the induction of domain-general problem schemas (e.g., Gick and Holyoak 1983; Loewenstein, Thompson, and Gentner, 2000; Novick and Holyoak 1991; Ross and Kennedy 1990). We believe that similar forces are at work during metaphor comprehension. The process of structural alignment allows for the induction of metaphoric categories, which may come to be lexicalized as secondary senses of metaphor base terms (Bowdle and Gentner 1995, 1999, in preparation; Gentner and Wolff 1997).

This kind of progressive abstraction can be computationally modeled by storing the common schema that SME derives from a comparison. We have used an extension of SME called SEQL to carry out this kind of schema abstraction (Skorstad, Gentner, and Medin 1988). In this model, the common schema that SME derives from carrying out a comparison is stored as an abstraction and carried forward. It can then be aligned with further exemplars. This process typically results in a progressively more abstract relational structure, with fewer and fewer surface details. Such abstractions could serve as metaphoric category representations. We suggest that the deriving and retaining of structural abstractions is the basic mechanism by which metaphors become conventionalized.

When a metaphor is first encountered, both the target and base terms refer to specific concepts from different semantic domains, and the metaphor is interpreted by aligning the two representations and importing further predicates from the base to the target. One result of this mapping is that the common relational structure that forms the metaphor interpretation will increase in salience relative to nonaligned aspects of the representations. If the same base term is repeatedly aligned with different targets so as to yield the same basic interpretation, then the highlighted system may become conventionally associated with the base as an abstract metaphoric category.

The gist of these claims is illustrated in figure 6.3, which shows the evolution from novel to conventional metaphor. *Novel metaphors* involve base terms that refer to a domain-specific concept, but are not (yet) associated with a domain-general category. They are interpreted as comparisons: direct structural alignments between the literal base and target concepts. *Conventional metaphors* involve base terms that refer both to a literal concept and to an associated metaphoric category. At this point in its evolution, the base term is polysemous, having both a domain-specific meaning and a related domain-general meaning. For

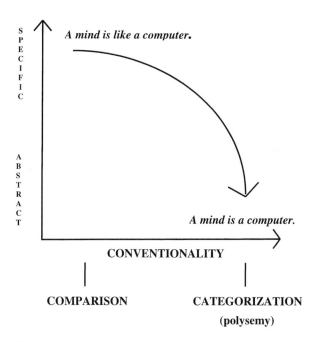

Figure 6.3.
The career of metaphor from novel to conventional metaphor.

instance, Sweetser (1990) suggests that many standard terms for mental processes are derived from terms for sensory perception: for example, *discernment, focus, point of view*, and so on (see also Holyoak and Thagard 1995; Murphy 1996).

Implications for Metaphor Comprehension

Research on metaphor comprehension has usually treated metaphor as an undifferentiated class. However, a number of theorists have recently argued that how a metaphor is processed may depend on its level of conventionality (e.g., Blank 1988; Blasko and Connine 1993; Giora 1997; Turner and Katz 1997). Our account of the relationship between metaphor and polysemy is in line with these claims. Specifically, we suggest that novel metaphors are processed by aligning the literal senses of both terms. In contrast, conventional base terms are often polysemous, with both literal and metaphoric meanings. Thus they may be interpreted either by aligning the target concept with the literal base concept, or by aligning the target concept with the base's abstract metaphoric category. We could think of the first as comparison and the second as categorization.[10]

Thus, the career of metaphor hypothesis predicts that as metaphors become increasingly conventional, there is a shift from comparison to categorization (Bowdle and Gentner 1995, 1999, in preparation; Gentner and Wolff 1997, 2000; Wolff and Gentner, forthcoming). This is consistent with recent proposals that the interpretation of novel metaphors involves sense creation, but the interpretation of conventional metaphors involves sense retrieval (e.g., Blank 1988; Blasko and Connine 1993; Giora 1997; Turner and Katz 1997); and likewise for idioms (Cacciari and Tabossi 1988; Gibbs 1980, 1994; Swinney and Cutler 1979; Williams 1992). On the present view, the senses retrieved during conventional metaphor comprehension are abstract metaphoric categories.

Bowdle and Gentner (1995, 1999, in preparation) tested five predictions of the career of metaphor account. The first two predictions took advantage of a proposed form-process link whereby the simile form (e.g., *A child is like a snowflake*) invites comparison and the metaphor form (e.g., *A child is a snowflake*) invites categorization (Bowdle's grammatical concordance assumption). This predicts that giving subjects the same pairs of terms in either simile or metaphor form should invite different forms of processing. Specifically, the predictions are: (1) novel figurative statements should be easier to process as similes than as metaphors. This is because the simile form invites comparison processing whereas the metaphor form invites subjects to search for a prestored category (which in the case of novel statements does not exist). (2) novel figurative statements should be preferred in the simile (comparison) form rather than the categorization form. Both these predictions were borne out.

To test the prediction that novel figuratives should be easier to process in the comparison form (e.g., *A mind is like a kitchen*) than in the categorization form (*A mind is a kitchen*) Bowdle and Gentner gave subjects a timed comprehension task. We found that novel figuratives were read faster in comparison (simile) form than in categorization (metaphor) form. The reverse was true for conventional figuratives; these were processed faster in categorization form (*An opportunity is a doorway*) than in comparison form (*An opportunity is like a doorway*). To test the second prediction, that novel figuratives should be preferred in the comparison form, we asked subjects to rate their preference for simile vs. metaphor form for a range of figurative statements. As predicted, participants strongly preferred the simile form for novel figuratives; they showed no preference between the simile and metaphor forms for conventional figuratives.

We also found evidence for two further predictions, one rather humdrum and one quite surprising, at least from the point of view of class-inclusion theories. The humdrum result is that people rated novel figurative statements as more metaphorical than conventional figuratives. This follows from the idea that the perception of metaphoricity reflects active construction of new alignments and inferences, such as occur for novel metaphors. The more surprising result is that people considered similes *more metaphorical* than metaphors overall. Specifically, similes were rated more metaphorical than metaphors for conventional figuratives, and equally metaphorical for novel figuratives. We believe this is because similes invite a fresh alignment between literal senses, even for conventional metaphors. For example, the stock metaphor *Fred is a gorilla* calls forth the standard "large, aggressive, and dangerous" abstraction; but in simile form—*Fred is like a gorilla*—it invites ideas such as "gentle despite strength, limited to a specific environmental niche, and vulnerable to extinction."

Finally, we directly tested the process account postulated in the career of metaphor hypothesis. We asked whether we could achieve conventionalization in vitro, by giving participants several parallel novel figurative statements using the same base term (Bowdle and Gentner 1999; in preparation). Participants were given two novel similes and asked to create a third that was similar in meaning to the first two: for example,

Doubt is like a tumor.

A grudge is like a tumor.

——— *is like a tumor.*

Each participant saw eight such sets, as well as other sets containing literal similarity statements, metaphors, and categorizations. Then participants were given test sentences containing the same bases in both simile and metaphor form and asked to say which they preferred—for example,

An obsession is a tumor.   *An obsession is like a tumor.*

Subjects who received the in vitro conventionalization condition (i.e., those who saw two novel similes) were significantly more likely to prefer the metaphor form than subjects who simply saw the test sentences with no prior manipulation, or who had seen the same base terms in literal similarity statements. It appears that carrying out a series of parallel figurative alignments led to the creation of an abstraction that favored the metaphor form.

Metaphor and Polysemy

Many linguists have proposed a link between metaphor and polysemy. A common proposal is that lexical extensions (e.g., the use of *see* in *I see your point*) are comprehended via a mapping from a (typically concrete) domain of experience to another (typically abstract) domain of experience (e.g., Lakoff and Johnson 1980; Lehrer 1990; Sweetser 1990); the concrete domain is invoked to explain phenomena in the abstract or less familiar domain. On this view, the metaphoric meaning of a polysemous word is understood directly in terms of its literal meaning.

Bowdle and Gentner (1995, 1999, in preparation) suggested a related but somewhat different relationship between metaphor and polysemy, one that follows naturally from considerations of analogical processing. The process of structural alignment allows for the induction of metaphoric categories, which then may be lexicalized as secondary senses of metaphor base terms (Bowdle and Gentner 1995, 1999, in preparation; Gentner and Wolff 1997). Such processes provide ways of creatively extending the lexicon (Gerrig and Gibbs 1988; Lehrer 1990). On this account, it is not necessary to return to the base to process conventional metaphors. Indeed, the metaphoric sense may persist even after the literal sense disappears, as discussed below.

From Comparison to Categorization

The career of metaphor hypothesis can be related to the proposal that metaphor is a species of categorization (e.g., Glucksberg and Keysar 1990; Glucksberg, McGlone, and Manfredi 1997; Honeck, Kibler, and Firment 1987; Kennedy 1990). As discussed earlier, Glucksberg and his colleagues have proposed that metaphors are processed as class inclusions: the base concept is used to access or derive an abstract metaphoric category to which the target concept is assigned. Our results suggest that this account is fundamentally wrong for novel metaphors, but that it may apply well to some conventional metaphors. Highly conventional metaphor bases are just those that have associated metaphorical abstractions—*dual representations* in Glucksberg and Keysar's (1990) terms.

What about intermediate stages of conventionalization? One appealing account is a race model (see Cacciari and Tabossi 1988 for idioms; Gentner and Wolff 1997 for metaphor). In this model, the literal and figurative interpretations are accessed in parallel and the first one to achieve a satisfactory interpretation wins. If it is faster to retrieve and apply a stored figurative interpretation than to create a new interpretation by aligning a base and target representation, then the stored figurative interpretation will prevail. The more conventionalized the base term, the more likely it is that the stock interpretation will prevail. The more similar the literal representations of the base and target, the more likely it is that the process will be one of alignment of literal senses.

The centrality of comparison. What all this implies is that comparison is the fundamental process that drives metaphor. Novel metaphors are understood *only* by comparison. Conventional metaphors can be understood by accessing stored abstractions, but these metaphoric abstractions are a *product* of past comparisons. Thus, although conventional metaphors can be seen as category-inclusion statements, the categories themselves are derived from prior alignment processes. To use one of Turner's procreative metaphors, one could say that comparison begets categorization.

There are three further reasons to emphasize comparison and alignment as central in metaphor interpretation. First, Bowdle and Gentner's results suggest that conventional metaphors can readily be processed either in comparison (simile) form or in categorization (metaphor) form, whereas novel metaphors are far more understandable in comparison form. Comparison is thus the more universal process for metaphor. Second, the career of metaphor account suggests that the class-inclusion stage occurs fairly late in the life of a metaphor. Third, even for conventional metaphors the *process* of comprehension may be structural alignment. The results of the Wolff and Gentner (2000) metaphor interference studies suggest that even for conventional metaphors, the initial process is alignment: even for highly conventional metaphors, reversed and forward metaphors were indistinguishable in initial processing. Thus, the career of metaphor from comparison to categorization may involve a change in *representation* rather than a change in *process*.[11]

Metaphor Senescence and Death: Conventionality and Idiomaticity

Research into real-time idiom processing can shed light on the processes used in highly conventional "stock" metaphors. One prominent view of idioms is that their figurative interpretations are stored in memory as single lexical items (Cacciari and Tabossi 1988; Ortony et al. 1978). This *idiom as dead metaphor* hypothesis posits that, at least in the lexicon, idioms' stored figurative meanings are interpretations stripped of their base to target mappings. Accessing the figurative meaning of the idiom *pop the question*, then, would tell one that the idiom referred to a marriage proposal; it would not tell one about the action of popping or the nature of questions.

Gibbs, Nayak, and Cutting (1989) distinguish between *decomposable idioms*, whose meanings can be deduced from their parts (e.g., *pop the question*), and *nondecomposable idioms*, whose meanings cannot be so deduced (e.g., *chew the fat*). Nondecomposable idioms seem relatively identifiable as idioms, while decomposable idioms, which may be linked to conceptual metaphors, seem less so. Gibbs, Nayak, and Cutting's findings suggest that people do not always analyze the literal meanings of idioms; rather, they perform a componential analysis that assigns a figurative interpretation to each of an idiom's components. Thus, someone reading *pop the question* would ascribe to it the meanings *suddenly say* and *a marriage proposal*. No explicitly "literal" interpretations of the idiom need be produced. Likewise, McGlone (forthcoming) suggests that idioms may be psychologically processed in units smaller than the whole phrase.

However, Gibbs and O'Brien (1990) have contested the claim that idioms are entirely stripped of their base-to-base target mappings. In a study analyzing protocols, they found considerable regularity in participants' descriptions of their mental images of idioms (e.g., *lose your cool*), a regularity lacking in other participants' descriptions of similar literal phrases (e.g., *lose your wallet*), or in descriptions of figurative interpretations (e.g., *to get angry*). They interpreted this regularity as indicating that these idioms remain connected to conceptual metaphors such as ANGER IS HEAT or THE MIND IS A CONTAINER (Lakoff and Johnson 1980). While their results suggest that idioms *can* regain their base-to-target mappings, Gibbs and O'Brien explicitly reject the idea that conceptual metaphors play an on-line role in normal idiom processing, given (a) that idioms are understood so rapidly and (b) the evidence reviewed earlier that the figurative meanings of idioms are stored in memory (Cacciari and Tabossi 1988).

In summary, the *career of metaphor* proposal traces metaphors from early alignment and mapping between literal meanings (the novel metaphor stage) to a later stage of dual representation in which the metaphor may be understood either by a novel alignment or by accessing an abstract representation (the conventional metaphor stage), to a stage in which the metaphoric representation has become a standard word sense for the base (the polysemy stage). At this point, the sense of metaphoricity disappears, and only polysemy remains. Sometimes, a still further stage occurs, in which the literal meaning disappears entirely, leaving only the (formerly) metaphoric sense as the meaning of the base term.

General Discussion

Analogy research offers a set of psychologically and computationally tested processes that can serve to illuminate both the processing of individual metaphors and extended systems of metaphors. Further, structure-mapping offers a way in which metaphorical and literal comparisons can be captured within a single mechanism.

Addressing the Classic Problems of Metaphor

We have suggested that structure-mapping can serve as an account of metaphor processing. To make good on this argument we must ask whether this framework can handle the central phenomena of metaphor, and how it deals with the classic challenges. The following four issues are points on which any theory of metaphor must take a stand:

1. *Metaphor recognition*: how and when metaphoric (as opposed to literal) processing is initiated
2. *Metaphoric meaning*: do metaphors create meaning or do they simply reflect parallels
3. *Metaphoric induction*: how (and how *much*) property inference occurs
4. *Directionality*: why metaphors are preferred in one direction over the other

The approach from analogy to metaphor offers some solutions.

1. *Metaphor recognition: How and when is metaphoric processing initiated?* A thorny problem in metaphor has been how people distinguish metaphors from literal statements so that they know to initiate metaphoric processing. What signals us to initiate metaphoric processing for *Genghis Khan was a butcher*, but not for *My neighbor is a butcher*? The classic proposal that metaphor is initiated only after literal processing fails has been rejected, but no new consensus has emerged. In SME, this problem does not arise. As noted above, SME normally produces at least two simultaneous interpretations of a comparison. In par-

ticular, it can derive literal and metaphorical interpretations simultaneously. If I tell you *My neighbor is a butcher*, for example, you might entertain both the possibility that his profession is slaughtering animals and the metaphoric possibility that he butchers something else—perhaps hedges? Which interpretation you choose will depend on (a) which has the largest and deepest common structure, as discussed above; (b) which best fits other knowledge about the target; and (c) which is more relevant to the current context. Likewise, if given *Genghis Khan was a butcher*, you might briefly imagine a literal interpretation—that his profession was slaughtering animals—but prior knowledge would quickly lead you to reject it in favor of the correct metaphorical alignment—that he slaughtered human beings.

2. *Metaphoric structure: Do metaphors create meaning, or merely reflect structural parallels?* The account offered by Lakoff and his colleagues (Lakoff 1990; Lakoff and Johnson 1980; Lakoff and Turner 1989) has it that metaphors create meaning: conceptual systems are projected from one domain to another, typically more abstract, domain. In contrast, Murphy (1996) proposes that metaphors do not provide new structure for the target domain, but rather reflect structural parallelism between two domains. Structure-mapping incorporates aspects of both these accounts. It begins with structural alignment (as in Murphy's account) but also allows for further candidate inferences—that is, for a constrained kind of meaning creation.

3. *Property induction. If metaphor is a comparison, then how does one account for property induction?* The fact that metaphors can convey new information is sometimes used to argue against comparison theories, on the grounds that merely highlighting common properties does not allow for new information (Glucksberg and Keysar 1990; Glucksberg, McGlone, and Manfredi 1997). But, as discussed above, inference projection naturally arises out of alignment. Indeed, it is far from clear that a pure projection theory can be made computationally tractable.

4. *Directional asymmetry: How can a comparison approach account for the strong directionality of metaphors?* People show strong directional preferences in metaphor. Thus, people tend to think that (1) is an intelligible metaphor, but that (2) is not:

(1)   Some jobs are jails.

(2)   Some jails are jobs.

As discussed earlier, the strong directionality of metaphors is a classic challenge to comparison models, and has been used to argue that metaphors are essentially class-inclusion statements rather than comparisons. Our evidence indicates that asymmetry in comprehension arises after the initial alignment stage. Inferences are directionally projected from the base to the target. This predicts that both speaker and hearer should prefer to have the more informative term in the base position.

Bowdle and Gentner (1997) verified that informativity can determine directionality, even for literal comparisons, which are less asymmetric than metaphors. Subjects read two brief passages, which were similar except that one passage contained a systematic causal structure linking the events and the other did not. When asked to generate any inferences they chose between the passages, subjects were overwhelmingly more likely to project inferences from the more systematic passage to the less systematic one. In another study, subjects were given two comparison statements—"A is similar to B" or "B is similar to A"—and asked to choose which direction they preferred. They consistently preferred the more systematic passage as base, and considered this direction more informative.[12] These findings establish a connection between inferential potential and preferred direction, as predicted by structure-mapping.

We suggest that systematicity imbalance can explain the directional asymmetry of metaphor. This would fit with the preponderance of embodiment metaphors noted by Lakoff and his colleagues. We rely heavily on mappings from experiential domains such as spatial relations and bodily force dynamics, because our models in these domains are sufficiently systematic to provide inferential structure for other domains.

Implications for Metaphor Research

Metaphor is related on the conventional side to idiom and on the novel side to analogy. But metaphor research has focused disproportionately on conventional metaphors. Indeed, Bowdle and Gentner (in preparation) surveyed the metaphors used in a sample of psychology research papers and found that most were of high conventionality. The current findings underscore the importance of conventionality as a factor in experiments. We need to reexamine claims about metaphoric processing that are based only on conventional metaphors.

Implications for Models of Analogy
This research has both local and global implications for models of analogical processing. At the local level, Wolff and Gentner's findings offer support for alignment-first models such as SME over projection-first models such as IAM. We found evidence for initial role-neutral processing. Even for strongly directional metaphors, forward and reversed orders appear to be initially equivalent in processing, consistent with SME's initial symmetric-alignment process. Our finding of directional superiority at longer deadlines is consistent with SME's later process of directed projection of inferences. In contrast, models that begin by directionally projecting information from base to target, such as IAM (Keane and Brayshaw 1988) and LISA (Hummel and Holyoak 1997) (though see note 9), should predict directional superiority from the start. Thus the initial equivalence of forward and reversed metaphors is a serious challenge to these models. Overall, the results support alignment-based models of analogy and metaphor.

At the global level, the finding of metaphoric consistency effects across extended metaphor systems drives home the importance of systematicity in human analogical processing. These results are consistent with prior findings that people make analogical inferences based on higher-order connecting relations (Clement and Gentner 1991; Lassaline 1996; Markman 1997).

At present, only a handful of models of analogy and similarity incorporate the ability to use higher-order relations to constrain interpretation and inference (e.g., Falkenhainer, Forbus, and Gentner 1989; Holyoak and Thagard 1989; Keane and Brayshaw 1988). Of course, there are alternatives to higher-order relations. Relational connectivity can be modeled by defining groups of assertions that are processed together (Hummel and Holyoak 1997), and relational complexity can be modeled in terms of numbers of arguments to a relation, rather than the depth of the relational structure (Halford, Wilson, and Phillips 1998). However, our findings suggest that the phenomena of analogy and metaphor—and even similarity—can best be captured by representing and using higher-order relations between relations.

Another link from metaphor to analogy is progressive abstraction. We have suggested that highlighting and storing the common schema is the chief mechanism by which novel metaphors become conventionalized. This process may also be central in learning ordinary categories. For example, the SEQL extension of SME, which simulates progressive abstraction of a common category (Skorstad, Gentner, and Medin 1988), has been used to simulate infants' regularity learning and adults' abstraction of story categories (Kuehne, Gentner, and Forbus 2000; Kuehne et al. 2000). We suggest that both metaphoric categories and literal categories (Kotovsky and Gentner 1996; Ross, Perkins, and Tenpenny 1990) can be derived by progressive abstraction across exemplars.

How Metaphors Are Different from Analogies

We have been stressing the commonalities between metaphor and analogy. There are also some differences. First, as we discussed at the outset, metaphors can be more structurally variable than analogies: They can be attribute matches, relation matches, or both; they can even violate structurally consistency (Gentner, Falkenhainer, and Skorstad 1988). As Fauconnier and Turner (1998) have noted, metaphors include complex blends that combine structure-mapping with metonymy and other processes. A second point is that the term *metaphor* is often used for novel and vivid nonliteral comparisons (Ortony 1975). For example, the subjects in Bowdle and Gentner's metaphor studies considered novel comparisons more metaphorical than conventional ones. However, as noted above, the term *metaphor* can also apply to systems of extended meanings that are so familiar as to be almost invisible (Lakoff and Johnson 1979; Nagy 1974).

Another dimension of difference is the pragmatic function of the figurative language. Gentner (1982) suggested that metaphors are typically used for expressive-affective purposes, and analogies for explanatory-predictive purposes. But we often speak of metaphors in science, so it might be more accurate to say that *analogy* is used in explanatory-predictive contexts, while *metaphor* can be used more broadly, in either explanatory-predictive or expressive-affective contexts.

From Comparison to Conceptual Systems: Metaphoric Systems in Reasoning

The process of conventionalization can result in stock metaphors, and finally in dead (or bleached, or frozen) local metaphorical senses. However, some metaphors take a different route, and end as conventionalized systems of reasoning. One case is which this occurs is in theory development in a domain. For example, in the history of theories of cognition, a common conceptualization of the mind is as a physical space (Roediger 1980). In this mapping, memories are objects in mental space, and recall involves spatial search. As cognitive theories evolved (and as technological advances created a greater set of potential bases), the set of metaphors enlarged. Gentner and Grudin (1985) surveyed the metaphors used in psychology over the ninety years since 1895 and traced a shift from general spatial metaphors to more complex systems metaphors—physics metaphors such as *associative force* and *goal gradient*, telephone switchboard metaphors, circuitry metaphors, and, eventually, computer metaphors. Boyd (1979) identified a number of terms derived from the "mind is a computer" metaphor, including "information processing," "encoding," "decoding," "indexing," "feedback," and "memory stores." (See also Fauconnier's discussion of the computer virus metaphor in chapter 7 of this volume.) Metaphors like this derive their force not from a local resemblance between physical objects and memory traces but rather from mapping the *system* of relationships in which these objects are embedded.

Some conventional analogical models in the physical domain also show systematic relational mappings despite conventionality. For example, Gentner and Gentner (1983) found in the domain of electricity that people extended their analogical models of electricity—typically, either a *water flow* metaphor or a *moving crowd* metaphor—to reason about new circuits. Despite their conventionality, these folk analogical models retained some relational generativity (diSessa 1983).

Finally, space-time metaphors are a striking example of a conventional metaphor that retains a systematic generative structure (Bierwisch 1996; Boroditsky 2000; Clark 1973; Gentner forthcoming; Gentner and Imai 1992; Gentner, Imai, and Boroditsky in preparation; McGlone and Harding 1998; Traugott 1978). In many languages, including English, there are two different metaphoric *space → time* systems: the *ego-moving* metaphor, wherein the observer's context progresses along the timeline toward the future, and the *time-moving* metaphor, wherein time is conceived of as a river or conveyor belt on which events are moving from the future to the past. To test whether these metaphors are psychologically processed as global systems, Gentner, Imai, and Boroditsky asked whether the metaphor-consistency effect found by Gentner and Boronat would occur here. Participants read statements about time, stated in terms of spatial metaphors—e.g., *Joe's birthday is approaching (Time-moving)* or *We are approaching the holidays (Ego-moving)*—and had to indicate whether a specified event was past or future relative to the other. Consistent with Gentner and Boronat's studies, processing was slowed by a shift from one space-time metaphor to the other—evidence for their psychological coherence. Likewise, McGlone et al. found that participants interpreted an ambiguous statement—such as *Wednesday's meeting was moved one day forward*—as either Thursday or Tuesday, depending on whether the preceding metaphoric context was ego-moving or time-moving. As further evidence for the existence of space-time generative mappings, Boroditsky (2000) showed that hearing sentences about spatial relations primes analogous sentences in the time domain, but not the reverse.

Why do some metaphors, such as space-time metaphors, become conventionalized as systems, while others turn into local categories? One possibility is that metaphors evolve as into conventional systems when they continue to support new reasoning that requires concatenating relations. Thus one factor in the evolution of metaphorical systems might be the needs of the target domain: metaphors retain system properties if they are needed for close reasoning. A second factor is the nature of the base domain. The metaphors that evolve into conventional systems are often taken from space—which perhaps deserves "universal donor" status—or from other well understood, highly systematic base domains such as flowing water or device causality. These two factors are presumably connected: the intention to carry out sustained reasoning about the target favors the selection of a systematic base domain.

Summary

We have suggested that metaphor is like analogy—that the basic processes of analogy are at work in metaphor. Specifically, we suggest that structural alignment, inference projection, progressive abstraction, and re-representation are employed in the processing of metaphor. Viewing metaphor as analogy offers a unified account of many important phenomena and helps resolve some current conflicts.

We further propose that individual metaphors evolve over the course of their lives from alignment-based processing in the early stages to projection-based processing as they become conventionalized. Conventionalization often results in local metaphoric categories, but it can also take the form of large-scale conventional systems of metaphors. Finally, the ubiquitousness of metaphor demonstrates again our human capacity for seeing and using common relational patterns—in short, for analogical insight.

Acknowledgments

Please address correspondence and reprint requests to Dedre Gentner, Northwestern University, Department of Psychology, 2029 Sheridan Rd., Evanston, IL 60208-2710. This work was supported by ONR grant N00014-92-J-1098 and NSF grant SBR-9511757 to the first author.

This chapter was partially prepared while the first author was a Fellow at the Center for Advanced Study in the Behavioral Sciences. We are grateful for the financial support provided by the William T. Grant Foundation, award #95167795. We thank Ken Forbus, Arthur Markman, Ken Kurtz and Jeff Loewenstein for comments on this paper, and Kathleen Braun for help with the research and analyses.

Notes

1. Metaphors are often defined as nonliteral similarity comparisons. Metaphors are distinguished from similes by the inclusion of explicit comparison forms such as *like* in similes, but not metaphors. Thus examples 1, 4, and 5 are technically similes, and 2 and 3 are metaphors. However, the term *metaphor* is often used to encompass both forms. We will use the term *metaphor* in this broad sense and mark cases where it contrasts with *simile*.

2. To avoid confusion, we will use the term *metaphor* to refer to an individual figurative phrase, and *global metaphor* to refer to an extended mapping between two domains.

3. The metaphors used earlier were designed to be individually fairly novel (even though many of them belonged to known conceptual metaphors).

4. Local-to-global is not the same as bottom-up, a point that occasionally engenders confusion (e.g., Love, Rouder, and Wisniewski 1999). In SME, processing starts by identifying matching nodes at *any level* of the structure, from higher-order relations to concrete perceptual attributes. These local identities are then coalesced into global system-mappings (Falkenhainer, Forbus, and Gentner, 1989; Forbus, Gentner, and Law 1995).

5. We make the theoretical assumption that similarity of relational predicates can be expressed as partial identity. This avoids the circularity of defining similarity in terms of similarity. (If we define two things to be similar if their predicates are similar, this merely pushes the problem of defining similarity to the predicate level.) The partial-identity assumption is also psychologically advantageous in modeling the phenomenon of re-representation (e.g., Gentner et al. 1997; Gentner et al. 1995). Thus for two situations to be analogous means that they must have some set of identical relations.

6. The original SME exhaustively produced all possible interpretations, but this is psychologically implausible. Although the interpretations found by the greedy merge algorithm cannot be guaranteed to be maximal, the algorithm does very well. Forbus and Oblinger (1990) tested the greedy algorithm on a large set of analogies; on fifty-two out of fifty-six pairs, its top interpretation was identical to the best interpretation found in an exhaustive merge.

7. However, there was one exception: Gentner and Wolff (1997) found a base advantage for metaphors having highly conventional meanings and low (metaphorical) similarity (i.e., similarity of relations). No base advantage was found for novel metaphors, regardless of metaphorical similarity. This pattern led us to suggest a race between horizontal alignment (promoted by high similarity) and vertical matching with the base abstraction (promoted by high base conventionality).

8. The metaphor interference effects in these studies cannot be attributed to local lexical effects. Although there was no difference in processing time between forward and reversed metaphors, both required longer to reject than scrambled metaphors (that is, re-pairings of the terms from the metaphors).

9. In LISA, information is directionally projected from a driver to a recipient. This would seem to place it among the projection models. However, because LISA can shift between the two terms of an analogy as to which is driver and which is recipient, its processing predictions are not clear.

10. This requires modeling categorization as an alignment process between an abstract representation and a more concrete one. We think this may be a viable account, as discussed later.

11. This invites a further conjecture. If conventional metaphoric categories are processed as alignments, then what about standard categories? We speculate that categories in general are processed via structural alignment and mapping between abstract representations and concrete ones (see Ramscar and Pain 1996).

12. Interestingly, these directionality effects held only if the two passages were alignable. When the two items were not alignable (as independently rated), subjects showed no directional preference regardless of the relative coherence of the passages. This is consistent with our claim that analogical inference depends on alignment.

References

Allbritton, D. W., McKoon, G., and Gerrig, R. (1995). Metaphor-based schemas and text representations: Making connections through conceptual metaphors. *Journal of Experimental Psychology: Learning, Memory, and Cognition* **21**:1–4.

Bierwisch, M. (1996). How much space gets into language? In P. Bloom, M. A. Peterson, L. Nadel, and M. F. Garrett, Eds., *Language and space*, pp. 31–76. Cambridge, MA: MIT Press.

Black, M. (1962). Metaphor. In M. Black, Ed., *Models and metaphors*, pp. 25–47. Ithaca, NY: Cornell University Press.

Blank, G. D. (1988). Metaphors in the lexicon. *Metaphor and Symbolic Activity* **3**:21–26.

Blasko, D. G., and Connine, C. M. (1993). Effects of familiarity and aptness on metaphor processing. *Journal of Experimental Psychology: Learning, Memory and Cognition* **12**:205–308.

Boroditsky, L. (2000). Metaphoric structuring: Understanding time through spatial metaphors. *Cognition* **75**(1):1–27.

Boronat, C. B. (1990). *Effects of base shift and frequency in extended metaphor processing*. M.A. thesis, University of Illinois at Urbana-Champaign.

Boronat, C., and Gentner, D. (in preparation). Novel metaphors are processed as generative domain-mappings.

Bowdle, B., and Gentner, D. (1995). The career of metaphor. Paper presented at the meeting of the Psychonomics Society, Los Angeles, CA.

Bowdle, B., and Gentner, D. (1997). Informativity and asymmetry in comparisons. *Cognitive Psychology* **34**(3):244–286.

Bowdle, B., and Gentner, D. (1999). Metaphor comprehension: From comparison to categorization. *Proceedings of the twenty-first annual conference of the Cognitive Science Society*. Hillsdale, NJ: Erlbaum.

Bowdle, B., and Gentner, D. (in preparation). *The career of metaphor*.

Boyd, R. (1979). Metaphor and theory change: What is "metaphor" a metaphor for? In A. Ortony, Ed., *Metaphor and thought*, pp. 356–408. Cambridge: Cambridge University Press.

Burstein, M. H. (1983). Concept formation by incremental analogical reasoning and debugging. *Proceedings of the International Machine Learning Workshop*, 19–25.

Burstein, M. H. (1986). Concept formation by incremental analogical reasoning and debugging. In R. S. Michalski, J. G. Carbonell, and T. M. Mitchell, Eds., *Machine learning: An artificial intelligence approach*, vol. 2, pp. 351–369. Los Altos, CA: Kaufmann.

Cacciari, C., and Tabossi, P. (1988). The comprehension of idioms. *Journal of Memory and Language* 27:668–683.

Camac, M. K., and Glucksberg, S. (1984). Metaphors do not use associations between concepts, they are used to create them. *Journal of Psycholinguistic Research* 13:443–455.

Clark, H. H. (1973). Space, time, semantics, and the child. In T. E. Moore, Ed., *Cognitive development and the acquisition of language*, pp. 27–63. New York: Academic Press.

Clark, H. H., and Lucy, P. (1975). Understanding what is meant from what is said: A study in conversationally conveyed requests. *Journal of Verbal Learning and Verbal Behavior* 14:56–72.

Clement, C. A., and Gentner, D. (1991). Systematicity as a selection constraint in analogical mapping. *Cognitive Science* 15:89–132.

diSessa, A. A. (1983). Phenomenology and the evolution of intuition. In D. Gentner and A. L. Stevens, Eds., *Mental models*, pp. 15–33. Hillsdale, NJ: Erlbaum.

Falkenhainer, B., Forbus, K. D., and Gentner, D. (1989). The structure-mapping engine: Algorithm and examples. *Artificial Intelligence* 41:1–63.

Fauconnier, G. (1990). Domains and connections. *Cognitive Linguistics* 1-1:151–174.

Fauconnier, G., and Turner, M. (1998). Conceptual integration networks. *Cognitive Science* 22(2):133–187.

Forbus, K. D., Ferguson, R. W., and Gentner, D. (1994). Incremental structure-mapping. *Proceedings of the sixteenth annual conference of the Cognitive Science Society*, pp. 313–318. Mahwah, NJ: Erlbaum.

Forbus, K. D., and Gentner, D. (1989). Structural evaluation of analogies: What counts? *Proceedings of the eleventh annual conference of the Cognitive Science Society*, pp. 341–348. Mahwah, NJ: Erlbaum.

Forbus, K. D., Gentner, D., and Law, K. (1995). MAC/FAC: A model of similarity-based retrieval. *Cognitive Science* 19(2):141–205.

Forbus, K. D., and Oblinger, D. (1990). Making SME greedy and pragmatic. *Proceedings of the twelfth annual conference of the Cognitive Science Society*, pp. 61–68. Mahwah, NJ: Erlbaum.

Gentner, D. (1975). Evidence for the psychological reality of semantic components: The verbs of possession. In D. A. Norman, D. E. Rumelhart, and the LNR Research Group, Eds., *Explorations in cognition*, pp. 211–246. San Francisco: W.H. Freeman.

Gentner, D. (1982). Are scientific analogies metaphors? In D. Miall, Ed., *Metaphor: Problems and perspectives*, pp. 106–132. Brighton: Harvester.

Gentner, D. (1983). Structure-mapping: A theoretical framework for analogy. *Cognitive Science* 7:155–170.

Gentner, D. (1988). Metaphor as structure mapping: The relational shift. *Child Development* 59:47–59.

Gentner, D. (1992). Metaphor as mapping. Paper presented at the meeting of the Cognitive Science Society, Chicago.

Gentner, D. (forthcoming). Spatial metaphors in temporal reasoning. In M. Gattis, Ed., *Spatial schemas in abstract thought*. Cambridge, MA: MIT Press.

Gentner, D., and Boronat, C. B. (1992). Metaphor as mapping. Paper presented at the Workshop on Metaphor, Tel Aviv.

Gentner, D., and Boronat, C. (in preparation). Metaphors are (sometimes) processed as generative domain-mappings.

Gentner, D., and Bowdle, B. (1994). The coherence imbalance hypothesis: A functional approach to asymmetry in comparison. *Proceedings of the sixteenth annual meeting of the Cognitive Science Society*, 351–356. Hillsdale, NJ: Erlbaum.

Gentner, D., Brem, S., Ferguson, R. W., Markman, A. B., Levidow, B. B., Wolff, P., and Forbus, K. D. (1997). Analogical reasoning and conceptual change: A case study of Johannes Kepler. *The Journal of the Learning Sciences* 6(1):3–40.

Gentner, D., and Clement, C. A. (1988). Evidence for relational selectivity in the interpretation of analogy and metaphor. In G. H. Bower, Ed., *The psychology of learning and motivation*, pp. 307–358. New York: Academic.

Gentner, D., Falkenhainer, B., and Skorstad, J. (1988). Viewing metaphor as analogy. In D. H. Helman, Ed., *Analogical reasoning: Perspectives of artificial intelligence, cognitive science, and philosophy*, pp. 171–177. Dordrecht: Kluwer.

Gentner, D., and France, I. M. (1988). The verb mutability effect: Studies of the combinatorial semantics of nouns and verbs. In S. L. Small, G. W. Cottrell, and M. K. Tanenhaus, Eds., *Lexical ambiguity resolution: Perspectives from psycholinguistics, neuropsychology, and artificial intelligence*, pp. 343–382. San Mateo, CA: Kaufmann.

Gentner, D., and Gentner, D. R. (1983). Flowing waters or teeming crowds: Mental models of electricity. In D. Gentner and A. L. Stevens, Eds., *Mental models*, pp. 99–129. Hillsdale, NJ: Erlbaum.

Gentner, D., and Grudin, J. (1985). The evolution of mental metaphors in psychology: A 90-year retrospective. *American Psychologist* 40:181–192.

Gentner, D., and Imai, M. (1992). Is the future always ahead? Evidence for system-mappings in understanding space-time metaphors. *Proceedings of the fourteenth annual meeting of the Cognitive Science Society*, pp. 510–515. Mahwah, NJ: Erlbaum.

Gentner, D., Imai, M., and Boroditsky, L. (in preparation). As time goes by: Evidence for two systems in processing space-time metaphors.

Gentner, D., and Jeziorski, M. (1993). The shift from metaphor to analogy in western science. In A. Ortony, Ed., *Metaphor and thought* (2d ed.), pp. 447–480. Cambridge: Cambridge University Press.

Gentner, D., and Markman, A. B. (1997). Structure mapping in analogy and similarity. *American Psychologist* 52:45–56.

Gentner, D., Rattermann, M. J., and Forbus, K. D. (1993). The roles of similarity in transfer: Separating retrievability from inferential soundness. *Cognitive Psychology* 25:524–575.

Gentner, D., Rattermann, M. J., Markman, A. B., and Kotovsky, L. (1995). Two forces in the development of relational similarity. In T. J. Simon and G. S. Halford, Eds., *Developing cognitive competence: New approaches to process modeling*, pp. 263–313. Hillsdale, NJ: Erlbaum.

Gentner, D., and Wolff, P. (2000). Metaphor and knowledge change. In E. Dietrich and A. B. Markman, Eds., *Cognitive dynamics: Conceptual and representational change in humans and machines*, pp. 295–342. Mahwah, NJ: Erlbaum.

Gentner, D., and Wolff, P. (1997). Alignment in the processing of metaphor. *Journal of Memory and Language* 37:331–355.

Gerrig, R. J., and Gibbs, R. W. (1988). Beyond the lexicon: Creativity in language production. *Metaphor and Symbolic Activity* 3:1–19.

Gibbs, R. (1985). On the process of understanding idioms. *Journal of Psycholinguistic Research* 14:465–472.

Gibbs, R. W., Jr. (1979). Contextual effects in understanding indirect requests. *Discourse Processes* 2:149–156.

Gibbs, R. W., Jr. (1980). Spilling the beans on understanding and memory for idioms in conversations. *Memory and Cognition* 8:449–456.

Gibbs, R. W., Jr. (1990). Comprehending figurative referential descriptions. *Journal of Experimental Psychology: Learning, Memory, and Cognition* 16:56–66.

Gibbs, R. W., Jr. (1994). *The poetics of mind: Figurative thought, language, and understanding*. New York: Cambridge University Press.

Gibbs, R. W., Jr. (1996). Why many concepts are metaphorical. *Cognition* 61:309–319.

Gibbs, R., Nayak, N. P., and Cutting, C. (1989). How to kick the bucket and not decompose: Analyzability and idiom processing. *Journal of Memory and Language* 28:576–593.

Gibbs, R., and O'Brien, J. E. (1990). Idioms and mental imagery: The metaphorical motivation for idiomatic meaning. *Cognition* 36(1):35–68.

Gick, M. L., and Holyoak, K. J. (1983). Schema induction and analogical transfer. *Cognitive Psychology* 15:1–38.

Gildea, P., and Glucksberg, S. (1983). On understanding metaphors: The role of context. *Journal of Verbal Learning and Verbal Behavior* 22:577–590.

Giora, R. (1997). Understanding figurative and literal language: The graded salience hypothesis. *Cognitive Linguistics* 8(3):183–206.

Glucksberg, S., Brown, M., and McGlone, M. S. (1993). Conceptual analogies are not automatically accessed during idiom comprehension. *Memory and Cognition* 21:711–719.

Glucksberg, S., Gildea, P., and Bookin, H. B. (1982). On understanding nonliteral speech: Can people ignore metaphors? *Journal of Verbal Learning and Verbal Behavior* 21:85–98.

Glucksberg, S., and Keysar, B. (1990). Understanding metaphorical comparisons: Beyond similarity. *Psychological Review* 97:3–18.

Glucksberg, S., McGlone, M. S., and Manfredi, D. (1997). Property attribution in metaphor comprehension. *Journal of Memory and Language* 36:50–67.

Goldstone, R. L. (1994). Similarity, interactive activation, and mapping. *Journal of Experimental Psychology: Learning, Memory, and Cognition* 20(1):3–28.

Goldstone, R. L., and Medin, D. L. (1994). Similarity, interactive-activation and mapping: An overview. In K. J. Holyoak and J. A. Barnden, Eds., *Advances in connectionist and neural computation theory*, vol. 2, *Analogical connections*, pp. 321–362. Norwood, NJ: Ablex.

Greiner, R. (1988). Learning by understanding analogies. *Artificial Intelligence* 35:81–125.

Gruber, H. E. (1995). Insight and affect in the history of science. In R. J. Sternberg and J. E. Davidson, Eds., *The nature of insight*, pp. 397–432. Cambridge, MA: MIT Press.

Halford, G. S., Wilson, W. H., and Phillips, S. (1998). Processing capacity defined by relational complexity: Implications for comparative, developmental, and cognitive psychology. *Behavioral and Brain Sciences* 21:803–864.

Hobbs, J. R. (1979). Metaphor, metaphor schemata, and selective inferencing. Technical Note 204, SRI Projects 7910 and 7500. Menlo Park, CA: SRI International.

Hoffman, R. R., and Kemper, S. (1987). What could reaction-time studies be telling us about metaphor comprehension? *Metaphor and Symbolic Activity* 2:149–186.

Holyoak, K. J., and Thagard, P. (1989). Analogical mapping by constraint satisfaction. *Cognitive Science* 13(3):295–355.

Holyoak, K. J., and Thagard, P. R. (1995). *Mental leaps: Analogy in creative thought.* Cambridge, MA: MIT Press.

Honeck, R. P., Kibler, C. T., and Firment, M. J. (1987). Figurative language and psychological views of categorization: Two ships in the night? In R. E. Haskell, Ed., *Cognition and symbolic structures: The psychology of metaphoric transformation,* pp. 103–120. Norwood, NJ: Ablex.

Hummel, J. E., and Holyoak, K. J. (1997). Distributed representations of structure: A theory of analogical access and mapping. *Psychological Review* 104(3):427–466.

Keane, M. T., and Brayshaw, M. (1988). The incremental analogical machine: A computational model of analogy. In D. Sleeman, Ed., *Third European working session on machine learning,* pp. 53–62. San Mateo, CA: Kaufmann.

Keane, M. T., Ledgeway, T., and Duff, S. (1994). Constraints on analogical mapping: A comparison of three models. *Cognitive Science* 18(3):387–438.

Kedar-Cabelli, S. (1988). Toward a computational model of purpose-directed analogy. In A. Prieditis, Ed., *Analogica,* pp. 89–107. Los Altos, CA: Kaufmann.

Kelly, M. H., and Keil, F. C. (1987). Metaphor comprehension and knowledge of semantic domains. *Metaphor and Symbolic Activity* 2:33–51.

Kennedy, J. M. (1990). Metaphor—Its intellectual basis. *Metaphor and Symbolic Activity* 5:115–123.

Keysar, B. (1989). On the functional equivalence of literal and metaphorical interpretations in discourse. *Journal of Memory and Language* 28:375–385.

Keysar, B., and Bly, B. (1995). Intuitions of the transparency of idioms: Can one keep a secret by spilling the beans? *Journal of Memory and Language* 34(1):89–109.

Kintsch, W. (1974). *The representation of meaning in memory.* Hillsdale, NJ: Erlbaum.

Kittay, E. F. (1987). *Metaphor: Its cognitive force and linguistic structure.* Oxford: Clarendon.

Kittay, E. F., and Lehrer, A. (1981). Semantic fields and the structure of metaphor. *Studies in Language* 5(1):31–63.

Kotovsky, L., and Gentner, D. (1996). Comparison and categorization in the development of relational similarity. *Child Development* 67:2797–2822.

Kuehne, S. E., Forbus, K. D., Gentner, D., and Quinn, B. (2000). SEQL: Category learning as incremental abstraction using structure mapping. In *Proceedings of the twenty-second annual conference of the Cognitive Science Society.* Hillsdale, NJ: Erlbaum.

Kuehne, S. E., Gentner, D., and Forbus, K. D. (2000). Modeling infant learning via symbolic structural alignment. *Proceedings of the twenty-second annual Conference of the cognitive science society.* Hillsdale, NJ: Erlbaum Associates.

Lakoff, G. (1990). The invariance hypothesis: Is abstract reason based on image-schemas? *Cognitive Linguistics* 1(1):39–74.

Lakoff, G. (1993). The contemporary theory of metaphor. In A. Ortony, Ed., *Metaphor and thought*, 2nd ed., pp. 202–251. New York: Cambridge University Press.

Lakoff, G., and Johnson, M. (1980). *Metaphors we live by*. Chicago: University of Chicago Press.

Lakoff, G., and Turner, M. (1989). *More than cool reason: A field guide to poetic metaphor*. Chicago: University of Chicago Press.

Lassaline, M. E. (1996). Structural alignment in induction and similarity. *Journal of Experimental Psychology: Learning, Memory, and Cognition* 22(3):754–770.

Lehrer, A. (1990). Polysemy, conventionality, and the structure of the lexicon. *Cognitive Linguistics* 1(2):207–246.

Loewenstein, J., Thompson, L., and Gentner, D. (1999). Analogical encoding facilitates knowledge transfer in negotiation. *Psychonomic Bulletin and Review* 6(4):586–597.

Love, B. C., Rouder, J. N., and Wisniewski, E. J. (1999). A structural account of global and local processing. *Cognitive Psychology* 38:291–316.

Malgady, R., and Johnson, M. (1980). Measurement of figurative language: Semantic feature models of comprehension and appreciation. In R. Honeck and R. Hoffman, Eds., *Cognition and figurative language*, pp. 239–258. Hillsdale, NJ: Erlbaum.

Markman, A. B. (1997). Constraints on analogical inference. *Cognitive Science* 21(4):373–418.

Markman, A. B. (1999). *Knowledge representation*. Mahwah, NJ: Erlbaum.

Markman, A. B., and Gentner, D. (1993). Structural alignment during similarity comparisons. *Cognitive Psychology* 25:431–467.

Marschack, M., Katz, A., and Paivio, A. (1983). Dimensions of metaphor. *Journal of Psycholinguistic Research* 12:17–40.

McGlone, M. S. (forthcoming). Concepts as metaphors. In S. Glucksburg, Ed., *Metaphor and allusion: Studies of figurative language comprehension*. Oxford: Oxford University Press.

McGlone, M. S., and Harding, J. (1998). Back (or forward?) to the future: The role of perspective in temporal language comprehension. *Journal of Experimental Psychology: Learning, Memory, and Cognition* 24(5):1211–1223.

Medin, D. L., Goldstone, R. L., and Gentner, D. (1993). Respects for similarity. *Psychological Review* 100(2):254–278.

Miller, G. A. (1979). Images and models, similes and metaphors. In A. Ortony, Ed., *Metaphor and thought*, pp. 202–250. Cambridge: Cambridge University Press.

Miller, G. A. (1993). Images and models, similes and metaphors. In A. Ortony, Ed., *Metaphor and thought* (2d ed.), pp. 357–400. Cambridge: Cambridge University Press.

Murphy, G. L. (1996). On metaphoric representation. *Cognition* 60(2):173–204.

Murphy, G. L. (1997). Reasons to doubt the present evidence for metaphoric representation. *Cognition* 62:99–108.

Nagy, W. (1974). *Figurative patterns and redundancy in the lexicon.* Ph.D. dissertation, University of California at San Diego.

Nayak, N. P., and Gibbs, R. W. (1990). Conceptual knowledge in the interpretation of idioms. *Journal of Experimental Psychology* 119(3):315–330.

Nersessian, N. J. (1992). How do scientists think? Capturing the dynamics of conceptual change in science. In R. N. Giere and H. Feigl, Eds., *Cognitive models of science: Minnesota studies in the philosophy of science*, pp. 3–44. Minneapolis: University of Minnesota Press.

Novick, L. R., and Holyoak, K. J. (1991). Mathematical problem solving by analogy. *Journal of Experimental Psychology: Learning, Memory, and Cognition* 17(3):398–415.

Ortony, A. (1975). Why metaphors are necessary and not just nice. *Educational Theory* 25:45–53.

Ortony, A. (1979). Beyond literal similarity. *Psychological Review* 86:161–180.

Ortony, A., Schallert, D. L., Reynolds, R. E., and Antos, S. J. (1978). Interpreting metaphors and idioms: Some effects of context on comprehension. *Journal of Verbal Learning and Verbal Behavior* 17:465–477.

Ortony, A., Vondruska, R. J., Foss, M. A., and Jones, L. E. (1985). Salience, similes, and the asymmetry of similarity. *Journal of Memory and Language* 24:569–594.

Quinn, N. (1987). Convergent evidence for a cultural model of American marriage. In D. Holland and N. Quinn, Eds., *Cultural models in language and thought*, pp. 173–192. New York: Cambridge University Press.

Ramscar, M., and Pain, H. (1996). Can a real distinction be made between cognitive theories of analogy and categorisation? *Proceedings of the eighteenth annual conference of the Cognitive Science Society*, pp. 346–351. Mahwah, NJ: Erlbaum.

Roediger, H. (1980). Memory metaphors in cognitive psychology. *Memory and Cognition* 8:231–246.

Ross, B. H., and Kennedy, P. T. (1990). Generalizing from the use of earlier examples in problem solving. *Journal of Experimental Psychology: Learning, Memory, and Cognition* 16:42–55.

Ross, B. H., Perkins, S. J., and Tenpenny, P. L. (1990). Reminding-based category learning. *Cognitive Psychology* 22:460–492.

Rumelhart, D. E., and Abrahamson, A. A. (1973). A model for analogical reasoning. *Cognitive Psychology* 5:1–28.

Searle, J. R. (1976). A classification of illocutionary acts. *Language in Society* 5(1):1–23.

Shen, Y. (1992). Metaphors and categories. *Poetics Today* 13:771–794.

Skorstad, J., Gentner, D., and Medin, D. (1988). Abstraction processes during concept learning: A structural view. *Proceedings of the tenth annual conference of the Cognitive Science Society*, pp. 419–425. Mahwah NJ: Erlbaum.

Steen, G. J. (1989). Metaphor and literary comprehension: Towards a discourse theory of metaphor in literature. *Poetics*, 18:113–141.

Sweetser, E. (1990). *From etymology to pragmatics*. Cambridge: Cambridge University Press.

Swinney, D., and Cutler, A. (1979). The access and processing of idiomatic expressions. *Journal of Verbal Learning and Verbal Behavior* 18:523–534.

Tourangeau, R., and Rips, L. (1991). Interpreting and evaluating metaphors. *Journal of Memory and Language* 30:452–472.

Tourangeau, R., and Sternberg, R. (1981). Aptness in metaphor. *Cognitive Psychology* 13:27–55.

Tourangeau, R., and Sternberg, R. (1982). Understanding and appreciating metaphors. *Cognition* 11:203–244.

Traugott, E. C. (1978). On the expression of spatio-temporal relations in language. In J. H. Greenberg, Ed., *Universals of human language*, vol. 3, *Word structure*, pp. 369–400. Stanford: Stanford University Press.

Turner, M. (1987). *Death is the mother of beauty: Mind, metaphor, and criticism*. Chicago: University of Chicago Press.

Turner, M. (1991). *Reading minds: The study of English in the age of cognitive science*. Princeton, NJ: Princeton University Press.

Turner, N. E., and Katz, A. N. (1997). The availability of conventional and of literal meaning during the comprehension of proverbs. *Pragmatics and Cognition* 5:199–233.

Williams, J. (1992). Processing polysemous words in context: Evidence for interrelated meanings. *Journal of Psycholinguistic Research* 21:193–218.

Wolff, P., and Gentner, D. (1992). The time course of metaphor comprehension. *Proceedings of the fourteenth annual conference of the Cognitive Science Society*, pp. 504–509. Mahwah, NJ: Erlbaum.

Wolff, P., and Gentner, D. (2000). Evidence for role-neutral initial processing of metaphors. *Journal of Experimental Psychology: Learning, Memory, and Cognition* 26(2):529–541.

Wolff, P., and Gentner, D. (in preparation). From symmetric to asymmetric processing: Two stages in the comprehension of metaphors.

7
Conceptual Blending and Analogy

Gilles Fauconnier

The structure-mapping approach to analogy and metaphor was a turning point in cognitive science. It shifted focus from the rule-based generation of structures to the topology of mental models, the efficiency of partial matches, and the projection from one domain to another of conceptual and perceptual organization (Gentner 1983; Hofstadter 1985; Holyoak and Thagard 1994; Lakoff and Johnson 1980). As other authors in this volume make clear, the capacity of organisms to carry out such projections lies at the heart of cognition in its many forms. Far from being confined to problem-solving and conscious reasoning, structure-mapping is inherent in all of our thought processes, and especially in the permanent construction of meaning that we engage in effortlessly as we conceive the world around us, act upon it, talk about it, and stray beyond it in wild leaps of imagination, fantasy, and creativity.

Research on analogical mappings has strongly focused on processes of inference transfer from a source (or base) to a target. The gist of such processes lies in partially mapping and aligning structures and elements in the source and target, and then using the alignment and partial mappings to project additional structure present in the source onto the target, thereby creating additional structure in the target. This additional structure can in turn be dynamically manipulated, yielding further relations and connections. Building up the target in this fashion is a way to enrich its conceptualization, to generate novel inferences, and to make predictions about the world.

In 1993, Mark Turner and I began to study in some detail another cognitive operation, conceptual blending, which also depends centrally on structure projection and dynamic simulation (Fauconnier and Turner

1998). Like standard analogical mapping, blending aligns two partial structures (the inputs). But in addition, blending projects selectively to form a third structure, the blend. The blend is not a simple composition of the inputs. Through pattern completion and dynamic elaboration, it develops an emergent organization of its own. The blend can be used to provide inferences, emotional content, rhetorical force, and novel conceptualization. A major aspect of research on conceptual blending is the study of the different types of integration networks and of the competing optimality constraints that guide their emergence.

Conceptual blending plays a role in many types of cognitive phenomena. In-depth studies and analyses have been carried out in areas such as morphology and syntax (Mandelblit 1997), sign language (Liddell 1998), literature (Oakley 1998; Freeman 1997; Turner 1996), meaning (Sweetser (1997), music (Zbikowski 1999), humor (Coulson 2001), cinema (Veale 1996), and mathematics (Robert 1998; Lakoff and Nunez 2000).[1] A mathematically based approach to blending is developed by Goguen (1998). Aspects of blending have been modeled computationally by John Barnden and Tony Veale (Veale 1998).

The study of conceptual integration is closely tied to that of analogy for at least three reasons: (1) the function of some (but by no means all) conceptual integration networks is analogical, (2) conceptual integration networks whose function is not analogy still align two or more partial structures, typically by means of an analogical mapping, and (3) standard examples of analogy and metaphor often turn out to be cases of conceptual blending with analogical or metaphorical cross-space alignment. One purpose of this chapter is to point out the important respects in which analogy and blending can overlap or coexist within cognitive processing.

Let us first review some stock examples of conceptual blending (explored in far greater detail elsewhere). The examples belong to different formal types, and their status with respect to analogy differs.

Examples of Conceptual Blending and Types of Networks

A famous example of blending is "the boat race" or "regatta" (Fauconnier and Turner 1994, 1998). A modern catamaran is sailing from San

Francisco to Boston in 1993, trying to go faster than a clipper that sailed the same course in 1853. A sailing magazine reports on the event in the following way:

As we went to press, Rich Wilson and Bill Biewenga were barely maintaining a 4.5 day lead over the ghost of the clipper *Northern Light*, whose record run from San Francisco to Boston they're trying to beat. In 1853, the clipper made the passage in 76 days, 8 hours.—"Great America II," *Latitude 38*, vol. 190 (April 1993), p. 100.

Informally, there are two distinct events in this story, the run by the clipper in 1853 and the run by the catamaran in 1993 on (approximately) the same course. In the magazine quote, the two runs are merged into a single event, a race between the catamaran and the clipper's "ghost." In the terminology of conceptual blending theory, the two distinct events correspond to two input mental spaces, which reflect salient schematic aspects of the events: the voyage, the departure and arrival points, the period and time of travel, the boat, its positions at various times. There is a straightforward way to map the inputs onto each other (see fig. 7.1).

This mapping itself is possible by virtue of the more schematic frame (shared by the two events) of a boat sailing from San Francisco to Boston. This frame appears in a third space that we call the generic space.

Blending consists in projecting (partially) from the two input spaces into a fourth space, the blended space (see fig. 7.2). Because the same day (ordinally) is projected from both inputs, the two positions projected (i, j) are different. In the blended space, we have two boats on the same course, that left the starting point, San Francisco, on the same day. Pattern completion allows us to construe this situation as a race (by importing the familiar background frame of racing). This construal is emergent in the blend. The motion of the boats is structurally constrained by the mappings. The clipper becomes a ghost ship in the blend, another property licensed by a (fantastic) cultural model. By "running the blend," that is, by unfolding the race through time, we have the relative positions of the boats and their dynamics.

Crucially, the blended space remains connected to the inputs by the mappings, so that real inferences can be computed in the inputs from the imaginary situation in the blended space. For example, we can deduce that the catamaran is going faster overall in 1993 than the clipper did

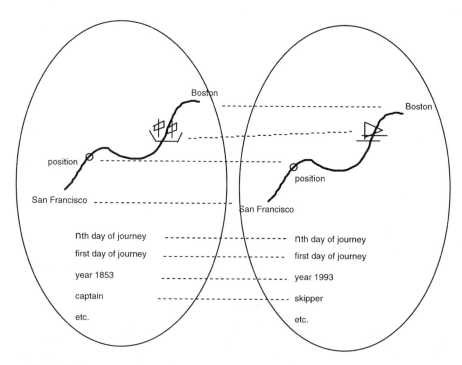

Figure 7.1

in 1853, and more precisely, we have some idea ("four and a half days") of their relative performances. We can also interpret the emotions of the catamaran crew in terms of the familiar emotions linked to the frame of racing.

The "boat race" example is a simple case of blending. Two inputs share organizing frame structure. They get linked by a cross-space mapping and projected selectively to a blended space. The projection allows emergent structure to develop on the basis of composition, pattern completion (based on background models), and elaboration ("running the blend") (see fig. 7.3).

This general scheme fits many cases of elementary blending. It can be further extended to allow multiple and successive blends (Fauconnier and Turner, in preparation). In order for integration to happen in our boat race example, there needs to be a cross-space mapping between the input spaces of the network. The mapping is licensed by the shared frame of

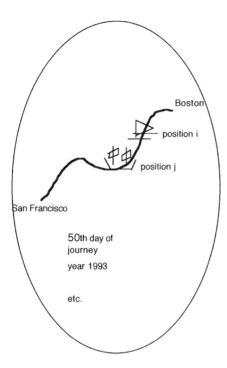

Figure 7.2

the inputs, very much as in standard cases of analogy (Markman 1997; Hofstadter 1985) where inferences are transferred from a source to a target on the basis of a shared frame, or more generally a shared schematic structure (Gick and Holyoak 1983). But the purpose and function of the statement in the yachting magazine is not analogical. It is not to transfer inferences from the input of the clipper to the input of the catamaran. In fact, the analogy between the two inputs in this case is trivial and obvious and taken for granted (the two boats sail from San Francisco to Boston).

In the appendix to this chapter, I have listed a number of examples that have been used by Turner, myself, and others to illustrate the great diversity of conceptual blending phenomena. Each example is a case of a particular type of conceptual integration network. The main categories are simplex networks, mirror networks, single-scope networks, and double-scope networks; further distinctions are made within each of the

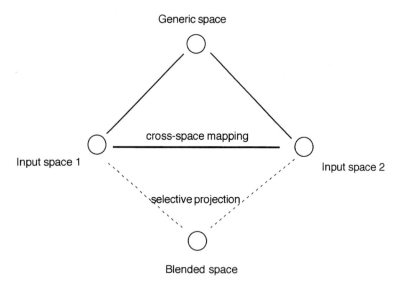

Figure 7.3

broad categories. The typology, along with optimality principles that govern it, is studied in some detail in Fauconnier and Turner (1998, in preparation), and I will not repeat that material here. But I will appeal to the same examples, because it is convenient to use the same stock examples to examine the various formal possibilities inherent in conceptual blending. In the typology, the boat race example is called a *mirror network* because the same organizing frame (boat sailing from San Francisco to Boston) is common to all the spaces in the network. That common frame drives the cross-space mapping needed to carry out blending. Other examples of mirror networks appear in the "Buddhist monk" and the "debate with Kant." By looking at those examples, the reader can check intuitively (and more rigorously in the references cited) that the blends require cross-space structure mapping, just as analogy typically does, but that they are not analogical in purpose and function. In the "debate with Kant," for instance, the feasibility of the blend depends on partially mapping Kant's activities as a thinker and writer in the eighteenth century onto the modern philosophy teacher's activities in the classroom. To be sure, there is analogy between the two, and that is why the mapping succeeds. But as in the boat race case, this analogy is obvious and taken for granted; it is not the point of the rhetorical blend.

Consider now the following action blend[2]: a ski instructor was trying to teach a novice (who happened to be French) to hold his arms correctly and look down the slope (rather than in the direction of the skis). The instructor told the novice to imagine that he was a waiter in Paris carrying a tray with champagne and croissants. By focusing his attention on the tray and trying to avoid spilling the champagne, the novice was able to produce something approaching the right integrated motion on the slope. The inputs in this case are the ski situation and the restaurant situation, with arm and body positions mapped onto each other. The generic space has only human posture and motion, with no particular context. But in the blend, the skier is also actually carrying the champagne tray. The blend is of course a fantasy, but it does map the right motion back onto the ski input. Rather remarkably, this pedagogical feat requires no actual champagne and croissants. Just thinking of them is enough. This blend is not a mirror network, because the two organizing frames in the inputs (skiing and waiting on tables respectively) are entirely distinct. The point is not to develop a strong analogy between the two; in fact, in this case it is their obvious dissimilarity that enhances the learning efficiency. But as opposed to the boat race or Kant examples, we do find analogical transfer operating here. The instructor is astutely using a hidden analogy between a small aspect of the waiter's motion and the desired skiing position. This analogy, however, makes little sense out of context and independently of the blend; the instructor is not suggesting that a good skier moves "just like" a competent waiter. It is only within the blend—when the novice tries to mentally carry the tray while physically skiing—that the intended structure (the improved body position) emerges. In this case, as in all others, we still have a cross-space mapping (crucial to the construction of the blend), but its function is not analogical reasoning: we are not drawing inferences from the domain of waiting on tables and projecting them to the domain of skiing. Rather, the point of the blend, within the frame of an instructor teaching a novice, is directly the integration of motion. Once the right motion has emerged through integration, and once it has been mastered by the novice, the links to croissants and champagne can be abandoned. The skier need not continue forever to think about carrying trays in order to perform adequately.

Turning now to metaphor, we can make distinctions there too between simple structure projection or structural alignment and the more complex projections at work in a conceptual integration network. In the simpler cases of metaphor, there is partial structural alignment between a source (or base) and a target. New structure is exported to the target either by transferring inferences available in the source into corresponding inferences for the corresponding elements in the target, or by actually adding to the target counterpart elements for what is in the source. So the computer virus metaphor in its simple form yields the inferences (transferred from the biological domain) that a "computer virus" is harmful, replicates, and so on, and the metaphor can add concepts of "vaccines," "disinfectants," and "safe interfaces" to the target domain of computer operation. But metaphor also arises routinely in more complex integration networks where the alignment between inputs is conflicted. The stock example often discussed in this regard is the conventional metaphor "to dig one's own grave." As discussed in detail by Fauconnier and Turner (1998) and Coulson (2001), it is inadequate to explain this type of metaphor by only invoking inference transfer from a source of "dying and grave-digging" to a target of "failure and misguided action." In the putative source domain, the death of one person causes and precedes the digging of a grave by another. In the target, it is the action of one person that causes and precedes the failure of that same person. Because death and failure on one hand and digging and action on the other hand are counterparts, there is a mismatch of the relevant temporal, causal, and referential structures. There is no easily available inference in the source that digging one's grave causes death (it does not), that could be projected to the desired target inference that misguided actions will cause failure. Instead, the expression "digging one's own grave" is a double-scope blend: the organizing frame of death and graves comes from one input; the causal and temporal structure comes from the other. We construct such a blend easily and automatically and do not find it odd that within the blend, digging graves causes death and can be done inadvertently. In using such metaphors (and they are the rule rather than the exception), we are not exploiting analogical transfer from the domain of "dying and graves" to the domain of "action and failure," because in fact the two domains in question are *not* structurally analogical in the relevant respects. Yet the power of the metaphor is as great as, or greater than, in cases of simple transfer. An even more transparent example of efficient emergent structure in a metaphorical blend, which cannot be attributed to source domain structure and transfer, is the following quote from the Reuters news service noted by Mark Turner[3]:

U.S. stocks ended sharply lower on Wednesday after an attempt to extend a one-day rally was quashed. Market players said investors were unwilling to return to the market amid fears that rising interest rates would lead to further losses in the days ahead. "Everybody has their horns pulled in," said Arnie Owen, director of equities at Kaufman Brothers.

A blend is constructed here in which bulls have retractable horns. The length of the horns varies in proportion to the degree of confidence and investment of the investors in the target domain of the stock market. Clearly, the variability in the blend is imported from the target (not from the source).[4] It provides a richer metaphorical way of talking about the stock market, but the relevant structure is not transferred analogically from available preexisting structure in the domain of charging bulls, because bulls do not in fact have retractable horns.

In Fauconnier (1997), I offer a great deal of evidence showing that counterfactuals in language, a supremely human thought process, it would seem, are the product of conceptual integration networks, and that their function is often to construct analogy or disanalogy. The stock example here is *In France, Watergate would not have hurt Nixon.* The conceptual blend is one which inherits the French mentality and political setting along with Nixon as president and the Watergate scandal (selectively projected of course: Watergate is now somehow in France, Nixon speaks French, and so on). Running this "impossible" blend provides inferences about the actual French political setting. Some counterfactual blends are routine (conventional)—*If I were you, I would . . .* [blends my dispositions with your situation], others are more spectacular, such as the "philosopher in a coma" [see appendix]. The literal impossibility of many such blends is striking out of context, but goes by unnoticed in actual use, because it is the entire network, not just the blended space, that is being manipulated.

Integrated Action

In developing a theory of blends, attention has been focused on the optimality constraints that guide their construction, the cross-space mappings and common schemas that serve to launch them, and the dynamic emergent structure that runs the blend and provides inferences and novel concepts. Their efficency in developing new types of integrated action, noted earlier in the ski example, deserves additional research. It bears in crucial ways with issues of embodiment and creativity that are central to cognitive science. To illustrate the hidden complexity of such integrations, I will evoke in this section the succession of blends that enter into the apparently simple activity of using a computer mouse. I am interested here only in the actual manipulation of "rectangles" on a vertical screen, using the mouse on a horizontal plane external to the computer terminal itself. I am not interested in the functional reasons for doing this (storing and editing information, etc.) or in the metaphors ultimately used to frame the manipulation (office work, files, folders, trash cans, and the like).

Before discussing what I see as revealing aspects of mouse-controlled interfaces, I will comment on some of the general issues. My efforts in this passage are prompted by comments of two reviewers for the present chapter.

Both reviewers were quite receptive to the idea of conceptual blending and deemed it a cognitive operation worthy of study. But their comments suggested that the case of the interface itself was relatively trivial, and could even perhaps be explained by appealing only to analogy and not to blending. I, on the contrary, along with others who have studied blending, see the interface example as anything but trivial and in fact as deeply representative of the fluid neural and psychological embodiment that characterizes successful conceptual integrations. Or to put things another way, the fact that conceptual blending in examples of this kind is invisible and unnoticed makes it paradoxically all the more interesting. I blame myself for not being able to bring this out more clearly. Here then are some general points that I hope will help.

First, conceptual blending is not an exotic phenomenon. It shows up in many apparently simple phenomena like adjective-noun or noun-noun combinations, *of*-constructions, successive developments of science and mathematics, sexual fantasies, pretend-play, and so on. Presumably, then, it is a readily available human capacity, not one that "costs" more cognitively than, say, analogy or framing. As noted above, conceptual blending is not something that you do *instead* of analogy. Rather, the cross-space mappings at work in blending are most often analogical, and the projections between mental spaces in a network (e.g., input to blend, or generic to input) are also structure-mappings of the type discovered for analogy. In standard analogy and blending alike, such mappings are often very partial (e.g., the skiing waiter). Conceptual blending adds to simple analogy the dimension of the blended space, its connections to the other spaces in the integration network, and imaginative cognitive work within the blended space itself. Integrated action or thought can emerge without loss of conceptual access to the initial input spaces. In the skiing example, skiing has not been reconceptualized in terms of waiting at tables and carrying bottles. In the sailing example, we remain lucidly aware that a single boat is making the run from San Francisco to Boston, even as we operate on the blended racing scenario in which there are two boats and two crews engaged in earnest competition. In the same way, the computer interface phenomenon will illustrate the user's ability to operate simultaneously in mental spaces constructed for the purpose of maximizing the efficiency and familiarity of the interface without being confused or deluded about what is going on. It is offered to show how automatic and cognitively effortless the integration of successive blends can be, and how they can lead to novel, creative integrated action that goes far beyond a simple juxtaposition of partial similarities.

There is little doubt, as we shall see, that massive blending is at work even (or perhaps especially) in what looks at first glance like the most straightforward component of human-computer interface. And yet in the vast literature on HCI, metaphor and analogy, but not blending, have been explicitly recognized and discussed.

Consider, then, a desktop environment, limited to various kinds of rectangles on the screen, the arrow, and its control by a user moving a mouse. Here are some of the blends that need to be constructed in order to become competent in this activity. I separate them here for expository purposes, but they need not actually be learned in the discrete order used here. In fact, the manipulation of the interface is typically learned quickly and the various blends will reenforce each other and be learned together as part of a total construction of meaning for the interface.

Object Blend
The rectangles on the screen are of course not really at all exactly like the three-dimensional objects of our everyday world. But they will fit into an extended notion of object, created by a blend. One input of this blend contains ordinary objects and their most obvious (commonsense) properties: *invariance* (the object is "the same" regardless of its position), *coherence* (a typical object holds together, is in one piece, has continuity, etc.), *stability* (does not change spontaneously), *nonubiquity* (cannot be in two places at the same time). The other input has the white or black rectangles and an arrow on the screen. Technically, they are different illuminations of the screen at different times, two-dimensional, without substance, cannot be grasped, held in your hand, and so on. But perceptually, they too have the properties of invariance (a rectangle is the same size and color no matter what its position), coherence (shape and color is continuous), stability (does not undergo spontaneous change), and nonubiquity (perceived, not quite correctly as it turns out, as being either in one position or in another). The shared perceptual properties between these two physically very different inputs are the basis for a straightforward cross-space mapping between the familiar input domain of three-dimensional-objects and the illuminations on the screen (see fig. 7.4).

In the blended space, we project from one input the perceived reality of the pixels on the computer screen, and from the other the everyday notion of object. The blend is a conceptualization of the rectangular and arrowlike illuminations on the screen as everyday objects. It is of course a natural (perhaps almost automatic) blend for humans to construct, given the salience of cognitively crucial objectlike properties in this

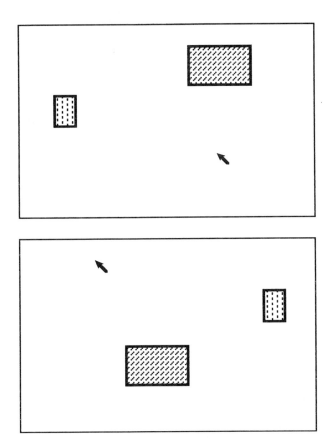

Figure 7.4
A screen with the same "objects" at two different times.

situation. But such an extension of the notion of object would be extremely bizarre if only the "objective" properties of the input domains were taken into account. The blend depends crucially on a cross-space mapping which is a very partial analogy.

Why do we invoke a third (blended) mental space here instead of just saying that the target has received additional structure from the source? The reason, as in other cases of blending, is that the conceptualizer (the user of the interface) must keep active all the spaces in the integration network, that is, be conscious on the one hand that she is dealing with a two-dimensional illuminated computer screen (input space 1, made available by the technology), and at the same time be able to manipulate it with some of the properties imported from input space 2 (three-dimensional objects) without being deluded into thinking that the illuminations actually are three-dimensional objects. It is in the blended space, but not in either of the input mental spaces, that the conceptualizer develops the emergent structure and dynamics to do this. But more about this below.

Arrow and Mouse Blend

Ignore the rectangles on the screen for now, and consider only the arrow. One input of this network is the ception[5] of the screen with the arrow moving in a vertical plane (this description assumes the conceptualization in terms of the *object blend*, although, as mentioned before, a learner would typically not learn the blends in succession). The other input is the ception of the motion of the mouse (a real three-dimensional object, typically held by the user) on a horizontal plane). The technology determines a correlation between the horizontal motion of the mouse on the table, and the vertical motion of the arrow on the screen. Such correlation is typical of remote-control situations. The mental cross-space mapping is between the arrow and the mouse, and between their respective motions. In everyday life, there is the following correlation between visual and tactile experience: when I look at an object and move it at the same time, I see a change in the object's spatial position that correlates with the motion I am performing. Children must learn to control such correlations. The ways in which a hand and arm are used to place an object in a desired location constitute an extremely difficult problem, in terms of body mechanics, brain activity, correlation, and feedback. Now in the case of the mouse and arrow, something additional goes on. I perceive a systematic correlation between my controlled motion of the three-dimensional-mouse in one input, and the motion of its counterpart, the two-dimensional arrow, in the other input. In the blend, my body mechanics are projected from the "mouse" input, while the object being moved, the arrow, and its plane of motion, are projected from the "screen" input. In the blend, the user's attention and awareness are focused on the arrow as the object being moved.

This embodied capacity to integrate the manipulation of the mouse with the motion of the arrow—to *feel* that one is moving the arrow—is remarkable. It is different from long-distance remote control, where the controlled object is not perceived, and there is only knowledge about the transfer of certain dynamics: if I move A, its counterpart A′ will end up moving in some correlated way. Studies of analogy typically concentrate on the transfer aspect of analogical mappings (an inference in the source corresponds to an inference in the target, a change in the source (e.g., motion) corresponds to a change in the target (e.g., counterpart motion of the counterparts). I am stressing here the *integration* aspect of cases that also crucially involve partial mapping. Integration produces a new activity, not just an analogy or systematic correlation between two old ones.

The example also illustrates that in an objective sense, the correspondence between inputs can be highly imperfect, but that once the integration is achieved, this imperfection is hardly accessible to consciousness any longer. The mouse input has properties quite different from the screen input. The mouse can be in contact with the horizontal surface or not. Only when there is such contact will there be a corresponding motion of the arrow on the screen. This property allows the relative motion of the mouse to count, not its absolute position on the pad or desk, whereas on the screen, the absolute position of the arrow is essential. Once mouse manipulation has been mastered, all these discrepancies are disregarded conceptually. The user has developed a novel emergent notion of how to move an object by performing certain physical bodily acts.

Grasping and Moving Blend

The "object" and "mouse" blends give us a conceptual means of moving an arrow on the screen, with coherent action from one type of input (moving the mouse on the pad) and perception from another type of input (seeing the arrow move on the screen). The technology further enables us to move other objects on the screen. But for this to be experienced as a case of willfully moving objects around, another blend must be constructed for "grasping" and "moving." This time, one input is the everyday world where we grasp three-dimensional objects and then by moving our body parts (hand, arm, feet, etc.) and holding on to the object, we end up moving the object. We can often visually perceive the motion of the object, as we cause it to move by performing motor actions. The other input for the blend is the computer screen with object/rectangles and a moving arrow controlled by the user, as structured by the previous object and mouse blends. The cross-space mapping for the new blend associates the user's hand with the arrow on the screen, physical contact with visual contact on the screen (arrow "on" the rectangle), grasping with clicking (and holding the click position), releasing with unclicking. When the clicked arrow moves to another position on the screen, the rectangle on which it was clicked finds itself in the same new location. This is naturally associated by the mapping with the fact that when a hand grasps an object and then moves, the object finds itself in the same location as the hand that moved. The grasping/moving blended space is formed by selectively projecting the frame of moving and grasping objects from one input (everyday world as conceived and perceived), and projecting the counterparts of the hand and objects, namely the arrow and the rectangles, from the other input. As in the previous case, this blend makes it possible to experience the clicking on the rectangle as a form of grasping, and the motion of the clicked mouse as deliberately moving an object. This may look easy, but it demands highly complex correlations and integrations at many levels: neural, perceptual, motor, and conceptual.

Now if we look at the actual implementation of this blend as a computer interface in the Macintosh desktop, we find a number of strange and interesting things. First, there are glaring mismatches in the cross-space mapping that underlies the blend. Clicking on an object in the screen input will change its color (see figs. 7.5, 7.6).

In the other input (everyday world), grasping objects does not make them change color. The difference between touching and grasping is now associated with a difference in color.

Now consider the motion itself. On the desktop interface, it is not the colored rectangle itself which is directly "moved." Rather, as the arrow is moved, with the mouse clicked, a "phantom" object (dotted, uncolored, outline of the rectangle) is moved on the screen, while the object itself (the

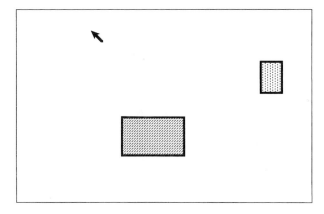

Figure 7.5
Arrow and two objects.

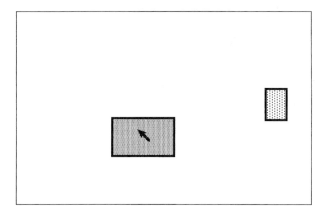

Figure 7.6
Arrow has moved onto an object and clicking has been subsequently performed, changing the object's color.

colored rectangle) remains in its position. When the mouse is unclicked, the phantom disappears, and the colored rectangle appears in its place. The colored rectangle in the original position disappears (see fig. 7.7).

So in fact, in the grasping and moving blend, the nonubiquity and uniqueness properties of objects have been relaxed. In the cross-space mapping between the input of moving three-dimensional objects and the screen input of perceived rectangles, the initial position of an object is mapped onto the stationary colored rectangle, while the moving object itself is mapped onto the "moving" phantom. This is a glaring mismatch, it would seem. In the blended space, however, perception (the double object with a moving phantom, and a stationary anchor) is projected from one input, while conception (moving a single object) is projected from the other. That is, the user experiences motion of a single object, while really perceiving a complex array of phantom, initial, and final rectangles. Perceiving the phantom is clearly conscious at one level, but at another, it is hardly conscious at all. A user typically remembers moving the rectangle but does not remember the detailed separation of the phantom and the reappearance of the object in a different position. This is quite extraordinary, given the accessibility of the process. In terms of conceptual blending, the explanation for this is that although all spaces

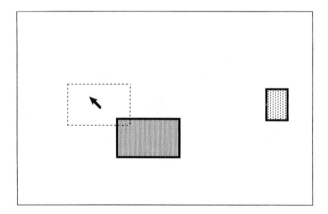

Figure 7.7
Arrow moves, "dragging" along a phantom of the "grasped" object (which remains in its original position until the mouse is released).

in the network remain connected, the conscious experience of moving the object in the blended space is ultimately framed conceptually by only the three-dimensional object input.

As before, but even more glaringly in the present case of the motion blend, the three mental spaces corresponding to conceptualization of "ordinary" three-dimensional objects, perception of the "objects" on the screen, and perception + conceptualization of the interface manipulation (the blended space) need to be kept apart, and connected at the same time. What the user is perceiving and manipulating at one level must include the dotted phantoms and the colored/uncolored rectangles. And so that must project into the blended space together with partial projection from the other input (nonubiquitous, non-color-changing three-dimensional objects). A traditional "source/base to target" account current in metaphor theory and analogy theory will not do here: for instance, saying only that the interface is understood in terms of motion of three-dimensional objects would not make sense, since the experience with the interface differs in *crucial* respects from the purported source/base domain of three-dimensional objects (ubiquity, noncontinuity of motion, instability of shape and color, etc.).

A full analysis of the mapping and blending process in this case would require explicit specification of all the correspondences, mismatches, selective projection, and a study of the violation of some of the optimality constraints under pressure from others. I will not do this here, but I hope that the essential elements are clear from the brief outline above. With respect to the theme of the present paper, we see that "obvious" analogies ("moving" rectangles on the screen and everyday three-dimensional objects) are exploited in implementing the blend technologically, but that violations of structure mapping and homomorphism are tolerated: a moving element in one space (three-dimensional objects) has *two* counterparts in the other, one of which (the dotted phantom) does not preserve original appearance (colored, solid line) and the other (the initial rectangle to be moved) which does not move during the operation, but then suddenly "magically" appears in another location (where it replaces the phantom). In spite of this important disanalogy, the integration proceeds smoothly.

Containment Blend

A further elaboration of the interface introduces the notion that some of the rectangles are "inside" others, can be put in, taken out, opened and closed. Assume for expository purposes that the other blends have already been constructed. One input space to the *containment blend* is the blended space that results from the *moving and grasping blend*. We have just seen how that space is structured perceptually and conceptually. It includes objects that can be "grasped" and moved willfully on the screen. That blended space becomes one of the inputs to a novel blend, the *containment blend*. The other input is the space corresponding to the everyday notion of containers. The cross-space mapping that connects the two spaces will use correspondences like the following:

• A container usually occludes a contained object from view (the container is visible, but the object inside is not); correspondingly, on the screen, the "contained object" will not be visible, while the container is visible.
• A contained object occupies part of the same portion of space as its container; correspondingly, a "contained" screen object will be moved to the location of its "container" object.
• A container is bigger than the object it contains.
• A container has an inside, in which the contained object is visible.
• Containers have boundaries; on the screen, the contained object is moved to a position included within the boundaries of the container object; in a view of the inside of an object, the contained objects are visible within the boundaries of the inside of the container.

Now, in the technological implementation of the blended space of the containment blend, we see what appears in figure 7.8.

The small object is moved (via its phantom) to the position of the large object. Both objects are *selected* (colored), the small object first during "motion," and the large object later, when the phantom has made substantial contact with it.

When the tip of the arrow is within the boundaries of the large object, and the mouse is unclicked the two manifestations of the small object (phantom and solid line colored) "disappear." They are no longer seen on the screen (see fig. 7.9).

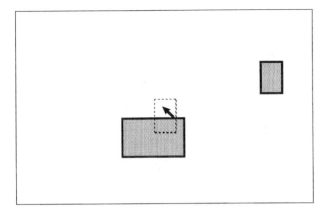

Figure 7.8
The small object is moved (via its phantom) to the position of the large object.
Both objects are *selected* (colored), the small object first during "motion", and
the large object later, when the phantom has made substantial contact with it.

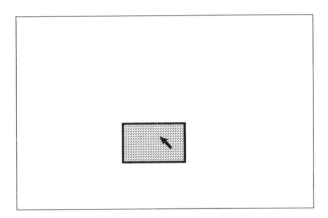

Figure 7.9
Object has been "moved into" the "container", and the mouse is released.

This sequence of motion, overlapping portions of space, and nonvisibility corresponds in obvious ways to the sequence in three-dimensional space of moving objects into containers. But again, there are glaring discrepancies, such as the double manifestation of the contained object, the disappearance of the stationary counterpart of the contained object without an intervening path into the container, and the fact that this happens when the phantom is not yet entirely occluded by the container object.

Double-clicking on the container will yield access to the "inside." But in the interface, this inside is typically a much larger object (a window). The contained object does show up within the boundaries of this "inside."[6] The smaller "outside" of the container coexists on the screen with the much larger "inside." The single object in the familiar three-dimensional domain of containment is mapped onto two distinct screen "objects," which both show up in the interface. The interface corresponds to the new blended space. In that space, the conceptual notions of single object, inside, and outside are projected from ordinary containment, while the actual perceptual array is projected from a screen input with two distinct objects of very different sizes (see figs. 7.10 and 7.11).

There are many other details that I will skip here. The main point is that in some crucial respects, the topologies of the two input spaces do

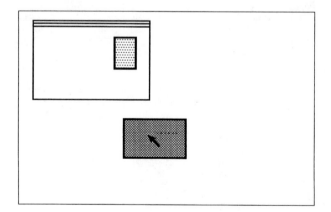

Figure 7.10
Opening the container and viewing its contents.

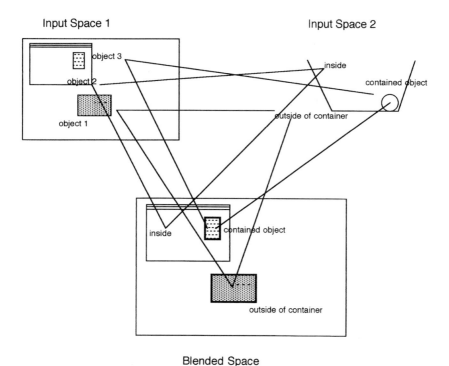

Figure 7.11
Some connections in the containment blend.

not match, and yet the blended space is easily constructed and its peculiar emergent structure is conceived by the user effortlessly as containment, opening, moving into and out of. The conceptual structure of ordinary containment is projected to the blend, in spite of the topological mismatches. The important thing for present purposes is that the understanding of the interface in terms of the familiar notion of containers is not achieved by simply projecting a schema from one domain onto another.

Conclusion

A fundamental component of analogical reasoning and of metaphorical conceptualization is undoubtedly the partial mapping of a source to a target and the transfer of inferences and structure that it creates. These are mappings from one mental space to another, and much of the power of analogy and metaphor stems from the fact that the source and target mental spaces may belong to superficially very different conceptual domains. Such cross-space mappings, however, are not restricted to analogy in the usual sense. They play a more general and central role in meaning construction and discourse management, where we find mental space mappings operating routinely in phenomena such as reference, tense and mood, counterfactuals, or fictive motion.

In particular, we find that a general operation of conceptual blending is at work in many linguistic and nonlinguistic situations and makes extensive use of cross-space mappings. The most remarkable character-istic of this cognitive operation is the creation of novel blended spaces with emergent structure that is grounded by connections to preexisting, more familiar input spaces. What is achieved in conceptual integration networks in addition to structure and inference transfer is the coherent, integrated, constitution of novel forms of thought and action. In this chapter, I have focused attention on the emergence of such integration. The example of the mouse-driven interface was discussed at length in order to bring out the remarkable human capacity for building novel conceptual/physical domains. When viewed in terms of objective prop-erties of the physical world, mouse manipulation and screen illumina-tion have precious little in common with the grasping and moving of three-dimensional objects. The possibility of building cross-space map-pings between extremely partial aspects of the domains depends heavily on properties made salient only by our own cognitive system and ex-perience in the world (visibility, containment, correlation of visual and motor activities). Such mappings, as explained earlier, are extremely partial and can be imperfect in many respects (topological and ontolog-ical violations). And yet they give rise to very smooth integrations, through successive blending. In the example, we saw how the notion of "object" could be brought into the interface, then "motion," then con-trolled motion, grasping, and then containment, "putting in," "taking out," and so on. The integration was not the simple product of ordinary analogy for two important reasons: (1) there are many discrepancies and mismatches in the mappings that associate the inputs; (2) the blended space has a dynamic, coherent, life of its own that is integrated and autonomous in ways that a mere alignment between structures is not. This should correspond to the configuration of genuinely novel neural patterns and dynamics as opposed to simple binding of old patterns.

Appendix: Examples of Conceptual Blends

The Debate with Kant (Rhetoric)

A philosophy teacher presents his ideas to the class in the following way: "I claim that reason is a self-developing capacity. Kant disagrees with me on this point. He says it's innate, but I answer that that's begging the question, to which he counters, in *Critique of Pure Reason*, that only innate ideas have power. But I say to that, what about neuronal group selection? And he gives no answer." (mirror network; from Fauconnier and Turner 1996)

The Buddhist Monk (Reasoning)

Riddle of the Buddhist monk and the mountain: A Buddhist monk begins walking up a mountain at dawn one day, reaches the top at sunset, meditates at the top for several days until one dawn he begins to walk back to the foot of the mountain, which he reaches at sunset. Making no assumptions about his starting or stopping or about his pace during the trips, prove that there is a place on the path that he occupies at the same hour of the day on the two separate journeys. (mirror network; from Fauconnier and Turner 1998)

Action Blends

I'm driving, and someone is sitting in the front passenger seat, talking to me, but I have trouble hearing what they say. I turn the volume knob on the car radio (which is off, of course). I've blended the frames for listening to the radio and for conversing with a passenger. (double-scope network; from Fauconnier and Turner 1994)

Trashcan Basketball

Children in a dormitory inventing a game, based on basketball, in which you must throw a crumpled-up sheet of paper into a wastepaper basket. One input is partial knowledge of basketball, the other input is the trash disposal situation with crumpled paper, a wastepaper basket, and so on. The partial mental mapping relates a ball to crumpled paper, a basketball basket to a wastepaper basket, players to children. In the new game, as defined by the blend, some properties are projected from the "basketball" input (scoring points when the ball falls into the basket, opponents in a game, winning and losing, etc.), some properties are projected from the "trash disposal" input (the basket is on the floor, not high up in the air, the ball has specific properties of crumpled paper, etc.), and some properties are shared by the two inputs (throwing a projectile into a receptacle). Many other properties of the game will emerge from affordances of the context (particular ways of throwing, conventions for scoring, fouls, etc.). (double-scope network; from Coulson 2001)

Science

The substance here treated of does not possess any of the properties of ordinary fluids except that of freedom of motion. It is not even a hypothetical fluid which is introduced to explain actual phenomena. It is simply a collection of imaginary properties, which may be employed for establishing certain theorems in pure mathematics in a way more intelligible to ordinary minds than that in which algebraic symbols are used. The use of the word *fluid* will not lead us into error if we remember that it simply denotes an imaginary substance with the properties.
[*Maxwell 1855*—Electricity, Heat, Magnetism, Galvanism]
(*from work by Jeff Lansing*)
Several scientists insisted that the term *virus* is more than a nice metaphor. . . . Although computer viruses are not fully alive, they embody many of the char-acteristics of life, and it is not hard to imagine computer viruses of the future that will be just as alive as biological viruses.
(*New York Times*, 2/25/90)
Complex numbers: cross-space mapping maps real numbers to one-dimensional space, maps "imaginary" numbers to two-dimensional space (Wallis). In the blend, numbers have number properties (addition, multiplication, square roots, etc.), vector properties (angle, magnitude), and point properties (coordinates). Angles come only from "spatial" input. Multiplication comes only from "number" input. In the blend, multiplication includes addition of angles (emer-gent structure).
(from Fauconnier and Turner 1998)

Metaphor

Boxing business competitors: Rupert Murdoch knocked out Iacocca. (*single-scope*)

George Bush was born on third base and thinks he hit a triple. (*double-scope*)

Dan Quayle was born on third base and thinks he kicked a field goal. (*multiple*)

The stork dropped George Bush on third base with a silver spoon in his mouth. (*multiple blend*)

Max is digging his own grave. (*conventional double-scope, with projected organizing frame*)

He's driving his mother into her grave. (*double-scope*; example provided by G. Lakoff)

The U.S. is in a position to exhume itself from the shallow grave that we've dug for ourselves. (*innovative complex double-scope*; from Coulson 2001)

Elmer was so angry, the smoke was coming out of his ears. (*double-scope*; G. Lakoff)

Bertran de Born

[Context: In the Inferno (canto 28, lines 139–142), Dante presents Bertran de Born, who while living had instigated strife between the king of England and the king's son. In hell, Bertran carries his head in his hand, and says:]

Perch'io parti' così giunte persone,	Because I parted people so joined,
partito porto il meo cerebro, lasso!	I carry my brain, alas, separated
dal suo principio ch'è in questo toncone.	from its root, which is in this trunk.
Così s'osserva in me lo contrapasso.	Thus is to be seen in me the retribution.

"So foul a sky clears not without a storm. Pour down thy weather."

[*Context: King John speaks to a troubled-looking (and perhaps tongue-tied) messenger who appears before him. Shakespeare*, King John, *act 4, scene 2, lines 108–109.*]

(examples from Turner 1996)

Analogical Counterfactuals

In France, Watergate would not have harmed Nixon.

"Why punish me for the sins of my father?" (*Coulson 2000—abortion rhetoric*)

"If I were his wife, I would have been his widow long ago." (*N. Mandelblit*)

If I were you, I wouldn't get pregnant.

Philosopher in a coma: A woman, who had been in a coma for ten years, was raped by a hospital employee and gave birth to a child. A debate ensued concerning whether the pregnancy should have been terminated. The *Los Angeles Times* article reporting the case ended with a comment by law professor Goldberg. She said, "Even if everyone agrees she [the comatose woman] was pro-life at 19, she is now 29 and has lived in PVS [persistent vegetative state] for ten years. Do we ask: 'Was she pro-life?' Or do we ask more appropriately: 'Would she be pro-life as a rape victim in a persistent vegetative state at 29 years of life?'" In the blend, the woman is in a persistent vegetative state, but has the reasoning capacities and general information that she would have had at age 29 under ordinary circumstances.

Multiple Blends

"What President Clinton did, bravely and brilliantly, I think, was to gamble that the repertory actors of the health care industry have frightened Americans so badly that we are willing to accept anything, including higher taxes, rather than to continue being extras in a medical melodrama that resembles nothing so much as an endless "Dracula" movie where the count always wins, right up to the last drop." [Written by Richard Reeves, in a *Los Angeles Times* article titled "Best Performance by a Politician."] (*example discovered by Bill Gleim*)

Humor

Menendez Brothers Virus: Eliminates your files, takes the disk space they previously occupied, and then claims that it was a victim of physical and sexual abuse on the part of the files it erased. (*Coulson 1996*)

Jay Leno on Sidney Biddle Barrows's new job as "expert" commentator for the Heidi Fleiss trial at one of the cable channels:
Instead of hiring a legal expert, they got a woman who made her name as a madam. They figured it's a few bucks cheaper, and she essentially does the same thing.

Why God won't get tenure
1. Only published one book.
2. It was in Hebrew.
3. It had no references.
4. He did not publish it in referenced journals.
5. Some doubt He even wrote it Himself.
6. He is not known for His cooperative work.
7. Sure, He created the world, but what has He done lately?
8. He did not get permission from any review board to work with human 9.
9. When one experiment went awry, He tried to cover it up by drowning all the subjects.
10. When sample subjects do not behave as predicted, He deletes the whole sample.
11. He rarely comes to class—just tells His students to read the Book.
12. It is rumored that He sometimes lets His Son teach the class.
13. Although He only has 10 requirements, His students often fail His tests.
14. He expelled His first two students for learning.
15. His office hours were infrequent and usually held on a mountain top. subjects.

Notes

1. A detailed bibliography of work on these topics can be found on the blending Web site at http://www.wam.umd.edu/~mturn/WWW/blending.html
2. This example is discussed briefly in Fauconnier (1998).

3. The example is analyzed in Turner and Fauconnier (1999).

4. More precisely, what is projected is the varying degree of confidence and investment.

5. I borrow this term from Len Talmy to indicate that perception and conception are both involved (with no necessary clear separation between the two).

6. As Boicho Kokinov notes, the problem here is not with the change of size per se, since we experience that in everyday life all the time through perspective effects (zooming in and zooming out). The mismatch (inconsequential in the construction of an integrated activity) comes from instantaneity of the change (on the screen, by clicking) and the resulting simultaneous presence on the screen of two objects of very different size which are in fact the same object (the inside and the outside). That ubiquity, disparity, and simultaneous view from incompatible points of view is of course not part of our everyday experience of containers.

References

Coulson, S. (1996). Menendez brothers virus: Blended spaces and internet humor. In Adele Goldberg, Ed., *Conceptual structure, discourse, and language*, pp. 67–82. Stanford: Center for the Study of Language and Information.

Coulson, S. (2001). *Semantic leaps: Frame-shifting and conceptual blending in Meaning Construction*. New York: Cambridge University Press.

Fauconnier, G. (1997). *Mappings in thought and language*. New York: Cambridge University Press.

Fauconnier, G. (1998). Mental spaces, language modalities, and conceptual integration. In M. Tomasello, Ed., *The new psychology of language: Cognitive and functional approaches to language structure*, pp. 251–279. Mahwah, NJ: Erlbaum.

Fauconnier, G., and Turner, M. (1994). Conceptual projection and middle spaces. Department of Cognitive Science Technical Report 9401, University of California at San Diego. [Available online from http://cogsci.ucsd.edu and http://www.wam.umd.edu/~mturn]

Fauconnier, G., and Turner, M. (1996). Blending as a central process of grammar. In Adele Goldberg, Ed., *Conceptual structure, discourse, and language*, pp. 113–129. Stanford: Center for the Study of Language and Information.

Fauconnier, G., and Turner, M. (1998). Conceptual integration networks. *Cognitive Science* 22(2):133–187.

Fauconnier, G., and Turner, M. (in preparation). *The Way We Think*.

Freeman, M. (1997). Grounded spaces: Deictic-self anaphors in the poetry of Emily Dickinson. *Language and Literature* 6(1):7–28.

Freeman, M. (in preparation). "Mak[ing] new stock from the salt": Poetic metaphor as conceptual blend in Sylvia Plath's "The Applicant."

Gentner, D. (1983). Structure-mapping: A theoretical framework for analogy. *Cognitive Science* 7:155–170.

Gick, M., and Holyoak, K. (1983). Schema induction and analogical transfer. *Cognitive Psychology* 15:1–38.

Goguen, J. (1998). An introduction to algebraic semiotics, with application to user interface design. In C. Nehanive, Ed., *Computation for metaphors, analogy, and agents*, pp. 242–291. Berlin: Springer-Verlag.

Hofstadter, D. 1985. Analogies and roles in human and machine thinking. In *Metamagical themas*. New York: Bantam.

Hofstadter, D., and the Fluid Analogies Research Group (1995). *Fluid concepts and creative analogies*. New York: Basic Books.

Holyoak, K. J., and Thagard, P. (1994). *Mental leaps: Analogy in creative thought*. Cambridge, MA: MIT Press.

Lakoff, G., and Johnson, M. (1980). *Metaphors we live by*. Chicago: University of Chicago Press.

Lakoff, G., and Núñez, R. (2000). *Where mathematics comes from: How the embodied mind brings mathematics into being*. New York: Basic Books.

Liddell, S. (1998). Grounded blends, gestures, and conceptual shifts. *Cognitive Linguistics* 9(3):283–314.

Mandelblit, N. (1997). *Grammatical blending: Creative and schematic aspects in sentence processing and translation*. Ph.D. dissertation, University of California at San Diego.

Markman, A. (1997). Constraints on analogical inference. *Cognitive Science* 21(4):373–418.

Oakley, T. (1998). Conceptual blending, narrative discourse, and rhetoric. *Cognitive Linguistics* 9(4):321–360.

Robert, A. (1998). Blending and other conceptual operations in the interpretation of mathematical proofs. In Jean-Pierre Koenig, Ed., *Discourse and cognition*, pp. 337–350. Stanford: Center for the Study of Language and Information.

Sweetser, E. (1999). Compositionality and blending: Semantic composition in a cognitively realistic framework. In G. Redeker and T. Jansen, Eds., Cognitive linguistics: Foundations, scope, and methodology, pp. 129–162. Hawthorne, NY: Mouton de Gruyter.

Turner, M. (1996). *The literary mind*. New York: Oxford University Press.

Turner, M., and Fauconnier, G. (1999). Life on Mars: Language and the instruments of invention. In R. Wheeler, Ed., *The workings of language*. New York: Praeger.

Veale, T. (1996). Pastiche: A metaphor-centred computational model of conceptual blending, with special reference to cinematic borrowing. Manuscript.

Veale, T. (1998). Pragmatic forces in metaphor use: the mechanics of blend recruitment in visual metaphors. In C. Nehanive, Ed., *Computation for metaphors, analogy, and agents*, pp. 37–51. Berlin: Springer-Verlag.

Zbikowski, L. (1999). The blossoms of 'Trockne Blumen': Music and text in the early nineteenth century. *Music Analysis* 18(3):307–345.

8

Setting Limits on Analogy: Why Conceptual Combination Is Not Structural Alignment

Mark T. Keane and Fintan Costello

There is an emerging view that analogy, or more precisely structure-mapping or structural alignment, is a fundamental mechanism at the heart of many different cognitive processes.[1] Apart from being implicated in analogical thinking, it has been proposed that mechanisms of structural alignment and analogy lie behind phenomena such as metaphor, similarity, and conceptual combination (see fig. 8.1). Our premise in this chapter is somewhat cheeky in the context of a book on analogy: we argue that one particular phenomenon, namely conceptual combination, is not based on analogy and cannot be explained by mechanisms such as structural alignment. In a sense, our aim is to "burst the bubble" of a grand unified theory of thought and language based on structural alignment and analogy. Although structural alignment can account for results in a number of different domains, it is not a universal theory: in particular, there are a number of results in conceptual combination which it is unable to explain.

There are several reasons for thinking that conceptual combination and analogy via structural alignment are two quite separate processes. The interpretation of a concept combination (e.g., *soccer mom, river chair, Republican Party reptile*) is generally a rapid, "once off" task: people encounter a new compound, interpret it quickly, and move on. Indeed, combinations are so common that they have to be processed in this way. Analogy, on the other hand, appears to be a more considered process. Analogies tend to be extended over time: an analogy can be returned to again and again to elaborate further inferences from it (under time constraints in comparison judgments people avoid the full rigor of

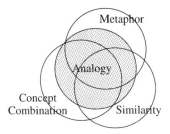

Figure 8.1
How different phenomena might overlap and be explained by a unifying analogy mechanism like structural alignment.

analogical processing; e.g., Goldstone and Medin 1994). Further, compound phrases and analogies serve different functions in language: compounds are names that identify a category, whereas analogies are descriptions rather than names. Compound phrases can have alternate meanings which analogies may not have (a *jail job* could be a prison warder's or police officer's job, or it could be a job which is like a jail; the analogy "my job is like a jail" could not literally mean "I work as a prison warder"). Analogies seem more productive than conceptual combinations: the analogy "my job is like a jail" licenses the structural mapping "my computer is like a pair of handcuffs," but the combination *jail job* does not license a new combination such as *handcuff computer*. The pragmatic context in which compound phrases are used is quite circumscribed: they are used to convey information in a compact fashion that is concise yet comprehensible. In contrast, the pragmatic contexts in which analogies are used are hugely diverse (e.g., problem-solving, learning, argumentation, illustration). Finally, we have found many specific empirical reasons for thinking that conceptual combination does not involve analogy or structural alignment. At the risk of being the "specters" at the analogy feast, we present the alternative argument that has been forced upon us by the results of our research.

Structural Alignment as a Unifying Principle

Originally proposed as a mechanism underlying analogy, the tenets of structural alignment have been well supported by empirical work on analogy (see e.g., Clement and Gentner 1991; Gentner 1983; Gentner and Toupin 1986; Gick and Holyoak 1980, 1983; Keane 1985, 1988, 1996, 1997; Keane, Ledgeway, and Duff 1994; Markman 1997; Spellman and Holyoak 1997). *Structural alignment* is a process that matches the relational structure of two domains of knowledge (e.g., concepts or stories) guided by the systematicity principle (Gentner 1983). Although the idea has been restated in a number of different ways since its inception, its three main components are (1) *one-to-one correspondence*, which proposes that the comparison process is one that maintains an isomorphism between elements of both domains, (2) *parallel connectivity*, that if two statements are matched then their arguments should be placed in correspondence, too, and (3) *systematicity*, that larger systems of shared matches are preferred over smaller systems of matches or fragmented, isolated matches (most commonly cast as the *systematicity principle*). This theoretical specification of structural alignment has been implemented in many different algorithms; including, the structure-mapping engine (Falkenhainer, Forbus, and Gentner 1986, 1989; Forbus and Oblinger 1990; Forbus, Ferguson, and Gentner 1994), the incremental analogy machine (Keane 1990, 1997; Keane and Brayshaw 1988; Keane, Ledgeway, and Duff 1994), Sapper (Veale and Keane 1994, 1997, 1998a, 1998b), ACME (Holyoak and Thagard 1989, 1995), and LISA (Hummel and Holyoak 1992, 1997). Even though all of these models characterize the process of analogizing in slightly different ways, they are all still algorithmic variations on the computational-level theme of structural alignment (see Keane, Ledgeway, and Duff 1994; Veale and Keane 1998b).

In recent years, the reach of structure-mapping as an explanatory construct has extended beyond its home territory of analogy to metaphor, similarity and conceptual combination. *Metaphor*, given its closeness to analogy, has quite naturally been proposed to be a phenomenon that also involves structural alignment (see e.g., Gentner 1982; Gentner and Clement 1988; Gentner and Wolff 1998; Veale and Keane 1994, 1997). For instance, Gentner and Wolff (1998) have shown, using a priming technique, that the time course of metaphor comprehension is most consistent with accounts in which the conceptual domains are aligned before candidate inferences are made; although, they point out that this process may only be used to understand novel metaphors, with conventional metaphors being dealt with differently. Also, in a computational vein, Veale and Keane (1997) have argued that noun-noun metaphors (like "Surgeons are butchers") can be characterized as structure-mapping within a semantic network of connected concepts.

Similarity can also be characterized as structural alignment (see, e.g., Goldstone 1994; Goldstone and Medin 1994; Markman and Gentner 1993a, 1993b; Markman and Wisniewski 1997). Markman and Gentner (1993b) used pictures with cross-mappings; that is, pairs of pictures in which perceptually similar objects played different roles in like relational structures. Although controls indicated the perceptually similar object match to a target match when questioned immediately, the experimental group were more likely to override this perceptual choice and map the object using relational roles, after they had been asked to rate the similarity of both pictures (but see Davenport and Keane 1999). That is, the similarity comparisons appeared to promote a structural alignment of both pictures. It should be pointed out that Medin, Goldstone, and Gentner (1993) take a pluralistic view on similarity; arguing that it may be computed in many different ways but that one of the important ways is through structural alignment. This view is supported by response-time studies that show that under time pressures the perceptual attributes of stimuli take precedence in similarity judgements but that, with more time, the alignment of relational structures has a greater impact (see Goldstone and Medin 1994).

Conceptual combination is, perhaps, the most recent area in which structural alignment has been proposed to play a role (Wisniewski 1996, 1997a, 1997b; Wisniewski and Gentner 1991; Wisniewski and Love 1998; Wisniewski and Markman 1993). Conceptual combination is the process that enables people to interpret novel combinations like *horse bird, river chair, Republican Party reptile* and so on. From one perspective, concept combinations can be viewed as a microcosm of language generativity; as one instance of people's amazing ability to extract meaning from collections of words they have never seen combined before. It is also a process that plays an important role in language change; Cannon (1987) reports that 55 percent of entries in a corpus of new words are compounds of existing words. The work we examine is limited to noun-noun combinations rather than the many other syntactic possibilities for combination. As we shall see, people can produce many different interpretations to these word pairs, the key analogy proposal being that some of these interpretations are produced by a structural-alignment process.

For the most part, we would defend the use of structure-mapping in the context of analogy, metaphor and similarity. However, we believe that it is inappropriate to extend this account to conceptual combination.[2] Our argument is laid out in the remainder of the paper. First, we outline some of the empirical aspects of conceptual combination that have to be handled by any adequate theory. Second, we describe the dual-process theory, the theory that uses structural alignment, in some detail. Third, we propose an alternative account called the constraint theory. Fourth, we describe some critical evidence favoring the constraint theory over dual-process theory. In conclusion, we consider alternative arguments that may be made against constraint theory from a structure-mapping perspective. Unsurprisingly, perhaps, we consider such alternatives to lack a certain force.

Interpreting Conceptual Combinations

It is possible to get a good feel for what people do when they interpret noun-noun combinations from a series of experiments performed by Costello and Keane (1997) in which participants typically read a novel, noun-noun compound and were asked to say "what the phrase could plausibly mean and if you can think of more than one possible meaning to report them." Given a novel combination like *bed pencil*, for example, participants proposed a variety of interpretations including:

(1) a pencil that you put beside your bed for writing some messages

(2) a special pencil used by a carpenter in making beds

(3) a pencil used to draw patterns on bed-clothes

(4) a pencil shaped like a bed

(5) a place for putting pencils

(6) a thin bed

(7)   a bed made out of pencils

(8)   a big, flat pencil that is a bed for a doll

Even though all of these interpretations were not produced by a single subject, they do give a good feel for the diversity of interpretations produced by people. This diversity has been captured, in part, by two taxonomies for interpretations; using classifications based on types of interpretation and the focus of an interpretation (see, e.g., Gagné and Shoben 1997; Levi 1978; Shoben 1993, for more fine-grained content classifications).

Types of Interpretation

Interpretations can be classified into at least four main types: relational, property-mapping, conjunctive, and known-concept interpretations (see, e.g., Hampton 1987; Murphy 1988; Smith et al. 1988; Wisniewski 1996; Wisniewski and Gentner 1991).

Relational interpretations establish some relationship between the *modifier* concept (i.e., the concept denoted by the first word) and the *head* concept (i.e., the concept denoted by the second word; Cohen and Murphy 1984; Murphy 1988, 1990); in the bed pencil example most of the interpretations explicitly relate the bed and pencil concepts in some way:

(1)   a pencil that you *put beside* your bed for writing some messages

(2)   a special pencil *used by* a carpenter in making beds

(3)   a pencil *used to draw patterns on* bed-clothes

where the main relationships are in italics. This interpretation type is one of the most common, accounting for between 30 percent and 50 percent of interpretations produced (Wisniewski and Gentner 1991).

Property interpretations have a different structure in that they involve a property of one concept being asserted of the other. Wisniewski and Gentner (1991) showed that this type of interpretation is also very common, occurring between 30 percent and 50 percent of the time (see also Costello and Keane 1997, forthcoming; Markman and Wisniewski 1997; Wisniewski 1996; Wisniewski and Markman 1993): Examples for the *bed pencil* case would be:

(4)   a pencil *shaped* like a bed

(6)   a *thin* bed

where the asserted property is in italics. The frequency of property mapping interpretations tends to increase with the similarity of the concepts in the combination (Markman and Wisniewski 1997; Wisniewski and Markman 1993).

Conjunctive or Hybrid Interpretations conjoin both concepts in some way, the interpretation is *both* the modifier-concept and the head-concept (see, e.g., Hampton 1987, 1988). These interpretations include examples like "a colorful fish that is also a pet" for *pet fish*. In the *bed pencil* case, the closest we have to such an interpretation is:

(8)   a big, flat pencil that is a bed for a doll

where the interpretation describes something that is both a *bed* and a *pencil*.

Known-concept interpretations, in which the interpretation of the combination is an existing, known concept; for example, a participant might interpret *horse house* to be a "stable." We do not have an instance of such an interpretation for *bed pencil*, but one was produced to *pencil bed*:

(9)   a pencil-case

Known-concept interpretations have been shown to occur about 10 percent of the time (see Costello 1996; Costello and Keane 1997).

These four categories do not exhaust the range of possible interpretation types which people produce, as there are many variations on these interpretation types, and often interpretations do not fall neatly into one or other of these general categories. At the very least, however, an adequate theory of combination should be able to account for how these four main types of interpretation are produced.

Interpretation Focus
Semantically, one part of an interpretation has privileged status as the focal concept of the interpretation: that is, the concept that the interpretation is about. For example, the focal concept of the interpretation "an *apartment dog* is a small dog which lives in city apartments" is the

concept *dog*; the interpretation is about a dog, not an apartment or a city. In the *bed pencil* case, *pencil* is the focal concept of the following interpretations:

(1)   a *pencil* that you put beside your bed for writing some messages

(2)   a special *pencil* used by a carpenter in making beds

(3)   a *pencil* used to draw patterns on bed-clothes

(4)   a *pencil* shaped like a bed

The focal concept contributes most semantic information to an interpretation, with the other parts of an interpretation limited to modifying one particular aspect of the focal concept. The focal concept identifies the general category of which the combined concept is a member; and is typically the first mentioned in a verbal description of the combined concept. When asked to describe an interpretation, people usually list properties of the focal concept only, and do not mention properties of other parts of the interpretation. For example, when describing their interpretation for the phrase "apartment dog," people might mention attributes such as SMALL, FOUR-LEGGED, or ANIMATE, which belong to the focal concept *dog*, but would not mention attributes such as HAS-BEDROOMS or MADE-OF-BRICK, which might belong to the *apartment* part of the interpretation.

In most interpretations of compound phrases the focal concept is simply the concept named by the head word of the phrase (as in "apartment dog"). Some compounds, however, do not follow this pattern. Exocentric compounds (Bauer 1983) have as their focal concept some concept other than the head, as in the case "a jellybean shovel is a type of *spoon* for dispensing jellybeans." Wisniewski (1996) has identified similar cases, which he terms *construals*. In other interpretations the pattern of focus is reversed, with the focal concept being the modifier of the phrase being interpreted. For example, *bed* can be the focal concept in some interpretations of *bed pencil*:

(6)   a thin *bed*

(7)   a *bed* made out of pencils

While these *focus reversals* are rare they have been found both in experimental investigations of conceptual combination (Costello 1996;

Costello and Keane 1997; Gerrig and Murphy 1992; Wisniewski and Gentner 1991), and in everyday discourse; for instance, in a Disney Chip-and-Dale story in which the phrase "slipper bed" was interpreted as "a slipper in which a chipmunk can sleep." In this interpretation, the modifier "slipper" plays the role of focal concept, contributing most to the new combined concept, best identifying the category in which the combined concept is a member, and being mentioned first in the description. Our view is that the change of focus in exocentric compounds and in focus reversals represent an extension of the usual focal concept (the head) to cover the modifier or some other concept.

The observed variations of interpretation type and focal concept in concept combinations stand as a challenge for theories of conceptual combination. As we shall see, these empirical phenomena have been important targets for structure-mapping accounts of conceptual combination, in the form of dual-process theory, and our own constraint theory.

Dual-Process Theory

Dual-process theory (Wisniewski 1997a, 1997b) proposes that two main mechanisms underlie conceptual combination: structural alignment and scenario construction. Each of these processes is responsible for explaining the different types of interpretation that people produce. Structural alignment is proposed to explain property interpretations where a property from one concept is asserted of the other (e.g., an *elephant fish* is a big fish). It also accounts for conjunctive interpretations in which the interpretation is some combination of the properties of both concepts; for example, a drill screwdriver is two-in-one tool with features of both a drill and a screwdriver. Scenario construction is very like Murphy's (1988; Cohen and Murphy 1984) concept-specialization mechanism and is used to explain relational interpretations (e.g., a night flight is a flight taken at night). We will concentrate on the structural-alignment mechanism here inasmuch as it is our main concern.

The structural alignment process is essentially analogical structure-mapping (Gentner 1983; see Keane 1993, for a review). To interpret a given compound phrase the structural alignment process compares the two constituent concepts, and on the basis of that comparison selects an alignable difference to transfer from one concept to the other. When two concepts are compared a number of different relationships can be found between their parts: commonalities (where both slots and values match), alignable differences (where slots match, but values do not) and non-alignable differences (where neither slots nor values match; see figure 8.2). According to dual-process theory, it is the values that are found in alignable differences that are used in property interpretations; for example, "an *elephant fish* is a big fish" is produced by comparing the concepts "elephant" and "fish," noticing that the "elephant" and "fish" share the dimension SIZE but have different values on that dimension, and transferring the alignable difference BIG from "elephant" to "fish." When a single aligned property is selected for transfer, a property interpretation is produced; if multiple properties are transferred, a hybrid interpretation results. The diagnosticity of a property may have a role in choosing between competing alignable differences, if more than one is available (Wisniewski 1997a).

It is important to note that the concept representations used in dual-process theory consist of schemas which can have quite complex internal structures. A representational schema can contain typical properties of a concept. These properties are paired with the dimensions on which they typically occur, giving slot-value structures such as <COLOR, RED>. A representational scenario can be structured in terms of relations between parts, for example, each part being represented in terms of properties and dimensions (a fish could have parts, tail, fins, and so on, with each part having properties of its own on the dimensions shape, color,

	Elephant			Fish		
Commonalities {	class	:	living thing	class	:	living thing
Alignable differences {	size color	: :	big gray	size color	: :	small silver
Nonalignable differences {		:	has trunk			
					:	has fins

Figure 8.2
The different relationships that occur when two concepts are aligned.

and so on). Finally, a representational schema can also contain roles or scenarios, corresponding to verbs describing actions, events, or states.

Empirical Support for Dual-Process Theory

One important prediction made from this alignment mechanism is that property interpretations should increase in frequency when the constituent concepts of a combination are similar (and hence, easy to align). Evidence for structural alignment comes from an observed correlation between alignability, similarity, and the production of property interpretations.

Wisniewski and Markman (1993) have found evidence for the specific use of alignable differences in property interpretations. Participants were asked to produce interpretations for combinations taken from the materials used by Markman and Gentner (1993a). Markman and Gentner (1993a) gathered commonality and (nonalignable and alignable) difference listings for a set of concept pairs that were subsequently used in an interpretation task by Wisniewski and Markman. Wisniewski and Markman found that the property interpretations produced for the concept pairs were more likely to contain properties classified as an alignable difference (78%) than a nonalignable difference (3%).

Markman and Wisniewski (1997) examined the frequency of property interpretations produced for combinations with constituent concepts that systematically differed from one another: basic/basic-same combinations (containing two basic-level concepts from the same superordinate category), basic/basic-different combinations (two basic-level concepts from different superordinates), and super/super combinations (two different superordinate concepts). They found that participants rated the constituent concepts in basic/basic-same combinations as most similar to each other, while the constituent concepts in basic/basic-different or super-super combinations were rated as less similar. Similarly, participants listed more commonalities and alignable differences for basic/basic-same combinations than for basic/basic-different or super/super combinations. Furthermore, when participants produced interpretations for these combinations, they produced more property interpretations for basic/basic-same combinations than for basic/basic-different or super/super combinations. Thus, as the alignability (similarity) of the constituent concepts increases, so too does the rate of property interpretations produced.

Summary

Dual-process theory is a well-developed account that makes several novel and interesting predictions about the interpretation of conceptual combinations, many of which have been confirmed empirically. However, we believe that structural alignment is *not* used in conceptual combination and have advanced an alternative theory that can generate property, relational, conjunctive, and known-concept interpretations using a very different set of mechanisms guided by certain high-level constraints. In the next section, we outline this theory before describing some evidence that supports it.

The Constraint Theory

Constraint theory (Costello 1996; Costello and Keane 1997, 1998a, 1998b, 2000) describes conceptual combination as a process that constructs representations that satisfy the three constraints of diagnosticity, plausibility, and informativeness. These constraints derive from the pragmatics of compound interpretation and use (Grice 1975; see Costello and Keane 2000, for details). In this section we describe these three constraints and the specific algorithm for building representations that satisfy these constraints.

The *diagnosticity constraint* requires the construction of an interpretation containing diagnostic properties from each of the concepts being combined. The diagnostic properties of a concept are those which occur often in instances of that concept and rarely in instances of other concepts (similar to Rosch 1978 on cue validity). Diagnosticity predicts that the interpretation "a cactus fish is a prickly fish" is preferable to "a cactus fish is a green fish" because PRICKLY is more diagnostic of cactus than GREEN. Diagnosticity also identifies the focal concept or central concept which an interpretation is about; the focal concept of an interpretation is defined to be that part of the interpretation that possesses the diagnostic properties of the head noun of the phrase being interpreted.

The *plausibility constraint* requires the construction of an interpretation containing semantic elements that are already known to co-occur on the basis of past experience. The plausibility constraint ensures that interpretations describe an object (or collection of objects) that could plausibly exist. Plausibility would predict that the interpretation "an *angel pig* is a pig with wings on its torso" would be preferable to "an *angel pig* is a pig with wings on its tail," because prior experience suggests that wings are typically attached to the center of gravity of an object (see also Downing 1977).

The *informativeness constraint* requires the construction of an interpretation which conveys a requisite amount of new information. Informativeness excludes feasible interpretations that do not communicate anything new relative to either constituent concept; for example, "a *pencil bed* is a bed made of wood" is a feasible interpretation for "pencil bed" but none of the participants in our studies presented with this compound has ever produced it as an interpretation (see Costello and Keane 1997). Together these three constraints account for the range of different combination types that have been observed: each combination type represents a different way of satisfying the constraints.

Representationally, like dual-process theory, constraint theory uses schemas with complex internal structures, containing attributes, relations and roles. However, unlike dual-process theory, constraint theory assumes that the combination process has access to a wide range of heterogeneous knowledge, including prototypes of the concepts being combined, specific instances of those concepts, prototypes and instances of related concepts, general domain theories, and specific event representations involving these and other concepts. In short, constraint theory assumes that, from the beginning of the combination process, there is direct access to many different sources of knowledge. This position is to be contrasted with that of dual-process theory; namely, that the combination process is initially limited to summary, prototype information, with other types of knowledge only being used to elaborate a combined concept initially constructed from these prototypes (a position originally espoused in Murphy's [1988] concept-specialization theory).

The C³ Model

The preceding description of constraint theory is a computational level description that has been elaborated in a clear formulaic fashion (see Costello and Keane 2000). The theory has also been specified in a running computational model, the C³ model (Constraints on Conceptual Combination). The C³ model uses constraint-satisfaction techniques to efficiently sift through a range of possible interpretations for a given phrase to find the best interpretation. The model performs a constrained search of the space of possible interpretations. This search ends when the best interpretation for the phrase in question has been found. At each stage of the search, possible interpretations are constructed by first putting diagnostic properties of the combining concepts together in various different ways, to produce a partial interpretation (the exact mechanism forms subsets of selected predicates using a type of unification). Further plausible properties and relations from diverse knowledge sources are added to those partial interpretations in a controlled fashion to produce full interpretations (see Costello and Keane 2000, for more details). The mechanism proposed by the model is significant because it deals with the inherent intractability of the task of combining two complex concept descriptions.

Empirical Support for Constraint Theory

Empirical support for constraint theory comes from analyses of the rates of different interpretation-types produced to combinations involving constituents of different classes (e.g., artifacts, natural kinds, superordinates, and basic-level concepts; see Costello and Keane 1997, forthcoming). The theory also makes novel predictions about the frequency of property interpretations in so-called *focus reversal* interpretations; for instance, "a *chair ladder* is a chair that is by necessity used as a ladder" (see also Gerrig and Murphy 1992; Wisniewski and Gentner 1991). In constraint theory, the focal concept of an interpretation is identified by the diagnostic properties of the head concept of the phrase being interpreted. Therefore, the theory predicts that focus reversals should involve the diagnostic properties of the head being applied to the modifier; in short, that focus reversals will be property interpretations. Costello and Keane (1997) have found that this is indeed the case, that while property interpretations were in general less frequent (around 30%) than relational interpretations (around 50%), for focus reversals this pattern was reversed: around 50 percent of them were property-mappings, with only 30 percent being relational interpretations (see also Costello and Keane 1998b)

Evidence Against Structural Alignment

Both the dual-process theory and constraint theory speak to a common corpus of empirical evidence, and each makes its own predictions about certain novel phenomena. The difficulty is in finding evidence that decides between the two theories. We have recently completed just such a study (see Costello and Keane 1998, forthcoming). This study presents some difficulties for dual-process theory.

Costello and Keane's (1998, forthcoming) study examined people's comprehension and production of property interpretations that were systematically varied in terms of their alignability and diagnosticity. In a judgment experiment, participants were asked to rate the goodness of a set of property interpretations to noun-noun compounds varied in terms of their alignability and diagnosticity. For the novel combination "bumblebee moth," for example, participants received the following four possible interpretations:

Bumblebee moths are:

moths that are black and yellow   (aligned diagnostic)

moths that are the size of a bumblebee   (aligned nondiagnostic)

moths that sting   (nonaligned diagnostic)

moths that fertilize plants   (nonaligned nondiagnostic)

Participants then rated the goodness of these meanings for the combination, using a seven-point scale (from −3 to +3). The interpretations used in this main experiment were constructed based on analyses from two pre-test experiments. In pre-test 1, alignable and nonalignable differences for the concepts in each noun-noun phrase were gathered (using Markman and Wisniewski's [1997] methodology). In pre-test 2, the diagnosticity of these selected alignable and nonalignable properties were determined in a rating study. The results showed that people prefer property interpretations using nonalignable properties (if they are diagnostic) to alignable differences (if they are not diagnostic; see figure 8.3). Notably, this experiment clearly shows that diagnostic, nonalignable properties support good property interpretations. This structural alignment account predicts that alignable properties will always be preferred.[3]

One reasonable objection to this study is that it involves the rating of experimenter-produced interpretations rather than the production of interpretations to presented combinations. However, Costello and Keane (forthcoming) have also shown that this dominance of diagnosticity over alignability also holds for a production experiment (see figure 8.3b). So, when participants are given the combinations from the comprehension study (e.g., bumblebee moth) and asked to generate an interpretation for them, they tend to produce property interpretations based on diagnostic properties rather than nondiagnostic ones and to avoid using properties that are alignable per se. This study constitutes strong evidence against the dual-process theory, while being quite supportive of constraint theory.

Counterarguments from the Structure-Mapping School

Thus far we have presented dual-process theory's structural-alignment account of conceptual combination, our alternative constraint theory and some empirical evidence that attempts to test them in a competitive fashion. Naturally, we would argue that the weight of the evidence suggests that structural alignment is not implicated in the combination process. But, what might be the counter from the structure-mapping perspective? A number of empirical and theoretical counterpoints suggest themselves.

Constraint Theory Is Empirically Deficient, Too

One possible empirical argument, which incidentally does not refute the preceding findings, is that constraint theory fails to deal with the structural-alignment predictions found in other studies (Markman and Wisniewski 1997; Wisniewski and Markman 1993). Recall that these studies found that (1) people generate more property interpretations for similar (easily alignable) concepts than for dissimilar concepts (less

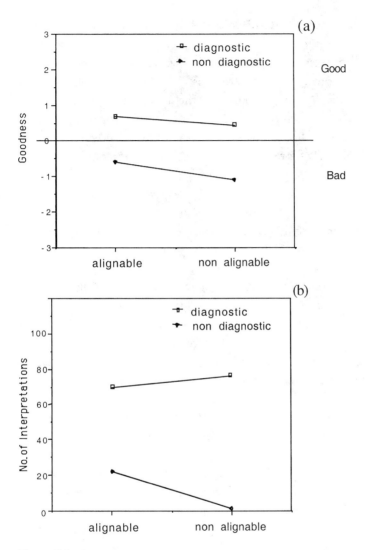

Figure 8.3
The (a) mean goodness ratings for different property interpretations and (b) frequency of production of interpretations (from Costello and Keane forthcoming).

alignable; Markman and Wisniewski 1997); and (2) in a random sample of property interpretations, more alignable differences were used than nonalignable differences (Wisniewski and Markman 1993). We would argue that this contrary evidence to constraint theory is apparent rather than *real*. In the first case, constraint theory has an alternative non-alignment account for the effects of similarity on the frequency of property interpretations. In the second case, the observed predominance of alignable differences may arise because of a failure to control for diagnosticity in the specific materials used.

Similarity and Property Interpretations

The observed correlation between similarity and property interpretations does not necessarily mean that property interpretations are formed by alignment. Constraint theory gives an alternative account, in which the correlation arises as a side effect of the constraints controlling combination. Stated briefly, constraint theory maintains that property interpretations between similar concepts will be more frequent because these interpretations are more likely to meet the plausibility constraint (containing semantic elements that co-occur). A plausible property interpretation is one in which the transferred property "makes sense" relative to the conceptual structure of the target concept. For example, the HAS-POUCH property of *kangaroo* is more plausible when asserted of *monkey* (i.e., "a *kangaroo monkey* is a monkey with a pouch") than it is when asserted of *floor* (i.e., "a *kangaroo floor* is a floor with a pouch") because the conceptual content of *monkey* better allows POUCH to be asserted of it than *floor* does. When concepts are similar, they are more likely to accommodate an asserted property plausibly in this way, hence the increased frequency of property interpretations for similar concepts.

Constraint theory's account of the link between similarity and frequency of property interpretations differs from dual-process theory's account in two important ways. First, dual-process theory proposes a comparison process between the concepts being combined; constraint theory does not. Constraint theory checks to see if the asserted diagnostic property fits plausibly with the target concept without aligning the structure of the two constituent concepts. Second, constraint theory will often allow dissimilar concepts to accommodate a transferred property plausibly. For example, the interpretation "a *kangaroo jacket* is a jacket with a pouch" seems reasonable because the property HAS-POUCH plausibly fits with the concept *jacket*, even though the concepts involved are relatively dissimilar. The observed correlation between similarity and property interpretations could thus arise as a side effect of the requirement to ensure that a property fits plausibly. A good fit is more likely to occur when similar concepts are combined; but it can also happen when specific dissimilar concepts come together.

The Predominance of Alignable Differences

The second apparent conflict is the observed predominance of alignable differences in a random sample of property interpretations (Wisniewski and Markman 1993). We would argue that this effect is an artefact of the materials used, arising because Wisniewski and Markman did not control for diagnosticity. Many of Wisniewski and Markman's materials involved alignable differences that were also the most diagnostic properties for the given concept. For example, one of the materials used is the combination "bluebird robin." Subjectively, it seems likely that the most diagnostic property of the concept *bluebird* would be the property COLORED-BLUE, which also happens to be an alignable difference of the concepts *bluebird* and *robin*. It is not unreasonable to assume that participants would interpret "bluebird robin" as "a robin that is colored blue," thus producing a large number of property interpretations predominantly containing alignable differences. To control for this conflation of alignability and diagnosticity Wisniewski and Markman could have used pairs of combinations where the diagnostic properties were either alignable or nonalignable differences (in a manner reminiscent of Costello and Keane forthcoming). One such pair could be "bluebird robin" (COLORED-BLUE being a diagnostic and alignable property of *bluebird*) and "cuckoo robin" (LAYS-EGGS-IN-OTHER-NESTS being a diagnostic and nonalignable property of *cuckoo*). We would predict that for the diagnostic and alignable combination (i.e., "bluebird robin") people would produce property interpretations with alignable differences ("a *bluebird robin* is a robin that is colored blue"); for the diagnostic and nonalignable combination (i.e., "cuckoo robin") people would produce property interpretations with nonalignable differences ("a *cuckoo robin* is a robin that lays its eggs in other birds' nests"). The observed predominance of alignable differences in property interpretations would then disappear.

Hence, the two empirical objections to constraint theory from the structural-alignment camp do not stand up to scrutiny. They can either be accounted for by constraint theory as it stands (but in a different way) or are due to confounds in the materials that, when resolved, would produce different results. Indeed, Costello and Keane's (forthcoming) study provides strong evidence that, when the confounds *are* resolved, the findings do not favor an alignment account.

The Plausibility Constraint Is Structural Alignment in Disguise
There is also a more subtle theoretical counterpoint that hinges on accepting constraint theory but reinterpreting one of its constraints as being structural alignment. One might accept that the overall mechanism for conceptual combination is not structural alignment (as proposed in the dual-process theory) but rather that some other subprocess of constraint theory is indeed structure-mapping. The most likely candidate for this treatment would be the plausibility component: The argument being that the plausibility of different candidate interpretations is established by structurally aligning its concepts in memory (Markman, personal communication).

We view this as an intriguing idea which is certainly theoretically feasible. However, we would point out that the C^3 model does not compute plausibility in this fashion; rather it selects predicates incrementally from concepts in memory, adding them to an interpretation incrementally, and assessing the plausibility of that interpretation by determining the co-oc-currence of these predicates in existing concepts. At no point does the model structurally align the interpretation and the concepts in memory. Of course, the model does match relational structure when it determines plausibility (as some of the predicates are relational predicates) but the mere matching of relational structure is not itself equivalent to structure-mapping.

Conclusions

Grand unified theories are very attractive. We would had preferred to present a chapter in this book that showed that, yet again, structure-mapping carried the day; that conceptual combination and all of its attendant phenomena could be accounted for by analogical mechanisms. Unfortunately, our conclusion is that this is unwarranted.

If there is a unification between analogy and concept combination it should be sought among the higher-level constraints of the two phenomena (see Keane, Ledgeway, and Duff 1994 on the meta-theoretical analysis of analogy). Currently, there is a recognized set of constraints that shape analogy (i.e., structural, similarity, and pragmatic constraints) and another set of constraints that shape conceptual combination (i.e., diagnosticity, plausibility, and informativeness constraints). It may indeed be the case that the phenomena share some constraints but differ in others. Analogy may be a phenomenon that is especially sensitive to structural constraints, whereas other phenomena like conceptual combination are shaped more by constraints that reflect aspects of the nature of knowledge in memory (like diagnosticity, plausibility, and informativeness). We believe that this constraint satisfaction view is, potentially, a more productive perspective unifying these diverse phenomena.

For instance, it allows one to turn the present argument on its head, to ask "Do the constraints that are active in concept combination help to explain aspects of analogy?" One possible contact point is in area of plausibility; evidence suggests that in the adaptation of analogies plausibility may play a critical role (see Keane 1990, 1996). Keane (1996) found that inferences made by analogy are more easily found if they are plausible; that is, if they "make sense" in the context of known experience. This suggests a whole host of analogy effects based on making candidate inferences in familiar as opposed to unfamiliar domains (Keane 1990). The diagnosticity constraint should also play some role in analogical mapping. One of the key issues in analogy is what drives the selection of information in a base domain. Models like IAM and LISA can exploit structural and pragmatic characteristics of the base domain, to select some piece of knowledge over another (see Keane 1997; Kubose, Holyoak, and Hummel 1998). Diagnostic aspects of a base domain may also play an important selective role, highlighting some parts of a domain over others for mapping purposes.

We believe that such considerations could be very productive for the field of analogy. So, rather than be specters at the analogy feast, we would like to be viewed as princes in disguise who bring rare treats from far-off lands.

Notes

1. Throughout, we use structure-mapping and structural alignment interchangeably.

2. There are circumstances under which analogy is certainly used to interpret combinations; for instance, it is hard to explain how Irangate could be interpreted without using Watergate by analogy (see Shoben 1989; Thagard 1997). However, this type of interpretation is uncommon and cannot account for most of the interpretations normally produced.

3. The tendency for alignable interpretations to be rated better than nonalignable ones in figure 8.3 is not reliable, as it is a materials-only effect that appears to be due to a confound with plausibility (see Costello and Keane 1998b for details).

References

Bauer, L. (1983). *English word formation*. Cambridge: Cambridge University Press.

Cannon, G. (1987). *Historical change and English word-formation*. New York: Lang.

Clement, C. A., and Gentner, D. (1991). Systematicity as a selection constraint in analogical mapping. *Cognitive Science* 15:89–132.

Cohen, B., and Murphy, G. L. (1984). Models of concepts. *Cognitive Science* 8:27–58.

Costello, F. J. (1996). *Noun-noun conceptual combination: The polysemy of compound phrases*. Ph.D. dissertation, University of Dublin.

Costello, F. J., and Keane, M. T. (1997). Polysemy in conceptual combination: Testing the constraint theory of combination. In *Proceedings of the nineteenth annual conference of the Cognitive Science Society*, pp. 137–142. Hillsdale, NJ: Erlbaum.

Costello, F. J., and Keane, M. T. (1998). Alignment versus diagnosticity in conceptual combination. Seventh Irish Conference on AI and Cognitive Science. University College, Dublin, Ireland.

Costello, F. J., and Keane, M. T. (2000). Efficient creativity: Constraints on conceptual combination. *Cognitive Science* 24:299–349.

Costello, F. J., and Keane, M. T. (forthcoming). Testing two theories of conceptual combination: Alignment versus diagnosticity in the comprehension and production of combined concepts. *Journal of Experimental Psychology: Learning, Memory, and Cognition*.

Davenport, J., and Keane, M. T. (1999). Similarity and structural alignment: You can have one without the other. In *Proceedings of the twenty-first annual conference of the Cognitive Science Society*, pp. 142–147. Hillsdale, NJ: Erlbaum.

Downing, P. (1977). On the creation and use of English compound nouns. *Language* 53(4):810–842.

Falkenhainer, B., Forbus, K. D., and Gentner, D. (1986). Structure-mapping engine. *Proceedings of the annual conference of the American Association for Artificial Intelligence*, pp. 272–277. Washington, DC: AAAI.

Falkenhainer, B., Forbus, K. D., and Gentner, D. (1989). Structure-mapping engine. *Artificial Intelligence* 41:1–63.

Forbus, K. D., Ferguson, R. W., and Gentner, D. (1994). Incremental structure mapping. In *Proceedings of the sixteenth annual conference of the Cognitive Science Society*. Hillsdale, NJ: Erlbaum.

Forbus, K. D., and Oblinger, D. (1990). Making SME greedy and pragmatic. *Proceedings of the twelfth annual conference of the Cognitive Science Society*. Hillsdale: Erlbaum.

Forbus, K. D., Gentner, D., and Law, K. (1994). MAC/FAC: A model of similarity-based retrieval. *Cognitive Science* 19:141–205.

Gagné, C. L., and Shoben, E. J. (1997). Influence of thematic relations on the comprehension of modifier-noun combinations. *Journal of Experimental Psychology: Learning, Memory and Cognition* 23(1):71–87.

Gentner, D. (1982). The role of analogy in science. In D. S. Miall, Ed., *Metaphor: Problems and perspectives*. Brighton: Harvester.

Gentner, D. (1983). Structure-mapping: A theoretical framework for analogy. *Cognitive Science* 7:155–170.

Gentner, D., and Clement, C. A. (1988). Evidence for relational selectivity in the interpretation of analogy and metaphor. In G. H. Bower Ed., *The psychology of learning and motivation*, vol. 22, pp. 302–358. New York: Academic Press.

Gentner, D., and Toupin, C. (1986). Systematicity and surface similarity in the development of analogy. *Cognitive Science* 10:227–300.

Gentner, D., and Wolff, P. (1997). Metaphor and knowledge change. In A. Kasher and Y. Shen, Eds., *Cognitive aspects of metaphor*. Amsterdam: North Holland.

Gerrig, R. J., and Murphy, G. L. (1992). Contextual influences on the comprehension of complex concepts. *Language and Cognitive Processes* 7(3–4): 205–230.

Gick, M. L., and Holyoak, K. J. (1980). Analogical problem solving. *Cognitive Psychology* 12:306–355.

Gick, M. L., and Holyoak, K. J. (1983). Schema induction in analogical transfer. *Cognitive Psychology* 15:1–38.

Goldstone, R. L. (1994). Similarity, interactive activation and mapping. *Journal of Experimental Psychology: Language, Memory and Cognition* 20:3–28.

Goldstone, R. L., and Medin, D. L. (1994). Time course of comparison. *Journal of Experimental Psychology: Language, Memory and Cognition* 20:29–50.

Grice, H. P. (1975). Logic and conversation. In P. Cole and J. L. Morgan, Eds., *Syntax and semantics*, vol. 3, *Speech acts*. New York: Academic Press.

Hampton, J. A. (1987). Inheritance of attributes in natural concept conjunctions. *Memory and Cognition* 15:55–71.

Hampton, J. A. (1988). Overextension of conjunctive concepts: Evidence for a unitary model of concept typicality and class diagnosticity. *Journal of Experimental Psychology: Learning, Memory, and Cognition* 14:12–32.

Holyoak, K. J., and Thagard, P. R. (1989). Analogical mapping by constraint satisfaction. *Cognitive Science* 13:295–355.

Holyoak, K. J., and Thagard, P. R. (1995). *Mental leaps: Analogy in creative thought.* Cambridge, MA: MIT Press.

Hummel, J. E., and Holyoak, K. J. (1992). Indirect analogical mapping. In *Proceedings of the fourteenth annual conference of the Cognitive Science Society* Mahwah, NJ: Erlbaum.

Hummel, J. E., and Holyoak, K. J. (1997). Distributed representations of structure: A theory of analogical access and mapping. *Psychological Review* 104:427–466.

Keane, M. T. (1985). On drawing analogies when solving problems: A theory and test of solution generation in an analogical problem solving task. *British Journal of Psychology* 76:449–458.

Keane, M. T. (1988). *Analogical problem solving.* Chichester: Ellis Horwood.

Keane, M. T. (1990). Incremental analogising: Theory and model. In K. J. Gilhooly, M. T. Keane, R. Logie, and G. Erdos, Eds., *Lines of thinking: Reflections on the psychology of thought*, vol. 1, pp. 221–235. Chichester: John Wiley.

Keane, M. T. (1993). The cognitive processes underlying complex analogies: Theoretical and empirical advances. *Ricerche di Psicologia* 17:9–36.

Keane, M. T. (1996). On adaptation in analogy: Tests of pragmatic importance and adaptability in analogical problem solving. *Quarterly Journal of Experimental Psychology* 49:1062–1085.

Keane, M. T. (1997). What makes an analogy difficult? The effects of order and causal structure in analogical mapping. *Journal of Experimental Psychology: Language, Memory and Cognition* 23:946–967.

Keane, M. T., and Brayshaw, M. (1988). The Incremental Analogy Machine: A computational model of analogy. In D. Sleeman Ed., *Third European working session on learning*, pp. 53–62. London: Pitman.

Keane, M. T., Ledgeway, T., and Duff, S. (1994). Constraints on analogical mapping: A comparison of three models. *Cognitive Science* 18:287–334.

Kubose, T., Holyoak, K. J., and Hummel, J. E. (1998). Strategic use of working memory in analogical mapping. Manuscript.

Levi, J. N. (1978). *The syntax and semantics of complex nominals.* New York: Academic Press.

Markman, A. B. (1997). Constraints on analogical inference. *Cognitive Science* 21:373–418.

Markman, A. B., and Gentner, D. (1993a). Splitting the differences: A structural alignment view of similarity. *Journal of Memory and Language* 32(4):517–535.

Markman, A. B., and Gentner, D. (1993b). Structural alignment during similarity comparisons, *Cognitive Psychology* 25(4):431–467.

Markman, A. B., and Wisniewski, E. J. (1997). Same and different: The differentiation of basic-level categories. *Journal of Experimental Psychology: Language, Memory and Cognition* 23:54–70.

Medin, D. L., Goldstone, R. L., and Gentner, D. (1994). Respects for similarity. *Psychological Review* 100:254–278.

Murphy, G. L. (1988). Comprehending complex concepts. *Cognitive Science* 12(4):529–562.

Murphy, G. L. (1990). Noun phrase interpretation and conceptual combination. *Journal of Memory and Language* 29:259–288.

Rosch, E. (1978). Principles of categorization. In E. Rosch and B. B. Lloyd, Eds., *Cognition and categorization.* Hillsdale, NJ: Erlbaum.

Shoben, E. J. (1993). Non-predicating conceptual combinations. *The Psychology of Learning and Motivation* 29:391–409.

Smith, E. E., Osherson, D. N., Rips, L. J., and Keane, M. (1988). Combining prototypes: A selective modification model. *Cognitive Science* 12:485–527.

Spellman, B. A., and Holyoak, K. J. (1996). Pragmatics in analogical mapping. *Cognitive Psychology* 31:307–346.

Thagard, P. (1997). Coherent and creative conceptual combinations. In T. B. Ward, S. M. Smith, and J. Vaid, Eds., *Creative thought: An investigation of conceptual structures and processes.* Washington, DC: APA Press.

Veale, T., and Keane, M. T. (1994). Belief modelling, intentionality and perlocution in metaphor comprehension. *Proceedings of the sixteenth annual meeting of the Cognitive Science Society*, pp. 910–915. Hillsdale, NJ: Lawrence Erlbaum.

Veale, T., and Keane, M. T. (1997). The competence of sub-optimal structure mapping on "hard" analogies. *IJCAI'97: International Joint Conference on Artificial Intelligence*, pp. 200–205. Los Altos, CA: Morgan Kaufmann.

Veale, T., and Keane, M. T. (1998a). Principle differences in structure mapping. *Analogy'98.* Sofia: New University of Bulgaria.

Veale, T., and Keane, M. T. (1998b). Principles of sub-optimal structure mapping: Competence and performance. Manuscript.

Wisniewski, E. J. (1996). Construal and similarity in conceptual combination. *Journal of Memory and Language* 35(3):434–453.

Wisniewski, E. J. (1997a). Conceptual combination: Possibilities and esthetics. In T. B. Ward, S. M. Smith, and J. Vaid, Eds., *Creative thought: An investigation of conceptual structures and processes.* Washington DC: American Psychological Association.

Wisniewski, E. J. (1997b). When concepts combine. *Psychonomic Bulletin and Review* 4(2):167–183.

Wisniewski, E. J., and Gentner, D. (1991). On the combinatorial semantics of noun pairs: Minor and major adjustments to meaning. In G. B. Simpson, Ed., *Understanding word and sentence.* Amsterdam: North Holland.

Wisniewski, E. J., and Love, B. C. (1998). Relations versus properties in conceptual combination. *Journal of Memory and Language* 38:177–202.

Wisniewski, E. J., and Markman, A. B. (1993). The role of structural alignment in conceptual combination. *Proceedings of the fifteenth annual conference of the Cognitive Science Society.* Mahwah, NJ: Erlbaum.

9

The Analogical Paradox: Why Analogy Is so Easy in Naturalistic Settings, Yet so Difficult in the Psychological Laboratory

Kevin Dunbar

A subject walks into a psychological laboratory at 2:00 P.M. She is told a story about a problem and is given the solution to the problem. Then she is given a list of words to remember. Five minutes later (at 2:18 P.M.) she is given new problems to solve, one of which shares superficial similarity to the first problem and the second shares structural similarity with the first problem. She does not use the first problem to solve the second when the two problems only share structural similarity, but does use the first problem when it shares superficial similarity.

A scientist is investigating the way that HIV works. She obtains a very strange result. To explain what happened she spontaneously draws an analogy to a genetic mechanism found in heat-resistant bacteria.

A politician is trying to convince people to vote against independence in the Canadian province of Quebec. He says that voting for independence "would be like leaving an ocean liner for a lifeboat, without paddles, on a stormy sea."

These three examples exemplify what I term the *analogical paradox*. Subjects in many psychology experiments tend to focus on superficial features when using analogy, whereas people in nonexperimental contexts, such as politicians and scientists, frequently use deeper more structural features. What is the cause of these different findings? How can we account for this apparent paradox? On one hand, the results of the past twenty years of research on analogical reasoning have found that unless subjects are given extensive training, examples, or hints, they will be much more likely to choose superficial features than deep structural features when using analogies (e.g., Forbus, Gentner, and Law 1994; Gick and Holyoak 1980, 1983; Novick 1988). On the other hand, such results are at odds with the data that we have collected from naturalistic settings. In both science and politics, we have found that structural analogies are not a rare event. People very frequently access structural and relational features when using analogy.[1] The differences between the ways that analogy is used in naturalistic versus laboratory settings provide important insights for all models of analogical reasoning and shed new light on the nature of complex thinking.

The finding that people focus on superficial features in laboratory experiments is also paradoxical in relation to current theories of analogy. As can be seen in many chapters of this book, most theories of analogy have structural or higher-order sets of relations as a central component of the model (e.g., Holyoak, chap. 5, and Gentner, chap. 6, this volume). What the models do is find and select analogies based upon sets of relations or structural features. The way these "true analogs" are retrieved varies from model to model and is highly influenced by the results of experiments. Given that the laboratory studies have shown that people tend to focus on superficial features, these models have had to incorporate mechanisms that make the models find superficial matches, even though the power of these analogical reasoning engines used in these models is that they can find higher order relations that are similar between a source and a target. Thus, models of analogy provide another facet of the "analogical paradox."

In this chapter, I will first provide a summary of our research on the use of analogy in science and politics. This research demonstrates that people outside the psychological laboratory frequently use analogies based on structural features and higher-order relations rather than mostly using superficial matches. I will then present one possible explanation for these findings: that when generating analogies people search memory for structural relations, but when they are asked to choose between different sources they will focus on superficial features. I will discuss some recent work that Isabelle Blanchette and I have conducted to test this hypothesis. I will then probe the paradox deeper. One possible reason that generation of analogies is more structural has to do with *both* the way the subjects encode the source *and* the way that they search memory to retrieve a source. I conclude that the joint interaction of encoding and retrieval provides a good fit to both naturalistic and experimental approaches to analogical reasoning and helps us untangle the mystery underlying the Analogical Paradox.

The Paradox Unfolds: "In Vivo" Investigations of Analogy in Science and Politics

Many of the contributors to this volume note that analogy is a key component of human mental life (see especially Hofstadter, chap. 15). Our in vivo cognitive studies also highlight the importance of analogy. I begin the discussion of our in vivo work with an overview of our findings of analogy in science.

Analogy in Science

For the past decade we have been investigating the way that scientists think, reason, and make discoveries (Dunbar 1993, 1995, 1997, 1999, forthcoming). I have been investigating reasoning as it unfolds "live" at laboratory meetings. I found that the most representative, and spontaneous, cross-section of the ways scientists think and reason is the weekly laboratory meeting. Thus, we have videotaped and audiotaped leading molecular biologists and immunologists as they think and reason at their laboratory meetings. We then analyze, sentence by sentence, the types of thinking and reasoning that they use when formulating theories, analyzing data, and designing experiments. We have investigated leading laboratories in the United States, Canada, and Italy. Each laboratory we have followed from three months to a year. We supplement the meetings with interviews and other documents such as grant proposals, drafts of papers, and one-on-one meetings. Using this novel approach, we are able to capture science as it happens and see what really goes on in science. This approach I have called the "in vivo" cognitive approach, where we investigate science "live." Another approach that we have used is what I term the "in vitro" cognitive approach, where we conduct experiments on scientific thinking in our own cognitive laboratory. As we will see, the in vivo/in vitro distinction is also important for understanding analogical thinking.[2]

Our in vivo analyses of scientists reasoning in their laboratories reveals that analogical thinking is a key component of all aspects of scientific reasoning, ranging from hypothesis generation to experimental design, data interpretation, and explanations. Analogy not only permeates all aspects of scientific thinking, but is a key component of the ways that scientists reason about unexpected findings. Here, I will provide an outline of our basic findings. We have focused on the use of analogy in four laboratories and have found that there were anywhere from two to fourteen analogies at every laboratory meeting. In Dunbar (1997) I provided a breakdown of the goals that scientists have when making analogies. As can be seen from table 9.1, we found that analogies serve three major goals—formulating theories, designing experiments, and giving explanations to other scientists. We also coded the distance between the source and the target and found that very few analogies were when the source and target were from radically different domains even when formulating theories. Instead, we found that most analogies were either from highly similar domains (e.g., HIV to HIV), or domains from common superordinate categories (e.g., one type of virus to another type of virus[3]). We found that when scientists were attempting to fix experimental problems, they tended to use "local analogies"—analogies to very similar experiments or organisms (we call these within-organism analogies: see table 9.1), but when the scientists were attempting to formulate new models or concepts, they tended to make analogies to concepts in other related domains. Note that even the analogies that were to similar experiments or the same organism were dependent on higher-order relational or structural similarities rather than being based upon superficial features. Indeed, if we break down all the analogies used in terms of whether they share literal similarity, we found that around 25 percent of the analogies consisted of mappings between superficial features. For example, one scientist when looking at some data might say, "yes in my

Table 9.1
Goals that scientists have for within-organism, other organism, and nonbiological analogies (Reprinted with permission from Dunbar 1997)

	Within organism	Other organism	Nonbiological
Form hypothesis	3	20	0
Design experiment	9	12	0
Fix experiment	5	5	0
Explain	23	20	2

experiment I got a band that looks like that, I think it might be degradation . . . I did . . . and the band went away." Here the scientist draws an analogy between two sets of experimental results, shows how he changed his method to deal with the result and suggests that the other scientist can use the same method to solve the problem.

One important place where analogy is frequently used is where unexpected findings occur. What we have found, in all the labs that we have studied, is that over half of the findings that scientists obtain are unexpected. Thus, one important problem that scientists must cope with is both interpreting the unexpected findings and deciding what to do next. Scientists' initial reaction to an unexpected finding is that the finding is due to some sort of methodological error. Analogy is one of the first cognitive tools that they use when reasoning about these unexpected findings. Following an unexpected finding, the scientists frequently draw analogies to other experiments that have yielded similar results under similar conditions, often with the same organism—they use within-organism analogies. Using within-organism analogies is the first type of analogical reasoning that scientists use when they obtain unexpected findings and is an important part of dealing with such findings. Note that by making the analogy they also find a solution to the problem. For example, the analogy between two experiments with similar bands (discussed in the previous paragraph) led one scientist to use the same method as the other scientist and the problem was solved. Thus, use of these within organism analogies can be a powerful reasoning tool that is used to solve problems. Scientists rarely mention these types of analogies in their autobiographies because they appear to be uninteresting, yet these types of analogies are one of the first mechanisms that are used in dealing with unexpected findings. Another important point here is that using analogies based upon superficial similarities can indeed be helpful. Rather than being a deficient form of reasoning, these superficial analogies are a useful way of fixing problems.

The way that scientists used analogy changes when they obtain a *series* of unexpected findings. This usually occurred when the scientist continued to obtain unexpected findings despite having modified the method, attempted to replicate the finding, or when they obtained a whole series of unexpected findings in related conditions. It is at this point that a major shift in the reasoning occurs; the scientists begin to offer new more general models, hypotheses, or theoretical explanations. In this situation, they drew analogies to different types of mechanisms and models in other organisms rather than making analogies to the same organism. We called these "between-organism analogies." This also involves making analogies to research conducted outside their lab. The scientists switched from using local analogies to more distant analogies, but still within the domain of biology. For example, a scientist working on a novel type of bacterium might say that *"IF3* in *E.coli* works like this, maybe your gene is doing the same thing." Thus, the way that analogies are used changes now. At this point a complicated sequence of analogy, generalization, and deduction often occurs. This will result in both the formulation of new models and theories, as well as the design of new experiments. It is important to note that analogy works in concert with a whole host of cognitive processes, rather than working alone when discoveries are made. Another important point is that many different analogies are used, each local in nature, but resulting in large-scale changes in representations. In some instances, we saw strings of different cognitive processes such as generalization-analogy-deduction-analogy-generalization. The mechanisms by which these different forms of reasoning interact is one of the current research topics that we are investigating in my laboratory. The finding that more distant analogies are used following a set of unexpected findings is interesting for two main reasons. First, analogy use changes with the current goal; a series of unexpected findings act as a trigger for the wider search for sources and provide a new mechanisms for expanding the search process. Second, analogy use does not occur in isolation; it works in conjunction with other psychological processes.

One interesting feature of our results is that the scientists have little memory of the reasoning processes that have gone into a particular scientific finding. For example, when I returned to one of the labs six months after its staff had made a discovery, the postdoc who had conducted the experiments that led to the discovery remembered little of what went on at the meeting, but could remember the final interpretation of the data. In particular, the scientists had little memory of the analogies that they made in response to the unexpected findings. While analogy was an important component of the reasoning process, the analogies were forgotten. This result indicates that to gain an understanding of the way analogy is used in science it is necessary to collect data live, and treat scientists' retrospective reports with caution. Another important finding here was that analogies from a totally different domain (nonbiological analogies) were very rare, and were used mainly to give explanations.

Overall, the results of our analyses of scientists reasoning live or in vivo reveal a number of important features of the analogical reasoning process. First, analogy is common. Second, while the scientists do make analogies based on superficial features, they frequently and spontaneously generate analogies based deep structural features and higher-order relations. Third, the goals that the scientists have influence the range over which an analogy is applied. Fourth, the scientists appear to be using the analogies as scaffolding. Once the analogies serve their purpose of building new explanations and models they are discarded and this is why they forget them.

Analogy in Politics

Having investigated the use of analogy in one context—science—Isabelle Blanchette and I decided to investigate analogy use in another naturalistic context—politics (Blanchette and Dunbar 1997, 1999). Politics is an interesting area to investigate the use of analogy, inasmuch as analogies are frequently used, in political speech and by collecting a database of analogies, we could discover the types of features and ranges over which analogies are applied. This analysis thus provides us with a new database of the ways that analogy is used in naturalistic contexts that can make it possible to build general models of analogical reasoning. Furthermore, we can compare the politicians' use of analogy with that of scientists and subjects in psychology experiments.

The particular political issue that we focused on was a referendum on independence that took place in Quebec in 1996. The electorate were presented with the choice of voting to keep the province of Quebec within the country of Canada or voting to make Quebec a new country.[4] We analyzed politicians' and journalists' use of analogy in newspaper articles during the final week of the referendum campaign. What we did was to take every newspaper story that appeared in three Montreal newspapers during the last week of the referendum campaign and search for all uses of analogy in the paper. Two of the newspapers were in French (*La Presse* and *Le Devoir*) and one was in English (*The Gazette*). We found more than four hundred articles referring to the referendum and then searched for every analogy that was used. This analysis resulted in the discovery of more than two hundred analogies. Next we categorized the analogies in terms of the semantic categories of the source and target, the emotional connotation of the source, and how distant the source and target were from each other—that is, whether the source and target were from the same domains, superficially similar domains, or only structurally similar domains. Any statement, or set of statements where two items were said to be similar, and features of one item were mapped onto the other item were coded as an analogy. Example analogies are "Quebec's path to sovereignty is like a hockey game. The referendum is the end of the third period." Another analogy that was used was "Separation is like a major surgery. It is important that the patient is informed by the surgeon and that the surgeon is impartial. The referendum is a way to inform the population. But in this case, the surgeons are not impartial and they really want their operation."

The analysis of semantic categories revealed that only 24 percent of the sources were from politics. Put another way, over 75 percent of the sources were not based on superficial features. Instead the analogies were based on higher-order relations and structural features. We compared the analogies made by journalists and by politicians and found no differences in either the categories of sources or the distance between the source and the target. Both politicians and journalists were equally likely to use sources and targets from nonpolitical domains. The range of source categories was fascinating, ranging from agriculture to the family, sport, magic, and religion. We also analyzed the semantic categories in terms of whether the analogies were used to support independence or to argue against independence. Again there were no differences. Thus, these analyses revealed that the politicians and journalists frequently use sources from domains other than politics. They were not basing their analogies on superficial features. In both science and politics we have found that rather than being a rare phenomenon, analogies based on higher-order relations are common.[5]

One feature of the politician's use of analogy that we found intriguing was the frequent reference to highly emotional sources. We decided to probe this phenomenon more deeply by asking subjects to categorize each source used in the referendum in terms of whether it had a positive or a negative connotation. We found that the nonpolitical analogies received much stronger ratings of emotionality than the political analogies. Furthermore, we found that the sources used in making an analogy for one's own side were rated as emotionally positive, but that the sources used when attacking the other side were rated as emotionally negative. These findings suggest that one of the reasons that the politicians were using analogies from nonpolitical domains was to map the emotional connotation of the source onto the political debate. Thus, for one's own side the politicians mapped well-being, happiness, and health onto their view, whereas they mapped fear, disgust, and anger onto the other side. Obviously the hope of the politicians was that by mapping a positive emotion onto a particular option, the likelihood that the general public will choose that option will increase.[6] The finding that analogy use can also involve the mapping of emotions, and not just "cold" cognitive states, demonstrates that analogy is much more than a mechanistic thought process. As both Paul Thagard and Douglas Hofstader argue in this volume, analogy is a powerful mechanism that is involved in all aspects of life.

The scientific and political use of analogy led us to an interesting conclusion. People frequently make analogies that are based on deep structural features and have little superficial overlap between the source and the target. How could this be possible? More than twenty years of research has shown repeatedly that subjects in psychology experiments will use superficial features when given the choice, or, when given an example with only deep structural similarity, will fail to notice the similarities. It is only when subjects are given extensive encoding or various hints that they will use structural or complex relational information. One important difference between the ways that people use analogy in the naturalistic contexts that we have investigated and the ways that subjects use analogy in psychology experiments is that the psychology subjects are given the sources and targets, whereas the scientists, journalists, and politicians generate the analogies themselves. Another obvious difference between the naturalistic studies and the classic psychology experiment is that people in these naturalistic settings have a vast pool of knowledge and expertise that can influence their analogical reasoning. Thus, it may be the expertise of the subjects that allows them to make these types of analogies (e.g., Novick 1988a, 1988b). In the next section I will look at these issues.

"In Vitro" Investigations of Analogical Reasoning

The in vivo–in vitro approach that I have been pursuing over the past decade necessitates going back and forth between naturalistic and laboratory settings. Our in vivo findings led us to conduct new sets of experiments that allowed us the design experiments that got the to the core of the analogical paradox. First, I will consider the role analogy generation and then the roles of encoding and retrieval in the analogical paradox.

Analogy Generation Hypothesis and Experiments

Our work on scientists and politicians and their use of structural features when making analogies suggested that there may be a number of reasons why subjects in standard psychology experiments tend to rely on superficial features. One possible reason for the difference is that the scientists and politicians are generating their own analogies rather than being asked to use various source analogs that are provided by the experimenter. Isabelle Blanchette and I (Blanchette and Dunbar 1998, 2000) have conducted a number of experiments to determine why laboratory and naturalistic studies have yielded different results. We have used a "production paradigm" in which subjects were asked to generate sources for a given target. The task that we used in these experiments was one of asking subjects to generate analogies to the zero-deficit problem. The zero-deficit problem refers to a problem that all Canadian governments had to deal with in the 1990s. Both the federal government and all the provincial governments had accumulated an enormous deficit that had to be cut. Governments reasoned that they had to cut their spending to cut the deficit. One view of this deficit problem is that the deficit must be cut no matter what the consequences. Another view is that social programs such as health and education must not be cut and that other ways of dealing with the deficit must be found. What we did was to ask subjects to generate analogies that would justify the "cut no matter what the consequences," or "save social programs" viewpoint. We did this by first explaining the deficit problem to subjects. Subjects were then told to pretend that they were working for a political action group that was lobbying for a particular way of dealing with the deficit. Subjects were told that psychologists had found that analogy is a very powerful way of changing opinion and that they had to generate analogies that could be used to change opinion on the deficit issue. One group of subjects was told that they were working for a group that wanted to cut the deficit no matter what the consequences. The other group was told that they were working for an interest group that wanted to save the social programs. Subjects were asked to generate as many analogies as they possibly could. What we were interested in was the type of analogy that the subjects generated. Would they pick analogs that shared superficial features only, shared structural and superficial features, or shared only structural features? We took every analogy that subjects generated, coded the domain from which it was taken, and determined its structure.

The results of these experiments were that subjects generated analogies that share few superficial features with the deficit problem. Overall, each subject produced around eleven analogies. Eighty percent of the analogies that the subjects produced were from domains other than politics or anything related to money. The types of analogies that they picked were from domains such as fables, domestic tasks, and animals. More than 40 percent of the analogies were from idiosyncratic sources. Thus, we have again found that people will use analogies with deep structural features bearing no superficial similarities to the target problem (see table 9.2).

The next question that we addressed was whether we obtained our results because subjects were "experts" on the problem or because they were generating the analogies themselves. Subjects could be "experts" on the deficit because it had been widely discussed in the media and was frequently debated in the many recent elections in Quebec. We tested this

Table 9.2
Percentage of retrievals of sources based upon superficial or structural similarity
(Adapted with permission from Blanchette and Dunbar (2000))

	Remind	Generate
Structural	19	79.8
Superficial	81	20.1

hypothesis by changing our task to a more standard "reception paradigm" where subjects are given various sources to read and then, at a
later point in time, are given new stories and asked which old stories
they are reminded of by the new stories. We reasoned that if using this
more standard paradigm subjects still use structural features, then it was
subjects' familiarity with the deficit problem that led to them to use structural features in the previous task. If, however, subjects use superficial
features when the task is changed to a reception task, then it must be
the task that is causing the subjects to choose superficial features. The
results of this experiment were that the subjects used superficial features.
Thus, when given the same materials that subjects generated in the first
experiment it was possible for subjects to switch from using structural
features to superficial features. The results of this series of experiments
suggest that one component of the reason why people in naturalistic contexts use structural features when making analogies is that they are generating the analogies themselves. Generating analogies leads people to
focus on structural features. But how? Like a Russian doll, the generation hypothesis leads us to ask a further question.

Experiments on Encoding and Retrieval
The results of the analogy production experiments led us back to the
issue of encoding and retrieval. Perhaps the generation of analogies is
structural because of the way that subjects encode the issue. More than
ten years ago Chris Schunn and I began investigating the role of encoding in analogical reasoning. I now see that what we were really doing is
investigating the analogical paradox. We hypothesized that one of the
reasons that subjects in psychology experiments tend to rely on superficial features is that they do not encode the source problem at a struc-

tural level. We reasoned that if subjects had to discover the answer to a problem, they would encode the problem at a structural level and have a much more abstract representation of the problem than simply being told the answer to the problem. We reckoned that subjects who solved the source problem would be much more likely to use that problem in an analogy than subjects who were merely told the answer to the problem. Our results demonstrated that solving the source problem does indeed facilitate performance on the target problem. Thus, the way that the source problem is encoded will influence whether the source is retrieved when working on a structurally similar problem. Surprisingly, subjects in this experiment did not make any explicit analogies to the source problem when they solved the target problem, yet solving the source problem benefited performance. We argued that because the subjects had previously learned the to-be-used concept in their psychology courses, the source problem primed the concept. When subjects were given the target problem to solve, the primed concept was available in memory to be used and subjects retrieved the concept. The process by which this happens still is not clear. However, what these results demonstrated is that the way that source information is encoded will have important effects on whether the source is retrieved when working on similar problems. Thus, we and various other researchers have concluded that the way that source information is encoded is important to analogical reasoning.

Encoding alone does not resolve the analogical paradox. Many researchers have demonstrated that even with a rich encoding of the source, subjects will not necessarily use the source when working on a structurally related problem (e.g., Catrambone 1997). Furthermore, work by other researchers such as Dedre Gentner and her colleagues has demonstrated that type of retrieval cue given to subjects has an effect on whether they will retrieve analogies based on superficial or relational features. Thus, both encoding and retrieval are important factors in understanding analogy use. These various results converge on the hypothesis that the interaction between encoding operations and retrieval cues will determine whether people will retrieve a source based on superficial or relational similarity. Research on attention and memory from the 1970s and 1980s has shown that the types of operations that are performed at encoding *and* at retrieval will determine the types of items that are recalled (Bransford et al. 1979; Craik and Lockhart 1972; Fiske and Schneider 1984; Tulving and Thompson 1973). We hypothesized that one of the reasons that there are differences between naturalistic and laboratory investigations of analogical reasoning is a complex set of relations between the conditions prevailing at encoding and the conditions under which retrieval occurs. If encoding does not stress relational features of the source or highlight these features and neither do the retrieval conditions, then subjects will retrieve only superficial matches. If, however, encoding stresses relational features, then subjects will be able to retrieve relational matches, particularly when the retrieval conditions stress relational features. We see encoding and retrieval conditions as lying along a continuum from superficial to relational and that, ideally, both encoding and retrieval conditions must match for successful analogical reasoning to occur.

This hypothesis was tested by my student Tia Chung (Dunbar, Blanchette, and Chung, in preparation). She conducted an experiment using the Karla the Hawk stimuli of Rattermann and Gentner (1987).[7] Subjects read a story and a week later were brought back to the lab and given a new set of stories that might be structurally similar bearing no superficial similarity, or be only superficially similar to the original stories. What we did is to vary both the types of encoding and retrieval conditions that subjects were asked to perform. We used three types of encoding conditions. The first was telling the subjects to read the story. This Read-Story condition is the same type of encoding condition as used in many analogy studies. The second encoding condition was what we called sham-analogy. Here the subjects were told that at some later point in time they would have to generate an analogy for the story that they were reading. In fact, they never had to generate an analogy at all, but anticipated that they might have to do so. We expected this encoding manipulation to highlight relational and structural features of the source. The third type of encoding condition was where the subjects were told to generate an analogy to the source story. We called this the generate-analogy condition. Here, the subjects really did have to generate analogies to the source stories. We expected this condition to strongly highlight the relational features of the source. Subjects returned a week later and were given various stories to read. They were asked about the relationship of these new stories to the initial stories. Half the subjects were asked, "which story does this remind you of"—the remind condition. The other half of the subjects were asked "which of the initial stories is this new story thematically similar to"—the thematic condition. We expected that the remind retrieval cue would be a superficial retrieval cue (see also Wharton et al. 1995), whereas the thematically similar cue would stress relational features. By factorially manipulating the encoding and retrieval features, we wanted to gain a clearer picture of how encoding and retrieval are related in analogical reasoning.

As can be seen from figure 9.1, the results of this experiment were straightforward. Subjects in the read-story condition retrieved the fewest

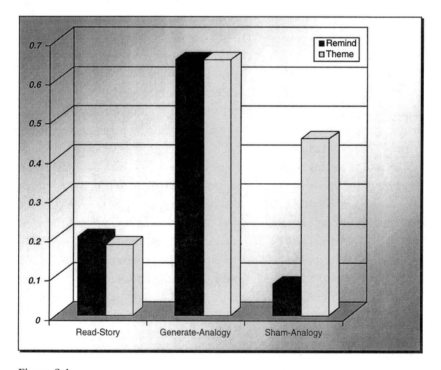

Figure 9.1
Proportion of times higher-order source is selected as a function of type of encoding and retrieval cue.

analogical matches and it did not matter whether they were given the remind or thematic retrieval cues. Conversely, subjects in the generate-analogy condition retrieved the most analogies and again it did not matter whether they received the remind or the thematic retrieval cue. At this point, it might be possible to conclude that the type of retrieval cue that is given is irrelevant and all that matters is the way that the source is encoded. However, the results of the sham-analogy condition demonstrate that the relationship between encoding and retrieval does indeed matter, albeit under specific conditions. When the encoding was sham-analogy and the retrieval cue was remind, then a small number of analogies were retrieved. However, when the retrieval cue was thematic, then there were a large number of analogies retrieved. These results reveal that there is a complex relation between encoding and retrieval conditions. When encoding strongly highlights relational features of a source, then regardless of the retrieval cue given, subjects will be able to retrieve analogically similar matches. When encoding is superficial, even when a relational retrieval cue is given, this will not help subjects retrieve the relational analogs. When there is a moderate level of relational information highlighted at encoding, then the type of retrieval cue does matter. A superficial retrieval cue will not help, whereas a relational retrieval cue will help.

The results of this experiment have helped us understand some of the conditions under which relational analogies can be retrieved. In naturalistic settings, people have encoded both the source and the target problems in a relational way. A scientist attempting to understand the way that viral DNA interacts and integrates itself into the DNA of a cell has a relational understanding of the mechanisms of a virus and searches for other types of biological mechanisms that have similar relational mechanisms. Thus, in many naturalistic settings the analogizer is in the position of the subjects in our generate-analogy/Thematic condition. There is a match between the relational encoding of the source and the relational goal of the analogizer. However, subjects in many analogy experiments are akin to the subjects in the read-story/remind condition. There is neither a relational encoding of the source nor a relational retrieval cue. I suspect that the subjects in our analogy generation experiments (Blanchette and Dunbar 1998, 2000) are somewhat similar to the subjects in the Sham-Analogy conditions. The subjects have a relational understanding of the source problem and when asked to generate analogies they are essentially given a relational retrieval cue. Thus, they will retrieve relational analogies having few superficial features in common with the target problem. When, however, subjects are asked what these analogies remind them of, they are much less likely to retrieve structurally similar sources and retrieve superficial matches. In this condition, they are like the subjects in the sham-analogy/remind condition.

Conclusion: Analogy Unplugged

The goal of this chapter was both to highlight the analogical paradox as an important issue for research on analogy and to propose a resolution of the paradox. By investigating analogy use in naturalistic contexts and comparing these results to those of analogical reasoning experiments a paradox is apparent: Analogy seems easy in naturalistic contexts, yet difficult in the psychological laboratory. By going back into the lab and conducting experiments, the paradox can be resolved. Both encoding and retrieval conditions underlie the paradox: Naturalistic environments make it possible for people to use structural features and higher order relations because information is encoded in a richer way. Furthermore, naturalistic settings influence the retrieval conditions, often stressing the search for higher-order analogs rather than analogs that share superficial features. Experiments on analogy have tended to use conditions that do not stress a rich encoding of the information, nor stress structural information at retrieval. Other researchers also have noted that analogical reasoning can be based on structural rather than superficial features (e.g., Faries and Reiser 1988), these results have often been interpreted as a product of expertise: Experts have more relational and structural knowledge than novices therefore they can make analogies based on higher-order structural relations. Although this view is certainly consistent with the findings that we have obtained, the point that I am making is different: both experts and novices are capable of generating true structural analogies if the circumstances permit (see also Faries and Reiser 1990). If the encoding and retrieval conditions highlight structural features, then both novices and experts can generate analogies based on structural features. To generate an analogy, people do not need the training that is needed for true expertise (e.g., Ericsson 1994), but must be in a context that highlights structural relations. Subjects must have a minimal amount of understanding of the source and target, but do not need the extensive knowledge of experts to use higher-order structural relations. All human beings possess at least a minimal knowledge of myriads of issues and are able to make analogies based on structural features and higher-order relations. To be sure, both scientists and politicians in naturalistic settings can generate superficial mappings between sources and targets (and many times these superficial mappings are useful!). Placing people in naturalistic settings does not automatically guarantee elegant analogical reasoning. However, what our research has demonstrated is that structural analogies are a frequent, rather than a rare phenomenon. Overall, subjects in psychology experiments are just like rock musicians in the "unplugged" series[8]; they can perform well without the usual props, but at least need to be given a guitar!

Acknowledgments

I would like to thank Isabelle Blanchette and Chris Schunn for the many discussions that we have had on analogical reasoning that underlie the work reported in this chapter. Comments from Laura Ann Petitto, Keith Holyoak, Dedre Gentner, David Klahr, and a chance conversation with Ed Wisniewski have greatly improved it. Grants from the Spencer Foundation, Natural Sciences and Engineering Council of Canada and the Social Sciences Research Council of Canada made this research possible. I would like to thank Massimo Piatelli-Palmarini for making it possible to write this paper at the Università Vita-Salute San Raffaele in Milan.

Notes

1. Using historical analyses, Gentner et al. (1997), and Holyoak and Thagard (1995) have also documented numerous cases where scientists, politicians, and even generals have used analogies based on structural features and higher-order relations.

2. It is important to note that the InVivo/InVitro methodology (Dunbar 1995, 1997, forthcoming a) is different from "situated cognition." The assumption of

the InVitro/InVivo Cognitive approach is that by going back and forth between naturalistic and laboratory investigations of cognitive processes it is possible to build a more complete and detailed account of human cognition than either approach alone would give. The in vivo/in vitro approach does not presuppose that either laboratory or naturalistic investigations of cognition are inherently superior. The underlying rationale for in vivo/in vitro is itself based on an analogy with biology research. Many biologists conduct both in vivo and in vitro research and go back and forth between the two domains. What works in the test tube may not work in the organism and vice versa. By doing both types of research the biologists gain a more complete and robust understanding of the phenomena that they are investigating.

3. Note that, to a molecular biologist, comparing one type of virus to another type of virus could be like comparing one type of vehicle such as skis, to another type of vehicle, such as a Stealth bomber. To a nonbiologist the difference between one type of virus and another seems minimal, but to a biologist it can seem enormous. One virus will have vastly different biological properties to another virus, but share certain other biological mechanisms and genes.

4. Strictly speaking, the choice that the electorate faced was more complicated than this, but both the public and the politicians believed that the referendum was about staying in Canada or forming a new country.

5. The finding that over three quarters of the analogies used were nonpolitical might be because the journalists who wrote the articles filtered out the analogies lacking good structural qualities or analogies that were based on superficial features. Currently, Isabelle Blanchette is checking this hypothesis. She attended a number of speeches by politicians in a recent election campaign, tape-recorded them, analyzed them for use of analogy, and compared what the politicians said with what was reported in the newspapers. She found that the politicians made few, if any, analogies based on superficial similarity. Analogies that did not make it into the newspaper tended to be the ones that were vague in their mappings. Thus, it does not appear to be the case that the predominance of nonpolitical analogies is a by-product of the filtering of analogies by the newspapers.

6. It appears that politicians and journalists are making the assumption that the general public will understand these nonsuperficial analogies. An interesting question is whether these types of analogies are indeed understood by the general public, and do they have an effect on behavior?

7. I thank Dedre Gentner and Mary Jo Rattermann for graciously providing us with the stories for this experiment.

8. In the "unplugged" series rock musicians are asked to perform without using electric guitars and all the other electrical instruments that they normally use when they give a concert. Here the musicians are allowed use an acoustic guitar and often perform alone without their band. The point here is that the musician without her or his electrical instruments is similar to a subject in a psychology experiment: the subject must perform without the usual props and does not have a social support structure to back up the cognitive processing. However, in the

"unplugged" series, the musicians are allowed have a musical instrument such as an acoustic guitar and can perform extremely well. Participants in psychology experiments similarly need to be supplied with something that will allow them to perform well, such as a rich encoding, expertise, or adequate retrieval cues.

References

Blanchette, I., and Dunbar, K. (1997). Constraints underlying analogy use in a real-world context: Politics. *Proceedings of the nineteenth annual conference of the Cognitive Science Society.* Mahwah, NJ: Lawrence Erlbaum Associates.

Blanchette, I., and Dunbar, K. (1998). Superficial and structural features in the generation of analogies. *Proceedings of the twentieth annual conference of the Cognitive Science Society.* Mahwah, NJ: Lawrence Erlbaum Associates.

Blanchette, I., and Dunbar, K. (2000). How analogies are generated: The roles of structural and superficial Similarity. *Memory and Cognition* 28:108–124.

Bransford, J. D., Franks, J. J., Morris, C. D., and Stein, B. S. (1979). Some general constraints on learning and memory research. In L. S. Cermak and F. I. M. Craik, Eds., *Levels of processing in human memory,* pp. 331–354. Hillsdale, NJ: Erlbaum.

Catrambone, R. (1997). Reinvestigating the effects of surface and structural features on analogical access. *Proceedings of the nineteenth annual meeting of the Cognitive Science Society.* Mahwah, NJ: Lawrence Erlbaum Associates.

Craik, F. I. M., and Lockhart, R. S. (1972). Levels of processing: A framework for memory research. *Journal of Verbal Learning & Verbal Behavior* 11:671–684.

Dunbar, K. (1993). In vivo cognition: Knowledge representation and change in real-world scientific laboratories. *Paper presented at the Society for Research in Child Development.* New Orleans, LA.

Dunbar, K. (1995). How scientists really reason: Scientific reasoning in real-world laboratories. In R. J. Sternberg and J. E. Davidson, Eds., *The nature of insight,* pp. 365–395. Cambridge, MA: MIT Press.

Dunbar, K. (1997). How scientists think: On-line creativity and conceptual change in science. In T. B. Ward, S. M. Smith, and S. Vaid, Eds., *Conceptual structures and processes: Emergence, discovery and change.* Washington, DC: APA Press.

Dunbar, K. (forthcoming). What scientific thinking reveals about the nature of cognition. In Crowley, K., Schunn, C. D., and Okada, T., Eds., *Designing for science: Implications from everyday, classroom, and professional settings.* Hillsdale, NJ: Lawrence Erlbaum Associates.

Dunbar, K. (1999). The scientist in vivo: How scientists think and reason in the laboratory. In Magnani, L., Nersessian, N., and Thagard, P., Eds., *Model-based reasoning in scientific discovery,* pp. 89–98. New York: Plenum Press.

Dunbar, K., Blanchette, I., and Chung, T. (in preparation). Goals, encoding, and analog retrieval.

Dunbar, K., and Schunn, C. D. (1990). The temporal nature of scientific discovery: The roles of priming and analogy. *Proceedings of the twelfth annual meeting of the Cognitive Science Society*, pp. 93–100. Mahwah, NJ: Lawrence Erlbaum Associates.

Ericsson, A. K. (1994). Expert performance: Its structure and acquisition. *American Psychologist* 49:725–747.

Faries, J. M., and Reiser, B. J. (1988). Access and use of previous solutions in a problem-solving situation. *Proceedings of the tenth annual meeting of the Cognitive Science Society*, pp. 433–439. Hillsdale, NJ: Erlbaum.

Faries, J. M., and Reiser, B. J. (1990). Terrorists and spoiled children: Retrieval of analogies for political arguments. *Proceedings of the 1990 AAAI Spring Symposium on Case-Based Reasoning*. Stanford University.

Fiske, A. D., and Schneider, W. (1984). Memory as a function of attention, level of processing, and automatization. *Journal of Experimental Psychology: Learning, Memory, and Cognition* 10:181–197.

Forbus, K., Gentner, D., and Law, K. (1994). MAC/FAC: A model of similarity-based retrieval. *Cognitive Science* 19:141–205.

Gentner, D. (2000). Metaphor is like analogy. In D. Gentner, K. J. Holyoak, and B. N. Kokinov, Eds., *Analogy: Perspectives from cognitive science*. Cambridge, MA: MIT Press.

Gentner, D., Rattermann, M. J., and Forbus, K. (1993). The roles of similarity in transfer: Separating retrievability from inferential soundness. *Cognitive Psychology* 25:524–575.

Gick, M. L., and Holyoak, K. J. (1980). Analogical problem solving. *Cognitive Psychology* 12:306–355.

Gick, M. L., and Holyoak, K. J. (1983). Schema induction and analogical transfer. *Cognitive Psychology* 15:1–38.

Hofstadter, D. R. (2000). Analogy as the core of cognition. In D. Gentner, K. J. Holyoak, and B. N. Kokinov, Eds., *Analogy: Perspectives from cognitive science*. Cambridge, MA: MIT Press.

Holyoak, K. J., and Hummel, J. (2000). Toward an understanding of biological symbol systems. In D. Gentner, K. J. Holyoak, and B. N. Kokinov, Eds., *Analogy: Perspectives from cognitive science*. Cambridge, MA: MIT Press.

Holyoak, K. J., and Thagard, P. (1989). Analogical mapping by constraint satisfaction. *Cognitive Science* 13:295–355.

Holyoak, K. J., and Thagard, P. (1995). *Mental leaps: Analogy in creative thought*. Cambridge, MA: MIT Press.

Holyoak, K. J., and Thagard, P. (1997). The analogical mind. *American Psychologist* 52:35–44.

Novick, L. R. (1988). Analogical transfer, problem similarity, and expertise. *Journal of Experimental Psychology: Learning, Memory, and Cognition* **14**:510–520.

Rattermann, M. J., and Gentner, D. (1987). Analogy and similarity: Determinants of accessibility and inferential soundness. In *Proceedings of the ninth annual meeting of the Cognitive Science Society*, pp. 22–34. Hillsdale, NJ: Erlbaum.

Thagard, P., and Shelley, C. (2000). Emotional analogies and analogical inference. In D. Gentner, K. J. Holyoak, and B. N. Kokinov, Eds., Analogy: Perspectives from Cognitive Science. Cambridge, MA: MIT Press.

Tulving, E., and Thompson, D. M. (1973). Encoding specificity and retrieval processes in episodic memory. *Psychological Review* **80**:352–373.

Wharton, C. M., Holyoak, K. J., Downing, P. E., Lange, T. E., Wickens, T. D., and Melz, E. R. (1994). Below the surface: Analogical similarity and retrieval competition in reminding. *Cognitive Psychology* **26**:64–101.

10

Emotional Analogies and Analogical Inference

Paul Thagard and Cameron Shelley

10.1 Introduction

Despite the growing appreciation of the relevance of affect to cognition, analogy researchers have paid remarkably little attention to emotion. This paper discusses three general classes of analogy that involve emotions. The most straightforward are analogies and metaphors *about* emotions, for example, "Love is a rose and you better not pick it." Much more interesting are analogies that involve the transfer of emotions, for example, in empathy in which people understand the emotions of others by imagining their own emotional reactions in similar situations. Finally, there are analogies that generate emotions, for example, analogical jokes that generate emotions such as surprise and amusement.

Understanding emotional analogies requires a more complex theory of analogical inference than has been available. The next section presents a new account that shows how analogical inference can be defeasible, holistic, multiple, and emotional, in ways to be described. Analogies about emotions can to some extent be explained using the standard models such as ACME and SME, but analogies that transfer emotions require an extended treatment that takes into account the special character of emotional states. We describe HOTCO (hot coherence), a new model of emotional coherence that simulates transfer of emotions, and show how HOTCO models the generation of emotions such as reactions to humorous analogies. Finally, we supplement our anecdotal collection of emotional analogies by discussing a more comprehensive sample culled from Internet wire services.

336 P. Thagard and C. Shelley

10.2 Analogical Inference: Current Models

In logic books, analogical inference is usually presented by a schema such as the following (Salmon 1984:105):

Objects of type X have properties G, H, etc.

Objects of type Y have properties G, H, etc.

Objects of type X have property F.

Therefore: Objects of type Y have property F.

For example, when experiments determined that large quantities of the artificial sweetener saccharine caused bladder cancer in rats, scientists analogized that it might also be carcinogenic in humans. Logicians additionally point out that analogical arguments may be strong or weak depending on the extent to which the properties in the premises are relevant to the property in the conclusion.

This characterization of analogical inference, which dates back at least to John Stuart Mill's nineteenth-century *System of Logic*, is flawed in several respects. First, logicians rarely spell out what "relevant" means, so the schema provides little help in distinguishing strong analogies from weak. Second, the schema is stated in terms of objects and their properties, obscuring the fact that the strongest and most useful analogies involve relations, in particular causal relations (Gentner 1983; Holyoak and Thagard 1995). Such causal relations are usually the key to determining relevance: if, in the above schema, G and H together cause F in X, then analogically they may cause F in Y, producing a much stronger inference than just counting properties. Third, logicians typically discuss analogical arguments and tend to ignore the complexity of analogical inference, which requires a more holistic assessment of a potential conclusion with respect to other information. There is no point in inferring that objects of type Y have property F if you already know of many such objects that lack F, or if a different analogy suggests that they do not have F. Analogical inference must be defeasible, in that the potential conclusion can be overturned by other information, and it must be holistic in that everything the inference maker knows is potentially relevant to overturning or enhancing the inference.

Compared to the logician's schema, much richer accounts of the structure of analogies have been provided by computational models of analogical mapping such as SME (Falkenhainer, Forbus, and Gentner 1989) and ACME (Holyoak and Thagard 1989). SME uses relational structure to generate candidate inferences, and ACME transfers information from a source analog to a target analog using a process that Holyoak, Novick, and Melz (1994) called copying with substitution and generation (CWSG). Similar processes are used in case-based reasoning (Kolodner 1993), and in many other computational models of analogy.

But all of these computational models are inadequate for understanding analogical inference in general and emotional analogies in particular. They do not show how analogical inference can be defeasible and holistic, or how it can make use of multiple-source analogs to support or defeat a conclusion. Moreover, the prevalent models of analogy encode information symbolically and assume that what is inferred is verbal information that can be represented in propositional form by predicate calculus or some similar representational system. (One of the few attempts to deal with nonverbal analogies is the VAMP system for visual analogical mapping; Thagard, Gochfeld, and Hardy 1992.) As section 10.5 documents, analogical inference often serves to transfer an emotion, not just the verbal representation of an emotion. We will now describe how a new model of emotional coherence, HOTCO, can perform analogical inferences that are defeasible, holistic, multiple, and emotional.

10.3 Analogical Inference in HOTCO

Thagard (2000, chap. 6) proposes a theory of emotional coherence that has applications to numerous important psychological phenomena such as trust. This theory makes the following assumptions about inference and emotions:

1. All inference is coherence based. So-called rules of inference such as *modus ponens* do not by themselves license inferences, because their conclusions may contradict other accepted information. The only rule of inference is: Accept a conclusion if its acceptance maximizes coherence.

2. Coherence is a matter of constraint satisfaction, and can be computed by connectionist and other algorithms (Thagard and Verbeurgt 1998).
3. There are six kinds of coherence: analogical, conceptual, explanatory, deductive, perceptual, and deliberative (Thagard et al., forthcoming).
4. Coherence is not just a matter of accepting or rejecting a conclusion, but can also involve attaching a positive or negative emotional assessment to a proposition, object, concept, or other representation.

From this coherentist perspective, *all* inference is defeasible and holistic and differs markedly from logical deduction in formal systems. Philosophers who have advocated coherentist accounts of inference include Bosanquet (1920) and Harman (1986).

The computational model HOTCO implements these theoretical assumptions. It amalgamates the following previous models of coherence:

- Explanatory coherence: ECHO (Thagard 1989, 1992);
- Conceptual coherence: IMP (Kunda and Thagard 1996);
- Analogical coherence: ACME (Holyoak and Thagard 1989);
- Deliberative coherence: DECO (Thagard and Millgram 1995).

Amalgamation is natural, because all of these models use a similar connectionist algorithm for maximizing constraint satisfaction, although they employ different constraints operating on different kinds of representation. What is novel about HOTCO is that representational elements possess not only activations that represent their acceptance and rejection, but also valences that represent a judgment of their positive or negative emotional appeal. In HOTCO, as in its component models, inferences about what to accept are made by a holistic process in which activation spreads through a network of units with excitatory and inhibitory links, representing elements with positive and negative constraints. But HOTCO spreads valences as well as activations in a similar holistic fashion, using the same system of excitatory and inhibitory links. For example, HOTCO models the decision of whether to hire a particular person as a baby-sitter as in part a matter of "cold" deliberative, explanatory, conceptual, and analogical coherence, but also as a matter of generating an emotional reaction to the candidate. The emotional reaction derives from a combination of the cold inferences made about the person and the valences attached to what is inferred. If you infer that a baby-sitting candidate is responsible, intelligent, and likes children, the positive valence of these attributes will spread to him or her; whereas if coherence leads to you infer that the candidate is lazy, dumb, and psychopathic, he or she will acquire a negative valence. In HOTCO, valences spread through the constraint network in much the same way that activation does (see Thagard 2000, for technical details). The result is an emotional Gestalt that provides an overall "gut reaction" to the potential babysitter.

Now we can describe how HOTCO performs analogical inference in a way that is defeasible, holistic, and multiple. HOTCO uses ACME to perform analogical mapping between a source and a target, and uses copying with substitution and generation to produce new propositions to be inferred. It can operate either in a *broad* mode in which everything about the source is transferred to the target, or in a more *specific* mode in which a query is used to enhance the target using a particular proposition in the source. Here, in predicate calculus formalization where each proposition has the structure (predicate (objects) proposition-name), is an example of a scientific analogy concerning the coelacanth, a rare fish that is hard to study directly (Shelley 1999).

Source 1: centroscymnus

  (have (centroscymnus rod-pigment-1) have-1)

  (absorb (rod-pigment-1 472nm-light) absorb-1)

  (penetrate (472nm-light deep-ocean-water) penetrate-1)

  (see-in (centroscymnus deep-ocean-water) see-in-1)

  (inhabit (centroscymnus deep-ocean-water) inhabit-1)

  (enable (have-1 see-in-1) enable-1)

  (because (absorb-1 penetrate-1) because-1)

  (adapt (see-in-1 inhabit-1) adapt-1)

Target: coelacanth-3

  (have (coelacanth rod-pigment-3) have-3)

  (absorb (rod-pigment-3 473nm-light) absorb-3)

  (penetrate (473nm-light deep-ocean-water) penetrate-3)

  (see-in (coelacanth deep-ocean-water) see-in-3)

(enable (have-3 see-in-3) enable-3)

(because (absorb-3 penetrate-3) because-3)

Operating in specific mode, HOTCO is asked what depth the coelacanth inhabits, and uses the proposition INHABIT-1 in the source to construct for the target the proposition

(inhabit (coelacanth deep-ocean-water) inhabit-new)

Operating in broad mode and doing general copying with substitution and generation, HOTCO can analogically transfer everything about the source to the target, in this case generating the proposition that coelacanths inhabit deep water as a candidate to be inferred.

However, HOTCO does *not* actually infer the new proposition, because analogical inference is defeasible. Rather, it simply establishes an excitatory link between the unit representing the source proposition INHABIT-1 and the target proposition INHABIT-NEW. This link represents a positive constraint between the two propositions, so that coherence maximization will encourage them to be accepted together or rejected together. The source proposition INHABIT-1 is presumably accepted, so in the HOTCO model it will have positive activation which will spread to provide positive activation to INHABIT-NEW, unless INHABIT-NEW is incompatible with other accepted propositions that will tend to suppress its activation. Thus analogical inference is defeasible, because all HOTCO does is to create a link representing a new constraint for overall coherence judgment, and it is holistic, because the entire constraint network can potentially contribute to the final acceptance or rejection of the inferred proposition.

Within this framework, it is easy to see how analogical inference can employ multiple analogies, because more than one source can be used to create new constraints. Shelley (1999) describes how biologists do not simply use the centroscymnus analog as a source to infer that coelacanths inhabit deep water, but also use the following different source:

Source 2: ruvettus-2

(have (ruvettus rod-pigment-2) have-2)

(absorb (rod-pigment-2 474nm-light) absorb-2)

(penetrate (474nm-light deep-ocean-water) penetrate-2)

(see-in (ruvettus deep-ocean-water) see-in-2)

(inhabit (ruvettus deep-ocean-water) inhabit-2)

(enable (have-2 see-in-2) enable-2)

(because (absorb-2 penetrate-2) because-2)

(adapt (see-in-2 inhabit-2) adapt-2)

The overall inference is that coelacanths inhabit deep water because they are like the centroscysmus and the ruvettus sources in having rod pigments that adapt them to life in deep water. Notice that these are deep, systematic analogies, because the theory of natural selection suggests that the two source fishes have the rod pigments because the pigments adapt them to life in deep ocean water environments. When HOTCO maps the ruvettus source to the coelecanth target after mapping the centroscysmus source, it creates excitatory links from the inferred proposition INHABIT-NEW with both INHABIT-1 in the first source and INHABIT-2 in the second source. Hence activation can flow from both these propositions to INHABIT-NEW, so that the inference is supported by multiple analogies. If another analog or other information suggests a contradictory inference, then INHABIT-NEW will be both excited and inhibited. Thus multiple analogies can contribute to the defeasible and holistic character of analogical inference.

The new links created between the target proposition and the source proposition can also make possible emotional transfer. The coelacanth example is emotionally neutral for most people, but if an emotional valence were attached to INHABIT-1 and INHABIT-2, then the excitatory links between them and INHABIT-NEW would make possible spread of that valence as well as spread of activation representing acceptance. In complex analogies, in which multiple new excitatory link are created between aspects of one or more sources and the target, valences can spread over all the created links, contributing to the general emotional reaction to the target. Section 10.5 provides detailed examples of this kind of emotional analogical inference.

10.4 Analogies about Emotions

The *Columbia Dictionary of Quotations* (available electronically as part of the Microsoft Bookshelf) contains many metaphors and analogies concerning love and other emotions. For example, love is compared to religion, a master, a pilgrimage, an angel/bird, gluttony, war, disease, drunkenness, insanity, market exchange, light, ghosts, and smoke. It is not surprising that writers discuss emotions nonliterally, because it is very difficult to describe the experience of emotions in words. In analogies about emotions, verbal sources help to illuminate the emotional target, which may be verbally described but which also has an elusive, non-verbal, phenomenological aspect. Analogies are also used about negative emotions: anger is like a volcano, jealousy is a green-eyed monster, and so on.

In order to handle the complexities of emotion, poets often resort to multiple analogies, as in the following examples:

Love was as subtly catched, as a disease;
But being got it is a treasure sweet.
—John Donne

O, my love is like a red, red rose,
That's newly sprung in June:
My love is like a melodie,
That's sweetly play'd in tune.

—Robert Burns

Love is a smoke made with the fume of sighs,
Being purged, a fire sparkling in lovers' eyes,
Being vexed, a sea nourished with lovers' tears.
What is it else? A madness most discreet,
A choking gall and a preserving sweet.

—William Shakespeare

In each of these examples, the poet uses more than one analogy or metaphor to bring out different aspects of love. The use of multiple analogies is different from the scientific example described in the last section, in which the point of using two marine sources was to support the same conclusion about the depths inhabited by coelacanths. In these poetic examples, different source analogs bring out different aspects of the target emotion, love.

Analogies about emotions may be general, as in the above examples about love, or particular, used to describe the emotional state of an individual. For example, in the movie *Marvin's Room*, the character Lee, played by Meryl Streep, describes her reluctance to discuss her emotions by saying that her feelings are like fishhooks—you can't pick up just one. Just as it is hard to verbalize the general character of an emotion, it is often difficult to describe verbally one's own emotional state. Victims of post-traumatic stress disorder frequently use analogies and metaphors to describe their own situations (Meichenbaum 1994: 112–113):

· I am a time bomb ticking, ready to explode.
· I feel like I am caught up in a tornado.
· I am a rabbit stuck in the glare of headlights who can't move.
· My life is like a rerun of a movie that won't stop.
· I feel like I'm in a cave and can't get out.
· Home is like a pressure cooker.
· I am a robot with no feelings.

In these particular emotional analogies, the target to be understood is the emotional state of an individual, and the verbal source describes roughly what the person feels like.

The purpose of analogies about emotions is often explanatory, describing the nature of a general emotion or a particular person's emotional state. But analogy can also be used to help deal with emotions, as in the following quote from Nathaniel Hawthorne: "Happiness is a butterfly, which, when pursued, is always just beyond your grasp, but which, if you will sit down quietly, may alight upon you." People are also given advice on how to deal with negative emotions, being told for example to "vent" their anger, or to "put a lid on it."

In principle, analogies about emotions could be simulated by the standard models such as ACME and SME, with a verbal representation of the source being used to generate inferences about the emotional target. However, even in some of the above examples, the point of the analogy is not just to transfer verbal information, but also to transfer an emotional attitude. When someone says, "I feel like I am caught up in a tornado," he or she may be saying something like, "My feelings are like the feelings you would have if you were caught in a tornado." To handle the transfer of emotions, we need to go beyond verbal analogy.

10.5   Analogies that Transfer Emotions

As we have already mentioned, not all analogies are verbal: some involve transfer of visual representations (Holyoak and Thagard 1995). In addition, analogies can involve transfer of emotions from a source to a target. There are at least three such kinds of emotional transfer, involved in persuasion, empathy, and reverse empathy. In persuasion, I may use an analogy to convince you to adopt an emotional attitude. In empathy, I try to understand your emotional reaction to a situation by transferring to you my emotional reaction to a similar situation. In reverse empathy, I try to get you to understand my emotion by comparing my situation and emotional response to it with situations and responses familiar to you.

The purpose of many persuasive analogies is to produce an emotional attitude, for example when an attempt is made to convince someone that abortion is abominable or that capital punishment is highly desirable. If I want to get someone to adopt positive emotions toward something, I can compare it to something else toward which he or she already has a positive attitude. Conversely, I can try to produce a negative attitude by comparison with something already viewed negatively. The structure of persuasive emotional analogies is:

You have an emotional appraisal of the source S.

The target T is like S in relevant respects.

So you should have a similar emotional appraisal of T.

Of course, the emotional appraisal could be represented verbally by terms such as "wonderful," "awful," and so on, but for persuasive purposes it is much more effective if the particular gut feeling that is attached to something can itself be transferred over to the target. For example, emotionally intense subjects such as the Holocaust or infanticide are commonly used to transfer negative emotions.

Blanchette and Dunbar (1997) thoroughly documented the use of persuasive analogies in a political context, the 1995 referendum in which the people of Quebec voted whether to separate from Canada. In three Montreal newspapers, they found a total of 234 different analogies, drawn from many diverse source domains: politics, sports, business, and so on. Many of these analogies were emotional: sixty-six were coded by Blanchette and Dunbar as emotionally negative, and seventy-five were judged to be emotionally positive. Thus more than half of the analogies used in the referendum had an identifiable emotional dimension. For example, the side opposed to Quebec separation said, "It's like parents getting a divorce, and maybe the parent you don't like getting custody." Here the negative emotional connotation of divorce is transferred over to Quebec separation. In contrast, the yes side used positive emotional analogs for separation: "A win from the YES side would be like a magic wand for the economy."

HOTCO can naturally model the use of emotional persuasive analogies. The separation-divorce analogy can be represented as follows:

Source: divorce

(married (spouse-1 spouse-2) married-1)

(have (spouse-1 spouse-2 child) have-1)

(divorce (spouse-1 spouse-2) divorce-1) negative valence

(get-custody (spouse-1) get-custody-1)

(not-liked (spouse-1) not-liked-1) negative valence

Target: separation

(part-of (Quebec Canada) part-of-2)

(govern (Quebec Canada people-of-Quebec) govern-2)

(separate-from (Quebec Canada) separate-from–2)

(control (Quebec people-of-Quebec) control-2)

When HOTCO performs a broad inference on this example, it not only computes the analogical mapping from the source to the target and completes the target using copying with substitution and generation, but also transfers the negative valence attached to the proposition DIVORCE-1 to SEPARATE-FROM-2.

Persuasive analogies have been rampant in the recent debates about whether Microsoft has been engaging in monopolistic practices by including its World Wide Web browser in its operating system, Windows 98. In response to the suggestion that Microsoft also be required to include the rival browser produced by its competitor, Netscape, Microsoft's chairman Bill Gates complained that this would be "like requiring Coca-Cola to include three cans of Pepsi in every six-pack it sells," or like "ordering Ford to sell autos fitted with Chrysler engines." These analogies are in part emotional, since they are intended to transfer the emotional response to coercing Coca-Cola and Ford—assumed to be ridiculous—over to the coercion of Microsoft. On the other hand, critics of Microsoft's near-monopoly on personal computer operating systems have been comparing Gates to John D. Rockefeller, whose predatory Standard Oil monopoly on petroleum products was broken up by the U.S. government in 1911.

Persuasive analogies suggest a possible extension to the multiconstraint theory of analogical reasoning developed by Holyoak and Thagard (1995). In that theory, similarity is one of the constraints that influence how two analogs are mapped to each other, including both the semantic similarity of predicates and the visual similarity of objects. We conjecture that emotional similarity may also influence analogical mapping and predict that people will be more likely to map elements that have the same positive or negative valence. For example, if you have a positive feeling about Bill Gates and a negative feeling about John D. Rockefeller, you will be less likely to see them as analogs, impeding both retrieval and mapping. A recent advertisement for a book on cancer compared the genetically mutated cell that initiates a tumor growth to Jesus initiating Christianity. Regardless of how structurally informative this analogy might be, the correspondences between cancer cells and Jesus and between tumors and Christianity produce for many people an emotional mismatch that renders the analogy ineffective. During the Kosovo war in 1999, comparisons were frequently made between the Serbian leader Slobodan Milosevic and Adolf Hitler; these comparisons were emotionally congruent for most people, but not for Milosevic's supporters.

Another, more personal, kind of persuasive emotional analogy is identification, in which you identify with someone and then transfer positive emotional attitudes about yourself to them. According to Fenno (1978:58), members of the U.S. congress try to convey a sense of identification to their constituents. The message is, "You know me, and I'm like you, so you can trust me." The structure of this kind of identification is:

You have a positive emotional appraisal of yourself (source).

I (the target) am similar to you.

So you should have a positive emotional appraisal of me.

Identification is a kind of persuasive analogy, but differs from the general case in that the source and target are the people involved. A full representation of the similarity involved in identification and other analogies requires specification of the causal and other higher-order relations that capture deep, highly relevant similarities between the source and target.

Empathy also involves transfer of emotional states between people; see Barnes and Thagard (1997) for a full discussion. It differs from persuasion in that the goal of the analogy is to understand rather than to convince someone. Summarizing, the basic structure is:

You are in situation T (target).

When I was in a similar situation S, I felt emotion E (source).

So maybe you are feeling an emotion similar to E.

As with persuasion and identification, such analogizing could be done purely verbally, but it is much more effective to actually feel something like what the target person is feeling. For example, if Thagard wants to understand the emotional state of a new graduate student just arrived from a foreign country, he can recall his emotional state of anxiety and confusion when he went to study in England. Here is a more detailed example of empathy involving someone trying to understand the distress of Shakespeare's Hamlet at losing his father by comparing it to his or her own loss of a job (from Barnes and Thagard 1997):

Source: you	Target: Hamlet
(fire (boss, you) s1-fire)	(kill (uncle, father) t1-kill)
(loss (you, job) s2-lose)	(lose (Hamlet, father) t2-lose)
	(marry (uncle, mother) t2a-marry)
(cause (s1-fire, s2-lose) s3)	(cause (t1-kill, t2-lose) t3)
(angry (you): s4-angry)	(angry (Hamlet) t4-angry)
(depressed (you) s5-depressed)	(depressed (Hamlet) t5-depressed)
(cause (s2-lose, s4-angry) s6)	(cause (t2-lose, t4-angry) t6)

(cause (s2-lose, s5-depressed) s7)   (cause (t2-lose, t5-depressed) t7)

(indecisive (you) s8-indecisive)

(cause (s5-depressed,
s8-indecisive) s9)

The purpose of this analogy is not simply to draw the obvious correspondences between the source and the target, but to transfer over your remembered image of depression to Hamlet.

Unlike persuasive analogies, whose main function is to transfer positive or negative valence, empathy requires transfer of the full range of emotional responses. Depending on his or her situation, I need to imagine someone being angry, fearful, disdainful, ecstatic, enraptured, and so on. As currently implemented, HOTCO transfers only positive or negative valences associated with a proposition or object, but it can easily be expanded so that transfer involves an *emotional vector* that represents a pattern of activation of numerous units, each of whose activation represents different components of emotion. This expanded representation would also make possible the transfer of "mixed" emotions.

Empathy is only one kind of explanatory emotional analogy. In section 10.4, we already saw examples of analogies whose function is to explain one's own emotional state to another, a kind of reverse empathy in that it enables others to have an empathic understanding of oneself. Here is the structure of reverse empathy:

I am in situation T (target).

When you were in a similar situation S, you felt emotion E (source).

So I am feeling an emotion similar to E.

Here is a final example of analogical transfer of emotion: "Psychologists would rather use each other's toothbrushes than each other's terminology." This analogy is complex, because at one level it is projecting the emotional reaction of disgust from use of toothbrushes to use of terminology, but it is also generating amusement. A similar dual role is also found in the following remark in *The Globe and Mail*: "Starbuck's coffee shops are spreading through Toronto faster than head lice through a kindergarten class." Both these examples convey an attitude, as does the remark of country music star Garth Brooks: "My job is like what people say about pizza and sex: When it's good, it's great; and even when it's bad, it's still pretty good." Note that this is a multiple analogy, for what it's worth. The writer Gusteve Flaubert also used an analogy to convey his attitude toward his work: "I love my work with a love that is frantic and perverted, as an ascetic loves the hair shirt that scratches his belly." Let us now consider analogies that go beyond analogical transfer of emotions and actually generate new emotions.

10.6 Analogies that Generate Emotions

A third class of emotional analogies involves ones that are not about emotions and do not transfer emotional states, but rather serve to generate new emotional states. There are at least four subclasses of emotion-generating analogies, including humor, irony, discovery, and motivation.

One of the most enjoyable uses of analogy is to make people laugh, generating the emotional state of mirth or amusement. The University of Michigan recently ran an informational campaign to get people to guard their computer passwords more carefully. Posters warn students to treat their computer passwords like underwear: make them long and mysterious, don't leave them lying around, and change them often. The point of the analogy is not to persuade anyone based on the similarity between passwords and underwear, but rather to generate amusement that focuses attention on the problem of password security.

A major part of what makes an analogy funny is a surprising combination of congruity and incongruity. Passwords do not fit semantically with underwear, so it is surprising when a good relational fit is presented (change them often). Other emotions can also feed into making an analogy funny, for example when the analogy is directed against a person or group one dislikes:

Why do psychologists prefer lawyers to rats for their experiments?

1. There are now more lawyers than rats.
2. The psychologists found they were getting attached to the rats.
3. And there are some things that rats won't do.

This joke depends on a surprising analogical mapping between rats in psychological experiments and lawyers in their practices, and on negative emotions attached to lawyers. Further surprise comes from the addendum that psychologists have stopped using lawyers in their experiments because the results did not transfer to humans. Another humorous analogy is implicit in the joke: "How can a single woman get a cockroach out of her kitchen? Ask him for a commitment."

Some analogical jokes depend on visual representations, as in the following children's joke: "What did the 0 say to the 8? Nice belt." This joke requires a surprising visual mapping between numerals and human dress. A more risqué visual example is. "Did you hear about the man with five penises? His pants fit like a glove." Here are some more humorous analogies, all of which involve mappings that generate surprise and amusement:

Safe eating is like safe sex: You may be eating whatever it was that what you're eating ate before you ate it.

Changing a university has all the difficulties of moving a cemetery.

Administering academics is like herding cats.

An associate dean is a mouse training to be a rat.

The juvenile sea squirt wanders through the sea searching for a suitable rock or hunk of coral to cling to and make its home for life. For this task, it has a rudimentary nervous system. When it finds its spot and takes root, it doesn't need its brain anymore, so it eats it! (It's rather like getting tenure.) (Dennett 1991: 177)

Bill James on Tim McCarver's book on baseball: But just to read the book is nearly impossible; it's like canoeing across Lake Molasses.

Red Smith: Telling a nonfan about baseball is like telling an eight-year-old about sex. No matter what you say, the response is, "But why?"

Melissa Franklin (Harvard physicist) on quarks: It's weird. You've got six quarks; five of them are really light, and the sixth is unbelievably heavy. It's as if you had Sleepy, Dopey, Grumpy, Happy, and Kierkegaard.

Note that Franklin only mentions four dwarves, so the mapping is not one-one, a fact that does not undermine the analogy. Failure of one-one mapping can even be funny, as in a 1998 cartoon that showed a ship labeled "Bill Clinton" about to hit an iceberg labeled "Bill Clinton."

In the emotional coherence theory of Thagard (2000), surprise is treated as a kind of metacoherence. When HOTCO shifts from coherent interpretation to another, with units that were previously activated being deactivated and vice versa, the units that underwent an activation shift activate a surprise node. In analogical jokes, the unusual mapping produces surprise because it connects together elements not previously mapped, but does so in a way that is still highly coherent. The combination of activation of the surprise node, the coherence node, and other emotions generates humorous amusement.

Analogies that are particularly deep and elegant can also generate an emotion similar to that produced by beauty. A beautiful analogy is one so accurate, rich, and suggestive that it has the emotional appeal of an excellent scientific theory or mathematical theorem. Holyoak and Thagard (1995, chap. 8) describe important scientific analogies such as the connection with Malthusian population growth that inspired Darwin's theory of natural selection. Thus scientific and other elegant analogies can generate positive emotions such as excitement and joy without being funny.

Not all analogies generate positive emotions, however. Ironies are sometimes based on analogy, and they are sometimes amusing, but they can also produce negative emotions such as despair:

HONG KONG (January 11, 1998 AF-P)—Staff of Hong Kong's ailing Peregrine Investments Holdings will turn up for work Monday still in the dark over the fate of the firm and their jobs. . . . Other Peregrine staff members at the brokerage were quoted as saying Sunday they were pessimistic over the future of the firm, saddled with an estimated 400 million dollars in debts. "I'm going to see the Titanic movie . . . that will be quite ironic, another big thing going down," the South China Morning Post quoted one broker as saying.

Shelley (in press) argues that irony is a matter of "bicoherence," with two situations being perceived as both coherent and incoherent with each other. The Peregrine Investments–Titanic analogy is partly a matter of transferring the emotion of despair from the Titanic situation to the company, but the irony generates an additional emotion of depressing appropriateness.

The final category of emotion-generating analogies we want to discuss is motivational ones, in which an analogy generates positive emotions involved in inspiration and self-confidence. Lockwood and Kunda (1997) have described how people use role models as analogs to themselves, in order to suggest new possibilities for what they can accomplish. For example, an athletic African American boy might see Michael Jordan as someone who used his athletic ability to achieve great success. By analogically comparing himself to Michael Jordan, the boy can feel good about his chances to accomplish his athletic goals. Adopting a role model in part involves transferring emotions, for example, transferring the positive valence of the role model's success to one's own anticipated success, but it also generates new emotions accompanying the drive and inspiration to pursue the course of action that the analogy suggests. The general structure of the analogical inference is:

My role model accomplished the goal G by doing the action A.

I am like my role model in various respects.

So maybe I can do A to accomplish G.

The inference that I may have the ability to do A can generate great excitement about the prospect of such an accomplishment.

10.7   An Internet Survey

The examples so far discussed were collected haphazardly, and thus amount to anecdotes rather than data. To compile analogies more systematically, Cam Shelley wrote a program to use the Internet to search for stories about analogy. Candidate news articles were collected by a keyword search for the term *analogy* and other comparative terms through Internet-based search engines, from February 1997 through September 1998. Many candidate articles were rejected due to lack of clarity. The others were classified by Shelley according to their primary practical function, including:

1. Clarification: to spell out or work through similarities between two things, often as an exercise in puzzle-solving;
2. Inference: to complete some target concept with information supplied from a source concept;
3. Description: to provide lively or colorful reading.

Inferential analogies were further divided into two types: "hot" and "cold." Hot analogies serve to transfer emotional tags or attitudes from the source to target, whereas cold analogies serve simply to transfer structured information without producing any particular affect.

Hot analogies were further broken down into the three types of emotional analogies discussed above, namely empathy, reverse empathy, and persuasion. Very often the analogies conveyed in each news article were complex and appeared to serve more than one of the functions listed here. However, we counted each analogy only once on the basis of its most salient function. Figure 10.1 displays the results. Note that well over half of the analogies had emotional content and purpose. Perhaps this result is not surprising, since news reports, particularly those of the major wire services such as the Associated Press or Reuters, tend to be sensational to attract readers.

Many of the nonemotional analogies came from reports of scientific advances, such as medical research on the origin of the human immune system. For example, when Dr. Gary Litman expresses an enthusiastic interest in the analogy between human and shark immune systems, the comparison serves largely to inform his research rather than to create excitement among his colleagues (from "Scientist goes fishing," 11 February 1998, *St. Petersburg Times*).

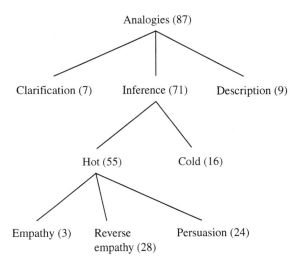

Figure 10.1
Classification of analogies found on Internet wire services.

Remarkably few of the emotional analogies seem to display the process of empathy. News reports were counted as examples of empathy where they showed people attempting to understand another person by analogies about their own emotional experiences. Given the interest that reporters have in recording people in the grip of highly emotional experiences, it appears surprising that so few examples of empathy should be present in the database. But there are at least two reasons to suppose that the lack of examples is illusory.

First, we might expect people to empathize based on their own personal experiences. But this expectation is implicitly based on the idea that our personal experiences are necessarily the most immediate or salient experiences that we might recall. This idea appears to be untrue. The examples of empathy in the database show people empathizing with others based on conventional or stereotypical experiences. For example, Dr. William Catalona expresses empathy with middle-aged men who are clamoring for the potency drug Viagra by comparing it to the demand for wrinkle cream (from "Baby Boomers fight aging in a variety of ways," by P. B. Librach, 1 June 1998, Scripps Howard News Service): "It's like the Fountain of Youth," said Catalona. "Viagra is analogous to anti-wrinkle cream. This is something that will turn back the clock and make men the way they were when they were young."

In other words, Catalona empathizes with middle-aged men by comparing their desire for Viagra with what he imagines to be the desire of middle-aged women for wrinkle cream. This source analog, although it does not represent Catalona's own experience, was selected due to (1) the surface similarity between Viagra as a drug and wrinkle cream as a cosmetic and (2) the representativeness of the wrinkle-cream situation as a stereotype of the (foolish?) desire to feel young. Because people tend to pick out stereotyped analogs when empathizing, it is not always clear whether they are truly empathizing instead of simply persuading the reporter that two emotional situations are indeed similar. Empathy and persuasion can be difficult to tell apart as they are reported in news articles.

The second reason why empathy appears to be rare is that it may serve as a first step in the process of persuasion or reverse empathy, both of which involve someone attempting to influence someone else's judgment of emotions. But, in order to affect people's judgments on such issues to a particular end, it is necessary to have some estimate of their emotional repertoire or their opinions on emotional situations. Getting the correct emotional response out of people requires some idea of their view of emotions and emotional topics. Empathy is an important means for getting such an idea about someone. (There are other means, of course, such as using a general set of rules about people's emotional responses.) For example, consider the analogy made by Israeli Prime Minister Benjamin Netanyahu, who compared the Palestinian Authority to "a regime facilitating terror" (from "U.S. raps Arafat, Netanyahu for rhetoric," 7 August 1998, Reuters):

Netanyahu equated economic pressure he exerted on the Palestinians since the bombing with economic sanctions Washington imposed on countries with alleged involvement in terrorism, like Libya. Albright said this analogy "does not work" and inflames the situation rather than lowering tensions. "The whole situation is totally different and while we respect the need for a prime minister, Prime Minister Netanyahu, to do what he can to protect the security of the people, using analogies that don't fit doesn't prove any point," she said.

Here Netanyahu compares Arafat's Palestinian Authority to Gaddafi's regime in Libya in order to project to his audience, which includes prominent Americans, his feelings about Arafat. However, Netanyahu's choice of Libya as the source analog is suggested not merely by any similarities between it and the Palestinian Authority, but also by his knowledge that Libya is particularly reviled by Americans. In other words, Netanyahu empathizes with Americans enough to know that mention of Libya and Gaddafi is likely to arouse strong, negative emotions in them. Certainly, U.S. Secretary of State Madeline Albright found his choice of source analog to be inflammatory.

Table 10.1 indicates the frequency with which emotions of positive and negative valence occur in the analogy database. Valences were assigned on a conventional basis, with emotional states suggesting fear, anger, disgust, sadness, and surprise counted as negative, whereas emotional states suggesting happiness, pride, admiration, calm, and trust counted as positive. Of course, the emotional states described in the news articles were typically complex and could not be completely captured simply as instances of happiness or anger, for example. We used the so-called basic emotions (anger, fear, disgust, surprise, and happiness) to

Table 10.1
Frequency of positive and negative emotions in emotional analogies

	Positive emotion	Negative emotion
Empathy	1	2
Reverse empathy	15	13
Persuasion	3	21

catalog each example of an emotional analogy. Where such a description was obviously impossible or inadequate, terms referring to more complex states were used, for example, pride and admiration. Eleven emotion terms were employed for the purposes of basic categorization: fear, happy, admiration, calm, disgust, anger, pride, trust, sad, surprise, and discomfort. Other terms were used to supplement these terms where they failed to completely capture the emotional content of an analogy.

The low number of examples of empathy precludes drawing any conclusions about that process, but the figures for reverse empathy and persuasion are more interesting. Instances of reverse empathy were fairly evenly distributed between positive and negative valences. As we described earlier, reverse empathy involves using an analogy in order to get someone else to understand your own emotional state. Consider the example given by Norman Siegel, executive director of the American Civil Liberties Union, who joined a twenty-eight-member task force created by New York Mayor Rudolph Giuliani to look into the problem of police brutality (from "Under fire, Giuliani forms panel on police," by Fred Kaplan, 20 August 1997, *Boston Globe*). "Although Siegel remained cautious about Guiliani's committment to the task force, he emphasized that he is willing for now to take the mayor at his word, saying Giuliani is in a unique position 'to, once and for all, confront the systemic problems of police brutality.' 'The analogy is Nixon going to China,' Siegel said in a telephone interview earlier yesterday." Just as President Nixon, who long was known as a foe of communism, could recognize China without facing accusations of being soft on communism, so Giuliani—a former US prosecutor who has supported the police at nearly every turn of his political career—can mount an attack on the police force without prompting charges of being soft on crime.

This analogy suggests that Guiliani is at least in a good position to undertake a review of police misbehavior. But it also conveys Siegel's emotional attitude toward the task force. Siegel explains why he trusts Guiliani (takes him at his word) in terms of the trust that people invested in Nixon due to his long-standing anticommunist activities when he recognized communist China. In both cases, the trust signals belief in a positive outcome of the activity concerned, although the choice of "Tricky Dick" as a source analog might also signal that Siegel's belief in Guiliani's sincerity remains qualified by doubt.

An excellent example of the projection of a positive emotion in reverse empathy is given by astronaut David Wolf's description of what it felt like when he began his mission on the Mir space station (from "Astronaut describes life on Mir in wry e-mail home," by Adam Tanner, 2 December 1997, Reuters):

Named NASA's inventor of the year in 1992, Wolf also describes feeling a wide array of emotions, including the moment when the U.S. space shuttle undocked from Mir, leaving him behind for his four-month mission.

"I remember the place I last felt it. Ten years old, as my parents' station wagon pulled away from my first summer camp in southern Indiana. That satisfying thrill that something new is going to happen and we don't know what it is yet."

Here, Wolf projects his feelings about being left behind on a space station by reference to his feelings about being left behind at summer camp as a youth. Besides conveying the structure of the event, Wolf's use of a source analog shared by many Americans helpfully conveys the positive thrill of anticipation that he felt during an event very few people have ever experienced themselves.

Persuasive emotional analogies usually serve not to communicate an emotion between people of varied experience, but to have one person transfer some emotional attitude from one concept to another. For example, in order to persuade people to feel calm about an apparently dangerous situation, you might remind them of analogous situations that they regard calmly. Such a case actually occurred in response to volcanic activity in the neighborhood of Mexico City (from an untitled article, 24 April 1997, Associated Press):

The picturesque Popocatepetl volcano that overlooks Mexico City spouted plumes of gas and ash 2 to 3 miles into the air on Thursday in what experts described as the geologic equivalent of a belch. Although it was the largest volcanic activity at the snow-covered peak in the last five to six months, Robert Quass of Mexico's National Center for Disaster Prevention said the flare-up did not portend a full-scale eruption. "The explosions are simply an opening up . . . of respirator tubes that have been blocked with magma since about March," Quass said. "It is better that this pressure be liberated than contained."

In this example, Quass attempts to persuade the public to feel calm regarding the volcanic activity of Popocatepetl by comparing it to a belch, an event no one presumably feels is too grave. Positive occurrences of persuasion tend to involve such humorous belittlement of some situation or concern.

Table 10.1 shows that there is a great asymmetry in the database between positive and negative valences in cases of persuasion. It appears that persuasive analogies are mostly used to condemn a person or situation. Consider the reaction of a *Boston Globe* reporter to a vegetarian burger being tested in McDonald's outlets in New York's Greenwich Village by its inventor, Jim Lewis (from "Will McDonald's beef up menu with veggie burger?" by Alex Beam, 10 June 1998, *Boston Globe*):

Ah, taste. Even Lewis concedes that taste is not the long suit of his custom-made, soybean-based, Archer Daniels Midland "meat analog" patty. Although it has more fat than the ordinary burger, it is curiously tasteless. Lewis explains that the patty was engineered to duplicate the tactile sensation of eating a burger, rather than to mimic the taste. Call it the inflatable blow-up doll of the hamburger world.

Here, Beam expresses disgust, or at least distaste and derision, for the vegetarian burger patty by comparing the act of eating it with the act of having sex with an inflatable doll. Beam does not need to elaborate on his source analog; it and the emotional attitude attached to it are readily available (or imaginable) to the reading audience.

It is not clear why negative emotions should dominate persuasive analogies. One possibility is bias in story selection, that is, it may be that news reporters are more interested in describing negative emotions. But this possibility does not gibe with the symmetry of positive and negative emotions in cases of reverse empathy. A second and more likely possibility is bias in the source itself, that is, it may be that the use of analogies for the purpose of persuasion lends itself better to negative emotions than to positive ones. But the reason for this situation is unclear: Do people simply have more negative experiences stored up for others to remind them of? Are negative experiences more readily recalled than positive ones? Are negative experiences more readily attached to new situations than positive ones? Is it more socially acceptable to persuade people that something is blameworthy rather than praiseworthy? The database suggests no clear answer, but the nature of reverse empathy suggests that social factors could play an important role. Of the three kinds of emotional analogies discussed here, persuasion is the one by which a speaker imposes on his or her audience to the greatest degree; that is, the speaker is deliberately trying to change other people's minds. The indirection achieved by evaluating something analogous to the real topic of discourse may serve to mitigate the imposition and make the audience more likely to adopt the speaker's opinion.

Social factors such as this one also tend to obscure the distinction between reverse empathy and persuasive analogies in practice. As Grice (1989) observed, much human communication and interaction depends on people adopting a cooperative stance in dealing with each other. Thus, to return to a classic example, someone might request a salt shaker not by asking for it directly but by stating something like "this lasagna could use some salt." Similarly, someone could employ an indirect method of persuasion by using reverse empathy. Consider the following analogy stated by Microsoft's William Neukom, senior vice president for law and corporate affairs, during a court appeal concerning Microsoft's practice of forcing computer makers to bundle its Internet Explorer with every installation of the Windows 95 operating system (from "Microsoft unveils defiant strategy in appeal," by Kaitlin Quistgaard and Dan Brekke, 16 December 1997, Reuters): "The central point of our position is that when a computer manufacturer licenses Windows, it should install the entire product, just as Ford requires that all its vehicles be sold with Ford engines. This is the only way to guarantee customers a consistent Windows experience." In this case, Neukom is attempting to persuade the court judge that the suit against Microsoft is as unreasonable as a suit against Ford would be. In so doing, Neukom does not directly urge the court to adopt Microsoft's position but rather simply states what their position is. In other words, he just states Microsoft's official attitude for the court in such as way as to invite the judge to adopt it—an indirect use of persuasion. This indirect approach is only one example of how social factors such as the exhibition of cooperative behavior tends to obscure the distinctions between the use of emotional analogies in persuasion and reverse empathy.

We cannot assume that the analogies found in the Internet survey are characteristic of emotional analogies in general. Perhaps a different methodology would find more instances of empathy and positive emotions. But the survey has served to collect many interesting analogies and to illustrate further the emotional nature of much analogical inference.

10.8   Conclusion

In this chapter, we have provided numerous examples of emotional analogies, including analogies about emotions; analogies that transfer emotions in persuasion, empathy, and reverse empathy; and analogies that generate emotions in humor, irony, discovery, and motivation. In order to understand the cognitive processes involved in emotional analogies, we have proposed an account of analogical inference as defeasible, holistic, multiple, and emotional. The HOTCO model of emotional coherence provides a computational account of the interaction of cognitive and emotional aspects of analogical inference.

Acknowledgments

Thagard's work on this project was supported by a grant from the Natural Sciences and Engineering Council of Canada and by a Canada Council Killam Research Fellowship. Shelley was supported by a doctoral fellowship from the Social Sciences and Humanities Research Council of Canada. We are grateful to Usha Goswami for comments on an earlier draft.

References

Barnes, A., and Thagard, P. (1997). Empathy and analogy. *Dialogue: Canadian Philosophical Review* **36**:705–720.

Blanchette, I., and Dunbar, K. (1997). Constraints underlying analogy use in a real-world context: Politics. In M. G. Shafto and P. Langley, Eds., *Proceedings of the nineteenth annual conference of the Cognitive Science Society*, p. 867. Mahwah, NJ: Erlbaum.

Bosanquet, B. (1920). *Implication and linear inference*. London: Macmillan.

Dennett, D. (1991). *Consciousness explained*. Boston: Little, Brown.

Falkenhainer, B., Forbus, K. D., and Gentner, D. (1989). The structure-mapping engine: Algorithms and examples. *Artificial Intelligence* 41:1–63.

Fenno, R. F. (1978). *Home style: House members in their districts*. Boston: Little, Brown.

Gentner, D. (1983). Structure-mapping: A theoretical framework for analogy. *Cognitive Science* 7:155–170.

Grice, H. P. (1989). *Studies in the way of words*. Cambridge, MA: Harvard University Press.

Harman, G. (1986). *Change in view: Principles of reasoning*. Cambridge, MA: MIT Press.

Holyoak, K. J., Novick, L. R., and Melz, E. R. (1994). Component processes in analogical transfer: Mapping, pattern completion, and adaptation. In K. J. Holyoak and J. A. Barnden, Eds., *Advances in connectionist and neural computation theory*, vol. 2, *Analogical connections*, pp. 113–180. Norwood, NJ: Ablex.

Holyoak, K. J., and Thagard, P. (1989). Analogical mapping by constraint satisfaction. *Cognitive Science* 13:295–355.

Holyoak, K. J., and Thagard, P. (1995). *Mental leaps: Analogy in creative thought*. Cambridge, MA: MIT Press.

Kolodner, J. (1993). *Case-based reasoning*. San Mateo, CA: Morgan Kaufmann.

Kunda, Z., and Thagard, P. (1996). Forming impressions from stereotypes, traits, and behaviors: A-parallel constraint-satisfaction theory. *Psychological Review* 103:284–308.

Lockwood, P., and Kunda, Z. (1997). Superstars and me: Predicting the impact of role models on the self. *Journal of Personality and Social Psychology* 73:91–103.

Meichenbaum, D. (1994). *A clinical handbook/practical therapist manual for assessing and treating adults with post-traumatic stress disorder (PTSD)*. Waterloo, Ontario: Institute Press.

Mill, J. S. (1970). *A system of logic*. (8th ed.). London: Longman.

Salmon, W. (1984). *Logic*. (3d ed.). Englewood Cliffs, NJ: Prentice-Hall.

Shelley, C. P. (1999). Multiple analogies in evolutionary biology. *Studies in History and Philosophy of Science, Part C, Studies in History and Philosophy of Biological and Biomedical Sciences* 30:143–180.

Shelly, C. (in press). The bicoherence theory of situational irony. *Cognitive Science*.

Thagard, P. (1989). Explanatory coherence. *Behavioral and Brain Sciences* 12:435–467.

Thagard, P. (1992). *Conceptual revolutions*. Princeton, NJ: Princeton University Press.

Thagard, P. (2000). *Coherence in thought and action*. Cambridge, MA: MIT Press.

Thagard, P., Eliasmith, C., Rusnock, P., and Shelley, C. P. (forthcoming). Knowledge and coherence. In R. Elio, Ed., *Common sense, reasoning, and rationality*, vol. 11. New York: Oxford University Press.

Thagard, P., Gochfeld, D., and Hardy, S. (1992). Visual analogical mapping, *Proceedings of the fourteenth annual conference of the Cognitive Science Society*, pp. 522–527. Hillsdale, NJ: Erlbaum.

Thagard, P., and Millgram, E. (1995). Inference to the best plan: A coherence theory of decision. In A. Ram and D. B. Leake, Eds., *Goal-driven learning*, pp. 439–454. Cambridge, MA: MIT Press.

Thagard, P., and Verbeurgt, K. (1998). Coherence as constraint satisfaction. *Cognitive Science* 22:1–24.

11

Analogy and Analogical Comparison in Choice

Arthur B. Markman and C. Page Moreau

A choice situation arises when a person, group, or organization identifies both an unsatisfied goal and a set of alternative ways to satisfy that goal. In order to make a choice, decision makers must identify a set of potential solutions (i.e., the consideration set), evaluate the options, and finally adopt a method for selecting one of the options (or deferring the decision). The decisions themselves may range in importance and scope. At one extreme are simple and relatively unimportant decisions such as selecting a brand of candy bar at a store counter. In the middle are moderately important choices such as buying a car or a house. At the other extreme are choices large in both scope and implication, such as a person's decision to take a new job or a country's decision about whether to go to war.

Given this diversity of choice situations, it is unlikely that a single method encompasses all of the cognitive processes required to make decisions. Some processes, however, are likely to be used across a wide variety of settings. This chapter focuses on one such process: the use of analogy and analogical comparison in choice. Most choice situations require people to apply their previous experience when making new decisions, and many accomplish this through the use of analogies. The processes underlying analogical reasoning are also active in choice situations when decision makers compare alternatives.

We begin this chapter by examining the role of analogies in choice. Many researchers have considered analogies to be important for generating and evaluating options in consumer behavior (Gregan-Paxton and Roedder John 1997; Gregan-Paxton 1998; Gregan-Paxton and Cote

1998), political strategy (Glad and Taber 1990; Khong 1992; May 1973), and legal decision-making (Holyoak and Thagard 1995; Holyoak and Simon 1999). We will examine how analogies can be used to frame a choice, to learn about options whose properties are unfamiliar, to construct a set of options, and to select a particular option.

While researchers have demonstrated the utility of analogies in a variety of aspects of decision making, the more general importance of analogical comparison processes has not been as widely recognized. Using an analogy in a choice task involves some comparison of a new situation to a stored experience. The structural alignment process that carries out these comparisons can be used to compare options to each other or to compare a new option to options seen before. These comparisons highlight the commonalities and differences of the options and influence what is learned about new options (Markman and Medin 1995; Zhang and Markman 1998). In this chapter, we will also review how choices involve the structural alignment process that is central to analogical comparisons, even when an explicit analogy is not being drawn.

Analogies are powerful determinants of decisions. They can be used to frame a choice situation, thereby constraining the set of options considered and influencing how those options are evaluated. In this section, we will consider examples of the use of analogy drawn from consumer behavior and political decision making. These examples demonstrate the importance of analogy both in individual and in group decision settings. We begin with a discussion of how general analogies (and metaphors) can influence the way decisions are framed and what is learned about novel options. Then, we discuss how analogies can lead to the construction of a consideration set.

Analogies as Framing Devices

Much research in decision making and consumer behavior is stimulus based, requiring people choose from among a set of options presented. However, there is also research on memory-based choice, which involves a more open-ended decision situation in which the options are not presented (for a review, see Alba, Hutchinson, and Lynch 1991). In memory-based choice tasks, the decision maker (a person or an organization) must first clarify the central goal in order to determine the set of options (the consideration set) and to evaluate those options. In general, a decision situation will be represented initially using background knowledge. In some cases, the choice process is straightforward. For example, purchasing tomato sauce is an open-ended decision. There are many possible options to choose from, and each satisfies a slightly different goal (e.g., different combinations of tastes and different price ranges). This choice is often made in a simple way by direct application of a highly similar previous episode. For example, consumers go to a supermarket (often a specific supermarket) because that is what they did the last time they purchased tomato sauce. The consideration set is constrained by the brands available at that store, and consumers frequently purchase the brand they bought the last time (or select from among a small number of brands they habitually buy; Hoyer 1984). Many researchers in marketing refer to this use of past experience as *brand loyalty* (Fader and Lattin 1993), and have demonstrated that it is typically the best predictor of people's future purchases in common purchase situations (Guidagni and Little 1983).

In other instances, decision situations are likely to be very different from previous situations. For example, in politics, it is rare that the same decision arises twice. Instead, new situations differ significantly from other relevant episodes from history. Further, in each situation, there are many possible courses of action, each of which could lead to very different outcomes. To conceptualize the choice task, the decision maker needs to find some way to use past experience effectively. Analogies can be useful for framing the terms of a debate in a political decision. Given the vast number of causal forces that bear on most complex issues, it is particularly important to rely on past experience in these situations (Klein 1987). An analogy can serve as a stand-in for this causal knowledge.

As one example, many historians (particularly those interested in political psychology) have examined the use of the "domino theory" in American politics in the 1950s and 1960s (Glad and Taber 1990; May 1973; Shimko 1994). Following World War II, politicians began to view the systems of government in neighboring countries (both in Europe and the

Far East) as interrelated. At the time, many European and Far Eastern countries had strong Communist elements that were in control of part of the country or were threatening to take control of the country. There were a number of possible options for U.S. foreign policy. The United States could have elected to stay out of the political decisions made in other countries. Conversely, they could have tried to intervene in a number of ways including providing military and financial aid to particular factions in the country or they could intervene directly by using military force.

Analogies were used frequently in the post–World War II era because the political landscape changed greatly in a short time. During the war, Germany and Japan were powerful countries, and Germany, in particular, had dominated politics in Europe since World War I. Following World War II, both Germany and Japan were decimated, and the United States and the USSR began to assume their roles as postwar powers. The United States began to view global politics as a struggle between countries aligned with them and Communist countries aligned with the USSR. Indeed, this tendency to view Communist countries as a single entity made it difficult for American politicians to recognize the split between China and the Soviet Union early in the Cold War.

One of the most potent analogies used to describe the interrelationship among countries was that of falling dominos.[1] The base domain of this analogy is a child's line of standing dominos. If one domino is tipped over, the entire line will fall over. Thus, if someone's goal is to keep the line of dominos standing, it is critical to make sure that no single domino falls over. In this way, all of the dominos are equally important. After the first domino falls, every other domino falls because of external forces applied to it.

In U.S. foreign policy, this analogy helped to conceptualize Communist revolutions around the world as an attempt to extend the global reach of Communism. Each country in which a Communist government came to power represented a falling domino that would lead to subsequent Communist revolutions in other countries. Thus, it was critical to make sure that no country fell to Communism, no matter how seemingly insignificant that country was. Communist revolutions were viewed as being caused by external forces acting on the country rather than as caused by internal forces. That is, these revolutions were viewed as being promulgated by outside governments (like the USSR), rather than as civil wars.

The domino analogy was extremely important in framing the political debate surrounding the Korean War. After World War II, the Korean peninsula was split into Communist North Korea and the South Korean republic. At the time, the United States had an occupying force in South Korea, which it wanted to withdraw because it did not believe that Korea was of strategic importance. In 1950, the North Korean army attacked South Korea. At the request of the United States, the United Nations security council ordered North Korea to withdraw. When this appeal was ignored, a multinational force (composed largely of American troops) was sent to Korea to repel the North Korean attack.

Prior to the attack, American politicians had acknowledged that Korea was not of strategic importance, and many had warned against getting involved in a war to save South Korea (May 1973). Despite this stance, the domino analogy had a strong influence on the reasoning of politicians who urged the United States to get involved the conflict. Given the domino analogy, the conflict could not be ignored, because just as any falling domino will cause the rest to fall, a Communist takeover of South Korea would ease Communist takeovers in other countries in the region. This inference suggested that the United States had to guard against Communist revolutions throughout the world. Thus, this analogy dictated the available options and suggested a metric for evaluating those options.

Furthermore, the domino analogy led people to conceptualize the forces acting on North Korea and South Korea as external to the countries (Shimko 1994). This interpretation of events was not required, and it would have been reasonable for the United States to consider the war in Korea to be a civil war (Glad and Taber 1990; May 1973). Under its charter, the United Nations has no role to play in civil wars, and thus it would not have gotten involved in the Korean conflict had it been viewed as a civil war. Because it was seen as a conflict between nations, the United Nations had a right to intervene.

While the domino analogy had important consequences for decisions made by the United States during the Cold War, it provided only a general framework for conceptualizing global politics. The relations carried from base to target in this analogy were abstract (e.g., that the United States had to guard against a Communist takeover in South Korea). The domino analogy could not be used to generate specific hypotheses about actions to carry out (e.g., the specific type of military, economic, or diplomatic force to use to stop the spread of Communism in Korea). As we will discuss in the next section, analogies can suggest more specific hypotheses, but only when the analogies come from reasonably close domains (see Dunbar 1997 for a similar argument in the context of scientific discovery).

Analogies and Learning about Options

Analogies can also be used to frame an individual's decisions. In this case, the analogy will often influence what is learned about options in a novel situation. This use of analogy can be seen in the domain of consumer behavior where people are learning about innovative products (Moreau, Markman, and Lehman, in press). An innovative product is one that does not fit into any known classes. Typically, the product is not wildly dissimilar from known products, because creative advances are often based on existing designs for familiar products (Ward 1995). Instead, the new product changes one or more central *immutable* features of known products. Love and Sloman (1995; Love 1996) define the mutability of a feature of an object as the extent to which the value of that feature can be changed without people feeling that the object is no longer a member of the category to which it belonged initially. A feature is relatively more immutable if it is frequent in a category and if it is connected via relations to other features of the category (see also Gentner and France 1988).

For example, in the mid-1990s, the digital camera was considered an innovative product. Digital cameras were generally assumed to be related to film-based cameras, as evidenced by the fact that many of the early manufacturers of digital cameras were companies specializing in film-based cameras such as Kodak and Olympus. Digital cameras were similar in size and shape to film-based cameras and had many of the same features, like zoom lenses and automatic flashbulbs. However, digital cameras changed a central and immutable feature of cameras: film. Other aspects of digital cameras also differed from the properties of film-based cameras such as the ability to compress images and to download images directly to a computer.

Because digital cameras were a novel innovative product, consumers needed a domain of background knowledge to conceptualize the new product. Moreau, Markman, and Lehman (in press) demonstrated that providing a base domain for an analogy to the novel target domain can influence how the new product is conceptualized. In this study, college students (a population not familiar with digital cameras at the time the study was conducted) were introduced to a new digital camera using one of two types of ads shown in figure 11.1. One type of ad compared the digital camera to a film-based camera using the ad headline, "Picture your world," text in the ad saying the digital camera was like a real camera, and a "thought bubble" rising from a picture of the digital camera with a picture of a film-based camera inside.[2] The other type of ad compared the digital camera to a scanner using the ad headline, "Scan your world," text in the ad saying the digital camera was like a scanner, and a "thought bubble" rising from the picture of the digital camera with a picture of a scanner in it.

After people were exposed to this ad, they were asked to answer a number of questions. To measure how they categorized the camera, subjects were shown a store layout with various departments labeled (including a camera department and a computer department) and were asked where they expected to find the camera. To measure their expectations of the camera's performance, subjects were shown six images at different levels of resolution (from grainy to clear) and were asked which was most likely to be the output of a digital camera. Finally, to measure their purchase intentions, subjects were given scales to measure their attitude toward the camera as well as descriptions of a number of situations for which they were asked if they might use the camera.

The results suggest that people were influenced by the analogy they saw in the ad. People who saw the ad comparing the digital camera to the film-based camera tended to expect to find the digital camera in the camera department of the store, whereas those who saw the ad comparing the digital camera to the scanner tended to expect to find the

PICTURE
YOUR
WORLD !!

SCAN
YOUR
WORLD !!

The DX-250 Works Like a Camera!

With a click of the button, you capture high-quality
color images, then publish or transmit them
right from your computer!

The DX-250 Works
Like a Scanner !

With a click of the button, you capture high-quality
color images, then publish or transmit them
right from your computer!

Figure 11.1
Ads instantiating an analogy between a digital camera and a film-based camera,
and between a digital camera and a scanner used by Moreau, Markman, and
Lehman (in preparation).

digital camera in the computer department of the store. The expected
location of the digital camera was then the best predictor of people's
judgments of picture quality. In general, subjects who expected to find
the digital camera in the camera department predicted better picture
quality than those who expected to find it in the computer department.
Finally, the judgments of picture quality were the best predictors of
people's rated intention to purchase the camera, where higher picture
quality was associated with greater intention to purchase the product.

Thus, analogy has a strong effect on the way people conceptualize
novel products. In the experiment just described, the subjects saw only
a single ad for a short period of time, and yet it influenced how they
classified the camera. This classification, in turn, influenced subjects'
beliefs about the camera's performance as well as their intentions to
purchase one.

What is the analogy doing in this situation? Gentner and Wolff (2000)
suggest that one important function of analogies is to provide a representational structure for a new concept. When a concept is new, people

will generally know a few features of the concept, but they will not know how the features are related. The base domain of an analogy contains a relational structure that binds together the features within the concept. If this relational structure can be carried over to the target concept, it can be used to structure the representation for the new concept. In this way, the analogy provides coherence (i.e., *systematicity*; Gentner 1983, 1989) to the representation of the innovative product.

One implication of having an analogy provide a relational structure for a new concept is that once an initial structure is provided, other base domains are unlikely to be good analogies for the newly structured concept. Other base domains are probably structured differently than the initial base domain. Thus, if the target domain has already taken its representational structure from the first domain, the second base domain will not be a good analog to the target. This analysis suggests that the first analogy provided as a base domain for a new concept will have a stronger influence on the representation of the new concept than will analogies presented later. Evidence for this point was obtained in a study in which people were exposed to both an ad comparing a digital camera to a film-based camera and once comparing it to a scanner (Moreau, Markman, and Lehman, in press). In this study, half of the people saw the film-based camera ad first, while the other half saw the scanner ad first. In the subsequent task in which people predicted where they expected to find the camera, people tended to expect the camera in the department consistent with the first ad they saw. As expected, the second ad had little influence on people's judgments about the camera. This finding suggests that after the first analogy provides a relational structure for the nascent concept, a new base domain no longer provides a good match and is no longer useful.

Comparisons to prior knowledge can also influence learning by affecting how people deal with missing information. Many studies of choice have demonstrated that missing information about options is discounted (e.g., Markman and Medin 1995; Slovic and MacPhillamy 1974). However, it has been demonstrated that experts in a domain are able to fill in missing information. Sanbonmatsu, Kardes, and Herr (1992) gave people descriptions of bicycles in which important information (like the weight of the bicycle) was missing for some options. Consistent with other research, novices gave little weight to this missing information. In contrast, experts who understood the importance of the missing information and the relationship between this information and other attributes of bicycles, attempted to fill in the missing information and then to use their guesses to evaluate the options.

In the context of analogy, situations in which options have missing information are similar to cases in which candidate inferences can be made. An analogical inference involves filling in missing information about one domain (the target) by carrying information from another domain (the base) through a process of structural completion. In particular, when there is a fact known about the base but not the target, it will be proposed as a candidate inference when that fact is connected via relations to matching information between base and target provided that it is consistent with the target (Clement and Gentner 1991; Markman 1997). Because inferences are rooted in relations, and experts are likely to know more relational information about products than are novices, they should be more likely to be able to fill in missing information than novices. Thus, it makes sense that experts are better able to deal with missing information than are novices.

Analogies and the Formation of Consideration Sets

When the base and target come from distant domains (e.g., dominos and geopolitics), then the analogy can provide a general frame for thinking about the target domain, but is unlikely to suggest specific courses of action in the target domain. In particular, the domains are likely to share only abstract relational similarities. There will (obviously) be no similar objects in the two domains, but there will also be few similar lower order relations. Plans for action require that both higher order relations and lower order relations to be worked through. For example, the domino analogy described earlier suggests general strategies such as keeping individual countries from being taken over by Communist governments. The analogy, however, does not suggest specific strategies, such as how to prevent a particular country from being taken over by a particular Communist government.

Nearer analogies are more likely to provide specific courses of action. For example, Dunbar (1995, 1997) has studied the way scientists reason by observing microbiologists doing research. He finds that scientists use analogies to suggest possible experiments and explanations for new patterns of data. The microbiologists prefer to use analogies from very close domains (e.g., forming an analogy from one bacterium to another) rather than from distant domains (e.g., a bacterium to a building). Presumably, this preference reflects the larger number of lower-order relations that are shared between close analogs than between far analogs. For this reason, explanations generated from pairs of close domains are more likely to be plausible than are explanations generated from pairs of distant domains.

One place where the influence of close analogies can be seen in decision making is in the formation of *consideration sets*. A consideration set is the set of options that a decision maker evaluates. Traditional studies of decision making give people a set of options and ask them to choose among them. For this reason, little research has focused on factors that determine the composition of the consideration set (for an exception see Roberts and Lattin 1991). It is critical to understand how consideration sets are formed, however, given that the composition of the consideration set critically determines which option is selected (Kardes et al. 1993; Shapiro, Macinnis, and Heckler 1997).

The role of analogy in consideration-set formation can be seen in the political decisions surrounding the entry of the United States into the Vietnam War (Khong 1992; May 1973).[3] Khong (1992) counted the number of analogies used by key decision makers in the Vietnam era both in public speeches and in private documents. The number of analogies that were used peaked in late 1964 and early 1965 at the time that the United States was developing a set of options to deal with Vietnam (i.e., the government was forming its consideration set). It could be argued that analogies used in public were primarily valued for their persuasiveness, inasmuch as the American public had to be convinced of the necessity of going to war in Vietnam. However, the use of analogies in private also suggests that they were contributing to the decision-making process.

Two analogies were used extensively by policymakers to privately formulate strategy during the pre-Vietnam era: (1) the U.S. role in the Korean War and (2) the French experience in Vietnam in the 1950s (Khong 1992). The analogy to the U.S. experience in Korea was typically used to justify sending American troops and air support into

Vietnam. Just as the United States had led a UN coalition into Korea to support the South Korean government, so too should it support the South Vietnamese government (although there was no UN coalition in this case). The Korean conflict constrained the range of options, however, because U.S. officials wanted to avoid drawing China into the Vietnam conflict. During the Korean War, Chinese troops had entered Korea after U.S. forces crossed the border between North and South Korea. Thus, many of the options considered for Vietnam were designed to be large enough to be successful, but small enough to avoid Chinese intervention. Because of the geographical similarities between Korea and Vietnam, it could be assumed that many of the same factors active in Korea would also occur for an American intervention in Vietnam. Thus, options constructed on the basis of the Korean War could carry over both abstract relations (e.g., enter the war to stave off a Communist takeover) and also more specific relations (e.g., avoid Chinese intervention by not attacking too many major sites in North Vietnam). Khong (1992) suggests that the preoccupation with avoiding Chinese entry into the Vietnam conflict led the United States to consider choices that were unlikely to lead to victory.

The second analogy used frequently during this decision making process was to the French experience in Vietnam. The French had great difficulty fighting in Vietnam because the North Vietnamese forces were intermixed into the local population, allowing them to carry out a guerrilla war. George Ball, a member of the Johnson administration and one of the most outspoken opponents of escalation in Vietnam, continually pointed to the French experience in Vietnam to suggest that the United States must avoid deeper involvement in the conflict. He recommended that the United States cut its losses and withdraw.

Two aspects of this analogy are interesting. First, like the Korea analogy, both abstract relations and more specific elements could be carried from base to target. At an abstract level, the analogy suggested that a war in Vietnam would be destined to fail. At a more specific level, the reasons for the failure (e.g., the use of guerrilla warfare, the difficulty of distinguishing between soldiers from North Vietnam and citizens of South Vietnam, and the difficulty of fighting in the jungle) could be carried over more or less directly from the base domain.

A second reason the French analogy is interesting is that it was used to argue against the appropriateness of the Korea analogy. This argument was carried out by comparing the two analogies to each other. Khong (1992) points out that Ball found five aspects of the analogies that differed. These differences arose from corresponding aspects of the analogies that manifested themselves differently in each domain (i.e., they were *alignable differences*; Gentner and Markman 1997; Markman and Gentner 1993). Among the crucial differences were the following: (1) the attacking army in Korea was a multinational force, but the attacking army in Vietnam would consist primarily of Americans; (2) the Korean government in 1950 was stable, but the Vietnamese government in 1965 was unstable; and (3) the Korean War was started by a North Korean invasion of South Korea, but the conflict in Vietnam would involve a more subtle insurgency in South Vietnam instigated by infiltrating forces from the North. Ball believed that these differences argued against the escalation of the war in Vietnam (at least as justified by the analogy to Korea).

This historical situation demonstrates the role analogies play in constraining the range of options considered when making a decision. Three aspects of the cognitive psychology of analogy are interesting here. First, in debating the entry of the United States into Vietnam, the analogies considered were all very similar to the Vietnam situation, and were typically analogies that came from the personal experience of the person suggesting the analogy (Khong 1992). Second, only a limited number of analogies were considered, with each player in the decision process typically putting forward only one or two analogies (May 1973). Finally, the role of analogy in constraining the Vietnam debate was not recognized fully by the decision makers themselves (Shimko 1994). We now elaborate on these three issues.

Types of Analogies Used

A number of factors limit the set of analogies used in choice situations to those analogies that are either familiar and/or similar to the current situation. First, as discussed earlier, close analogs are more likely to lead to the transfer of lower-order relations than are more distant analogs. For example, the prediction that China might enter the Vietnam conflict is based on the specific experience of the United States in the Korean War. Second, surface elements of target domains are often better retrieval cues than are connected relational systems (Gentner, Rattermann, and Forbus 1993; Gick and Holyoak 1980, 1983). Thus, the debate over U.S. involvement in Vietnam is likely to lead to remindings of past situations involving Korea and Vietnam rather than more distant situations like Napoleon's invasion of Russia. Third, elements related to an individual's personal experience are highly accessible (Higgins 1996). Many of the people making decisions about Vietnam were also part of the decision process (or at least part of the government) during the Korean War, so this base domain was clearly accessible for them. Finally, base domains that are part of someone's past experience are likely to have richly connected relational structures, and so will provide fertile ground for analogical inferences. As anecdotal support for these last two points, it is interesting that George Ball had worked with the French government during its Vietnam experience, so this domain was both accessible and richly represented for him. It may be that his arguments were not heeded because other participants in the debate did not share his experience.

Number of Analogies Used

May (1973) pointed out that one problem with reasoning from history is that people often draw on only a small number of base analogies that are not subjected to intense scrutiny. It seems to be a general facet of analogical reasoning that people retrieve and reason about only a small number of analogs. For example, one set of studies examined analogical retrieval when two relevant analogs were available in memory and found that people typically recalled only one of them (Wharton et al. 1994). Even studies that have focused on how multiple analogies can be used during learning and problem solving have focused on the use of a small number of base domains (e.g., Burstein 1988). To the extent that an analogy is being used to represent the target domain, people may find it difficult to use more than one analogy. Analogies are helpful because they provide a set of relations that structure the representation of the target domain. Once these relations are in place, the target domain is no longer likely to be a good relational match for other base domains (particularly base domains that are different from the first base domain used). Thus, once the representation of the target domain has been established, other analogs will no longer seem to be as relevant. This hypothesis is consistent with the finding described above that the first analogy presented to people learning about digital cameras was more effective than was the second analogy.

Awareness of Analogies Used

This latter point may also help explain why the influence of analogies is not always fully recognized by the participants in a decision. By determining how the target domain is represented, the analogy places strong constraints on what options are considered and on how these options are evaluated. However, these constraints are placed by the nature of the representation, and not by some external set of evaluation criteria. It can be quite difficult to recognize the factors that influence how a domain is represented, and hence the analogy can have its effects without the reasoners recognizing the extent of the influence of the analogy.

In this section, we have examined ways that an analogy can suggest courses of action. In this way, the formation of a consideration set can be determined in part by analogous situations from the past. This role of analogy has also been recognized as important by researchers in consumer behavior (Gregan-Paxton and Roedder John 1997). At present, however, no work has been done to suggest how analogies operate during consideration-set formation by consumers.

Analogical Comparisons among Options

In the preceding section, we focused on ways that analogies influence choice. In particular, when facing a novel situation, people can use some base domain to provide relations that bind together the elements in a target domain. Further, the analogy may suggest courses of action to be carried out. Because the base domains are often distant from the target domain, research on the role of analogies in choice focuses primarily on the influence of the analogy on choice rather than on the processes by which the base domain is compared to the target domain.

Current work in analogical reasoning (such as that described in other chapters in this volume) suggests that correspondences between a base and target domain involve an alignment of structured relational representations. The process of comparison used in analogy has also been implicated in ordinary similarity comparisons (Gentner and Markman 1997; Goldstone and Medin 1994; Markman and Gentner 1993). In the context of similarity, this process has been demonstrated to lead people to focus on the *commonalities* of a pair and their *alignable differences* at the expense of their *nonalignable differences.* Commonalities are the matching elements in the representations. For example, in comparing a sports car to a minivan, the fact that both are vehicles is a commonality. Alignable differences are aspects of the items that are placed in correspondence based on the commonalities of the pair but are dissimilar. For example, the fact that sports cars have good handling and that minivans have poor handling is an alignable difference. Finally, nonalignable differences are aspects of one item that have no correspondence at all in the other. For example, the fact that sports cars have rear spoilers while minivans do not is a nonalignable difference.

Alignable differences can be found between base and target domains or between different base domains used in analogies during choice. For example, in the previous section we discussed a comparison that George Ball made between the Korea analogy to Vietnam and the French analogy to Vietnam. The five major points of dissimilarity between these analogies were all alignable differences. The dissimilarities resulted from shared, rather than nonshared, elements that differed across the analogies. This focus on alignable differences is typical of people's use of differences in comparisons (Gentner and Markman 1994; Markman and Gentner 1993, 1997).

The structural alignment process can also be used to compare options within a consideration set. Comparing options should lead to a focus on the commonalities and alignable differences of the options rather than on the nonalignable differences. Because commonalities are not diagnostic when deciding among options, alignable differences are likely be central to choices. In the next section, we will discuss some evidence for the importance of alignable differences in choice situations where options are compared. Then, we will explore how structural alignment influences what is learned about new products.

Structural Alignment and Choice

If people compare options to each other in the process of making a choice, they should attend more to the alignable differences of options than to the nonalignable differences. In research on decision-making and consumer behavior, there is a reasonable amount of evidence for this prediction. In one set of studies, Slovic and MacPhillamy (1974) asked people to judge the freshman grade point average of two students, each of whom was described by two test scores. One of the test scores came from a test both students had taken, and the other came from a test taken by only one of the students. People performing this task systematically gave more weight to the scores from the shared test than from the scores on the unique test.

Johnson (1984, 1988) examined this issue in a different way by observing how people made choices between comparable and noncomparable sets of items. A comparable set would be a pair of objects from the same category (e.g., two toasters). A noncomparable set would be a pair of objects from different categories (e.g., a toaster and a smoke alarm). People were asked to think aloud while making their choices. For comparable consideration sets, people tended to focus on concrete attributes of the products. For example, they might compare the number of slots or settings of each of a pair of toasters. In contrast, for noncomparable consideration sets, people tended to focus on abstract attributes. For example, they might compare how much they needed a toaster or a smoke alarm. People could have used concrete aspects of the products, but the concrete aspects would have been primarily nonalignable differences (e.g., slots for a toaster or sensitivity of a smoke alarm). Rather than using these nonalignable differences, people preferred to rise to a higher level of abstraction where alignable differences between the products could be found.

As a third example of this phenomenon, Markman and Medin (1995) showed people pairs of paragraph descriptions of video games, and asked them to select the game they thought would sell best and to justify their decision. The descriptions of the games were set up so that there were four alignable differences in each pair of games. Between subjects, different sentences were removed from the descriptions of each game so that the pair had two alignable differences and two nonalignable differences. People's justifications mentioned alignable differences more often than nonalignable differences, suggesting that they were focusing on the alignable differences of the games. These results are striking, because the use of paragraph descriptions (as opposed to feature lists or an information grid) makes it difficult to find the corresponding aspects of the games.

In a set of follow-up studies, college students were shown paragraph descriptions of colleges and were asked which they would recommend to a younger sibling (Lindemann and Markman 1996). As in the video game study, the descriptions were created so that some of the attributes were alignable differences and some were nonalignable differences. The methodology of the earlier studies was extended in two ways. First, rather than write out justifications for their choices, participants thought aloud while making their decisions. Second, importance ratings of all attributes were obtained to see whether people would ignore attributes thought to be important, simply because they were nonalignable. The results of this study were similar to those obtained by Markman and Medin (1995), in that people talked about more alignable differences than nonalignable differences in their protocols. This finding suggests that the results of the previous study were not simply due to a belief that alignable differences make particularly good justifications. Further, the results show that people may discount information that is believed to be important if that information is not alignable with information about other options.

A final demonstration of the influence of alignable differences comes from studies examining the role of direction of comparison on choice. Houston, Sherman, and Baker (1989) demonstrated that people tend to focus on unique features of options when making choices. When options are presented sequentially, the second option is typically the referent of a comparison. If the options have unique properties that are negative, then people tend to prefer the first option, because the negative properties of the referent loom larger than do the negative properties of the first entrant. If the options have unique properties that are positive, then people tend to prefer the referent (i.e., the second option), because the positive properties loom larger. In an extension of this work, Sanbon-matsu, Kardes, and Gibson (1991) found that people were less likely to discount the features of the first option (which is not the referent) when the unique properties come from the same dimension (and hence are alignable differences) than when the unique properties come from different dimensions (and hence are nonalignable differences).

There are probably two reasons for the preference for alignable differences over nonalignable differences in choice. First, alignable differences are focal outputs of the comparison process and thus require less effort to access and use than nonalignable differences. Because people tend to minimize the amount of cognitive effort they expend making choices, they are more likely to use alignable differences than nonalignable differences (Payne, Bettman, and Johnson 1993; Russo and Dosher 1983). Second, in order for people to evaluate an alignable difference, they only need to know the relative goodness of the attribute, because they have values for all of the options. In contrast, to evaluate a nonalignable difference, they need to know the absolute level of goodness of the attribute. For example, if you are told that one computer has 48 Mb of RAM and another has 32 Mb of RAM, then you can guess that the first is better along that aspect than the second, even if you do not know the function of RAM in a computer. In contrast, if you only know that one computer has 48 Mb of RAM, then you must know the absolute level of goodness of that property in order to evaluate it.

There are two converging lines of evidence suggesting that the distinction between absolute and relative attribute values is important for choice. First, the consumer behavior literature makes a distinction between *attributes* and *benefits* (Conover 1982). An attribute is an aspect of a product stated in terms of its specific value (e.g., "This computer has 48 Mb of RAM"). A benefit is an aspect of a product stated in terms of a comparison to other brands (e.g., "This computer has the most RAM you can buy"). Studies have demonstrated that novices in a domain prefer to have properties of options stated as benefits, while experts prefer to have the properties stated as attributes. This finding suggests that as people gain more knowledge, they are better able to evaluate individual properties of options, and so they may be better able to evaluate the nonalignable differences.

A second line of evidence for this point comes from the work of Hsee (1996), who documented preference reversals for objects as a function of the ease of evaluating their attributes. In his materials, the options were each described by two dimensions. One dimension was easy to evaluate (e.g., any defects in a dictionary: no defects vs. a torn cover), while the other was difficult to evaluate (e.g., number of entries in a dictionary: 10,000 vs. 20,000). The options were designed so that the option that was easy to evaluate was less important than the option that was difficult to evaluate. When the options were presented individually, and people were asked to rate their goodness, subjects tended to focus on the dimension that was easy to evaluate and gave higher ratings to the option with the better value along that dimension. In contrast, when the options were presented together and people could evaluate both dimensions, they focused on the more important dimension and preferred the other option. This research suggests that the ease with which options can be evaluated influences people's preferences. To the extent that alignable differences are generally easier to evaluate, they should often be used in choices.

Taken together, these results support a core prediction of structural alignment, that alignable differences will be used in choice more frequently than will nonalignable differences. This focus on alignable differences reflects both that alignable differences are promoted over nonalignable differences by comparisons and also that alignable differences are easier to evaluate than are nonalignable differences.

Structural Alignment and Learning

Comparisons among options focus on the alignable differences of those options. In the previous section, we discussed the prediction that this focus would influence which attributes were used as the basis of choices and judgments of preference. Another influence that comparison can have is to determine what people learn about options in the course of forming preferences. In the following sections, we explore the role of structural alignment on learning that occurs during choice.

Preference and Category Learning

Much research on categorization has examined how people learn about new objects in the process of classifying them (e.g., Medin and Schaffer 1978; Nosofsky 1986, 1987). More recently, research has begun to focus on other ways that categories are learned including problem solving (Ross 1996, 1997), predictive inference (Ross and Murphy 1996; Yamauchi and Markman 1998) and communication (Markman and Makin 1998). People may also learn about categories in the world in the process of forming preferences and making choices (Zhang and Markman 1998).

Consider a situation in which consumers learn about a new product in an existing market (e.g., a new brand of microwave popcorn). Hearing about this new brand is likely to call to mind other brands that are similar to this one (namely, other brands of microwave popcorn). The attributes of the new brand can then be compared to the attributes of existing brands. This comparison will influence both what is learned about the new brand and also the preference for the new brand. Specifically, people should focus primarily on the alignable differences between the new brand and existing brands, and they should prefer new products with superior values on the alignable differences.

This proposal helps explain a seemingly paradoxical result in consumer behavior. This potential paradox comes from research on the *pioneer advantage*, which is the observation that early market leaders in a product category are often the dominant brand in that market for many years (Carpenter and Nakamoto 1989; Golder and Tellis 1993; Kardes et al. 1993). For example, Coca-Cola is currently the market leader in cola and has been for more than seventy-five years. Some of the factors leading to this pioneer advantage have to do with the economics of doing business (e.g., early market leaders tend to have better systems of distribution than do later entrants). However, consumer psychologists have examined cognitive factors that might underlie the pioneer advantage and have also searched for factors that would lead later entrants to be preferred to existing firms. This latter effort is an attempt to explain the manifest success of companies like Microsoft that are not first to market with a given product but are able to become market leaders.

Carpenter and Nakamoto (1989) suggest that successful competition with an early entrant requires that the later entrant differentiate itself from the early entrant. This hypothesis is consistent with the suggestion that later entrants must have differences (specifically alignable differences) with the early entrant. A study by Kardes and Kalyanaram (1992) casts doubt on this explanation, however, because it suggests that people are unable to recall the distinctive properties of early entrants. Thus, the authors suggest, the advantage that early market leaders have is driven by people's ability to recall the attributes of the early entrants better than the attributes of later entrants.

An examination of the materials used in the studies by Carpenter and Nakamoto and by Kardes and Kalyanaram suggests a possible resolution to these conflicting results. Carpenter and Nakamoto based their suggestion that later entrants must differentiate to be successful on studies in which all of the products were defined by five dimensions. That is, in their studies, all of the products had alignable differences with each other. In contrast, the studies of Kardes and Kalyanaram used products in which all of the differences were unique properties (i.e., nonalignable differences).

The discussion of consumer category acquisition presented above suggests that people learning about new products compare the new entrant back to previously learned products, and particularly to the early entrant, a salient item in memory. When the differences between the new product and existing products are alignable, people should be able to recall these properties and to prefer later entrants with superior alignable differences. In contrast, when the differences are nonalignable, people should have difficulty recalling these properties and should continue to prefer the early entrant.

This hypothesis was tested in a series of studies by Zhang and Markman (1998). In one study, three brands of microwave popcorn were presented to subjects in three sessions (each separated by two to five days). The set of brands (shown in table 11.1) consisted of a list of ten attributes: five commonalities and five differences. For half of the subjects, the differences were alignable, and for half of the subjects the differences were nonalignable. The brands were constructed so that two of the brands were approximately equal in preferability (as rated by an independent group of

Table 11.1
Stimulus attributes used in the studies by Zhang and Markman (1998)

Brand	Early entrant	Late entrant	Enhanced late entrant
	Fairly low level of sodium	Fairly low level of sodium	Fairly low level of sodium
	Easy to prepare	Easy to prepare	Easy to prepare
	Not salty	Not salty	Not salty
	Easy to store	Easy to store	Easy to store
	Fairly low cost per serving	Fairly low cost per serving	Fairly low cost per serving
Alignable differences			
	Uses Southwest corn	Uses Midwest corn	Uses Northwest corn
	Medium size kernels	Small size kernels	Very large kernels
	Requires a microwave bowl	Comes with disposable microwave bags	Pops in its own bag
	Calories equal to a tablespoon of sugar	Calories equal to 20 peanuts	Calories equal to a slice of bread
	Crunchiness lasts a long time	Crunchiness lasts for three hours	Crunchiness lasts within a specified time
Nonalignable differences			
	Kind of crispy	Few kernels left unpopped	Uses Northwest corn
	Not likely to burn	Some oil	Very large kernels
	Tastes a bit sweet	Comes in one package size	Pops in its own bag
	Easy to swallow	Not tough	Calories equal to a slice of bread
	Low in corn or grain flavor	Has fiber	Crunchiness lasts within a specified time

subjects) and the third was superior to the other two. The same set of attributes was used to describe this superior brand for both the stimulus sets (i.e., the alignable and nonalignable difference sets).

In the first session, people were shown only one entrant (called the first entrant). In the second session, people were shown all three entrants (the first entrant again, as well as the late entrant and the superior [or *enhanced*] late entrant). After a brief delay, they were asked to recall as many attributes of the entrants as possible, and to allocate 100 points across the entrants in proportion to their relative preference. In the third session, people carried out the recall and preference tasks again without re-exposure to the brands.

People shown brands with only nonalignable differences had difficulty recalling the distinctive attributes of the later entrants (as found by Kardes and Kalyanaram 1992). Further, these subjects allocated more points to the first entrant than to later entrants, thereby exhibiting a pioneer advantage. In contrast, people shown brands with alignable differences were able to recall many attributes of all of the entrants. Further, they allocated significantly more points to the superior enhanced late entrant than to the early entrants. This result suggests that when people learn about new items in the context of making choices, they compare the early entrant back to existing entrants.

The Importance of Structure in Structural Alignment
The key advance of structural alignment over featural theories of similarity like Tversky's (1977) influential contrast model is that structural alignment permits nonidentical representational elements to be placed in correspondence when they play the same role in a matching relational structure. For example, both the tires of a car and the legs of a bird play the role of supporting the objects to which they are attached, and so they form an alignable difference when a car and a bird are compared. On the featural view, nonidentical representational elements can never be placed in correspondence. There are only common features and distinctive features. The tires of a car and the feet of a bird cannot be seen as dissimilar manifestations of some common aspect of the objects.

This analysis highlights the fact that relations are critical for finding alignable differences. If a pair does not share some common relational structure, then there can only be nonalignable differences between them.

This point was demonstrated in another set of studies looking at the pioneer advantage, this time in unfamiliar product categories (Zhang and Markman, in preparation). In the experiment described in the previous section, participants were introduced to brands of microwave popcorn, a product familiar to them. In this experiment, participants learned about brands of electronic organizers, which are small handheld devices that are used to store scheduling information, phone numbers, and other personal data. At the time these studies were run, electronic organizers were not yet used by a substantial number of consumers.

Because people were not familiar with the product category, they did not know the relations among the attributes that would permit them to identify alignable differences when different brands were compared. The brands in this study each had nine attributes: four commonalities and five alignable differences (see table 11.2). The differences were designed to be treated as alignable differences if the person were expert enough in the product domain to be able to place contrasting values in correspondence. For example, one organizer might be described as recognizing handwritten data, while the second might be described as having a keyboard. A person is only likely to know that these attributes are contrasting values of an alignable difference if they know the functions that these attributes play in the product.

Prior to being exposed to the brands, people were given some information about the attributes. They were asked to copy three attributes into each of the five columns of a table. The attributes they copied into each column were the attributes that comprised a set of alignable differences across the three brands they would see later in the study. This task was done under the guise that a manufacturer wanted handwriting samples of the attributes to use in later packaging. The only thing that differed between conditions was the labels on the columns in this table. In the functional relation condition, the labels described the functions carried out by the attributes in that column (e.g., "Ways to do computing" or "Ways to input data"). In the preference condition, the labels described experts' judgments of preference for the features (e.g., "Features that are necessary" or "Good features but cost more"). The assumption was that functional relations, which relate properties of organizers to each other, would provide the relational structure necessary to find alignable differences during comparisons. In contrast, preference information, which provides

Table 11.2
Stimulus attributes used in the studies by Zhang and Markman (in preparation)

Brand		
Early entrant	Late entrant	Enhanced late entrant
address book with over 200 entries	address book with over 200 entries	address book with over 200 entries
scheduler and appointment book	scheduler and appointment book	scheduler and appointment book
are easy to use	are easy to use	are easy to use
good for travel	good for travel	good for travel
one year warranty	one year warranty	one year warranty
Differences		
with financial calculator	has calculator with scientific functions	with spreadsheet calculator
memo pad allows storage of images large keyboard to enter data	has relatively large memo pad has standard keyboard and numeric keypad for data entry	memo pad with search functions can recognize handwritten data
PC and Macintosh compatible	can exchange data with other organizers over infra-red link	has desktop-compatible connection
waterproof	shock resistant	with a protection jacket

relations between an attribute and an expert, would not support the determination of alignable differences.

As before, the brands were introduced sequentially, although they were presented in a single session in this study. First, subjects filled out the table and then they were shown the first brand. After a twenty-minute filler task, they were shown the first brand again as well as the other two brands. As before, one of the late brands was designed to be objectively superior to the first brand. After being exposed to all three brands, subjects recalled as many attributes of each brand as they could and allocated 100 points across the brands in proportion to their preference.

Subjects given the preference information were not expected to be able to place contrasting values of the attributes in correspondence, and so they were expected to act like people in the previous studies who were given brands with nonalignable differences. In contrast, people given the functional relations were expected to be able to recognize the differences of the products as alignable. Consistent with these predictions, people given the functional relations recalled more differences overall than did those given the preference information. Further, people in the preference condition allocated more points in the preference task to the first entrant than to the objectively superior late entrant. In contrast, people given functional relational information allocated more points to the superior late entrant than to the first entrant.

These results support the contention that relational knowledge is necessary for the comparison process to identify alignable differences. This finding raises some important issues that need to be addressed. First, we must explore how people come to learn about the relations in a domain. In the present study, people were simply given the relations. There are likely to be other mechanisms for learning relations. Second, these results suggest that very new product domains may be treated differently during choice than are familiar product domains. Further research needs to explore the differences between novel and familiar domains.

Learning about Nonalignable Differences

The discussion so far has focused on the importance of alignable differences in choice. Nonetheless, nonalignable differences are not irrelevant in the choice process. People can learn about unique properties of options. Further, these differences are often innovative aspects of a new product, and so it is important for marketers to find ways to get people to attend to the nonalignable differences of new products.

Understanding how nonalignable differences are involved in choices must go beyond research on structural alignment, which has focused on the claim that alignable differences are more central to similarity comparisons than are nonalignable differences. Focusing on differences related to the commonalities of a pair is often a good strategy, because this strategy filters out those differences that are unlikely to be relevant to the task being performed. For example, in a comparison of a similar pair of objects like a robin and a bluebird, most of the differences are likely to be alignable, and most are probably also relevant to reasoning tasks performed on this pair. In contrast, the differences of a dissimilar pair like robin and eggplant are generally going to be nonalignable. Thus, it is generally a good idea for the cognitive system to ignore these differences.

This analysis suggests that one reason nonalignable differences are ignored is that attending to them requires substantial cognitive resources, because the comparison process does not make nonalignable differences available. If consumers were willing to expend effort to process information about a domain, then they should give more weight to nonalignable differences than to alignable differences. This hypothesis was tested in a study by Zhang and Markman (in press). Participants were shown two brands of microwave popcorn (presented in table 11.3), each described by twelve attributes: four commonalities, four alignable differences, and four nonalignable differences. The brands were constructed so that the alignable differences of one brand were better than those of the other, but the nonalignable differences of the second brand were better than those of the first. Further, the nonalignable differences of the latter brand were superior to all of the attributes of all of the brands, so that this brand was objectively superior. Thus, if people attended to alignable differences, they should exhibit a preference for the brand with the better alignable differences, but if they attended to the nonalignable differences (or both the alignable and nonalignable differences) they should prefer the brand with the better nonalignable differences.

Table 11.3
Stimuli used in study of the role of involvement in product learning and preference (Zhang and Markman, in press)

Alignable better brand	Nonalignable better brand
Commonalities	
Low cost per serving	Low cost per serving
Low level of sodium	Low level of sodium
Not salty	Not salty
Easy to prepare	Easy to prepare
Alignable differences	
Large size kernels	Medium size kernels
Pops in its own bag	Requires a microwave bowl
Calories equal to a slice of bread	Calories equal to a tablespoon of sugar
Crunchiness lasts a long time	Crunchiness lasts for three hours
Nonalignable differences	
Slightly low in corn and grain flavor	Does not stick in teeth
Tastes a bit sweet	Not likely to burn
Has some citric acid	Few kernels left unpopped
With waterproof wrapping	Very crispy and easy to swallow

Half of the participants were put in a low involvement condition. This was done by telling them that their data would be averaged with those of a large number of other participants, and that the products being tested were in the early development stages (see Johar 1995 for a similar manipulation). The other half of the participants were put in a high involvement condition by telling them that they were one of a small number of people in the study and that the product would soon be introduced in their area. Subjects in the high involvement condition were expected to have more motivation to process information than subjects in the low involvement condition and thus were expected to be more likely than the low involvement subjects to attend to the nonalignable differences of the products.

Once again, subjects allocated 100 points across the brands in proportion to their preference. Subjects in the low involvement condition allocated more points on average to the brand with the better alignable differences than to the brand with the better nonalignable differences. This preference was observed, even though the brand with the better nonalignable differences was also the objectively superior brand. In contrast, subjects in the high involvement condition allocated more points to the brand with the better nonalignable differences, suggesting that they were able to attend to the nonalignable differences. This result is consistent with the suggestion that focusing on alignable differences saves cognitive effort, and that people who are willing to expend additional effort can attend to the nonalignable differences.

This interpretation is supported by a second study suggesting that people are more likely to attend to the nonalignable differences of new brands after they become familiar with brands in that domain than when they are first learning about brands in that domain (Zhang and Markman, in preparation). In this study, participants were exposed to brands of electronic organizers (an unfamiliar product class) with ten attributes: four commonalities, three alignable differences, and three nonalignable differences. In the first session, one group of subjects saw two brands (A and B), and later recalled attributes of the brands and performed a points allocation task as a measure of preference. In the second session, they saw the same two brands (A and B) again, and again did the recall and preference tasks. In the third session, they saw one of the brands that they saw during the first two sessions (A) as well as a new brand (C), and again performed the recall and preference tasks. A second group performed the same tasks, but saw brands A and C in the first two sessions, and were exposed to brand B for the first time in the third session. This design is summarized in table 11.4.

The key question in these studies involved the level of recall of the alignable and nonalignable differences of a brand as a function of when they initially saw it. In particular, the recall data for a brand were examined both when it was presented for the first time in the first session of the study and when it was presented for the first time in the third session of the study. Overall, people were more likely to recall the nonalignable differences of a brand when it was presented for the first time in the third session than when it was presented for the first time in the first session. In contrast, there was a small decrease in the number of alignable dif-

Table 11.4
Design of product familiarity study done by Zhang and Markman (in preparation)

	Session 1	Session 2	Session 3
Group 1	AB	AB	AC
Group 2	AC	AC	AB

ferences recalled for a brand when it was presented for the first time in the third session compared to when it was presented for the first time in the first session. This result suggests that as people get more comfortable learning about the products in a domain, they are better able to attend to the nonalignable differences of the brands.

An interesting facet of this result is that mere repetition of the brands across sessions does not have the same influence. In particular, there was only a very small increase in the number of nonalignable differences people could recall about a brand when it was repeated in the second session of the study after having been presented in the first session. Thus, the substantial increase in recall of nonalignable differences came only for brands presented for the first time after people had experience learning about products in that domain.

To summarize, nonalignable differences can be important aspects of new products, because they are often the innovative aspects of products. Thus, it is important to understand the conditions that permit nonalignable differences to be processed fluently. Researchers are just beginning to explore this topic. The early results suggest that being motivated to process information in a domain, or having experience learning about products in a domain, eases the acquisition and use of nonalignable differences of new products. Further research must focus on other ways that nonalignable differences can be used in choice.

Using Analogy in Choice

In this chapter, we have discussed two central ways that analogy influences the choice process. First, analogies to other domains can be used to provide a representation for a choice situation. In general, making a decision requires some familiarity with the choice setting. In cases where the domain of the choice is new, analogies can be used to relate the choice to previous experience. These analogies can be used to provide a general framework for thinking about a choice (as in the use of the domino analogy during the Cold War) or they can be used to generate options for making a choice (as in the Korea analogy to Vietnam). Because the role of the analogy in this case is to structure the representation of the choice situation, it exerts a strong influence on the outcome of the decision. In particular, it constrains the range of options considered and the evaluation of those options. Further, this influence may go unnoticed by the decision maker. Thus, when reasoning in new situations, it is critical to think about the analogies that may affect the choice.

The structural alignment processes involved in analogy also plays a role in choice through the comparison of options. New options can be learned through comparison to existing options. These comparisons will highlight both the commonalities and the alignable differences of the options at the expense of the nonalignable differences. Thus, alignable differences will typically be learned before nonalignable differences. Options whose attributes are already known may also be compared during choice. In these situations, alignable differences are used more frequently than nonalignable differences. Nonalignable differences of new options can be learned, however, when the decision maker is motivated to process information and when the decision maker is already generally familiar with the domain.

An examination of the role of analogy in decision-making highlights the parallels between categorization and choice. The study of categorization is focused on understanding how people's mental representations are learned, and how those representations are structured. Future work in this area will not only shed light on how people make choices, but also on how mental representations are formed in the process of determining preferences.

Notes

1. Some researchers have suggested that the falling-dominos description was a metaphor rather than an analogy (Shimko 1994). In general, the border between metaphor and analogy is fuzzy, and nothing in the present analysis rides on this

distinction (Gentner 1989). In this case, however, the falling dominos analogy did not give rise to a generative lexicon for talking about conflicts during the Cold War. Thus, this analogy was not used as a metaphorical system like those studied by Lakoff and Johnson (Lakoff 1987; Lakoff and Johnson 1980).

2. Half of the subjects in this study saw the ads without the thought bubbles. This manipulation did not change the basic pattern of data described here.

3. Holyoak and Thagard (1995) provide a brief readable overview of analogies used during the Vietnam era that synthesizes the work of a number of historians.

References

Alba, J. W., Hutchinson, J. W., and Lynch Jr., J. G. (1991). Memory and decision making. In T. Robertson and H. Kassarjian, Eds., *Handbook of consumer behavior*, pp. 1–49. Englewood Cliffs, NJ: Prentice-Hall.

Burstein, M. H. (1988). Incremental learning from multiple analogies. In A. Prieditis, Ed., *Analogica*, pp. 37–62. Los Altos, CA: Morgan Kaufmann.

Carpenter, G. S., and Nakamoto, K. (1989). Consumer preference formation and pioneering advantage. *Journal of Marketing Research* 26:285–298.

Clement, C. A., and Gentner, D. (1991). Systematicity as a selection constraint in analogical mapping. *Cognitive Science* 15:89–132.

Conover, J. N. (1982). Familiarity and the structure of product knowledge. *Advances in Consumer Research* 9:494–498.

Dunbar, K. (1995). How scientists really reason: Scientific reasoning in real-world laboratories. In R. J. Sternberg and J. E. Davidson, Eds., *The nature of insight*, pp. 365–396. Cambridge, MA: The MIT Press.

Dunbar, K. (1997). How scientists think: On-line creativity and conceptual change in science. In T. B. Ward, S. M. Smith, and J. Vaid, Eds., *Creative thought: An investigation of conceptual structures and processes*, pp. 461–493. Washington, DC: American Psychological Association.

Fader, P. S., and Lattin, J. M. (1993). Accounting for heterogeneity and nonstationarity in a cross-sectional model of consumer purchase behavior. *Marketing Science* 12(3):304–317.

Gentner, D. (1983). Structure-mapping: A theoretical framework for analogy. *Cognitive Science* 7:155–170.

Gentner, D. (1989). The mechanisms of analogical learning. In S. Vosniadou and A. Ortony, Eds., *Similarity and analogical reasoning*, pp. 199–241. New York: Cambridge University Press.

Gentner, D., and France, I. M. (1988). The verb mutability effect. In S. L. Small, G. G. Cottrell, and M. K. Tanenhaus, Eds., *Lexical ambiguity resolution: Perspectives from psycholinguistics, neuropsychology and artificial intelligence*, pp. 343–382. San Mateo, CA: Morgan Kaufmann.

Gentner, D., and Markman, A. B. (1994). Structural alignment in comparison: No difference without similarity. *Psychological Science* 5(3):152–158.

Gentner, D., and Markman, A. B. (1997). Structural alignment in analogy and similarity. *American Psychologist* 52(1):45–56.

Gentner, D., Rattermann, M. J., and Forbus, K. D. (1993). The roles of similarity in transfer: Separating retrievability from inferential soundness. *Cognitive Psychology* 25(4):524–575.

Gentner, D., and Wolff, P. (2000). Metaphor and Knowledge Change. In E. Dietrich and A. B. Markman, Eds., *Cognitive Dynamics*, pp. 295–342. Mahwah, NJ: Lawrence Erlbaum Associates.

Gick, M. L., and Holyoak, K. J. (1980). Analogical problem solving. *Cognitive Psychology* 12:306–355.

Gick, M. L., and Holyoak, K. J. (1983). Schema induction and analogical transfer. *Cognitive Psychology* 15(1):1–38.

Glad, B., and Taber, C. S. (1990). Images, learning, and the decision to use force: The domino theory of the United States. In B. Glad, Ed., *Psychological dimensions of war*, pp. 56–82. Newbury Park, CA: Sage Publications.

Golder, P. T., and Tellis, G. J. (1993). Pioneer advantage: Marketing logic or marketing legend? *Journal of Marketing Research* 30:158–170.

Goldstone, R. L., and Medin, D. L. (1994). Similarity, interactive-activation and mapping: An overview. In K. J. Holyoak and J. A. Barnden, Eds., *Advances in Connectionist and Neural Computation Theory*, vol. 2, *Analogical Connections*, pp. 321–362. Norwood, NJ: Ablex.

Gregan-Paxton, J., and Roedder John, D. (1997). Consumer learning by analogy: A model of internal knowledge transfer. *Journal of Consumer Research* 24:266–284.

Gregan-Paxton, J. (in preparation). The role of abstract and specific knowledge in the product evaluation process: An analogical learning perspective.

Gregan-Paxton, J., and Cote, J. (in preparation). How do investors make predictions? Insights from analogical reasoning research.

Guidagni, P. M., and Little, J. D. C. (1983). A logit model of brand choice calibrated on scanner data. *Marketing Science* 2:203–238.

Higgins, E. T. (1996). Knowledge activation: Accessibility, applicability, and salience. In E. T. Higgins and A. W. Kruglanski, Eds., *Social psychology: Handbook of basic principles*, pp. 133–168. New York: Guilford Press.

Holyoak, K. J., and Simon, D. (1999). Bidirectional reasoning in decision making. *Journal of Experimental Psychology: General* 128:3–31.

Holyoak, K. J., and Thagard, P. (1995). *Mental leaps: Analogy in creative thought*. Cambridge, MA: MIT Press.

Houston, D. A., Sherman, S. J., and Baker, S. M. (1989). The influence of unique features and direction of comparison on preferences. *Journal of Experimental Social Psychology* 25:121–141.

Hoyer, W. D. (1984). An examination of consumer decision making for a common repeat purchase. *Journal of Consumer Research* 11:822–829.

Hsee, C. K. (1996). The evaluability hypothesis: An explanation for preference reversals between joint and separate evaluations of alternatives. *Organizational Behavior and Human Decision Processes* 67(3):247–257.

Johar, G. V. (1995). Consumer involvement and deception from implied advertising claims. *Journal of Marketing Research* 32:267–279.

Johnson, M. D. (1984). Consumer choice strategies for comparing noncomparable alternatives. *Journal of Consumer Research* 11:741–753.

Johnson, M. D. (1988). Comparability and hierarchical processing in multialternative choice. *Journal of Consumer Research* 15:303–314.

Kardes, F. R., and Kalyanaram, G. (1992). Order-of-entry effects on consumer memory and judgment: An information integration perspective. *Journal of Marketing Research* 29:343–357.

Kardes, F. R., Kalyanaram, G., Chandrashekaran, M., and Dornoff, R. J. (1993). Brand retrieval, consideration set, composition, consumer choice, and the pioneering advantage. *Journal of Consumer Research* 20:62–75.

Khong, Y. F. (1992). *Analogies at war.* Princeton, NJ: Princeton University Press.

Klein, G. A. (1987). Applications of analogical reasoning. *Metaphor and Symbolic Activity* 2(3):201–218.

Lakoff, G. (1987). *Women, fire and dangerous things: What categories reveal about the mind.* Chicago: University of Chicago Press.

Lakoff, G., and Johnson, M. (1980). *Metaphors we live by.* Chicago: University of Chicago Press.

Lindemann, P. G., and Markman, A. B. (1996). Alignability and attribute importance in choice. Paper presented at the eighteenth annual meeting of the Cognitive Science Society, San Diego, CA.

Love, B. C. (1996). Mutability, conceptual transformation, and context. In G. Cottrell, Ed., *Proceedings of the eighteenth annual meeting of the Cognitive Science Society*, pp. 459–463. Mahwah, NJ: Lawrence Erlbaum Associates.

Love, B. C., and Sloman, S. A. (1995). Mutability and the determinants of conceptual transformability. Paper presented at the seventeenth annual conference of the Cognitive Science Society, Pittsburgh, PA.

Markman, A. B. (1997). Constraints on analogical inference. *Cognitive Science* 21:373–418.

Markman, A. B., and Gentner, D. (1993). Splitting the differences: A structural alignment view of similarity. *Journal of Memory and Language* 32(4):517–535.

Markman, A. B., and Gentner, D. (1997). The effects of alignability on memory. *Psychological Science* 8(5):363–367.

Markman, A. B., and Makin, V. S. (1998). Referential communication and category acquisition. *Journal of Experimental Psychology: General* 127:331–354.

Markman, A. B., and Medin, D. L. (1995). Similarity and alignment in choice. *Organizational Behavior and Human Decision Processes* **63**(2):117–130.

May, E. R. (1973). *"Lessons" of the past*. New York: Oxford University Press.

Medin, D. L., and Schaffer, M. M. (1978). Context theory of classification. *Psychological Review* **85**(3):207–238.

Moreau, C. P., Markman, A. B., and Lehman, D. R. (in press). 'What is it?' Categorization flexibility and consumers' responses to really new products. *Journal of Consumer Research*.

Nosofsky, R. M. (1986). Attention, similarity and the identification-categorization relationship. *Journal of Experimental Psychology: General* **115**(1):39–57.

Nosofsky, R. M. (1987). Attention and learning processes in the identification and categorization of integral stimuli. *Journal of Experimental Psychology: Learning, Memory, and Cognition* **13**(1):87–108.

Payne, J. W., Bettman, J. R., and Johnson, E. J. (1993). *The adaptive decision maker*. New York: Cambridge University Press.

Roberts, J. H., and Lattin, J. M. (1991). Development and testing of a model of consideration set composition. *Journal of Marketing Research* **28**:429–440.

Ross, B. H. (1996). Category representations and the effects of interacting with instances. *Journal of Experimental Psychology: Learning, Memory, and Cognition* **22**(5):1249–1265.

Ross, B. H. (1997). The use of categories affects classification. *Journal of Memory and Language* **37**:240–267.

Ross, B. H., and Murphy, G. L. (1996). Category-based predictions: Influence of uncertainty and feature associations. *Journal of Experimental Psychology: Learning, Memory, and Cognition* **22**(3):736–753.

Russo, J. E., and Dosher, B. A. (1983). Strategies for multiattribute binary choice. *Journal of Experimental Psychology: Learning, Memory, and Cognition* **9**(4): 676–696.

Sanbonmatsu, D. M., Kardes, F. R., and Gibson, B. D. (1991). The role of attribute knowledge and overall evaluations in comparative judgment. *Organizational Behavior and Human Decision Processes* **48**:131–146.

Sanbonmatsu, D. M., Kardes, F. R., and Herr, P. M. (1992). The role of prior knowledge and missing information in multiattribute evaluation. *Organizational Behavior and Human Decision Processes* **51**:76–91.

Shapiro, S., Macinnis, D. J., and Heckler, S. E. (1997). The effects of incidental ad exposure on the formation of consideration sets. *Journal of Consumer Research* **24**:94–104.

Shimko, K. L. (1994). Metaphors and foreign policy decision making. *Political Psychology* **15**(4):655–671.

Slovic, P., and MacPhillamy, D. (1974). Dimensional commensurability and cue utilization in comparative judgment. *Organizational Behavior and Human Performance* 11:172–194.

Tversky, A. (1977). Features of similarity. *Psychological Review* 84(4):327–352.

Ward, T. B. (1995). What's old about new ideas. In S. M. Smith, T. B. Ward, and R. A. Finke, Eds., *The creative cognition approach*, pp. 157–178. Cambridge, MA: MIT Press.

Wharton, C. M., Holyoak, K. J., Downing, P. E., Lange, T. E., Wickens, T. D., and Melz, E. R. (1994). Below the surface: Analogical similarity and retrieval competition in reminding. *Cognitive Psychology* 26(1):64–101.

Yamauchi, T., and Markman, A. B. (1998). Category learning by inference and classification. *Journal of Memory and Language* 39(1):124–148.

Zhang, S., and Markman, A. B. (1998). Overcoming the early entrant advantage via differentiation: The role of alignable and nonalignable differences. *Journal of Marketing Research* 35:413–426.

Zhang, S., and Markman, A. B. (in press). Processing product-unique features: Alignment and involvement in preference construction. *Journal of Consumer Psychology*.

Zhang, S., and Markman, A. B. (in preparation). Representational structure and the detection of alignable differences.

12
Semantic Alignments in Mathematical Word Problems

Miriam Bassok

Students of mathematics, physics, or economics are all too familiar with mathematical *word problems*—short and highly contrived story problems that describe quantitative properties of various objects (e.g., crayons, cars, or workers) and require mathematical solutions. For example, the following is a simple division word problem about Jane, apples, and baskets: "Jane wants to place sixty apples in five baskets such that each basket contains the same number of apples. How many apples should she place in each basket?" Mathematics educators use such "popular twentieth-century fables called word problems" (Hinsley, Hayes, and Simon 1977) as instructional tools that are supposed to help students relate their world knowledge to formal mathematical knowledge.

Word problems are used for two related purposes (see Nesher 1989 for a critical discussion of this dual use). First, they serve as concrete illustrations of the abstract mathematical concepts and rules students are expected to acquire (e.g., the mathematical operation of division is like the partitioning of apples among baskets). Second, they provide students with situations that can be successfully modeled by the previously learned mathematical knowledge (e.g., a problem about partitioning apples among baskets can be solved using the operation of division). In both cases, students are expected to reason by analogy. In the first case (i.e., illustration), the situation described in the problem is the familiar *base* and the mathematical structure the novel *target*; in the second case (i.e., modeling), the mathematical structure is the base and the situation the target.

In a recent analysis of textbook word problems (Bassok, Chase, and Martin 1998) we found that most word problems are designed in a way that is consistent with their instructional roles (illustration and modeling). Specifically, we found that the problems' cover stories describe, or imply, semantic relations between objects (*semantic structure*) that correspond to mathematical relations between abstract mathematical entities (*mathematical structure*). Based on their extensive experience with such problems, students seem to learn that they can safely use the problem's semantic structure (e.g., PLACE IN [apples, baskets]) to infer, by analogy, its mathematical structure (e.g., DIVIDE [dividend, divisor]). I refer to this inferential process with the term *semantic alignment*.

In this chapter I describe results from three related studies that document the impact of semantic alignments on people's reasoning about mathematical word problems. Before describing these results, I first situate the work on semantic alignments in the context of research on analogical reasoning and then describe some characteristics of word problems and of the instructional practices that appear to support or impede semantic alignments. After describing the semantic-alignment results, I discuss their implications for instruction and for research on analogical transfer.

The Relevance of Semantic Alignments to Research on Analogy

I chose the term *semantic alignment* to highlight the relation between the process that mediates the interpretation of word problems and the general process of "structural alignment" that has been proposed as the mechanism that mediates analogical reasoning and similarity judgments (see, e.g., review by Medin, Goldstone, and Gentner 1993). As in other cases of analogical reasoning, semantic alignments involve alignment of conceptual structures that allow people to draw mathematical inferences by analogy to the situations described in the problems (and vice versa). As such, semantic alignments provide a novel and ecologically valid domain for testing and applying our knowledge and understanding of analogical reasoning.

Despite these obvious similarities with analogical reasoning, there are at least two important ways in which semantic alignments differ from structural alignments that have been investigated in previous work on analogy. First, semantic alignments occur within a given problem, affecting how people represent the problem's mathematical structure (e.g., the inference that a problem about apples and baskets is probably a division problem). Second, they involve mappings between structures that differ in their levels of abstraction: a concrete semantic structure (e.g., placing apples in baskets) and an abstract mathematical structure (e.g., dividing a dividend by a divisor). By contrast, most studies on analogical reasoning have investigated alignments of distinct base and target analogs that were at a similar level of abstraction. For example, in Gick and Holyoak's (1980) study people had to align two semantic structures: army troops destroying a fortress (base) and X-rays destroying a tumor (target). These two distinct characteristics of semantic alignments make them an interesting test bed for the generality of the extant theoretical accounts of analogical mapping (e.g., Falkenhainer, Forbus, and Gentner 1989; Hummel and Holyoak 1997).

Another reason that makes semantic alignments relevant to research on analogy is that mathematical word problems are often used as the base and the target stimuli in research on analogical problem solving (e.g., Bassok and Holyoak 1993; Catrambone 1994; Novick 1988; Reed 1993; Ross 1987). In general, the pattern of transfer results obtained in such studies is consistent with that obtained for nonmathematical analogs. For example, the finding that similarities in the content covers of analogous base and target stimuli have a different impact on analogical access and mapping was initially documented with nonmathematical story problems (e.g., Gentner and Landers 1985; Holyoak and Koh 1987). This finding was then validated, extended and qualified with probability word problems (Ross 1987, 1989). As another example, the finding that schema abstraction facilitates analogical transfer was initially documented with analogs of Duncker's (1945) radiation problem (Gick and Holyoak 1983). This finding was then validated, extended, and qualified with word problems from algebra, physics, and economics (Bassok 1990; Bassok and Holyoak 1989).

The similarity in the pattern of transfer results between studies that used mathematical and nonmathematical story problems attests to the generality of the mechanisms that mediate analogical transfer.

Furthermore, it validates the relevance of basic research on analogical reasoning to the understanding of learning and transfer in ecologically valid educational tasks. Nonetheless, there are some important differences between word problems and nonmathematical analogs that are likely to affect analogical transfer. In particular, because each mathematical word problem has both a semantic and a mathematical structure, transfer performance can be affected by two distinct sources of structural similarity that may either support or compete with each other.

To the extent that people's interpretation of word problems is mediated by semantic alignments, the mathematical structures they infer for the base and the target problems using the semantic structures of the problem cover stories may either facilitate or impede analogical transfer (Bassok and Olseth 1995; Bassok, Wu, and Olseth 1995). As I will describe later in this chapter, when people attempt to understand word problems they sometimes infer and try to align semantic relations that cannot or should not be aligned with the problem's mathematical structure. As a result, they may infer (incorrectly) that mathematically isomorphic base and target word problems differ in their mathematical structures. In such cases, semantic alignments impede analogical transfer. In other cases, the semantic structures people infer for the base and the target problems help them realize that the problems share the same mathematical structures and thereby facilitate analogical transfer. It therefore follows that every comparison of transfer results obtained for word problems and nonmathematical stimuli, and every attempt to implement findings from research on analogical transfer to mathematical learning, requires careful attention to the potential interpretive effects of semantic alignments.

The Instructional Context of Semantic Alignments

I mentioned earlier that mathematical word problems are designed as analogies between their semantic and mathematical structures. This design is accompanied by unique text characteristics. It is my understanding that, consciously or unconsciously, mathematics educators construct word problems such that their texts omit any type of information that could potentially distract students' attention from the intended semantic alignments. In particular, word problems omit many typical story characteristics, such as the motives of the characters and the outcomes of their actions (Kintsch 1977). For example, the text of the previously described problem about Jane, who is placing apples in baskets, does not specify how or why Jane got the apples, why she wants to place them in five baskets, or why she wants to have an equal number of apples in each basket. Of course, there is no mention of Jane's age or the color of the apples. In general, word problem texts are short, contrived, and use highly standardized phrasing. These distinct text characteristics signal to students that they should be employing a specialized set of mathematically relevant comprehension rules (Hinsley, Hayes, and Simon 1977; Kintsch and Greeno 1985; Nesher and Katriel 1977; Nesher and Teubal 1975).

The specialized comprehension rules that allow students to interpret word problems are not self-evident. In fact, students often find it difficult to understand which aspects of the situations described in the problems should and which should not be mapped onto mathematical concepts and rules. For example, a teacher might say that fractions are like slices of pizza, but she also says that it does not matter what toppings are on the pizza, and that the child cannot cut "a bigger half" for herself because the slices have to be equal in size. Without knowing which aspect of mathematical knowledge is illustrated by a given word problem, or which aspect of a given situation has to be modeled by a mathematical structure, the task of mapping between the situations described in word problems and the relevant mathematical concepts and rules might be quite confusing even to very intelligent novices.

The generality of the learned mathematical rules is similarly unclear. For example, a teacher might say that the operation of division can be applied to any two arbitrary variables (A and B) and that the rules of mathematics do not dictate whether A should be the dividend and B the divisor or vice versa. At the same time, she might claim that the correct way to express the solution in a problem involving a group of children sharing pizzas is "pizzas/children" and not "children/pizzas." Such apparently contradictory statements lead some students to give up on their attempts to understand the relation between the cover stories and the mathematical structures of word problems, even though they can achieve reasonable alignments when solving realistic problems (Nunes, Schliemann, and Carraher 1993). Nonetheless, at least the better students manage to learn the rules of this school-specific "alignment game" (e.g., Greer 1993; Nathan, Kintsch, and Young 1992; Paige and Simon 1966).

An important aspect of word problem is that their standardized phrasing allows students to solve many problems correctly without understanding the problems' semantic or mathematical structures. This is because various keywords and phrases provide highly reliable *syntactic cues* to the correct solutions (Hinsley, Hayes, and Simon 1977). For example, students learn that "altogether" indicates that they should use addition whereas "less" indicates that they should use subtraction (Nesher and Teubal 1975), or that "times" indicates multiplication rather than division (English 1997). Because syntactic cues are highly positively correlated with mathematical operations, reliance on such cues leads to a high proportion of correct solutions. Only problems that undo or reverse the typical correlation (e.g., the keyword "less" appears in a problem that requires addition) reveal students' extensive use of such a syntactic-translation strategy.

Students tend to use syntactic cues as a convenient shortcut strategy. They are especially likely to engage is syntactic translation if they have difficulties with constructing correct semantic alignments. The difference between students with good and poor mathematical understanding is that the former, but not the later, can check the outcome of their syntactic translation solutions by attending to the semantic meaning of the problems. For example, Paige and Simon (1966) presented students with semantically anomalous word problems (e.g., a problem in which there were more quarters than dimes, but the value of dimes exceeded the value of the quarters). The better students, but not the poor ones, spontaneously noticed or corrected such anomalies (e.g., made the value of the quarters exceed the value of the dimes).

As Paige and Simon (1966) have shown, correct interpretation of mathematical word problems often depends on semantic information that is not explicated in the text. Rather, it has to be inferred from knowledge about the specific entities that instantiate the variable roles in the problems (e.g., the fact that the value of a quarter exceeds the value of a dime). Indeed, students who fail to draw such semantic inferences come up with nonsensical solutions even when they select and execute the correct mathematical operations (e.g., conclude that 4.12 buses be rented for a school trip; Silver, Shapiro, and Deutsch 1993). The studies on semantic alignments I will describe build on people's tendency to draw such object-based semantic inferences—to exploit object-based *semantic cues*.

In the following pages I describe results from three related studies in which semantic inferences about likely object relations affected, via semantic alignments, how people construct and solve mathematical word problems. All the studies I describe here varied the pairs of object sets that served as the arguments of mathematical word problems. The paired sets were selected to invoke either symmetric (taxonomic) or asymmetric (thematic) semantic relations (e.g., tulips-daffodils or tulips-vases, respectively). The studies examined whether people spontaneously infer how the paired object sets are semantically related and align the inferred semantic symmetry with the symmetry of the target mathematical relations (e.g., symmetric addition and asymmetric division). The first two studies document that semantic alignments affect how students generate and solve arithmetic word problems. The third study, which actually motivated our work on semantic alignments, presents evidence that such alignments affect analogical mapping between mathematically isomorphic probability word problems.

Semantic Alignments in Addition and Division Word Problems

In this section, I describe results from a study in which semantic alignments affected how people construct addition and division word problems (Bassok, Chase, and Martin 1998). As I noted in the previous section, people sometimes fail to align the semantic and mathematical structures of word problems. Such failures are especially likely when people have poor mathematical understanding, or when they can circumvent semantic alignments by exploiting syntactic cues that are provided by the problem's text. In order to prevent the impact of such potential obstacles to semantic alignments, Valerie M. Chase, Shirley A. Martin, and I asked undergraduate students to *construct* (rather than solve) simple addition or division word problems for pairs of object sets we provided. Because the participants in our study had extensive experience in using arithmetic operations, and because the construction task eliminated the possibility of reliance on syntactic cues, we expected that they would construct word problems that reflect semantic alignments. Specifically, as I explain below, we expected them to construct word problems in which the required arithmetic operation corresponds to the symmetry of the semantic relation invoked by the paired object sets.

The stimuli in our experiments were pairs of object sets (i.e., countable entities). Hence, the mathematical properties of addition and division that are relevant to semantic alignments in the construction task concern positive integers, a and b, that denote the number of elements in two distinct nonempty sets, S and T, such that $a = n\{S\}$ and $b = n\{T\}$. Note that the numerosities of the sets (a and b), and therefore the mathematical properties of addition and division, are independent of the specific elements in the sets ($s_i \, \varepsilon \, S$ and $t_j \, \varepsilon \, T$). That is, mathematically speaking (e.g., Campbell 1970), it is perfectly legitimate to perform arithmetic operations on the numbers of elements in such arbitrary sets as $S = \{$cat, boat, glove, carrot$\}$ and $T = \{$doctor, muffin$\}$, which are $a = 4$ and $b = 2$, respectively. However, as we found in this study, people care which objects comprise the sets they add and divide. For example, people readily add a apples and b oranges but avoid adding a apples and b baskets. This is because they tend to align the mathematical operation that relates the numerosities of the paired sets (a and b) with the semantic relation that they infer for the particular elements in the reference sets ($s_i \, \varepsilon \, S$ and $t_j \, \varepsilon \, T$).

The essence of the semantic alignments in our study was bringing into correspondence the *symmetry* and *asymmetry* of the mathematical relations between the arguments in the arithmetic operations and the semantic relations between the paired object sets. The operation of addition ($a + b = c$) is commutative ($a + b = b + a$). That is, the addends (a and b) play interchangeable or symmetric structural roles in the additive relation. By contrast, the operation of division ($a/b = c$) is not commutative ($a/b \neq b/a$). That is, the two arguments of division—the dividend (a) and the divisor (b)—play asymmetric structural roles. Semantic relations between object sets also differ in symmetry. In particular, the symmetric sets in our study were object sets from the same taxonomic category (e.g., tulips and daffodils). Taxonomically related objects play symmetric roles with respect to their joint superset (e.g., flowers); they also play inter-changeable roles in a variety of semantic relations. For example, tulips or daffodils (or both) can be placed in a vase. The asymmetric sets in our study were arguments of functionally asymmetric semantic relations, such as CONTAIN or SERVE. For example, vases can contain tulips but not vice versa.

Figure 12.1 presents a schematic representation of a partial semantic network for the pairs tulips-daffodils and tulips-vases. It shows how the objects in these pairs (represented by ovals) are aligned with the argu-ments of the addition and division operations (represented by squares).

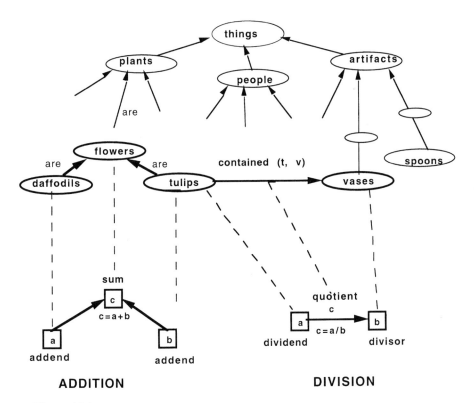

Figure 12.1
An illustration of semantic alignments for the mathematical operations of addi-tion (tulips-daffodils) and division (tulips-vases).

As can be seen in figure 12.1, the mathematically symmetric roles of addends (*a* and *b*) with respect to their sum (*c*) can be readily aligned with the semantically symmetric roles of two subsets (e.g., tulips and daffodils) with respect to their joint taxonomic category (e.g., flowers). That is, tulips and daffodils (or daffodils and tulips) can be placed in a one-to-one correspondence with the addends *a* and *b*, and the set of flowers can be placed in a one-to-one correspondence with the sum *c*.[1]

When the paired sets are not subsets of the same taxonomic category (e.g., tulips-spoons), semantic alignment should be quite difficult for at least two reasons. First, alignment of such sets demands traversing several levels of the semantic net to find a joint category that corresponds to their union ("things"). Second, each link in the semantic structure that must be traversed in order to achieve semantic alignment introduces a relational mismatch into the mapping with the additive mathematical structure, which lacks such intermediate links. Semantic alignment with addition for object sets from distinct taxonomic categories should be even more difficult when they are known to be arguments of an asymmetric semantic relation (e.g., tulips-vases). An asymmetric semantic relation between elements of such sets creates not only a relational mismatch with addition (where there is no corresponding relation between the addends), but also a relational match with division—an alternative and therefore potentially competing arithmetic operation.

Figure 12.1 also shows that, in the arithmetic operation of division, the mathematically asymmetric roles of dividend (*a*) and divisor (*b*) can be readily aligned with object sets that are arguments of asymmetric semantic relations. In particular, when the implied semantic relation is CONTAIN [contents, containers], the dividend (*a*) is aligned with contents (e.g., tulips) and the divisor (*b*) with containers (e.g., vases). Note that, unlike in the symmetric addition structure, semantic considerations constrain the structural roles that the paired sets assume in the asymmetric division structure (e.g., *a* tulips are contained in and therefore divided by *b* vases rather than vice versa). When the paired sets lack an asymmetric semantic relation (e.g., tulips-spoons), semantic alignment should be hindered by a relational mismatch. When the paired sets lack an asymmetric semantic relation and are also subsets of a joint taxonomic category (e.g., tulips-daffodils), alignment with division should be further hindered by the existence of a relational match with an alternative and therefore potentially competing operation of addition.

To summarize, object sets from the same taxonomic category (i.e., *symmetric sets*) create a good semantic alignment with the mathematically symmetric operation of addition and a poor semantic alignment with the mathematically asymmetric operation of division. At the same time, object sets that play asymmetric structural roles in semantic relations (i.e., *asymmetric sets*) create a good semantic alignment with the mathematically asymmetric operation of division and a poor semantic alignment with the mathematically symmetric operation of addition.

The construction task was designed to test whether people's reasoning about arithmetic word problems is affected by such potentially different semantic alignments. Participants received booklets consisting of equal number (either four or six) of symmetric sets (e.g., boys-girls, guitarists-drummers, or crayons-markers) and asymmetric sets (e.g., priests-parishioners, doctors-patients, or peaches-baskets). Each pair of object sets was typed at the top of a separate page. On the cover page participants were asked to construct a simple addition or division word problem involving each pair of sets. They worked at their own pace without any intervention from the experimenter.

The solution that fulfills the minimal requirements of the construction task is to relate the numerosities of members in the given sets directly by the required arithmetic operation of addition $(a + b)$ or division (a/b). I refer to such solutions as *mathematically direct* (MD). An example of an addition MD problem constructed for the pair doctors-lawyers is: "If there are two doctors and three lawyers in a room, how many people are there altogether?" An example of a division MD problem constructed for the pair boys-teachers is: "Three teachers want to evenly divide a class of sixty boys. How many boys should go with each teacher?"

If people ignore considerations of semantic alignment, there should be no difference in the frequency of MD problems constructed for the symmetric and asymmetric sets. If, however, people engage in semantic alignments, then the frequency of MD problems should be higher for semantically alignable than nonalignable object pairs. That is, matches between the mathematical and semantic relations should facilitate construction of MD problems for symmetric sets in the addition condition and asymmetric sets in the division condition. At the same time, mismatches between the mathematical and semantic relations should hinder construction of MD problems for asymmetric sets in the addition condition and symmetric sets in the division condition.

As we predicted, participants were much more likely to construct MD problems for semantically alignable than for semantically nonalignable pairs. In one experiment (experiment 2), the percentages of MD problems constructed for the alignable pairs, symmetric addition and asymmetric division, were 55 percent and 72 percent, respectively. The percentages of MD problems constructed for the nonalignable pairs, asymmetric addition and symmetric division, were significantly lower (9% and 29%, respectively).

Instead of constructing MD problems for the nonalignable object pairs, considerations of semantic alignment led participants to construct problems that reflected a variety of what we have called *semantic escape* strategies (SE). The most frequent semantic escapes were alignable operation and unrelated sets. In alignable-operation problems, the sets were related by the semantically alignable operation instead of being related by the requested but semantically nonalignable operation: division instead of addition or addition instead of division. An example of an alignable-operation SE problem is a direct division problem (a/b) constructed in the addition condition for the asymmetric pair peaches-baskets: "Two baskets hold thirty peaches; how many peaches does one basket hold?" or a direct addition problem ($a + b$) constructed in the Division condition for the Symmetric pair peaches-plums[2]: "If there is a basket with peaches and plums in it, and we know that the total number of pieces of fruit is twenty, and that there are five peaches, how many plums must there be in the basket?"

Note that these examples achieve semantic alignments at the expense of including the requested arithmetic operation. Other alignable-operation SE problems satisfied this requirement by inventing another set of objects and constructing a word problem that had a more complex mathematical structure. For example, one participant in the division condition constructed the following division problem for the symmetric pair tulips-daffodils ($(a + b)/q$): "Wilma planted 250 tulips and 250 daffodils and it took twenty days to plant them. How many flowers did she plant per day?" This problem involves addition of the given sets of flowers (i.e., alignable operation); the resulting sum is then divided by the invented set of days.

In the unrelated-sets SE problems, the given sets were not related in the computation by any arithmetic operation. The following problem constructed for the asymmetric pair doctors-patients in the addition condition is an example ($b_1 + b_2$): "One doctor sees five patients on Monday and six on Wednesday. How many patients has she seen all together?" This problem achieves semantic alignment at the expense of meeting the task requirement of including both sets in the computation (i.e., the number of doctors is irrelevant to the computation). Other unrelated-sets SE problems fulfilled this requirement via increased complexity: they consisted of two separate problems, one for each given set. For example, the following problem was constructed for the symmetric pair peaches-plums in the Division condition ($\max\{a/p, b/q\}$): "Every year Grandma's plum tree produces 45 less plums and her peach tree produces 110 less peaches. If she had 220 plums and 330 peaches this year, how long will it be before she has no produce?" Another example is a problem constructed for the symmetric pair guitarists-drummers in the division condition (a/p; b/p): "For six bands there are thirty guitarists and twelve drummers. How many of each are in each band?"

Consistent with our predictions, and complementing the distribution of mathematically direct problems, semantic escapes were much more frequent when participants had to construct addition problems for asymmetric sets or division problems for symmetric sets than when they had to add symmetric sets or divide asymmetric sets.

To further validate our analysis of semantic alignments for addition and division, in one experiment (experiment 2) we also included pairs of object sets that supported the set-subset semantic relation (e.g., tulips-flowers). The set-subset relation is an interesting in-between case because it is an asymmetric semantic relation (e.g., all tulips are flowers, but some flowers are not tulips) that affords semantic alignment with the MD structure of both addition and division. Figure 12.2 presents a schematic representation of alignment between the set-subset relation and the MD addition and division structures for the pair tulips-flowers. Object sets are represented by ovals, whereas the arguments of the addition and division operations are represented by squares.

As can be seen in figure 12.2, the set-subset relation affords an alignable MD solution to the addition construction task if one subtracts the subset (a = tulips) from the set (b = flowers). In this alignment, c is the complementary subset of flowers that are not tulips. At the same time, the set-subset relation affords an alignable MD solution to the division construction task. In this case, semantic considerations dictate that the subset, which is contained in the inclusive set, be aligned with the dividend (a) and the inclusive set with the divisor (b) rather than vice versa (a tulips/ b flowers = c proportion of tulips in the set of flowers).

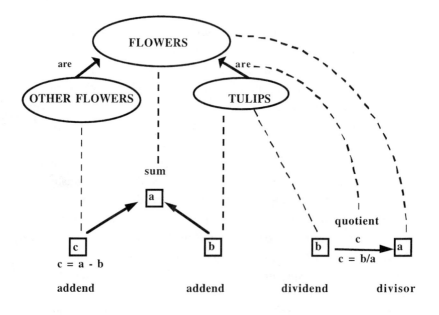

Figure 12.2
Alternative semantic alignments for the set-subset semantic relation (tulips-flowers) with the mathematical operations of subtraction and division.

We predicted that the double status of the set-subset relation with respect to alignability with the MD addition and division structures would lead to performance that falls between that for strictly symmetric sets (i.e., same taxonomic category) and strictly asymmetric sets (i.e., functionally asymmetric relations, such as CONTAIN). Indeed, the proportion of MD problems in the addition condition was highest for symmetric pairs, intermediate for set-subset pairs, and lowest for asymmetric pairs. Conversely, the proportion of MD problems in the division condition was highest for asymmetric pairs, intermediate for set-subset pairs, and lowest for symmetric pairs. In both the addition and division conditions, the frequency of SE problems constructed for the set-subset pairs fell in between the frequencies of SE problems constructed for strictly symmetric and strictly asymmetric pairs. In a follow-up study, Katja Borchert and I obtained a similar pattern of results for another type of double-status items: pairs of object sets from the same taxonomic category that were also related by an asymmetric functional relation (e.g., cars-tow trucks, ferries-lifeboats).

The construction task enabled us to test another aspect of performance that is indicative of semantic alignments. In order to construct word problems, participants had to invent the numerosities for the sets we provided (i.e., to invent *a* and *b*). We examined whether the relative numerosities participants assigned to the paired sets were consistent with their world knowledge. We constructed the materials such that one set (e.g., tulips) appeared in both a symmetric pair (e.g., tulips-daffodils) and an asymmetric pair (e.g., tulips-vases). In asymmetric sets, this *common* set was the one that we expected participants to make larger (e.g., more tulips than vases). In symmetric pairs, we did not expect a systematic tendency to make the common set either smaller or larger than the other set (e.g., the number of tulips might be made equal, smaller, or larger than the number of daffodils). As predicted, the common set was the larger in 84 percent of the 459 problems constructed for the asymmetric pairs (e.g., more muffins than trays) and in only 53 percent of the 397 problems constructed for the symmetric pairs (e.g., more muffins than brownies).

To summarize, the pattern of results in the construction task shows that adults with many years of mathematical schooling tend to align semantic relations that are afforded by pairs of object sets with mathematical relations between arguments of arithmetic operations. This tendency was reflected in the higher frequency of MD problems constructed for semantically alignable than nonalignable sets, and in the complementary distribution of semantic-escape problems. In addition to their tendency to construct word problems with a semantically alignable structure, participants made sure that the relative numerosities of the paired sets were consistent with their world knowledge.

Semantic Alignments in Division Word Problems

The pattern of semantic alignments in the previously described construction task is consistent with students' learning history. In Bassok, Chase, and Martin (1998, experiment 3), we examined the proportion of semantic alignments for the addition and division operations in textbook word problems. We analyzed all the chapter-review and test word problems for grades 1 through 8 in a popular textbook series (Eicholz et al. 1987), which was in use when the participants in our study attended elementary schools. All the paired objects that had to be related by addition were symmetric, and more than 95 percent of the paired objects that had to be related by division were asymmetric. Thus, it appears that mathematics educators very rarely expose their students to word problems with nonalignable entities.

The high positive correlation between semantic and mathematical relations in word problems provides students with reliable semantic cues for selecting the correct mathematical operations. Nonetheless, word problems may sometimes involve entities that invoke inconsistent, ambiguous, or neutral semantic cues. Consider, for example, the semantically neutral case in which a problem statement compares the numerosity of elements in two symmetric sets: "There are six times as many cupcakes as muffins." Semantic knowledge about cupcakes and muffins does not provide information about the relative numerosity of these sets. Without a pragmatic context, the fact that there are more cupcakes than muffins must be inferred solely from the syntactic phrasing of the comparison statement. To the extent that people try to interpret such comparison statements using object-induced semantic cues, they should be more likely to interpret correctly comparison statements involving semantically informative asymmetric sets, such as "There are six times as many cupcakes as trays," than comparison statements involving semantically uninformative symmetric sets. Shirley A. Martin, Katja Borchert, and I conducted several experiments that support this prediction (Bassok and Martin 1997; Bassok, Borchert, and Martin 1998).

We chose to examine the impact of semantic alignments on the interpretation of comparison statements because prior evidence suggests that such statements tend to induce a high proportion of syntactic translation errors. Clement, Lochhead, and Soloway (1979) asked engineering students to construct an algebraic equation that represents the following statement: "At a certain university, there are six times as many students (*S*) as professors (*P*)." A large minority of the subjects in their study (37%) constructed the incorrect equation $6S = P$ instead of $6P = S$, indicating that they were following the order in which the reference sets "students" and "professors" and the keyword "times" appeared in the comparison statement.

Note that the syntactic-translation error in the equation constructed for the students-professors statement (i.e., $6S = P$) leads to an answer that contradicts people's semantic knowledge, making professors more numerous than students. It is possible that mathematically capable college students exploit both syntactic cues (i.e., the "times" keyword and the order in which the sets appear in the statement) and semantic cues (i.e., knowledge about the relative numerosity of the objects in the comparison statement). If so, then syntactic translation errors should be more pronounced when the comparison statements involve semantically symmetric than semantically asymmetric sets. Our studies were designed to examine whether semantic information provided by the compared object sets affects the frequency of syntactic translation errors and the extent to which such effects hold true for students at different stages of their mathematical schooling (middle school through college).

We tested the relative impact of semantic and syntactic cues in two related tasks. One task replicated the procedure used by Clement, Lochhead, and Soloway (1979). Students were asked to construct equations that represent comparison statements involving either symmetric or asymmetric sets, similar to the paired sets we used in the word-problem construction task described in the previous section. The second task involved the solution of simple division word problems that contained the comparison statements from the equation-construction task. Table 12.1 presents one quadruplet of matched symmetric and asymmetric comparison statements and word problems that is representative of the stimuli we used in several related experiments.

We examined students' problem-solving performance, in addition to their performance on the equation-construction task because we wanted to ensure that the students who participated in our studies had sufficient mathematical knowledge to perform the required task. The youngest participants in our study (seventh graders) had extensive experience in solving simple division word problems, but they did not learn how to construct algebraic equations. Moreover, even high school and college students might have more difficulty with constructing equations than with solving simple division word problems, if only because they had more practice with the problem-solving task. Accordingly, we expected that students at all grade levels would be more successful in performing the problem solving than the equation construction task.

We also expected that the impact of the helpful semantic information implied by the asymmetric sets, relative to the neutral information in the symmetric sets, will be more pronounced when students solve word problems than when they construct algebraic equations. Two main

Table 12.1
An example of matched asymmetric and symmetric statements and word problems in Bassok, Borchert, and Martin (1998)

	Asymmetric	Symmetric
Statement	At a certain university, there are six times as many students (S) as professors (P).	A certain factory produces six times as many nails (N) as screws (S).
Word Problem	At a certain university, there are 3,450 students. If there are six times as many students as professors at this university, how many professors are there?	On a certain day, a factory produced 3,450 nails. If the factory produces six times as many nails as screws, how many screws did it produce that day?

reasons led us to this prediction. First, word problems provide more semantic context than single statements. Second, when students solve problems they obtain numerical results. These results, in turn, could help them recognize and therefore correct their initial translation errors. Numerical results should be especially helpful when the translation solution (e.g., $6S = P$) contradicts people's semantic knowledge (e.g., there are more students (S) than professors (P)). Numerical results should have little or no advantage when the paired sets do not provide semantic information about their relative numerosity (e.g., nails may be either more or less numerous than screws).

In one study (Bassok and Martin 1997), we examined whether students at different grade levels rely on semantic and syntactic cues in a problem solving and in an equation construction task. The participants were 736 students from several schools in the Chicago area (seventh, ninth, and eleventh graders) and undergraduates from the University of Chicago. Students either constructed equations or solved word problems that involved comparison of either symmetric or asymmetric sets. Figure 12.3 presents the percentages of correct solutions for each of the conditions in this 2 (task) × 4 (grade) × 2 (symmetry) between subjects experimental design.

Figure 12.3 shows that students at all grade levels were quite successful in solving the division word problems (76% correct), but they performed very poorly on the equation-construction task (35% correct). The effect of semantic cues (i.e., the symmetry of the compared sets) interacted with task. Students were much more successful solving word problems with asymmetric than with symmetric sets (89 vs. 64% correct, respectively). At the same time, there was virtually no difference in the frequency of correct equations they constructed for statements with asymmetric and symmetric sets (35 vs. 34% correct, respectively).

As one would expect, students' performance on word problems improved with grade. Surprisingly, their equation-construction performance remained very low from seventh grade through high school, rising to only 55 percent correct at the college level. This difference in the learning curve for word problems and equations was accompanied by a difference in the degree of sensitivity to the semantic information implied by the compared object sets. In the problem-solving task, there was a

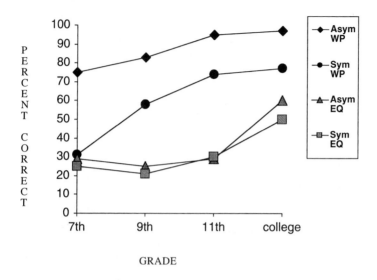

Figure 12.3
Percentage of correct responses for asymmetric and symmetric problems and equations in Bassok and Martin (1997).

significant semantic effect at every grade level, although the magnitude of this effect decreased as students increased their proficiency in solving word problems. The differences between the frequencies of correct solutions on problems with asymmetric and symmetric sets were 40, 29, 23, and 10 percent for students in the seventh, ninth, eleventh, and college grades, respectively. At the same time, students' poor performance in the equation-construction task was not affected by the symmetry of the compared sets in any of the grade levels.

The difference in students' performance on the two tasks was also reflected in the type of errors they committed. Most of the word-problem errors in all grades (79% of all errors), indicated syntactic translation of the order in which the sets appeared in the comparison statements (e.g., $6S = P$ for the statement "There are six times as many students as professors). Syntactic translation errors were less frequent in the equation-construction task (57% of all errors). Interestingly, many of the nontranslation errors were similar to the semantic escapes in the problem construction task described in the previous section. Specifically, students sometimes related the compared sets with the operation of addition (e.g., $N + S = 6$ for the statement "There are six times as many nails as screws"). Such errors occurred twice as often when the sets were Symmetric than when they were asymmetric (42 vs. 20% of all errors, respectively). Notably, the youngest students committed most of these semantic-alignment errors.

To summarize, we found that helpful semantic information (asymmetric sets) led to fewer syntactic translation errors than neutral semantic information (symmetric sets). However, semantic information affected students' performance only when they solved word problems, it did not affect the frequency of translation errors on the equation-construction task. This pattern of results held true for students with different levels of mathematical experience (i.e., seventh graders through college), and it was replicated in several follow-up studies (Bassok, Borchert, and Martin 1998). We are now in the process of collecting verbal protocols from college students who perform the equation-construction and the problem-solving tasks under a variety of experimental conditions. We hope that these data would help us understand when and how people incorporate semantic knowledge into their representations of mathematical statements and word problems. At this stage all we can say with certainty is that, in middle school through college students, object-based inferences have significant effects on problem solving and are powerful enough to override the effects of syntactic translation.

Effects of Semantic Alignments on Analogical Transfer

As I pointed out in the introduction, the interpretation of transfer results obtained for word problems requires careful attention to the correspondence between the problems' semantic and mathematical structures. In particular, when different objects serve as arguments of mathematically isomorphic word problems, semantic alignments may lead people to infer correctly that the problems share the same mathematical structure or to infer incorrectly that the problems differ in their mathematical structures. These two cases have different implications for analogical transfer. In the first case, mismatching objects are the only obstacles to transfer, but in the second case transfer may be also impaired by the inferred mismatches in the problems' mathematical structures (Bassok and Olseth 1995; Bassok, Wu, and Olseth 1995).

In this section, I describe the main results of Bassok, Wu, and Olseth (1995), which documents the impact of semantic-symmetry alignments on analogical transfer. Ling-Ling Wu, Karen Olseth, and I constructed probability word problems that had the same *objective mathematical structure* (and therefore could be solved in the same way), but induced, via semantic alignments, either symmetric or asymmetric *interpreted mathematical structures*. All the problems described a person who randomly assigned three elements from one set (of size n) to three elements from a different set (of size m) and asked for the probabilities of such random assignments. As in the arithmetic word problems I discussed earlier, the objects in the assigned set and in the set of assignees (denoted by n and m, respectively) were either symmetric or asymmetric. We expected that these two types of object sets would lead participants to infer that the problems have, respectively, either symmetric or asymmetric mathematical structures.

Box 12.1 presents two representative problems from experiment 1 in Bassok, Wu, and Olseth (1995). In the first problem (asymmetric sets), prizes are randomly assigned to students; in the second problem (symmetric sets), children from one school are randomly assigned to children from another school.

Note that, irrespective of whether a teacher assigns prizes to students or students to prizes (asymmetric sets), the outcome is that students get prizes rather than vice versa (i.e., an asymmetric semantic relation). By contrast, when a teacher assigns children from one school to children from another school (symmetric sets) the children end up being in a symmetric semantic relation, such as playing or working with each other. That is, the semantic outcome of the assignment process depends on the semantic symmetry of the two sets and is not affected by the direction of assignment.

To validate the effectiveness of our semantic manipulation, we first examined whether the symmetry of the paired sets affects how people represent the mathematical structures of these novel and rather complex word problems. We asked undergraduate students from the University

Box 12.1
Examples of asymmetric and symmetric mathematically isomorphic permutation word problems in Bassok, Wu, and Olseth (1995)

Asymmetric sets (Students and Prizes)

In a high school awards ceremony some students will receive prizes. There are 26 wrapped prizes, marked with the numbers one through 26. There are 30 honor students who would like to receive a prize in the ceremony. The names of the students are listed in the order of their GPA (grade point average), from highest to lowest. The teacher who organizes the ceremony randomly assigns prizes to students according to the order of the students' GPA. What is the probability that the first three students on the GPA list will receive the first three prizes (nos. 1 through 3), respectively?

Symmetric sets (Children and Children)

In a certain after-school program, kids from Sweetie Nursery School will get to work in pairs with kids from Paradise Nursery School. There is a list of 18 kids from Paradise, arranged in order of their height: from tallest to shortest. There are 22 kids from Sweetie that would like to work with the kids from Paradise. The names of the Sweetie kids are listed in order of their age: from oldest to youngest. The director of the after-school program randomly assigns kids from Paradise to kids from Sweetie according to the age order of the Sweetie kids. What is the probability that the three oldest kids from Sweetie will get to work with the three tallest kids from Paradise, respectively?

---

of Chicago and Northwestern University to solve either the symmetric or the asymmetric permutation word problems as best they could. To minimize the effects of familiarity with such problems, we analyzed only the incorrect solutions. We transformed each (incorrect) numerical solution into an algebraic equation, and examined whether the paired object sets (m and n) played symmetric or asymmetric structural roles in these equations.

We found that, indeed, the erroneous solutions to these unfamiliar word problems reflected semantic alignments. In the asymmetric condition (secretaries-computers), most participants (87%) placed the numbers representing the paired sets in mathematically asymmetric roles (e.g., $m^3/n!$, $1/n^3$). By contrast, in the symmetric condition (doctors-doctors), most participants (78%) placed the numbers representing the paired sets in mathematically symmetric roles (e.g., $(m + n)/(mn)^3$, $3/(m + n)!$). That is, participants inferred that the asymmetric and symmetric semantic relations (e.g., "get," "work with") correspond, respectively, to asymmetric and symmetric mathematical relations. Importantly, they inferred such subjectively distinct mathematical structures for mathematically isomorphic word problems.

After their initial attempt at solving these novel permutation problems, all participants received a short chapter that introduced them to the relevant probability concepts and provided them with the equation for solving such problems. For three random drawings, which was the case in all the word problems we used, the equation is $1/n(n - 1)(n - 2)$. Note that the only variable in this equation is the number of elements in the assigned set (n). In this sense, the mathematical equation is asymmetric (i.e., only one of the two sets mentioned in the problem's text is relevant to the problem's solution). The training session ended with participants studying a worked-out solution to the permutation word problem (the base) they had initially attempted to solve on their own. Following the training session, participants received a novel permutation problem (the target) together with the learned equation ($1/n[n - 1][n - 2]$) and were asked to instantiate the equation for the target problem. That is, they had to choose which of the two object sets in the target problem was the randomly assigned set (n).

The pattern of transfer results revealed large and significant effects of semantic alignments. For example, after learning a solution to an asymmetric base problem in which computers were assigned to secretaries, most participants (89%) solved correctly an asymmetric target problem in which prizes were assigned to students. However, only 60 percent of the participants solved correctly a symmetric target problem in which children from one school were assigned to children from another school. That is, the correctness of the solution to the target problem depended on the similarity between the interpreted mathematical structures participants inferred, via semantic alignments, for the formally isomorphic base and target problems.

Interestingly, some participants were so confident that the semantically asymmetric base problem differed in its mathematical structure from the semantically symmetric target problem that they crossed out the correct asymmetric equation we presented with the target problem and, instead, constructed an incorrect symmetric equation. In other words, they crossed out the one-set equation (n) and, instead, constructed an equation in which both sets, m and n, played symmetric mathematical roles. For example, one participant combined the two sets of children ($m + n$), and sampled pairs of children from the combined set. Following is an excerpt from this participant's verbal protocol:

What's that have to do with 16 kids from 20 kids? . . . So you have to take all the kids from one and all the kids from the other. . . . Sum of elements is 36, . . . so 36, 34, 32. . . . Every time you do this you take out 2.

Thus, just as the participants who constructed incorrect symmetric equations for the semantically symmetric base problems before the training session, participants who were trained on semantically asymmetric base problems constructed incorrect symmetric equations for the semantically symmetric target problems.

In addition to the inferred structural discrepancy between the semantically symmetric and asymmetric permutation problems, semantic knowledge affected participants' decisions about which of the two asymmetric sets should be the assigned set and which should be the set of assignees. For example, in one experimental condition participants received a worked-out solution to a permutation problem in which caddies were randomly assigned to golfers. Following this training, 94 percent of the participants solved correctly a mathematically isomorphic problem in which prizes were randomly assigned to students, but only 17 percent solved correctly a mathematically isomorphic problem in which students were randomly assigned to prizes. That is, participants were operating under the assumption that the direction of assignment in the base and target problems is compatible with the outcome of assignment. Because golfers get caddies and not vice versa (base), and because students get prizes and not vice versa (target), they understood that the direction of assignment in the target must be from prizes to students.

The same assumption guided participants' solutions when one of the paired sets appeared in both the base and the target problems. For example, after receiving a worked-out solution to a problem in which caddies were randomly assigned to golfers, some participants received a target problem in which caddies were randomly assigned to carts and others received a target problem in which carts were randomly assigned to caddies. Previous studies on analogical mapping have shown that people prefer to place similar objects in similar structural roles (Gentner and Toupin 1986; Ross 1989). Because in the base problem caddies were the assigned set, reliance on object similarity would dictate better performance on the "caddies assigned to carts" than on the "carts assigned to caddies" target problem. However, because participants engaged in semantic alignments, they understood that the direction of assignment is compatible with the outcome of assignment. In the base problem golfers got caddies and in the target problem caddies got carts. Hence, participants understood that carts were assigned to caddies. That is, contrary to what would be predicted by direct object similarity, 94 percent of the participants solved correctly the "carts assigned to caddies" problem, but only 24 percent solved correctly the "caddies assigned to carts" problem.

To summarize, the results of Bassok, Wu, and Olseth (1995) show that semantically symmetric and asymmetric object sets lead people to construct symmetric and asymmetric interpreted structures for mathematically isomorphic probability problems. Similarities and differences between such interpreted mathematical structures affected analogical transfer. The effects of semantic alignments were powerful enough to override the impact of direct object similarities on analogical mapping.

Discussion

The studies I describe in this chapter have shown that when school children and adults reason about mathematical word problems they (1) infer how the objects mentioned in the cover story tend to be related and (2) align the inferred semantic relation with a structurally isomorphic mathematical relation. Such semantic alignments were reflected in the mathematical structures of the addition and division word problems people constructed, in the frequency of syntactic translation errors in the division word problems people solved, and in the pattern of learning and transfer of solutions to probability word problems. That is, semantic alignments affected how people reasoned about word problems with both familiar and unfamiliar mathematical structures.

There is little doubt that the performance of the participants in our studies was affected by schooling, if only because they were exposed to textbook word problems with semantically alignable objects (Bassok, Chase, and Martin 1998). However, this explanation raises the question why textbook writers construct word problems in which the semantic relations between the specific objects are consistent with the required mathematical operations. One could try to explain the performance of textbook writers by tracing it back to their own learning history. Alternatively, or in addition, one could argue that such performance reflects their conscious attempts to construct word problems in which the semantic relations in the cover stories are analogous to the mathematical relations. Even if these explanations are correct, a learning history of exposure to alignable problems and a strategic attempt to construct semantically alignable word problems cannot explain how mathematics educators, and their students, select which object relations correspond to mathematical relations.

I suspect that such object-based semantic alignments are guided, or supported, by the general cognitive mechanism of structural alignment (e.g., Gentner 1983; Markman and Gentner 1993; Medin, Goldstone, and Gentner 1993), and that the effects of this mechanism are largely unconscious. I had an opportunity to discuss the semantic-alignment findings with several mathematics educators. My impression was that they were not aware that most textbook word problems align the semantic relations that are afforded by the specific objects in the cover stories with structurally isomorphic mathematical relations, or that students rely on such alignments to interpret and solve word problems.

One might wonder to what extent the mathematical knowledge of mathematicians and mathematics educators is separated from their everyday experiences. According to Lakoff and Nunez (1997), all mathematical concepts and theories are metaphorical constructs that are grounded in cognitive schemas and then linked with each other. To support their argument, Lakoff and Nunez present numerous illustrations of one-to-one mappings between mathematical ideas and cognitive schemas (e.g., set theory and the container schema). They also claim that most mathematicians are not aware of the metaphorical nature of mathematical theories. Lakoff and Nunez's argument suggests that word problems might be second-order metaphors, providing novel metaphorical mappings of situation schemas for previously established metaphorical mathematical constructs.

Whatever the origins of mathematical concepts and theories, there is little doubt that mathematics educators present students with problems that align the now abstract mathematical concepts with students' world knowledge. To the extent that educators are unaware that they expose students to object-based semantic alignments, the present findings might help them achieve better understanding of students' performance and assist them in designing instructional interventions that promote correct interpretation and use of mathematical knowledge. For example, one instructional intervention that is implicated by the studies I reported here is to present students with pairs mathematically isomorphic alignable and nonalignable word problems and ask them to compare the mathematical solutions to these problems. Shirley Martin, Katja Borchert, and I pilot-tested this procedure with college students, varying the order in which we presented the two problems. We found that students' overall performance was much better when they first solved the alignable problem and then the nonalignable one than when they first solved the nonalignable problem and then the alignable one.

Although all the studies I described here involved semantically symmetric and asymmetric object sets, semantic alignments are obviously not limited to the symmetry distinction. In Bassok and Olseth (1995) we presented college students with algebra, economics, and physics word problems involving constant change. For these problems, participants inferred whether the entities described in the cover stories changed discretely or continuously (e.g., ice deliveries to a restaurant vs. ice melting off a glacier, respectively) and aligned these semantic models of change with discrete and continuous mathematical structures (arithmetic progressions and linear functions, respectively). In addition to such broad semantic distinctions as symmetry-asymmetry or continuity-discreteness, it appears that people expect to find systematic correspondences between the roles particular objects tend to assume in real-life situations and the roles they assume in word problems. For example, one of the participants in a study that examined how people learn from examples (Chi et al. 1989) expected that a block hanging from a ceiling would be the physical "body" rather than the physical "force."

Clearly, more research is needed to establish the range of semantic alignments and their interaction with pragmatic consideration. Thus, for example, if you are deciding whether or not to get into the express lane at the supermarket, it makes sense to add up muffins and trays and a toothbrush to figure out how many "things" you have. Moreover, it is reasonable to assume that semantic alignments are not restricted to mathematics, but rather, mediate learning and application of other formal rules, such as logic or probability (e.g., Cheng and Holyoak 1985). If, as I believe, semantic alignments are guided by the same mechanism that mediates analogical reasoning (i.e., structural alignment), extant models of analogical mapping (e.g., Falkenhainer, Forbus, and Gentner 1989; Hummel and Holyoak 1997) could help us understand how people relate formal knowledge to their knowledge of objects, situations, and events.

In addition to providing a novel and challenging application domain, the unique properties of semantic alignments afford analogy researchers an interesting domain for testing the generality of the theoretical assumptions about the process that mediates analogical mapping. Semantic alignments might also shed new light on previous findings pertaining to analogical transfer. As I mentioned earlier, results of studies on analogical transfer that employed mathematically isomorphic word problems are similar to those obtained in studies that employed nonmathematical stimuli. However, the mathematical representations people construct for word problems (via semantic alignment) are probably more abstract and more general than the semantic representations they construct for nonmathematical story problems. Hence, transfer between two mathematically isomorphic word problems is probably more similar to the pattern of transfer following schema abstraction than following exposure to a single base analog (e.g., Gick and Holyoak 1983 vs. Gick and Holyoak 1980).

To summarize, semantic alignments of object-based inferences affect how people understand and solve mathematical word problems. Because people may infer and try to align semantic relations that cannot or should not be aligned with the mathematical structure, this interpretive process may sometimes lead to errors. However, by and large, semantic alignments of object-based inferences lead to correct solutions and ensure sensible application of abstract mathematical knowledge to real-life situations. For example, they account for the fact that people tend to divide apples among baskets rather than vice versa, or that they refrain from adding apples and baskets but are very likely to add apples and oranges. I have suggested that models of analogical reasoning could be extended to account for the interpretive process that mediates semantic alignments. At the same time, semantic alignments could be instrumental in testing the generality of the theoretical assumptions in extant models of analogical reasoning.

Notes

1. Mapping the union set of tulips and daffodils onto flowers is not one-to-one in the sense that the union set is subsumed by the set "flowers," which also includes other flowers (e.g., roses).
2. For this analysis, we did not distinguish between addition and subtraction.

References

Bassok, M. (1990). Transfer of domain-specific problem solving procedures. *Journal of Experimental Psychology: Learning, Memory, and Cognition* 16:522–533.

Bassok, M., Borchert, K., and Martin, S. A. (1998). Semantic and syntactic cues in mathematical problem solving. Paper presented at the 39th annual meeting of the Psychonomic Society, Dallas, TX.

Bassok, M., Chase, V. M., and Martin, S. A. (1998). Adding apples and oranges: Alignment of semantic and formal knowledge. *Cognitive Psychology* 35:99–134.

Bassok, M., and Holyoak, K. J. (1989). Interdomain transfer between isomorphic topics in algebra and physics. *Journal of Experimental Psychology: Learning, Memory, and Cognition* 15:153–166.

Bassok, M., and Holyoak, K. J. (1993). Pragmatic knowledge and conceptual structure: Determinants of transfer between quantitative domains. In D. K.

Detterman and R. J. Sternberg, Eds., *Transfer on trial: Intelligence, cognition, and instruction*, pp. 68–98. Norwood, NJ: Ablex.

Bassok, M., and Martin, S. A. (1997). Object-based interpretation of arithmetic word problems. Paper presented at the 38th annual meeting of the Psychonomic Society, Philadelphia, PA.

Bassok, M., and Olseth, K. L. (1995). Object-based representations: Transfer between cases of continuous and discrete models of change. *Journal of Experimental Psychology: Learning, Memory, and Cognition* 21:1522–1538.

Bassok, M., Wu, L., and Olseth, K. L. (1995). Judging a book by its cover: Interpretative effects of content on problem solving transfer. *Memory and Cognition* 23:354–367.

Campbell, H. E. (1970). *The structure of arithmetic*. New York: Appleton Century Crofts.

Catrambone, R. (1994). Improving examples to improve transfer to novel problems. *Memory and Cognition* 22:606–615.

Cheng, P. W., and Holyoak, K. J. (1985). Pragmatic reasoning schemas. *Cognitive Psychology* 17:391–416.

Chi, M. T. H., Bassok, M., Lewis, M. W., Reimann, P., and Glaser, R. (1989). Self-explanations: How students study and use examples in learning to solve problems. *Cognitive Science* 13:145–182.

Clement, J., Lochhead, J., and Soloway, E. (1979). Translating between symbol systems: Isolating a common difficulty in solving algebra word problems. Cognitive Development Project, Department of Physics and Astronomy. University of Massachusetts.

De Corte, E., and Verschaffel, L. (1985). Teaching word problems in the primary school. What research has to say to the teacher. In B. Greer and G. Mulhern, Eds., *New developments in teaching mathematics*, pp. 85–106. London: Routledge.

Duncker, K. (1945). On problem solving. *Psychological Monographs* 58(No. 270).

Eicholz, R. E., O'Daffer, P. G., Fleener, C. R., Charles, R. I., Young, S., and Barnett, C. S. (1987). *Addison-Wesley mathematics* (2d ed.). Menlo Park, NJ: Addison-Wesley.

English, L. (1997). Children's reasoning processes in classifying and solving computational word problems. In L. English, Ed., *Mathematical reasoning: Analogies, metaphors, and images*, pp. 191–220. Hillsdale, NJ: Erlbaum.

Falkenhainer, B., Forbus, K. D., and Gentner, D. (1989). The structure mapping engine: Algorithm and examples. *Artificial Intelligence* 41:1–63.

Gentner, D. (1983). Structure-mapping: A theoretical framework for analogy. *Cognitive Science* 7:155–170.

Gentner, D., and Landers, R. (1985). Analogical reminding: A good match is hard to find. *Proceedings of the International Conference on Systems, Man and*

Cybernetics, pp. 306–355. Tucson, AZ: International Conference on Systems, Man and Cybernetics.

Gentner, D., and Toupin, C. (1986). Systematicity and surface similarity in the development of analogy. *Cognitive Science* 10:277–300.

Gick, M. L., and Holyoak, K. J. (1980). Analogical problem solving. *Cognitive Psychology* 12:306–355.

Gick, M. L., and Holyoak, K. J. (1983). Schema induction and analogical transfer. *Cognitive Psychology* 15:1–38.

Greer, B. (1993). The modeling perspective on wor(l)d problems. *Journal of Mathematical Behavior* 12:239–250.

Hinsley, D. A., Hayes, J. R., and Simon, H. A. (1977). From words to equations: Meaning and representation in algebra word problems. In M. A. Just and P. A. Carpenter, Eds., *Cognitive processes in comprehension*, pp. 89–106. Hillsdale, NJ: Erlbaum.

Holyoak, K. J., and Koh, K. (1987). Surface and structural similarity in analogical transfer. *Memory and Cognition* 15:332–340.

Hummel, J. E., and Holyoak, K. J. (1997). Distributed representations of structure: A theory of analogical access and mapping. *Psychological Review* 104:427–466.

Kintsch, W. (1977). On comprehending stories. In M. A. Just and P. A. Carpenter, Eds., *Cognitive processes in comprehension*, pp. 33–62. Hillsdale, NJ: Erlbaum.

Kintsch, W., and Greeno, J. G. (1985). Understanding and solving word arithmetic problems. *Psychological Review* 92:109–129.

Lakoff, G., and Nunez, R. E. (1997). The metaphorical structure of mathematics: sketching out cognitive foundations for a mind-based mathematics. In L. English, Ed., *Mathematical reasoning: Analogies, metaphors, and images*, pp. 21–89. Hillsdale, NJ: Erlbaum.

Markman, A. B., and Gentner, D. (1993). Structural alignment during similarity comparisons. *Cognitive Psychology* 25:431–467.

Medin, D. L., Goldstone, R. L., and Gentner, D. (1993). Respects for similarity. *Psychological Review* 100:254–278.

Nathan, M. J., Kintsch, W., and Young, E. (1992). A theory of algebra-word-problem comprehension and its implications for the design of learning environments. *Cognition and Instruction* 9:329–389.

Nesher, P. (1989). Microworlds in mathematical education: A pedagogical realism. In L. B. Resnick, Ed., *Knowing, learning, and instruction: Essays in honor of Robert Glaser*, pp. 187–215. Hillsdale, NJ: Erlbaum.

Nesher, P., and Katriel, T. A. (1977). A semantic analysis of addition and subtraction word problems in arithmetic. *Educational Studies in Mathematics* 8:251–269.

Nesher, P., and Teubal, E. (1975). Verbal cues as an interfering factor in verbal problem solving. *Educational Studies in Mathematics* 6:41–51.

Novick, L. R. (1988). Analogical transfer, problem similarity, and expertise. *Journal of Experimental Psychology: Learning, Memory, and Cognition* 14:510–520.

Nunes, T., Schliemann, A. D., and Carraher, D. W. (1993). *Street mathematics and school mathematics.* Cambridge: Cambridge University Press.

Paige, J. M., and Simon, H. A. (1966). Cognitive processes in solving algebra word problems. In B. Kleinmuntz, Ed., *Problem solving: Research, method, and theory*, pp. 51–119. New York: John Wiley and Sons.

Reed, S. K. (1993). A schema-based theory of transfer. In D. K. Detterman and R. J. Sternberg, Eds., *Transfer on trial: Intelligence, cognition, and instruction*, pp. 39–67. Norwood, NJ: Ablex.

Ross, B. H. (1987). This is like that: The use of earlier problems and the separation of similarity effects. *Journal of Experimental Psychology: Learning, Memory, and Cognition* 13:629–639.

Ross, B. H. (1989). Distinguishing types of superficial similarities: Different effects on the access and use of earlier problems. *Journal of Experimental Psychology: Learning, Memory, and Cognition* 15:456–468.

Silver, E. A., Shapiro, A., and Deutsch, A. (1993). Sense making and the solution of division problems involving remainders: An examination of middle-school students' solution processes and their interpretations of solutions. *Journal of Research in Mathematics Education* 24:117–135.

III
Developmental and Comparative Approaches

13

Analogical Reasoning in Children

Usha Goswami

Analogical thinking lies at the core of human creativity. It has been argued that the very act of forming an analogy requires a kind of "mental leap," inasmuch as it necessitates seeing one thing as if it were another (Holyoak and Thagard 1995). Famous analogies in science frequently reveal their inventor's ability to make these mental leaps. However, as well as being an important cognitive mechanism in creative thinking, analogy is the basis of much of our everyday problem solving. Small-scale mental leaps are being made all the time by children and adults and form a core part of our everyday mental repertoire. This chapter examines the availability of analogical reasoning to young children. Far from being a sophisticated reasoning strategy characteristic of older children and adults, it will be argued that analogical reasoning is available from infancy onward. "Analogy pervades all our thinking, our everyday speech and our trivial conclusions as well as artistic ways of expression and the highest scientific achievements" (Polya 1957).

The Development of Analogical Reasoning

The study of analogical development was pioneered by Piaget, who examined analogical reasoning in children from five to twelve years of age (Piaget, Montangero, and Billeter 1977). More recently, analogical reasoning in children as young as one and two has been reported. There is still considerable debate about what constitutes a proper analogy, particularly in a toddler.

The Relational Similarity Constraint

Even though analogies require mental leaps, they are guided by certain basic constraints. The most important is the need for *relational* or *structural* similarity. In many analogies, the objects in the analogy are not similar at all. Their similarity is at a purely relational or structural level. A striking example of this is the analogy that led to Kekule's (1865) theory about the molecular structure of benzene (see Holyoak and Thagard 1995). In a dream, Kekule had a visual image of a snake biting its own tail. This gave him the idea that the carbon atoms in benzene could be arranged in a ring. The similarity between the snake and the carbon atoms was at a purely structural/relational level: circular arrangement. The fact that the objects being compared in an analogy should be linked by the *same* relations is widely accepted to be the hallmark of analogical reasoning, and has been called the "relational similarity constraint" by Goswami (1992).

Quite frequently, objects in the two situations being compared in an analogy do bear some resemblance to each other—they share "surface" similarity. This similarity of appearance can support the analogical mapping. An example is the invention of Velcro, which followed the observation by Georges de Mestral that burdock burrs stuck to his dog's fur (see Holyoak and Thagard 1995). The *surface similarity* in the appearance of the small hairs coating burdock burrs and the fuzz on Velcro supports the relational similarity of "effective sticking mechanism". These two factors—relational similarity and surface similarity—both affect analogical reasoning (e.g., Gentner 1989). Gentner's work shows clearly that surface similarities between objects can support relational mappings and hence affect analogical performance. In order to examine the development of "pure" analogical reasoning in children, therefore, we need to examine their understanding of the relational similarity constraint in the *absence* of surface similarity.

The Item Analogy Task

The standard test for analogical reasoning (used in IQ testing) is the "item analogy" task. In item analogies, two items A and B are presented to the child, a third item C is presented, and the child is required to generate a D term that has the same relation to C as B has to A. Successful generation of a D term requires the use of the relational similarity constraint. For example, if the child is given the items *cat is to kitten as dog is to . . . ?* she is expected to generate the solution term "puppy". The response "bone", which is a strong associate of dog, would be an error. Another example is the analogy *Bicycle is to handlebars as ship is to . . . ?* Here the relation constraining the choice of a D term is "steering mechanism", and so a child who offered the completion term "bird" would not be credited with understanding the relational similarity constraint.

The first developmental psychologist to study analogical reasoning, Piaget, used a pictorial version of the item analogy task, and his data suggested that understanding of the relational similarity constraint did not develop until early adolescence (Piaget, Montangero, and Billeter, 1977). Younger children tested by Piaget offered solutions like "bird" to the *bicycle/ship* analogy, giving reasons like "both birds and ships are found on the lake". Piaget concluded that younger children solved analogies on the basis of associations (see also Sternberg and Nigro 1980). He argued that children only became able to reason on the basis of relational similarity at around eleven to twelve years of age. This conclusion was accepted in developmental psychology for many years. Piaget's conclusions about analogical development fitted neatly into his influential theory of the development of logical reasoning in children. Analogies appeared to be characteristic of the final stage of logical development— the stage of "formal operational" reasoning. Formal operational reasoning required children to operate mentally on the results of simpler operations. A simpler operation was finding relations between objects ("first-order" relations). As analogies required children to reason about similarities *between* the relations between objects ("second-order" relations), it appeared to be a typical formal operational skill.

The Role of Relational Familiarity in Analogical Development
Closer inspection of Piaget's experimental methods, however, suggest that his conclusions about analogical development were too negative (Goswami 1991). A key methodological problem was that Piaget did not check whether the younger children in his experiments understood the relations on which his analogies were based (for example, the relation

"steering mechanism" in the *bicycle:handlebars::ship:rudder* analogy). This failure to ensure that the first-order relations were familiar means that the younger children's failure to solve the item analogies in Piaget's experiments could have arisen from a lack of knowledge of the relations being used. Item analogies based on *unfamiliar* relations would obviously *underestimate* analogical ability.

One way to test this possibility is to design analogies based on relations that are known to be highly familiar to younger children from other cognitive developmental research. Simple *causal* relations such as *melting, wetting* and *cutting* are known to be acquired early in development, and to be available for use in picture-based tasks by the ages of three and four years. Relations between real world objects such as *"trains go on tracks"* and *"birds live in nests"* are very familiar to four- and five-year-olds. Item analogies such as *"Playdoh is to cut Playdoh as apple is to cut apple"* and *"bird is to nest as dog is to doghouse"* can thus be used to examine whether three- to five-year-olds have the ability to reason by analogy.

For this young age group, a picture-based version of the item analogy task is required (Goswami 1989; Goswami and Brown 1989, 1990). The analogy task can then be presented as a "game" about matching pictures. In our studies, the children were shown a "game board" with four slots for pictures, the slots being grouped into two pairs for the A:B and C:D parts of the analogy (see figure 13.1). As the children watched, the experimenter presented the first three terms of a given analogy (e.g., pictures of a bird [A], a nest [B], and a dog [C]). As the pictures were presented, the child was asked to name each one to ensure that they were familiar. The child was then asked to predict the picture that was needed to finish the pattern. The prediction task was included to see whether the children could generate an analogical solution spontaneously, without seeing the solution pictures. This would be evidence for truly "mental" operations.

Following the request for a prediction, the experimenter showed the child a choice of solution terms. For the *bird/dog* analogy, these were pictures of a *doghouse*, a *cat*, another *dog*, and a *bone* (see figure 13.1). The different choices were designed to test different theories of analog-

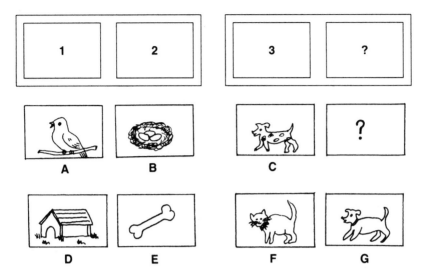

Figure 13.1
The game board (top row), analogy terms (middle row) and correct answer and distractors (bottom row) for the analogy *bird:nest::dog:doghouse* (Goswami and Brown 1990).

ical development. The correct choice, which would indicate analogical ability, was the *doghouse*. The associative choice was the *bone*. Selection of the bone would be expected if younger children rely on associative reasoning to solve analogies, as Piaget and Sternberg had claimed. The other choices were a "mere appearance match" choice (the second dog), and a category match (the cat). "Mere appearance" matching is a term coined by Gentner (1989) to refer to the matching of object or "surface" similarities when attempting to solve analogies (such as choosing another dog to match the dog in the C term, or choosing something that looks like a nest to match the B term). Gentner has suggested that younger children might rely quite heavily on object similarity in reaching analogical solutions (Gentner 1989).

The matching game showed that all children tested (four-, five-, and nine-year-olds) performed at levels significantly above chance in the analogy task, selecting the correct completion term 59 percent, 66 percent, and 94 percent of the time, respectively. There was no evidence of mere appearance matching. Although many younger children were shy of making predictions prior to seeing the solution choices, those who were more confident showed clear analogical ability on this measure as well. For example, when four-year-old Lucas was given the analogy *bird is to nest as dog is to . . . ?* he first predicted that the correct solution was *puppy*. He argued, quite logically, "Bird lays eggs in her nest [the nest in the B-term picture contained three eggs]—dog—dogs lay babies, and the babies are—umm—and the name of the babies is puppy!" Lucas had used the relation *type of offspring* to solve the analogy, and was quite certain that he was correct. He continued "I don't have to look [at the solution pictures]—the name of the baby is puppy!" Once he looked at the different solution options, however, he decided that the *doghouse* was the correct response.

The matching game also included a control task to ensure that the correct solution to the analogy was not simply the most attractive pictorial match for the C term picture. In the control task, the children were simply shown the C term picture along with the correct solution term and the distractors, and were asked to choose which picture "went best" with the C term picture. For example, the children were shown the picture of the dog, and were asked to choose the best match from the pictures of the doghouse, bone, second dog and cat. In this unconstrained task, the children were as likely to select the associative match (bone) as the analogy match (doghouse). Additionally, although the children readily agreed that another match could be correct in the control condition (nine-year-olds: 76%, four-year-olds: 82%), they were not so flexible in the analogy condition, where most of them said that only *one* answer could be correct (nine-year-olds: 89%, four-year-olds: 60%). This shows awareness of the relational similarity constraint that governs truly analogical responding. The children understood that the correct completion term for the analogy had to link the C and D terms by the *same* relation that linked the A and B terms. Notice also that Lucas was using the relational similarity constraint when he generated the solution "puppy" for the *bird/dog* analogy. This cognitive flexibility displays a full understanding of analogy, and provides evidence of truly mental operations, thereby meeting Piaget's original criteria for the presence of "true" analogical reasoning.

The Relationship between Relational Knowledge and Analogical Responding

From the picture analogy game, we know that the ability to reason by analogy is present by at least age four. However, the analogy game may *still* have underestimated analogical ability. This is because relational knowledge was not measured *independently* of analogical success. Instead, it was simply assumed that familiar relations had been selected for the analogies, leaving open the possibility that the younger children may have failed in some trials because the relations used in those particular analogies were unfamiliar to them. Alternatively, some children may have failed some analogies because they were actually reasoning about relations that were *different* from those intended by the experimenter—like Lucas.

The idea that children's analogical performance depends on their relational knowledge has been called the *relational familiarity hypothesis* (Goswami 1992). In order to establish whether children's use of analogical reasoning is knowledge-based, dependent on relational familiarity rather than analogical ability, relational knowledge *as well as* analogical ability needs to be assessed. This can be done by changing the control task in the picture matching game. The appropriate control task measures children's knowledge of the relations being used in the analogies that are presented in the item analogy task.

A second set of analogy experiments using the picture matching game were thus carried out to test the relational familiarity hypothesis. This time, item analogies based on physical causal relations like *melting*, *cutting*, and *wetting* were used. These relations are known to be available by three to four years of age (Bullock, Gelman, and Baillargeon 1982). Children aged three to six years were given analogies like *chocolate is to melted chocolate as snowman is to . . . ?* and *Playdoh is to cut Playdoh as apple is to . . . ?* This time the distractors were (1) a different object with the same causal change (e.g., cut bread for the *cutting* analogy), (2) the same object with a different causal change (e.g., a bruised apple), (3) a mere appearance match (e.g., a small ball), and (4) a semantic associate of the C term (e.g., a banana). Knowledge of the causal relations required to solve the analogies was measured in a control condition. Here the children were shown three pictures of items that had been causally transformed (e.g., cut Playdoh, cut bread, cut apple), and were asked to select the causal agent responsible for the transformation from a set of pictures of possible agents (e.g., a knife, water, the sun).

The results showed that both analogical success and causal relational knowledge increased with age. The three-year-olds solved 52 percent of the analogies and 52 percent of the control sequences,[1] the four-year-olds solved 89 percent of the analogies and 80 percent of the control sequences, and the six-year-olds solved 99 percent of the analogies and 100 percent of the control sequences. By far the most frequent error was to select the correct object with the wrong causal change (e.g., the bruised apple, a dirty snowman). This suggested that the children knew that a causal transformation was required, but did not always select the correct one. The next most frequent error was to select the correct causal transformation of the wrong object. There was also a significant *conditional* relationship between performance in the analogy condition and performance in the control condition, as would be predicted by the relational familiarity hypothesis. This conditional relationship arose because individual children's performance in the analogy task was linked to their knowledge of the corresponding causal relations (see Rattermann and Gentner 1998). Analogical reasoning in children is thus highly dependent on relational knowledge. This raises the possibility that children younger than three years may be able to reason by analogy—as long as they have the requisite relational knowledge.

Analogical Reasoning in Infants and Toddlers

It is difficult to use the item analogy format to demonstrate analogical competence in children younger than three because of the abstract nature of the task. Researchers working with very young children have thus devised ingenious *problem analogies* in order to show analogical reasoning at work. In problem analogies, a young child is faced with a problem that they need to solve. Let us call this problem B. The use of an analogy from a previously experienced problem, problem A, offers a solution. The measure of analogical reasoning is whether the children think of using the solution from problem A in order to solve problem B.

Chen and his colleagues devised a way of giving problem analogies to infants as young as ten months, using a procedure first developed by Brown (1989) for one and a half- to two-year-olds. Brown's procedure depended on seeing whether toddlers could learn how to acquire attractive toys that were out of reach. Different objects (such as a variety of tools, some more effective than others) were provided as a *means* to a particular *end* (bringing the desired toy within grasping distance). The analogy was that the means-to-an-end solution that worked for getting one toy in fact worked for all of the problems given, even though the problems themselves appeared on the surface to be rather different. Brown and her colleagues used this paradigm to study analogical reasoning in children aged seventeen to thirty-six months. Chen, Sanchez, and Campbell (1997) were able to extend it to infants.

In their procedure, the infants came into the laboratory and were presented with an Ernie doll that was out of their reach. The Ernie doll was also behind a barrier (a box), and had a string attached to him that was lying on a cloth (see figure 13.2). In order to bring the doll within reach, the infants needed to learn to perform a series of actions. They had to remove the barrier, to pull on the cloth so that the string attached to the

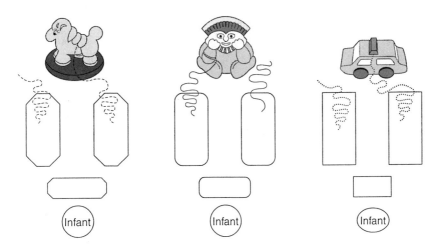

Figure 13.2
Depiction of the problem scenarios used to study analogical reasoning in infants by Chen, Campbell, and Polley 1995.

toy came within their grasp, and then to pull on the string itself so that they could reach Ernie. Following success on the first trial, two different toy problem scenarios were presented, each using identical tools (cloths, boxes, and strings). However, each problem appeared to be different to the problems that preceded it, as the cloths, boxes and strings were always dissimilar to those encountered before. In addition, in each problem *two* strings and *two* cloths were provided, although only one pair could be used to reach the toy.

Chen, Sanchez, and Campbell tested infants aged ten and 13 months in the Ernie paradigm. They found that although some of the older infants worked out the solution to reaching Ernie on their own, others needed their parents to model the solution to the first toy acquisition problem for them. Once the solution to the first problem had been modeled, however, the thirteen-month-olds readily transferred an analogous solution to the second and third problems. The younger infants (ten months) needed more salient perceptual support in order for reasoning by analogy to occur. They only showed spontaneous evidence of using analogies when the perceptual similarity between the problems was increased (for example, by using the same goal toy, such as the Ernie doll, in all three problems). Perceptual similarity between objects may be important in supporting analogical reasoning, particularly when relations are not well understood (see Goswami 1992; Rattermann and Gentner 1998).

Freeman (1996) devised a series of analogies for two-year-olds using real objects and models. Her analogies were based on the simple causal relations of *stretching, fixing, opening, rolling, breaking,* and *attaching.* For example, a child might watch the experimenter *stretching* a loose rubber band between two Plexiglas poles in order to make a "bridge" that she could roll an orange across ("Look what I'm going to do, I'm going to use this stuff to roll the orange! Stretch it out, put it on—wow, that's how I roll the orange!"). Following an opportunity to roll the orange by themselves, the children were given a transfer problem involving a loose piece of elastic, a toy bird, and a model with a tree at one end and a rock at the other. They were asked "can you use this stuff to help the bird fly?" The intended solution was to stretch the elastic from the tree to the rock, and to "fly" the bird along it. In a third analogy problem, the children were asked to "give the doll a ride" by stretching some ribbon between two towers of different heights that were fixed to a base board. Children in a control condition were simply asked to "help the bird fly" and "give the doll a ride" without first seeing the base analogy of rolling the orange.

Freeman found that whereas only 6 percent of the children in the control condition thought of the *stretching* solution to the transfer problem, 28 percent of thirty-month-olds in the analogy condition did so, and this figure rose to 48 percent following hints to use an analogy ("You know what? To help the bird fly, we have to change this," said while pointing to the elastic). When the same hint was given to the children in the control condition, only 14 percent thought of the *stretching* solution. Although these performance levels may appear modest, they are comparable to the spontaneous levels of analogical transfer found in adults. Problem analogy studies conducted with adults typically find spontaneous transfer levels of around 30 percent, at least in unfamiliar problem scenarios (e.g., Gick and Holyoak 1980).

The studies reviewed earlier suggest that analogical reasoning is available at one and two years of age. In some circumstances, the support of perceptual or surface similarity may be required if analogies are to be used successfully (as in the study with ten-month-old babies reported by Chen, Sanchez, and Campbell 1997). However, the degree of surface similarity required probably depends on the extent to which the relations relevant to the analogy have been represented, as surface similarity affects analogical reasoning across the life span (e.g., Goswami 1996; Holyoak and Koh 1987; Rattermann and Gentner 1998). When relations are highly salient, recent research evidence from studies of babies suggests that a focus on relations can be strong even in the first year of life, and even in the absence of surface similarity.

The Origins of Relational Reasoning

The knowledge that children have about objects and events in their worlds, and the knowledge that they have about the causal and explanatory structures underlying *relations* between these objects and events, is known to expand at a terrific rate from the very first months of infancy. Recent research has shown that young infants remember events that are causally related and forget events that are arbitrarily related, that they seek causal explanations for physical events and are surprised by physically "impossible" events, and that the search for causal relations to explain featural clustering in categories underlies the development of conceptual knowledge (see Goswami 1998 for a review). Infants and young children seek to *explain* their everyday worlds to themselves. The process of revising and restructuring the knowledge base is aided by the development of abstract knowledge structures (such as concepts that organize information about objects, and schemas and scripts that organize information about the temporal and causal frameworks of events). These conceptual frameworks facilitate the storage and organization of incoming information, and presumably also facilitate the application of analogy. However, the recognition of relational similarity may in itself also facilitate the development of abstract representations. For example, it has been pointed out that the process of drawing analogies has important similarities to the processes underlying the computation of categories and concepts, and that rather than being distinct processes a common mechanism may underlie both categorization and analogy (Ramscar and Pain 1996). The ability to compute categories by forming prototypes certainly appears to be present from very early in development. Evidence of this kind has led to the notion that relational processing may be active from early in infancy. This idea, which is controversial, has been called the "relational primacy" hypothesis (Goswami 1992, 1996).

Relational Processing in Infants: The Physical World
The roots of relational competence can be found in the mechanisms that infants use to process perceptual information. The early representation of categorical information in terms of perceptual *prototypes*, for example, appears to depend on the extraction of correlational information about visual features, suggesting sensitivity to the relations between those features (see Goswami 1996, 1998). For example, infants who were shown a series of "cartoon" animals attended not only to the distinctive features of these animals (e.g., their necks and legs), but to the

correlations between the features (long legs went with short necks, short legs went with long necks; see Younger and Cohen 1983). New exemplars were then categorized by the infants according to their relational similarity to the prototype (see Goswami 1992, 1996, 1998, for detail).

Structural similarities among perceptual stimuli can also be recognized by infants, and these may well form the basis of relational representations of those stimuli at a conceptual level (se Smith and Heise 1992 for an interesting analysis). For example, structural similarities in auditory and visual perceptual events can convey relational information. A tone of music may be ascending because of acoustic properties such as timbre. A visual stimulus may have properties that convey ascension, such as a locus of highest density at its uppermost point (e.g., an arrow). Infants who are shown a choice between two visual stimuli, an arrow pointing upward and an arrow pointing downward, and who hear an ascending tone of music coming from the midline, preferentially look at the "up" arrow (Wagner et al. 1981). This is a form of analogy. These inherent *perceptual* properties of rising tones of music and of arrows pointing upward could convey the shared relation "ascending", which is part of our mental *representation* of these physical events. Infants may first be sensitive to the similarity between the inherent structure of physical events, and then come to *represent* them as relationally similar (see Goswami 1998 for further discussion).

Another intriguing line of evidence for relational primacy comes from recent experimental work in speech processing. Marcus et al. (1999) showed that seven-month-old infants could represent abstract relational similarities between sequences of nonsense syllables via evidence from artificial grammar learning studies. For example, in one study the infants were habituated to either AAB grammatical strings like /ga ga ti/ or ABB grammatical strings like /ga ti ti/. At test, the infants received novel items that either shared the relational structure of the training stimuli (e.g., /wo wo fe/ for the AAB group) or did not (e.g., /wo fe fe/ for the AAB group). Marcus et al. reported that sixteen out of sixteen infants discriminated reliably between the relationally similar and the relationally dissimilar strings. As they noted, these results cannot be explained in terms of stored sequences of words (e.g., surface similarities with the learned sets of words) as both the consistent and the inconsistent items were completely novel. Only the relational structure of the nonsense strings was similar.

Further support for the notion that infants are sensitive to relational information from early in development comes from evidence that infants preferentially attend to *changes* in the visual scene. Change is informative, because change signals the occurrence of *events*. Events in the visual world are usually described by *relations* between objects (such as ball *collides with* teddy, child *pushes* friend). The ability to detect structural regularities in these relations (to notice relational similarity) would be cognitively powerful in terms of knowledge acquisition, as events in the visual world are frequently *causal* in nature. The detection of regularities in causal relations like *collide*, *push*, and *supports* between different objects (such as ball collides with teddy, toy car collides with toy garage, mommy collides with daddy) may involve a rudimentary form of analogical reasoning.

There is quite a lot of evidence that infants are sensitive to cause-effect relations by about six months of age (see Goswami 1998 for a review). Other types of relations, such as spatial relations (*above* and *below*) and quantitative relations (*more than* and *less than*) are also detected by this age. One way of measuring infants' ability to process and represent spatial, numerical, and causal relations is to introduce *violations* of typical regularities in the relations between objects, which then result in physically "impossible" events. For example, an object with no visible means of support can remain stationary in midair instead of falling to the ground. The experimental investigation of infants' ability to detect such violations is the main source of evidence for infants' ability to process relations between events.

Consider the causal relations involved in *support*. Adults are well aware that if they put a box of cookies down on a table and the box protrudes too far over the table's edge, the cookies will fall onto the floor. If only a small portion of the bottom surface of the box protrudes over the table's edge, the cookies will not fall. The recognition of how much contact is required to support an object in different situations must require a degree of relational comparison between one situation and the next. Baillargeon, Needham, and DeVos (1992) studied six and a half-month-old infants' expectations about when a box would fall off a platform. The infants were shown a box sitting at the left-hand end of a long platform, and then watched as the finger of a gloved hand pushed the box along the platform until part of it was suspended over the right-hand edge. For some infants, the pushing continued until 85 percent of the bottom surface of the box protruded over the platform, and for others the pushing stopped when 30 percent of the bottom surface of the box protruded over the platform. In a control condition the same infants watched the box being pushed to the right-hand end of the platform, but the bottom surface of the box remained in full contact with the platform. The infants spent reliably longer looking at the apparatus in the 85 percent protrusion event than in the full-contact control event. This suggests that they expected the box to fall off the platform (the box was able to remain magically suspended in midair via a hidden hand). The infants in the 30 percent protrusion event looked equally during the protrusion event and the control event. Baillargeon, Needham, and DeVos argued that the infants were able to judge *how much* contact was required between the box and the platform in order for the box to be stable. In fact, Baillargeon has repeatedly found that infants reason on the basis of relational information before they reason on the basis of absolute information when making judgments about the physical properties of objects. Bryant (1974) has reported a similar precedence for relational over absolute information in young children. The ease with which infants and young children process relational information suggests that relational processing is present in the cradle, and that relational comparisons are an important source of information about the physical world. No one has so far devised a direct experimental test of these ideas, however.

Relational Processing in Infants: The Psychological World

As noted above, one powerful aspect of relational information is that it frequently provides information about *causality*. Causal relations are not only particularly powerful relations for understanding the everyday world of objects and events, they also provide an insight into the psychological world. For example, recent work with infants has suggested that a sensitivity to causal relations may partly underlie the development of a notion of *agency*. Things that move on their own are agents, and things that move because of other things obey certain cause/effect, or mechanical, laws (see Leslie 1994). Infants' interest in things that move helps them to sort out the source of different cause-effect relations in the physical world. Again, this seems likely to require a form of relational comparison.

For example, Gergely et al. (1995) have shown that twelve-month-old infants can analyze the spatial behavior of an agent in terms of its actions toward a goal, and will apply an "intentional stance" to this behavior when it appears rational, thereby attributing a mental cause for the goal-directed behavior. The adoption of an "intentional stance" toward agents entails an assumption of rationality—that the agent will adopt the most rational action in a particular situation to achieve his or her goal. To examine whether twelve-month-old infants would generate expectations about the particular actions an assumed agent was likely to perform in a new situation to achieve a desired goal, Gergely et al. designed a visual habituation study in which a computer display gave an impression of agency to the behavior of circles. The infants saw a display in which two circles, a large circle and a small circle, were separated by a tall rectangle (see figure 13.3). During the habituation event, each circle in turn

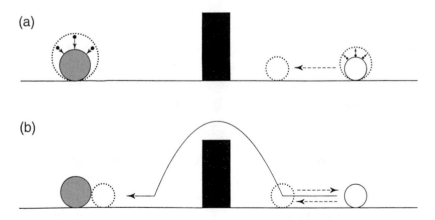

Figure 13.3
Schematic depiction of the habituation events shown to the infants in the rational approach group by Gergely et al. (1995), depicting (a) the expansion and contraction events and the first approach, and (b) the retreat, jump, and eventual contact events.

expanded and then contracted twice. The small circle then began to move toward the large circle. When it reached the rectangular barrier it retreated, only to set out toward the large circle a second time, this time jumping over the rectangle and making contact with the large circle. Both circles then expanded and contracted twice more. Adult observers of this visual event described it as a mother (large circle) calling to her child (small circle) who ran toward her, only to be prevented by the barrier, which she then jumped over. The two then embraced.

Following habituation to this event, the infants saw the same two circles making the same sequence of movements, but this time without a barrier being present. However, although the relations between these objects were the same, the absence of a barrier meant that the causal significance of the relations differed—in analogy terms, the "relational structure" was no longer comparable. In a "new action" event, the small circle simply took the shortest straight path to reach the large circle. Gergely et al. predicted that, if the infants were making an *intentional* causal analysis of the initial display, then they should spend more time looking at the "familiar action" event than the "new action" event, as even though the former event was familiar it was no longer *rational* (nor analogous). This was exactly what they found. A control group who saw the same habituating events without the rectangle acting as a barrier (it was positioned to the side of the screen) showed equal dishabituation to the old and new action events. This intriguing result shows just how powerful the ability to represent and compare causal relations between objects may be for the young infant. Causal analyses of the everyday world of objects and events supply information about the physical world of inanimate objects and *also* about the mental world of animate agents.

Relational Processing in Infants: Imitation

Relational processing and relational comparison may also lie at the heart of the early facial imitation of gestures such as tongue protrusion, which has been reported in infants as young as one to three days (e.g., Meltzoff and Moore 1983). Meltzoff and Moore (1997) describe the essential puzzle of facial imitation as follows: "Infants can see the adult's face but cannot see their own faces. They can feel their own faces move, but have no access to the feelings of movement in the other. By what mechanism can they connect the felt but unseen movements of the self with the seen but unfelt movements of the other?" (p. 180). Meltzoff and Moore suggest that the solution to this puzzle depends on the appreciation of the similarity of "organ relations". They suggest that infants might compute the configural relations between organs, such as "tongue-to-lips", and use these to represent *both* their own behavior and that of the adult. These perceived organ relations provide the targets that the infants attempt to match. On this account, imitation involves an early form of analogizing.

Interestingly, Piaget also suggested a role for analogy in explaining imitation behavior in infants. He noted the occurrence of "motor analogies" in his own babies, in which the infants imitated certain spatial relations that they had observed in the physical world with their own bodies. For example, they imitated the opening and closing of a matchbox by opening and closing their hands and mouths. Piaget suggested that this behavior showed that the infants were trying to *understand* the mechanism of the matchbox through a motor analogy, reproducing a kinesthetic image of opening and closing. Again, the infant is suggested to be representing *relations*, and analogy is suggested as a mechanism for knowledge acquisition and for explaining events in the everyday world.

The coding of "organ relations" proposed by Meltzoff and Moore (1997) would also allow infants to recognize when they are being imitated by an adult. Such recognition is found by at least fourteen months (Meltzoff, 1990). Recognizing that someone else is imitating you implies a recognition of the structural equivalence (or relational similarity) between another agent's behavior and your own (see also Meltzoff 1990; Meltzoff and Moore 1995). Again, this is a form of analogy. Such analogies may play an important role in the growth of psychological understanding. For example, Meltzoff has argued that imitation, broadly construed, serves as a discovery procedure for understanding persons. Although the links between imitation, analogy, and the development of an understanding of the psychological world noted here must remain speculative given the current absence of detailed research, it is perhaps not a coincidence that imitation, analogy, and the understanding of mental states ("theory of mind") are absent in the animal kingdom (with the possible exception of highly "language-trained" chimpanzees (e.g., Oden, Thompson, and Premack, chap. 14, this volume; Heyes 1996, 1998; Tomasello, Call, and Gluckman 1997; Visalberghi and Fragaszy 1990).

Analogies in Foundational Domains

Recently, a number of developmental psychologists have argued that the developing knowledge base can be divided into three foundational "domains" or sets of representations sustaining different areas of knowledge. These are the domains of naive biology, naive physics, and naive psychology (e.g., Wellman and Gelman 1997). Of course, many concepts will be represented in more than one of these foundational frameworks (for example, persons are psychological entities, biological entities *and* physical entities). Nevertheless, Wellman and Gelman suggest that children will use at least two levels of analysis within any framework, one that captures surface phenomena (mappings based on attributes) and another that penetrates to deeper levels (mappings based on relations). This means that analogies should be at work within foundational domains. We have already discussed evidence from infancy work that suggests that analogies play a role in helping the child to understand the physical and psychological worlds. We turn now to an examination of the role of analogies in developing knowledge in these foundational domains in early and later childhood.

Analogy as a Mechanism for Understanding Biological Principles
Evidence that analogy is an important mechanism for understanding biological principles comes from a series of studies by Inagaki and her colleagues (Inagaki and Hatano 1987; Inagaki and Sugiyama 1988). They were interested in how often children would base their predictions about biological phenomena on analogies to people: the *personification* analogy. As human beings are the biological kinds best known to young children, it seems plausible that children should use their biological knowledge about people to understand biological phenomena in other natural kinds. For example, Inagaki and Sugiyama (1988) asked four,

five, eight, and ten-year-olds a range of questions about various properties of eight target objects, including, "Does x breathe?" "Does x have
a heart?" "Does x feel pain if we prick it with a needle?" and "Can x
think?" The target objects were people, rabbits, pigeons, fish, grasshop-
pers, trees, tulips, and stones. Prior similarity judgments had established
that the target objects differed in their similarity to people in this order,
with rabbits being rated as most similar and stones being rated as least
similar. The children all showed a decreasing tendency to attribute the
physiological properties ("Does x breathe") to the target objects as the
perceived similarity to a person decreased. Apart from the four-year-olds,
very few children attributed physiological attributes to stones, tulips, and
trees, and even four-year-olds only attributed physiological properties to
stones 15 percent of the time. A similar pattern was found for the mental
properties ("Can x think?"). This study supports the idea that preschool-
ers' understanding of biological phenomena arises from analogies based
on their understanding of people.

Analogy as a Mechanism for Understanding Physical Principles
Evidence that analogy is an important mechanism for understanding
physical principles comes from a series of studies by Pauen and her colleagues. Pauen has studied children's understanding of the principles governing the interaction of forces by using a special apparatus called the
"force table" (Pauen 1996). The force table consists of an object that is
fixed at the center of a round platform. Two forces act on this object,
both represented by plates of weights. The plates of weights hang from
cords attached to the central object at 45, 75, or 105 degrees relative to
each other. The children's job is to work out the trajectory of the object
once it is released from its fixed position. The children's predictions concerning this trajectory are scored in terms of whether they consider only
a single force (one plate of weights), or whether they integrate both forces
in order to determine the appropriate trajectory. The force table problem
is presented to the children in the context of a story about a king (central
object) who has got tired of skating on a frozen lake (the platform) and
who wants to be pulled into his royal bed on the shore (see figure 13.4).
Children aged six, seven, eight, and nine years of age were tested.

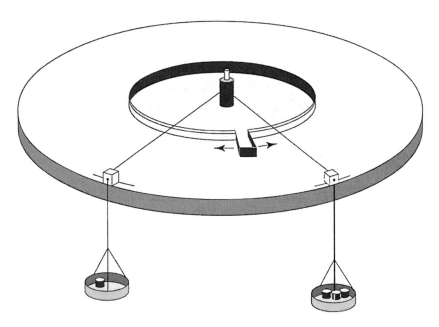

Figure 13.4
Schematic depiction of the force table used by Pauen (1996).

Pauen found that most of the younger children (80–85%) predicted that the king would move in the direction of the stronger force only (the larger plate of weights). An ability to consider the two forces simultaneously was only shown by some of the nine-year-olds (45%). Such integration rule responses were shown by the majority of the adults tested (63%). Pauen speculated that this may have been because the children who received the plates of weights applied a balance scale analogy to the force integration problem. A balance scale analogy gives rise to one-force-only solutions, which are incorrect.

This idea about the balance scale analogy was prompted by the comments of the children themselves, who said that the force table reminded them of a balance scale (presumably because of the plates of weights). This led Pauen to propose that the children were using spontaneous analogies in their reasoning about the physical laws underlying the force table, analogies that were in fact misleading. To investigate this idea further, Pauen and Wilkening (1997) gave nine-year-old children a training session with a balance scale prior to giving them the force table problem. One group of children received training with a traditional balance scale, in which they learned to apply the one-force-only rule, and a second group of children received training with a modified balance scale that had its center of gravity below the axis of rotation (a "swing boat" suspension). This modified balance scale provided training in the integration rule, as the swing boat suspension meant that even though the beam rotated toward the stronger force, the degree of deflection depended on the size of *both* forces.

Following the balance scale training, the children were given the force table task with the plates of weights. A third group of children received only the force table task, and acted as untrained controls. Pauen and Wilkening argued that an effect of the analogical training would be shown if the children who were trained with the traditional balance scale showed a greater tendency to use the one-force-only rule than the control group children, while the children who were trained with the modified balance scale showed a greater tendency to use the integration rule than the control group children. This was exactly the pattern that they found. The children's responses to the force table problem varied systematically with the solution provided by the analogical model. These results suggest that the children were using spontaneous analogies in their reasoning about physics, just as we have seen them do in their reasoning about biology. At the present time, studies of children's use of analogy in the domain of naive psychology (theory of mind) do not feature in the research literature, although a theoretical account of the role of relational complexity in the development of a theory of mind is offered by Halford (1993). However, given the promising developments noted in infancy research, this is surely only a matter of time.

Analogies in Piagetian Tasks

Traditionally, development psychology has measured children's intellectual progress in terms of their performance on different Piagetian tasks. These tasks are held to be characteristic of the different levels of logical reasoning postulated by Piaget's stage theory of logical development. Neo-Piagetian psychologists accept the basic observations about mental performance that led to Piaget's theory but propose alternative causal mechanisms to explain developmental change.

Halford's Structure Mapping Theory of Logical Development

Most neo-Piagetian theorists of cognitive development incorporate the concept of relational mapping (e.g., Case 1985; Halford 1987, 1993; Pascual-Leone 1987). However, Halford is the only neo-Piagetian who has formally proposed that analogy plays a central role in the development of logical reasoning, and who has linked analogical processes to performance in traditional Piagetian tasks. In his structure-mapping theory of cognitive development (1987, 1993), Halford proposed that most logical reasoning was analogical. He also proposed that limitations in primary memory (the memory system that holds any information that is currently being processed) constrained the kinds of analogy that children could use at different points in cognitive development. He suggested that this explained the relatively late emergence of the Piagetian "concrete operations". Piaget used the term *concrete operations* to refer to children's symbolic or representational understanding of the properties of concrete objects and the relations between them (such as transitivity and class inclusion). Halford's argument was that capacity limitations prevented children from representing and mapping transitive or class inclusion relations prior to approximately five years of age.

Halford suggested that the critical capacity limitations governing the use of analogy in logical reasoning concerned the number of relations that could be represented in primary memory at any one time (see also Halford, Wilson, and Phillips 1999). The number of relations determined the *processing load* entailed in solving the analogy, although processing load could be reduced in certain circumstances if concepts could be recoded into fewer dimensions ("conceptual chunking") and if tasks could be decomposed into serial steps which did not exceed processing capacity. A simple causal inference analogy of the kind used by Goswami and Brown (1989; e.g., *vase:pieces of vase::egg:broken egg*) was thought to entail a relatively low processing load, as it required the child to represent and map a *single* relation (breaking) from one object (vase) to another (egg.). These *relational mappings* were said to be within the information-processing capacity of children as young as two years. An analogy that required *two* relations to be processed jointly was thought to entail a higher processing load (e.g., *A above B above C :: Tom happier than Bill happier than John*). The information-processing capacity capable of supporting such *system mappings* was thought to emerge between four and five years of age. Prior to this, it was hypothesized that even *familiar* pairs of relations could not form the basis of an analogy, inasmuch as there was insufficient capacity in primary memory to hold and compare the representations of both relations simultaneously. Analogies based on pairs of relations were thought to be necessary for the successful solution of Piagetian concrete operational tasks. In order to test this theory, evidence that young children can solve analogies based on pairs of relations and evidence that they use analogies in Piagetian tasks such as transitive reasoning and class inclusion is required.

Analogies Based on Pairs of Relations

In order to examine whether young children can solve analogies based on pairs of relations, Goswami et al. (1998) designed a set of analogies based on pairs of physical causal relations (extending the technique used by Goswami and Brown 1989 described earlier). They asked three-, four-, five-, and six-year-old children to make relational mappings based on either single causal relations like *cut, paint,* and *wet,* or pairs of causal relations, like *cut + wet* and *mend + paint.* Their experiment had four conditions, a single-relation analogy condition (e.g., *apple: cut apple:: hair: cut hair*), a double-relation analogy condition (e.g., *apple: cut, wet apple:: hair: cut, wet hair*), a single-relation control condition and a double-relation control condition. The four distractors in both analogy conditions were the same (representing two double relational changes and two single relational changes respectively). The child was thus forced to attend to the A:B pairing in each condition in order to select the correct solution term to each analogy. In the control conditions, the children were asked to select the picture of the causal agent or the pair of causal agents responsible for the causal changes shown in the analogies, following Goswami and Brown (1989).

Children's performance in the analogy and the control conditions was then examined as a function of condition and age. The pattern of the results was remarkably similar to the pattern found in the causal-relations analogies used by Goswami and Brown (1989). There was a close correspondence between analogy performance and performance in the relational knowledge control conditions for both the single relation and the double relation analogies. For the single relation conditions, the three-year-olds solved 33 percent of the analogies and 46 percent of the control sequences, the four-year-olds solved 51 percent of the analogies and 63 percent of the control sequences, the five-year-olds solved 72 percent of the analogies and 76 percent of the control sequences, and the six-year-olds solved 89 percent of the analogies and 88 percent of the control sequences. For the double relation conditions, the three-year-olds solved 13 percent of the analogies and 31 percent of the control sequences, the four-year-olds solved 50 percent of the analogies and 50 percent of the control sequences, the five-year-olds solved 62 percent of the analogies and 74 percent of the control sequences, and the six-year-olds solved 78 percent of the analogies and 91 percent of the control sequences. Analyses demonstrated no interaction between age and number of relations, although the main effect of number of relations almost reached significance, reflecting the fact that children of all ages found the double relation analogies and control sequences more difficult than the single relation analogies and control sequences. Goswami et al. concluded that the ability to solve analogies based on pairs of relations was governed by relational familiarity. As long as familiar relational structures are chosen as a basis for analogy, therefore, young children should be able to use analogies to help them to solve Piagetian reasoning tasks.

Analogies in a Transitive Mapping Task

Halford has suggested that familiar ordered structures may provide useful analogies for transitive reasoning tasks. For example, a transitive sequence such as *Tom happier than Bill happier than John* may be solved by using an analogy to a familiar series of height relations such as *A above B above C*. Because relational familiarity is known to determine analogical reasoning in young children, we need a familiar instantiation of height relations for the children to use as a basis for analogy. The family provides a familiar example of an ordering structure based on size, as in most families the father is taller than the mother, and the mother is taller than the child or baby. According to Halford's structure-mapping theory, young children who have mentally represented the relational structure *Father > Mother > Baby* should be able to use this structure as a basis for analogies in transitive tasks using less familiar relations.

Goswami (1995) examined this hypothesis using Goldilocks and the Three Bears as a familiar example of family size relations (Daddy Bear > Mommy Bear > Baby Bear). Three- and four-year-old children were asked to use the relational structure represented by the Three Bears as a basis for solving transitive ordering problems involving perceptual dimensions such as temperature, loudness, intensity, and width. The transitive mapping test was presented by asking the children to imagine going to the Three Bears' house, and then to imagine looking at their different belongings. This imagination task constituted a fairly abstract test. For example, the imaginary bowls of the Three Bears' porridge could be either *boiling hot*, *hot*, or *warm*, and the child had to decide which bowl of porridge belonged to which bear. In order to give the correct answer, the child had to map the transitive height ordering of Daddy, Mommy, and Baby Bear to the different porridge temperatures, giving Daddy Bear the boiling hot porridge, Mommy Bear the hot porridge, and Baby Bear the warm porridge (these mappings do not follow the original fairy tale, in which Daddy Bear's porridge was too salty, and Mommy Bear's was too sweet).

The results showed that the percentage of correctly ordered mappings approached ceiling for the four-year-olds for most of the dimensions used. The lowest levels of performance occurred for *width* (of beds, 62% correct), and *hardness* (of chairs, 76% correct), and the highest occurred for *temperature* (of porridge, 95% correct). Performance with the width dimension (wide bed, medium bed, narrow bed) was possibly affected by worries that a baby could fall out of a narrow bed, as many children allocated the medium bed to Baby Bear. They were then left without a bed for Mommy Bear. The three-year-olds produced correctly ordered mappings for only some of the dimensions, performance being above chance (17%) for the dimensions of temperature of porridge (31% correct), pitch of voice (31% correct), and height of mirrors (62% correct, but an isomorphic relation). Relational familiarity and real-world knowledge about family size relations seem to have helped the three-year-olds with these particular dimensions. The children are unlikely to have based their correct mappings on the story, as none of these dimensions was mentioned in the *Three Bears* book that was read to them as part of the study. Note that this mapping task did not require a transitive *inference*, however. Evidence for the use of analogies by three- and four-year-olds in a "Daddy, Mommy, Baby" paradigm has also been demonstrated in a mapping task requiring the recognition of monotonic size ordering for successful performance (Gentner and Rattermann 1991; Ratterman and Gentner 1998).

Analogies in a Class Inclusion Task

Halford also suggested that families provide potentially useful analogues for class-inclusion tasks (Halford 1993). The logical concept of class inclusion involves understanding that a set of items can be *simultaneously* part of a combined set and part of an embedded set. For example, imagine a bunch of six flowers, four of which are red, and two of which are white. The *combined set* is the six flowers, and the *embedded sets* are the white flowers and the red flowers. In Piaget's class-inclusion task, the child's understanding is tested with the question "Are there more red flowers or more flowers here?" The correct answer is that there are more flowers.

Halford's argument concerning the class inclusion task was that families could be used as a basis for analogies to problems such as the flowers problem. He pointed out that families were very familiar entities to young children, that they fulfilled the criteria for inclusion of having two clearly defined subsets (parents and children), and that they typically had a small set size, making it easy for children to represent the relevant relations in order to make an analogy. In order to see whether the family could act as a basis for successful performance in Piagetian class inclusion tasks, Goswami, Pauen, and Wilkening (1996) devised the "create-a-family" paradigm.

The children in Goswami et al.'s study (four- to five-year-olds) had all failed the traditional Piagetian class inclusion task, which was given as a pretest ("Are there more red flowers or more flowers?"). In the "create-a-family" paradigm, children were shown a toy family, for example a family of toy mice (two large mice as parents, three small mice as children). Their job was to create analogous families (two parents and three children) from an assorted pile of toys (such as toy cars, spinning tops, balls and helicopters). After the children had correctly created four analogous families, they were given four new class-inclusion problems involving toy frogs, sheep, building blocks, and balloons. As "family" is also a collection term, and as collection terms are known to influence class inclusion reasoning, the class inclusion problems were posed using collection terms ("group", "herd", "pile", "bunch"). A control group of children received the same class inclusion problems using collection terms, but did not receive the "create-a-family" analogy training session.

Goswami et al. found that more children in the "create-a-family" analogy condition than in the control condition solved at least three of the four class-inclusion problems involving frogs, sheep, building blocks and balloons. This effect was particularly striking at age four, in which no improvement at all was found in the control group with the collection term wording, but criterion was reached by 50 percent of the experimental group. It should be remembered that all of the children had previously failed the standard Piagetian class inclusion task. Goswami et al. argued that this change was due to the use of analogies based on a representation of family structure. Goswami et al.'s data suggest that Halford's structure-mapping theory of how analogies might contribute to the development of logical reasoning is both powerful and plausible. However, further research is required, particularly regarding the developmental appropriateness of the notion of capacity limitation as an upper limit on children's use of analogies (see Gentner and Rattermann 1999; Goswami 1999).

Conclusion

It is not unusual in developmental psychology for researchers to demonstrate that apparent changes in children's cognition are in reality changes in the knowledge that children have available as a basis for exercising a particular skill. Analogical reasoning appears to be no exception. If measures of analogy are based on unfamiliar relations, then these measures seriously underestimate children's analogical skills. Hence early research concluded that analogical reasoning was absent until early adolescence because it depended on experimental tasks that used analogical relations that were unfamiliar to younger children. Later research has demonstrated that analogical reasoning is used by children as young as one, two, and three years of age. It has also been shown that forms of relational reasoning which probably involve relational comparisons are present in young infants.

Nevertheless, it is important to note that the nature of a cognitive skill measured at time 1 may differ completely from the nature of a cognitive skill measured at time 2. For example, Strauss (1998) has argued that the kind of analogies made by infants may be completely different from the kind of analogies made by older children. He suggests that the kind of analogies made by young infants are *perceptual* in nature, whereas those made by young children use *conceptual* knowledge. Such questions about the continuity of cognitive skills are important ones for answering the question of "what develops" in analogical reasoning.

In this chapter, I have argued that the early age at which analogies appear suggest that they provide a powerful logical tool for explaining and learning about the world. Analogies also contribute to both the acquisition and the restructuring of knowledge, and play an important role in conceptual change. As children's knowledge about the world becomes richer, the structure of their knowledge becomes deeper, and more complex relationships are represented, enabling deeper or more complex analogies. This means that, as children learn more about the world, the type of analogies that they make will change. Another important developmental question is whether these changes are driven solely by changes in the knowledge base, or whether information processing factors, such as the number of relations that can be represented in primary memory at any one time, determine these changes.

Finally, it may be worth noting that the developmental role of analogy in cognition is not limited to childhood. The role of analogy in the history of science can also be explained in a knowledge-based fashion. Scientific breakthroughs often depend on the right analogy (Gentner and Jeziorski 1993; Gordon 1979), but the scientists who make the breakthroughs seldom have extra information that is unavailable to their colleagues. Instead, the analogy occurs to them and not to their fellow scientists because of the way that their conceptual understanding of their field is structured, and the richness of their representations. This in turn may be correlated with their intelligence. If intelligence is important, then its importance may explain why classical analogy performance is a good correlate of IQ. It has been reported that more efficient processing of stimuli as a neonate (using a habituation paradigm) is related to performance on a test of analogical reasoning at age twelve (e.g., *bread* is to *food* as *water* is to *beverage*; Sigman et al. 1991). There is clearly still much research to be done before we can claim to understand the role of analogical reasoning in cognitive development in all its complexity.

Acknowledgments

I would like to thank Graeme Halford and Dedre Gentner for their valuable comments on the first draft of this chapter. This work was partially supported by a grant from the Spencer Foundation (199600149).

Note

1. Rattermann and Gentner (1998) have argued that these group means may be overestimates of three-year-old performance because of some carryover for some children from the control task. In Goswami et al. (1998), group performance for three-year-olds in the same task was measured without carryover effects, and was 33 percent correct. However, this was not significantly different from chance (25%). Formal multiple-choice tasks of this nature may thus lack sensitivity as group measures of analogical ability for such young children.

References

Baillargeon, R., Needham, A., and De Vos, J. (1992). The development of young infants' intuitions about support. *Early Development & Parenting* 1:69–78.

Brown, A. L. (1989). Analogical learning and transfer: What develops? In S. Vosniadou and A. Ortony, Eds., *Similarity and analogical reasoning*, pp. 369–412. Cambridge: Cambridge University Press.

Bryant, P. E. (1974). *Perception and understanding in young children*. London: Methuen.

Bullock, M., Gelman, R., and Baillargeon, R. (1982). The development of causal reasoning. In W. J. Friedman, Ed., *The developmental psychology of time*, pp. 209–254. New York: Academic Press.

Case, R. (1985). *Intellectual development: Birth to adulthood*. New York: Academic Press.

Chen, Z., Sanchez, R. P., and Campbell, T. (1997). From beyond to within their grasp: Analogical problem solving in 10- and 13-month-olds. *Developmental Psychology* 33:790–801.

Freeman, K. E. (1996). *Analogical reasoning in 2-year-olds: A comparison of formal and problem-solving paradigms*. Ph.D. dissertation, University of Minnesota.

Gentner, D. (1983). Structure-mapping: A theoretical framework for analogy. *Cognitive Science* 7:155–170.

Gentner, D. (1989). The Mechanisms of Analogical Learning. In S. Vosniadou and A. Ortony, Eds., *Similarity and analogical reasoning*, pp. 199–241. London: Cambridge University Press.

Gentner, D., and Jeziorski, M. (1993). The shift from metaphor to analogy in western science. In A. Ortony, Ed., *Metaphor and thought* (2d ed.), pp. 447–480. Cambridge: Cambridge University Press.

Gentner, D., and Rattermann, M. J. (1991). Language and the career of similarity. In S. A. Gelman and J. P. Byrnes, Eds., *Perspectives on thought and language: Interrelations in development*, pp. 225–277. London: Cambridge University Press.

Gentner, D., and Rattermann, M. J. (1999). Deep thinking in children: The case for knowledge change in analogical development. *Behavioural & Brain Sciences* 21(6):837–838.

Gergely, G., Nadasdy, Z., Csibra, G., and Biro, S. (1995). Taking the intentional stance at 12 months of age. *Cognition* 56:165–193.

Gick, M. L., and Holyoak, K. J. (1980). Analogical problem solving. *Cognitive Psychology* 12:306–355.

Gick, M. L., and Holyoak, K. J. (1983). Schema induction and analogical transfer. *Cognitive Psychology* 15:1–38.

Gordon, W. J. J. (1979). Some source material in discovery-by-analogy. *The Journal of Creative Behaviour* 8:239–257.

Goswami, U. (1991). Analogical reasoning: What develops? A review of research and theory. *Child Development* 62:1–22.

Goswami, U. (1992). *Analogical reasoning in children*. Hillsdale, NJ: Lawrence Erlbaum Associates.

Goswami, U. (1995). Transitive relational mappings in 3- and 4-year-olds: The analogy of Goldilocks and the Three Bears. *Child Development* 66:877–892.

Goswami, U. (1996). Analogical reasoning and cognitive development. *Advances in Child Development and Behaviour* 26:91–138.

Goswami, U. (1998). *Cognition in children*. Hove: Psychology Press.

Goswami, U. (1999). Is relational complexity a useful metric for cognitive development? *Behavioural & Brain Sciences* 21(6):838–839.

Goswami, U., and Brown, A. L. (1989). Melting chocolate and melting snowmen: Analogical reasoning and causal relations. *Cognition* 35:69–95.

Goswami, U., and Brown, A. L. (1990). Higher-order structure and relational reasoning: Contrasting analogical and thematic relations. *Cognition* 36:207–226.

Goswami, U., Pauen, S., and Wilkening, F. (1996). The effects of a "family" analogy on class inclusion reasoning in young children. Manuscript.

Goswami, U., Leevers, H., Pressley, S., and Wheelwright, S. (1998). Causal reasoning about pairs of relations and analogical reasoning in young children. *British Journal of Developmental Psychology* 16:553–569.

Halford, G. S. (1987). A structure-mapping approach to cognitive development. *International Journal of Psychology* 22:609–642.

Halford, G. S. (1993). *Children's understanding: The development of mental models.* Hillsdale, NJ: Erlbaum.

Halford, G. S., Wilson, W. H., and Phillips, S. (1999). Processing capacity defined by relational complexity: Implications for comparative, developmental and cognitive psychology. *Behavioural & Brain Sciences* 21(6):803–831.

Heyes, C. M. (1996). Genuine imitation? In C. M. Heyes and B. G. Galef, Eds., *Social learning in animals: The roots of culture*, pp. 371–389. San Diego: Academic.

Heyes, C. M. (1998). Theory of mind in non-human primates. *Behavioural & Brain Sciences* 21:101–134.

Holyoak, K. J., and Thagard, P. (1995). *Mental leaps: Analogy in creative thought.* Cambridge, MA: MIT Press.

Inagaki, K., and Hatano, G. (1987). Young children's spontaneous personifications as analogy. *Child Development* 58:1013–1020.

Inagaki, K., and Sugiyama, K. (1988). Attributing human characteristics: Development changes in over- and under-attribution. *Cognitive Development* 3:55–70.

Leslie, A. M. (1994). ToMM, ToBY and Agency: Core architecture and domain specificity. In L. A. Hirschfeld and S. A. Gelman, Eds., *Mapping the mind*, pp. 119–148. New York: Cambridge University Press.

Marcus, G. F., Vijayan, S., Rao, S. Bandi, and Vishton, P. M. (1999). Rule learning by seven-month-old infants. *Science* 283:77–80.

Meltzoff, A. (1990). Foundations for developing a concept of self: the role of imitation in relating self to other and the value of social mirroring, social modeling, and self-practice in infancy. In D. Cicchetti and M. Beeghly, Eds., *The self in transition: Infancy to childhood*, pp. 139–164. Chicago: University of Chicago Press.

Meltzoff, A. N. (1995). Understanding the intentions of others: Re-enactment of intended acts by 18-month-old children. *Developmental Psychology* **31**:838–850.

Meltzoff, A. N., and Moore, M. K. (1983). Newborn infants imitate adult facial gestures. *Child Development* **54**:702–709.

Meltzoff, A. N., and Moore, M. K. (1997). Explaining facial imitation: A theoretical model. *Early Development & Parenting* **6**:179–192.

Pascual-Leone, J. (1987). Organismic processes for neo-Piagetian theories: A dialectical causal account of cognitive development. *International Journal of Psychology* **22**:531–570.

Pauen, S. (1996). Children's reasoning about the interaction of forces. *Child Development* **67**:2728–2742.

Pauen, S., and Wilkening, F. (1996). Children's analogical reasoning about natural phenomena. *Journal of Experimental Child Psychology* **67**:90–114.

Piaget, J., Montangero, J., and Billeter, J. (1997). La formation des correlats. In J. Piaget, Ed., *Recherches sur L'Abstraction Reflechissante I*, pp. 115–129. Paris: Presses Universitaires de France.

Polya, G. (1957). *How to solve it.* Princeton, NJ: University Press.

Rattermann, M. J., and Gentner, D. (1998). The effect of language on similarity: The use of relational labels improves young children's performance in a mapping task. In K. Holyoak, D. Gentner, and B. Kokinov, Eds., *Advances in analogy research: Integration of theory and data from the cognitive, computational and neural sciences*, pp. 274–282. Sofia: New Bulgarian University Press.

Sigman, M., Cohen, S. E., Beckwith, L., Asarnow, R., and Parmelee, A. H. (1991). Continuity in cognitive abilities from infancy to 12 years of age. *Cognitive Development* **6**:47–57.

Smith, L. B., and Heise, D. (1992). Perceptual similarity and conceptual structure. In B. Burns, Ed., *Advances in psychology: Percepts, concepts and categories*, pp. 233–272. Amsterdam: Elsevier.

Sternberg, R. J., and Nigro, G. (1980). Developmental patterns in the solution of verbal analogies. *Child Development* **51**:27–38.

Strauss, S. (1998). Review of Goswami, U., Analogical reasoning in children. *Journal of Pragmatics* **29**:639–646.

Tomasello, M., Call, J., and Gluckman, A. (1997). Comprehension of novel communicative signs by apes and human children. *Child Development* **68**:1067–1080.

Visalberghi, E., and Fragaszy, D. (1990). Do monkeys ape? In S. Parker and K. Gibson, Eds., *Language and intelligence in monkeys and apes: Comparative developmental perspectives*, pp. 247–273. Cambridge: Cambridge University Press.

Wagner, S., Winner, E., Cicchetti, D., and Gardner, H. (1981). Metaphorical mapping in human infants. *Child Development* **52**:728–731.

Wellman, H. M., and Gelman, S. A. (1997). Knowledge acquisition in foundational domains. In D. Kuhn and R. S. Siegler, Eds., *Handbook of child psychology*, vol. 2, *Cognition, language and perception* (5th ed.), pp. 523–573. New York: Wiley.

Younger, B. A., and Cohen, L. B. (1983). Infant perception of correlations among attributes. *Child Development* **54**:858–867.

14

Can an Ape Reason Analogically?
Comprehension and Production of
Analogical Problems by Sarah, a Chimpanzee
(*Pan troglodytes*)

David L. Oden, Roger K. R. Thompson, and David Premack

Classical analogy problems involve perceptions and judgments about relations between relations. For example, the simple verbal analogy *dog:cat::puppy:kitten* reflects the same relation, *canine:feline*, within each side of the expression, and the same relation, *adult:juvenile*, across corresponding elements of the two sides. This fundamental pattern of relations between relations is also present or implicit in the powerful literary devices of metaphor and simile, and is a key element in the development of scientific models (e.g., Gentner 1998; Thagard 1992; Holyoak and Thagard 1997). Analogical reasoning is typically regarded as computationally complex and developmentally sophisticated (see, e.g., Goswami 1991; Holyoak and Thagard 1997; Piaget 1977; Sternberg 1977, 1982; Sternberg and Nigro 1980; Vosniadou and Ortony 1989).

The question of whether such sophisticated reasoning is unique to humans has been a perennial topic for debate (cf. Darwin 1871; Griffin 1992; James 1981/1890; Vauclair 1996; Weiskrantz 1985). Recently, techniques have been developed that allow a systematic examination of analogical reasoning and its component processes in species other than humans. For example, Premack and his colleagues (e.g., Premack 1978; Oden, Thompson, and Premack 1990) used a matching-to-sample (MTS) procedure with chimpanzees (*Pan troglodytes*) in which the sample and the choice alternatives consisted of pairs of objects or pictures of items. The stimulus pairs were composed of either two identical items—instantiating the relation of "identity" (I)—or two nonidentical items—instantiating the relation of "nonidentity" (NI). On a particular trial, either an I pair or an NI pair served as sample and the choice alternatives con-

sisted of one I pair and one NI pair. Because none of the items comprising the choice pairs were used in sample pairs, Premack labeled this
task "conceptual matching-to-sample."

Although the format of this task might not be immediately recognized
as requiring analogical reasoning, it is in essence an analogy problem in
which all the arguments are provided for the subject, along with irrelevant items. Successful performance on the conceptual matching to
sample task involves assessments of relations between relations. That is,
the relations reflected in the choice pairs (i.e., identity and nonidentity)
must be comprehended and compared to the relation (identity or nonidentity) reflected in the sample pair.

Returning to our earlier example of a verbal analogy, we could adopt
the matching procedure to explore a verbal human's reasoning by first
presenting our subject with the initial argument (i.e., sample)—*dog:cat*—
and then asking her or him to complete the expression by choosing
between the two arguments *puppy:kitten* vs. *horse:rider*. Obviously, as
noted, words are replaced with more concrete arguments consisting of
objects or pictures when exploring the reasoning of a nonverbal species.
Nevertheless, the cognitive demands of the conceptual matching task
remain the same. It follows, then, that any chimpanzee capable of performing the conceptual matching task possesses the computational cognitive foundations upon which formal analogical reasoning rests.

Gillan, Premack, and Woodruff (1981) reported that Sarah, a chimpanzee (*Pan troglodytes*) with a history of successful conceptual matching, succeeded also in completing partially constructed analogies
involving either complex geometric forms or functional relationships
between common objects. The elements of these analogies were presented to Sarah in a 2 × 2 matrix format where, as shown here, the
stimuli A and A' exemplified a certain relation, the stimuli B and B' exemplified the same relation but with different items, and "same" was the
plastic token or word for this concept from the chimpanzee's artificial
language (Premack 1976, Premack and Premack 1972).

A   B

   "Same"

A'   B'

As noted, the elements (A, A', B, and B') in some of these experiments were geometric forms and the relations on the vertical and horizontal dimensions involved transformations of physical properties, for example:

Large blue triangle   Large yellow crescent

"Same"

Small blue triangle   Small yellow crescent

In other experiments the elements were familiar objects and the relations were functional ones, for example:

Padlock   Tin can

"Same"

Key   Can opener

In one set of experiments, Sarah was presented with just three terms of an analogy (A, A', and B) positioned according to the format described above and was required to select the appropriate fourth term (B') when presented with two alternatives. In another set of experiments, four items were arranged in the 2 × 2 analogy format. Sarah was required to choose between her word for "same" and her word for "different" depending on whether the arrangement did or did not constitute a true analogy. Sarah succeeded in solving both types of problems.

Gillan, Premack, and Woodruff (1981) interpreted Sarah's successful performance on both geometric and functional analogy problems as reflecting her ability to reason analogically about relations-between-relations. That is, she presumably established the higher-order analogical relationship "same" (or "different") *between* the two sides of the analogy by first assessing the lower order relationships *within* each side and then comparing them. However, a close examination of the data reported by Gillan, Premack, and Woodruff suggests that at least some of her apparently analogical based performances could have reflected a far less sophisticated strategy.

This possibility was first brought to our attention by Sue Savage-Rumbaugh (personal communication, 1989) who provided a detailed analysis of Sarah's performance in the study by Gillan, Premack, and Woodruff (1981) on those problems that required her to select a fourth item to complete a partially constructed geometric analogy. This analysis indicated that Sarah's performance could have been the same even if she had not attended to the relationship instantiated by the A and A′ elements on the left-hand side of the matrix. Rather, Savage-Rumbaugh argued, Sarah's choices could have been determined solely by a hierarchical set of *featural* matching rules by which she identified the choice item *most similar*, if not identical, to the single item (i.e., B) on the right-hand side of the matrix. Savage-Rumbaugh's analysis was compelling because it predicted not only the chimpanzee's correct choices, but also her errors. Furthermore, independent studies of analogical reasoning in four- and five-year old children (Alexander et al. 1989; Goswami 1989; Rattermann and Gentner 1998) revealed that the less proficient of these young human reasoners frequently resorted to such strategies.

Although Savage-Rumbaugh's featural similarity matching analysis cannot account for Sarah's performance in other experiments in the Gillan, Premack, and Woodruff (1981) study (e.g., functional analogy problems) it is nevertheless important for two reasons. First, it alerts us to a variant of the *psychologist's fallacy* (James 1981/1890) wherein the experimenter confusing his or her perspective or understanding of a phenomenon with that of the subject confuses *product* with *process*. An experimental animal's, or for that matter child's, production of analogical relationships at a frequency greater than chance does not necessarily mean that either species necessarily uses analogical reasoning processes to complete the task. The cognitive revolution notwithstanding, Lloyd Morgan's Canon (1906) has served psychology well during the past century and should not be eschewed in the new. Morgan stated that "in no case may we interpret an action as the outcome of the exercise of a higher psychical faculty, if it can be interpreted as the outcome of the exercise of one which stands lower in the psychological scale" (Morgan 1906:53). Around the last quarter of the twentieth century more recent practitioners of animal behavior (e.g., Griffin 1976) suggested that it was time to take a more cognitively oriented perspective. But if one is to empirically rule out the use of simpler (i.e., associative) strategies in putatively cognitive tasks, then finer-grained analyses of performance than are typically the case are warranted.

Savage-Rumbaugh's analysis also raises a second fundamental question regarding the conditions necessary for the expression of analogical reasoning abilities (cf., Oden, Thompson, and Premack 1990). For example, Sarah's analogical reasoning ability may only have been expressed in situations where it was mandated by the structure of the task. Consider, for example, the case of functional analogies. Faced with the question *Padlock is to key as tin can is to . . . ?* Sarah could not have chosen a can-opener instead of a paintbrush other than by comparing functional relationships. The utility of associative strategies in this task was precluded by the experimental design. For example, the tin can in question was painted the same color as the bristles of the paintbrush. Hence, had Sarah been predisposed to choose items on the basis of physical identity or resemblance, she would have incorrectly selected the paintbrush rather than the can-opener, which was her actual choice.

Recent Advances in the Study of Analogies by a Chimpanzee

We present here a preliminary summary of ongoing extensive reanalyses of data from more recent research conducted with Sarah on analogical problem solving tasks (Oden, Thompson, and Premack, in preparation a; Oden, Thompson, and Premack, in preparation b). These experiments were conducted in part to determine the boundary conditions for Sarah's analogical reasoning. For example, would Sarah use analogical reasoning spontaneously in situations where a simpler associative strategy *would* suffice? If so, then one could argue that she is predisposed, as are we humans, to reason about relations between relations, seeking out metaphor even when it is not explicitly required.

Another goal of this research then was to determine whether Sarah could also *construct*, rather than merely *complete*, analogies. This task is substantially more demanding than those she faced in her earlier work. On the one hand, completing or evaluating analogies requires one to compare relations which have been previously established. On the other hand, constructing analogies, additionally requires one to seek out relations which reside among stimuli, but which have not been explicitly specified in advance.

The materials used in this series of analogy tasks were similar to those used in the Gillan, Premack, and Woodruff (1981) geometric analogy problems. Sarah worked with an analogy board: a blue cardboard rectangle with an attached white cardboard cross, the arms of which extended across the length and width of the rectangle. This provided, at each corner of the rectangle, a recess into which stimuli could be placed to construct an analogy. Sarah's plastic token for the concept "same" was placed at the intersection of the display board's arms (see figure 14.1).

The experimental stimuli were squares of white cardboard, each with a geometric form stenciled on it. The forms varied in color (4), shape (3), size (2), and whether they were filled in with color or simply a colored outline. All possible combinations of these properties were used to create a pool of forty-eight different items, which were used in the experiments reported here.

The following rules were used to select items for the analogies. A and A' differed with respect to a single dimension (size, color, shape, or fill). B and B' also differed in this single dimension. A differed from B (and thus A' differed from B') on two dimensions, each different from the property distinguishing A and A'. Hence, for example, if A' represented a size transformation of A, then B might differ from A with respect to color and shape or shape and fill. These were defined as 1 × 2 analogies (e.g., size × shape + fill), an example of which is shown in figure 14.1. Following these rules, a total of 612 unique combinations of four stimuli could be selected, which, when appropriately placed on the board, would

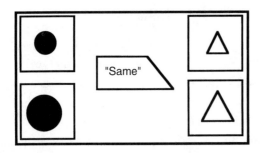

Figure 14.1
The 2 × 2 matrix format used by Gillan, Premack, and Woodruff 1981.

create an analogy. When experimental conditions required presentation of an additional (error) alternative choice item, this item (C) differed from B′ along the dimension that was not used in constructing the analogy. For example, if the analogy was a "size × shape + fill," then C differed from B′ in color only.

Sarah worked with these materials under four conditions. In two conditions, she was required to complete partially constructed analogies that were presented on the analogy board. In two other conditions, she was presented with an empty analogy board along with the appropriate stimulus items and had to construct an analogy from scratch. Throughout the study, a unique set of four analogy items was used on each trial.

General Test Procedures

A standard test procedure was used in all conditions. On each trial of a test session, the trainer placed the analogy board just inside the wire mesh of Sarah's home cage enclosure. The board contained either a partially-constructed analogy (completion conditions 1 and 2) or no stimuli at all (construction conditions 3 and 4). The stimuli that served as "answer" alternatives were contained in a covered cardboard box, which the trainer placed in front of the analogy board. After presenting the materials, the trainer left the room and recorded Sarah's behavior via a one-way mirror. Sarah's task was to open the alternatives box, make her selections, and place the items in the empty recesses of the analogy board. Any unused items were either left in the box or, at Sarah's discretion, placed in a pie tin adjacent to the testing area. She then rang a small bell inside her enclosure, summoning the trainer back into the room.

In those sessions where the design called for differential feedback (completion condition 1), Sarah was praised and given a piece of fruit after each trial when she had completed an analogy. When she erred, Sarah was mildly admonished and the trainer demonstrated the proper arrangement of stimuli but gave no food reward. In those sessions which called for nondifferential feedback (completion condition 2; construction conditions 3 and 4), Sarah was praised and given a food reward for every trial regardless of her accuracy, unless she had left an unfilled space on her analogy board. In that case, the trainer pointed to the empty recess and instructed Sarah, "Do better next time." No other feedback was given on such trials. Under nondifferential feedback, no particular problem-solving strategy is explicitly required, allowing the chimpanzee, if she is so inclined, to demonstrate spontaneous analogical reasoning (cf., Oden, Thompson, and Premack 1988).

Condition 1: Completion with two alternatives   This condition was a replication of the forced-choice task used by Gillan, Premack, and Woodruff (1981), in which Sarah was required to select a single item (B′) to complete a partially constructed analogy. This condition was intended to familiarize Sarah with the new analogy board and stimulus items, and to provide a performance baseline—regardless of the strategy or process used to generate it. The analogy elements A, A′, and B were placed in their appropriate positions on the board by the trainer. Two items, B′ and an error alternative (C), were placed in the alternatives box. One session of twelve trials was run using differential feedback.

Condition 2: Completion with three alternatives   This condition was run to determine whether Sarah could not only select items necessary to complete an analogy, but also position them on the board so that the final product reflected an analogical arrangement. In this condition, the trainer placed only A and A′ on the board. B, B′, and C were placed in the alternatives box. Sarah's task was to select and properly arrange B and B′ on the board. The arrangement of the items in the alternatives box was random. Four sessions of twelve trials each were run, using nondifferential feedback.

Condition 3: Construction with four alternatives   In this condition, Sarah was presented with her analogy board with only the "same" symbol on it. All four items necessary to construct an analogy were placed in her alternatives box. For two sessions of twelve trials each, the items were selected according to the construction rules followed in conditions 1 and 2. We wondered also whether increased similarity among items would help or hinder Sarah's performance. And so, in two other sessions of twelve trials each, A differed from B (and A′ from B′) in only one dimension instead of two ("1×1 analogies"). The two types of sessions (1×1 and 1×2 analogies) were run in an ABBA sequence, using nondifferential feedback.

Condition 4: Construction with five alternatives This condition was used to explore the effect of requiring an additional selection process as part of analogy construction. We were curious whether Sarah, faced with this additional complexity, would resort to a simpler associative strategy or perhaps abandon all strategies in favor of random selection and placement. In this condition, Sarah was presented with an empty analogy board and her box of alternatives which contained four elements that could be used to construct an analogy, and a fifth, unusable item (C, the error alternative). As in condition 3, Sarah's task was simply to fill the four empty spaces on the board. Six sessions of twelve trials each were run, using nondifferential feedback.

Results and Discussion
The results from all conditions are summarized in table 14.1. For each condition, the percentage of trials on which Sarah constructed an analogy are presented, along with the percentage expected on the basis of chance. Although Sarah's scores in all but condition 1 were somewhat lower than those reported by Gillan, Premack, and Woodruff (1981) her performance was nevertheless significantly greater than chance in all conditions.

This overall pattern of significant results strongly suggested that Sarah could indeed reason analogically both in completing partially constructed analogies and in creating her own analogies from scratch. Indeed, we drew this conclusion in an early report of these results (Oden and Thompson 1991). Our more recent concern, however, about the possibility of committing the previously noted fallacies has led us to reconsider that conclusion. First, as noted, one commits the psychologist's fallacy when one assumes that if we adult humans produce a particular result by reasoning analogically, then Sarah must do likewise. The second fallacy is to assume that because Sarah convincingly demonstrated analogical reasoning in the Gillan, Premack, and Woodruff (1981) *functional*

Table 14.1
Percentage of valid analogies constructed (Performance) and percentage of random arrangements of items that would result in valid analogies (Chance) under each experimental condition

Condition	Performance (% Correct)	Chance (% Predicted)
1 Completion (B′)	89*	50
2 Completion (B and B′)	46***	17
3 Construction (four item)		
1 × 1 analogies	58**	33
1 × 2 analogies	57*	33
4 Construction (five item)	21***	7

* = p < .05, ** = p < .01, *** = p < .001, Binomial tests.

analogy problems, she must also have used that ability to solve the *geometric* analogy problems in the present study. Heedful of these possibly fallacious assumptions, we have reexamined the details of Sarah's performance for evidence that would either confirm our early conclusion or alternatively provide clues of simpler, nonanalogical processes that may have produced the same results.

Condition 1: Completion with two alternatives   Three of the twelve trials in this condition could not be scored because one or more of the recesses on the analogy board were empty when the trainer was summoned by Sarah's bell. In two of these cases, this was the result of Sarah's having dismantled the partially constructed analogy to inspect the new stimulus materials closely. In the third case, both alternatives were laid on the floor beside the intact analogy board. Sarah succeeded in completing the analogy on eight of the nine trials that could be scored. This level of performance (89%) compares favorably with the 75 percent overall accuracy reported in the original analogy studies (Gillan, Premack, and Woodruff 1981) and provides a current behavioral baseline for performance using the new analogy materials. However, because this condition was intentionally similar to those of the Gillan, Premack, and Woodruff study, our results are also subject to a similarity-matching interpretation. That is, the B′ alternative was more similar to B (already on the right side of the analogy board) than was the C (error) alternative. Thus, a similarity-matching strategy using B as a sample would lead to an analogical product without the use of an analogical process.

Condition 2: Completion with three alternatives   Sarah completed an analogy on twenty-two of forty-eight trials (46%), significantly more often than the 17 percent expected by chance. She selected the analogy pair (B, B′) on twenty-seven of forty-eight trials (56%; chance = 33%). On twenty-two of these twenty-seven trials (81%; chance = 50%) the selected items were placed on the board in the B/B′ arrangement, which completed the analogy begun with A/A′.

Sarah's overall success at completing analogies under this second condition, while statistically significant, was substantially lower than in condition 1. An examination of her relative success on the two components of this task (item selection and analogical placement) indicates that, for Sarah, the first component was the more difficult of the two. That is, she selected the potential analogy choice pair on only 56 percent of the trials, but once this pair was selected, Sarah arranged them analogically 81 percent of the time. One reasonable interpretation of these data is that Sarah's performance was guided by her comprehending the *relations* between features in the A/A′ arrangement presented on her analogy board. With the psychologist's fallacy in mind, however, one might alternatively interpret these data as reflecting some elaborate series of similarity-matching processes, including, for example, independent similarity matches along either the diagonal or horizontal axes of the analogy board rather than the vertical axis as suggested by Savage-Rumbaugh. A detailed analysis of the sequence of Sarah's choice within each problem suggests, thus far, that Sarah was not inclined to use associative strategies of this type (Oden, Thompson, and Premack, in preparation, a).

Sarah's attention to relations then is particularly striking given that nondifferential reinforcement was used in condition 2. This meant that she could have used any strategy whatsoever (including random selection and placement) to fill the analogy board. Nevertheless, she appears to have spontaneously adopted the strategy of mapping relations between relations. The next two conditions were intended to determine whether Sarah could detect and use relations to *construct* an analogy when presented with the necessary elements and an empty analogy board.

Condition 3: Construction with four alternatives   In this condition, and in condition 4 with five alternatives, the criteria used for scoring Sarah's constructions were as follows. Sarah did not have to place the stimulus items originally designated by the investigators as A, A′, B, B′ in any particular recess. Any arrangement using these four elements was accepted as an analogy if A and B appeared together on one axis (row or column) of the board, and where A and A′ appeared together on the alternative axis (column or row). This scoring rule was based on the property of an analogy that its elements and arguments may be interchanged in certain ways and still maintain analogical relations. For example, the construction *dog:cat::puppy:kitten* is as valid as *cat:kitten::dog:puppy* even though the relations expressed are rearranged. However, *cat:puppy::kitten:dog* would not be accepted as a valid analogy.

There were twenty-four possible arrangements of the items for a given trial, eight of which (33%) would qualify as analogies according to the above scoring rule. Sarah constructed valid analogies on fourteen of twenty-four trials with 1 × 1 analogies and on twelve of twenty-one trials with 1 × 2 analogies (overall performance = 58%), significantly more often than expected by chance. On three of the trials with 1 × 2 analogies she left one or more recesses empty and thus her construction was not scored.

Insight into the processes involved in these constructions comes from an examination of Sarah's selection and placement of her first two choices. We were able to score Sarah's sequence of choices and placements on forty-five of the forty-eight trials. On all but three of the trials, Sarah placed her first two choices in the same row or column of the analogy board, thereby determining whether an analogy could be completed.

With four alternatives, there were twelve possible ways that the first two items could be chosen. Eight of these combinations, when placed in the same row or column of the analogy board, constituted a "potential analogy" (i.e., they could become part of a valid analogy if the remaining items were arranged properly). Thus, Sarah could create, randomly, a *potential* analogy 67 percent of the time. But, in fact, her first two choices and placements produced potential analogies 82 percent (37/45 trials) of the time. With 1 × 2 analogies, Sarah showed no preference for a pair with one featural difference between its elements compared to a pair involving two featural differences. This is difficult to reconcile with a similarity-matching hypothesis, but perfectly consistent with the analogical reasoning perspective.

We have here evidence that the relational properties of the final analogical product (rather than mere item similarity) engaged the corresponding analogical processes when Sarah began work on each trial. This exercise of apparent "foresight" enabled Sarah to create for herself the initial conditions that had been previously provided by the experimenters in condition 2 of the completion task.

In the present construction condition, Sarah completed the construction of a valid analogy on 76 percent (28/37) of those trials in which her first choices had created potential analogies. This level of success is comparable to her prior performances on the completion tasks reported here and by Gillan, Premack, and Woodruff (1981). Overall, the results from this condition suggest that Sarah not only reasoned analogically, but also, through her exercise of foresight, understood the nature of the task before her.

Condition 4: Construction with five alternatives   Recall that in condition 2, where Sarah was required to select and arrange two items from a group of three alternatives, the selection process proved to be more fragile than the arrangement process. As preliminary results discussed below demonstrate, this differential difficulty with selection as opposed to arrangement did not prove to be the case in the present condition, where the addition of a fifth, "error" alternative required Sarah to select, as well as arrange, four items in her constructions.

In this condition, Sarah constructed analogies on fifteen of seventy-two (21%) of the trials. This level of performance was substantially lower than performance in the three preceding conditions, but it was nevertheless still significant ($p < .001$, binomial test). As before, we examined the sequence of Sarah's selections and placements to determine whether her performance truly reflected analogical reasoning or if it was the accidental byproduct of some simpler strategy.

Possible Nonanalogical Strategies

We considered two possible nonanalogical strategies. One such strategy might involve Sarah attempting to minimize featural differences between the items she arranged on the analogy board. A second possible strategy could entail Sarah excluding the error alternative item because it possessed a unique featural property.

Strategy 1: Minimizing featural differences   Perhaps Sarah was guided by an appreciation of the global pattern of similarities among items in an analogy, rather than the relations between particular pairs of items. If so, she may have adopted the strategy, "minimize featural differences on the board." Tables 14.2 and 14.3 help clarify this possibility.

In table 14.2 we have tabulated the number of featural differences *between each of the five items* which we used to construct a 1 × 2 analogy with a single error alternative. For example, consider the top row of table 14.2. Item A, might differ from A′ in size (one featural difference) and A might differ from B in shape and fill (two featural differences). B′ would thus necessarily differ from A in size, shape, and fill (three featural differences) and C would differ from A in size, shape, fill and color (four featural differences). From table 14.2, one can compute the *total number of featural differences among members of four-item sets* drawn

Table 14.2
Number of featural differences between individual items used to construct a 1 × 2 analogy with one error alternative in condition 4

	A	A′	B	B′	C
A		1	2	3	4
A′	1		3	2	3
B	2	3		1	2
B′	3	2	1		1
C	4	3	2	1	

Table 14.3
Total featural differences within groups of four items in condition 4

Sets	Items	Total featural differences	Number of times selected in 72 trials
1	A A′ B B′	12	33
2	A A′ B C	15	10
3	A A′ C B′	14	10
4	A C B B′	13	10
5	C A′ B B′	12	9

from the five alternatives presented. These totals are shown in table 14.3, along with the frequency of Sarah's selections of each set indicated in the last column. Note that set 1, which could be used to construct an analogy (A, A′, B, B′), involved a minimum number of featural differences. However, set 5 (C, A′, B, B′) also minimized the number of featural differences between its members.

A strategy of minimizing featural differences on the board would have led to completion of analogies in condition 1 which entailed Sarah's completing an analogy with two alternatives. In condition 2, this strategy would have led to the appropriate selection, but not necessarily to the appropriate arrangement, of items needed to construct an analogy. In the present condition, this strategy would have led to the selection of set 1, the potential analogy set. However, it should also have led equally often to the selection of set 5, containing item C, the error alternative. In fact, Sarah selected the potential analogy set thirty-three times in seventy-two trials and chose set 5, with an equal number of featural differences, only nine times. Thus, Sarah was clearly not trying to simply maximize overall similarity among the four items placed on the board. It would be tempting, therefore, to conclude that the relationship between particular items (a prerequisite of analogical reasoning) was of significance to Sarah. However, an alternative strategy must be considered before accepting this conclusion.

Strategy 2: Exclusion of C, the odd man out   It could be that Sarah indirectly maximized similarity among the items in her constructions by *excluding* alternative C that possessed a single property (size, shape, color, or fill) that was *not* shared with any other of the five items. This particular strategy would have predisposed Sarah to select those four items, which, if arranged appropriately on the board, would produce an analogy. As noted, Sarah in fact selected such a "potential analogy" set thirty-three times over seventy-two trials. The statistical question then becomes: Did the actual analogies constructed by Sarah on fifteen of these thirty-three trials result simply from chance arrangements of these four "potential analogy" elements?

Given a selection of the appropriate items, one-third of their possible arrangements would meet *our* criteria, described previously, for an analogy. If one uses this proportion as an estimate of chance success, then Sarah's construction of fifteen analogies on thirty-three trials was not statistically significant. This finding suggests, therefore, that Sarah had *not* attended to relations between relations in this fourth condition. However, as described below, a more detailed analysis of the temporal sequence in which Sarah placed the four items on the board in condition 4 has led us to reject this pessimistic conclusion.

Sarah's Analogical Strategy: Equating Within-Pair Differences

As Sarah selected items and placed them on the board, she seems to have followed a strategy of equating the *number* of within-pair featural differences, independently of the *physical nature* of those differences. This strategy is illustrated in figure 14.2a–d. Sarah consistently placed her first two choices on the same horizontal or vertical axis of the analogy board, as illustrated in figure 14.2a. Here, B' (choice 2) and A (choice 1) have been placed respectively in the upper and lower recesses (i.e., a vertical axis) on the left-hand side of the board. We can now describe Sarah's third and fourth choices as being placed adjacent to either her first or her second choices. In this example Sarah placed item C (choice 3) in the upper right-hand recess adjacent to her second choice (see figure 14.2b). Sarah's fourth choice (A') was then placed in the lower right-hand recess adjacent to her first choice (see figure 14.2c). Thus, Sarah's last two placements of her third and fourth choices could be described as creating two pairs as shown in figure 14.2d. The *number* of featural differences within

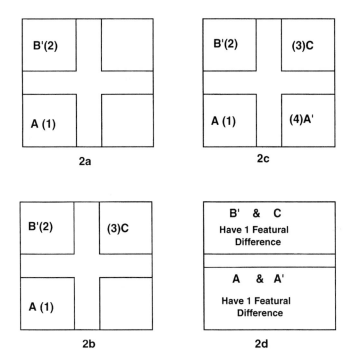

Figure 14.2
An illustrative sequence of Sarah's choices and placements in condition 4: analogy construction with five alternatives.

each pair is the same. That is, there is one featural difference in the B′ and C pair created by Sarah's placements of her second and third choices. The A and A′ pair created by her placements of her first and fourth choices similarly contains a single featural difference.

Each trial from condition 4 of the analogy construction was analyzed in the manner described above (Oden, Thompson, and Premack, in preparation b). The expected frequencies of each combination of featural differences were obtained by determining the six possible outcomes given her two initial choices. The observed frequencies of pairings which equated within-pair differences exceeded their expected frequencies. Sarah constructed twenty-two arrangements in which there was a single featural difference between pairs (expected frequency (Exp Frq = 12)) and she also arranged fifteen and ten arrangments in which there were, respectively, two (Exp Frq = 10) and three (Exp Frq = 10) featural differences between pairs. As noted, fifteen of these forty-seven arrangements—from a total of seventy-two—met the criteria for an analogy based also on the nature of the transformations between pairs.

Sarah apparently followed a strategy of numerically equating within-pair featural differences as she made her last two selections and placed them on the board. When Sarah placed her third choice next to one of the items already on the board, the resulting number of within-pair featural differences tended to be subsequently matched within the pair created by her placing her fourth choice next to the remaining item.

We argue that this pattern of results reveals analogical reasoning; it involves reasoning about relations between relations. There is a difference, of course, between the strategy employed by Sarah and the a priori rules we used to construct analogies. Whereas we had attended to the nature of *specific* features, as well as their number, Sarah attended only to the number of featural differences. For example, we regarded a (color + shape) transformation as differing from a (size + fill) transformation. In Sarah's eyes these transformations were equivalent because they both entailed two featural differences. Thus, compared to our reasoning, Sarah's may lack rigor, but fundamentally, she still reasoned about relations between relations. We do not believe that Sarah's failure to attend to featural details beyond number reflects a fundamental constraint on her reasoning abilities. Recall that the results from condition 2 of the completion task indicated that selection of items was a more difficult task than their arrangement. We believe that the decline in Sarah's performance in the present condition of the construction task resulted from the inherent complexity of the five-item stimulus array with which she was presented.

Summary

Collectively, the results from the four conditions reported here not only confirm that an adult chimpanzee can solve analogies (Gillan, Premack, and Woodruff 1981), but also demonstrate that she does so spontaneously, even in situations where a simpler associative strategy would suffice.

In condition 1 we replicated Gillan, Premack, and Woodruff (1981) earlier findings, which demonstrated that when faced with a partially constructed analogy problem, Sarah, the same adult chimpanzee subject, successfully selected from two available choices that item which would complete the analogy. In condition 2 of the completion task, Sarah demonstrated conclusively that her performance was mediated by analogical relationships and not a simple associative similarity matching strategy. When presented with only the two base elements of a classical analogy problem she successfully chose from three alternatives the two elements necessary to complete the target pair of the problem. More importantly however, was the finding that Sarah's spatial arrangement of these choices was guided by the relation initially established by the experimenters and not on the basis of mere similarity along any single physical dimension.

In conditions 3 and 4 we further demonstrated that the same chimpanzee, Sarah, could not only complete but also construct analogies. When presented with a randomized grouping of elements from which an analogy could be constructed she proceeded to do so spontaneously. When presented with the minimum of four elements, Sarah proceeded to arrange all of them in analogical fashion. When presented with five elements she arranged four of the five items analogically. However, Sarah did so in a manner analogous to, but not identical with that of her human experimenters. On one hand, we had attended to both specific physical factors and their number in each within-pair transformation. Sarah, on the other hand, had attended primarily to only the latter numerical dimension. Nevertheless, the resulting patterns produced by Sarah's arrangements were analogical. Our anthropocentric emphasis led to our initially underestimating Sarah's capacity for analogical reasoning.

Precursors for Analogical Reasoning

Some investigators have argued that analogical reasoning is the common foundation (denominator) of much of human reasoning, including logical inference (e.g., Halford 1992). Our results confirm earlier reports (Gillan, Premack, and Woodruff 1981) that it is well within the capabilities of at least one adult chimpanzee. Might this capacity be expected in chimpanzees other than Sarah? And if so, what about other nonhuman primates?

Our answer to the first question is a qualified yes. As previously noted, prior to her experience with formal analogical problem solving Sarah had mastered a conceptual matching task which, at the age of thirty-nine years, she still successfully performed under conditions of nondifferential reinforcement (Thompson, Oden, and Boysen 1997). Recall that in the conceptual matching task a subject is required to match a pair of physically identical sample items (e.g., a pair of locks) with another pair of identical items (e.g., a pair of cups) as opposed to a pair of physically nonidentical items like, for example, a pencil and an eraser. Conversely, this latter nonidentical pair would be the correct match given another nonidentical sample pair such as a shoe and ball.

Successful performance of the conceptual matching task as described above involves the matching of relations between relations and hence, as noted above in our introduction, it is itself, therefore, an analogy problem in which all the arguments are provided for the subject. It follows then that any chimpanzee or nonhuman subject capable of performing the conceptual matching task possesses the computational cognitive foundations upon which formal analogical reasoning rests.

There is good evidence, however, that not all chimpanzees, let alone any other nonhuman primate species, can match relations between relations despite their success on physical matching tasks (Thompson and Oden, forthcoming). Prior experience with tokens, analogous to words, that symbolize abstract same/different relations is a powerful facilitator enabling a chimpanzee or child to explicitly express in judgment tasks, like conceptual matching, their otherwise implicit perceptual knowledge about relations between relations (Premack 1983; Rattermann and Gentner 1998, forthcoming; Thompson and Oden 1993; Tyrrell, Stauffer, and Snowman 1991).

Interestingly, these analogical perceptual and conceptual capacities have been documented only in chimpanzees and humans. Unlike chimpanzee or human infants, Old World macaque monkeys (*Macaca mulatta*) trained with symbols for same and different with procedures comparable to those experienced by chimpanzees, subsequently failed to judge the analogical equivalence of stimulus pairs in a conceptual-matching task (Washburn, Thompson, and Oden 1997, in preparation). As yet, there is no compelling evidence that Old World monkeys spontaneously perceive, let alone judge, analogical relations. Neither adult nor infant macaque monkeys (*Macaca mulatta, Macaca neminstrina*) spontaneously perceive analogical or relational identity when tested using the same preference for novelty procedures employed with chimpanzees and human infants (Oden, Thompson, and Premack 1990; Maninger, Gunderson, and Thompson 1997; Thompson and Oden 1996, 1998, forthcoming; Thompson, Oden, and Gunderson 1997; Tyrrell, Stauffer, and Snowman 1991). Thus far, this disparity holds true regardless of the task (paired-comparison and habituation/dishabituation) and hence time available for information processing, or whether visual gaze or object handling is the dependent measure (Chaudhri et al. 1997; Thompson 1995; Thompson and Oden 1996; Thompson et al. 1997). Nevertheless, regardless of the dependent measure, the same monkeys give every indication that like chimpanzee and child they perceive objects to be the same or different based on physical properties alone.

Taken together, this pattern of findings indicates that analogical reasoning cannot emerge from a *tabula rasa*. Rather the facilitative effects of symbolic tokens analogous to words on the expression of analogical reasoning can only operate on preexisting perceptual competencies. Experience with an external symbolic relational labeling system in some way provides child and chimpanzee, if not monkey, with the requisite representational scaffolding for the complex computational operations necessary to solve problems involving conceptually abstract similarity judgments as in analogies (Clark and Thornton 1997; Gentner and Markman 1997; Gentner et al. 1995; Sternberg and Nigro 1980).

Some may wish to argue instead that Sarah's capacity for analogical reasoning is likely simply a functional outcome of a rich and varied history of complex problem-solving (e.g., Roitblat 1985). We disagree with this interpretation, as we have argued at length elsewhere (Thompson et al. 1997). Furthermore, it is an interpretation that runs contrary to current findings in the human developmental literature. Developmental research provides a compelling argument for the facilitative effects of words on the expression and judgment of a diverse set of abstract categorical and conceptual capacities including analogical reasoning (e.g., Rattermann and Gentner 1998; Xu and Carey 1996; Waxman and Markow 1995). We concur with Clark's (1998) conclusion that "learning such a set of arbitrary tags and labels . . . renders certain features of our world concrete and salient . . . a new domain of basic objects . . . (that can be) . . . attended to in ways that quickly reveal further otherwise hidden patterns, as in the case of relations-between-relations" (Clark 1998:175–176).

Conclusion

Analogical reasoning may indeed be a hallmark of human reasoning. Nevertheless, the results on completion and construction of analogical problem-solving by Sarah, a representative of the common chimpanzee species *Pan troglodytes*, demonstrate that this uncommon individual is predisposed, as are humans, to reason about relations between relations. Perhaps a cautionary note is called for here. Our reading of the developmental literature suggests that some if not all developmental psychologists equate "predisposed" with an innate capacity (e.g., Spelke 1994). Clearly—as indicated by our preceding discussion—analogical reasoning cannot emerge from a *tabula rasa*, but clearly, to paraphrase Butterworth (1996), as cited in Haith (1998), implicitly perceiving and explicitly judging properties of the world are not the same thing. For many comparative psychologists, like us, "predisposition" is intended here simply to refer to a behavioral/cognitive tendency the origins of which are a separate issue.

The data summarized here provide a cautionary tale for psychologists as to the potential traps and snares of the psychologist's fallacy discussed above. When constructing both the base and target relations of an analogy from four of five elements in condition 4, Sarah did so in a manner analogous to, but not identical with that of her human experimenters. As we have emphasized throughout this discussion, an anthropocentric bias can blind one to an animal's or, for that matter, a child's alternative, but no less successful strategies. Our cautionary tale is perhaps the analogical "other side of the coin" to Haith's (1998) warning to developmental psychologists that uncritical projections of an adult's understanding of a phenomenon onto that of human infants or children may lead to overly rich intepretations of their cognitive capacities. In the present case, however, the potential problem of projection was one which would have led us to underestimate the conceptual capacities of Sarah, a chimpanzee.

The analyses of Sarah's selection and arrangement of items on her analogy board in both types of analogy task provide no evidence that she attempted to use a less efficient associative strategy, as can occur with young children (Alexander et al. 1989). We can only be confident in this conclusion because of our exhaustive reanalyses of Sarah's response patterns. We concur with the recent recognition by some developmental psychologists of the theoretical and empirical utility of such detailed "microgenetic" analysis (Siegler and Crowley 1991).

Acknowledgments

We thank Bonnie Dennis and Teresa Anderson for their assistance in data collection. We also thank M. J. Rattermann for her helpful comments. The research reported here and preparation of this paper were supported by funds from the National Science Foundation (NSF-BNS 8418942 and NSF-IBN 9420756).

References

Alexander, P. A., Willson, V. L., White, C. S., Fuqua, J. D., Clark, G. D., Wilson, A. F., and Kulikowich, J. M. (1989). Development of analogical reasoning in 4- and 5-year-old children. *Cognitive Development* 4:65–88.

Butterworth, G. (1996). Infant perception from a non-conceptual point of view. Paper presented at the International Conference on Infant Studies, Providence.

Chaudhri, N., Ghazi, L., Thompson, R. K. R., and Oden, D. L. (1997). Do monkeys perceive abstract relations in handled object pairs? Paper presented at the annual meeting of the Eastern Psychological Association, Washington, DC.

Clark, A. (1998). Magic words: How language augments human computation. In P. Carruthers and J. Boucher, Eds., *Language and thought: Interdisciplinary themes*, pp. 162–183. Cambridge: Cambridge University Press.

Clark, A., and Thornton, C. (1997). Trading spaces: Computation, representation, and the limits of uniformed learning. *Behavioral and Brain Sciences* 20:57–90.

Darwin, C. (1871). *The descent of man and selection in relation to sex.* London, U.K.: Murray.

Gentner, D. (1998). Analogy. In W. Bechtel and G. Graham, Eds., *A companion to cognitive science*, pp. 107–113. Malden, MA: Blackwell Publishers.

Gentner, D., and Markman, A. B. (1997). Structural mapping in analogy and similarity. *American Psychologist* 52:45–56.

Gentner, D., Rattermann, M. J., Markman, A., and Kotovsky, L. (1995). Two forces in the development of relational similarity. In T. Simon and G. Halford, Eds., *Developing cognitive competence: New approaches to process modeling*, pp. 263–313. Hillsdale, NJ: Erlbaum.

Gillan, D. J., Premack, D., and Woodruff, G. (1981). Reasoning in the chimpanzee: I. Analogical reasoning. *Journal of Experimental Psychology: Animal Behavior Processes* 7:1–17.

Goswami, U. (1989). Relational complexity and the development of analogical reasoning. *Cognitive Development* 4:251–268.

Goswami, U. (1991). Analogical reasoning: What develops? A review of research and theory. *Child Development* 62:1–22.

Griffin, D. R. (1976). *The question of animal awareness.* New York: Rockefeller University Press.

Griffin, D. R. (1992). *Animal thinking.* Chicago: University of Chicago Press.

Haith, M. M. (1998). Who put the cog in infant cognition? Is rich interpretation too costly? *Infant Behavior & Development* 21:167–179.

Halford, G. S. (1992). Analogical reasoning and conceptual complexity in cognitive development. *Human Development* 35:193–217.

Holyoak, K. J., and Thagard, P. (1997). The analogical mind. *American Psychologist* 52(1):35–44.

James, W. (1981/1890). *The principles of psychology*, vol. I. Cambridge, MA: Harvard University Press.

Maninger, N., Gunderson, V. M., and Thompson, R. K. R. (1997). Perception of identity and difference relations in infant pigtailed macaques (*Macaca nemestrina*). Paper presented at the annual meeting of the American Primatological Society, San Diego, CA.

Morgan, C. L. (1906). *An introduction to comparative psychology.* (Rev. ed.). New York: Scribner's.

Oden, D. L., and Thompson, R. K. R. (1991). The construction of analogies by a chimpanzee. Paper presented at the meeting of the Psychonomic Society, San Francisco, CA.

Oden, D. L., Thompson, R. K. R., and Premack, D. (1988). Spontaneous transfer of matching by infant chimpanzees (*Pan troglodytes*). *Journal of Experimental Psychology: Animal Behavior Processes* 14:140–145.

Oden, D. L., Thompson, R. K. R., and Premack, D. (1990). Infant chimpanzees (*Pan troglodytes*) spontaneously perceive both concrete and abstract same/different relations. *Child Development* 61:621–631.

Oden, D. L., Thompson, R. K. R., and Premack, D. (In preparation a). A chimpanzee completes analogy problems analogically.

Oden, D. L., Thompson, R. K. R., and Premack, D. (In preparation b). Construction of analogies by a chimpanzee.

Piaget, J., Ed. (1977). *L'Abstraction reflechissante*. Paris: Presses Universitaires de France.

Premack, D. (1976). *Intelligence in ape and man*. Hillsdale, NJ: Erlbaum Associates.

Premack, D. (1978). On the abstractness of human concepts: Why it would be difficult to talk to a pigeon. In S. Hulse, H. Fowler, and W. K. Honig, Eds., *Cognitive processes in animal behavior*, pp. 423–451. Hillsdale, NJ: Erlbaum Associates.

Premack, D. (1983). The codes of man and beast. *Behavioral and Brain Sciences* 6:125–137.

Premack, A. J., and Premack, D. (1972). Teaching language to an ape. *Scientific American* 227:92–99.

Rattermann, M. J., and Gentner, D. (1998). The effect of relational language on children's performance in an analogical mapping task. In K. Holyoak, D. Gentner, and B. Kokinov, Eds., *Advances in analogy research: Integration of theory and data from the cognitive, computational, and neural sciences*, pp. 274–282. Sofia: New Bulgarian University Press.

Rattermann, M. J., and Gentner, D. (forthcoming). The effect of language on similarity: The use of relational labels improves young children's performance in a mapping task. *Cognitive Psychology*.

Roitblat, H. L. (1985). *Introduction to comparative cognition*. New York: W. H. Freeman.

Siegler, R. S., and Crowley, K. (1991). The microgenetic method: A direct means for studying cognitive development. *American Psychologist* 46:606–620.

Spelke, E. S. (1994). Initial knowledge: Six suggestions. *Cognition* 50:431–445.

Sternberg, R. J. (1977). *Intelligence, information processing, and analogical reasoning*. Hillsdale, NJ: Erlbaum.

Sternberg, R. J. (1982). Reasoning, problem solving, and intelligence. In R. J. Sternberg, Ed., *Handbook of human intelligence*, pp. 225–307. New York: Cambridge University Press.

Sternberg, R. J., and Nigro, G. (1980). Developmental patterns in the solution of verbal analogies. *Child Development* 51:27–38.

Thagard, P. (1992). *Conceptual revolutions*. Princeton, NJ: Princeton University Press.

Thompson, R. K. R. (1995). Natural and relational concepts in animals. In H. Roitblat and J. A. Meyer, Eds., *Comparative approaches to cognitive science*, pp. 175–224. Cambridge, MA: MIT Press.

Thompson, R. K. R., and Oden, D. L. (1993). "Language training" and its role in the expression of tacit propositional knowledge in chimpanzees (*Pan troglodytes*). In H. L. Roitblat, L. M. Herman, and P. E. Nachtigall, Eds., *Language and communication: Comparative perspectives*, pp. 365–384. Hillsdale, NJ: Erlbaum Associates.

Thompson, R. K. R., and Oden, D. L. (1996). A profound disparity revisited: Perception and judgment of abstract identity relations by chimpanzees, human infants, and monkeys. *Behavioral Processes* 35:149–161.

Thompson, R. K. R., and Oden, D. L. (1998). Why monkeys and pigeons, unlike certain apes, cannot reason analogically. In K. Holyoak, D. Gentner, and B. Kokinov, Eds., *Advances in analogy research: Integration of theory and data from the cognitive, computational, and neural sciences*, pp. 269–273. Sofia: New Bulgarian University Press.

Thompson, R. K. R., and Oden, D. L. (forthcoming). Categorical perception & conceptual judgments by nonhuman primates: The paleological monkey and the analogical ape. *Cognitive Science*.

Thompson, R. K. R., Oden, D. L., and Boysen, S. T. (1997). Language-naive chimpanzees (*Pan troglodytes*) judge relations between relations in a conceptual matching-to-sample task. *Journal of Experimental Psychology: Animal behavior processes* 23:31–43.

Thompson, R. K. R., Oden, D. L., Boyer, B., Coleman, J. F., and Hill, C. C. (1997). Test for the perception of abstract relational identity and nonidentity by macaque monkeys in an habituation/dishabituation task. Paper presented at the annual meeting of the Eastern Psychological Association, Washington, DC.

Thompson, R. K. R., Oden, D. L., and Gunderson, V. M. (1997). Adult and infant monkeys do not perceive abstract relational similarity. Paper presented at the 38th annual meeting of the Psychonomic Society, Philadelphia, PA.

Tyrrell, D. J., Stauffer, L. B., and Snowman, L. G. (1991). Perception of abstract identity/difference relationships by infants. *Infant Behavior and Development* 14:125–129.

Vosniadou, S., and Ortony, A., Eds. (1989). *Similarity and analogical reasoning*. Cambridge: Cambridge University Press.

Vauclair, J. (1996). *Animal cognition: An introduction to modern comparative psychology*. Cambridge, MA: Harvard University Press.

Washburn, D. A., Thompson, R. K. R., and Oden, D. L. (1997). *Monkeys trained with same/different symbols do not match relations.* Paper presented at the 38th Annual Meeting of the Psychonomic Society, Philadelphia, PA.

Waxman, S. R., and Markow, D. B. (1995). Words as invitations to form categories: Evidence from 12- to 13-month-old infants. *Cognitive Psychology* **29**:257–302.

Weiskrantz, L., Ed. (1985). *Animal intelligence.* Oxford: Clarendon Press.

Xu, F., and Carey, S. (1996). Infants' metaphysics: The case of numerical identity. *Cognitive Psychology* **30**:111–153.

15

Epilogue: Analogy as the Core of Cognition

Douglas R. Hofstadter

Grand Prelude and Mild Disclaimer

Once upon a time, I was invited to speak at an analogy workshop in the legendary city of Sofia in the far-off land of Bulgaria. Having accepted but wavering as to what to say, I finally chose to eschew technicalities and instead to convey a personal perspective on the importance and centrality of analogy-making in cognition. One way I could suggest this perspective is to rechant a refrain that I've chanted quite oft in the past, to wit:

One should not think of analogy-making as a special variety of *reasoning* (as in the dull and uninspiring phrase "analogical reasoning and problem-solving," a long-standing cliché in the cognitive-science world), for that is to do analogy a terrible disservice. After all, reasoning and problem-solving have (at least I dearly hope!) been at long last recognized as lying far indeed from the core of human thought. If analogy were merely a special variety of something that in itself lies way out on the peripheries, then it would be but an itty-bitty blip in the broad blue sky of cognition. To me, however, analogy is anything but a bitty blip—rather, it's the very blue that fills the whole sky of cognition—analogy is *everything*, or very nearly so, in my view.

End of oft-chanted refrain. If you don't like it, you won't like what follows.

The thrust of my chapter is to persuade readers of this unorthodox viewpoint, or failing that, at least to give them a strong whiff of it. In that sense, then, my article shares with Richard Dawkins's eye-opening book *The Selfish Gene* (Dawkins 1976) the quality of trying to make a scientific contribution mostly by suggesting to readers a shift of viewpoint—a new take on familiar phenomena. For Dawkins, the shift was to turn causality on its head, so that the old quip "a chicken is an egg's way of making another egg" might be taken not as a joke but quite seriously. In my case, the shift is to suggest that every concept we have is essentially nothing but a tightly packaged bundle of analogies, and to suggest that all we do when we think is to move fluidly from concept to concept—in other words, to leap from one analogy-bundle to another—and to suggest, lastly, that such concept-to-concept leaps are themselves made via analogical connection, to boot.

This viewpoint may be overly ambitious, and may even—horrors!—be somewhat wrong, but I have observed that many good ideas start out by claiming too much territory for themselves, and eventually, when they have received their fair share of attention and respect, the air clears and it emerges that, though still grand, they are not quite so grand and all-encompassing as their proponents first thought. But that's all right. As for me, I just hope that my view finds a few sympathetic readers. That would be a fine start.

Two Riddles

We begin with a couple of simple queries about familiar phenomena: "Why do babies not remember events that happen to them?" and "Why does each new year seem to pass faster than the one before?"

I wouldn't swear that I have the final answer to either one of these queries, but I do have a hunch, and I will here speculate on the basis of that hunch. And thus: the answer to both is basically the same, I would argue, and it has to do with the relentless, lifelong process of chunking—taking "small" concepts and putting them together into bigger and bigger ones, thus recursively building up a giant repertoire of concepts in the mind.

How, then, might chunking provide the clue to these riddles? Well, babies' concepts are simply too small. They have no way of framing entire events whatsoever in terms of their novice concepts. It is as if babies were looking at life through a randomly drifting keyhole, and at each moment could make out only the most local aspects of scenes before them. It would be hopeless to try to figure out how a whole room is organized, for instance, given just a keyhole view, even a randomly drifting keyhole view.

Or, to trot out another analogy, life is like a chess game, and babies are like beginners looking at a complex scene on a board, not having the faintest idea how to organize it into higher-level structures. As has been well known for decades, experienced chess players chunk the setup of pieces on the board nearly instantaneously into small dynamic groupings defined by their strategic meanings, and thanks to this automatic, intuitive chunking, they can make good moves nearly instantaneously and also can remember complex chess situations for very long times. Much the same holds for bridge players, who effortlessly remember every bid and every play in a game, and months later can still recite entire games at the drop of a hat.

All of this is due to chunking, and I speculate that babies are to life as novice players are to the games they are learning—they simply lack the experience that allows understanding (or even perceiving) of large structures, and so nothing above a rather low level of abstraction gets perceived at all, let alone remembered in later years. As one grows older, however, one's chunks grow in size and in number, and consequently one automatically starts to perceive and to frame ever larger events and constellations of events; by the time one is nearing one's teen years, complex fragments from life's stream are routinely stored as high-level wholes—and chunks just keep on accreting and becoming more numerous as one lives. Events that a baby or young child could not have possibly perceived as such—events that stretch out over many minutes, hours, days, or even weeks—are effortlessly perceived and stored away as single structures with much internal detail (varying amounts of which can be pulled up and contemplated in retrospect, depending on context). Babies do not have large chunks and simply cannot put things together coherently. Claims by some people that they remember complex events from when they were but a few months old (some even claim to remember being born!) strike me as nothing more than highly deluded wishful thinking.

So much for question number one. As for number two, the answer, or so I would claim, is very similar. The more we live, the larger our repertoire of concepts becomes, which allows us to gobble up ever larger coherent stretches of life in single mental chunks. As we start seeing life's patterns on higher and higher levels, the lower levels nearly vanish from our perception. This effectively means that seconds, once so salient to our baby selves, nearly vanish from sight, and then minutes go the way of seconds, and soon so do hours, and then days, and then weeks . . .

"Boy, this year sure went by fast!" is so tempting to say because each year is perceived in terms of chunks at a higher, grander, larger level than any year preceding it, and therefore each passing year contains fewer top-level chunks than any year preceding it, and so, psychologically, each year seems sparser than any of its predecessors. One might, somewhat facetiously, symbolize the ever-rapider passage of time by citing the famous harmonic series:

$$1 + 1/2 + 1/3 + 1/4 + 1/5 + 1/6 + 1/7 + 1/8 + \ldots$$

by which I mean to suggest that one's nth year feels subjectively n times as short as one's first year, or $n/5$ times as short as one's fifth year, and so on. Thus when one is an adult, the years seem to go by about at roughly a constant rate, because—for instance—$(1/35)/(1/36)$ is very nearly 1. Nonetheless, according to this theory, year 70 would still shoot by twice as fast as year 35 did, and seven times as fast as year 10 did.

But the exact numerical values shown above are not what matter; I just put them in for entertainment value. The more central and more serious idea is simply that relentless mental chunking makes life seem to pass ever faster as one ages, and there is nothing one can do about it. So much for our two riddles.

Analogy, Abstract Categories, and High-level Perception

Before I go any further, I would like to relate all this to analogy, for to some the connection may seem tenuous, if not nonexistent. And yet to me, by contrast, analogy does not just lurk darkly here, but is right up there, front and center. I begin with the mundane observation that vision takes an input of millions of retinal dots and gives an output of concepts—often words or phrases, such as "duck," "Victorian house," "funky chair," "Joyce Carol Oates hairdo," or "looks sort of like

President Eisenhower." The (visual) perceptual process, in other words, can be thought of as the triggering of mental categories—often standard lexical items—by scenes. Of course, high-level perception can take place through other sensory modalities: we can hear a low rumbling noise and say "helicopter," can sniff something and remark "doctor's office," can taste something and find the words "okra curry" jumping to our tongue, and so on.

In fact, I should stress that the upper echelons of high-level perception totally transcend the normal flavor of the word "perception," for at the highest levels, input modality plays essentially no role. Let me explain. Suppose I read a newspaper article about the violent expulsion of one group of people by another group from some geographical region, and the phrase "ethnic cleansing," nowhere present in the article, pops into my head. What has happened here is a quintessential example of high-level perception—but what was the input medium? Someone might say it was vision, since I used my eyes to read the newspaper. But really, was I perceiving ethnic cleansing visually? Hardly. Indeed, I might have heard the newspaper article read aloud to me and had the same exact thought pop to mind. Would that mean that I had aurally perceived ethnic cleansing? Or else I might be blind and have read the article in braille—in other words, with my fingertips, not my eyes or ears. Would that mean that I had tactilely perceived ethnic cleansing? The suggestion is absurd.

The sensory input modality of a complex story is totally irrelevant; all that matters is how it jointly activates a host of interrelated concepts, in such a way that further concepts (e.g., "ethnic cleansing") are automatically accessed and brought up to center stage. Thus "high-level perception" is a kind of misnomer when it reaches the most abstract levels, but I don't know what else to call it, because I see no sharp line separating it from cases of recognizing "French impressionism" in a piece of music heard on the radio or thinking "Art Deco" when looking at a typeface in an advertisement.

The triggering of prior mental categories by some kind of input—whether sensory or more abstract—is, I insist, an act of analogy-making. Why is this? Because whenever a set of incoming stimuli activates one or more mental categories, some amount of slippage must occur (no instance of a category ever being precisely identical to a prior instance).

Categories are quintessentially fluid entities; they adapt to a set of incoming stimuli and try to align themselves with it. The process of inexact matching between prior categories and new things being perceived (whether those "things" are physical objects or bite-size events or grand sagas) is analogy-making par excellence. How could anyone deny this? After all, it is the mental mapping onto each other of two entities—one old and sound asleep in the recesses of long-term memory, the other new and gaily dancing on the mind's center stage—that in fact differ from each other in a myriad of ways.

The Mental Lexicon: A Vast Storehouse of Triggerable Analogies

We humans begin life as rather austere analogy-makers—our set of categories is terribly sparse, and each category itself is hardly well-honed. Categories grow sharper and sharper and ever more flexible and subtle as we age, and of course fantastically more numerous. Many of our categories, though by no means all, are named by words or standard phrases shared with other people, and for the time being I will concentrate on those categories—categories that are named by so-called lexical items. The public labels of such categories—the lexical items themselves—come in many grades, ranging more or less as follows:

• *Simple words*:   chair, clock, cork, cannon, crash, clown, clue, cloak, climber . . .
• *Compound words*:   armchair, alarm clock, corkscrew, cannonball, skyscraper, station wagon, sexpot, salad dressing, schoolbus, jukebox, picket line, horror movie, wheeler-dealer . . .
• *Short phrases*:   musical chairs, out of order, Christmas tree ornament, nonprofit organization, business hours, foregone conclusion, rush-hour traffic, country-Western music, welcome home, tell me about it, give me a break, and his lovely wife, second rate, swallow your pride . . .
• *Longer phrases*:   stranded on a desert island; damned if you do, damned if you don't; praise the Lord and pass the ammunition; not in the foreseeable future; to the best of my knowledge; and they lived happily ever after; if it were up to me; haven't seen her since she was knee-high to a grasshopper; you could have knocked me over with a feather; thank you for not smoking; handed to him on a silver platter . . .

Such lists go on and on virtually forever, and yet the amazing fact is that few people have any inkling of the vastness of their mental lexicons (I owe a major debt here to Joe Becker—see Becker 1975). To be sure, most adults use their vast mental lexicons with great virtuosity, but they have stunningly little explicit awareness of what they are doing.

It was Roger Schank, I believe, who pointed out that we often use proverbs as what I would call "situation labels," by which I mean that when we perceive a situation, what often springs to mind, totally unbidden, is some proverb tucked away in our unconscious, and if we are talking to someone, we will quote that proverb, and our listener will in all likelihood understand very clearly how the proverb "fits" the situation—in other words, will effortlessly make the mapping (the analogy, to stress what it is that we are talking about here) between the phrase's meaning and the situation. Thus the following kinds of phrases can easily be used as situation labels:

That's the pot calling the kettle black if I ever saw it!

It just went in one ear and out the other . . .

Speak of the devil!

When the cat's away the mice will play!

The Common Core behind a Lexical Item

I now make an observation that, though banal and obvious, needs to be made explicitly nonetheless—namely, things "out there" (objects, situations, whatever) that are labeled by the same lexical item have something, some core, in common; also, whatever it is that those things "out there" share is shared with the abstract mental structure that lurks behind the label used for them. Getting to the core of things is, after all, what categories are for. In fact, I would go somewhat further and claim that getting to the core of things is what thinking itself is for—thus once again placing high-level perception front and center in the definition of cognition.

The noun "shadow" offers a good example of the complexity and subtlety of structure that lurks behind not just some lexical items, but behind every single one. Note, first of all, the subtle difference between "shadow" and "shade": we do not speak of cattle seeking shadow on a hot day, but shade. Many languages do not make this distinction, and thus they offer their native speakers a set of categories that is tuned slightly differently.

In many parts of the world, there are arid zones that lie just to the east of mountain ranges (e.g., the desert in Oregon just to the east of the Cascade mountains); these regions are standardly referred to as the mountain chain's "rain shadow."

What does one call the roughly circular patch of green seen underneath a tree after a snowfall? It could clearly be called a "snow shadow"—the region where snow failed to fall, having been blocked by an object.

A young woman who aspires to join her high-school swimming team, but whose mother was an Olympic swimmer, can be said to be "in the shadow of her mother." In fact, if she joins the team and competes, she might even be said to be "swimming in the shadow of her mother." And if she performs less well than her mother did, she will be said to be "overshadowed" by her mother.

One might say about a man who has had a bout with cancer but has recovered and is now feeling more secure about his health, "He is finally feeling more or less out of the shadow of his cancer." Along similar lines, many countries in Europe have recovered, to a large extent, from the ravages of World War II, but some might still be said to lie "in the shadow of World War II."

Another type of shadow cast by World War II (or by any war) lies in the skewed population distribution of any decimated group; that is, one imagines the human population as constituting a kind of flow of myriad tiny entities (individual people) down through the years (like that of photons or snowflakes through space), but long after the war's end, there are certain "regions" of humanity (e.g., certain ethnic groups) where the flow of births has been greatly reduced, much as if by an "obstacle" (namely, the millions of deaths in prior generations, whose effect continues to reverberate for many decades before gradually fading away, as a group's population replenishes itself).

There is of course no sharp line between cases where a word like "shadow" is used conventionally and cases where it is used in a novel manner; although "rain shadow" is something of a standard phrase, "snow shadow" (even though it is far easier to see) is less common. And notions like that of "population shadow" mentioned at the end are probably novel to most readers of this article, even though a closely related notion like "in the shadow of the war" is probably not new.

In short, the domain of the word "shadow" is a blurry region in semantic space, as is any human category, and—here I hark back to my initial refrain—that blur is due to the subtleties of mapping situations onto other situations—due, in other words, to the human facility of making analogies. The point is, a concept is a package of analogies.

Complex Lexical Items as Names of Complex Categories

Over the next few pages I will present a potpourri of mental categories (via proxies—namely, their English-language lexical-item representations); I invite you to think, as you consider each item, just what it is that very different exemplars of the category in question tend to have in common. Thus:

· dog
· backlog
· probably
· probab-*lee*!

I interrupt the list momentarily to comment on the last two entries, which of course are not nouns. (Who says nouns are the only mental categories? Obviously, verbs represent categories as well—but the same holds true, no less, for adjectives, adverbs, and so forth.) Some situations call forth the word "probably"; most do not. To some situations, the concept behind the word "probably" simply fits, while to most, it does not fit. We learn how to use the word "probably" over the course of years in childhood, until it becomes so ingrained that it never crosses our mind that "probably" is the name that English speakers give to a certain category of situations; it simply is evoked effortlessly and rapidly by those situations, and it is uttered without any conscious thought as to how it applies. It just "seems right" or "sounds right."

What, then, about the word below it: "probab-*lee*"? This, too, is a lexical item in the minds of most native speakers of contemporary

American English—perhaps not often used, perhaps more commonly heard than uttered by readers of this article, but nonetheless, we native speakers of American English all relate to hearing the word "probably" accented on its final rather than its initial syllable, and we all somehow realize the connotations hidden therein, though they may be terribly hard to articulate. I won't try to articulate them myself, but I would merely point out that this phonetic variant of the word "probably" fits only certain situations and not others (where the "situation" includes, needless to say, not just what is being talked about but also the mood of the speaker, and the speaker's assessment of the mood of the listener as well). Example: "Are our stupid leaders ever going to learn their lesson?" "Who knows? Maybe they're doomed to keep on repeating the mistakes of the past." "Mmm . . . Probab-*lee* . . ."

My point, with all the phrases cited above, is to bring to your conscious awareness the fact that there are certain situations that one could call "probab-*lee*! situations" no less than there are certain situations that are "musical-chairs situations" or "speak-of-the-devil situations." In short, lexical items can be very abstract categories evoked by special classes of situations and not by others. This applies to adjective, adverbs, prepositions, interjections, short and long phrases, and so on. Thus let me continue my list.

· Come on!
· Go for it!
· It's about time!
· Well, excuuuuuuuuuuuse me!
· Let's not stand on ceremony!
· without batting an eyelash
· ain't

Lest the lowest item above seem puzzling, let me point out that the notorious contraction "ain't," although it is in a certain sense ungrammatical and improper, is nonetheless used very precisely, like pinpoint bombing, by politicians, reporters, university presidents, and the like, who carefully and deliberately insert it into their speech at well-timed moments when they know their audience almost expects it—it fits the context perfectly. For example, a general trying to justify a bombing raid might say, in describing the series of deadly skirmishes that provoked it, "I'm sorry, but a Sunday picnic it just ain't." This is just one of many types of "ain't" situations. We native speakers know them when we hear them, and we likewise have a keen ear for improper uses of the word "ain't" by educated people, even if we ain't capable of putting our finger on what makes them inappropriate. (Curiously enough, shortly after drafting this paragraph, I came across an article in the *New York Times* about the failure of a test missile to hit its target, and a perfectly straight photo caption started out, "Two out of four goals ain't bad . . ." As I said above, even the most highly placed sources will use this "ungrammatical" word without batting an eyelash.)

"Suggestions" Imparted on the Soccer Field

As a nonnative speaker of Italian watching the 1998 Soccer World Cup on Italian television, I was struck by the repeated occurrence of a certain term in the rapid-fire speech of all the commentators: the word *suggerimento* (literally, "suggestion"). They kept on describing players as having given *suggerimenti* to other players. It was clear from the start that a *suggerimento* was not a verbal piece of advice (a suggestion in the most literal sense), but rather some kind of pass from one player to another as they advanced downfield. But what kind of pass was it exactly? By no means were all passes called *suggerimenti*; this term was clearly reserved for events that seemed to have some kind of scoring potential to them, as if one player was wordlessly saying to another, "Here now— take this and go for it!"

But how does a sports announcer unconsciously and effortlessly distinguish this kind of pass from other passes that in many ways look terribly similar? When is this kind of nonverbal "suggestion" being given by one player to another? I sensed that this must be a subtle judgment call, that there's no black-and-white line separating *suggerimenti* from mere *passaggi*, but that nonetheless there is a kind of core to the concept of *suggerimento* that all Italian announcers and keen Italian observers of soccer would agree on, and that there are fringes of the category, where some people might feel the word applied and others would not. Such blurriness is the case, of course, with every mental category, ranging from "chair" to "wheeler-dealer" to "pot calling the kettle black," but since *suggerimento* was not in my native language and thus I had been forced to grapple with it explicitly and consciously, it was an excellent example of the view of lexical items that I am herein trying to impart to my readers.

Polysemy and the Nonspherical Shapes of Concepts

It would be naive to imagine that each lexical item defines a perfectly "spherical" region in conceptual space, as pristine as an atomic nucleus surrounded by a spherical electron cloud whose density gradually attenuates with increasing distance from the core. Although the single-nucleus spherical-cloud image has some truth to it, a more accurate image of what lies behind a typical lexical item might be that of a molecule with two, three, or more nuclei that share an irregularly shaped electron cloud.

Suggerimento provides a perfect example of such a molecule, with one of its constituent atoms being the notion of a verbal piece of advice, another the notion of prompting on a theater stage, yet a third being the notion of a certain type of downfield soccer pass, and so forth. There is something in common, of course, that these all share, but they are nonetheless distinguishable regions in conceptual space.

Often native speakers of a language have a hard time realizing that two notions labeled identically in their language are seen as highly distinct concepts by speakers of other languages. Thus, native speakers of English feel the verb "to know" as a monolithic concept, and are sometimes surprised to find out that in other languages, one verb is used for knowing facts, a different verb for knowing people, and there may even be a third verb for knowing how to do things. When they are first told this, they are able to see the distinction, although it may seem highly finicky and pointless; with practice, however, they build up more refined categories until a moment may come when what once seemed an unnatural and gratuitous division of mental space now seems to offer a useful contrast between rather distinct notions. And conversely, speakers of a language where all three of these notions are represented by distinct lexical items may find it revelatory, fascinating, and perhaps even elegant to see how they are all subsumed under one umbrella-word in English.

My main point in bringing this up is simply to make explicit the fact that words and concepts are far from being regularly shaped convex regions in mental space; polysemy (the possession of multiple meanings) and metaphor make the regions complex and idiosyncratic. The simplest concepts are like isolated islands in a sea; the next-simplest are like pairs of islands joined by a narrow isthmus; then there are trios with two or three isthmuses having various widths; and so on. Caveat: When I say "simplest concepts," I do not mean those concepts that we pick up earliest in life, but in fact quite the contrary. After all, the majority of concepts planted in earliest childhood grow and grow over a lifetime and turn into the most frequently encountered concepts, whose elaborate ramifications and tendrils constitute the highest degree of twistiness! What I mean by "simplest concept" is merely "concept with maximally simple shape"; such a "simple" concept would most likely owe its simplicity precisely to its low frequency, and thus would seem like a sophisticated adult concept, such as "photosynthesis" or "hyperbola."

Conceptual Families and Lexical Rivalry

Walking down the corridors of a building in Italy in which I have worked over several summers, I have been faced innumerable times with an interesting problem in high-level perception that has to be solved in real time—in a couple of seconds at most, usually. That is, how do I greet each person who I recognize as we approach each other in the hall, and then pass? Here are five sample levels of greeting (there are dozens more, needless to say):

· *Buon giorno!* ("Hello!" or perhaps "Morning.")
· *Salve!* ("Howdy!" or perhaps "How are you.")
· *Buondì!* (Perhaps "Top o' the mornin'!" or "How ya doin'?")
· *Ciao!* ("Hi!" or "Hi there!")
· *Come stai?* ("How are you doing?" or perhaps "What's up?")

Each of them conveys a particular level of mutual acquaintance and a particular position along the formality/informality spectrum. And of course it frequently happens that I recognize someone but can't even remember how often I've met them before (let alone remember what their name is or what their role is), and so I have to make a decision that somehow will allow me to cover at least two different levels of friendliness (since I'm really not sure how friendly we are!). The choice is incredibly subtle and depends on dozens if not hundreds of variables, all unconsciously felt and all slightly contributing to a "vote" among my neurons, which then allow just one of these terms (or some other term) to come bubbling up out of my dormant Italian mental lexicon.

Consider the following spectrum of phrases all having in a certain sense "the same meaning," but ranging from very vulgar to somewhat incensed to quite restrained to utterly bland:

· He didn't give a flying f***.
· He didn't give a good God damn.
· He didn't give a tinker's damn.
· He didn't give a damn.
· He didn't give a darn.
· He didn't give a hoot.
· He didn't care at all.
· He didn't mind.
· He was indifferent.

For many native speakers, there are situations that correspond to each of these levels of intensity. To be sure, some speakers might be loath to utter certain of these phrases, but true native-level mastery nonetheless entails a keen awareness of when each of them might be called for in, say, a movie, or simply coming out of the mouth of someone else. After all, a large part of native mastery of a language is deeply knowing how other people use the language, regardless of whether one oneself uses certain phrases. And thus, to reiterate our theme, there are "He-didn't-give-a-good-God-damn situations" and there are situations of a very different sort, which could be called "He-didn't-care-at-all situations," and so forth. Each of the above expressions, then, can be thought of as the name of a particular type of situation, but since these categories are much closer to each other than just randomly chosen categories, they constitute potential rivalries that may take place during the ultra-fast high-level perceptual act that underlies speech.

Lexical Blends as a Window onto the Mind

Lexical blends, which are astonishingly common though very seldom noticed by speakers or by listeners, reveal precisely this type of unconscious competition among close relatives in the mental lexicon. A lexical blend occurs when a situation evokes two or more lexical items at once and fragments of the various evoked competitors wind up getting magically, sometimes seamlessly, spliced together into the vocalized output stream (see, for example, Hofstadter and Moser 1989). Occasionally the speaker catches such an error on its way out and corrects it, though just as often it goes totally unheard by all parties. Thus people make blends of the following sorts:

- Word-level blends: mop/broom ⇒ brop
- Phrase-level blends: easygoing/happy-go-lucky ⇒ easy-go-lucky
- Sentence-level blends: We'll leave no stone unturned/We'll pull out all the stops ⇒ We'll pull no stops unturned.

Blends reveal how much goes on beneath the surface as our brains try to figure out how to label simpler and more complex situations. In a way, what is amazing is that blends are not more common. Somehow, through some kind of cerebral magic, speakers light most of the time upon just one lexical label despite the existence of many potential ones, rather than coming out with a mishmosh of several—much as when a good pianist plays the piano, it is very seldom that two keys are struck at once, even though it might seem, a priori, that striking two neighboring keys at once ought to happen very often.

A Lexical Item as One Side of a Perceptual Analogy

At the risk of boring some readers, I shall now continue with my rather arbitrary sampler of lexical items, just to drive the point home that every lexical item that we possess is a mental category, and hence, restating what I earlier claimed, every lexical item, when used in speech (whether received or transmitted), constitutes one side of an analogy being made in real time in the speaker's/listener's mind. I thus urge readers to try on for size the mindset that equates a lexical item with the "name" of a certain blurry set of situations centered on some core. Though this sounds quite orthodox for nouns, it is less so for verbs, and when applied to many of the following linguistic expressions, it is highly unorthodox:

· slippery slope
· safety net
· shades of . . .
· Been there, done that.
· Forget it!
· It was touch-and-go.
· take a turn for the worse
· Be my guest!
· Make my day!
· Fancy that!
· Put your money where your mouth is!
· I mean, . . .
· Well, . . .
· Don't tell me that . . .
· It's fine to [do X] and all, but . . .
· kind of [+ adj.]
· when it comes to the crunch . . .
· You can't have it both ways!
· . . . that's for sure!
· the flip side [of the coin] is . . .
· You had to be there.
· It's high time that . . .
· Whatever!

Consider the teenager's favorite rejoinder, "Whatever!" If one were to try to capture its meaning—its range of applicability—one might paraphrase it somewhat along these lines: "You think such and so, and I disagree, but let's just agree to disagree and move on . . ." It takes a good number of years before one has acquired the various pieces of cognitive equipment that underpin the proper usage of such a phrase (which again ties in with the fact that one cannot remember events from one's babyhood).

High-Level Mental Chunks That Lack Labels

Although long stock phrases like "Put your money where your mouth is!" might seem to stretch the notion of mental chunking to the limit, that's hardly the case. Indeed, such phrases lie closer to the beginning than to the end of the story, for each one of use also remembers many thousands of events in our personal lives that are so large and so idiosyncratic that no one has ever given them a name and no one ever will, and yet they nonetheless are sharp memories and are revealed for the mental categories they are by the fact that they are summoned up cleanly and clearly by certain situations that take place later, often many years later. Thus take this one sample mental chunk, from my own personal usually dormant repertoire:

that time I spent an hour or two hoping that my old friend Robert, who I hadn't seen in two years but who was supposed to arrive from Germany by train sometime during that summer day in the little Danish fishing village of Frederikssund (which in a series of letters he and I had mutually picked out on maps, and in which I had just arrived early that morning after driving all night from Stockholm), might spot me as I lurked way out at the furthest tip of the very long pier, rather than merely bumping into me at random as we both walked around exploring the stores and streets and parks of this unknown hamlet

As its length suggests, this is a very detailed personal memory from many years ago (and indeed, I have merely sketched it for readers here— I could write pages about it), and might at first seem to be nothing at all like a mental category. And yet, how else can one explain the fact that the image of myself standing at pier's end tingling with unrealistic hope jumped instantly to mind some fifteen years later as I was idly seeking to rearrange the eight letters in the last name of Janet Kolodner, a new acquaintance, in such a way that they would spell a genuine English word? Without success, I had tried dozens of fairly "obvious" pathways, such as "rendlook," "leodronk," and "ondorkle," when out of the blue it occurred to me that the initial consonant cluster "kn", with its cleverly silent "k," might be the key to success, and I started excitedly trying this "brilliant idea." However, after exploring this strategy for a while, I realized, to my chagrin, that no matter how lovely it would be if the silent "k" were to yield a solution, the probabilities for such a clever coup were rapidly diminishing. And at the precise instant that this realization hit, the Frederikssund-pier image came swooshing up out of memory, an image to which I had devoted not even a split second of thought for many years.

There was, of course, a perfectly logical reason behind this sudden resurfacing—namely, a strong and rich analogy in which the mundane idea of merely walking around the fishing village mapped onto the mundane exploration of "rendlook" and cousins, in which the "romantic" idea of lingering way out at the tip of the pier mapped onto the "romantic" hope for an anagram beginning with the tricky "kn" cluster, and in which the growing recognition of the likelihood of failure of the more unlikely, more "romantic" strategies was the common core that bound the two otherwise remote events together.

The Central Cognitive Loop

Abstract remindings of this sort have been noted here and there in the cognitive-science literature, and some attempts have been made to explain them (e.g., Roger Schank's *Dynamic Memory* [1982]), but their starring role in the phenomenon of cognition has not, to my knowledge, been claimed. It is my purpose to stake that claim.

To make the claim more explicit, I must posit that such a large-scale memory chunk can be thought of as being stored in long-term memory as a "node"—that is, something that can be retrieved as a relatively discrete and separable whole, or to put it metaphorically, something that can be pulled like a fish out of the deep, dark brine of dormant memory. Once this "fish" has been pulled out, it is thrown in the "bucket" of short-term memory (often calling "working memory"), where it is available for scrutiny.

Scrutiny consists in the act of "unpacking" the node to some degree, which means that inside it are found other nodes linked together by some fabric of relationships, and this process of unpacking can then be continued recursively, given that the contents of unpacked nodes themselves are placed in short-term memory as well, and hence are themselves subject to more detailed scrutiny, if so desired. (I suppose one could extend the fishing analogy by imagining that smaller fish are found in the stomach of the first fish caught, as it is "cleaned"—and so forth, recursively. But that fanciful and somewhat gory image is not crucial to my story.)

Thus, if it is placed under scrutiny, inside the "Frederikssund pier" node can be found nodes for the exchange of letters that preceded Robert's and my Danish reunion, for Frederikssund itself, for my Stockholm drive, for Robert's train trip, for a few of the town's streets and shops, for the pier, for my growing disappointment, and so on. Not all of these will be placed into short-term memory each time the event as a whole is recalled, nor will the inner structure of those nodes that are placed there necessarily be looked into, although it is quite possible that some of their inner structure will be examined.

Thus the unpacking process of this kind of high-level unlabeled node (such as the "Frederikssund pier" node or the "Kolodner anagram" node) can fill short-term memory with a large number of interrelated structures. It must be stressed, however, that the unpacking process is highly context-dependent (i.e., sensitive to what concepts have been recently activated), and hence will yield a somewhat different filling-up of short-term memory on each occasion that the same high-level node is pulled up out of the ocean of long-term memory.

Once there are structures in short-term memory, then the perceptual process can be directed at any of them (this is, in fact, the kind of high-level perception that forms the core of the Copycat and Tabletop models of analogy-making—see Hofstadter and FARG 1995), the upshot of which will be the activation—thanks to analogy—of further nodes in long-term memory, which in turn causes new "fish" to be pulled out of that brine and placed into short-term memory's bucket. What we have described is, in short, the following central cognitive loop:

A long-term memory node is accessed, transferred to short-term memory and there unpacked to some degree, which yields new structures to be perceived, and the high-level perceptual act activates yet further nodes, which are then in turn accessed, transferred, unpacked, etc., etc.

An Illustration of the Central Cognitive Loop in Action

The foregoing may seem too abstract and vague, and so to make the ideas more concrete, I now will present a dialogue most of which actually took place, but some of which has been added on, so as to make some points emerge a little more clearly. The fact, however, that it all sounds perfectly normal is what matters—it certainly could pass for spontaneous cognition in the minds of two speakers. The dialogue exemplifies all the processes so far described, and—at least to my mind—shows how these processes are what drives thought. So here is the dialogue.

A and B are walking by a church when A looks up and notices that on the steeple, there are some objects that look like emergency-warning sirens attached to the base of the cross.

A: Hey, fancy that! Shades of "Praise the Lord and pass the ammunition!"

B: What do you mean?

A: Well, it's kind of amusing to me. On the one hand, the cross implies a belief in protection by the Lord, but on the other hand, the sirens suggest the need for a backup system, some kind of safety net. I mean, it's fine to believe in divine protection and all, but when it really comes to the crunch, religious people's true colors emerge . . .

B: Well, sooner safe than sorry, no?

A: Sure, but isn't a cross wrapped in danger sirens kind of hypocritical? I mean, why don't religious people put their money where their mouth is? If they really believe in God's benevolence, if they really have the courage of their own convictions, then how come it doesn't suffice to speak softly—why do they need to carry a big stick as well? Put it this way: Either you're a believer, or you ain't.

B: That's a bit black-and-white, isn't it?

A: Of course! As it should be! You can't have it both ways. Somehow this reminds me of when I had to leave my bags in a hotel in Italy for a few days, and the hotel people stored them in a tiny little chapel that was part of the hotel. A friend joked, "Well, this way they'll be protected." But why is such a remark so clearly a joke, even to religious people? Aren't churches houses of God? Shouldn't a sacred place be a safer place?

B: Yes, but being sacred doesn't make churches immune to disaster. We've all heard so often of churches whose roofs collapse on the assembled parishioners . . .

A: Exactly. And then pious people always say, "The Lord works in mysterious ways . . . It's beyond our comprehension." Well, how they can continue to believe after such an event is beyond my comprehension, that's for sure.

B: You're talking about people who claim to believe but in some sense act as if they don't really believe, deep down. But then there's the flip side of the coin: people who claim not to believe but act in a way as if they do. The reverse type of hypocrite, in sort.

A: Do you have an example in mind?

B: Yes—Niels Bohr, the great Danish physicist. I once read that in his house there was a horseshoe hanging over one door, and someone asked him, "What's this all about?" Bohr answered, "Well, horseshoes are supposed to bring good luck, so we put it up there." The friend then said, "Come now—surely you don't believe it brings good luck, do you?" Bohr laughed and said, "Of course not!" And then he added, "But they say it works even if you don't believe in it."

A: I see your point—in a way Bohr's remark is the flip side of "Praise the Lord and pass the ammunition." In the trench-warfare case, you have a believer whose actions reveal deep doubts about their proclaimed belief, and in the Bohr case, you have a skeptic whose actions reveal that he may doubt his own skepticism. But that cross with the sirens—I just can't believe that they would wrap them around the cross, of all things— that's the height of irony! I mean, it's like some priest who's going into a dangerous area of town and doesn't just carry a handgun along in case of need, but in fact a cross that doubles as a handgun.

B: You've made the irony rather clear, I agree. But tell me—would you propose that the pope, simply because he's a big-time believer in God, should travel through the world's cities without any protection? Would you propose that true believers, if they are to be self-consistent, shouldn't put locks on their churches?

A: Well, won't God take care of his flock? Especially the pope?

B: It's not that simple.

A: Come on—if God doesn't look after the pope, who does he look after?

B: Come on, yourself! They crucified Jesus, didn't they? If anyone should have had divine immunity, it was Jesus—but he didn't. And yet that in itself doesn't mean that Jesus wasn't God's son.

This exchange illustrates all of the themes so far presented. In the first place, it shows A and B using ordinary words—bite-size lexical items such as "cross," "sirens," "bags," "hotel," "when," "people," and dozens more—nouns, verbs, adjectives, adverbs, prepositions, and so forth. Nothing unusual here, of course, except that readers are being exhorted to picture each of these words as the tip of an iceberg that hides a myriad hidden analogies—namely, the analogies that collectively allowed the category to come into being in the first place in the speaker's or listener's or reader's mind.

In the second place, the dialogue shows a good number of the shorter phrases cited in lists above being used in realistic situations—smallish stock phrases such as "Fancy that!" "kind of," "I mean," "ain't," "that's for sure," and many more. These phrases are used by speakers because they meet the rhetorical needs of the particular context, and when perceived by listeners they activate familiar rhetorical-context categories.

In the third place, the dialogue illustrates high-level perception—the retrieval of high-level labels for perceptions—such as A's opening statement, in which the lexical item "Praise and Lord and pass the ammunition" is the effortlessly evoked label for a church cross with warning sirens attached to it. In fact, all through the dialogue, the participants use large lexical items to label situations that are being categorized in real time in their minds. Thus we hear "backup system," "safety net," "when it really comes to the crunch," "flip side of the coin," "put your money where your mouth is," "sooner safe than sorry," "speak softly and carry a big stick," "black-and-white," and many more.

In the fourth place, we have large-scale remindings. First there is the shift from the cross-wrapped-in-sirens scene to the suitcases-left-in-hotel-chapel situation, then the sift to the collapsing-churches scenario, after which comes the shift, mediated by a kind of conceptual reversal, to Niels Bohr's horseshoe-that-works-despite-skepticism (probably an apocryphal story, by the way). Following that image comes a different kind of shift—an analogy where a given, known scenario is compared with a spontaneously concocted hypothetical scenario—thus, for instance, the cross-wrapped-in-sirens scene is compared with a hypothetical cross/handgun blend. This is swiftly followed by a trio of further concocted analogues: first the pope traveling without protection, then churches that are left unlocked, and finally God not even taking care of his own son.

The Central Cognitive Loop in Isolation and in Interaction

The broad-stroke pathway meandering through the limitless space of potential ideas during the hypothetical conversation of A and B is due to various actual scenes or imagined scenarios being reperceived, in light of recently activated concepts, in novel fashions and thereby triggering dormant memories, which are then fished up from dormancy to center stage (i.e., short-term memory), where, partially unpacked, they are in turn subjected to the exact same context-dependent reperception process. Around and around in such a loop, alternating between fishing in long-term memory and unpacking and reperceiving in short-term memory, rolls the process of cognition.

Note that what I have just described is not problem-solving, which has traditionally played such a large role in modeling of thought and been tightly linked with "analogical reasoning"; no, everyday thought is not problem-solving or anything that resembles it at all; rather, it is a nonrandom stroll through long-term memory, mediated by high-level perception (which is simply, to echo myself, another name for analogy-making).

To be sure, thought does not generally take place in a sealed-off vat or an isolation chamber; most of the time, external events are constantly impinging on us. Therefore the purely self-driven flow that the "central loop" would suggest is just half of the story—it is the contribution from within one's private cognitive system. The other half—the contribution from outside—comes from inanimate objects impinging on one's senses (skyscrapers and sunsets and splashes, for instance), from animate agents seen mostly as objects (mosquitos that one swats at, people that one tries not to bang into as one hastens down a crowded sidewalk), or from other cognitive agents (conversations with friends, articles read in the paper, email messages, scenes in movies, and so on).

This buzzing, booming confusion in which one is immersed most of the time tends to obscure the constant running of the private inner loop—but when one retreats into solitude, when one starts to ponder or daydream, when one tries to close oneself off from these external impingements and to be internally driven, that is when the above-posited "central loop of cognition" assumes the dominant role.

Goal-Drivenness and the Central Loop

Where do goals enter this picture? How does the deeply goal-driven nature of human thought emerge from what might seem to be the randomness of the posited central loop? The answer resides in the enormously biased nature of each individual's perception.

Each person, as life progresses, develops a set of high-level concepts that they tend to favor, and their perception is continually seeking to cast the world in terms of those concepts. The perceptual process is thus far from neutral or random, but rather it seeks, whenever possible, to employ high-level concepts that one is used to, that one believes in, that one is comfortable with, that are one's pet themes. If the current perception of a situation leads one into a state of cognitive dissonance, then one goes back and searches for a new way to perceive it. Thus the avoidance of mental discomfort—the avoidance of cognitive dissonance—constitutes a powerful internal force that helps to channel the central loop in what amounts to a strongly goal-driven manner.

The Sapir-Whorf Hypothesis: Language and the Central Loop

The viewpoint I have been proposing here—in most ways quite unrevolutionary!—can be rephrased in terms of "perceptual attractors," which are long-term mental loci that are zoomed into when situations are encountered (see Kanerva 1988). We all have many thousands of such attractors in our dormant memories, only a tiny fraction of which are accessed when we encounter a new situation. Where do such attractors come from? How public are they? Do they have explicit labels? Here I list three main types:

• Standard lexical items (words, names, phrases, proverbs, etc.) provided to a vast public through a shared linguistic environment
• Shared vicarious experiences provided to a vast public through the media (e.g., places, personages, and events of small and large scale in books, movies, television shows, and so on), the smaller of which have explicit linguistic labels, the more complex of which have none
• Unique personal memories, lacking any fixed linguistic labels (such chunks are generally very large and complex, like the Frederikssund memory discussed above, or even far larger events, such as a favorite high-school class, a year spent in a special city, a protracted divorce, and so on)

Since a sizable fraction of one's personal repertoire of perceptual chunks is provided from without, by one's language and culture, this means that inevitably language and culture exert powerful, even irresistible, channeling influences on how one frames events. (This position is related to the "meme's-eye view" of the nature of thought, as put forth in numerous venues, most recently in Blackmore 1999.)

Consider, for instance, such words as "backlog," "burnout," "micromanaging," and "underachiever," all of which are commonplace in today's America. I chose these particular words because I suspect that what they designate can be found not only here and now, but as well in distant cultures and epochs, quite in contrast to such culturally and temporally bound terms as "soap opera," "mini-series," "couch potato," "news anchor," "hit-and-run driver," and so forth, which owe their existence to recent technological developments. So consider the first set of words. We Americans living at the millennium's cusp perceive backlogs of all sorts permeating our lives—but we do so because the word is there, warmly inviting us to see them. But back in, say, Johann Sebastian Bach's day, were there backlogs—or more precisely, were backlogs perceived? For that matter, did Bach ever experience burnout? Well, most likely he did—but did he know that he did? Or did some of his Latin pupils strike him as being underachievers? Could he see this quality without being given the label? Or, moving further afield, do Australian aborigines resent it when their relatives micromanage their lives? Of course, I could have chosen hundreds of other terms that have arisen only recently in our century, yet that designate aspects of life that were always around to be perceived but, for one reason or another, aroused little interest, and hence were neglected or overlooked.

My point is simple: we are prepared to see, and we see easily, things for which our language and culture hand us ready-made labels. When those labels are lacking, even though the phenomena may be all around us, we may quite easily fail to see them at all. The perceptual attractors that we each possess (some coming from without, some coming from within, some on the scale of mere words, some on a much grander scale) are the filters through which we scan and sort reality, and thereby they determine what we perceive on high and low levels.

Although this sounds like an obvious tautology, that part of it that concerns words is in fact a nontrivial proposition, which, under the controversial banner of "Sapir-Whorf hypothesis," has been heatedly debated, and to a large extent rejected, over the course of the twentieth century. I myself was once most disdainful of this hypothesis, but over time came to realize how deeply human thought—even my own!—is channeled by habit and thus, in the last accounting, by the repertoire of mental chunks (i.e., perceptual attractors) that are available to the thinker. I now think that it is high time for the Sapir-Whorf hypothesis to be reinstated, at least in its milder forms.

Language, Brains, and "Just Adding Water"

The usual goal of communication is, of course, to set up "the same thought" in the receiver's brain as is currently taking place in the sender's brain. The mode by which such replication is attempted is essentially a drastic compression of the complex symbolic dance occurring in the sender's brain into a temporal chain of sounds or a string of visual signs, which are then absorbed by the receiver's brain, where, by something like the reverse of said compression—a process that I will here term "just adding water"—a new symbolic dance is launched in the second brain. The human brain at one end drains the water out to produce "powdered food for thought," and the one at the other end adds the water back, to produce full-fledged food for thought.

Take, for instance, the paragraph given a few pages back:

that time I spent an hour or two hoping that my old friend Robert, who I hadn't seen in two years but who was supposed to arrive from Germany by train sometime during that summer day in the little Danish fishing village of Frederikssund (which in a series of letters he and I had mutually picked out on maps, and in which I had just arrived early that morning after driving all night from Stockholm), might spot me as I lurked way out at the furthest tip of the very long pier, rather than merely bumping into me at random as we both walked around exploring the stores and streets and parks of this unknown hamlet

Obviously, this set of black marks on a white background is not similar to the time I spent in Frederikssund, nor is any part of it similar to a pier, a drive from Stockholm, a body a water, or dashed hopes. And yet these marks triggered in your brain a symbolic dance so vivid that you saw, in your mind's eye, a fishing village, two young friends, their joyful anticipation of a semirandom reunion, a pier stretching far out into a gulf, a barely visible person anxiously pacing at its tip, and so on. A never-before-danced dance inside your brain, launched by a unique set of squiggly shapes, makes you feel almost as if you had been there; had I spelled it out with another page or two of intricate black-on-white patterns, it would feel all the more vivid. This is a wonderful kind of transportation of ideas between totally different media—uprooting ideas from one garden and replanting them in a garden never even imagined before, where they flourish beautifully.

Transportation

In his book *The poetics of translation* (Barnstone 1993), poet and translator Willis Barnstone has a section called "The Parable of the Greek Moving Van," where he points out that on the side of all Greek moving vans is written the word μεταφορά (phonetically "metafora" and semantically "transportation"). He then observes:

To come to Greece and find that even the moving vans run around under the sun and smog of greater Athens with advertisements for transportation, for metaphor, and ultimately with signs for translation should convince us that every motor truck hauling goods from one place to another, every perceived

metamorphosis of a word or phrase within or between languages, every deci-
pherment and interpretation of a text, every role by each actor in the cast, every
adaptation of a script by a director of opera, film, theater, ballet, pantomime,
indeed every perception of movement and change, in the street or on our tongues,
on the page or in our ears, leads us directly to the art and activity of translation.

I pack my mental goods down into tight, neat bundles, I load them as
carefully as I can into the metafora truck of language, it drives from my
brain to yours, and then you unpack. What a metaphor for communication! And yet it has often been said that all communication, all language, is metaphorical. Since I believe that metaphor and analogy are
the same phenomenon, it would follow that I believe that all communication is via analogy. Indeed, I would describe communication this way:
taking an intricate dance that can be danced in one and only one
medium, and then, despite the intimacy of the marriage of that dance to
that medium, making a radically new dance that is intimately married
to a radically different medium, and in just the same way as the first
dance was to its medium.

Trans-Sportation

To make this all a little more concrete, let us consider taking a complex
dance done in the medium of the sport of basketball and trans-sporting
that dance into the rather different medium of the sport of soccer. Indeed,
imagine taking the most enthralling basketball game you ever watched—
perhaps a championship game you saw on television—and giving a
videotape of that game to a "soccer choreographer," who will now stage
all the details of an artificial soccer game that is in some sense analogous
to your basketball game. Of course this could be done in many ways,
some conservative and some daring.

Some choreographers, citing irreconcilable differences between the
two sports (for instance, the difference in the number of players per team,
the lack of any counterpart to a goalie in basketball, the low frequency
of scoring in soccer relative to basketball, and on and on), might severely
bend the rules of soccer, creating a game with only five players on a team,
taking away the goalies, vastly reducing the size of the field (and the
goals), and so forth, thus effectively creating a hybrid soccer–basketball

game that looks very much like basketball, only it is played on grass and involves propelling the ball with the lower rather than the upper limbs. When one watched the reenactment of one's favorite basketball game in this artificial medium, one would not have the sense of watching a soccer game but of watching a very distorted basketball game.

Other choreographers, more willing to go out on a limb, would retain the normal rules of soccer but would attempt to stage a game whose every play felt like a particular play of the original basketball game, even though eleven players were retained on a side, even though the goals remained huge compared to baskets, even though there were still goalies, even though the goals might be coming a little too thick and fast, and so forth. There would be plays that would be essentially like slam-dunks while at the same time looking every bit like normal soccer plays. In such a case, one would feel one was watching a genuine soccer game—perhaps a peculiar one in some ways, but nonetheless genuine. In the ideal case, one could have the two counterpart games running on side-by-side television screens, and a "neutral" commentator using only terms that apply to both sports could be effectively heard as describing either of the games.

Anything in between these two extreme philosophies of "transsportation" can also be imagined—and just such a bizarre scenario is what I think everyday communication is actually like. Two brains are, in general, far more unalike than are the sports of soccer and basketball—and yet our society is predicated on mutual comprehensibility mediated by language.

Translation

It is astonishing to me how often people—even linguistically sophisticated people, such as philosophers, writers, linguists, translators, and cognitive scientists—will speak as if communication among members of a single language community were total and perfect, with serious communication gaps only taking place at the interface between different languages—as if translation were needed only between languages, never within a language community. Thus it is taken as obvious and indisputable that Russians all read, say, a novel by Pushkin in one and the same way, but that no one who reads an anglicized version of that novel could possibly get anything like "that same experience" (as if the reading of that novel engendered just one experience in the vast world of all different Russian speakers). My retort would be that what matters is not the dried linguistic powder that is used to transport the dance between brains—what matters is the dance set up inside a brain by whatever dried powder is used for the transport. Linguists (I exempt those in the very recent cognitive-linguistics movement) concentrate so hard on the overt dried powder that they wind up largely ignoring the covert dances that engender it, and that it engenders. As an ironic consequence, the standard model of language that has been built up this century by linguists is hugely impoverished.

Most people's (and most linguists') model of translation is as dry as the powder that carries dehydrated ideas from brain to brain; indeed, they conceive of translation as a mapping from one purely dehydrated chain of symbols to another dehydrated chain of symbols, without any need for "adding water" at any stage of the process. The whole process happens purely at the level of the dry symbols. Translation would thus be an activity for drones—and hence ideal for computers to carry out. Here—courtesy of my Sofia hotel—is an example of the "drone" theory of translation:

Please   don't   disturb

$\updownarrow$ $\updownarrow$ $\updownarrow$

Bitte   nicht   stören

Or, as the early machine-translation pioneer Warren Weaver once wrote (Weaver 1955), "When I look at an article in Russian, I say, 'This is really written in English, but it has been coded in some strange symbols. I shall now proceed to decode.'"

Since translation is but the challenge of communication rendered crystal-clear, and since communication is but metaphor, and since metaphor is but analogy, I shall spend the rest of this article on analogy focusing on translation and showing how at its core translation is analogy, and indeed, is analogy at its most sublime and enchanting.

Evgénii Onégin

When, a few paragraphs back, I wrote the phrase "a novel by Pushkin," my choice was not as flippant as I tried to make it seem. Indeed, as a recent translator of Alexander Pushkin's novel in verse *Eugene Onegin*, I have been totally absorbed over the past year or so in the delicious but daunting task of reincarnating Pushkin's sparkling poetry in the medium of contemporary English—or rather, contemporary American. It has not, needless to say, been a process that looked anything like the Sofia-hotel model, with the two-headed vertical arrows connecting words. In order to give a sense of what was involved, I must first describe the building blocks of the novel, usually called "Onegin stanzas." Each sonnet (of which there are nearly four hundred) is a "crystal"—a pattern to transplant from one medium to another. What is the nature of these crystals?

To begin with, each one consists of fourteen lines of strict iambic tetrameter (which means—at least in Russian—that stresses never fall on odd-numbered syllables). The rhyming pattern is always as follows:

A B A B C C D D E F F E G G

and within this framework, the "A," "C," and "E" line-pairs have the special property of being feminine rhymes, while the "B," "D," "F," and "G" line-pairs are masculine. The distinction is as follows: "return/discern" is a masculine rhyme, because the final syllables not only rhyme but are stressed, whereas "returning/discerning" is a feminine rhyme, because the penultimate syllables rhyme and are stressed, while the final syllables are not only unstressed but identical. In other words, in feminine rhymes, the "rhyming action" takes place before the line's final syllable (which is unstressed), whereas in masculine rhymes, the rhyming action takes place on the final syllable (which is stressed).

As a consequence of this intricate design, an Onegin stanza's lines have varying numbers of syllables, depending on whether they are feminine or masculine. The six "A," "C," and "E" lines have nine syllables apiece, while all others have eight, as follows:

9 8 9 8 9 9 8 8 9 8 8 9 8 8

All four hundred crystals in the original Russian have this property, and thus all four hundred crystals in the counterpart work in English should—should they not?—have this same property. The crucial question is, of course, what kind of compromises should be made in the transportation of Pushkin's virtuoso game into the new medium. One type of translator (Nabokov 1964) might insist on retaining the most literal possible rendering of each word and even much of the Russian word order, in which case all rhyming and rhythmic properties would have to be sacrificed. This would seem rather akin to the word-for-word Sofia-hotel model, and quite uninspired as a translation philosophy.

Another type of translator would insist on retaining the medium-message marriage that well-wrought poetry inevitably is, and thus on looking behind the scenes, looking beyond the dry dust on the paper, looking at the sparkling mental dance to which the dry powder gives rise, once water is added to it. To such a translator, what matters is that each semantic chunk of the original poetry (whether contained within a single line or spread across several) gives rise to a scene in the mind's eye of a reader (not to mention that of Pushkin), and this type of translator, having tried to envision that scene as clearly, fully, and faithfully as possible, then uses it as a source for English words and phrases that can be used in lines of English poetry that obey the formal constraints. Such a translator, in short, is inspired by the inner dance and not merely by the dry powder.

Since the scene conjured up by a line or two of the original goes far beyond the literal words in those lines (i.e., since "just adding water" adds such richness!), there is much more to draw on as potential material for a new poem in English, and so one is enormously freed up. There remain, of course, all the rhythmic and rhyming hoops to jump through, but by adding water, one has at least given oneself a fighting chance at finding a solution satisfying all the relevant constraints.

Of course satisfying those constraints is not a simple task, nor is it by any means a black-and-white matter to judge whether (or to what degree) the constraints have actually been met. There are many pressures vying with each other, and by no means are they all explicit, although some are. One might cite the following sets of pressures under which a translator must work:

· Content: the image evoked by the words and phrases in a semantic chunk

· Structural pattern: the above-described features that define the phonetic nature of an Onegin stanza
· Tone: an intangible brew of subliminally felt qualities suggested by the following oppositions: humorous vs. serious; straightforward vs. ironic; heavy vs. light; old-fashioned vs. modern; meditative vs. peppy; sweet vs. sad; resigned vs. delighted; highbrow vs. lowbrow; etc.

The only one of these constraints that has a sharp, black-and-white feel to it is that of the structural pattern, since it is generally fairly objective whether two words rhyme or not, how many syllables are in a word, where stress should fall, and whether a given two-syllable chunk is an iamb or not (although, in truth, these matters are surprisingly often quite blurry—does "midnight" make a true feminine rhyme with "slid right"? is "finally" bisyllabic or trisyllabic?).

The other constraints are anything but sharp, since the content of any lexical item is (as has been the thrust of this paper) determined by a host of prior analogies, and hence is tremendously blurry, and since tone is not only vague but also highly multidimensional, allowing for any conceivable combination of degree of irony, degree of modernity, degree of sadness, and so on, ad infinitum.

Given the complexity of this range of competing pressures, it is hardly surprising that there will occur, in the translation of nearly every single line, smaller or larger creative slippages, typified by, but by no means limited to, the following list:

· The "perfect" literal translation of a word is abandoned in favor of a slightly less perfect choice, because of (say) phonetic constraints
· A syntactic reversal, slightly unusual in English, is resorted to for (say) reasons of metric purity
· An idea or image is shifted from one line to another because English grammar works that way
· An alliterative pattern is dropped in one stanza but is introduced out of the blue in another, in order to replicate fairly accurately the overall density of alliteration in the original
· A modern-seeming word is used in a passage that has an older tone, or vice versa, because of (say) certain extra connotations that are gained thereby

• A word strongly evocative of something linked tightly to the target culture but not the original culture (e.g., "jive") is used, even if the effect creates a very short-lived subliminal shift of venue from source to target culture

• A perfect rhyme is sacrificed for a near-rhyme, in order to gain an extra set of connotations or to conjure up a precise image that would otherwise not be attainable

• A word is used in a highly metaphorical manner, stretching it even beyond its normal degree of plasticity

• A metaphor is dropped or is replaced by a different metaphor, because the original metaphor makes no sense in the target culture

• A metaphor is introduced out of the blue, perhaps because it is implicit in a stock phrase or proverb that fits aptly and that also rhymes very strongly;

• Etc., etc., etc.

The amusing fact about the result of all these kinds of creative slippage is that what emerges can often be so powerfully evocative of the original that it seems—at least on some levels—perfectly plausible to refer to the English-language Onegin stanza thereby produced as being "by Alexander Pushkin," and therefore to write those three words on the front cover and spine and title page of the book, perhaps even relegating the translator's name to nothing more than a line in fine print on the copyright page.

We shall now take a look at the results of all these kinds of slippages caused by multiple rival pressures in the minds of different translators with different philosophies of translation. I have selected one stanza, the 29th from chapter II, to illustrate what kinds of things can occur. (See also chapters 8, 9, and 13 of Hofstadter 1997.)

First I display Pushkin's original Russian and, next to it, a literal translation by Vladimir Nabokov; thereafter, in order, stanzas by the following translators (in the chronological order of publication of their translations): Babette Deutsch, Oliver Elton, Walter Arndt, Charles Johnston, James Falen, and Douglas Hofstadter.

Александр Пушкин (1825)

Ей рано нравились романы;
Они ей заменяли всё;
Она влюблялася в обманы
И Ричардсона и Руссо.
Отец её был добрый малый,
В прошедшем веке запоздалый,
Но в книгах не видал вреда;
Он, не читая никогда,
Их почитал пустой игрушкой
И не заботился о том,
Какой у дочки тайный том
Дремал до утра под подушкой.
Жена ж его была сама
От Ричардсона без ума.

Vladimir Nabokov (1964)

She early had been fond of novels; for
her they replaced all;
she grew enamored with the fictions
of Richardson and of Rousseau.
Her father was a kindly fellow
who lagged in the precedent age
but saw no harm in reading books;
he, never reading,
deemed them an empty toy,
nor did he care
what secret tome his daughter had
dozing till morn under her pillow.
As to his wife, she was herself
mad upon Richardson.

Babette Deutsch (1936)

She found in a romantic story
All one might care to be or know;
Living the chapters through, she'd glory
In Richardson as in Rousseau.
Her father saw no harm in reading
(He was a decent chap, conceding
He lived in quite another age);
But then he never read a page.
He did not know that books could say things
To move you even while you slept;
He thought the tomes his daughter kept
Beneath her pillow, empty playthings;
While, on the other hand, his wife
Held Richardson as dear as life.

Oliver Elton (1937)

Romances were her only passion,
And all the world to her; and so
She fell in love, the dupe of fashion,
With Richardson, and with Rousseau.
Quite a good fellow was her father,
Of the last age, belated rather;
He saw no mischief in a book,
Though in one he would never look;
Thought it a toy, and held it lightly,
And cared not what his daughter did
When she a private volume hid
Beneath her pillow, slumbering nightly.
His lady wife was mad upon
The tales of Samuel Richardson.

Walter Arndt (1963)

But novels, which she early favored,
Replaced for her all other treats;
With rapturous delight she savored
Rousseau's and Richardson's conceits.
Her honest father, though old-fashioned,
Last century's child, grew not impassioned
About the harm that books might breed;
He, who was never known to read,
Regarded them as empty thrillers
And never thought to bring to light
Which secret volume dreamt at night
Beneath his little daughter's pillows.
His wife had had a crush herself
On Richardson—still on her shelf.

Charles Johnston (1977)

From early on she loved romances,
they were her only food . . . and so
she fell in love with all the fancies
of Richardson and of Rousseau.
Her father, kindly, well-regarded,
but in an earlier age retarded,
could see no harm in books; himself
he never took one from the shelf,
thought them a pointless peccadillo;
and cared not what his daughter kept
by way of secret tome that slept
until the dawn beneath her pillow.
His wife, just like Tatyana, had
on Richardson gone raving mad.

D. R. Hofstadter

James Falen (1990)	Douglas Hofstadter (1999)
From early on she read romances,	*From early on, she read romances;*
And novels set her heart aglow;	*True life they were for her, not show.*
She loved the fictions and the fancies	*She fell for all the moods and trances*
Of Richardson and of Rousseau.	*Induced by authors like Rousseau*
Her father was a kindly fellow—	*And Richardson. A friendly fellow,*
Lost in a past he found more mellow;	*Her father was old-fashioned, mellow,*
But still, in books he saw no harm,	*And saw in books no cause for dread;*
And, though immune to reading's charm,	*Instead, because he never read,*
Deemed it a minor peccadillo;	*He thought of them as dull and boring,*
Nor did he care what secret tome	*And didn't give a tinker's damn*
His daughter read or kept at home	*What brand of frivolous flim-flam*
Asleep till morn beneath her pillow;	*His daughter clutched all night while snoring.*
His wife herself, we ought to add,	*But on the other hand, his wife*
For Richardson was simply mad.	*Thought Richardson the spice of life.*

Each of these compact fourteen-line verbal packets is a structure that bears to the original packet the relation of analog in the medium of the English language. Each one is clearly the result of myriad tradeoffs involving preservation of imagery, strictness of meter, perfection of rhyme, phonetic patternedness, era exuded by words and phrases, degree of humor, degree of catchiness, degree of familiarity of lexical items, ease of syntactical flow, sequential order of ideas, and much more.

Take, for instance, the word "instead" on line 8 of my translation. Initially, I had line 8 beginning with "indeed," which in some ways is stronger (because "indeed" carries a more emphatic flavor than "instead," and also because, more subtly, the comma-signaled pause that would follow "indeed" strikes me as ever-so-slightly longer and more charged than its counterpart with "instead"), and yet despite these lures, the internal rhyme of "instead" with "dread" preceding it and with "read" following it somehow carried the day in my mind. This is typical of the multidimensional internal conflicts that occur routinely in translation, and each time, one has to weigh all the factors and make a decision.

On a more blatant semantic level, you may note that the imagery in my stanza is that of the daughter sleeping—nay, snoring!—while clinging tightly to a favorite book, whereas the imagery in the original is of the book itself sleeping (or dreaming) beneath the girl's pillow. To what extent is one entitled to manipulate imagery this way and then to claim that the resulting book is "by Alexander Pushkin"?

To what extent did the nonanglophone Russian poet Alexander Pushkin ever say, in describing the girl's father, "and didn't give a tinker's damn"? On the other hand, to what extent did Pushkin ever write the line "nor did he care"? Using the former as line 10 provides a clear whiff of Pushkinesque humor (not to mention having the proper meter, rhyme, and so on), while using the latter as line 10 is bland and flat (and is but four syllables long, where Pushkin's line had, of course, four full iambs on it).

By what right did I feel entitled to insert an alliterative and flippant phrase like "frivolous flim-flam" into the lyrical mouth of Alexander Pushkin? On the other hand, by what right did Vladimir Nabokov feel entitled to insert the graceless and nonidiomatic phrase, "As to his wife, she was herself mad upon Richardson" into the mouth of Russia's greatest poet? For that matter, by what right did James Falen think he could get away with a pseudorhyme like "romances" and "fancies"? As for Walter Arndt, by what right did think he could get away with a non-rhyme like "thrillers" and "pillows"? And by what right did Charles Johnston think he was entitled to portray the girl's novels as "her only food"? By what right did Babette Deutsch rearrange the order of Pushkin's ideas, so as to make the father's old-fashionedness follow (and in parentheses, to boot!) his seeing no harm in books? And how in the world did Oliver Elton feel he was being faithful to Pushkin by using the bizarrely redundant phrase "his lady wife"?

Of course I am feigning outrage here; I have great respect for most of these translators, despite the fact that I see compromises ubiquitously riddling the productions of each of them. The questions just raised were raised purely rhetorically, my intention being to provoke readers into pondering which of these seven rival English-language stanzas might be seen as the most analogous to Pushkin's original stanza (without claiming there is any "correct" answer).

Winding Up: On Associationism and the Cartesian Theater

We have come a long way, starting out by seeing single words as analogs to perceived situations, and ending up by seeing sonnets in different languages as each other's analogs. Somewhere near the midpoint came the crux of this essay, however, which claimed that thinking (at least when isolated from external influences) is a series of leaps involving high-level perception, activation of concepts in long-term memory, transfer to short-term memory, partial and context-dependent unpacking of chunks, and then further high-level perception, and so forth.

This may sound like no more than the age-old idea of associationism—that we think by jumping associatively from one thing to another. If that's all it came down to, my thesis would certainly be a sterile and vapid noncontribution to cognitive science. But the mechanisms I posit are more specific, and in particular they depend on the transfer of tightly packed mental chunks from the dormant area of long-term memory into the active area of short-term memory, and on their being unpacked on arrival, and then scrutinized. Both transfer and perception are crucial, and in that respect, my thesis departs significantly from associationism.

Some readers, such as the author of *Consciousness explained* (Dennett 1991), might feel they detect in this theory of thinking an insidious residue of the so-called Cartesian theater—a hypothetical theater in which an "inner eye" watches as various images go parading by on a "mental screen," and becomes "aware" or "conscious" of such imagery. Such a notion of thinking leads very easily down the slippery slope of nested homunculi, and thus to an infinite regress concerning the site of consciousness.

I would gladly plead guilty to the accusation of positing a "screen" upon which are "projected" certain representations dredged up from long-term memory, and I would also plead guilty to the accusation of positing an "inner eye" that scans that screen and upon it posts further representational structures, which trigger a descent via analogy into the dormant depths of long-term memory. I would insist, however, that the label "perception," as applied to what the "inner eye" does, be sharply distinguished from visual or any other kind of sensory perception, since in general it involves no sensory modality in any normal sense of the term (recall the perception of "ethnic cleansing" in a newspaper story). The nature of such abstract or high-level perceptual processing has been sketched out in work done by my students and myself over the years (see Hofstadter and FARG 1995), and I will not attempt to describe it here.

Clearly, since it has been implemented as a computer program (at least to a first approximation), such a model does not succumb to snagging on the fatal hook of infinite regress.

To those who would scoff at the very notion of any "inner screen" involved in cognition, I would point to the large body of work of perceptual psychologist Anne Treisman (e.g., Treisman 1988), which in my view establishes beyond any doubt the existence of temporary perceptual structures created on the fly in working memory (she calls them "object files")—a stark contrast to the connectionist-style thesis that all cognition takes place in long-term memory, and that it consists merely of simultaneous conceptual activations (possibly with attached temporal phases, so as to handle the "binding problem") without any type of transfer to, or structure-building in, a distinct working area. Although this more distributed view of the essence of cognition might appeal to opponents of the Cartesian theater, it does not seem to me that it comes anywhere close to allowing the richness of thought that back-and-forth flow between long-term and short-term memory would allow.

I hope that my speculative portrayal of analogy as the lifeblood, so to speak, of human thinking, despite being highly ambitious and perhaps somewhat overreaching, strikes a resonant chord in those who study cognition. My most optimistic vision would be that the whole field of cognitive science suddenly woke up to the centrality of analogy, that all sides suddenly saw eye to eye on topics that had formerly divided them most bitterly, and naturally—indeed, it goes without saying—that they lived happily ever after. Whatever.

References

Barnstone, W. (1993). *The poetics of translation: History, theory, practice*. New Haven: Yale University Press.

Becker, J. D. (1975). The phrasal lexicon. In R. Schank and B. Nash-Webber, eds., *Theoretical Issues in Natural Language Processing*. Cambridge, MA: Bolt Beranek and Newman.

Blackmore, S. (1999). *The meme machine*. New York: Oxford University Press.

Dawkins, R. (1976). *The selfish gene*. New York: Oxford University Press.

Dennett, D. C. (1991). *Consciousness explained*. Boston: Little, Brown.

Hofstadter, D. (1997). *Le ton beau de Marot*. New York: Basic Books.

Hofstadter, D., and the Fluid Analogies Research Group (1995). *Fluid concepts and creative analogies*. New York: Basic Books.

Hofstadter, D., and Moser, D. (1989). To err is human, to study error-making is cognitive science. *Michigan Quarterly Review*. **28**(2):185–215.

Kanerva, P. (1988). *Sparse distributed memory*. Cambridge, MA: MIT Press.

Pushkin, A. S. (1832). *Eugene Onegin: A novel in verse*.

W. Arndt, trans. (1963). Ann Arbor, MI: Ardis Editions.

B. Deutsch, trans. (1998). New York: Dover.

O. Elton, trans. (1995). London: Everyman.

J. Falen, trans. (1995). New York: Oxford University Press.

D. Hofstadter, trans. (1999). New York: Basic Books.

C. Johnston, trans. (1977). New York: Penguin Books.

V. Nabokov, trans. (1964). Princeton, NJ: Princeton University Press.

F. Sobotka (1991). London: Bristol Classical Press.

Schank, R. (1982). *Dynamic memory*. New York: Cambridge University Press.

Treisman, A. (1988). Features and objects: The fourteenth Bartlett Memorial Lecture. *Quarterly Journal of Experimental Psychology* **40A**:201–237.

Weaver, W. (1955). Translation. In W. N. Lock and A. D. Booth, eds., *Machine translation of languages*. Cambridge, MA: MIT Press.

Index